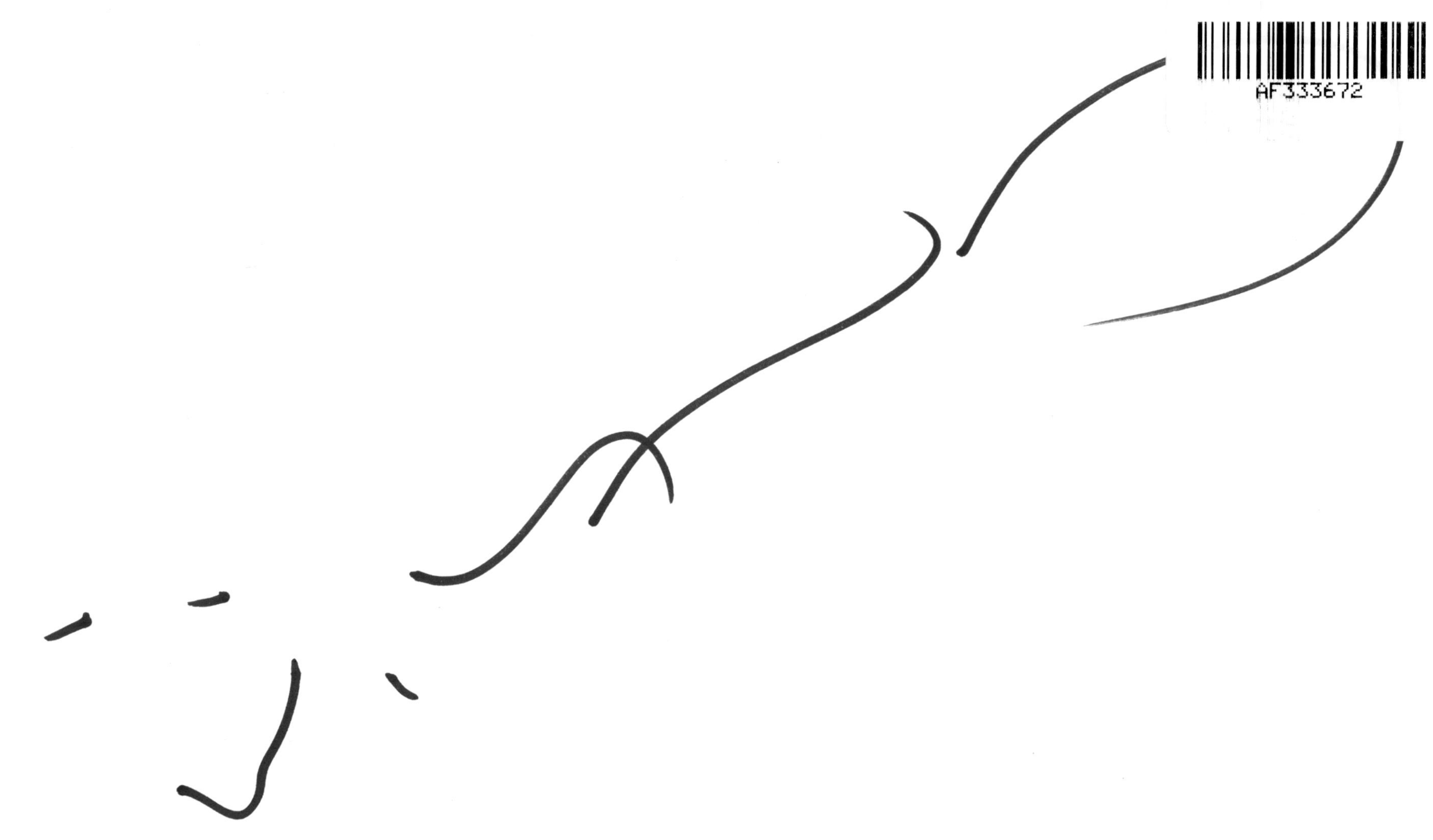

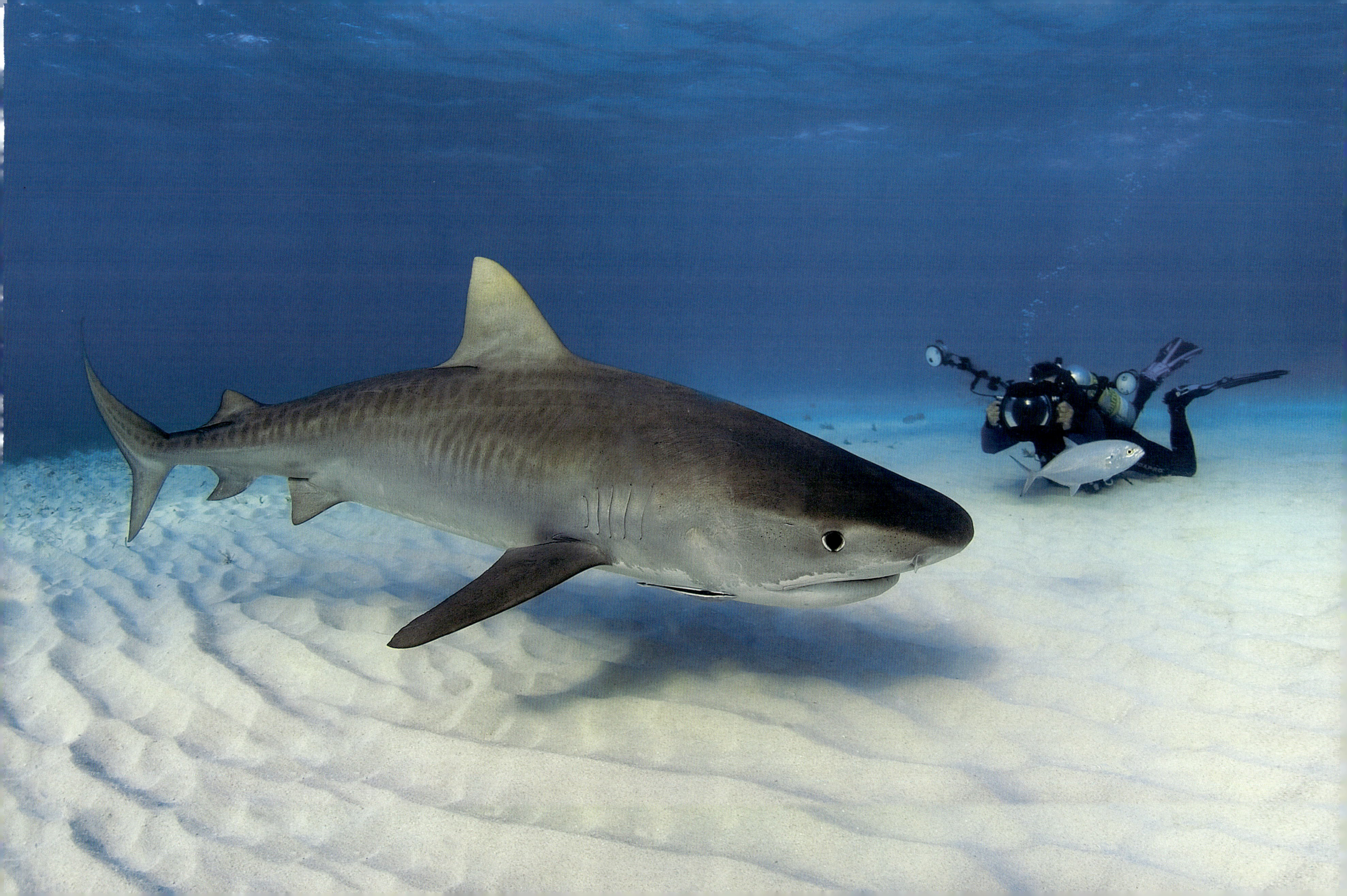

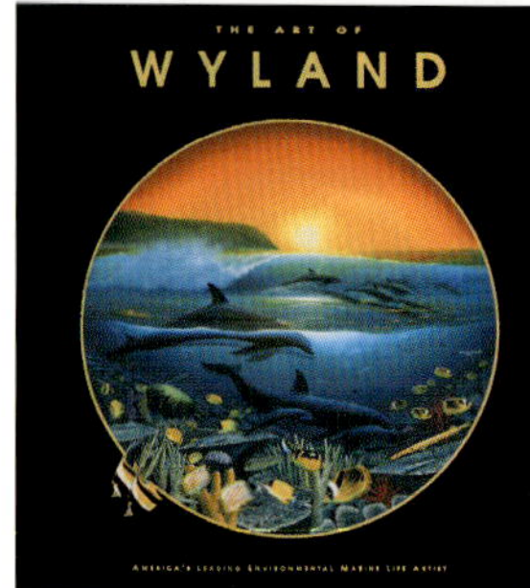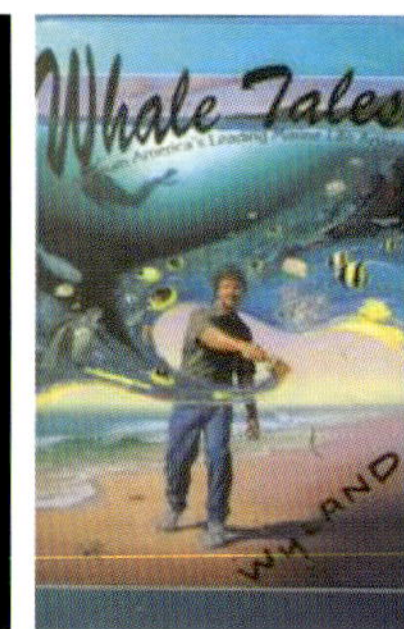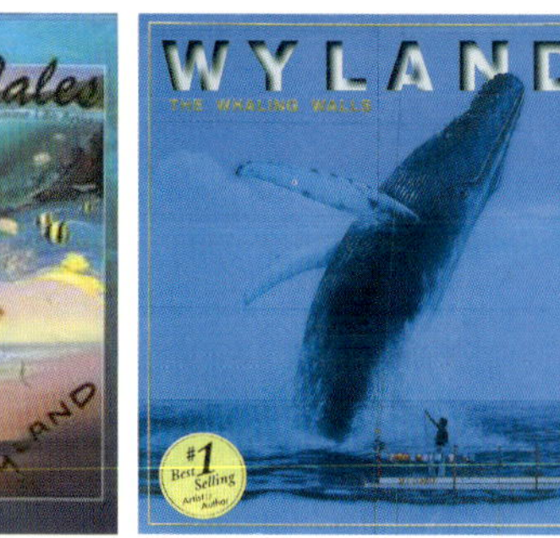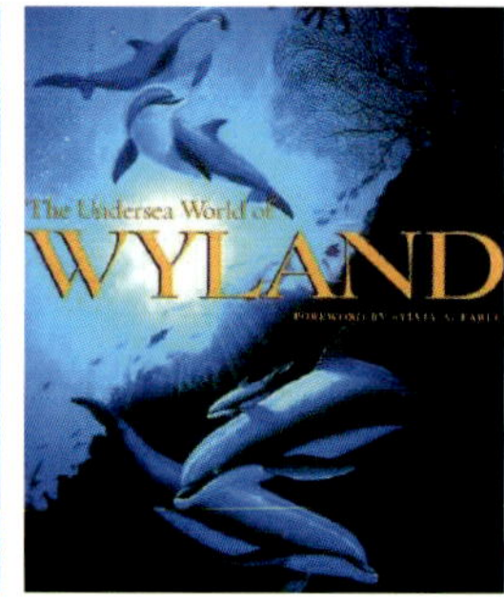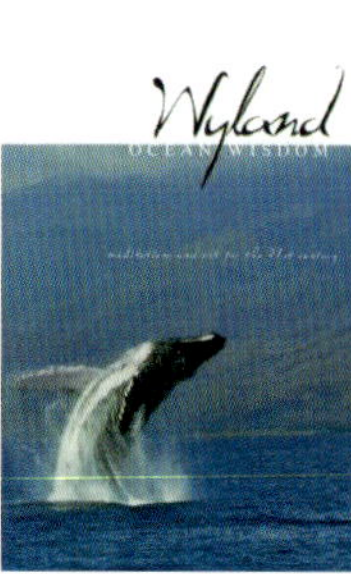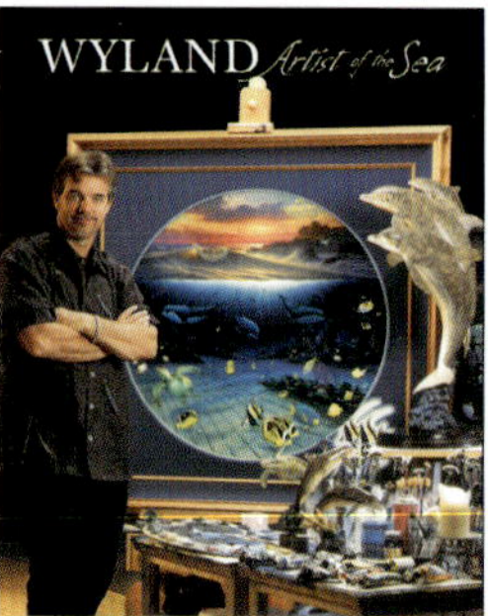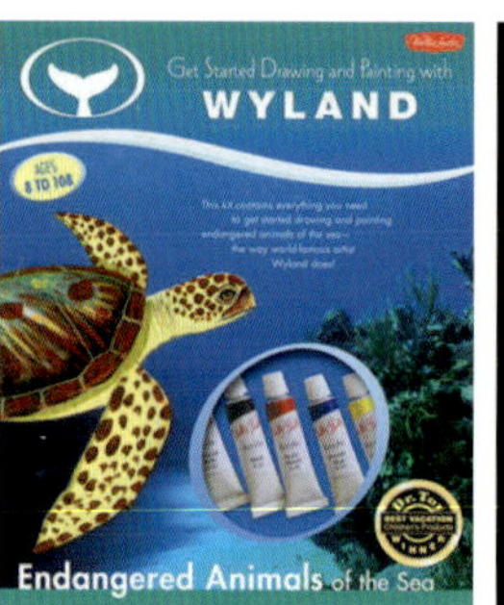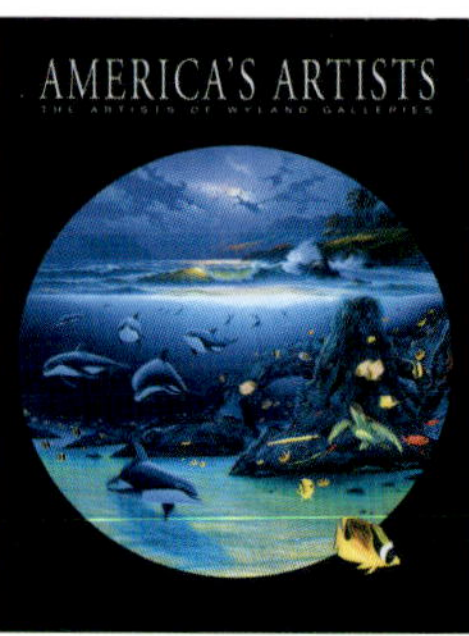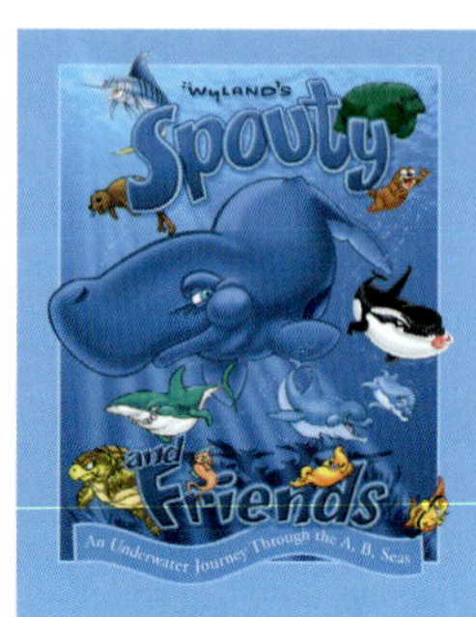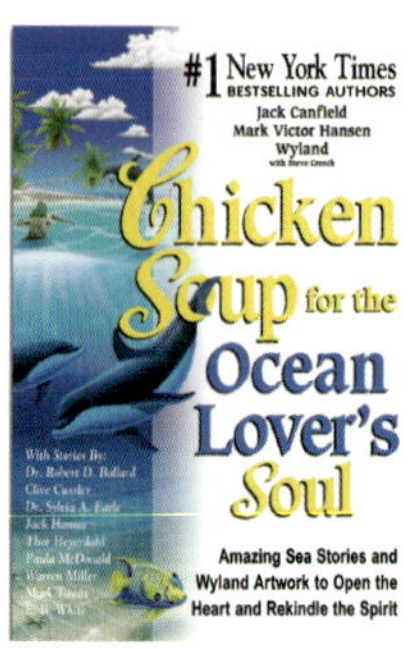

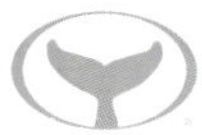

Wyland Worldwide, LLC
5 Columbia
Aliso Viejo, CA 92656
Phone 949-643-7070
Fax 949-643-7099
www.wyland.com
customerservice@wyland.com

Produced by:
Wyland Worldwide, LLC
5 Columbia
Aliso Viejo, CA 92656

1 3 5 7 9 10 8 6 4 2

Library of Congress Cataloging-in-Publication Data

Wyland, 1956
Wyland: Visions of the Sea

ISBN 978-1884840029 (Limited Edition)
ISBN 978-1884840012 (Standard Edition)

Special thanks to Wyland Design, Gino Beltran,
Steve Creech, Gregg Hamby, Karla Kipp, Tiffany Meairs,
and Jennifer Martin

Creative Production: Wyland Design
Printing: 2008 Everbest Printing Co.,Ltd
Marketing and Distribution: Angela Needham

Wyland Books

The Art of Wyland © 1992

Whale Tales © 1995

Wyland: The Whaling Walls © 1997

The Undersea World of Wyland © 1998

Wyland: Ocean Wisdom © 2000

Wyland: Artist of the Sea © 2002

Chicken Soup for the Ocean Lover's Soul © 2003

America's Artists: The Artists of Wyland Galleries © 2004

Spouty and Friends: An Underwater Journey
Through the A, B, Seas © 2004

Hold Your Water, 68 Things You Need To Know

To Keep Our Planet Blue © 2006

Wyland, 25 Years at Sea © 2006

Learn to Draw and Paint with Wyland © 2006

How to Draw Wyland's Spouty™ & Friends © 2006

How to Draw Wyland's Spouty™ and Friends © 2006

Animals of the Sea © 2006

Swimming Lessons: Natures Mothers, Sea Lions © 2007

Marine Life: Learn to Paint Step by Step with Wyland

(How To Draw/Paint Kit) © 2007

Acrylic Painting Kit Layer by Layer™:

Dolphin Mates © 2007

Acrylic Painting Kit Layer By Layer™:

In the Company of Orcas © 2007

Wyland

Visions of the Sea © 2008

Wyland - Water Signs — Fall 2008
Wyland - 100 Whaling Walls — Fall 2008
TO ORDER ANY OF THESE WYLAND BOOKS VISIT
WYLAND.COM OR CALL 1-800-WYLAND-0

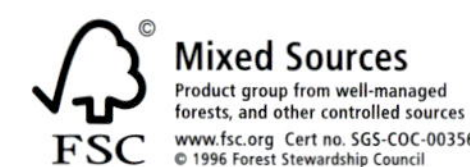

cover: whale sunset
back cover: newborn sea
previous: photo of Wyland with tiger shark by Annette Robertson

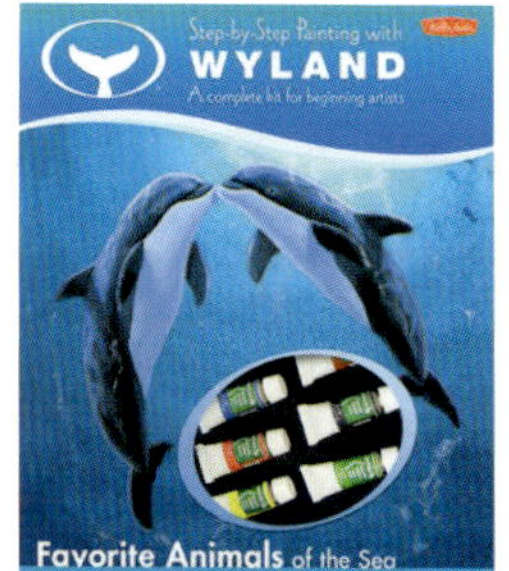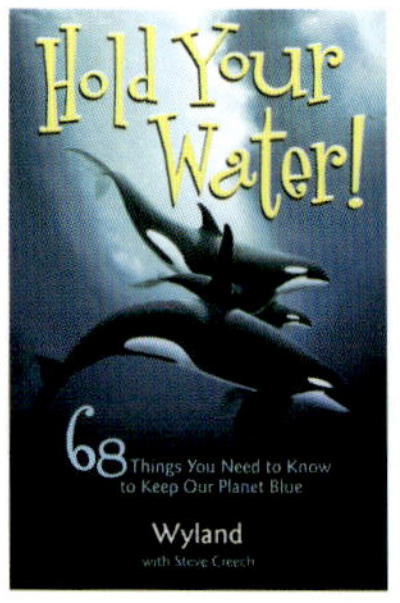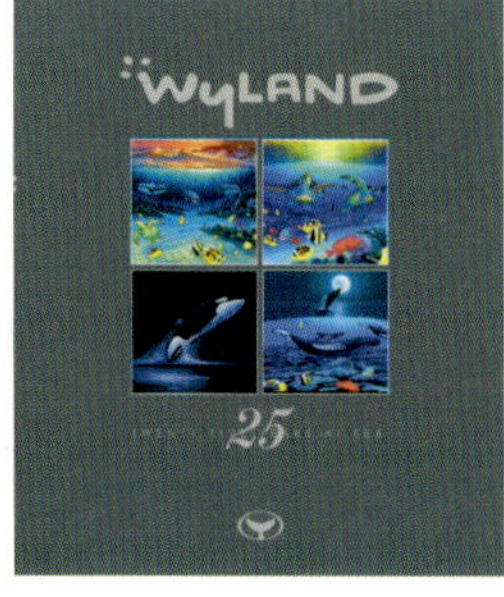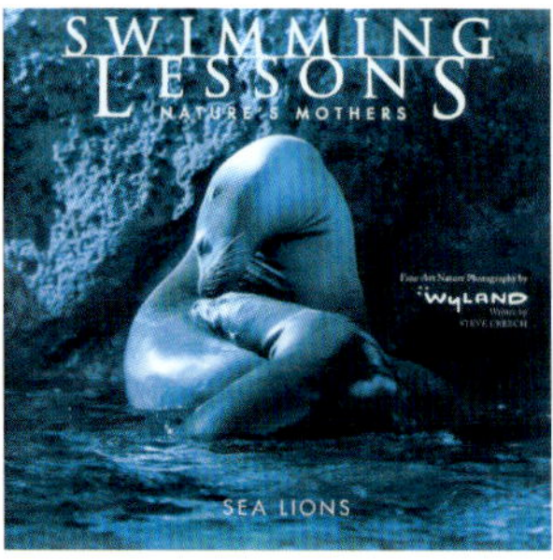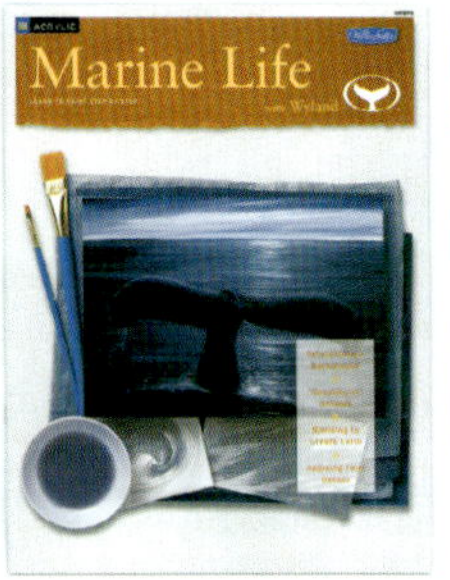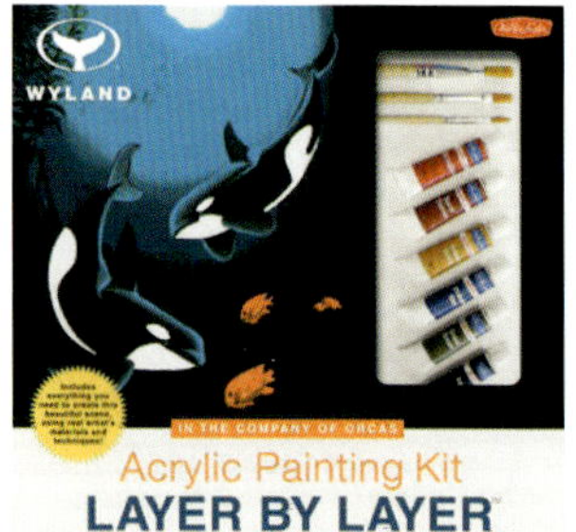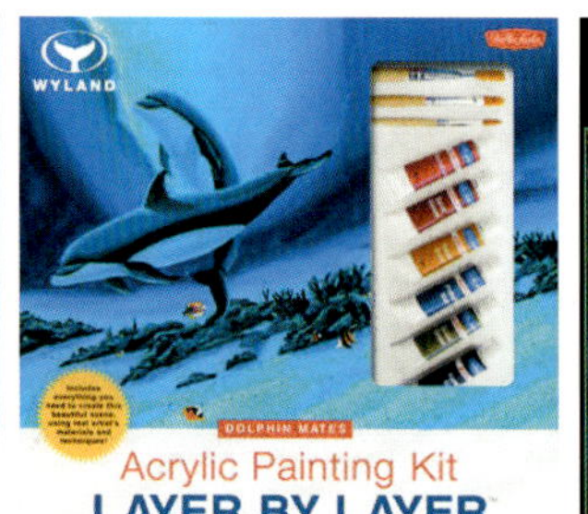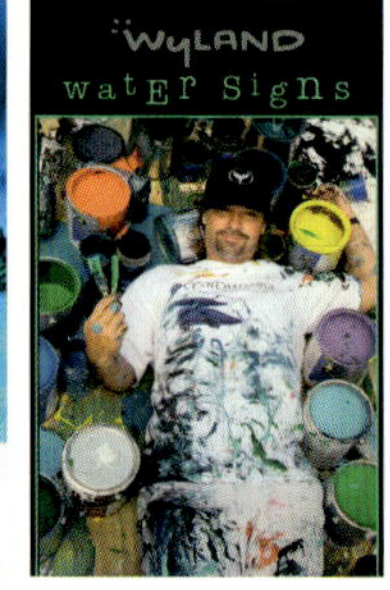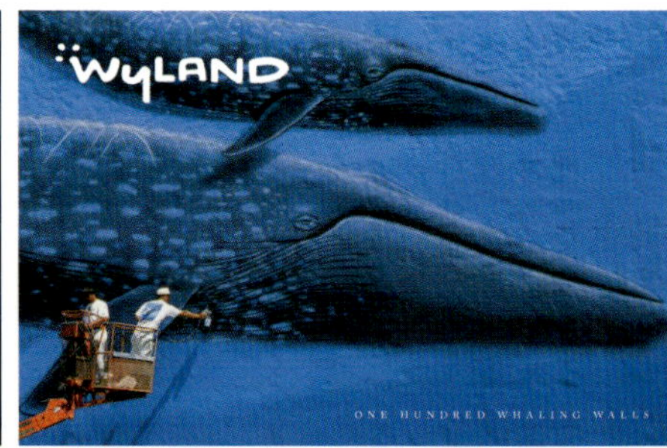

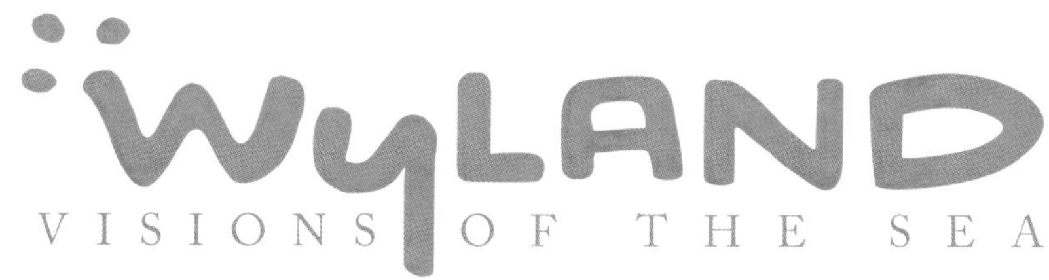

WYLAND
VISIONS OF THE SEA

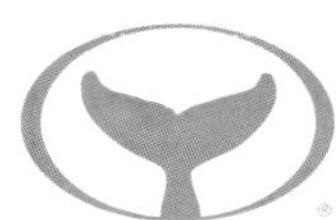

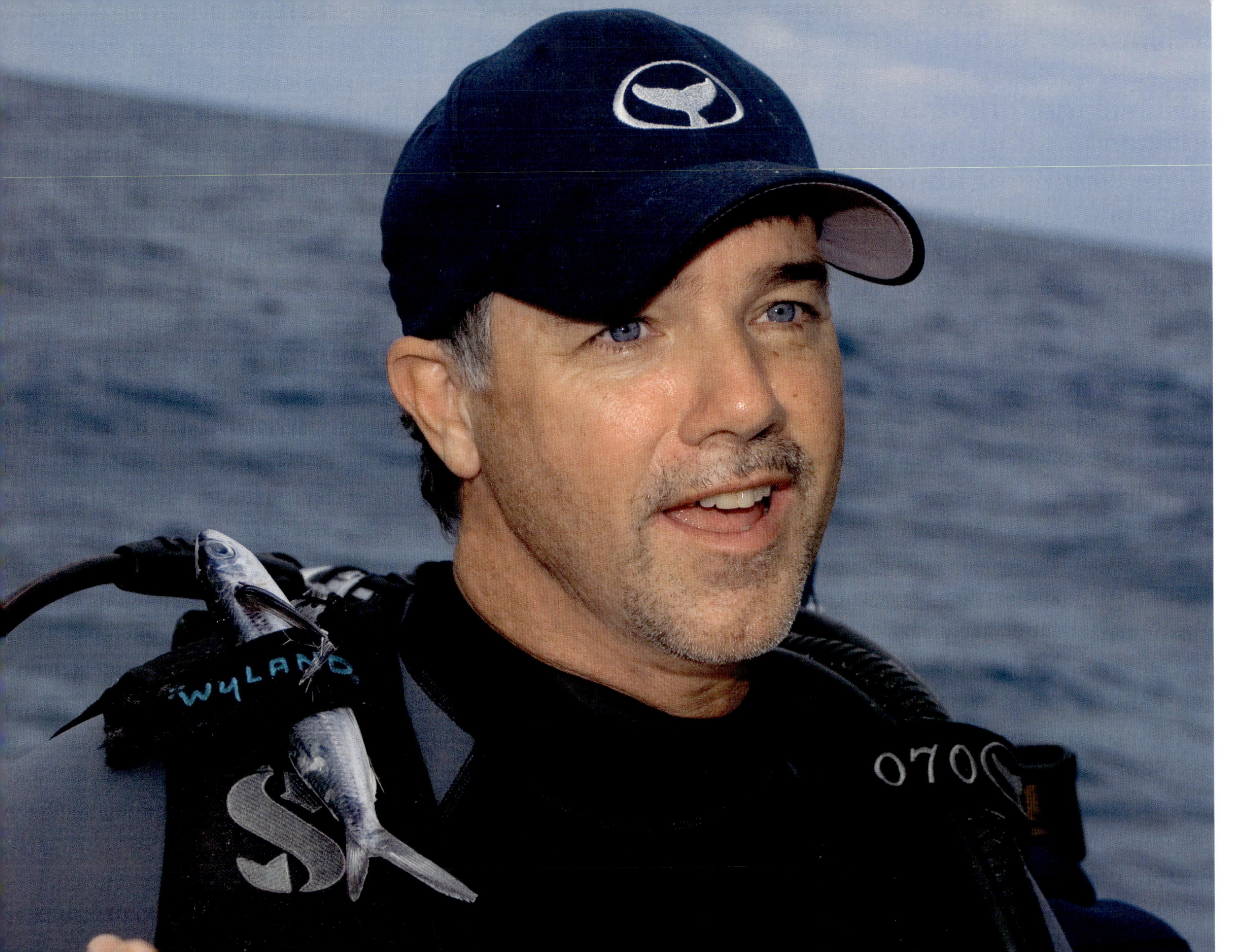

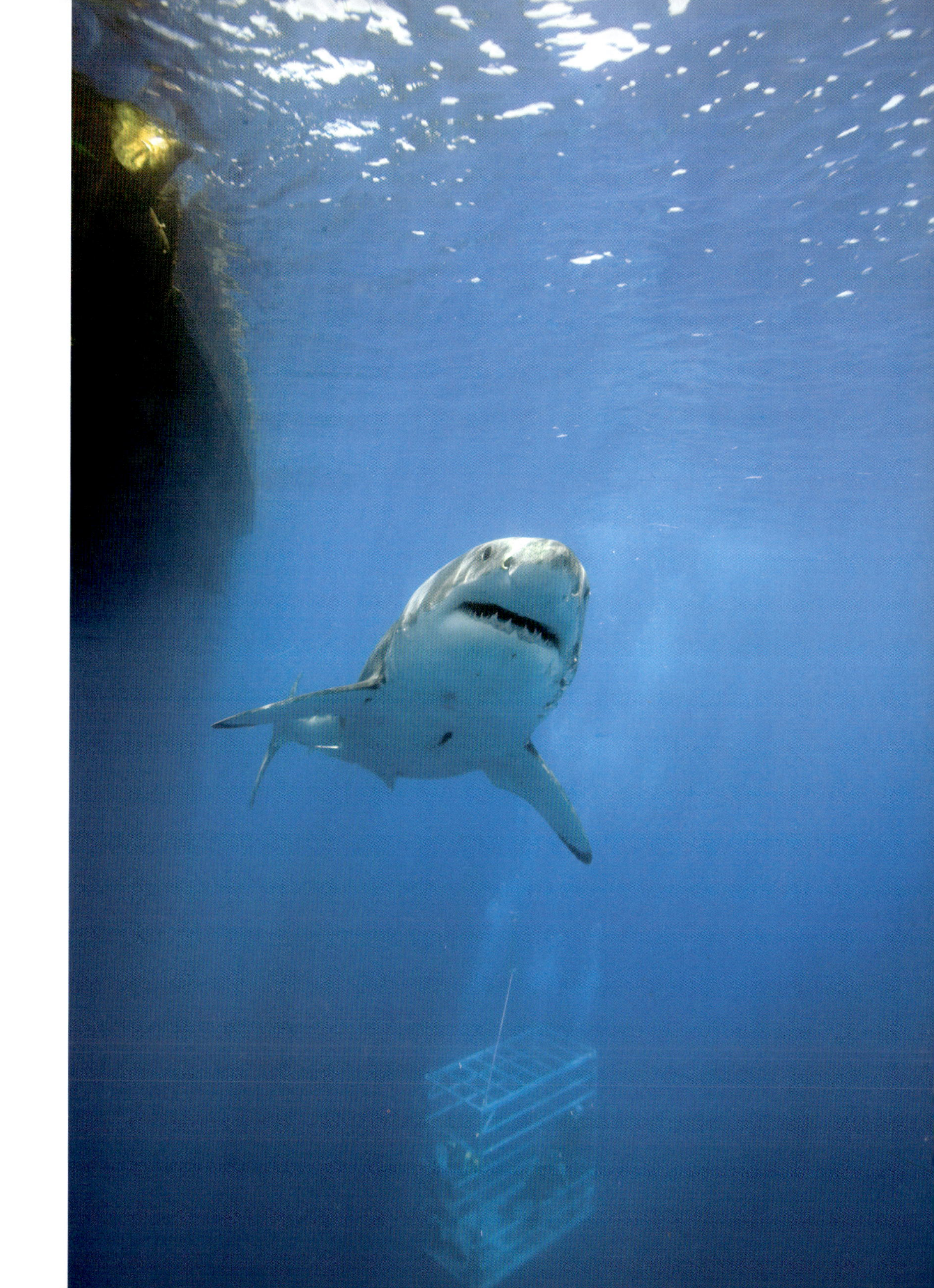

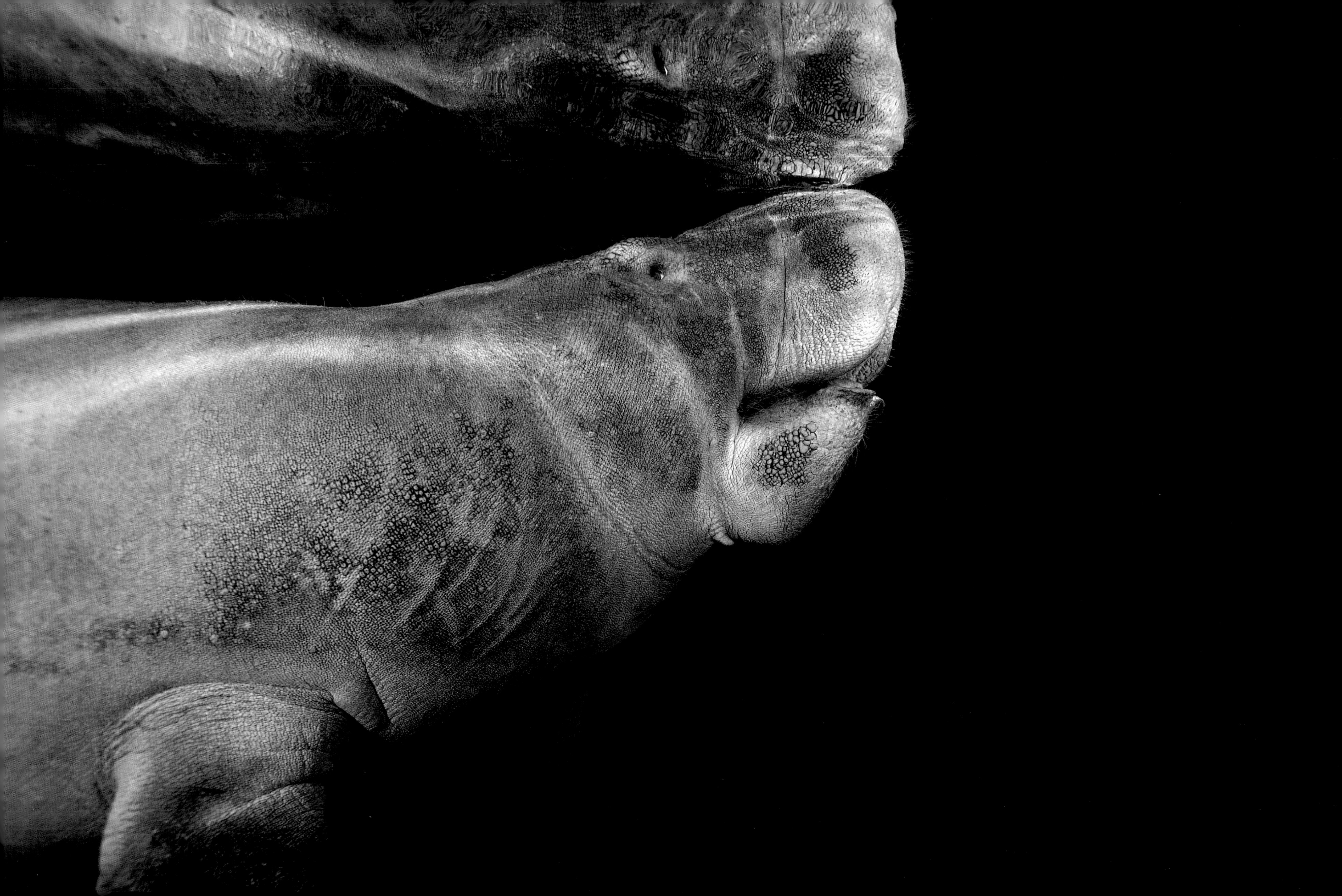

There will be moments in your life when a single photographic image will change everything you have read and heard about a subject. There may be a time when you will stop what you are doing to just earn a living and begin to live your dream.

The single image that determined the course of my life was Ansel Adams' "Moonrise over Hernandez" in black and white. I later viewed the photography of Ernst Hass, Ansel Adams, Armando Salas Portugal, and underwater photographers Lewis Marden and Hans Hass. If I could learn their techniques of exposure, development and working on the edge of light, I wondered: would I be able to make a visual statement of underseascapes to match Adam's style?
That was 45 years ago.

I had the good fortune to be born into a family of photographers. My grandmother was a portraitist in the early 1920s, my father a flower photographer in the 1940s and 50s and my uncle a landscape photographer. And, true to my heritage, my journey led me to combine a documentary art form with my love of the sea. Photography allowed me to share the feelings of peace and beauty that I had while diving. The ocean became the focus of my life. It was my playground with family, friends and students.

The magic of the photographic process is a painter's world where one can highlight the subject with the enduring spirit of life underwater. Just the other day a magnificent photograph arrived addressed to Ernie Brooks. It was a black and white image of a manatee touching the interface between water and air to create a mirror image of itself. Its eye contained a catch-light as if the photographer was a portraitist. Its unbroken reflection creates a feeling of serenity and portrays the gentleness of the creature. It takes the eye of an artist to capture this kind of moment. Before turning the image over to reveal the maker's signature, I noticed a compete tonal range of the twenty-one steps in photography from black to white. This photographer appeared to have studied the works of my mentors. The signature was Wyland and the event was to honor environmental awareness through educational programs, public art projects and a world of ocean awareness. It had a graceful stroke of a pen signed just Wyland. The image touched my heart.

Photography is in its truest sense, painting with light. *Visions of the Sea* focuses on the rebirth of the remarkable marine artist Wyland as a fine art nature photographer. His new canvas is unlike the old — not a white material stretched flat over a framework bordered by staples. Rather, it is a black, limitless framework awaiting the precious light of day. That same light that illuminates his well-known oil and acrylic artworks is now found in his masterful underwater photography.

There are few artists in our world who can create masterful paintings, sculptures, and now photographic canvases that reflect the true values

within our seas. I have known the artworks of Wyland for many years and have admired his endless drive to bring awareness of the beauty and richness of the ocean to all people.

Wyland entertained our hearts with his Whaling Wall projects around the world. As a fine art nature photographer, *Visions of the Sea* is his statement. A look at the world through his eyes.

Visions of the Sea comes at a critical moment, when we urgently need to look inside the water column and witness the life beneath its surface to realize that its beauty and onetime bounty are under assault. What were once resilient communities have been pummeled to near extinction. Here, photography is the reflection of the fragile beauty that remains. In this century of greater awareness, preservation and sustainable harvest are essential. We must act globally to end the destructive practices that destroy and stress our marine environments. Our own survival depends upon it. Wyland's work reminds us of the invaluable treasures we must maintain.

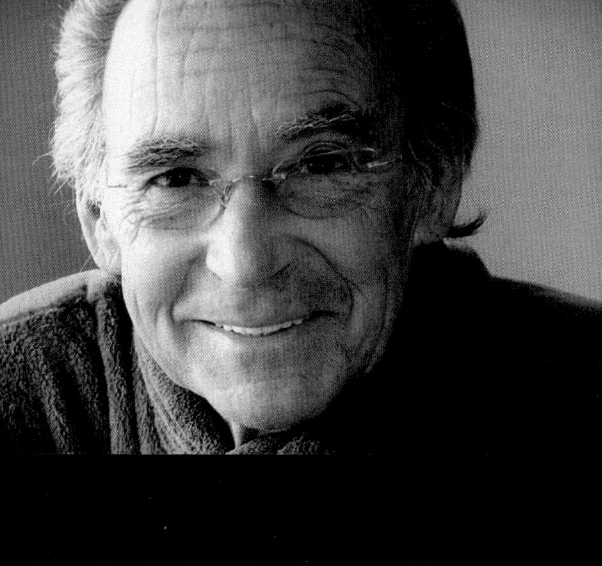

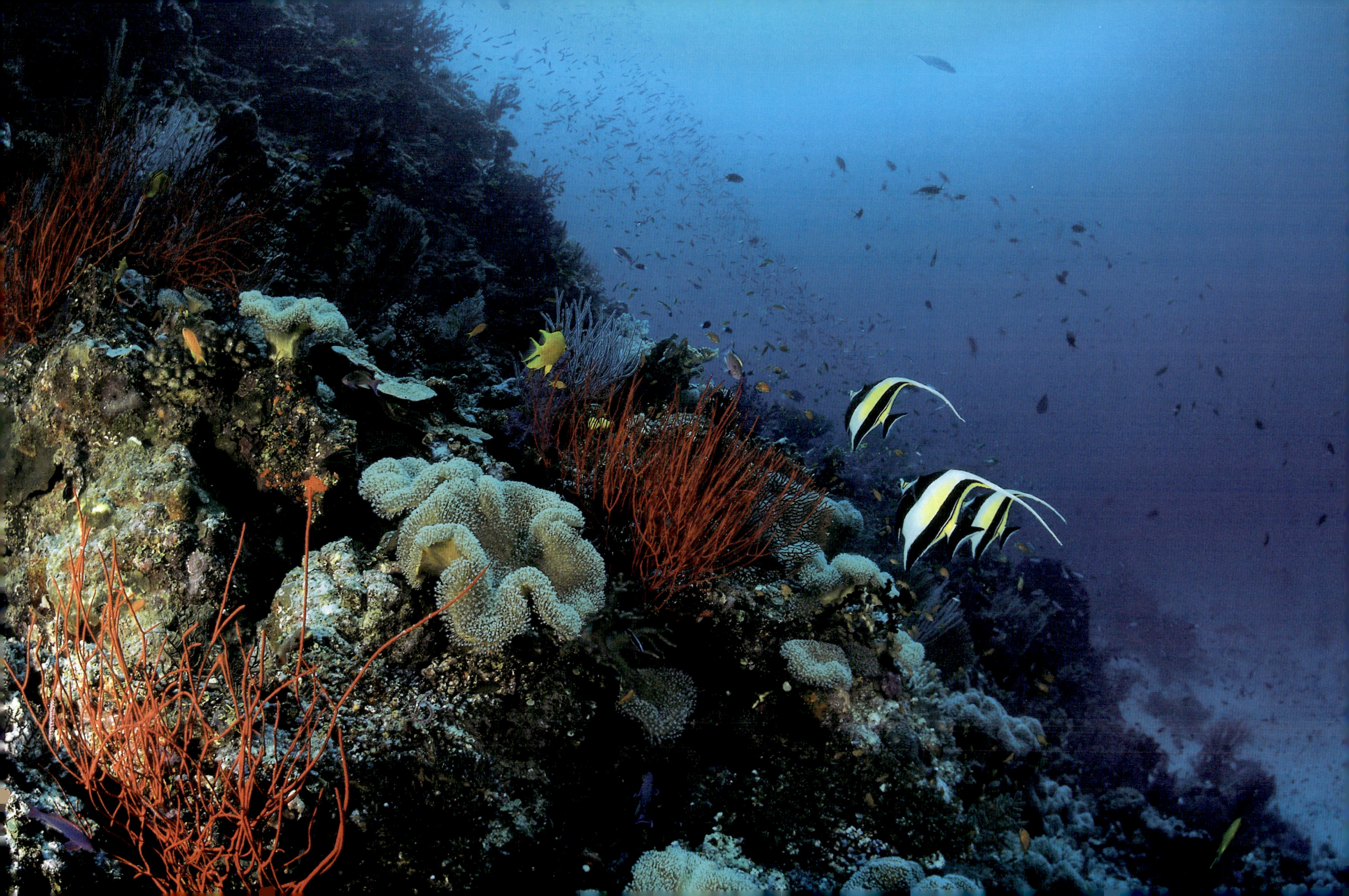

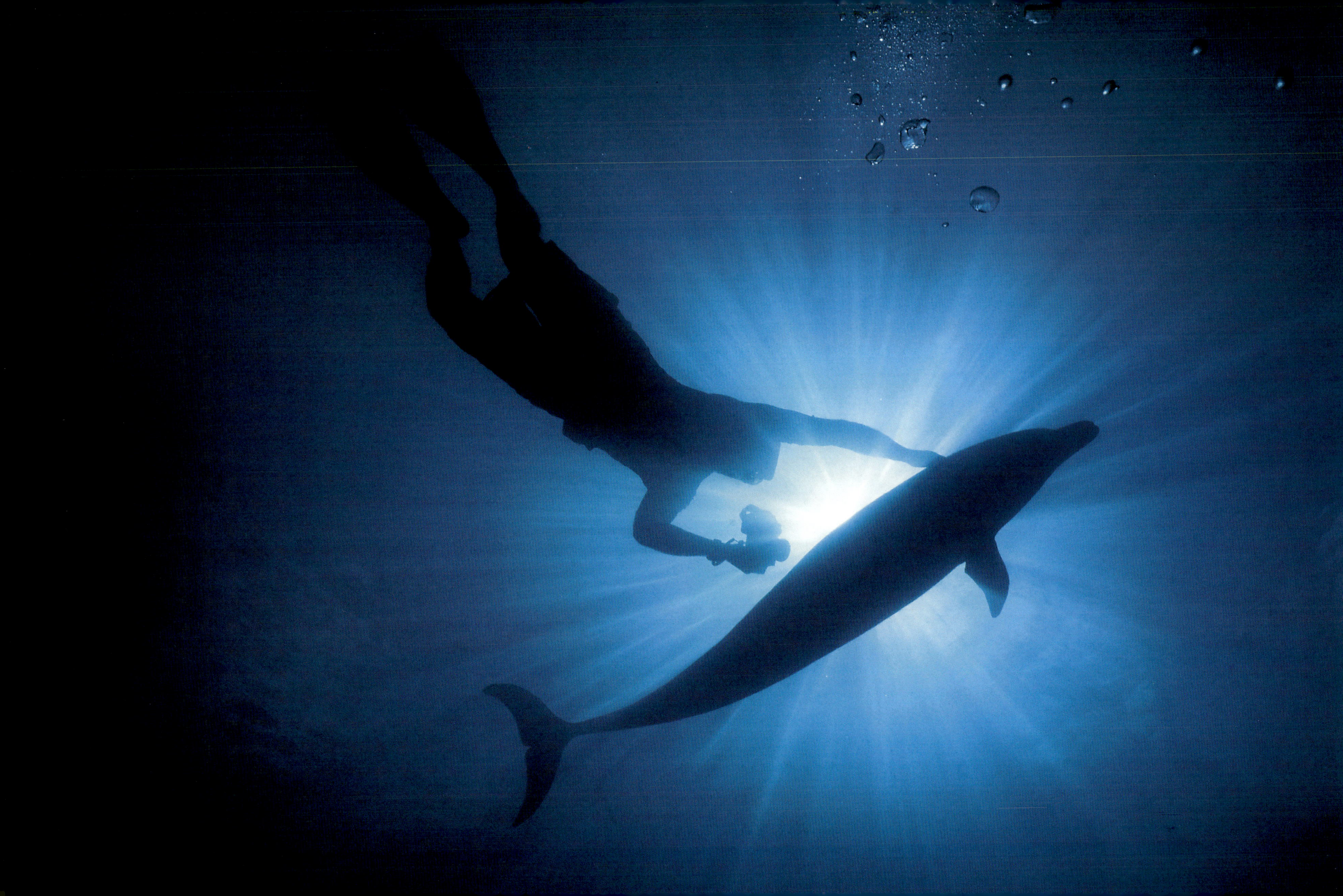

Wyland the artist paints fast. Amazingly, he has little fear of the most frustrating thing in this universe — a blank canvas. He plants his blue and white surfer sneakers in a wide, powerful stance and uses his whole body to paint. I have seen him complete a more formal painting on a 10-foot canvas in less than four hours. Blue whales that are the actual size of blue whales take slightly longer. Some of my favorite works are his ink and paper line drawings. It's wonderful to watch him capture the essence of a creature with a single thick brush stroke.

Wyland paints "with his mind's eye". He knows his subjects intimately because he spends time with them in the sea. He swims with the great whales, peers at Butterfly fish, and drifts in silence with manatees. Unknown to many, he has also photographed for the last two decades. He has made pictures in color and black and white. For a photographer the most difficult thing to capture is the drama of light as it works its way through the sea. For a painter the most difficult thing to recreate on canvas is water itself, not just the color, but also its texture, its very viscous, emotional feel.

An artist can bend time, add or subtract itinerant creatures and gracefully manipulate light and mood. An artist can put an inner dream onto a piece of canvas and control reality. A photographer swims though the sea, and instead of a brush he swims with an underwater camera housing sometimes fitted with spider crab arms that hold mallet-sized strobes. The photographic contraption is the size of a mini-microwave and, as such, swims like an underwater lawn mower. The underwater photographer is supposed to pirouette with the athletic grace of a sea lion and capture the magic that is the decisive moment.

Wyland the photographer swims through the sea floating and dreaming. The blue world becomes his floating studio and he often uses natural light, liberating him to move with fluid gesture like his subjects. His pictures are like his canvas, strong and dreamlike images that stand alone as superb photographs. They are not pre-sketches or visual exercises for his paintings or sculptures. All of Wyland's skill, his ability to paint water and light, as well as capture gestures and subtle movements of whales and sea creatures, and record the dancing shadows and light of the sea are incorporated into his photographs. On dry land these memories and moments in the sea transfer with consummate skill from Wyland's eye to his mind, arm, brush and finally from his brush to canvas or brick.

A photograph produced by a photographer is a formal affair. It captures truth at a precise moment in time with all of the attendant atmosphere. Wyland, the artist and photographer is not bound by eons of technical photographic constraints that photographers carry with them into the sea – as an artist he allows himself to enjoy the gift of visual freedom. Wyland's photographs have become stepping-stones towards his personal vision of the sea.

One hundred years ago the human vision of our planet's undersea universe was very Victorian. It was a world of ornate mythology. There were mermaids, sunken ships with skeletons at the helm and tattered sails blowing in the current. Since humans have been going underwater and looking through diving masks we have discovered

an absolute truth: Reality in the sea is more bizarre and beautiful than the edge of Victorian imagination.

Even though human vision underwater is less than three generations old we have had to bear witness to the destruction of our oceans. The teeming fish populations have collapsed, sharks have vanished from much of the world's oceans, coral reefs struggle for survival in the constantly warming tropical seas. Whales and dolphins once protected are pursued once again. The pictures that Wyland has made — and will make — are a living treatise of a time and place that we may not be able to preserve.

Swimming underwater in a clear ocean is one of the great joys of our planet. We glide over coral reefs and hang motionless against the blue canvas of the open sea. With weightless grace the largest and most elegant creatures on earth, the great whales, move across this infinite stage. As humans in the oceans our first job is to record, then later to interpret. Wyland's photography does this, illuminating old dreams and new visions.

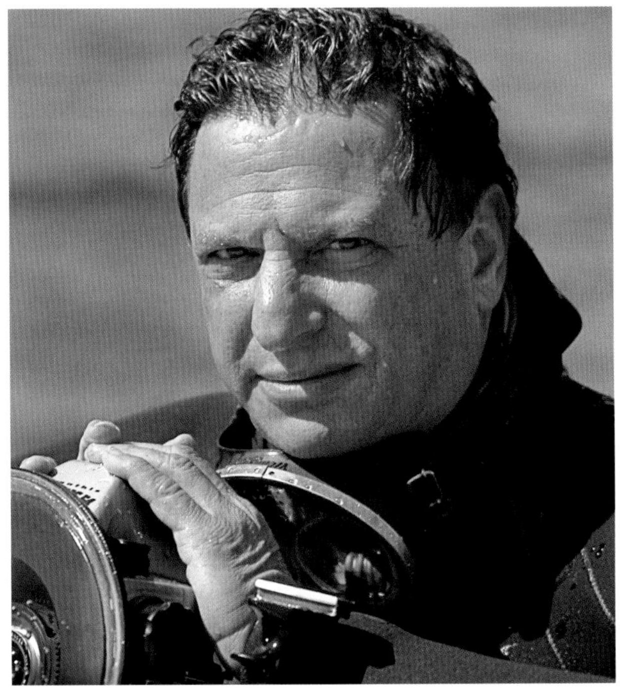

◄ David Doubliet
▶ great white shark encounter

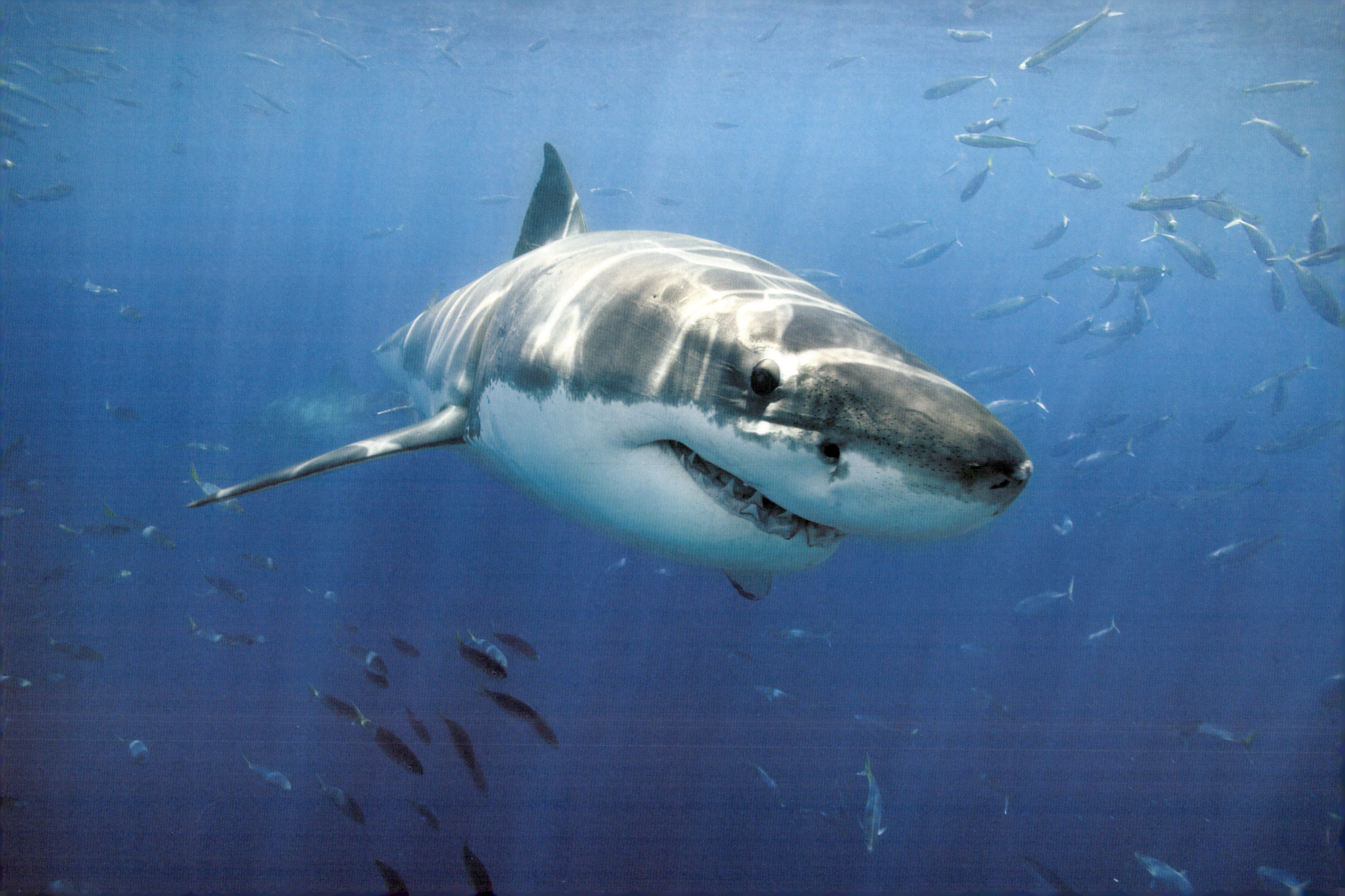

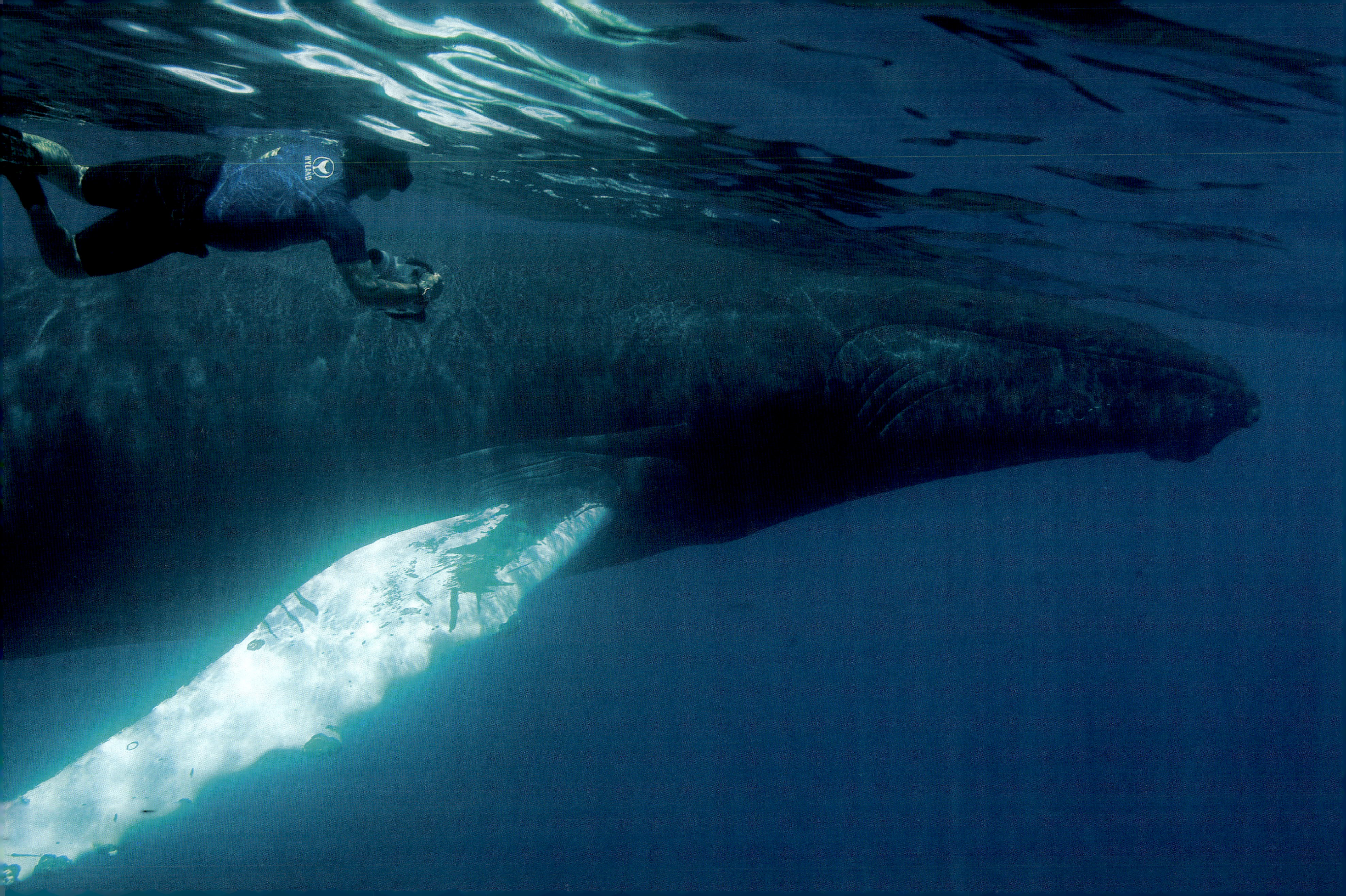

When I first saw her, I fell in love. Her beauty and spirit captivated me. We first met in Southern California when I was fourteen. I had dreamt of her for many years and was introduced to her by ocean icon Jacques Yves Cousteau. I had admired her beauty from afar, and now I was finally going to get a chance to see her face to face. Our first meeting took place in the beautiful coastal town of Laguna Beach, California. It was a sunny day, and I raced towards her and leapt into her embrace. It was widescreen, epic. Like a romantic movie. But, for me, it was real. My heart was pounding, and I felt reborn. At last, we joined, and it has been a love affair that has continued to this day.

The Pacific Ocean changed my life that fateful day. Ironically, the ocean — as she often does — revealed something magical and mysterious: two gray whales broke the surface in front of me. It was as if two dinosaurs suddenly appeared, the spray reaching toward the heavens, the barnacle encrusted backs, everything in slow motion. The flukes raised high above the surface with water cascading off their glistening tails. They were gone in a moment. But they live forever in my mind.

I often say that if you see a whale you are somehow changed. The sea embraced me and then shared one of her secrets. And this first encounter forever inspired me to love her and dedicate my art to her preservation.

I first began learning of the ocean and its amazing marine life in the early 1970s. I dived into libraries, watched the *Undersea World of Jacques Cousteau*, and listened to his wisdom and inspiration about conservation. I, too, felt like he did. And I also felt **strongly that art could play a role in protecting the**

◄ humpback whale photographer

oceans and life in the sea. Later, I began diving and swimming with great whales, getting close to them in their natural habitat. Seeing the whales in the buoyant sea changed my view of them and my art forever. Great whales swim gracefully and effortlessly. They have no fear of man. And in my personal encounters, I have felt their presence and spirit as they looked deep into my eyes and shared their world … if even for a small time. Did they sense that I was there to share their beauty and world with people? I may never know. But one thing is for sure: the whales allowed me to observe their beauty so that I may later share it through my art.

For the last twenty-five years, I have had the honor of photographing some of the most spectacular aquatic animals on the planet. Many of the encounters were rare and unique. And through sheer luck and timing I have been able to capture nature's wonders. I like to use my underwater camera as a paint brush, capturing the light, color, and subject. Fine art nature photography and underwater images are painted with light. And artists must compose each shot to reflect their vision of the sea. For me, I prefer to be a barnacle on a whale – and let the marine life become curious to this new aquatic species … me.

This approach is called a "Soft-In-Water" encounter and after these animals acclimate to you and decide that you are not a threat, many times they become curious and swim right over to you. That is when you get the best images. It is also a matter of respect. Everyone knows when you chase an animal, it just moves away from you. I have always found it better to do the opposite. After some time, you become part of the environment, and the animals decide that you are not a threat and go on about their lives

My greatest encounter was probably in the Sea of Cortez with a 90-foot blue whale that had been feeding on clouds of krill. This incredible animal swam just below me, turned ever so slightly, then disappeared into the deep. Very few people on earth have swam with a blue whale. And I felt compelled to paint a life-size portrait of the earth's greatest giant on canvas, the very next day.

Behind the lens
Technology has developed amazing digital cameras and underwater housings. I have been shooting the Canon EOS IDs Mark II, with a sea cam housing

and laser strobes. I use an 8 gigabyte card and each of the images are 16.7 million megapixels – a far superior alternative, in my mind, to the 35 millimeter films before. It also allows me to shoot 444 shots in one dive. In the old days, I used a Nikonos V and RS. This only allowed me to take 36 images on color slides. Most of my early photography was achieved in this way, but like most photographers today, those cameras are in a drawer somewhere. For me, it's all digital, and shooting in raw files offers many artistic options to manipulate images in your own style.

I have admired the great underwater photography of Hans Hass, who created some of the first underwater images using the cameras he invented. His images still hold up. I had a chance to meet him a few years ago and tell him how much his photography inspired my art. We immediately became fast friends. Great photographers like David Doubilet, Ernie Brooks, Bob Talbot, Chris Newbert, Jim Watt, and many others have elevated the art form to a new level. In fact, it was only in the last fifteen years or so that there has ever been an underwater photograph of a living blue whale. Each year the photography seems to get better.

Of course, technology has helped, but it is still the photographer-artist who captures the ultimate image that has elevated the art form. One of the greatest today is National Geographic photographer-in-residence David Doubilet. I have admired David's photography for over thirty years and consider him one of the great artists of the 21st century. Ernie Brooks who I consider the Ansel Adams of underwater photography creates distinctive images that have a style that he has pioneered.

In no way, would I ever try to compete against such masters, but as an artist I have a unique way of seeing nature above and below the surface painting the images with my camera and sometimes adding to them with a brush. I have the luxury of using artistic license with my photography. I hope everyone will enjoy the images as much as I enjoyed creating them, and I hope this book will inspire generations to come to appreciate our aquatic world and find a way to help preserve it for the future.

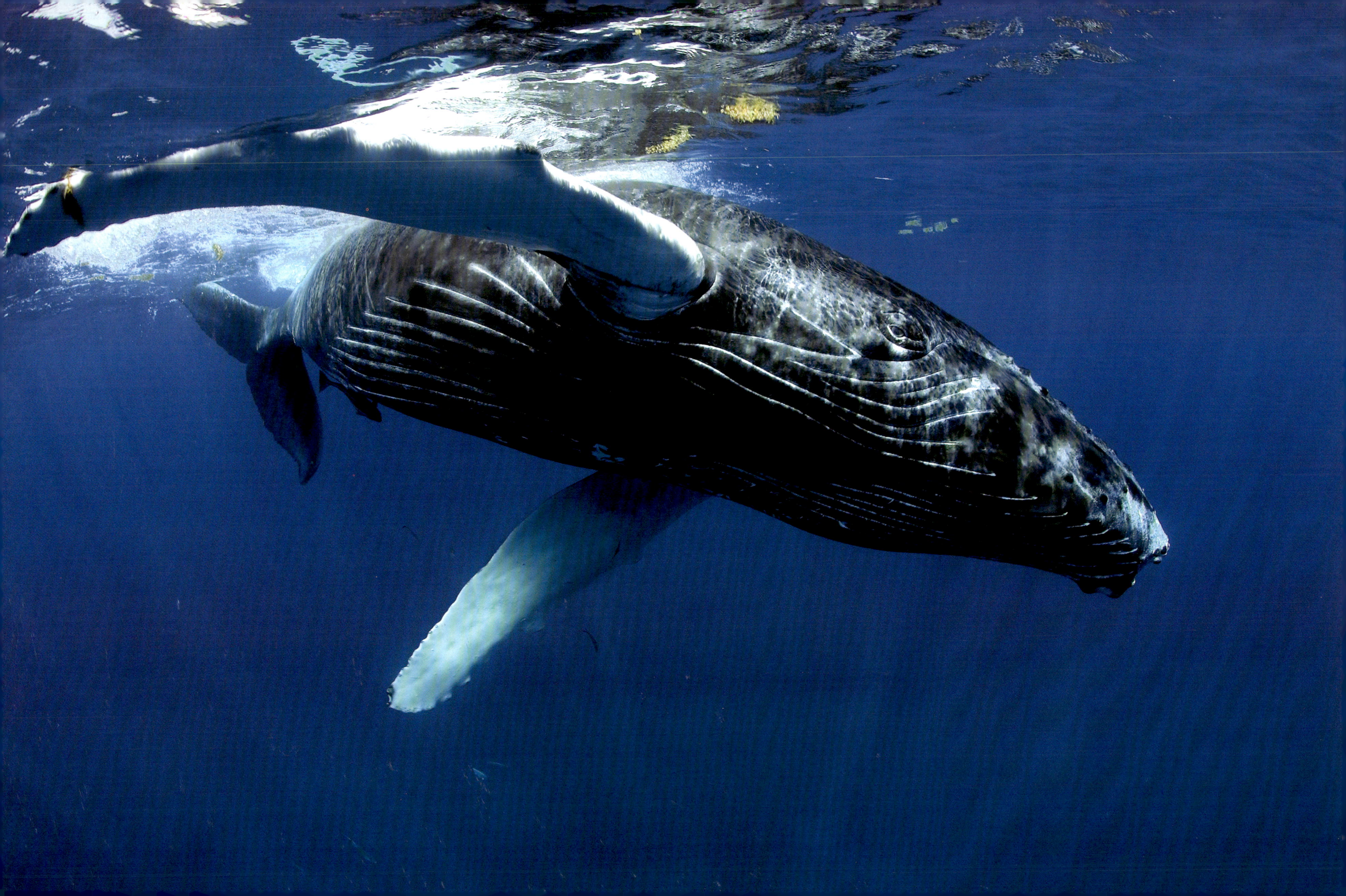

Anyone who has a passion for photography knows the feeling when they have captured a moment that will live forever. Nature provides us with an incredible array of dramatic scene — endless colors, animals large and small, and habitats so pristine and beautiful, they leave you breathless. Artists are sometimes given a rare gift to see a painted image unfold before them. The challenge is trying to capture that image, or as I like to say, paint it with our cameras in very short span of time. Often, it is a combination of many things — and a lot of luck — to get that perfect image.

My favorite part of photographing animals and wild places is when an animal decides you are not a threat and approaches you on its own terms. American Indians have told me that being eye-to-eye with a bald eagle is the highest level of consciousness. I believe, in the same way, that a person can reach that state by being eye-to-eye with a great whale. It has inspired me to dedicate my art and life to sharing the beauty of our planet with everyone, and my hope that the undersea colors captured here may inspire a new generation.

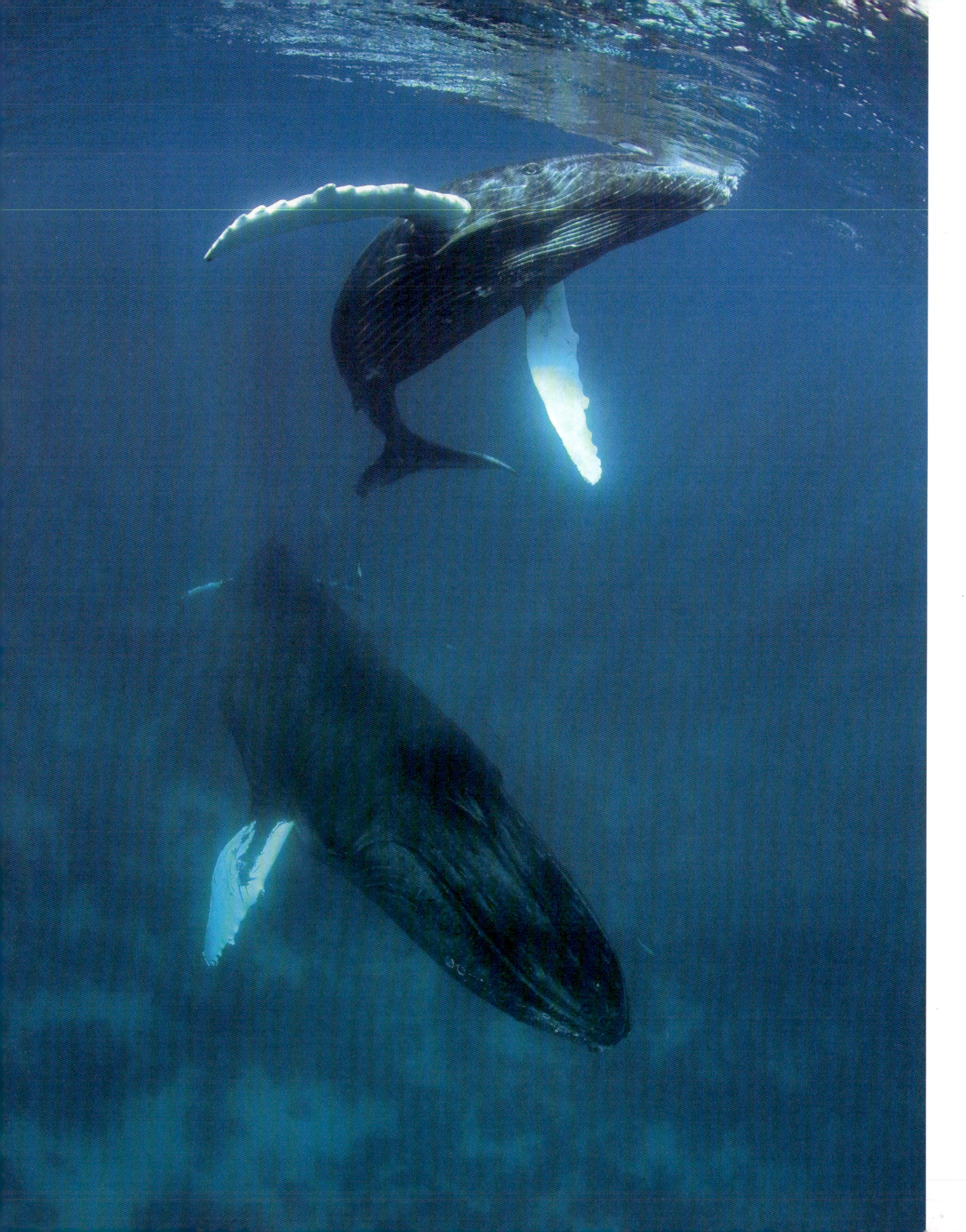

◀ mother and calf
▶ endangered green sea turtle

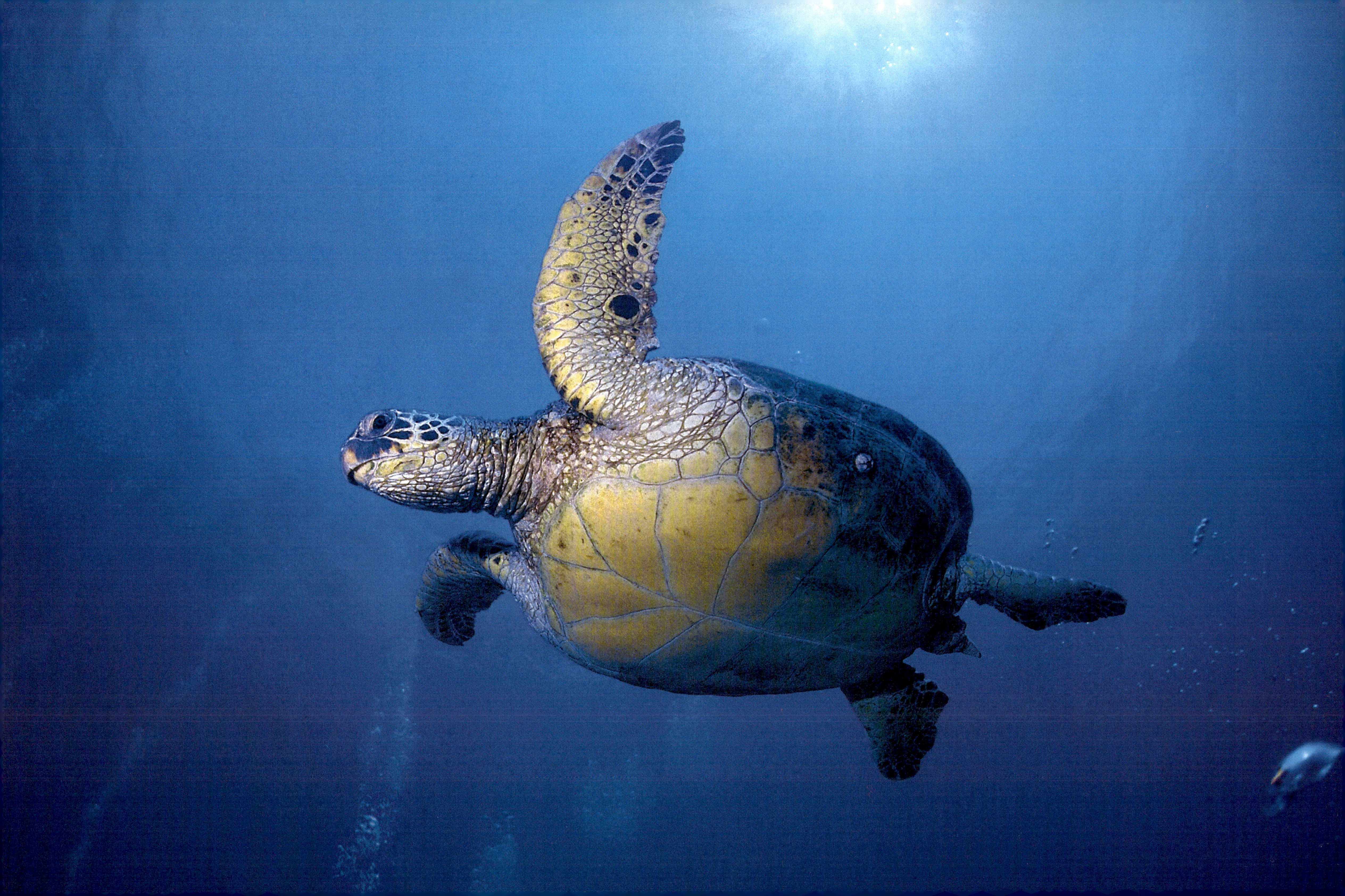

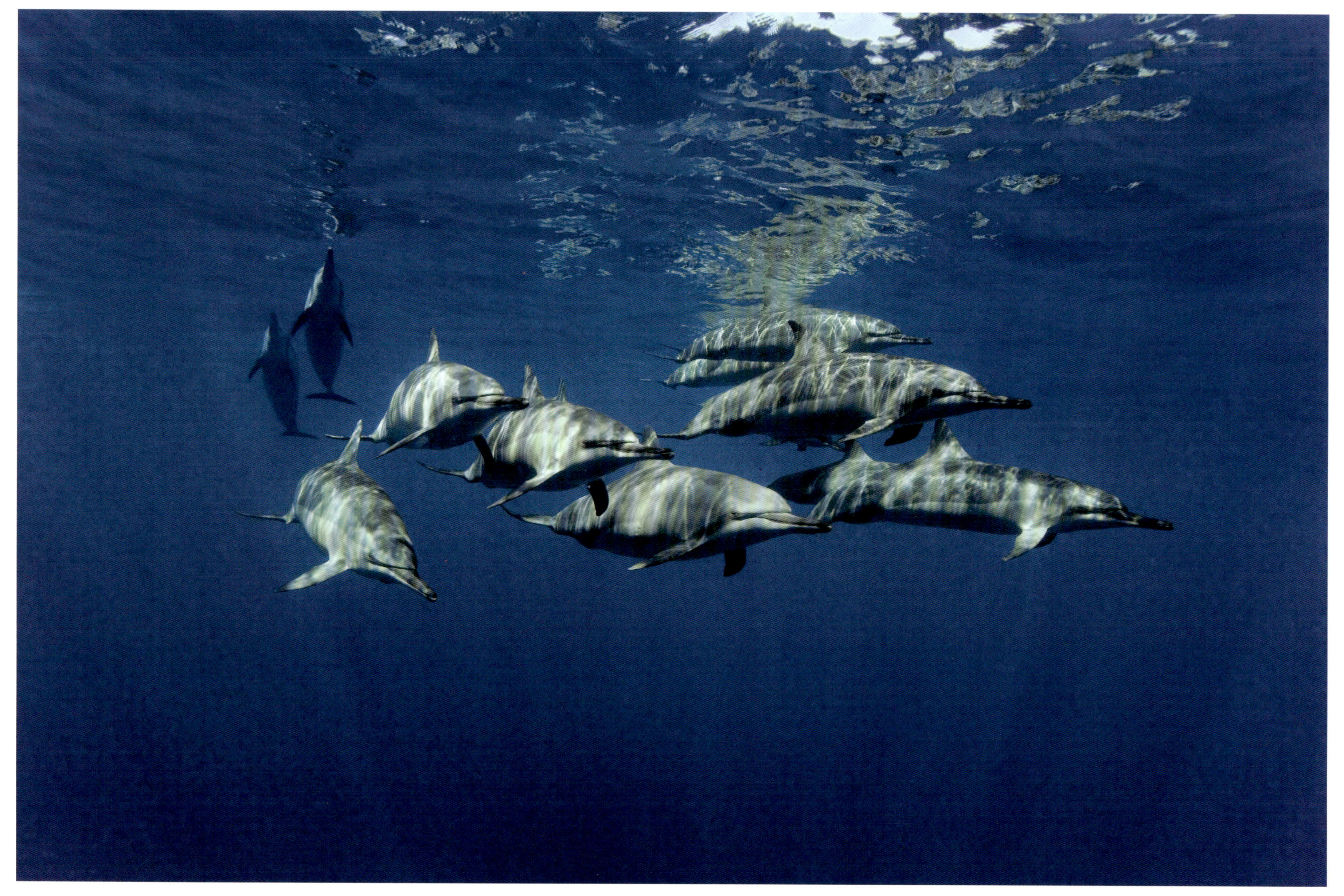

◀ spinner encounter
▶ giant breaching

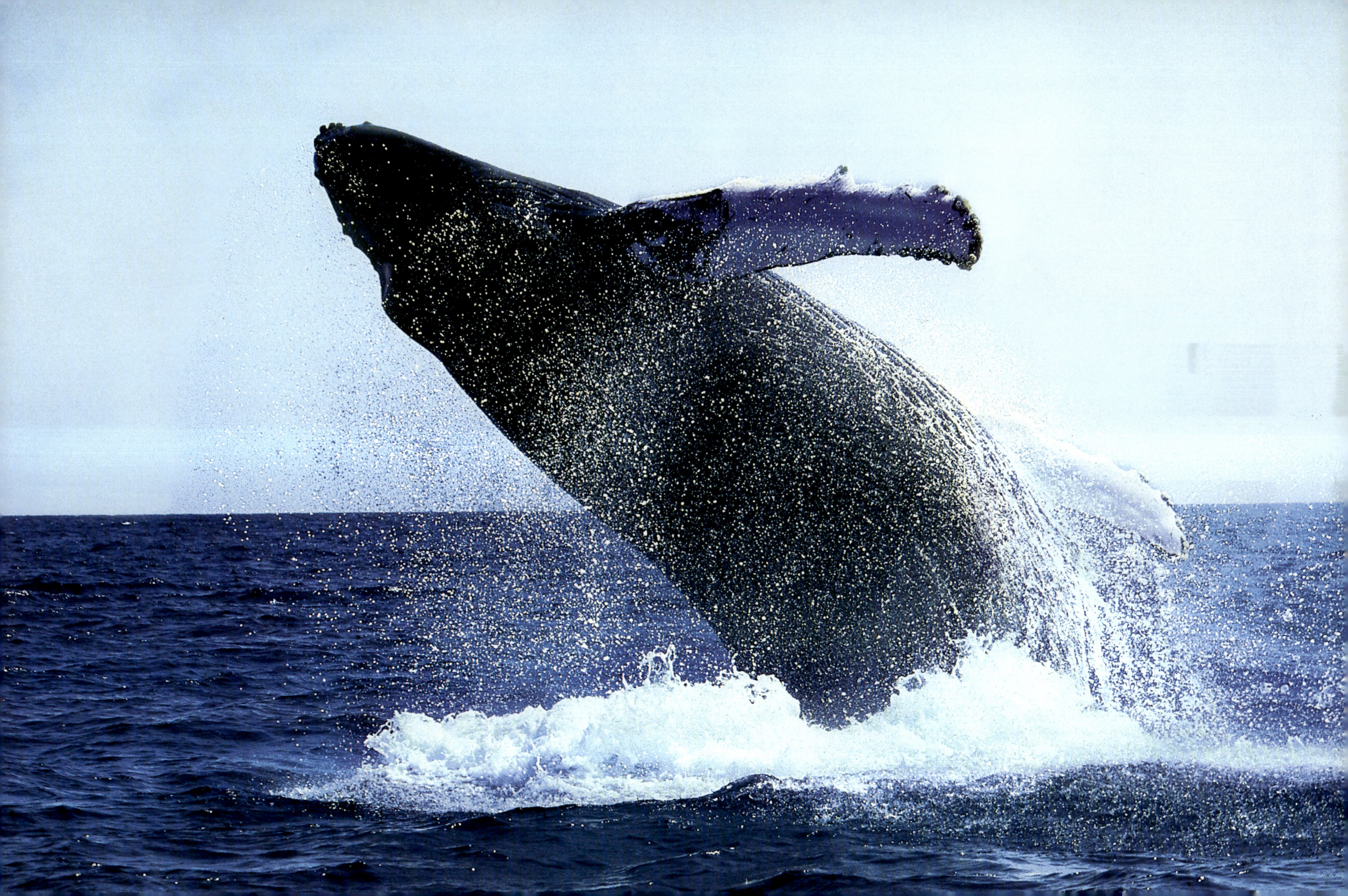

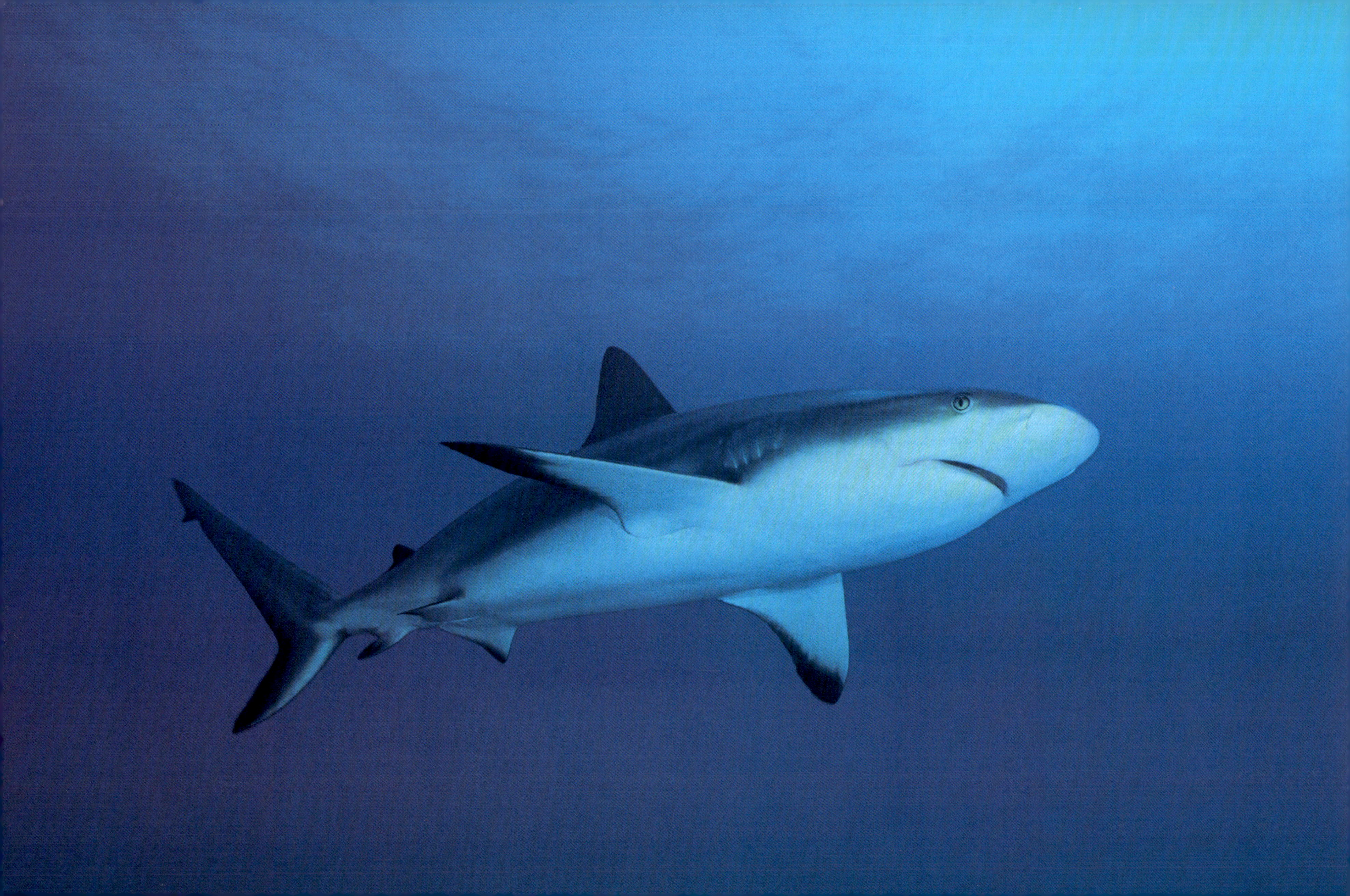

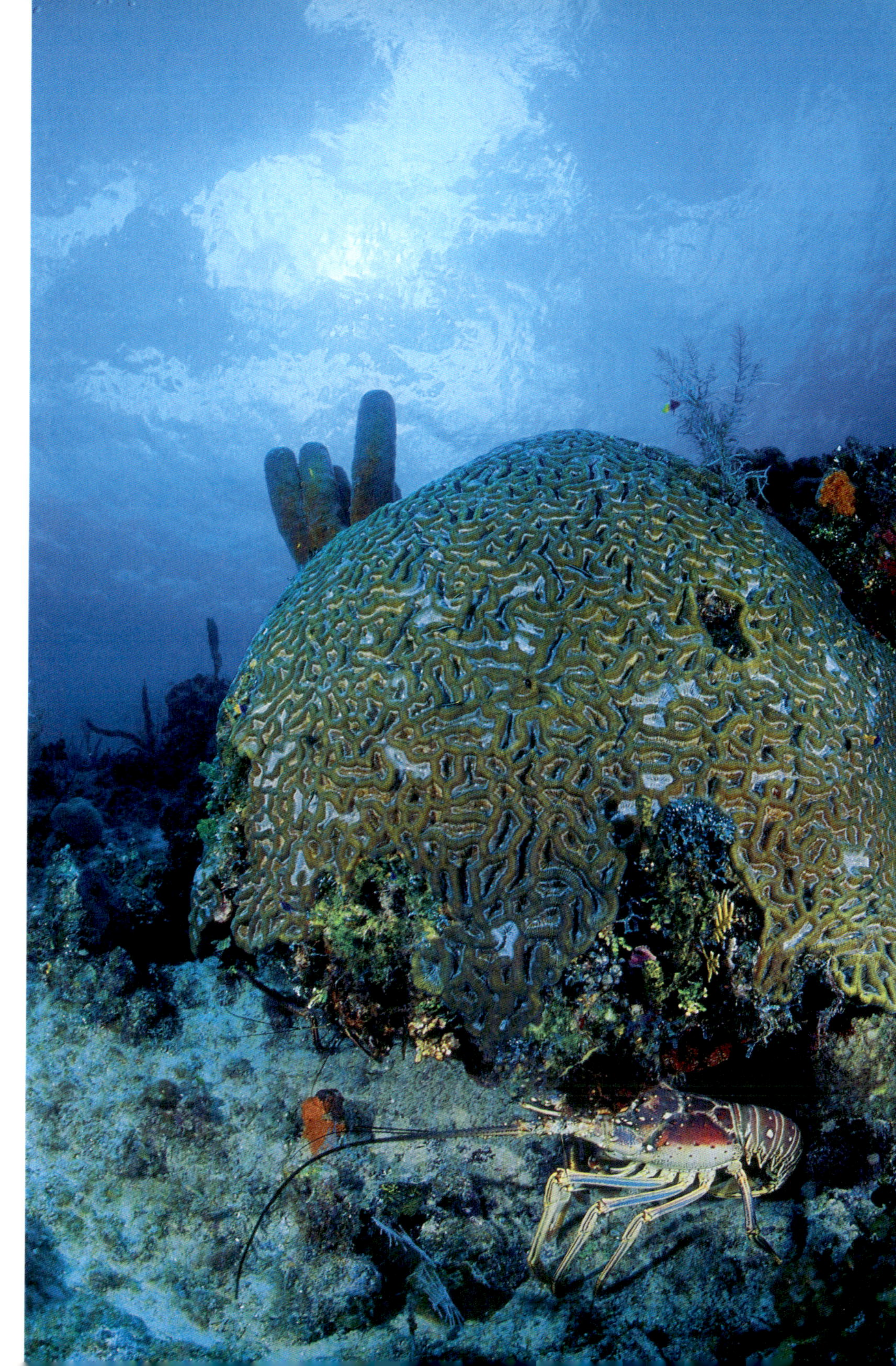

shark sea
reef bug

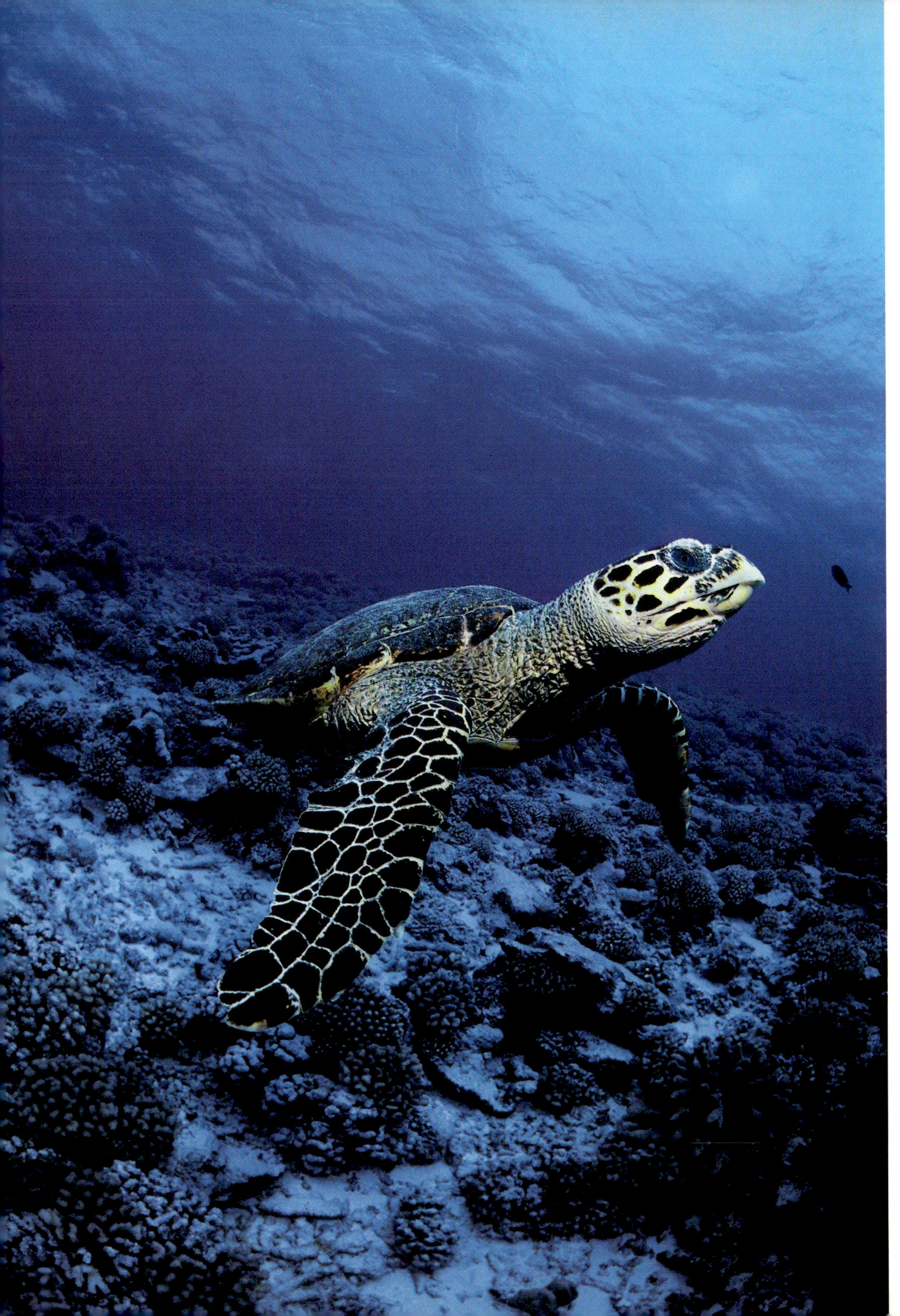

hawksbill reef
lion of the reef

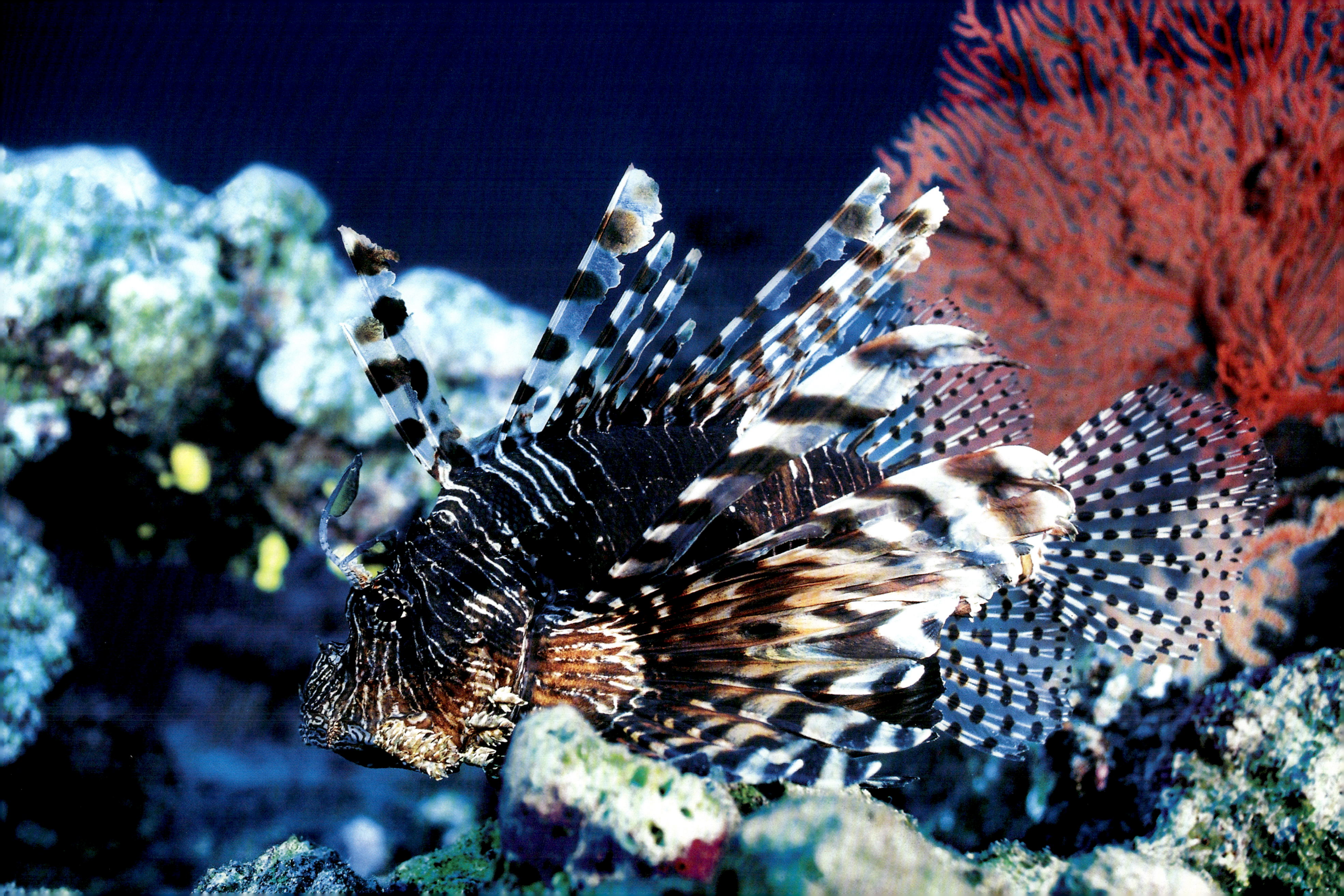

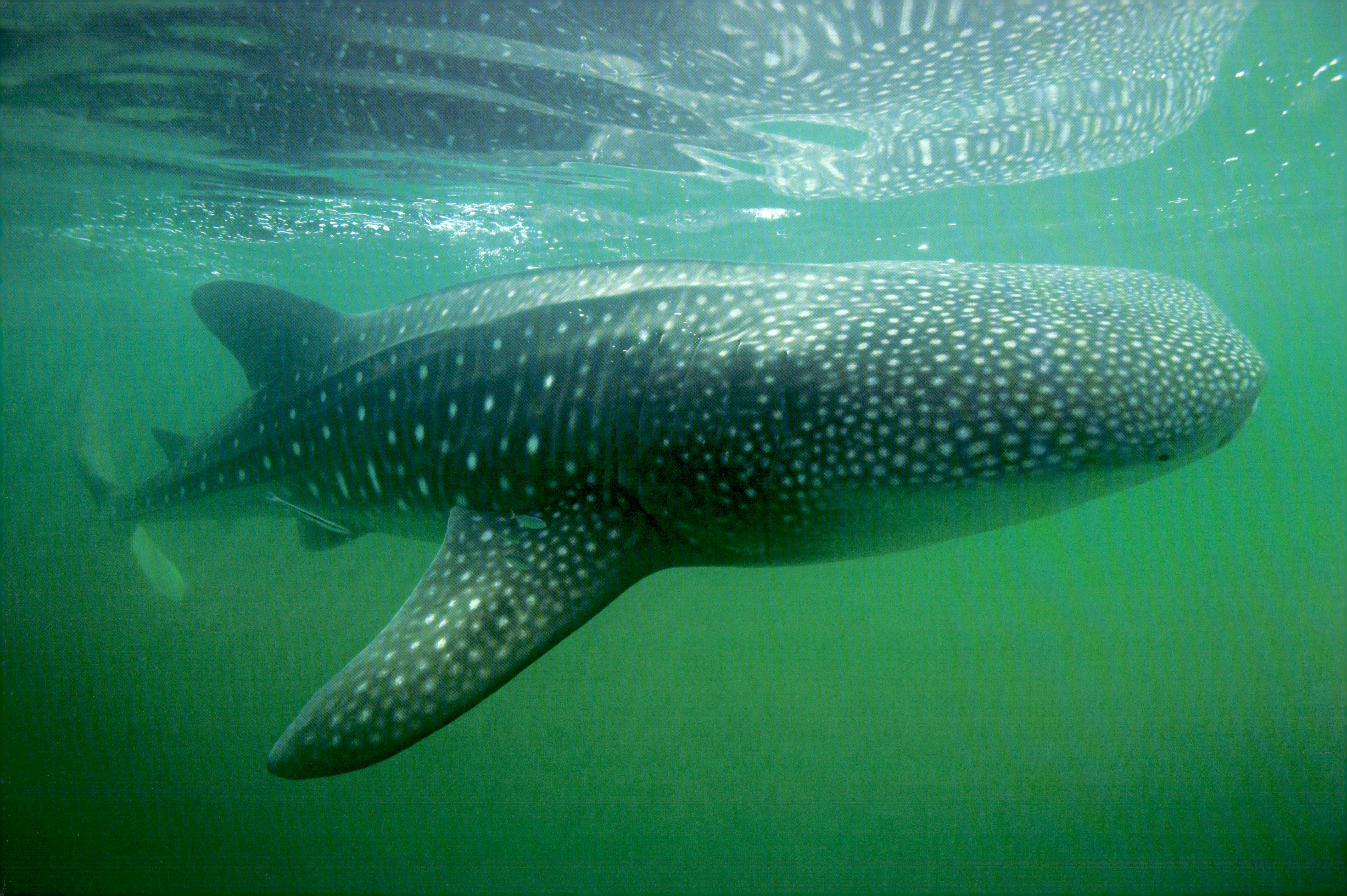

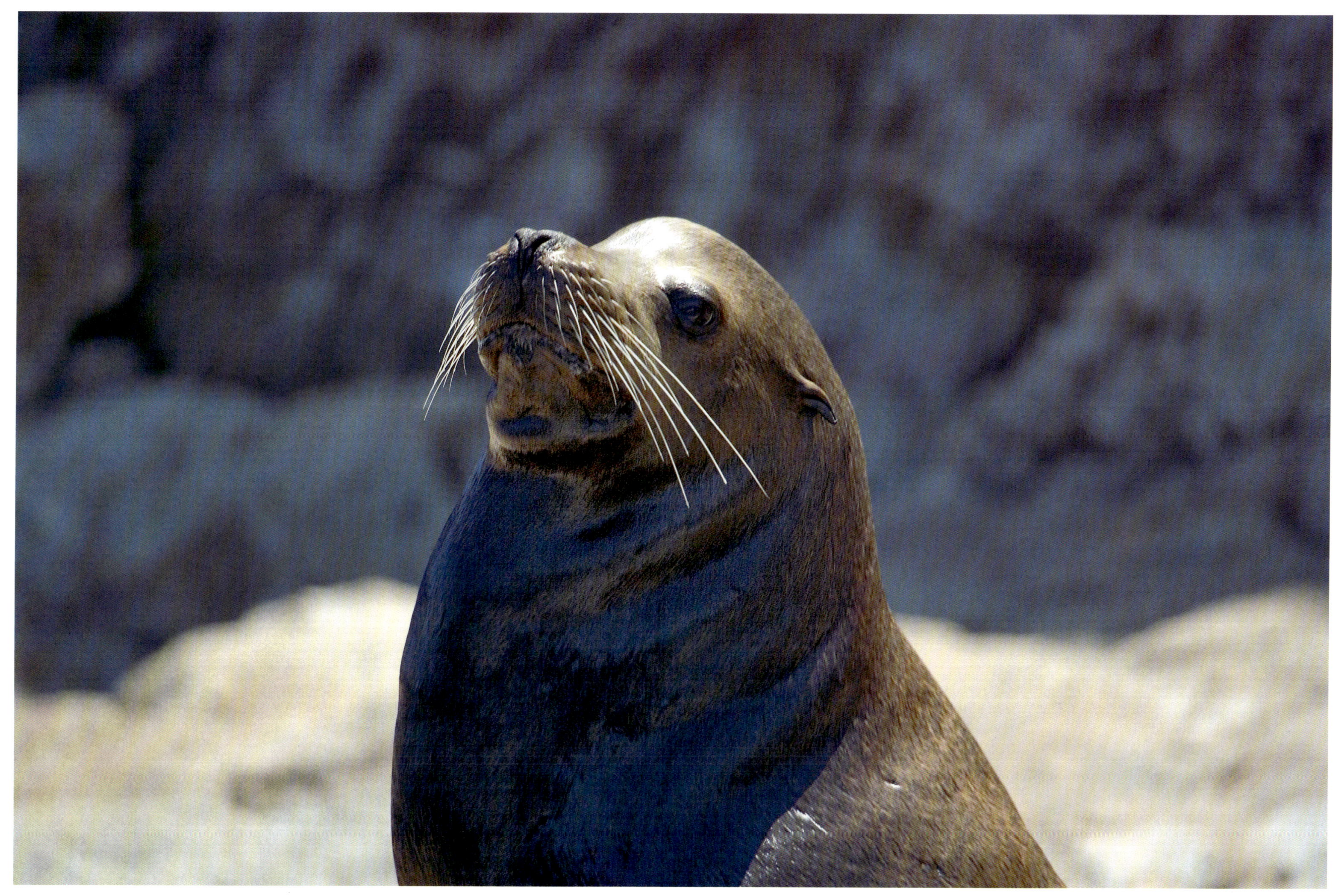

◄ gentle whale shark
► bull sea lion

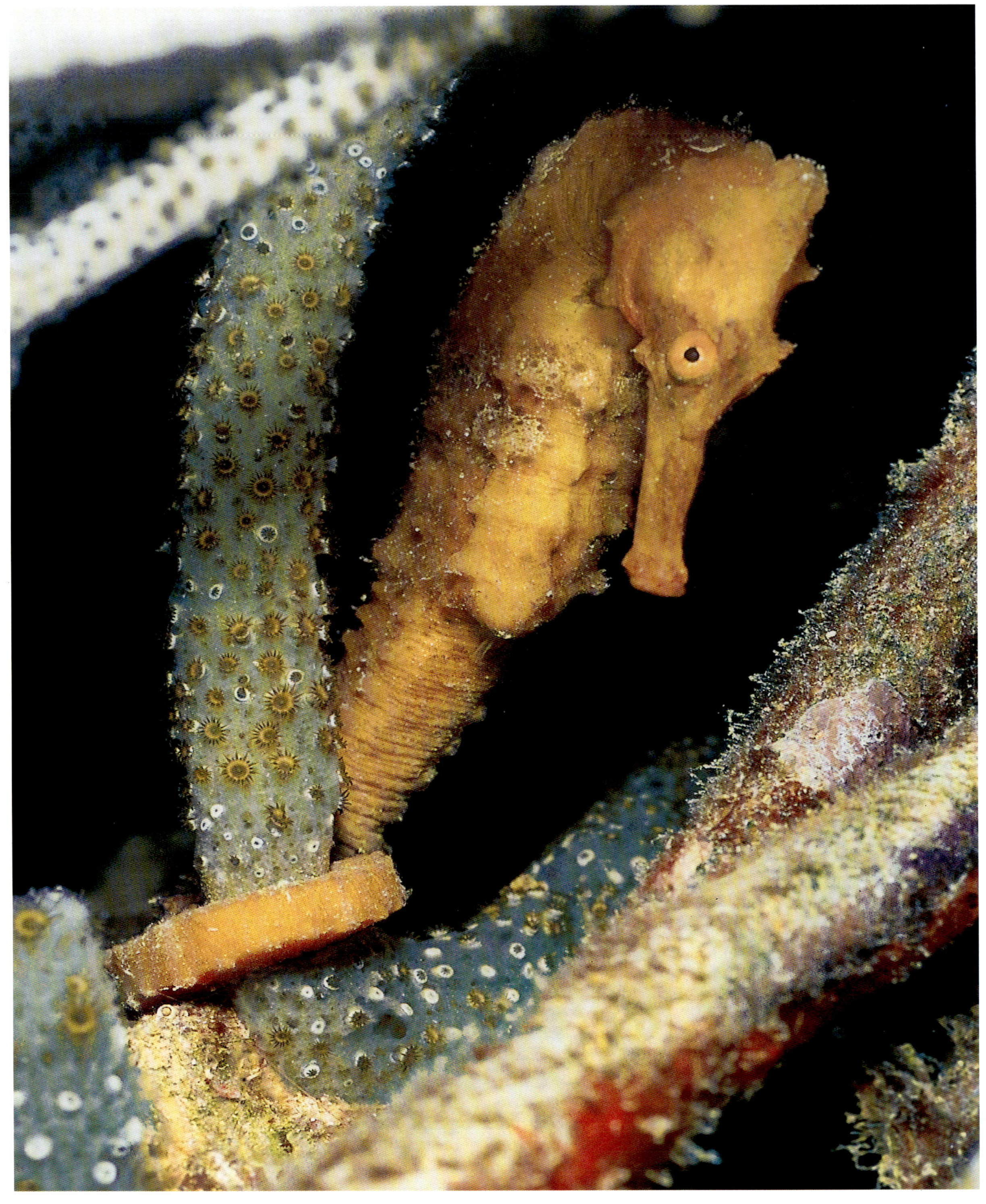

◄ sea horse reef
► sea horse soft coral

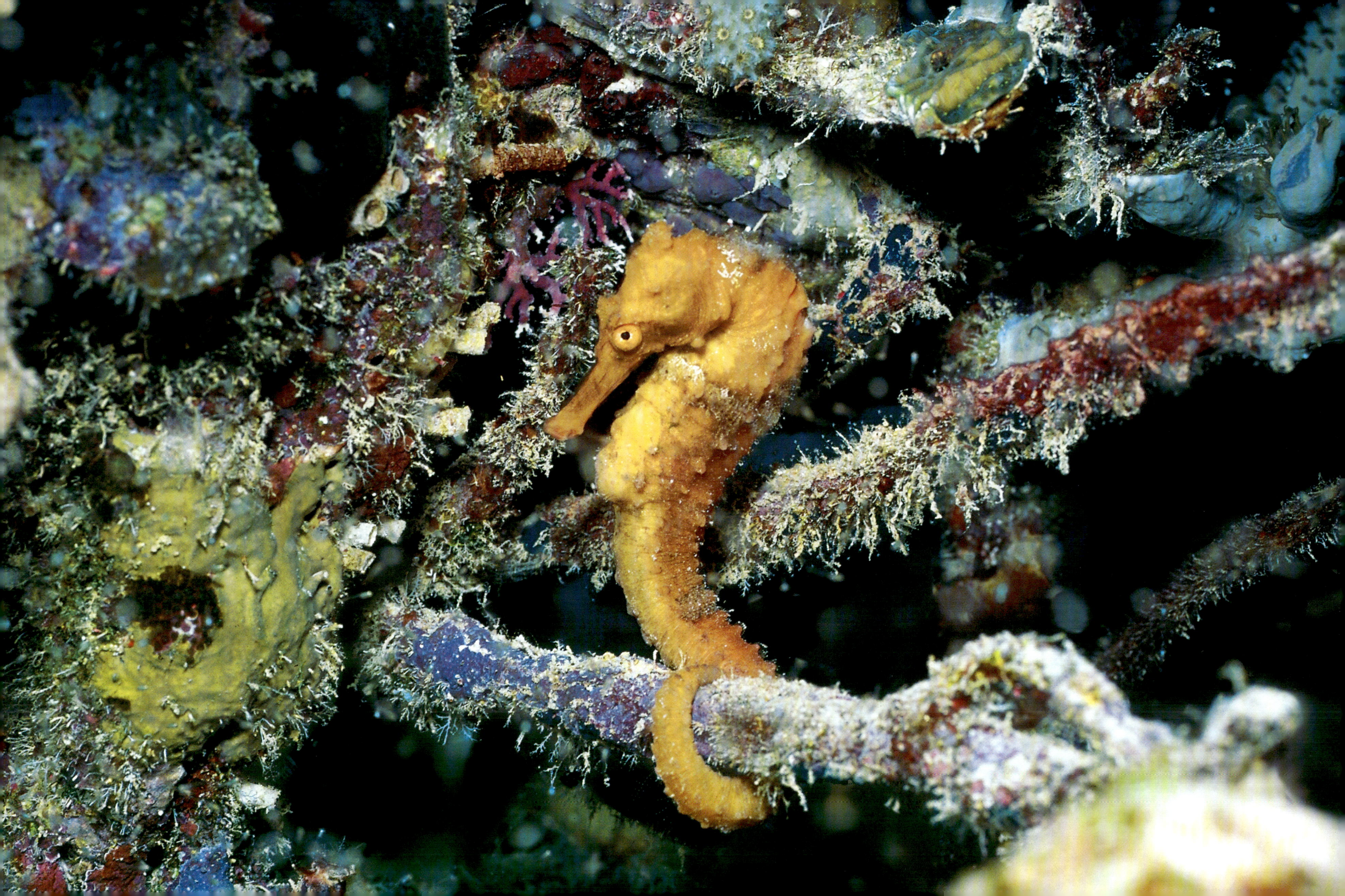

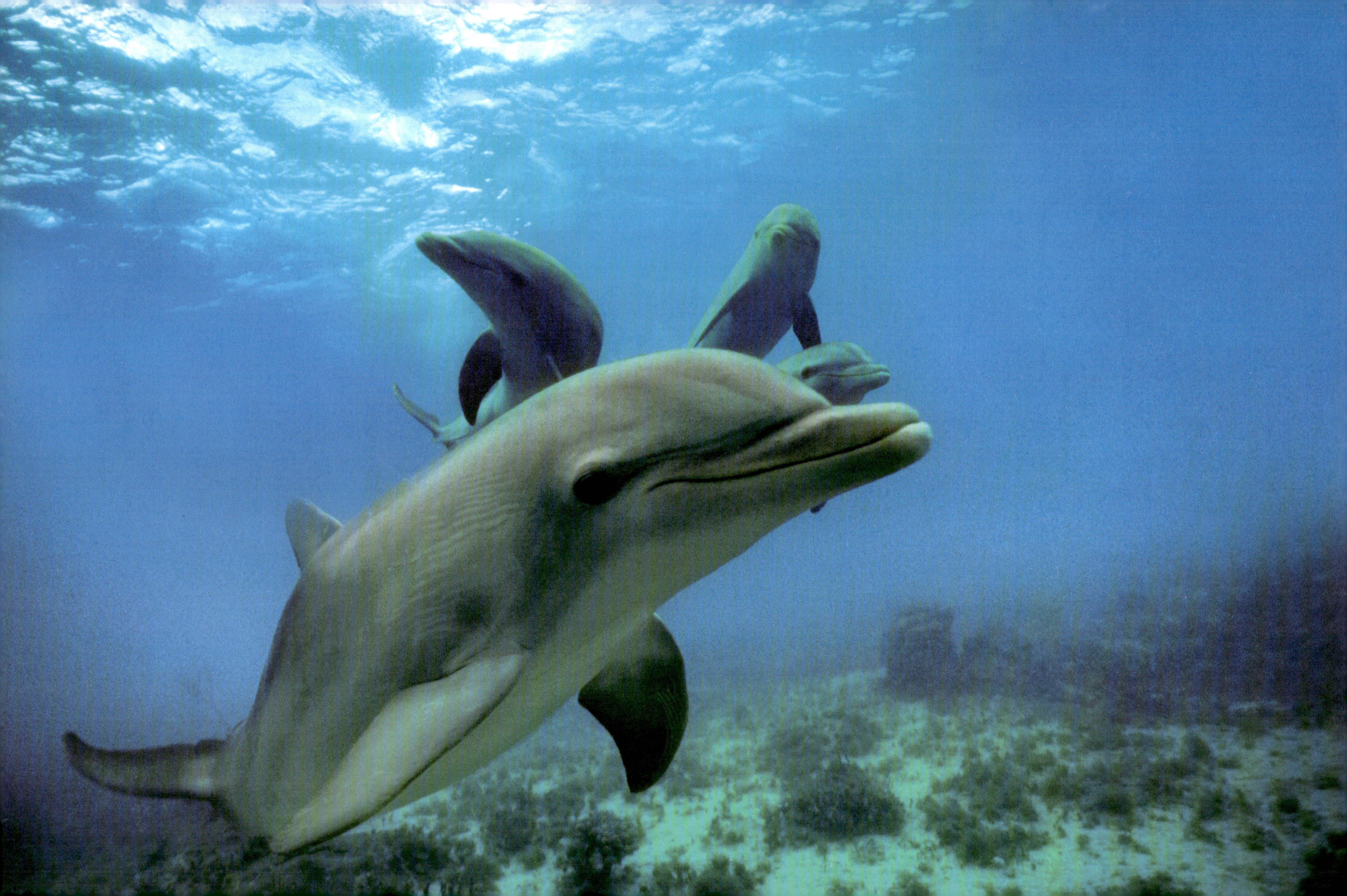

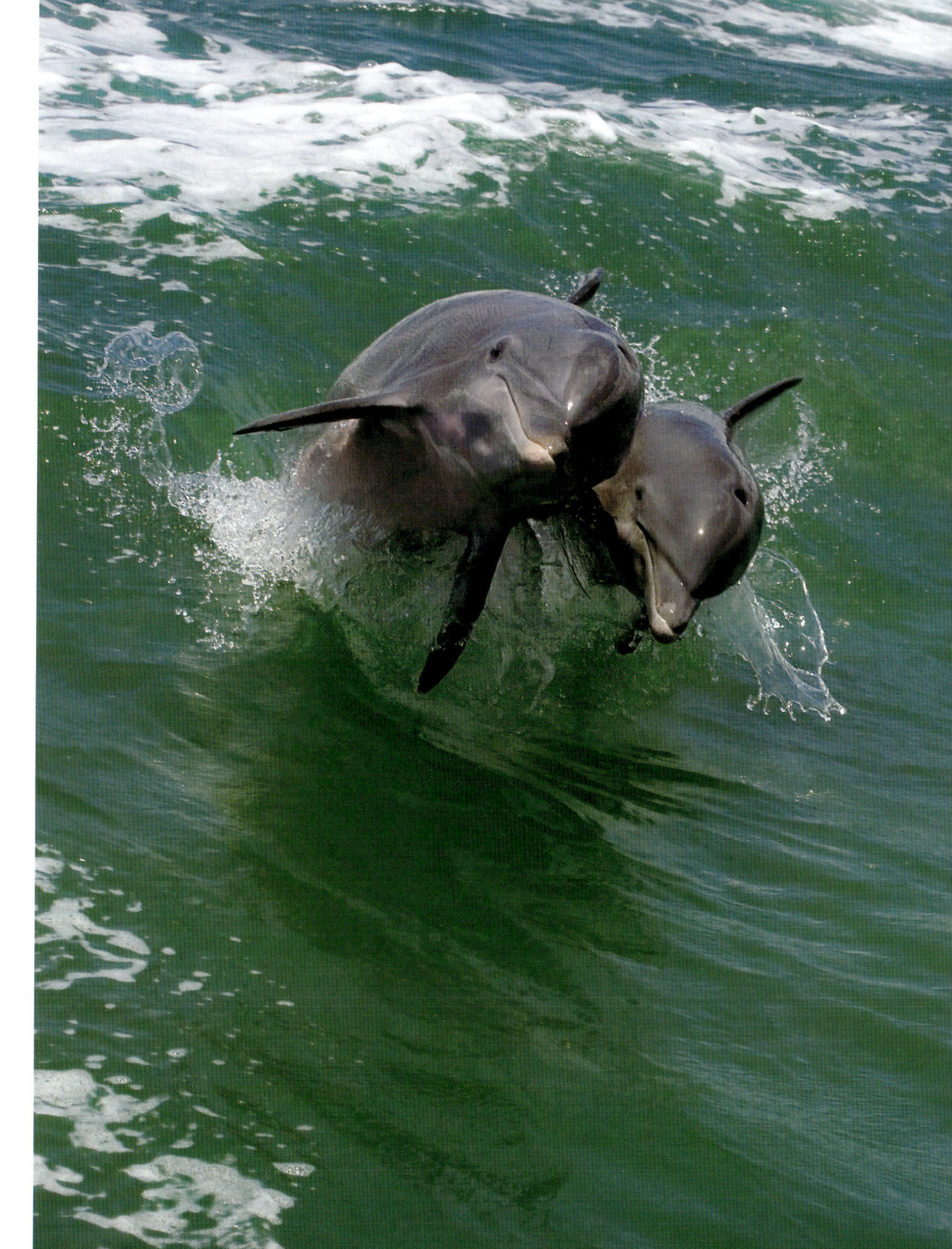

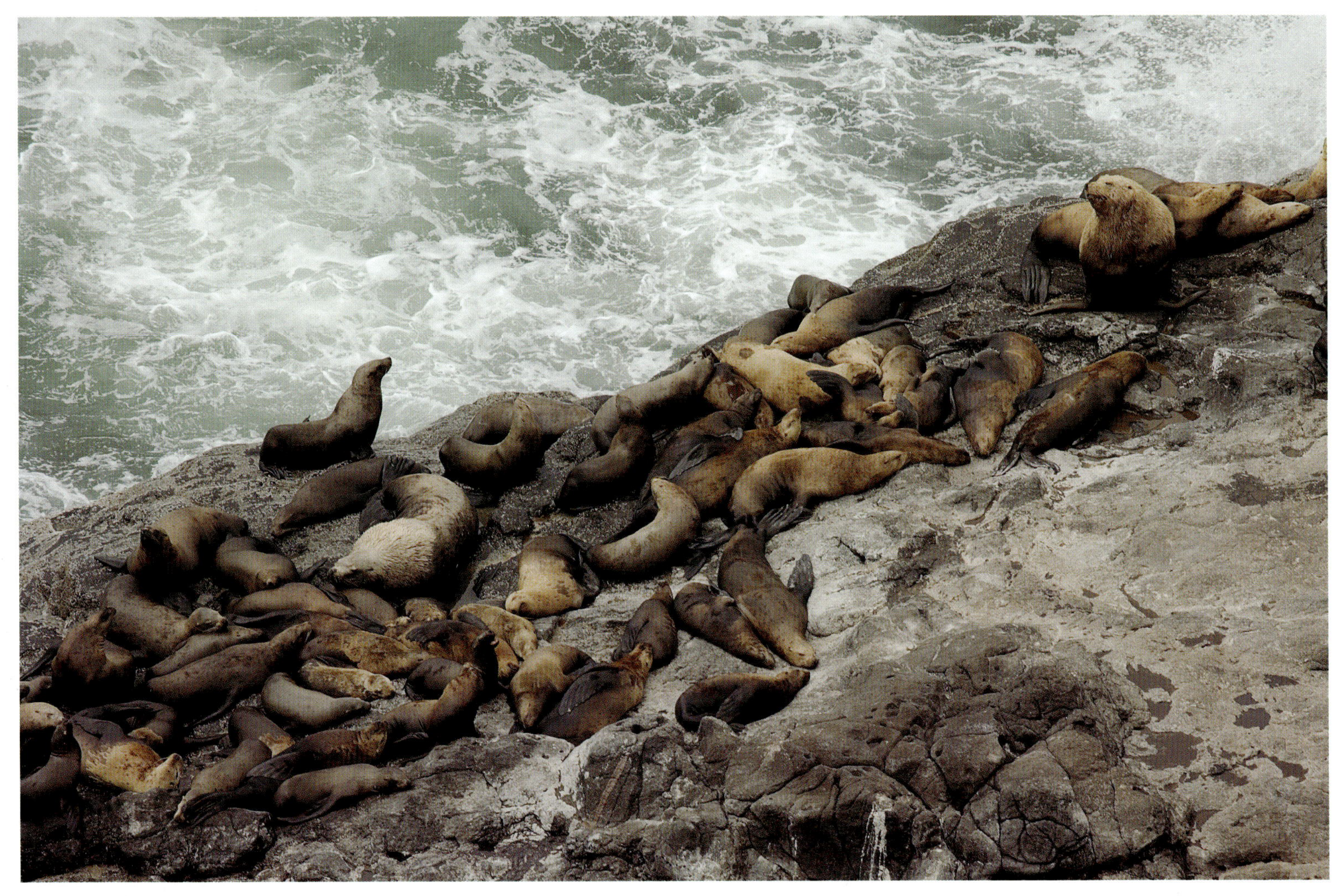

◀ sea lion rookery
▶ call of the wild ocean

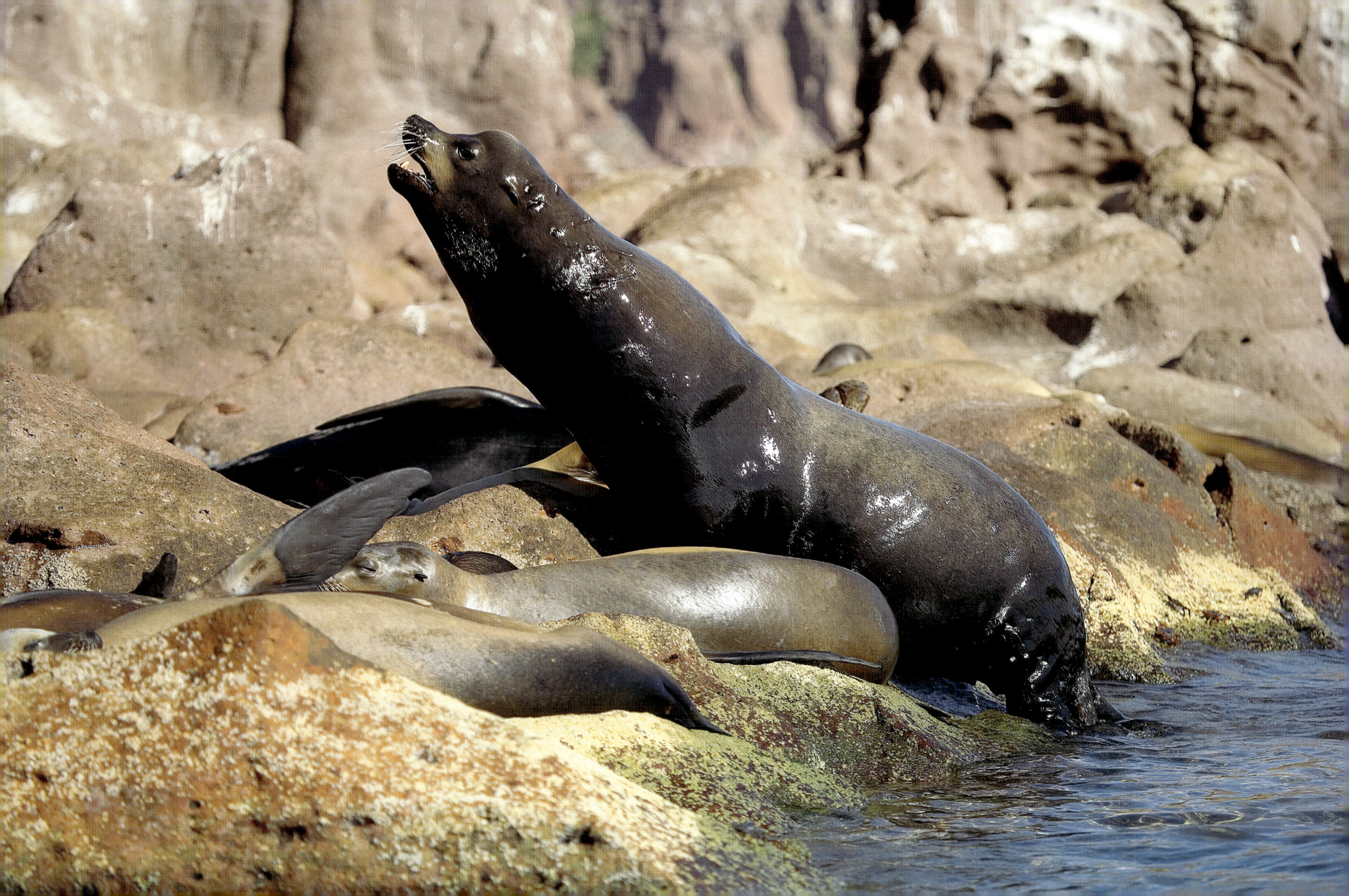

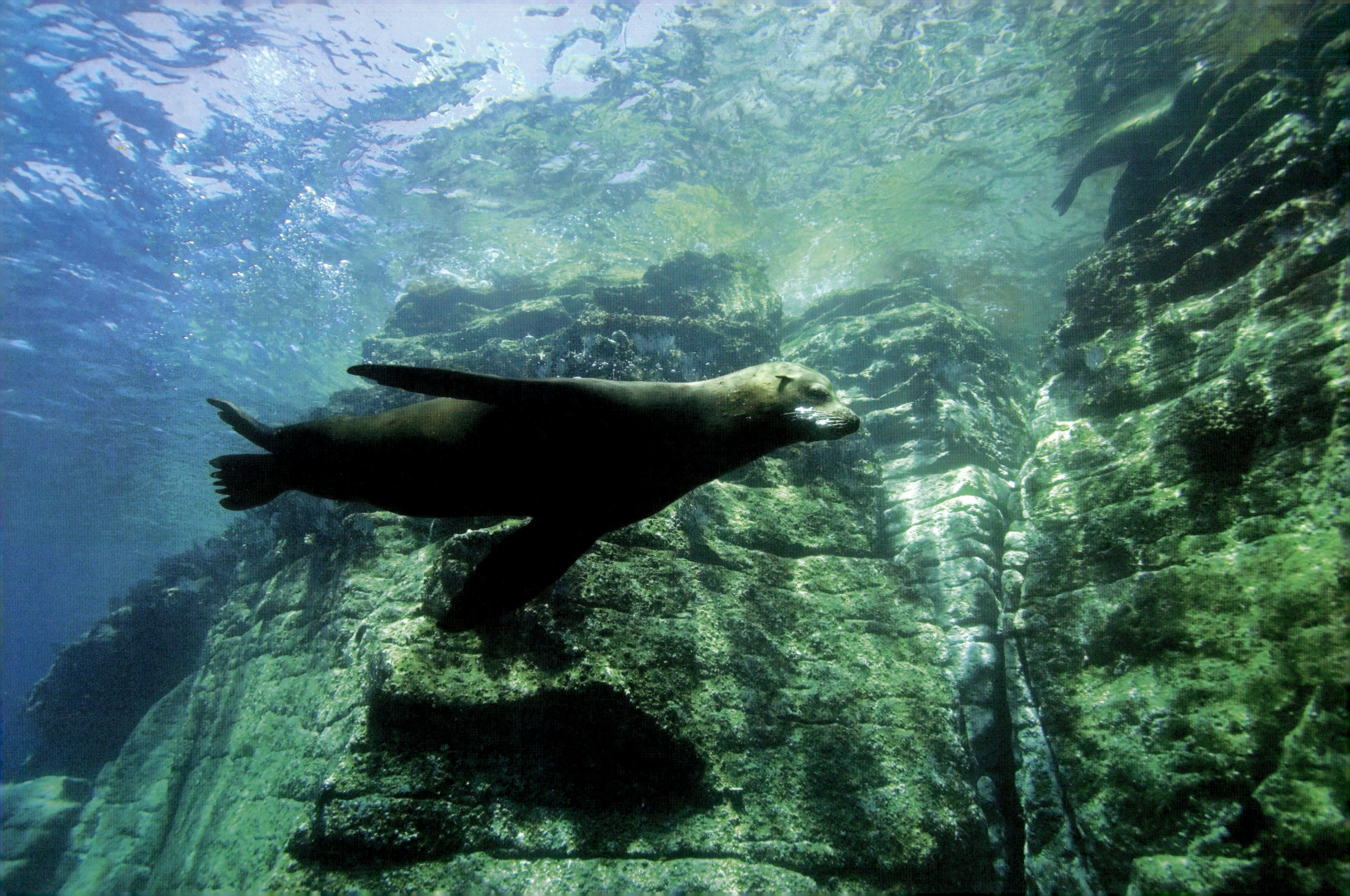

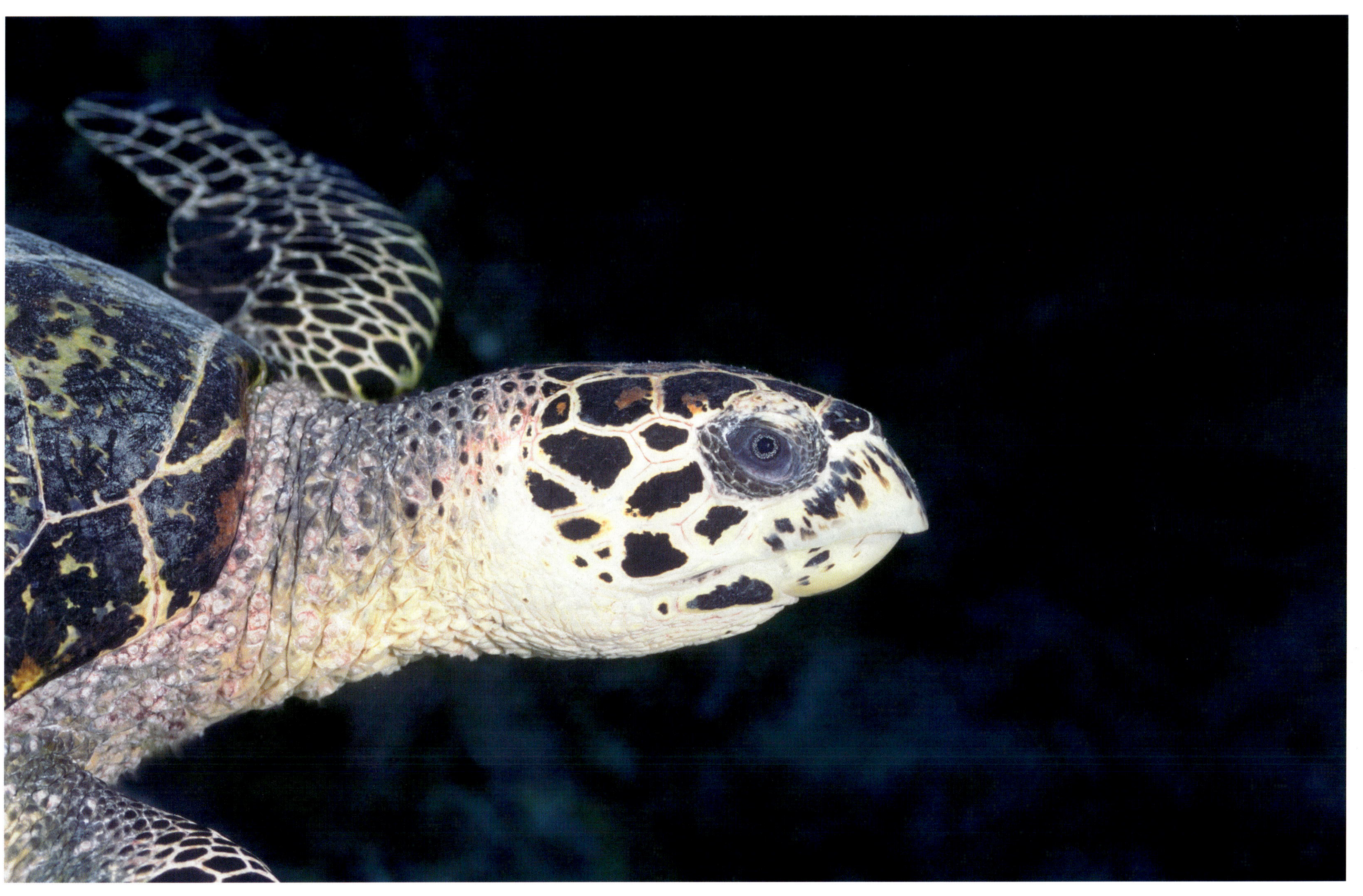

◀ undersea walls
▶ hawksbill sea turtle

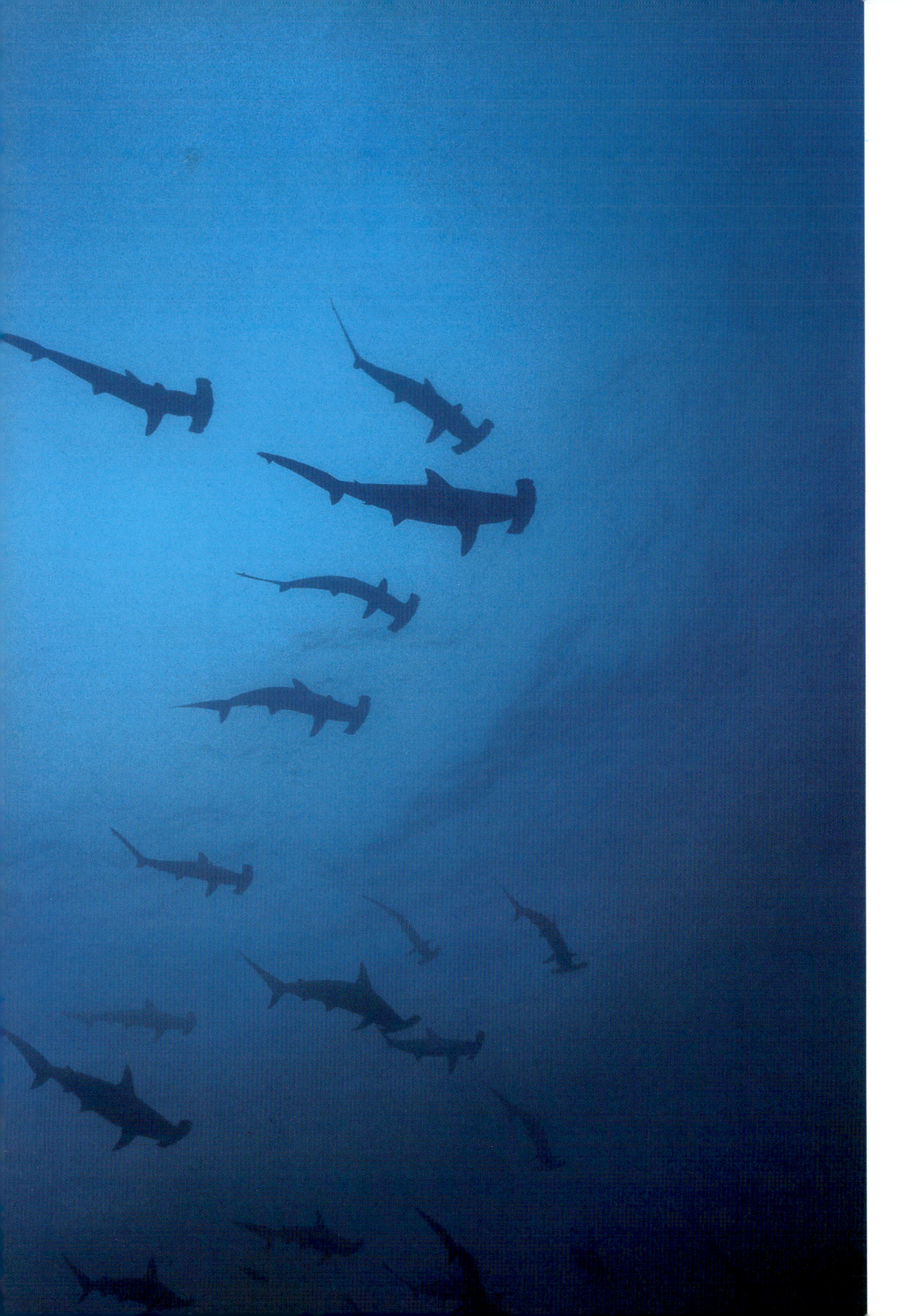

◀ hammerhead dive buddies
▶ cocos island hammerhead

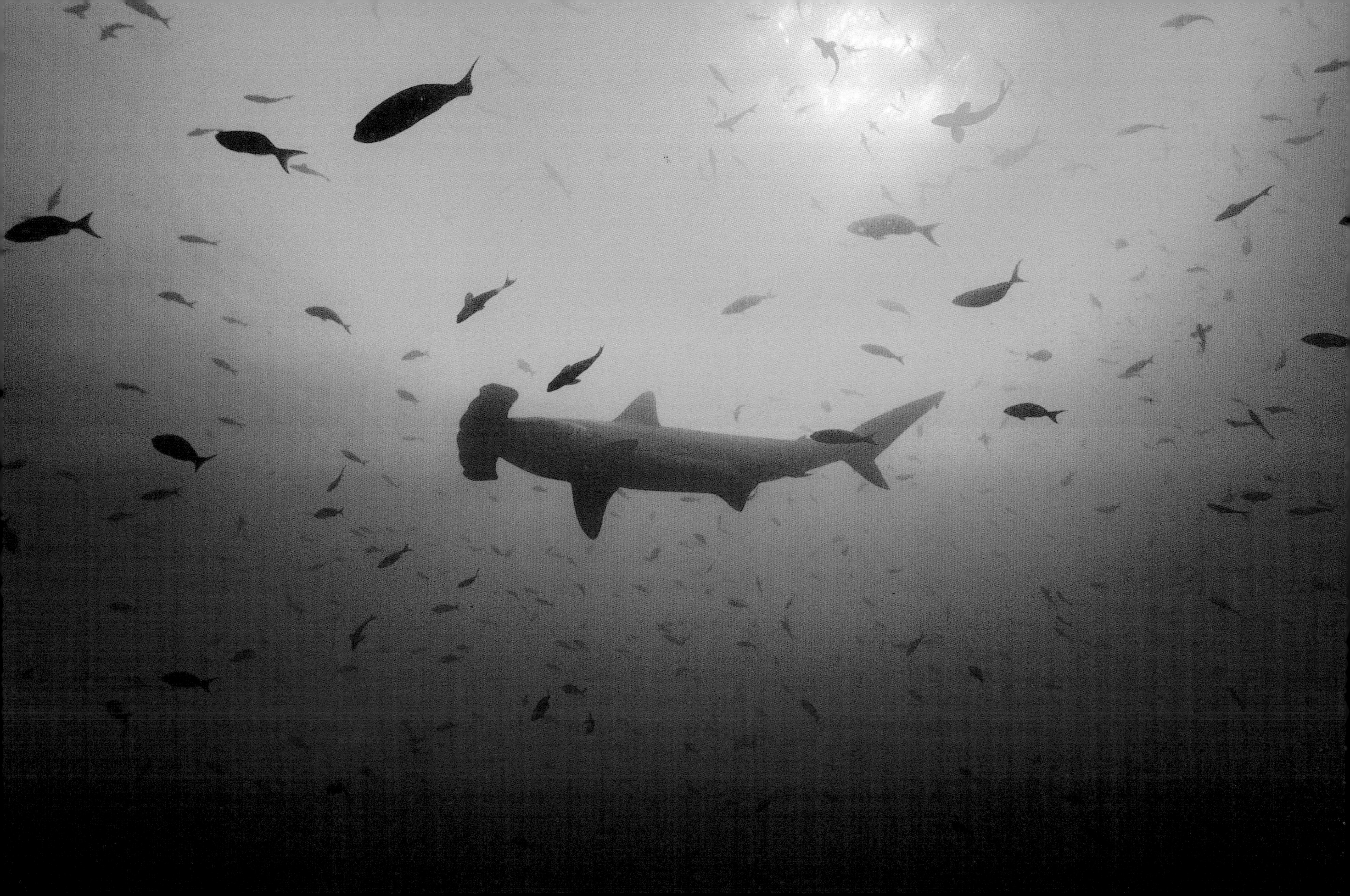

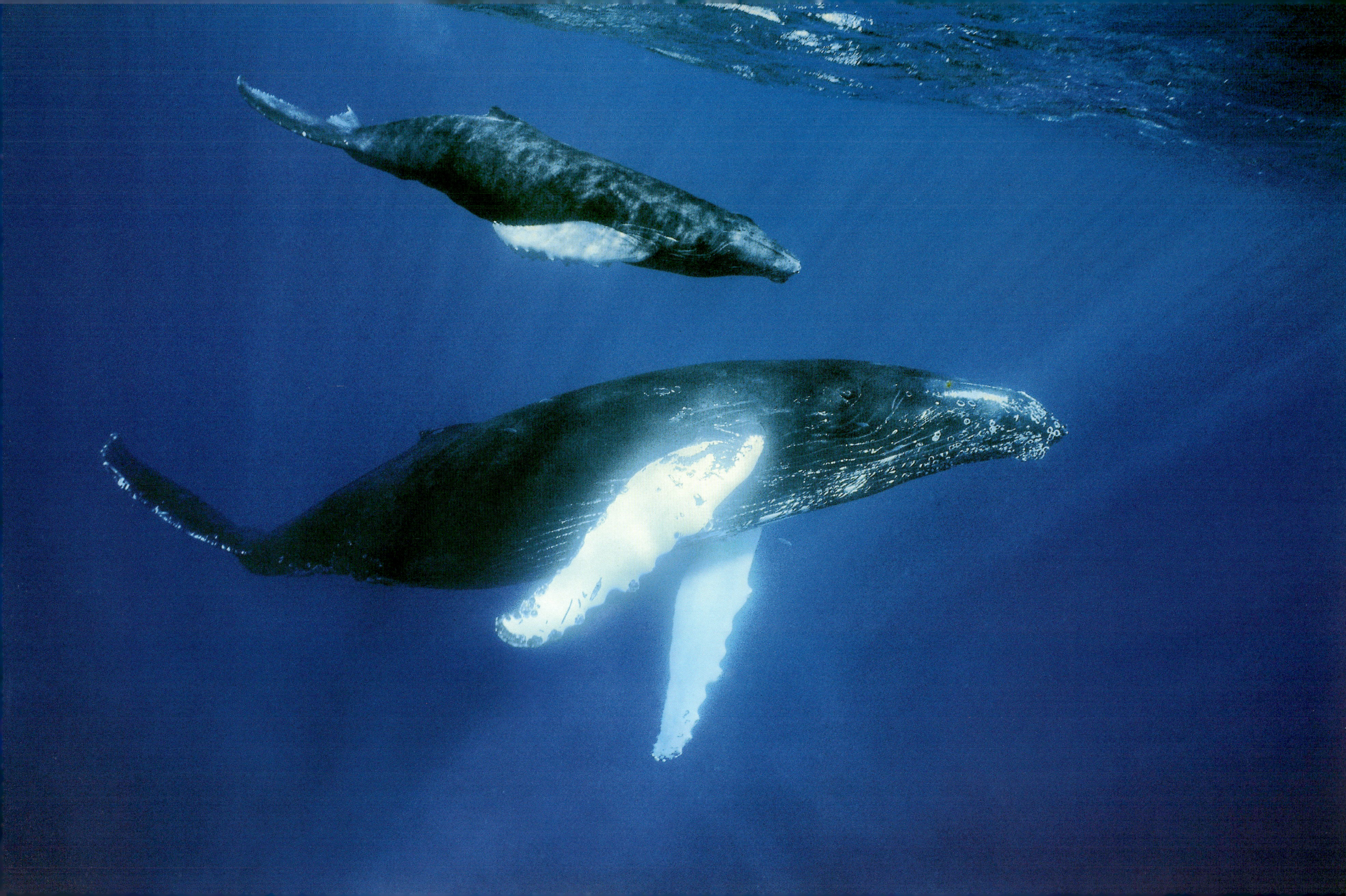

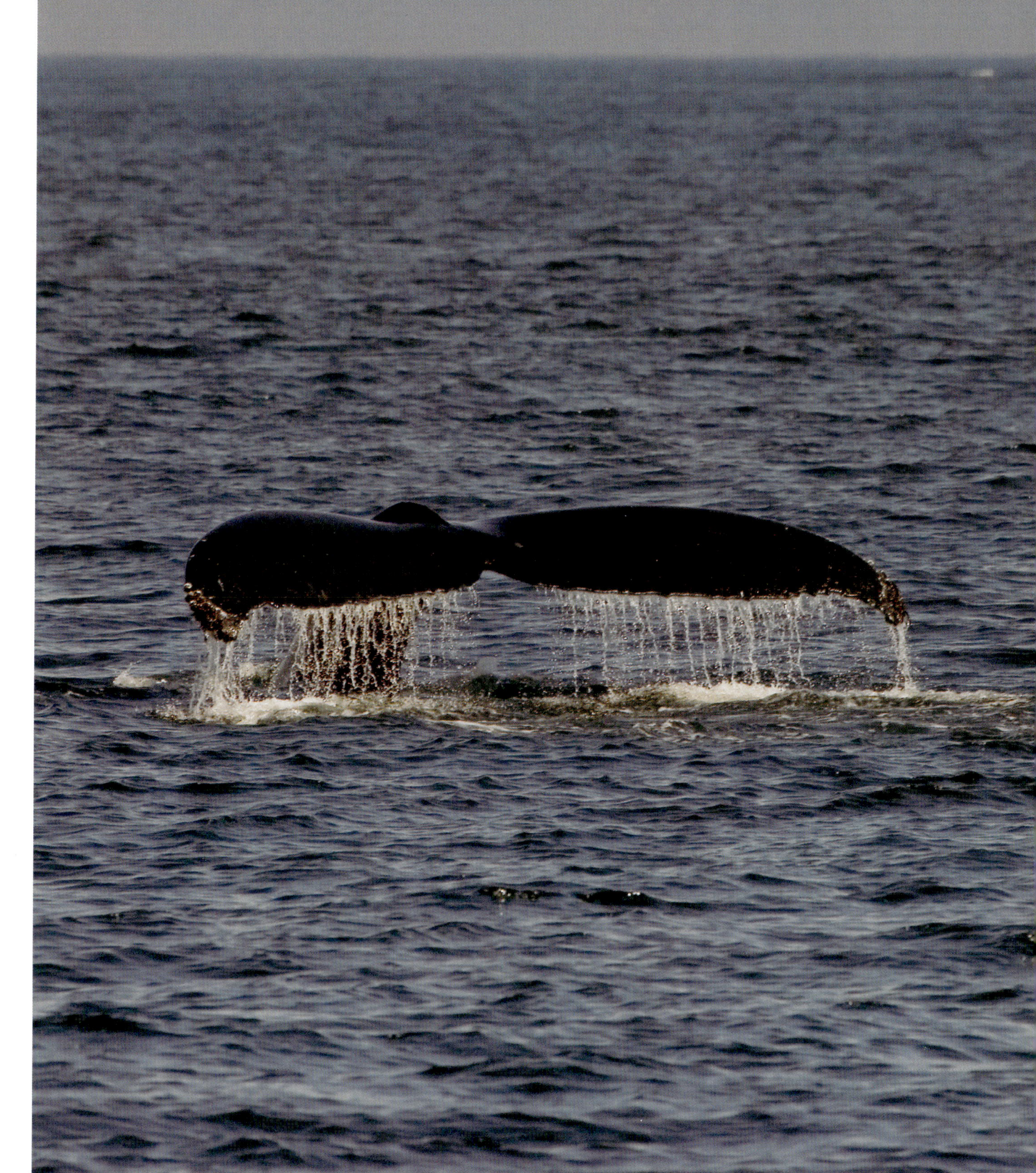

◀ whale encounter
▶ watching whales

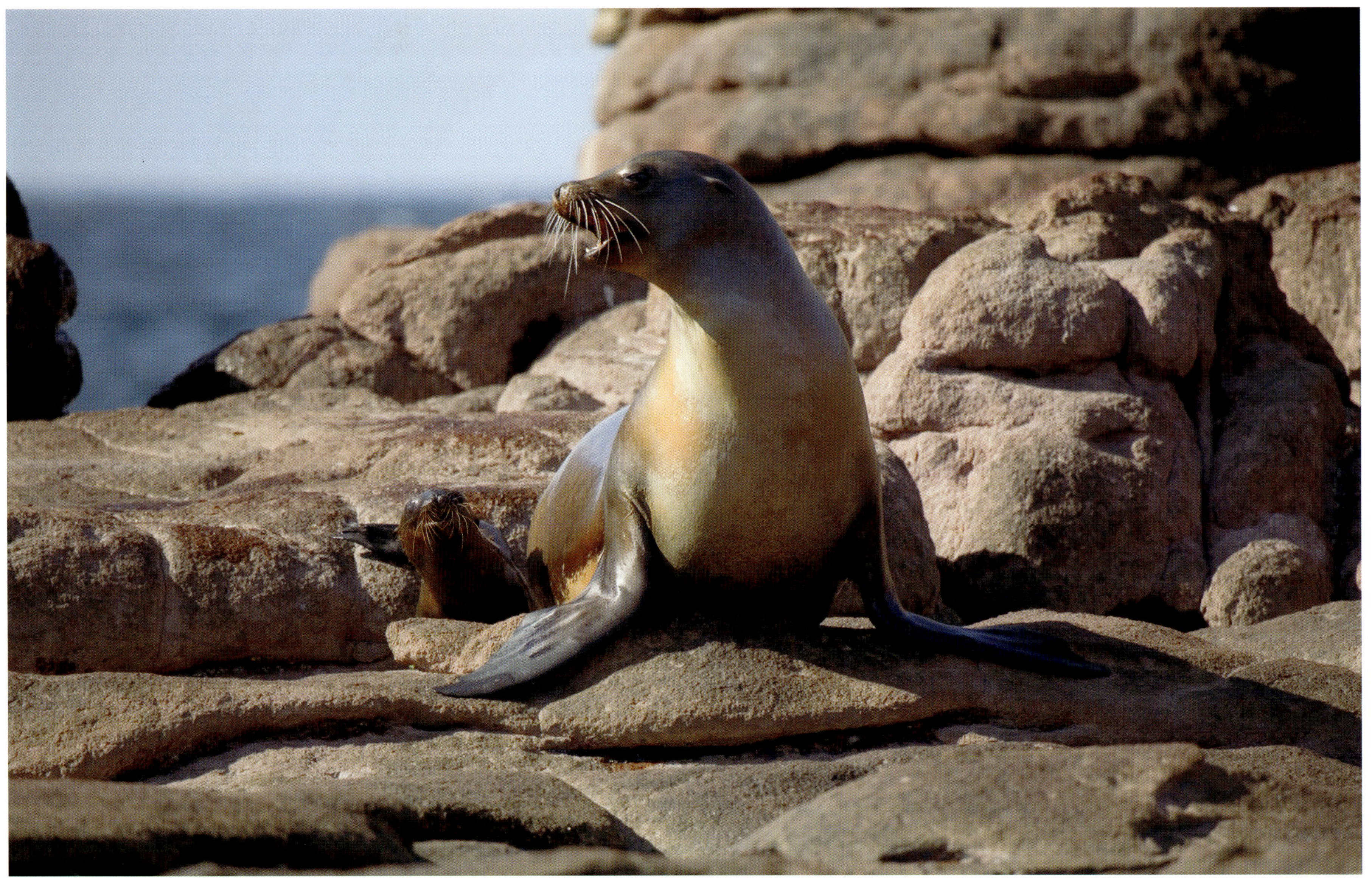

◄ mother and pup
► sea lion travelers

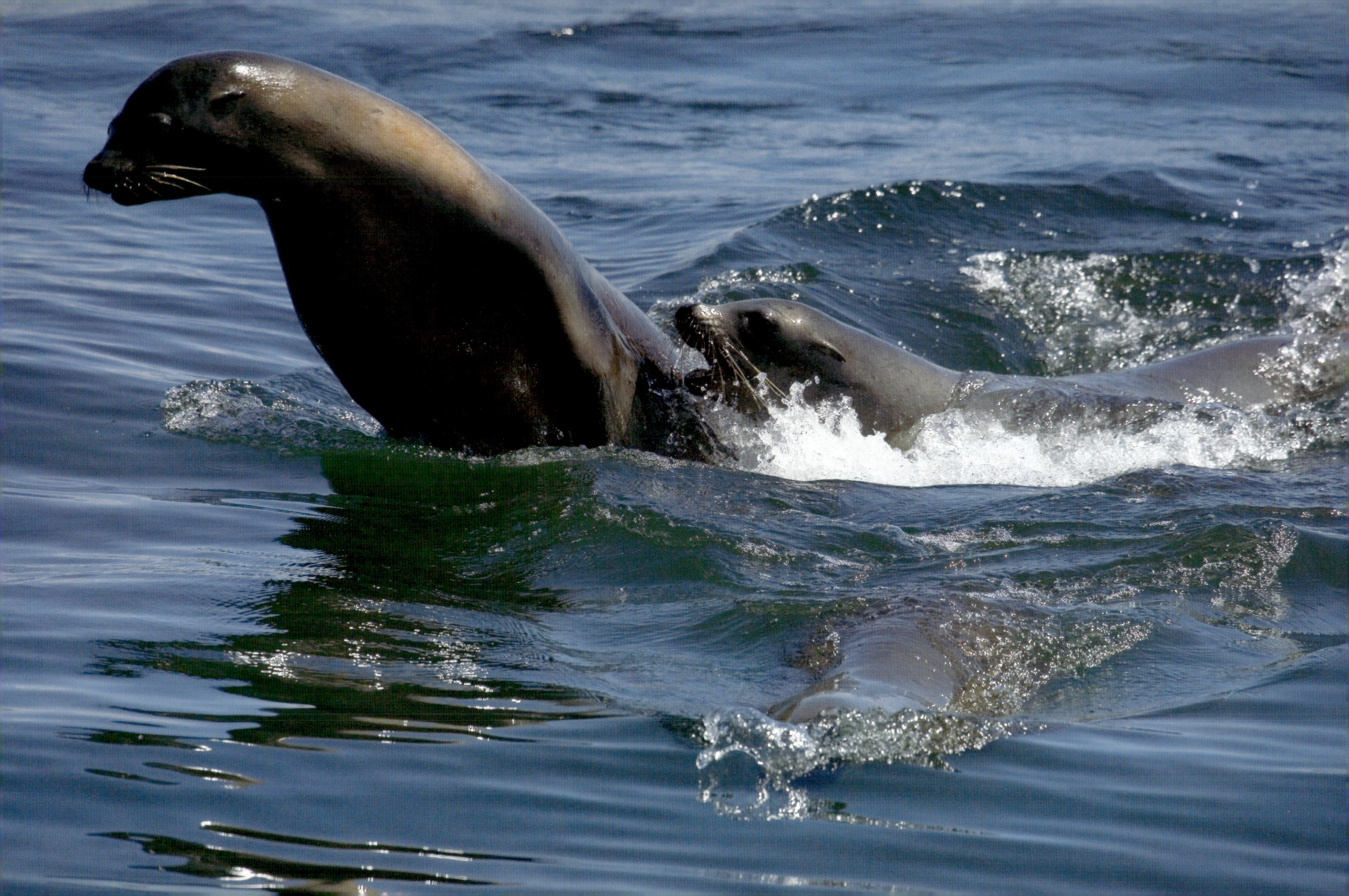

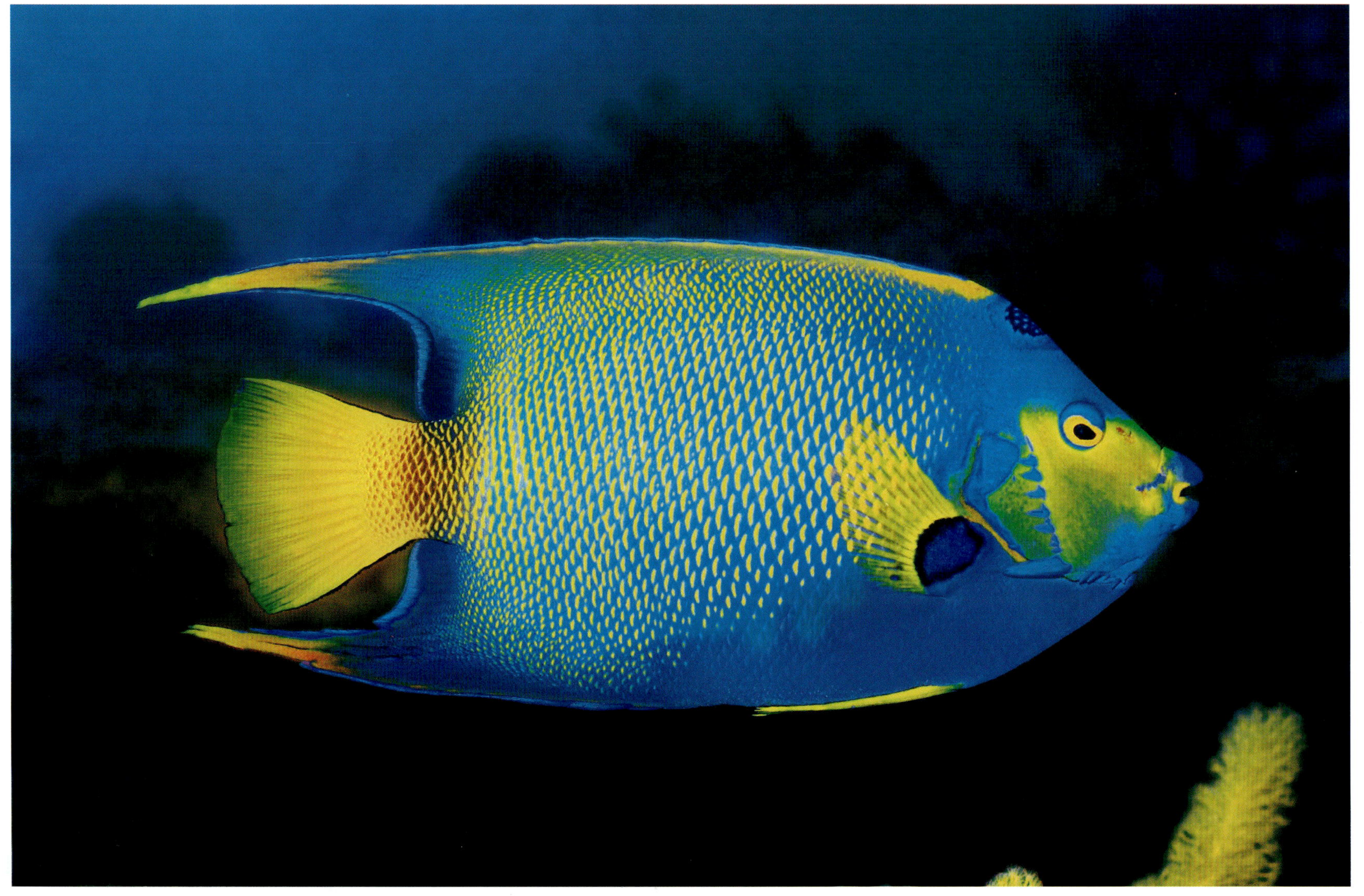

◄ queen angel of the sea
► maui style reef

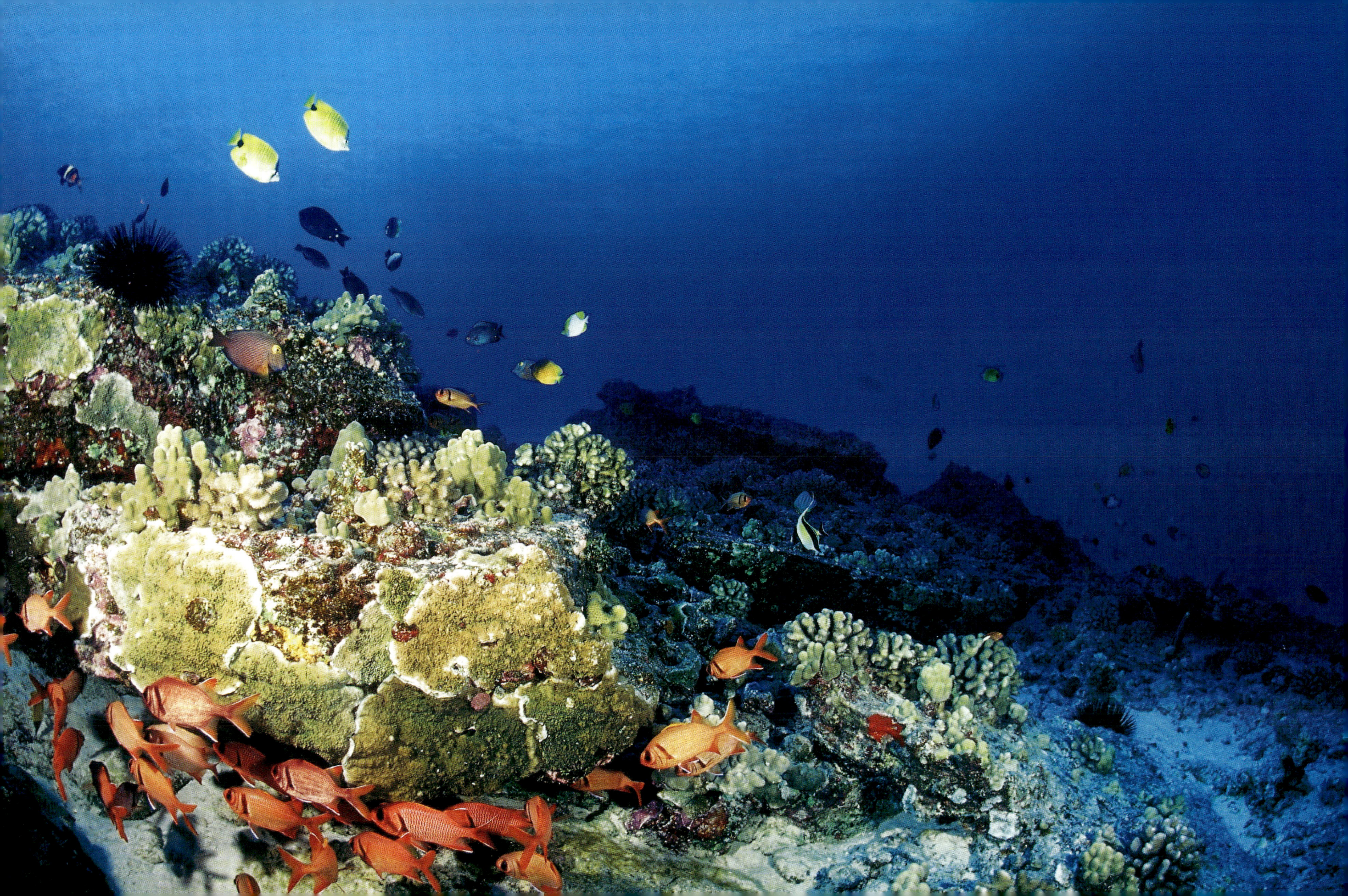

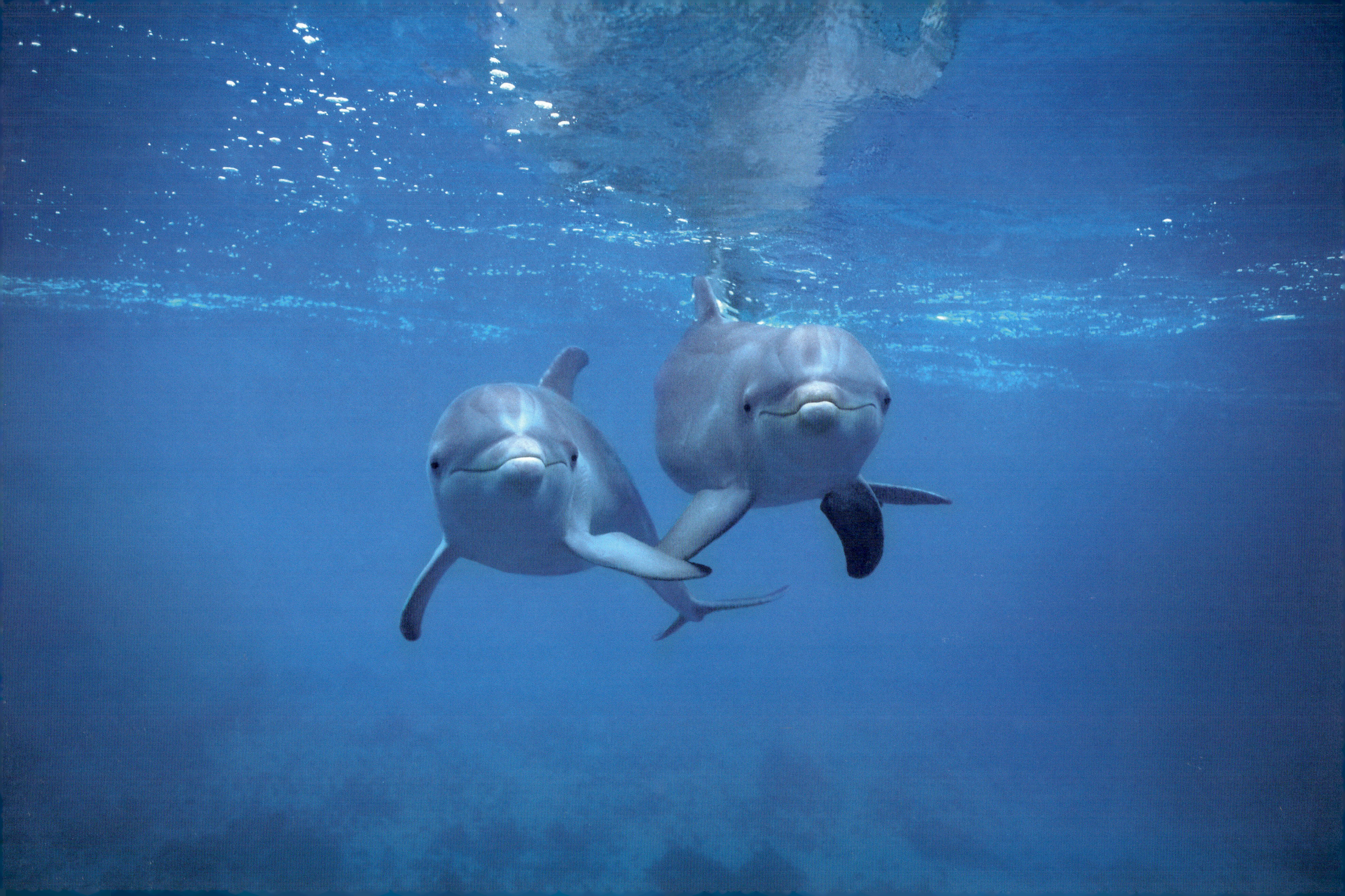

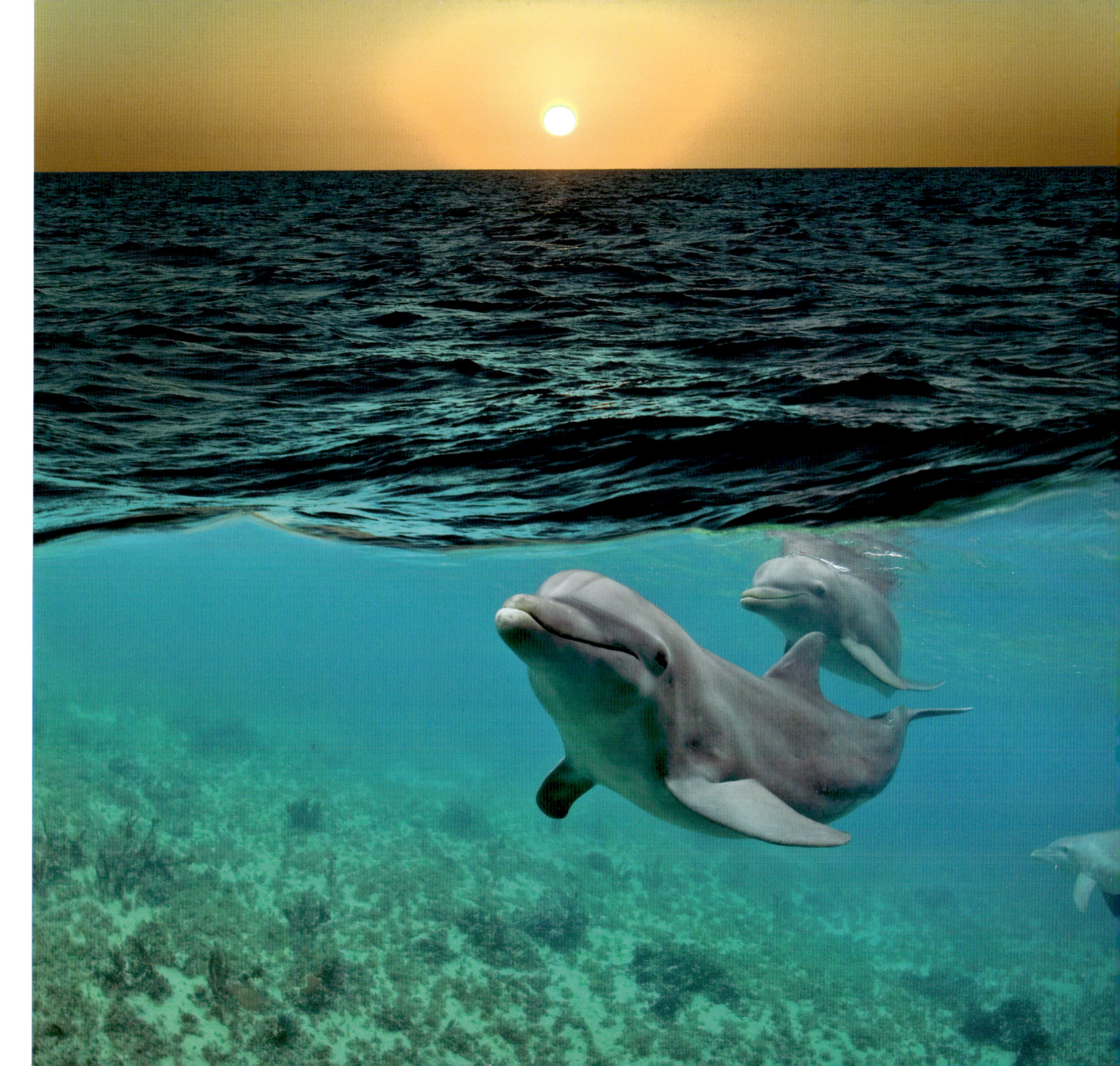

◄ dolphin aquatic
► two worlds of the dolphin

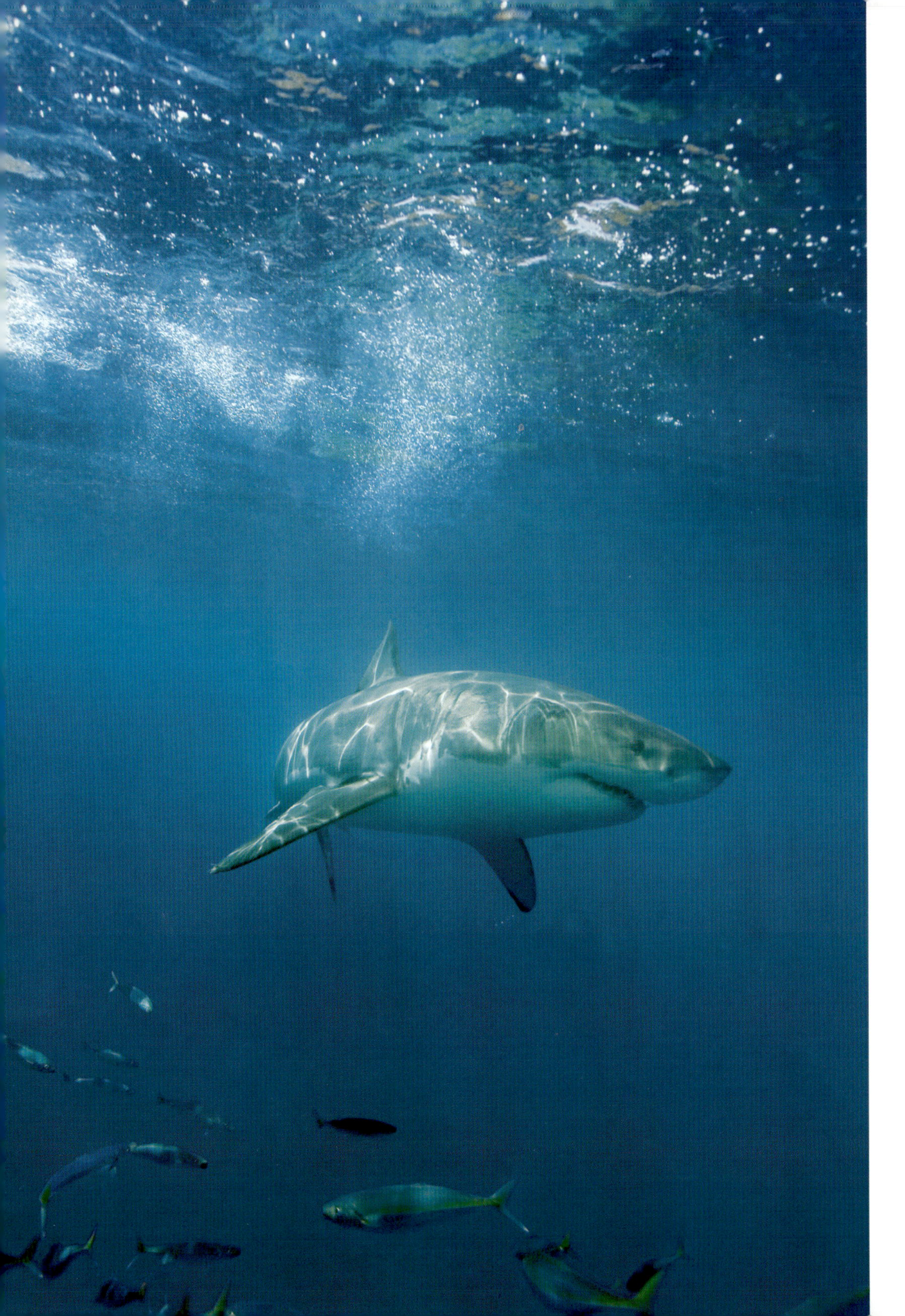

◀ great white below
▶ invisible predator

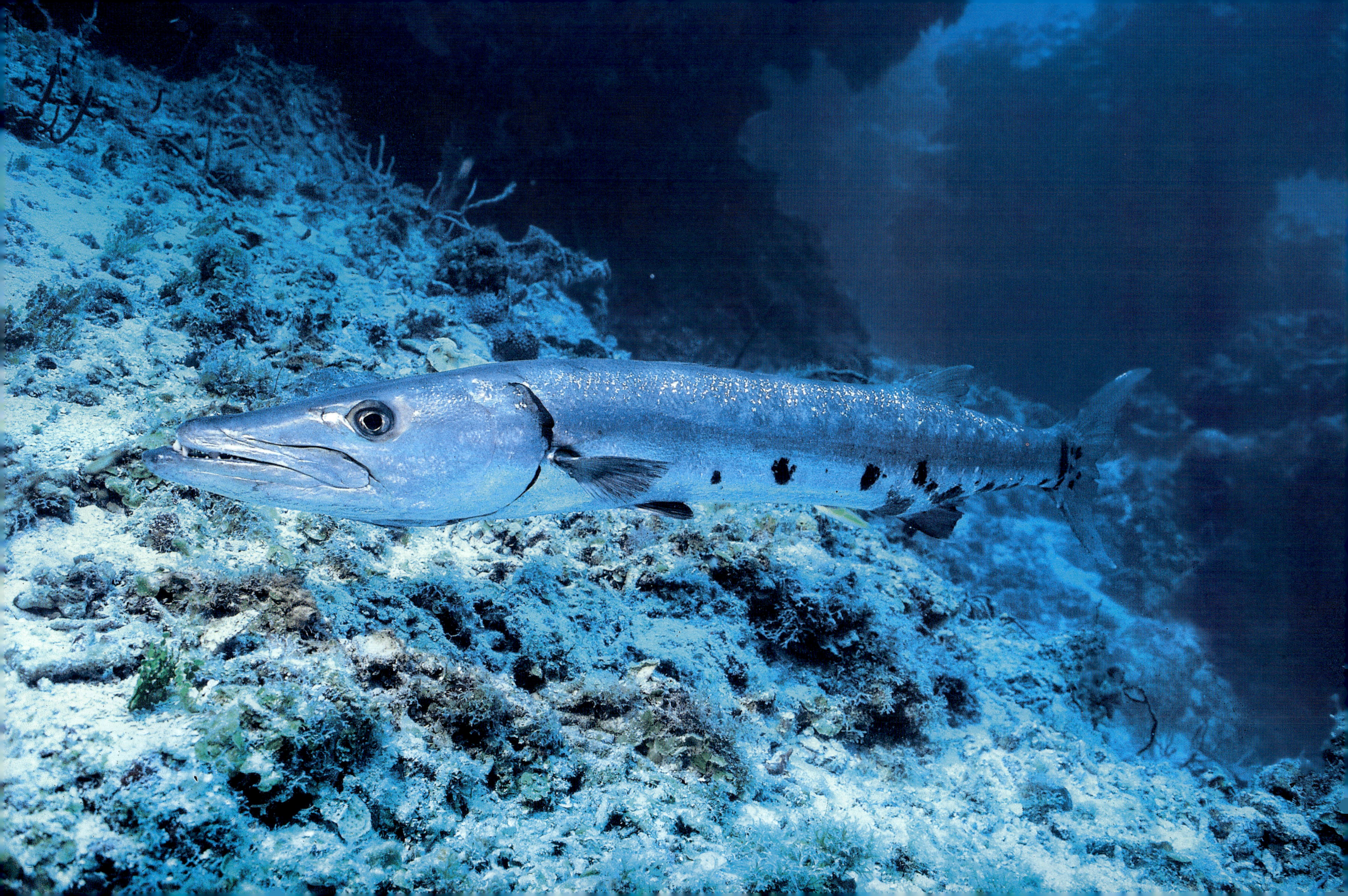

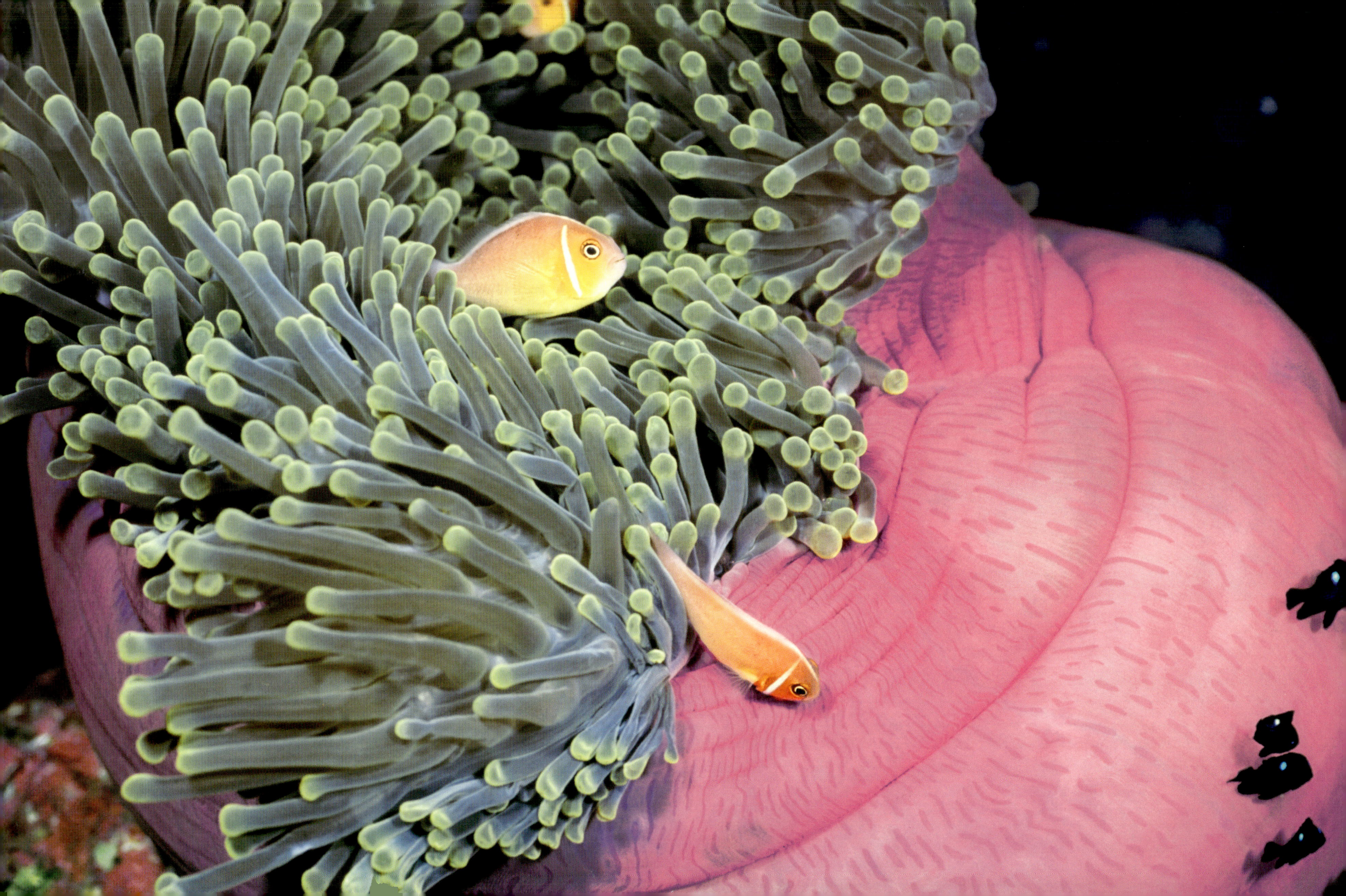

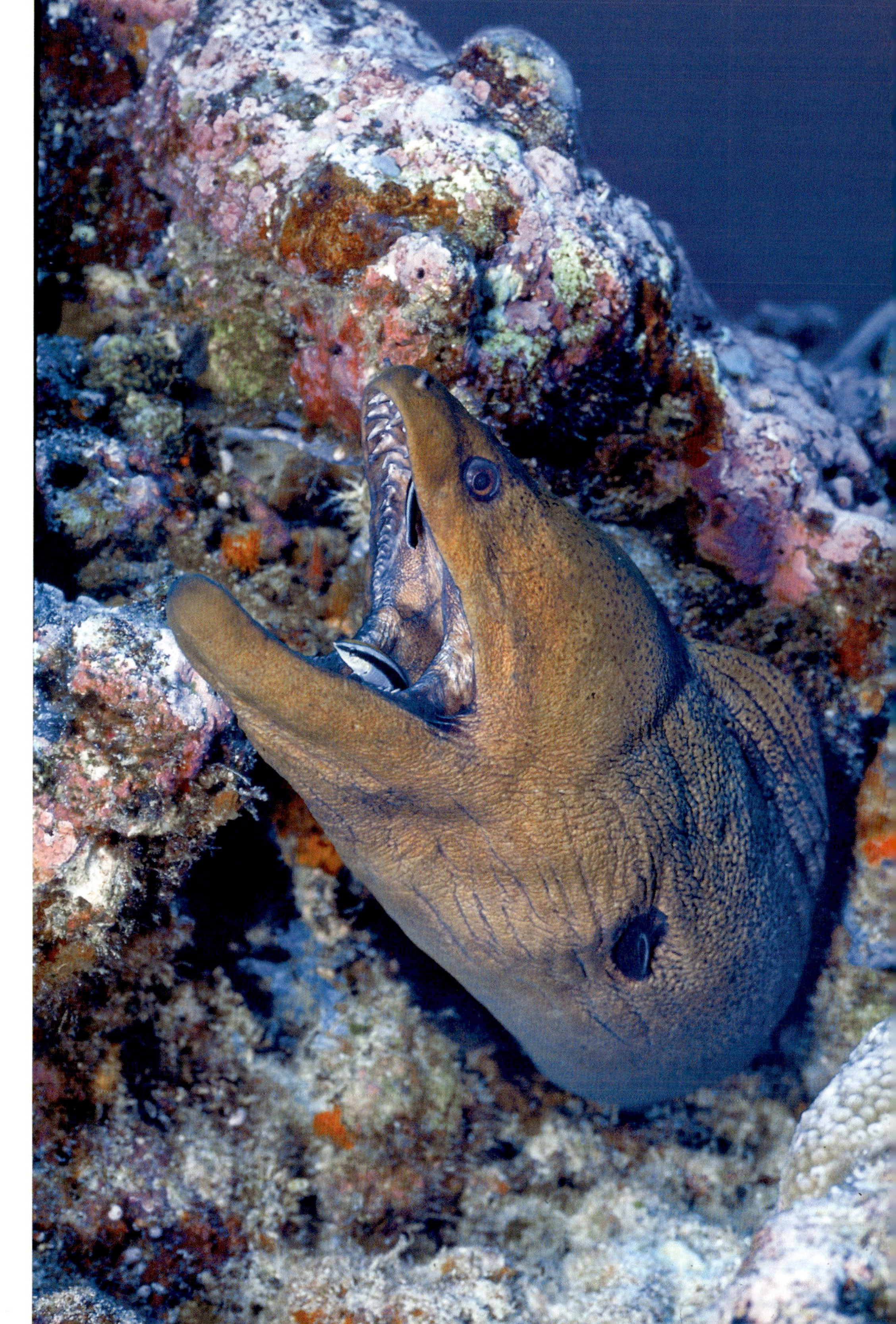

◀ sea anemone clowns
▶ eel cleaning

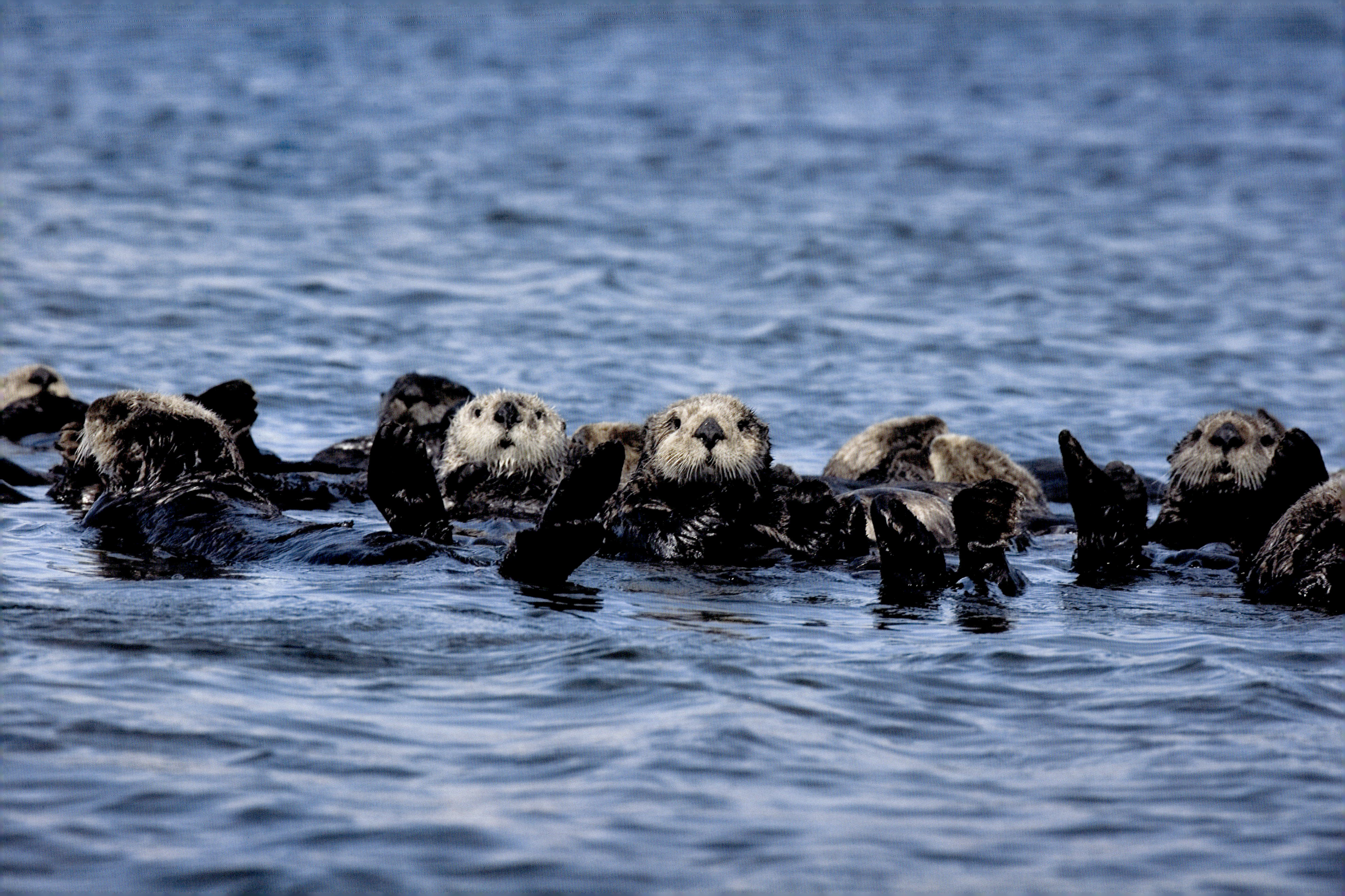

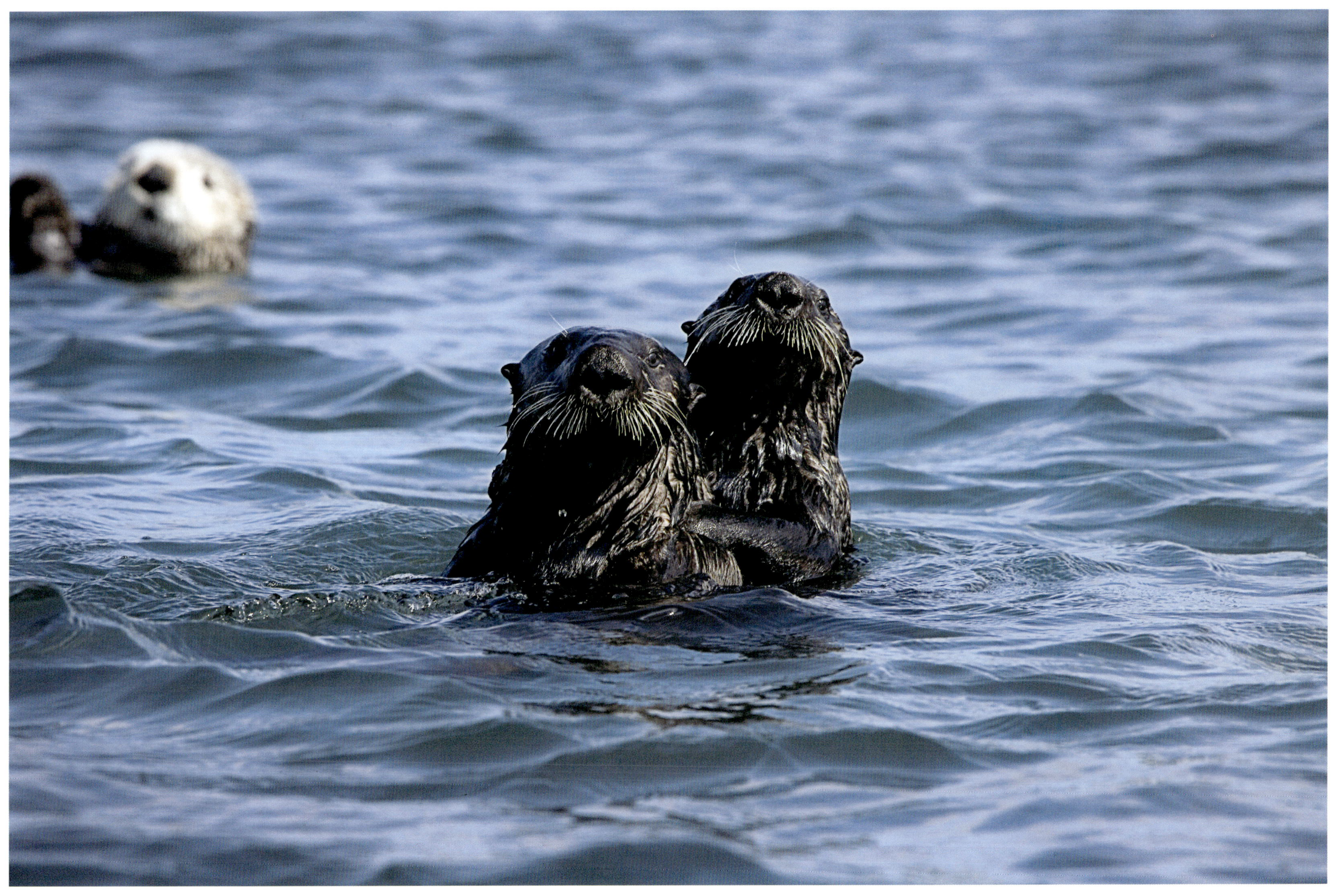

◄ sea otter raft
► hold on

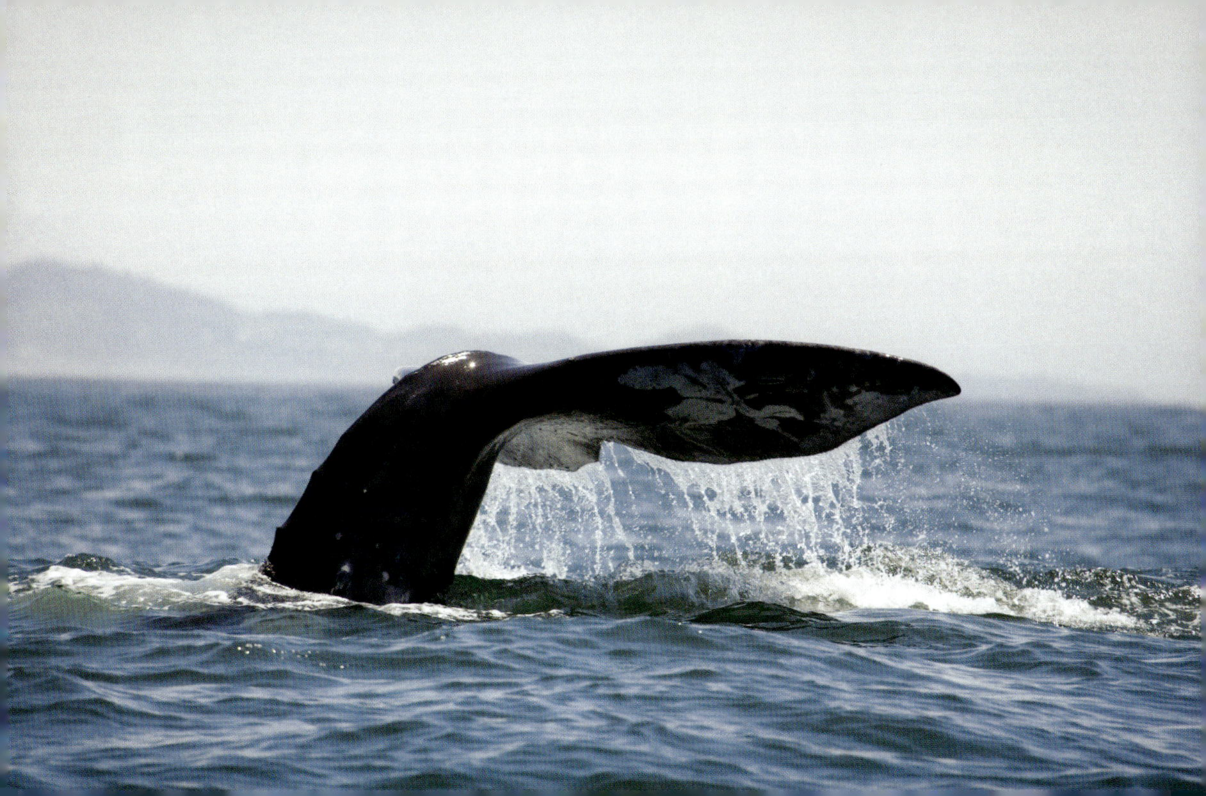

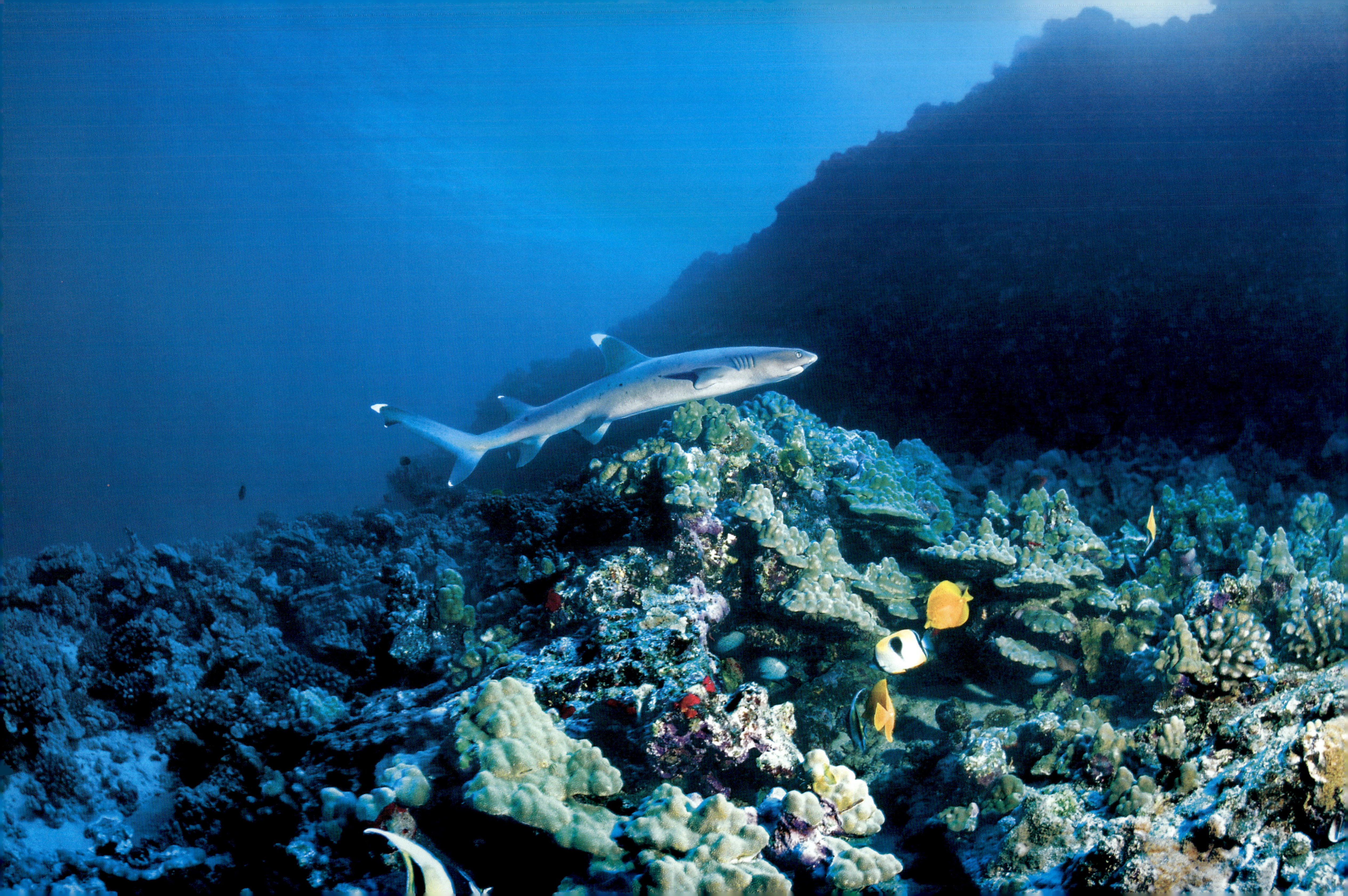

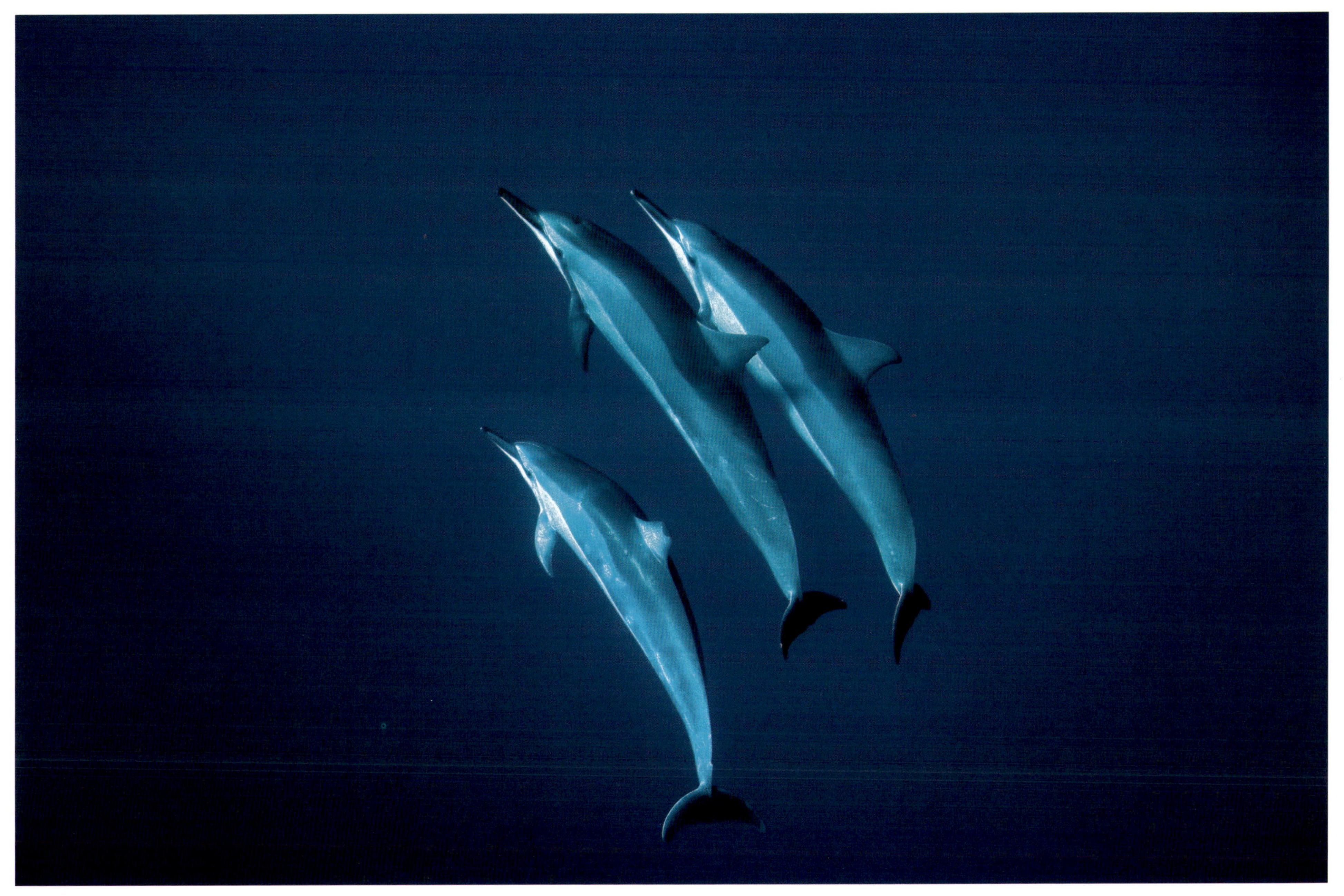

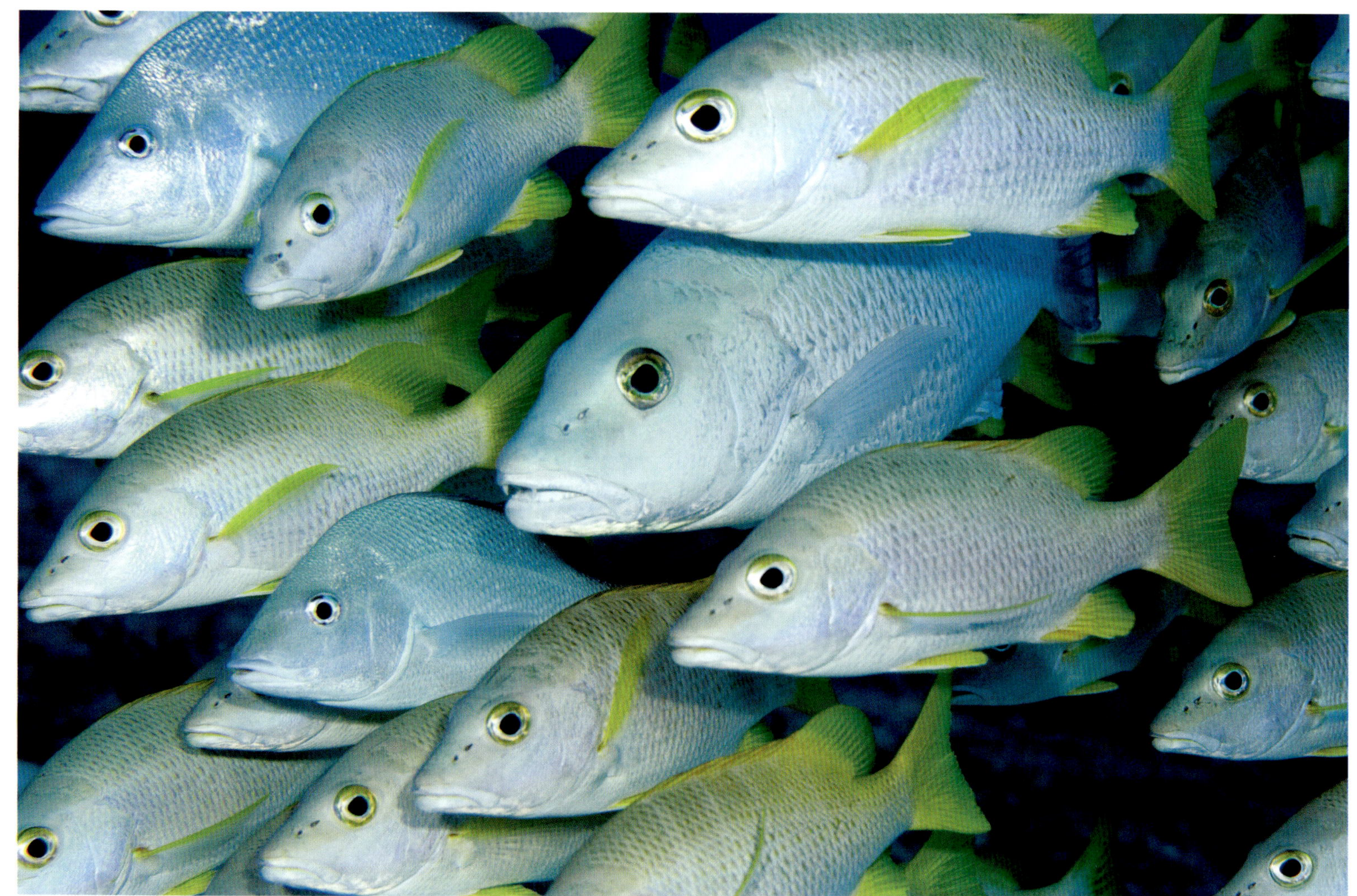

◀ fishe school
▶ nurse reef

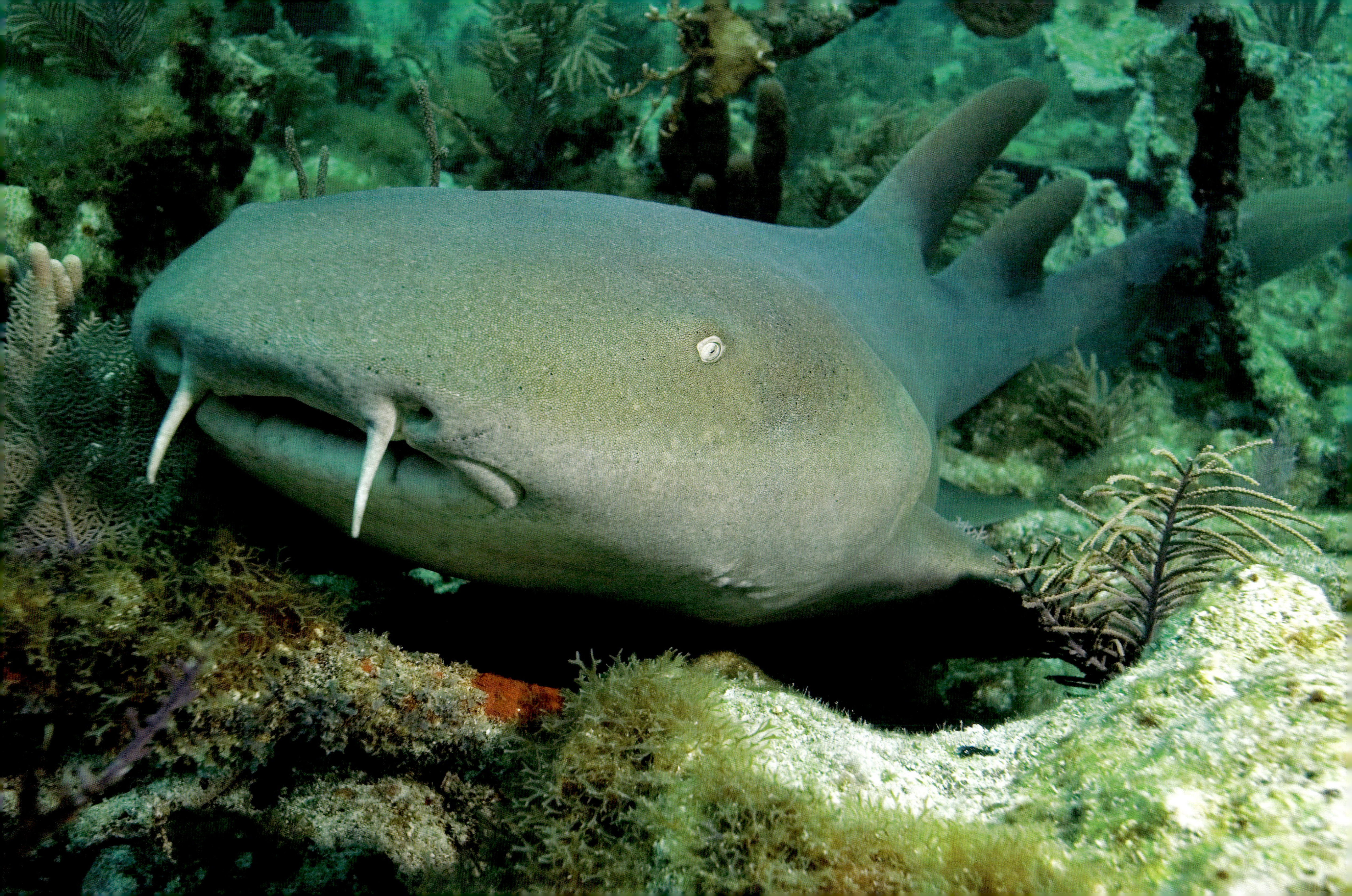

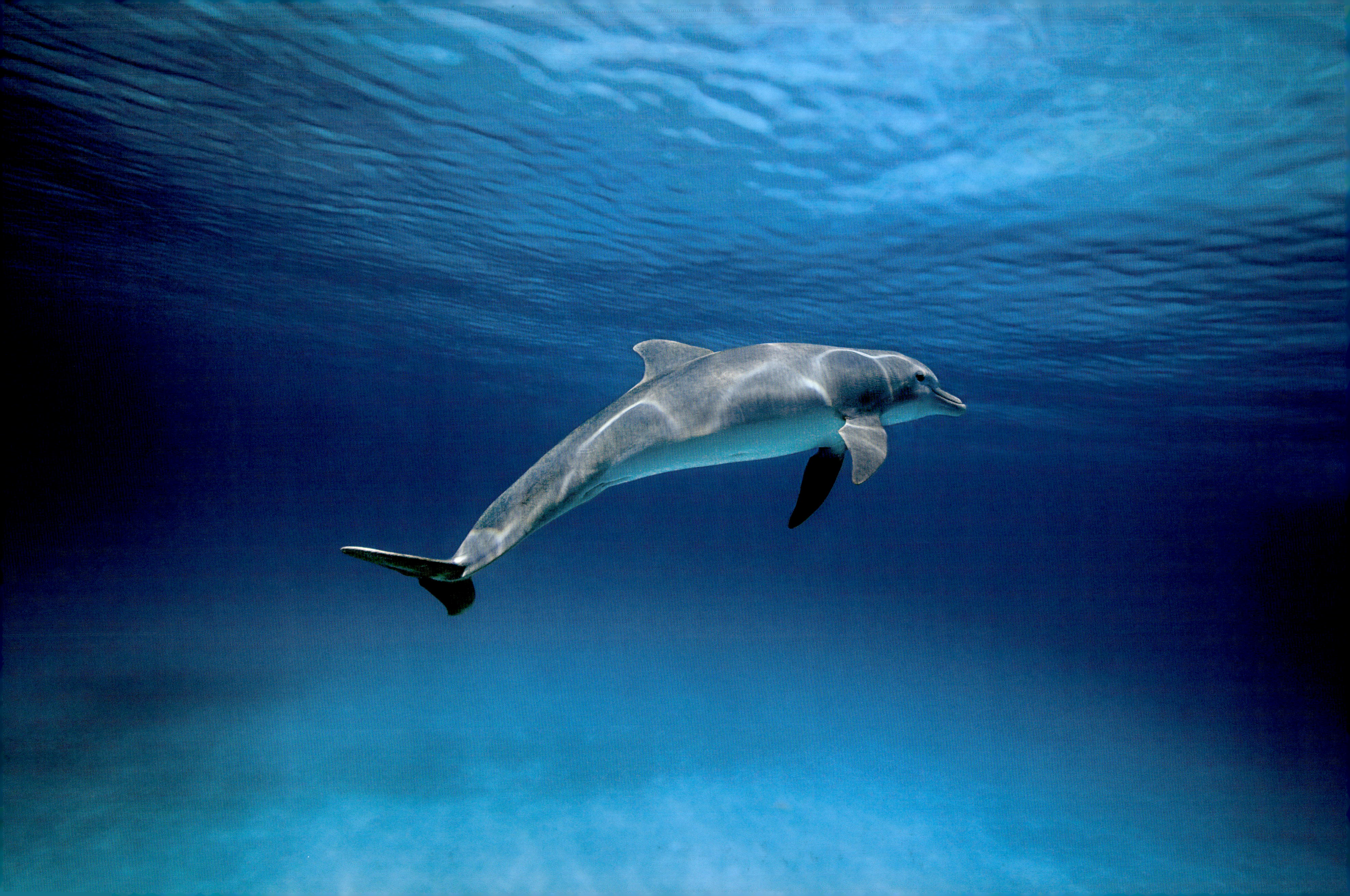

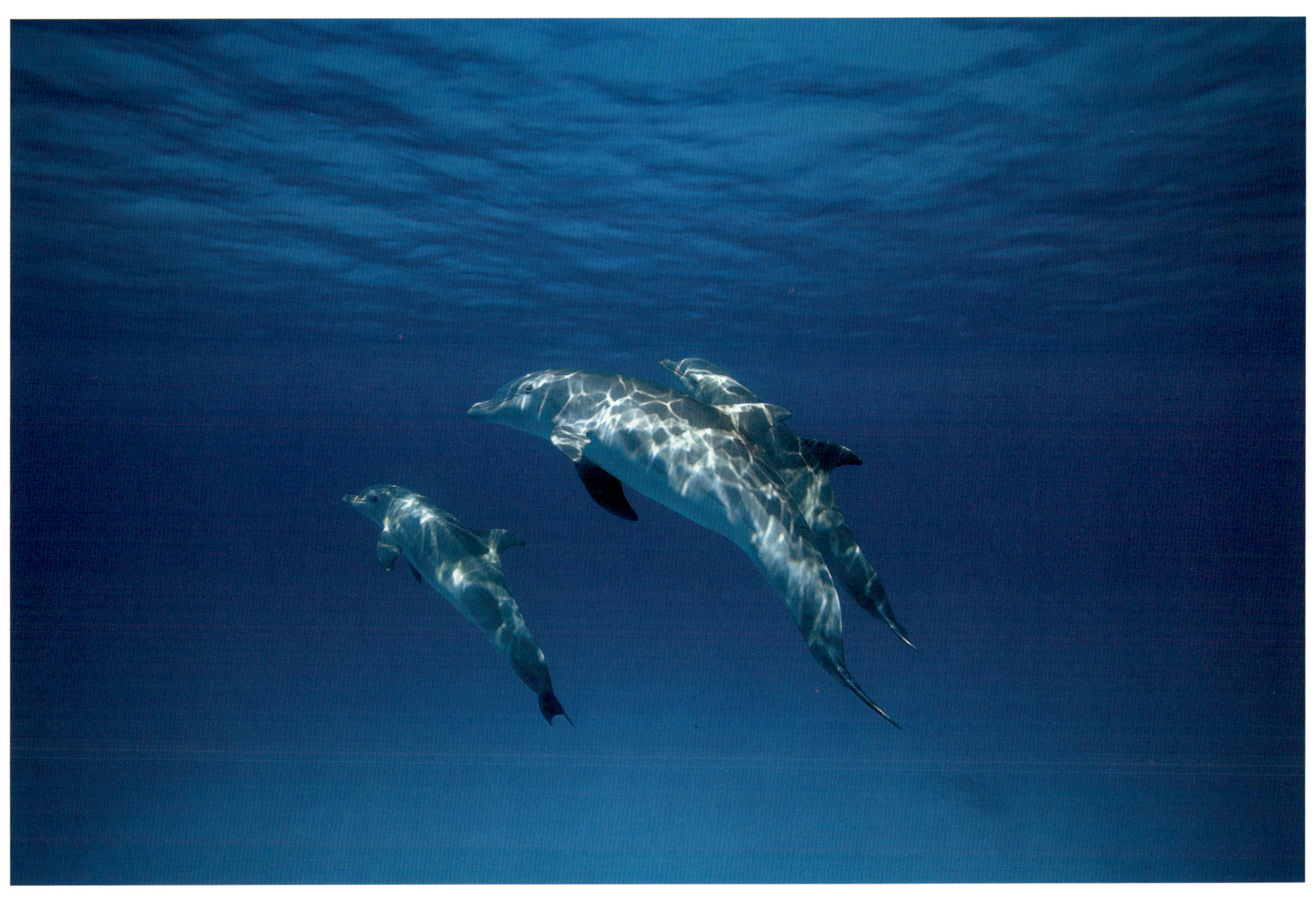

◀ silent sea
▶ weightless

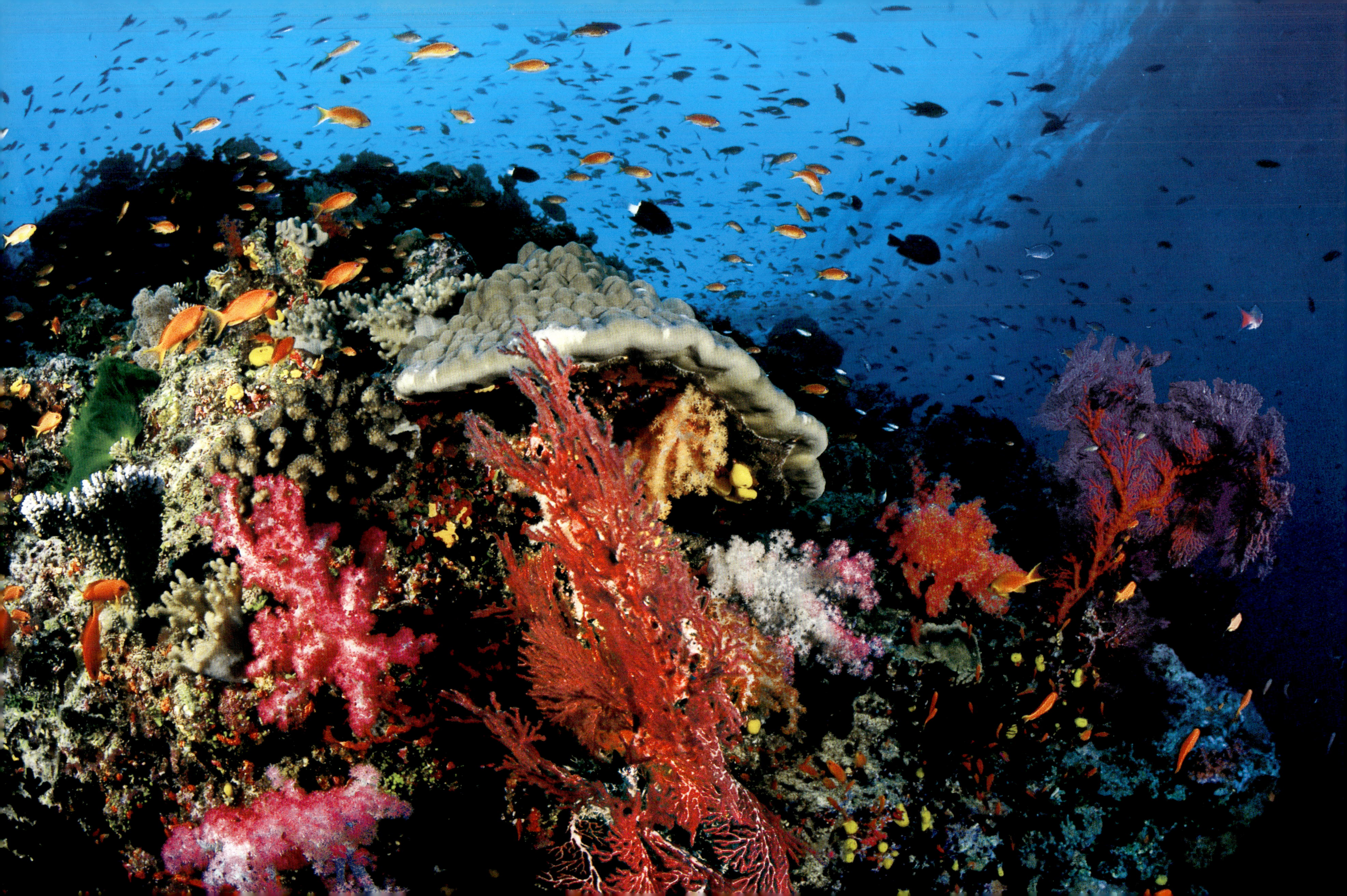

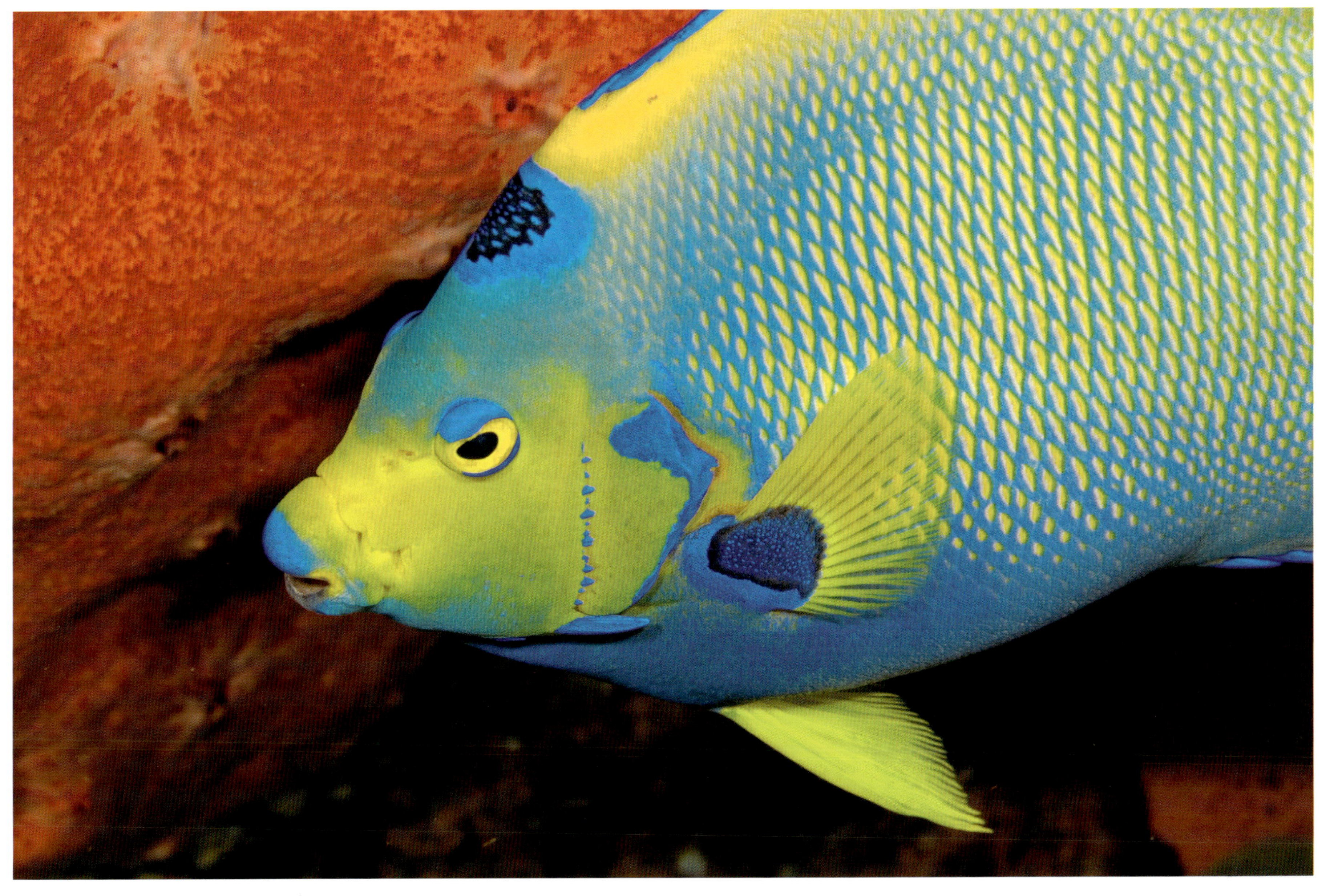

◀ radiance below
▶ queen angel colors

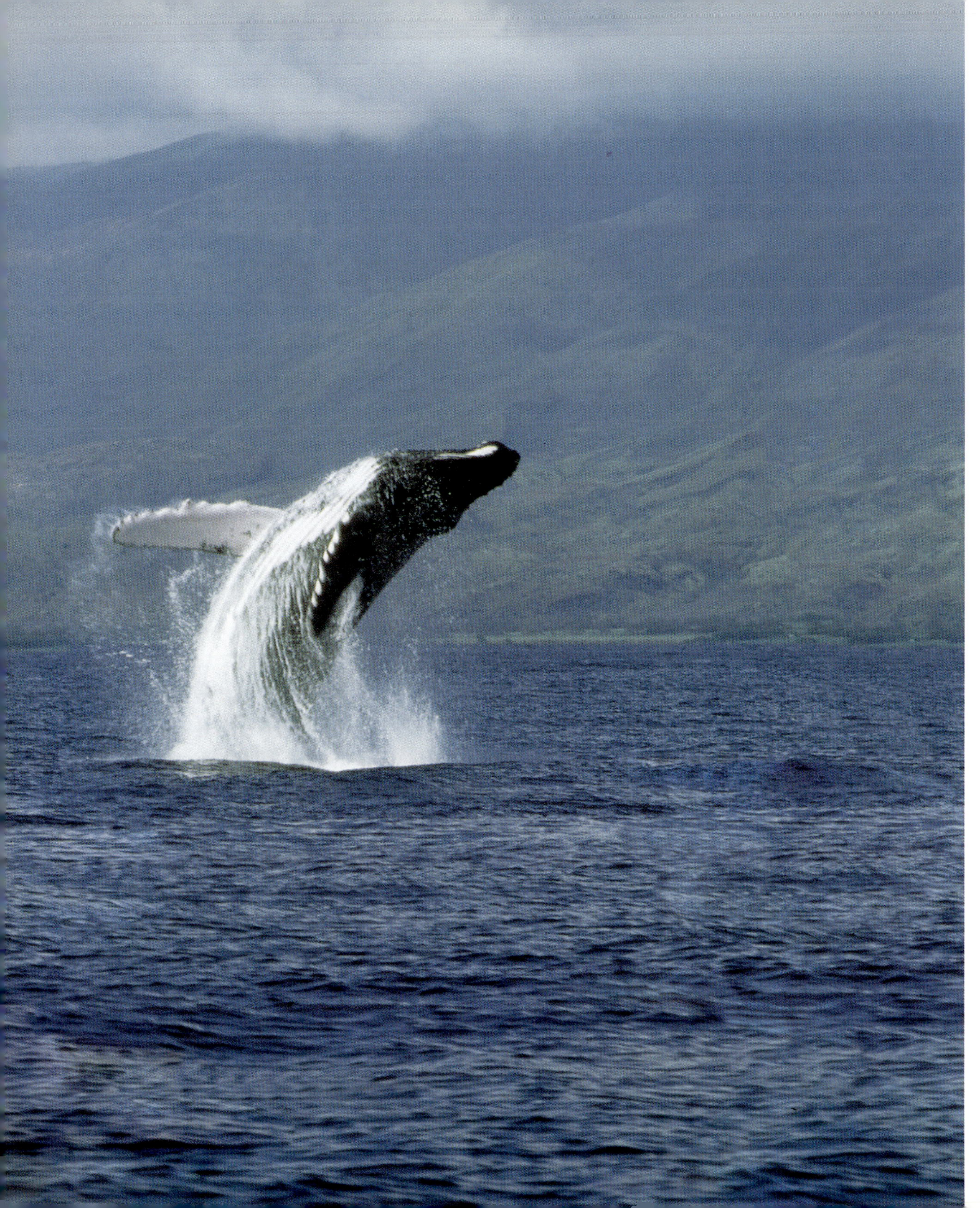

◄ whale flight
► waimea shore break

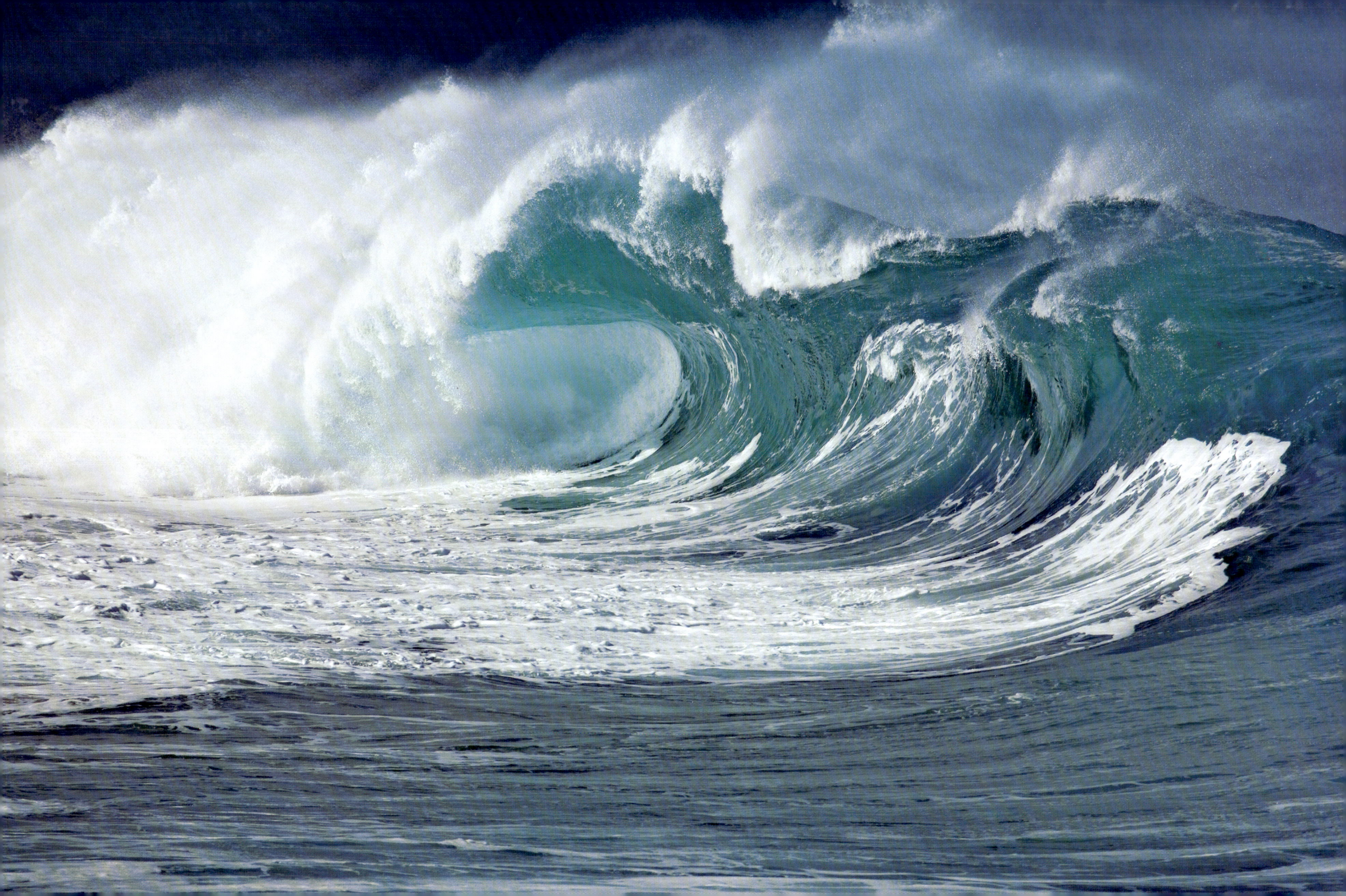

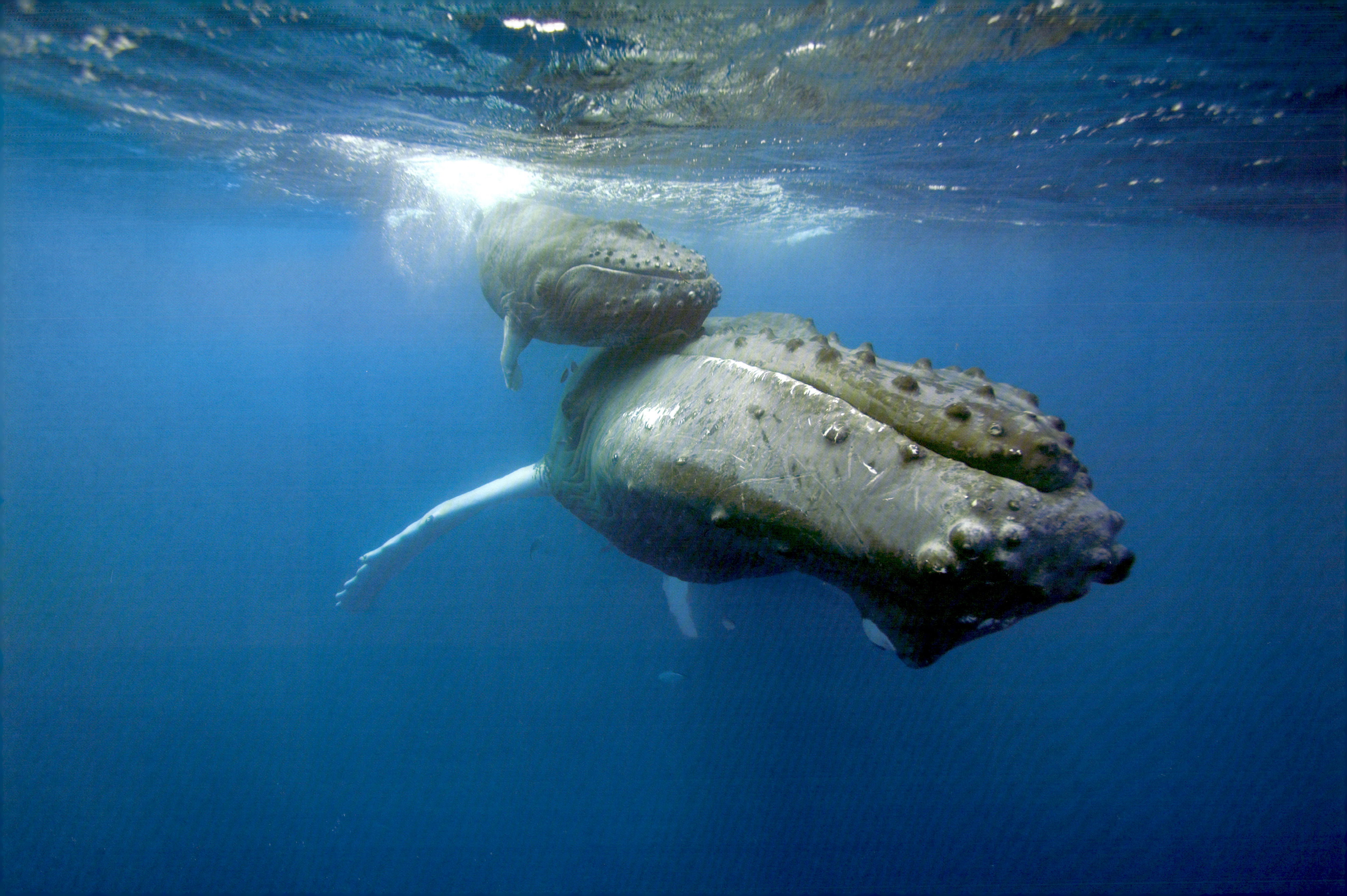

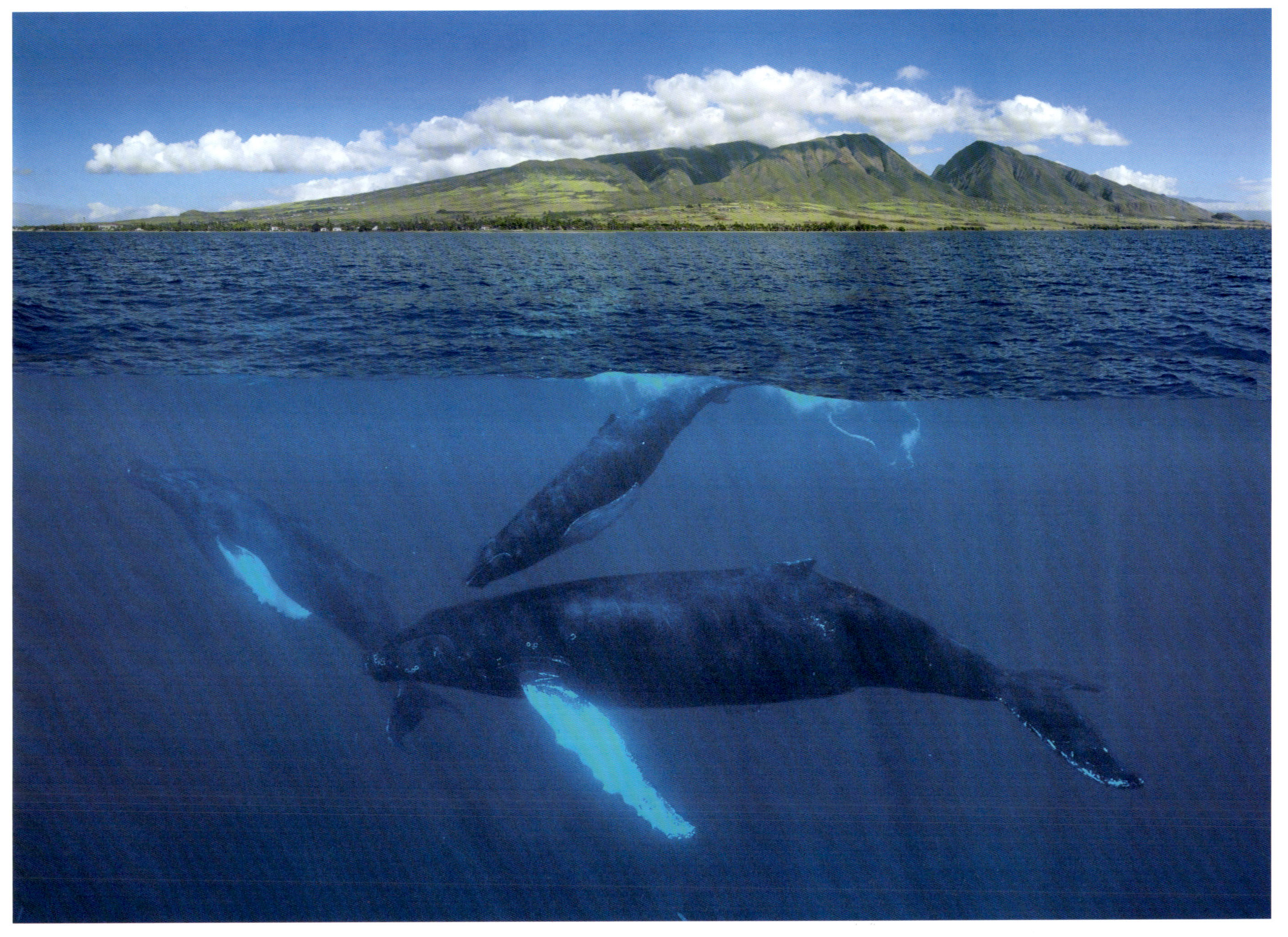

close encounter
maui whale waters

69

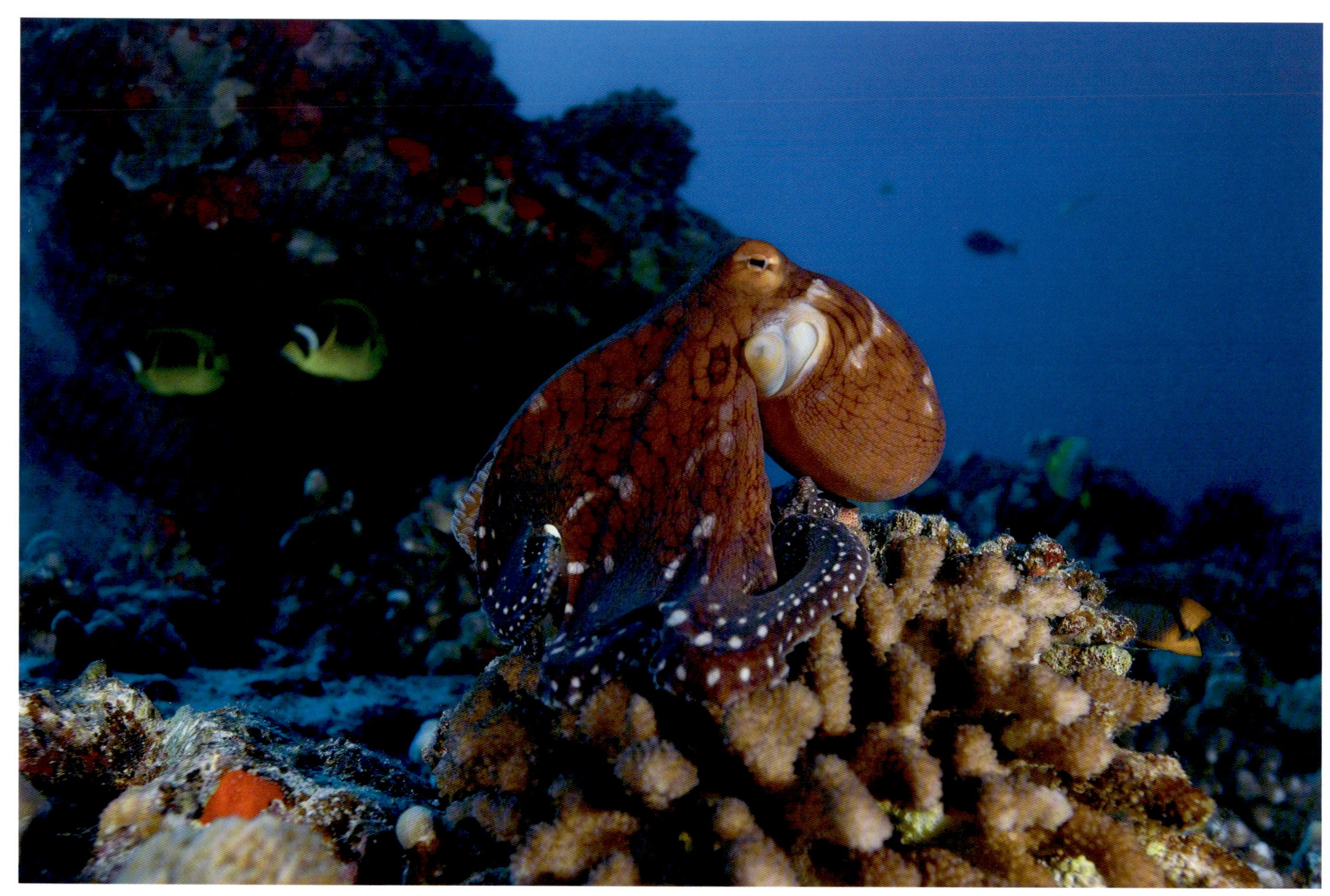

◄ noble octopus
► clown fish anemone

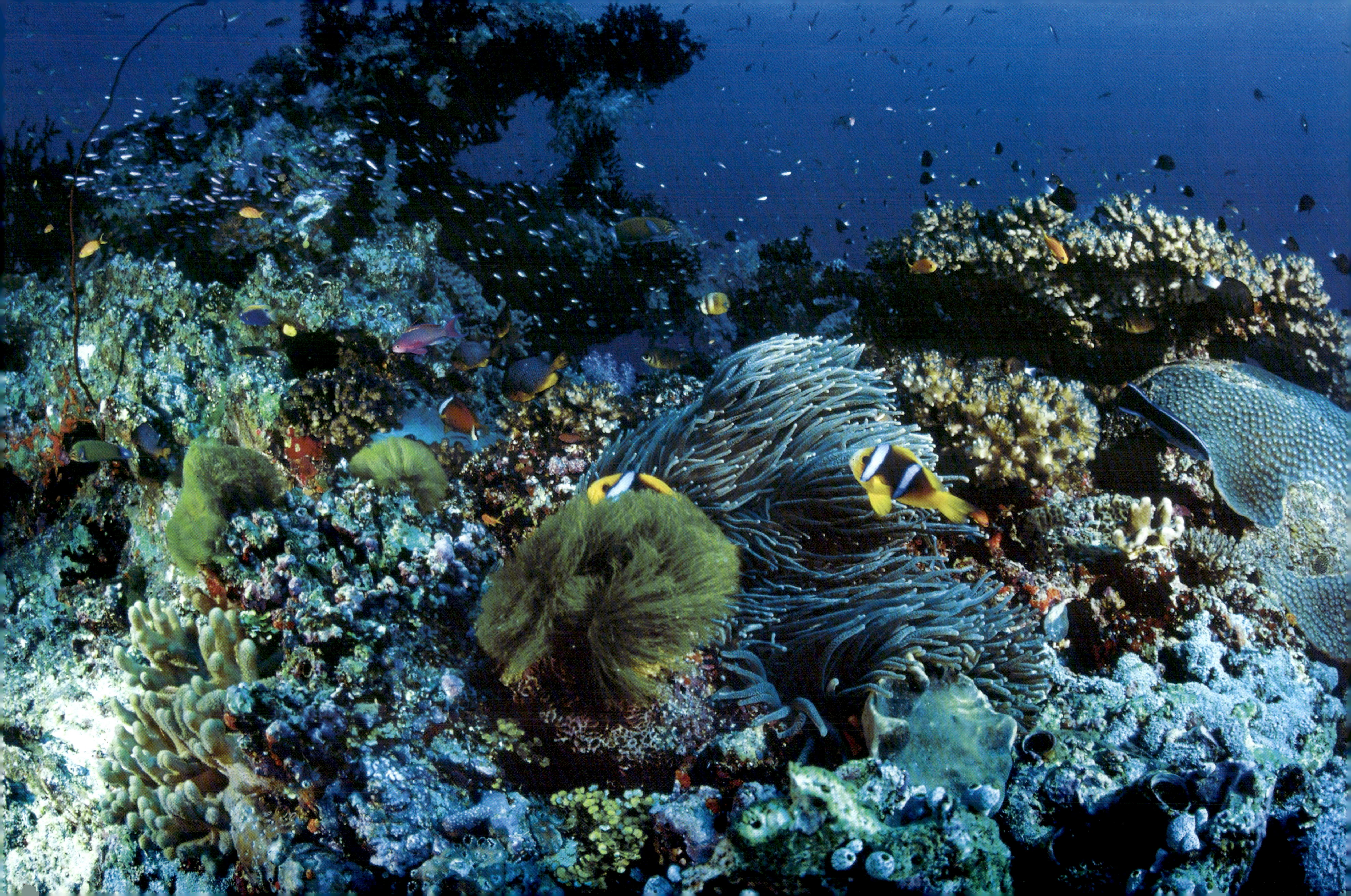

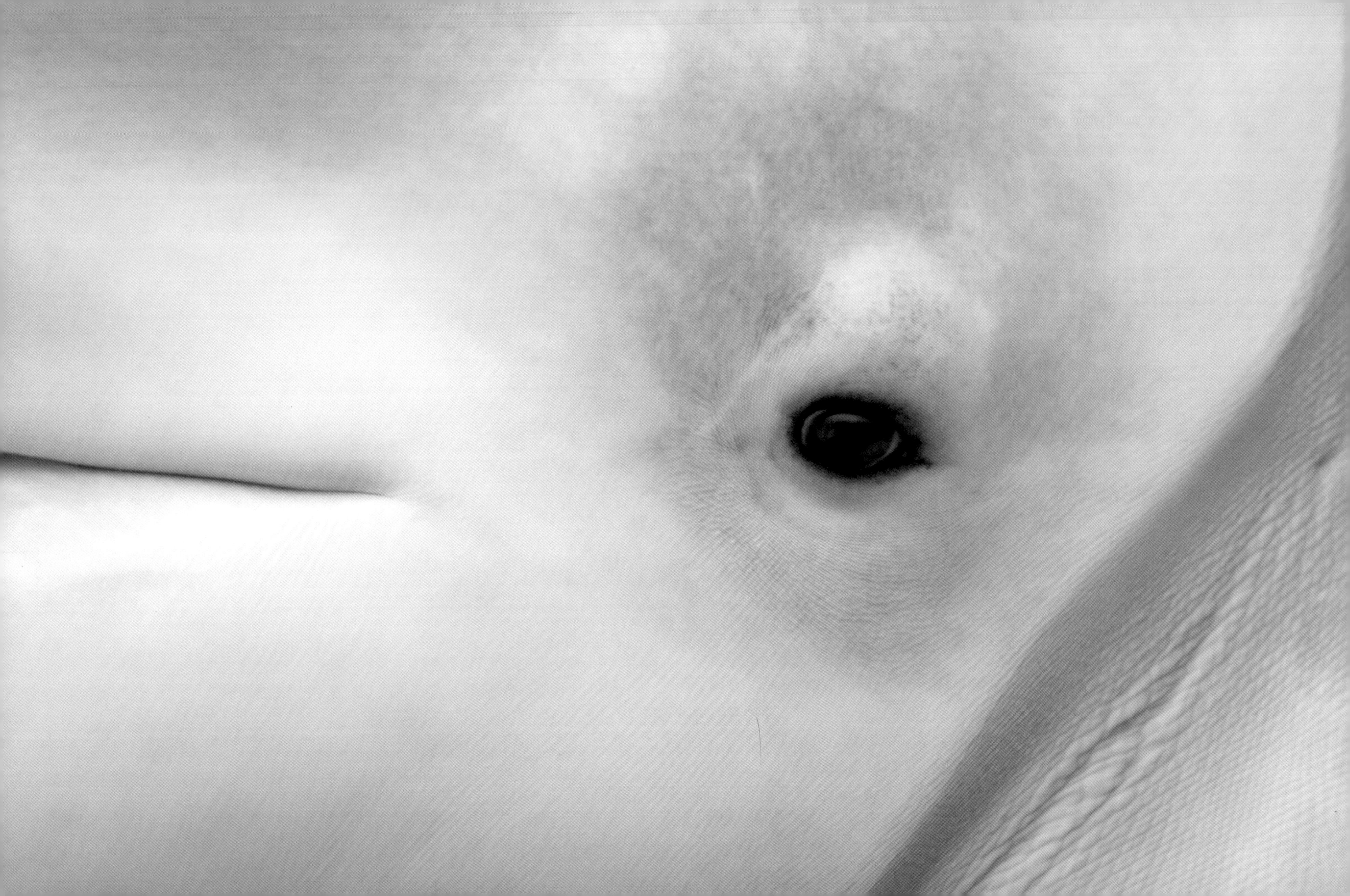

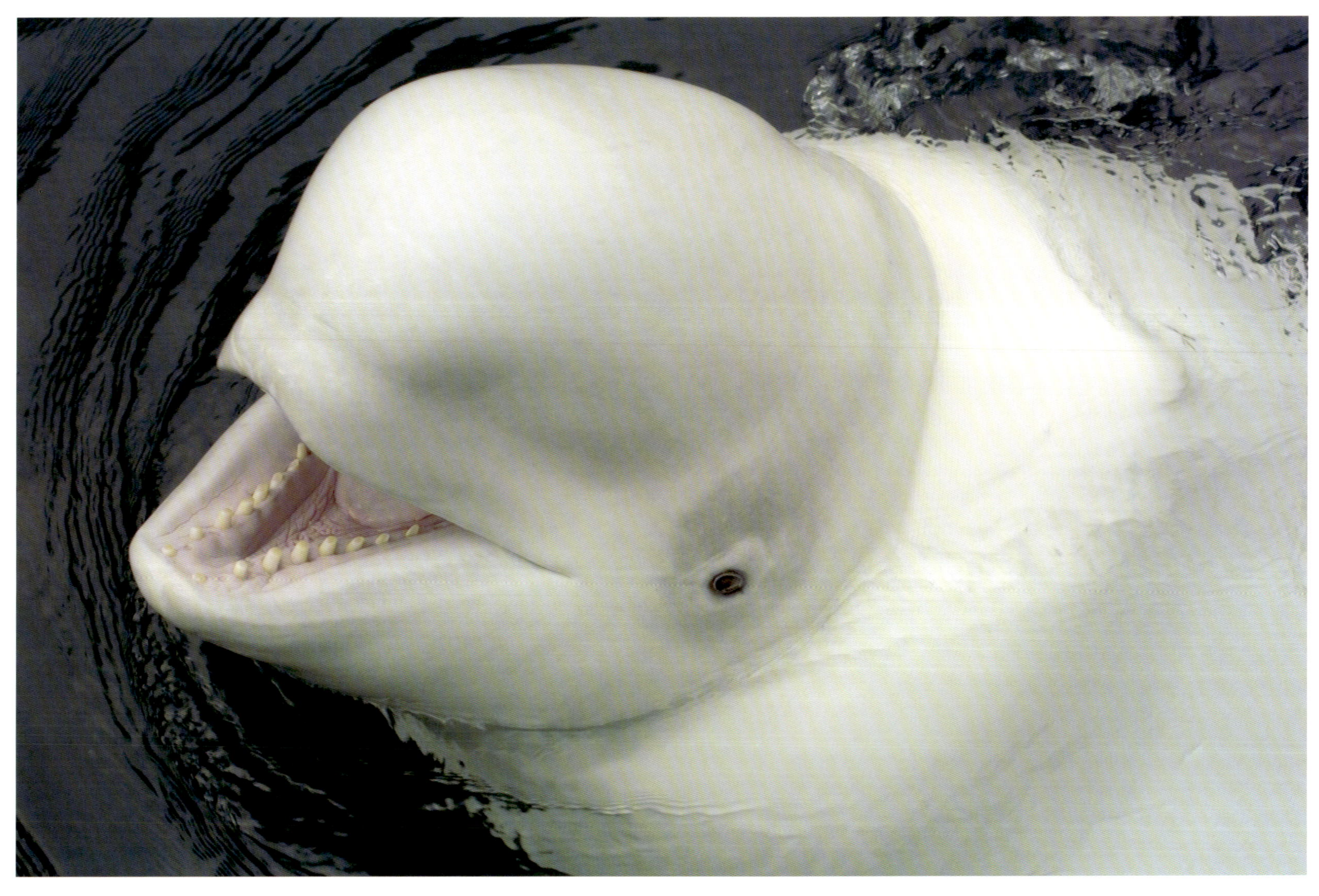

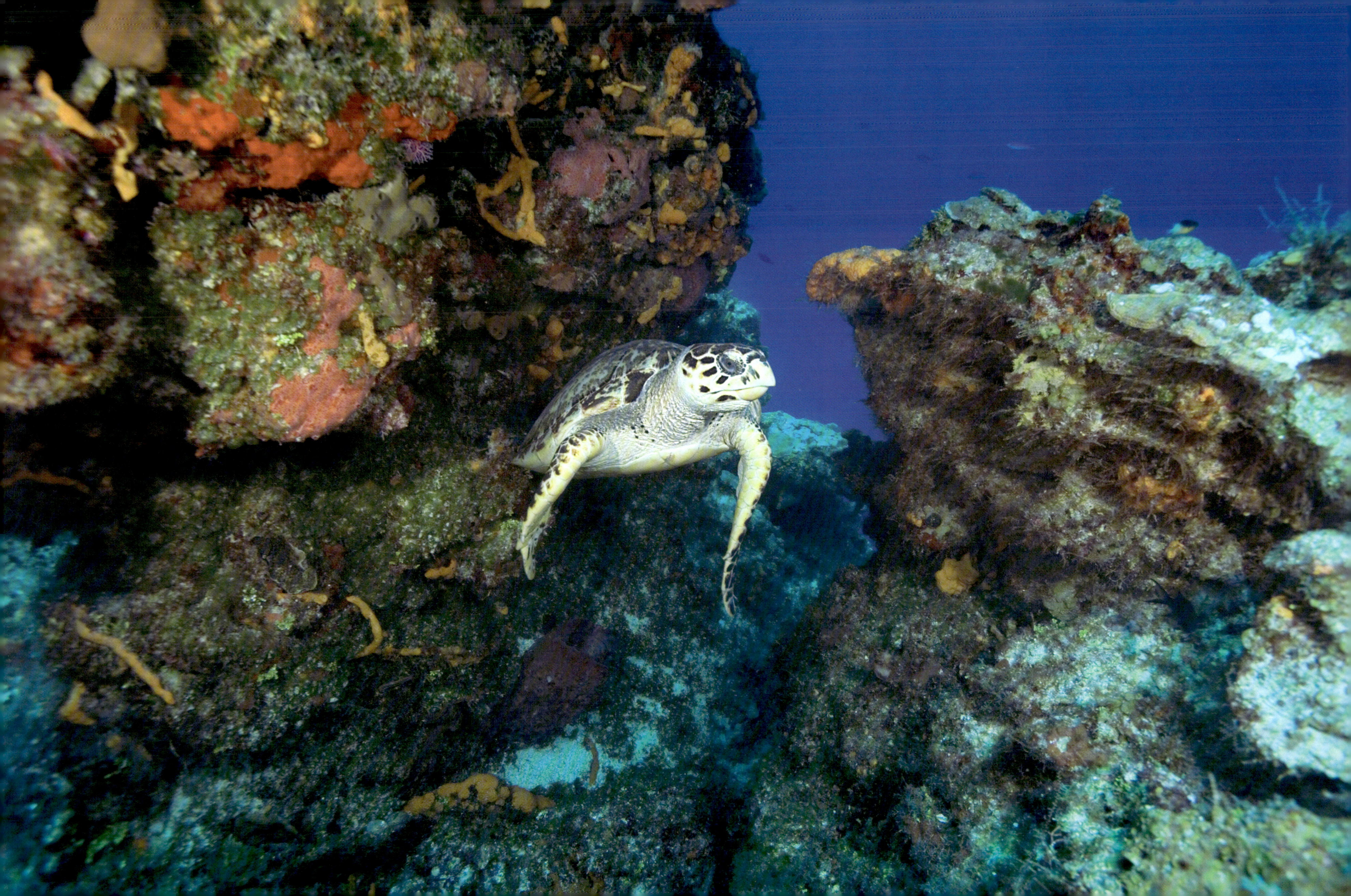

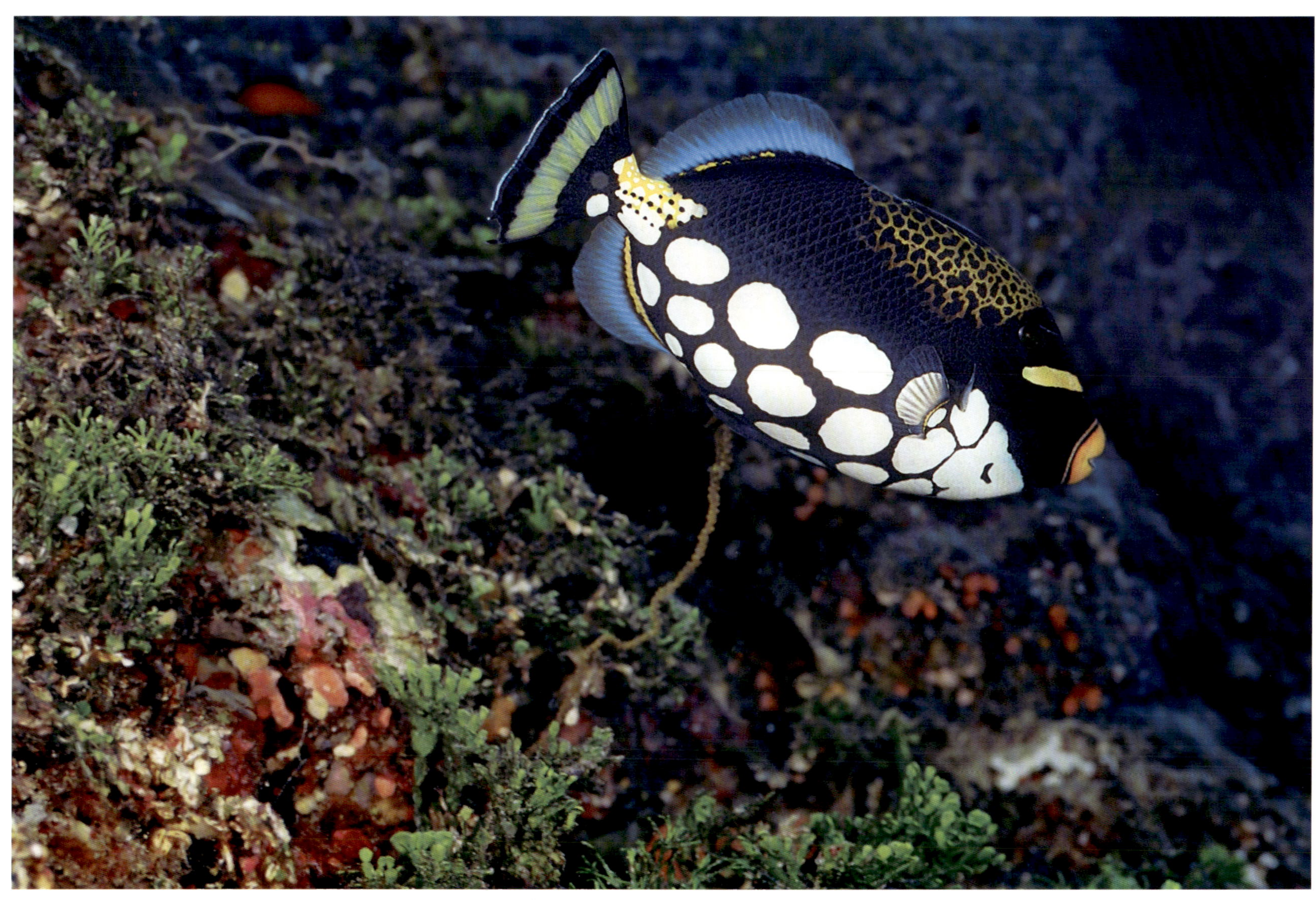

◀ turtle reef home
▶ clown trigger fish

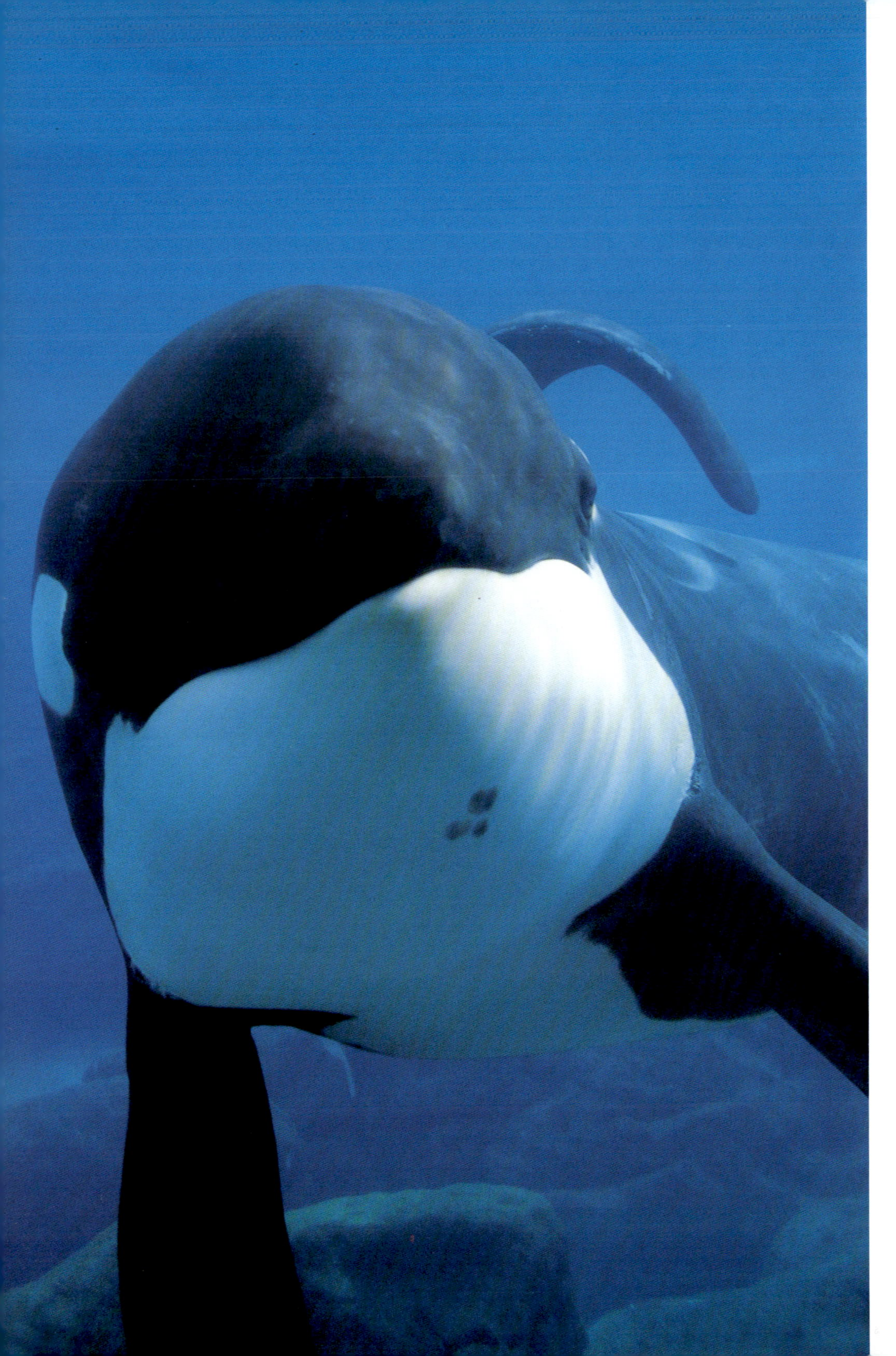

◀ keiko's world
▶ orca family

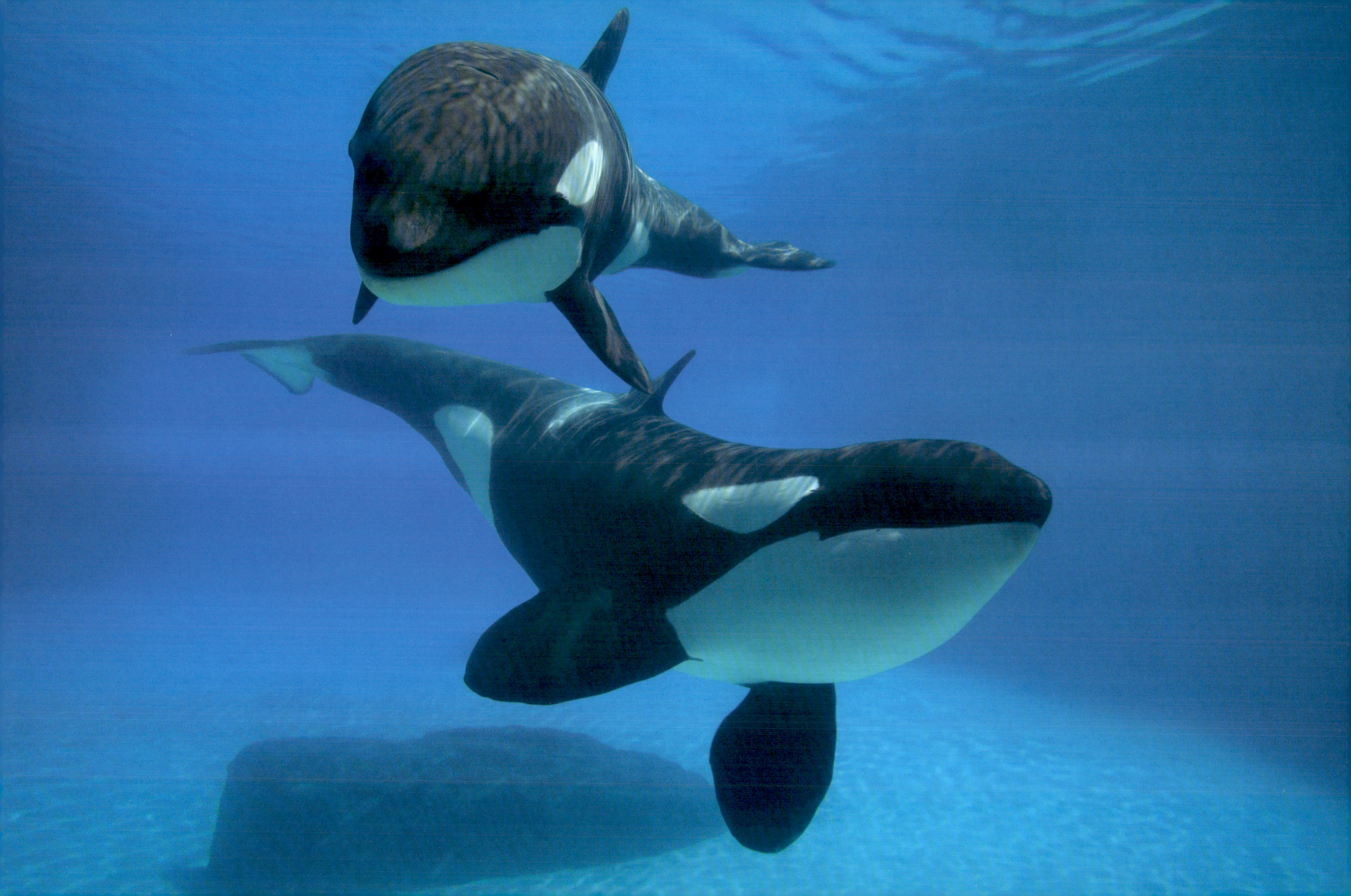

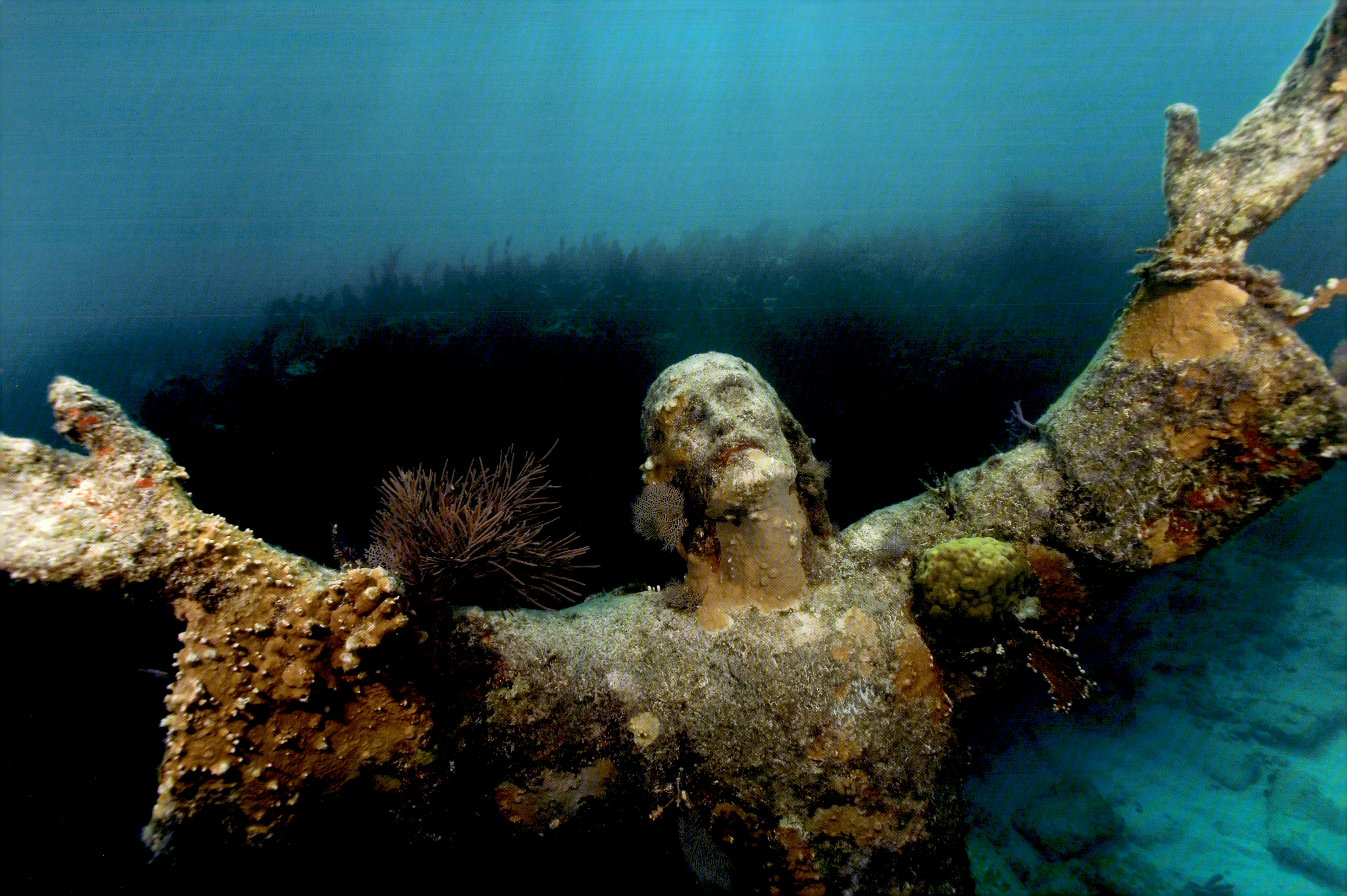

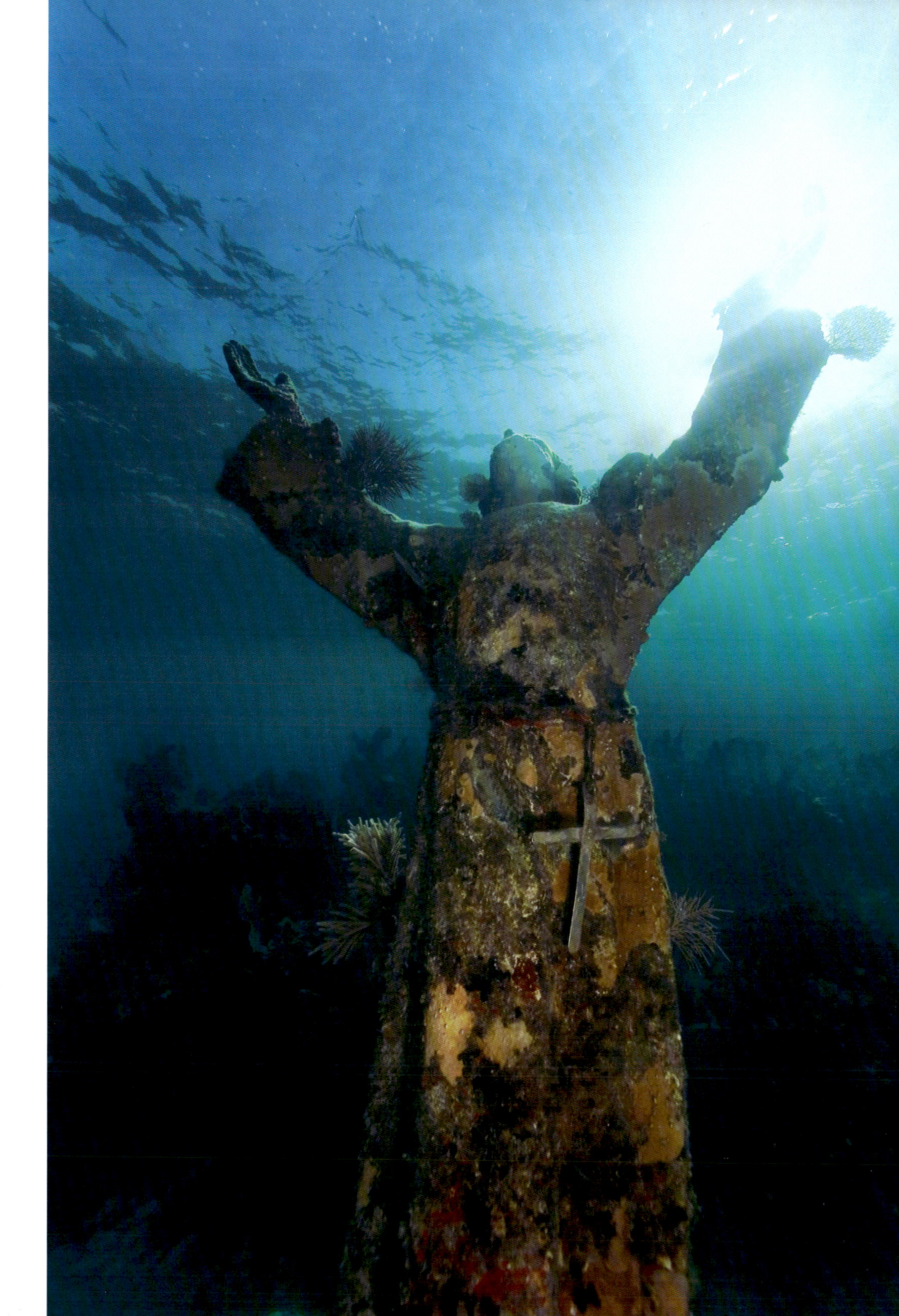

◄ christ of the abyss
► heaven below key largo

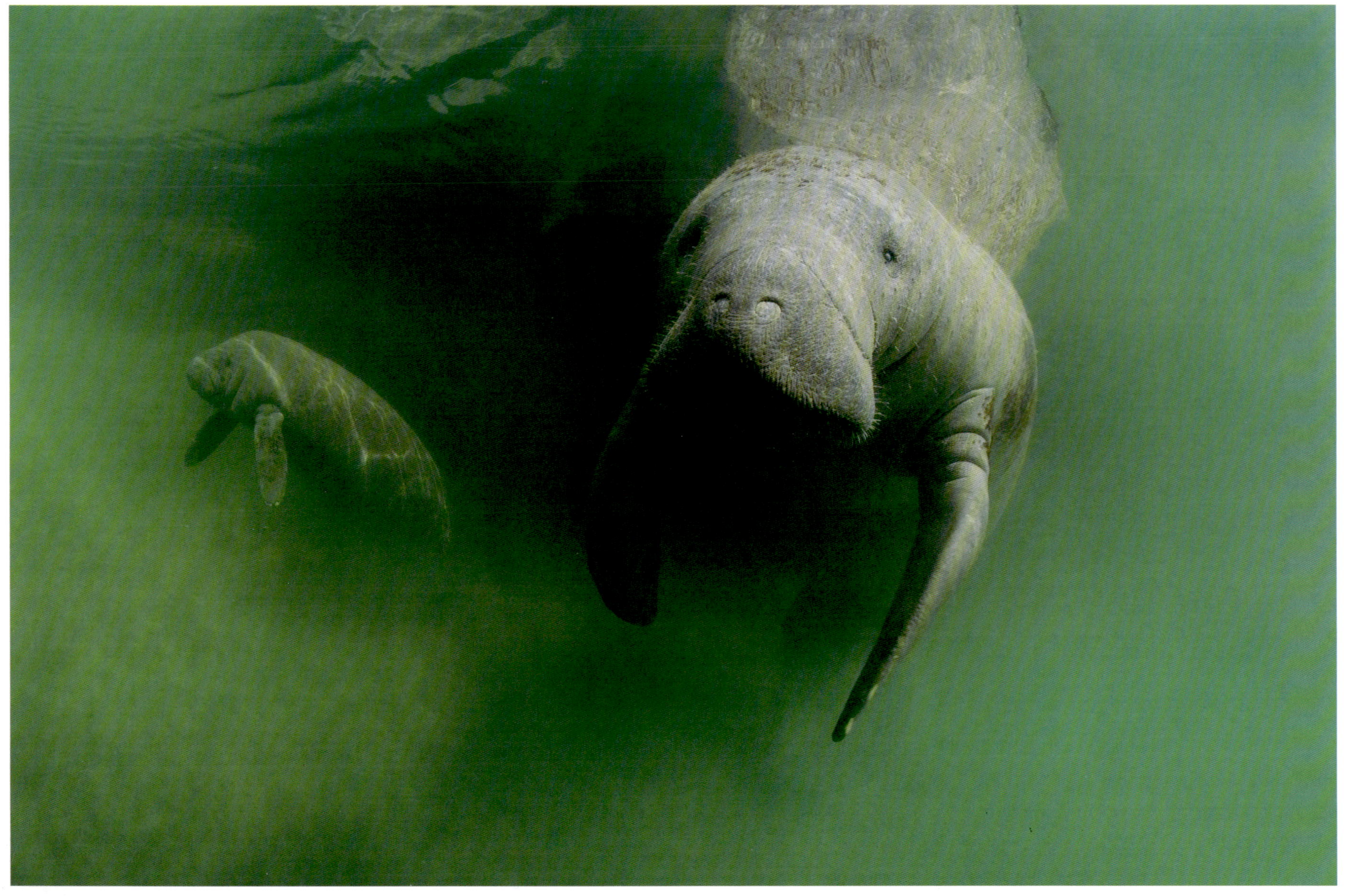

◄ sea cow and calf
► manatee waters

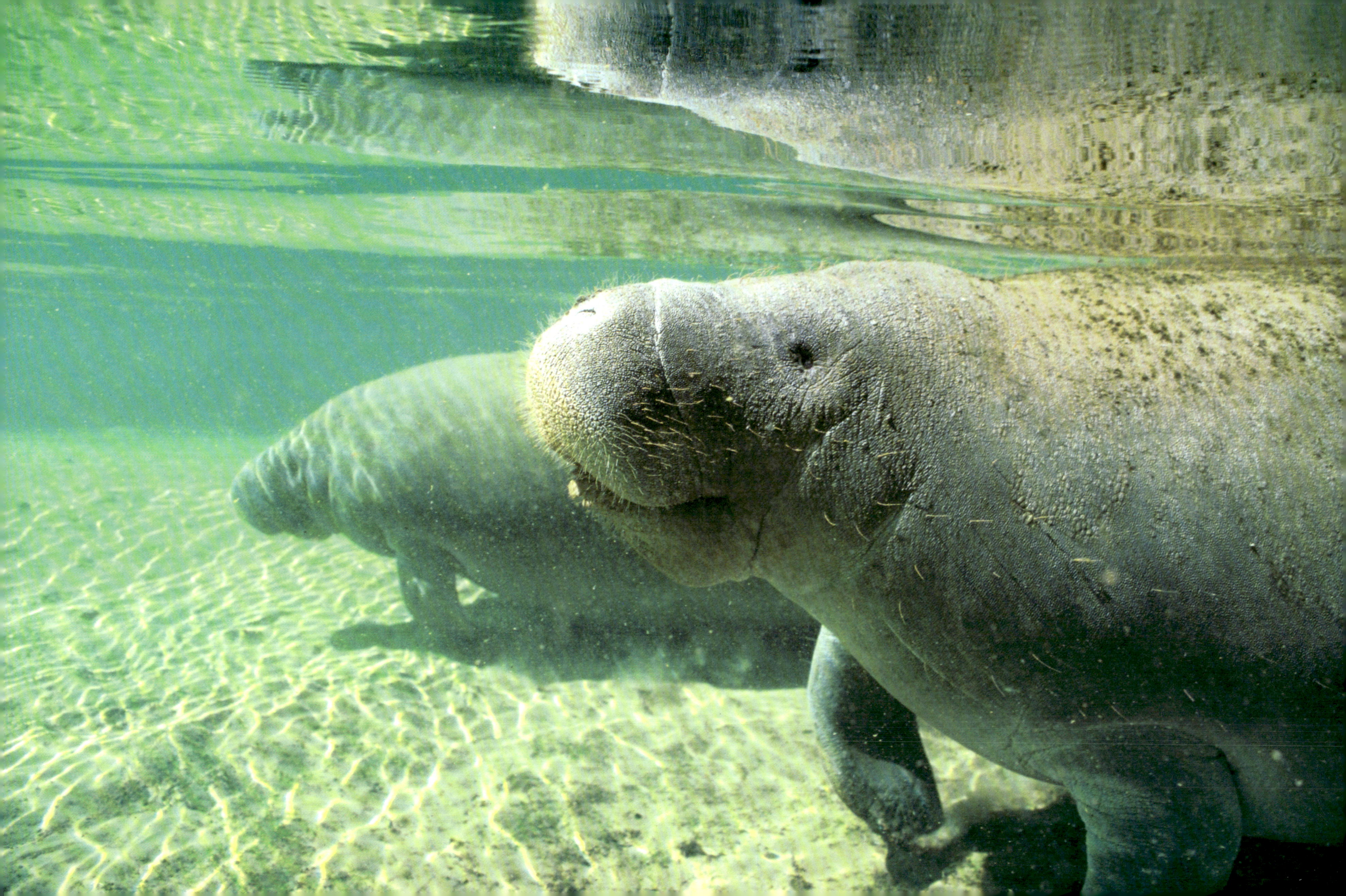

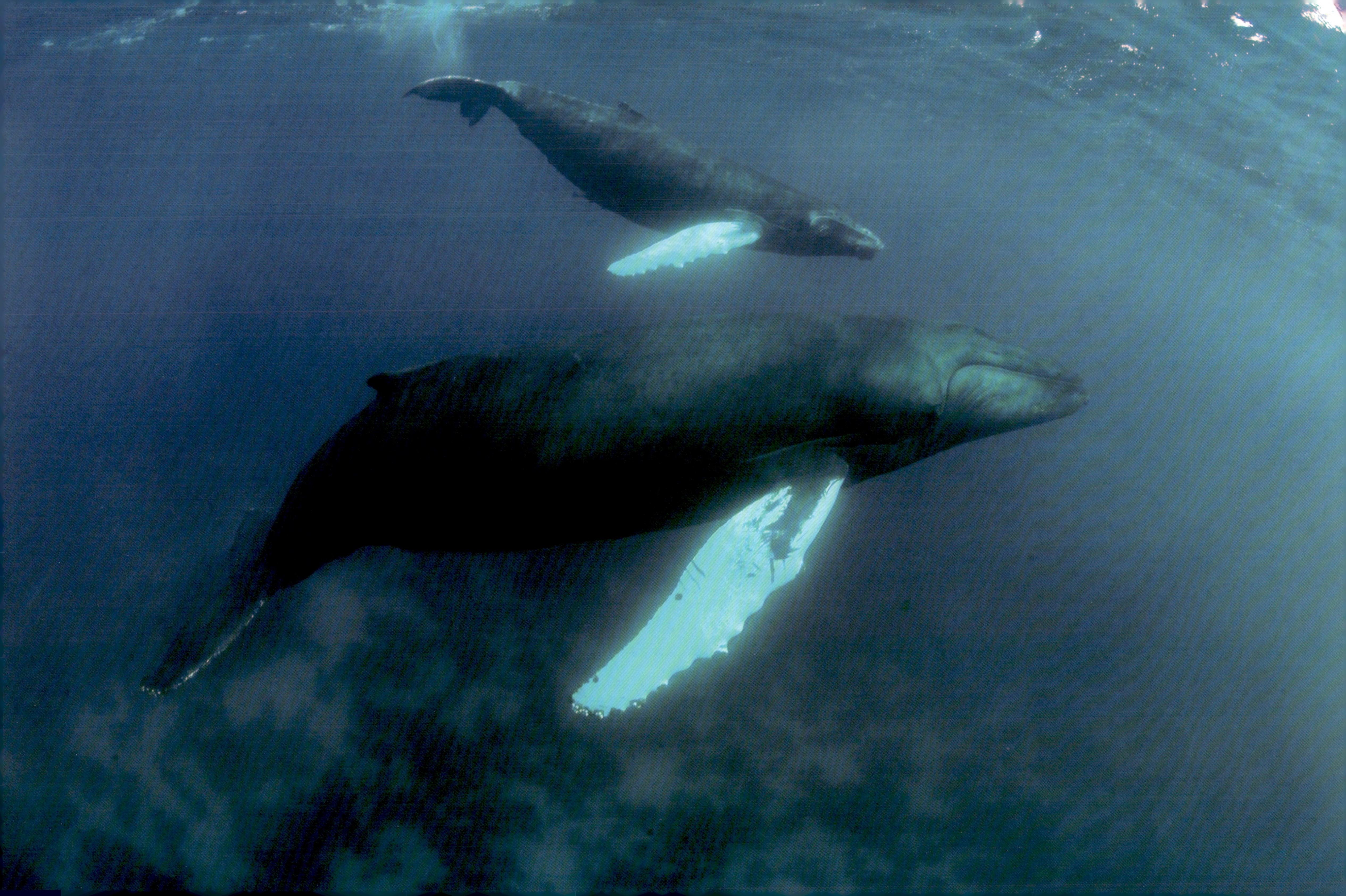

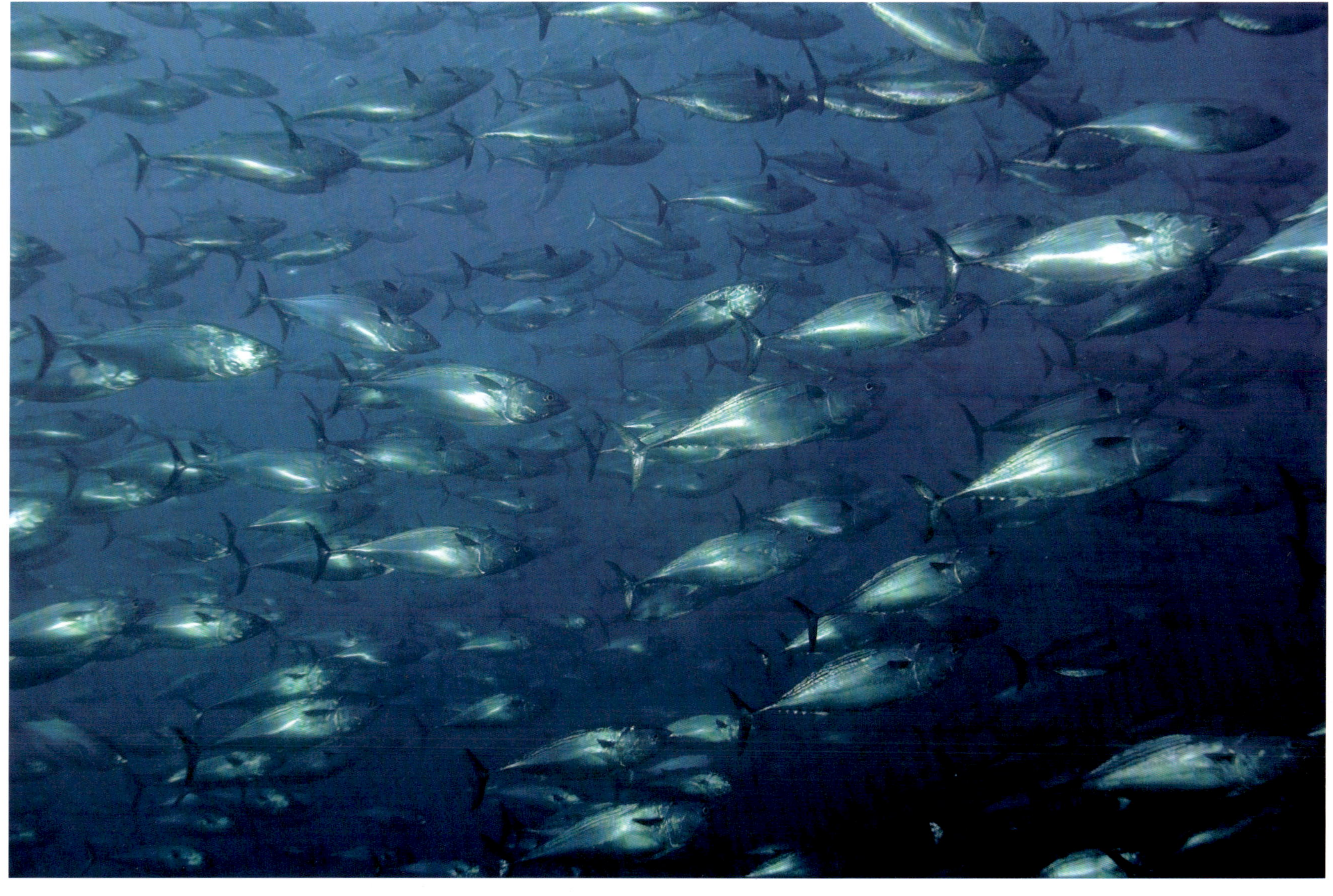

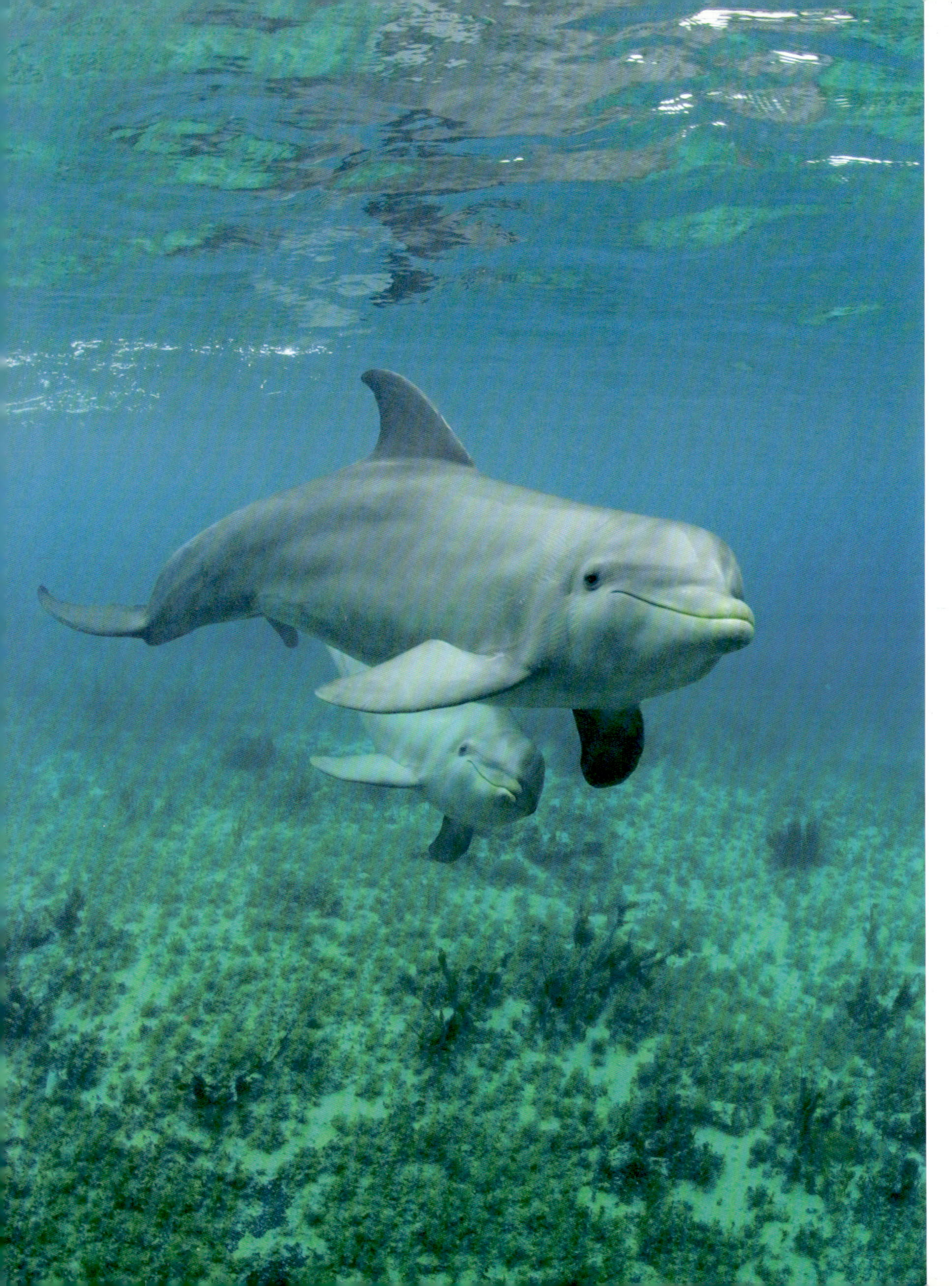

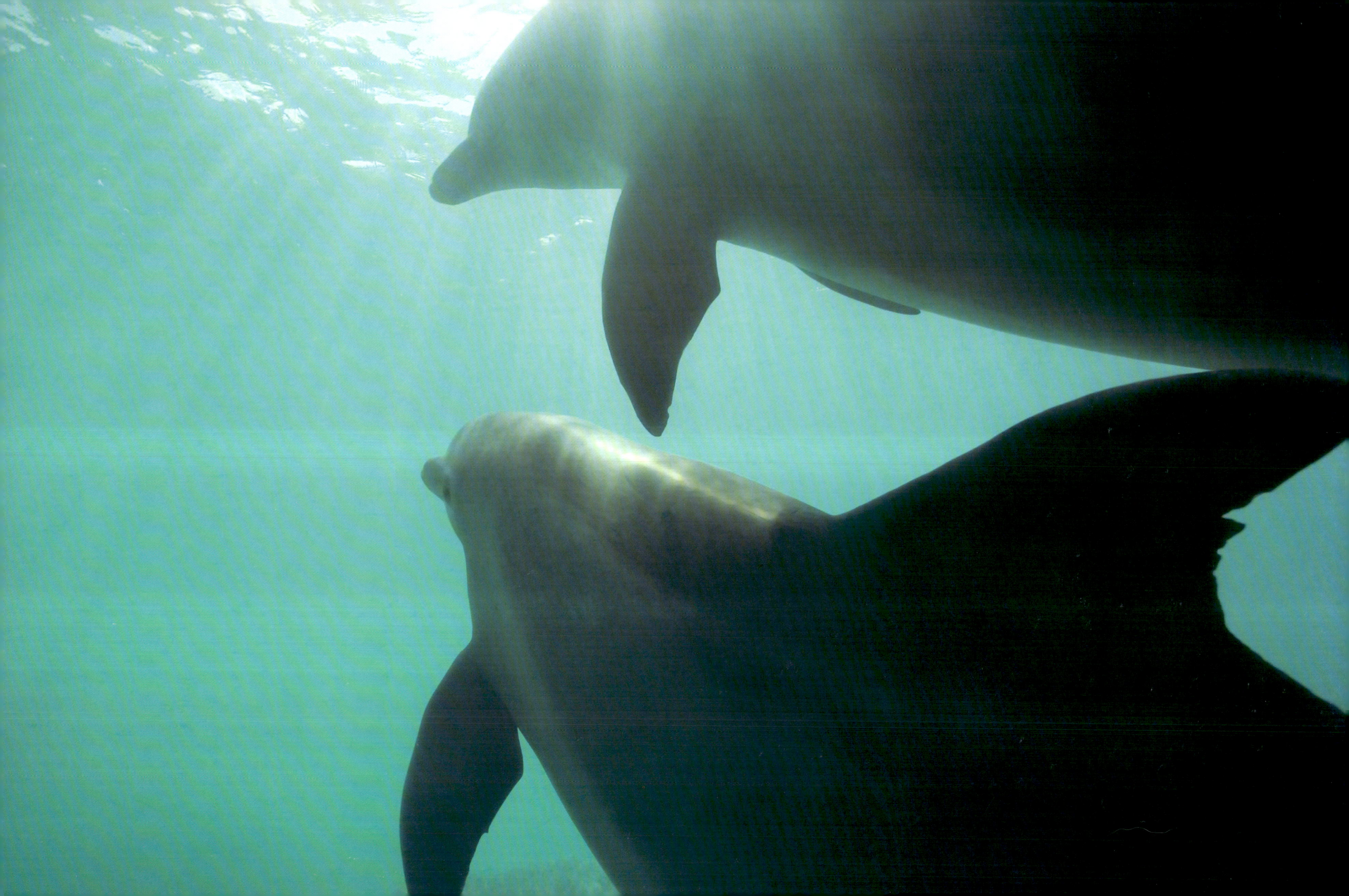

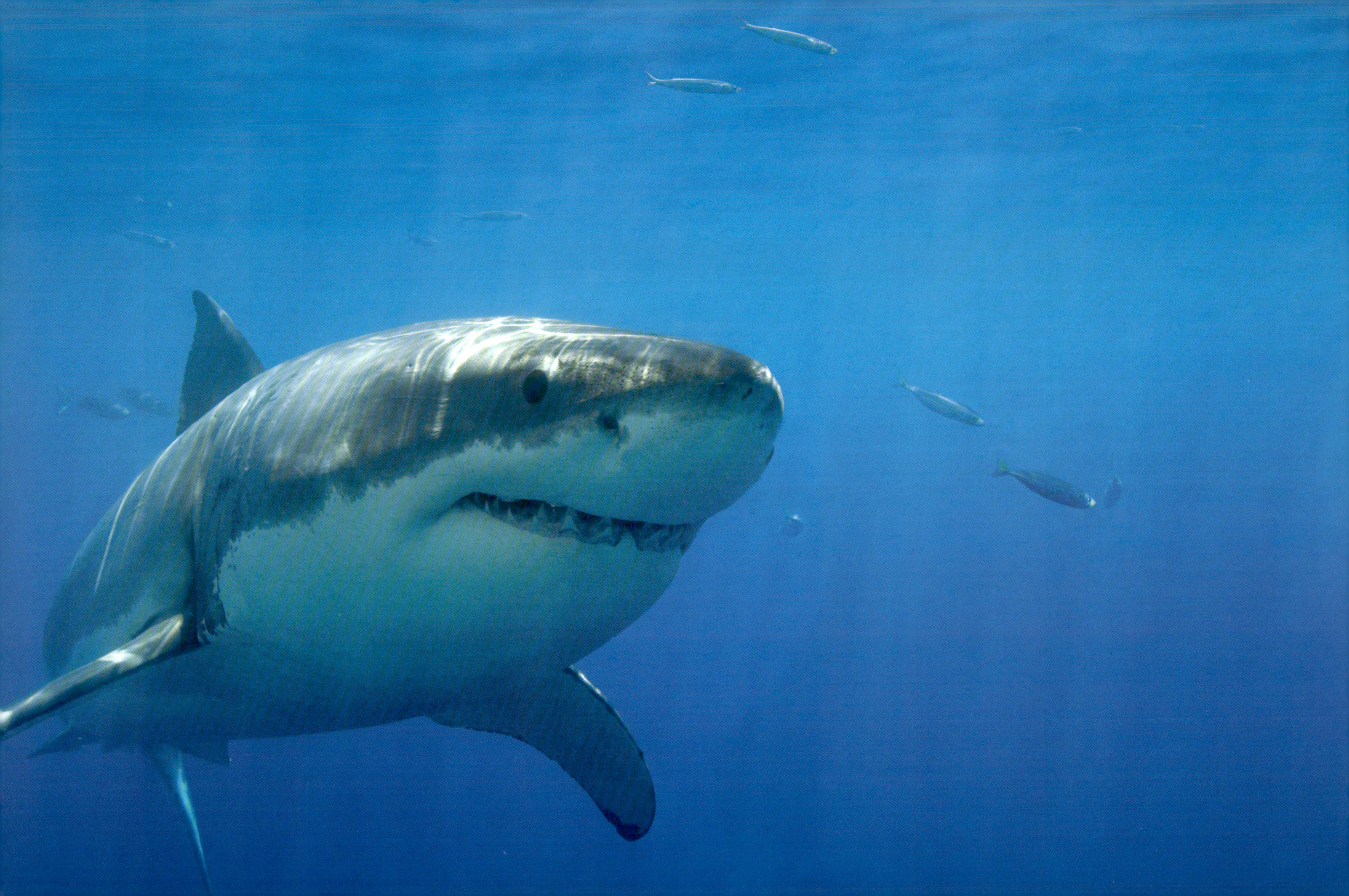

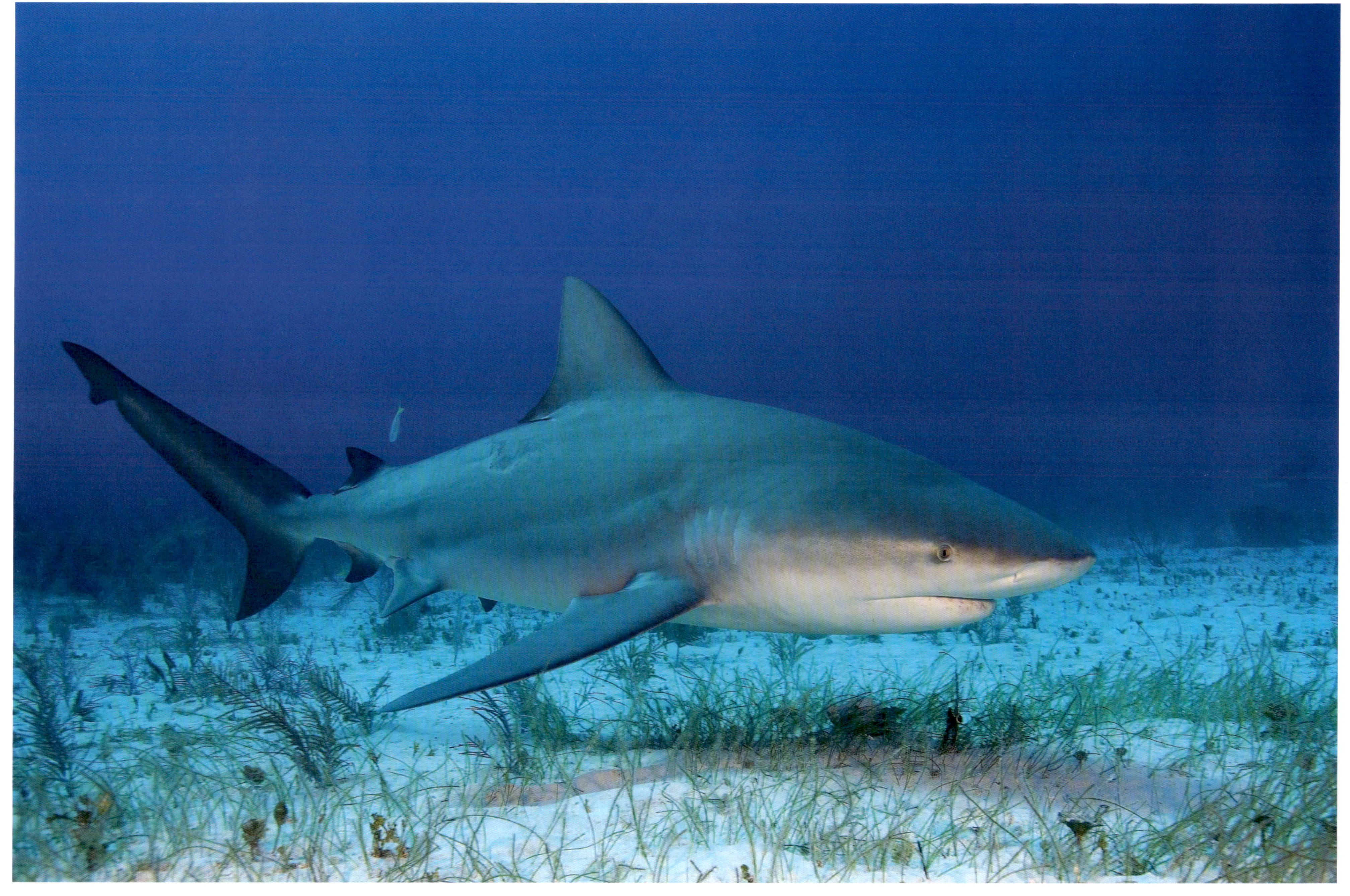

◄ shark view
► bull shark sea

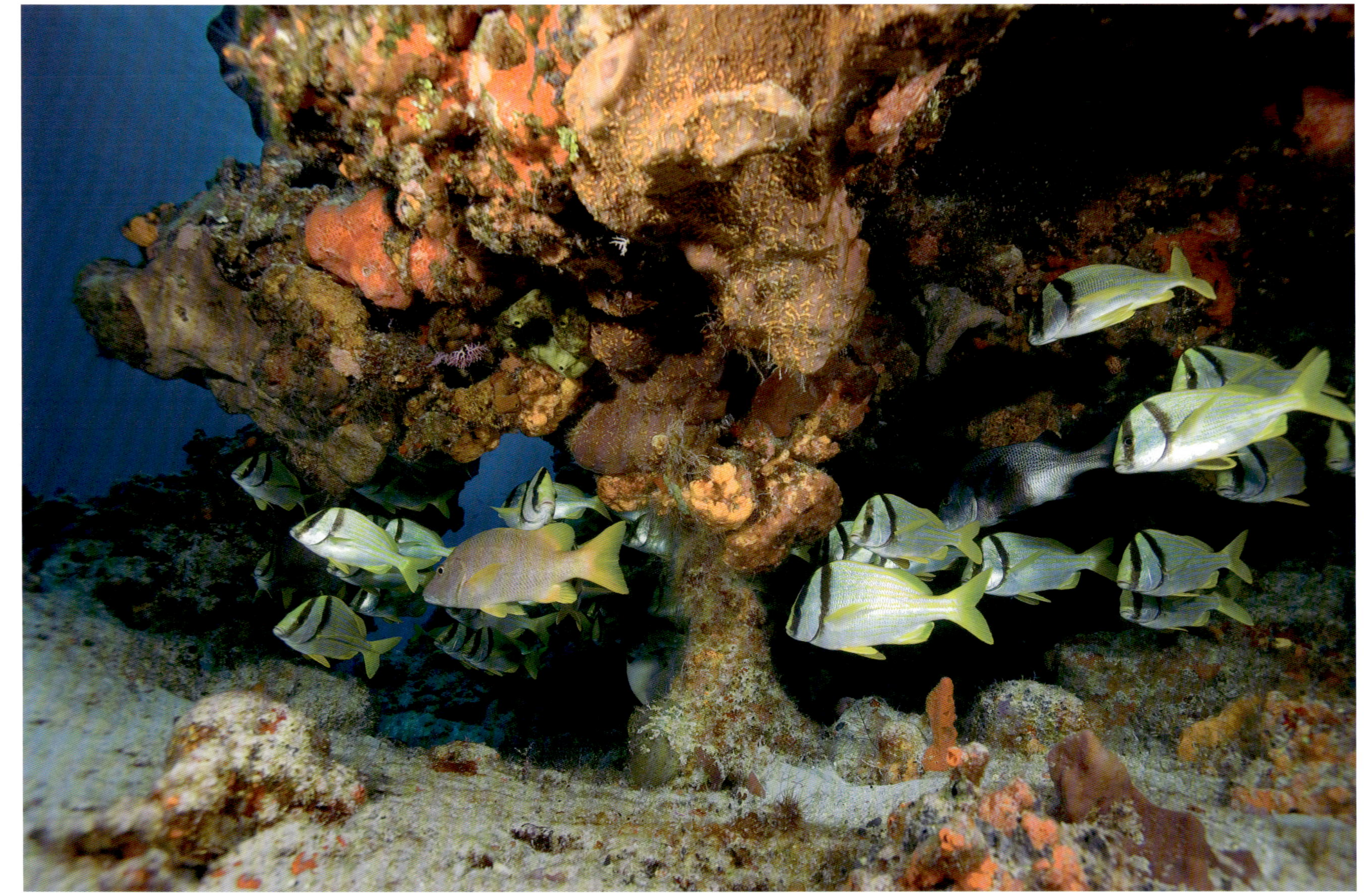

◄ pork fish reef
► goliath grouper

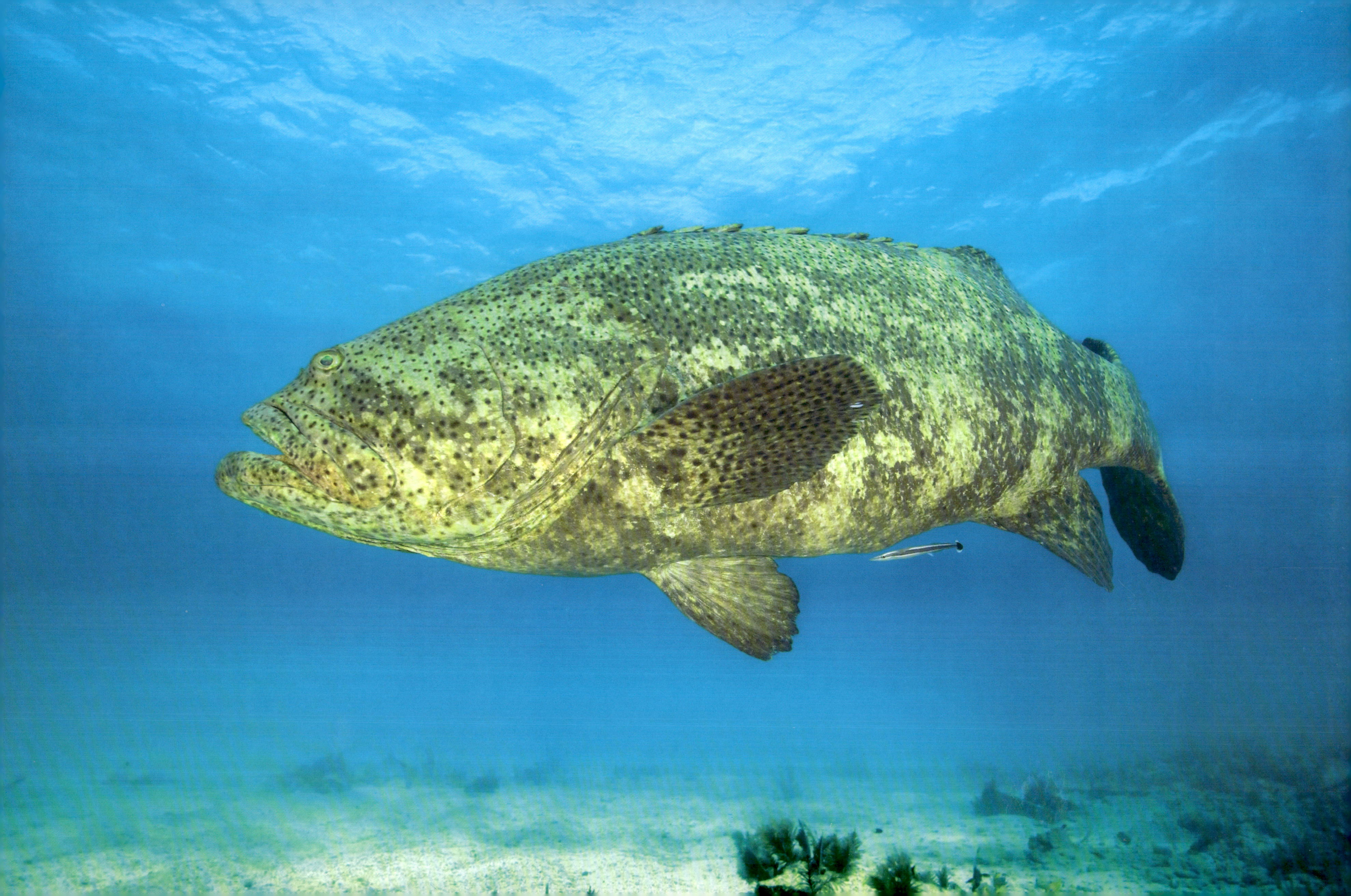

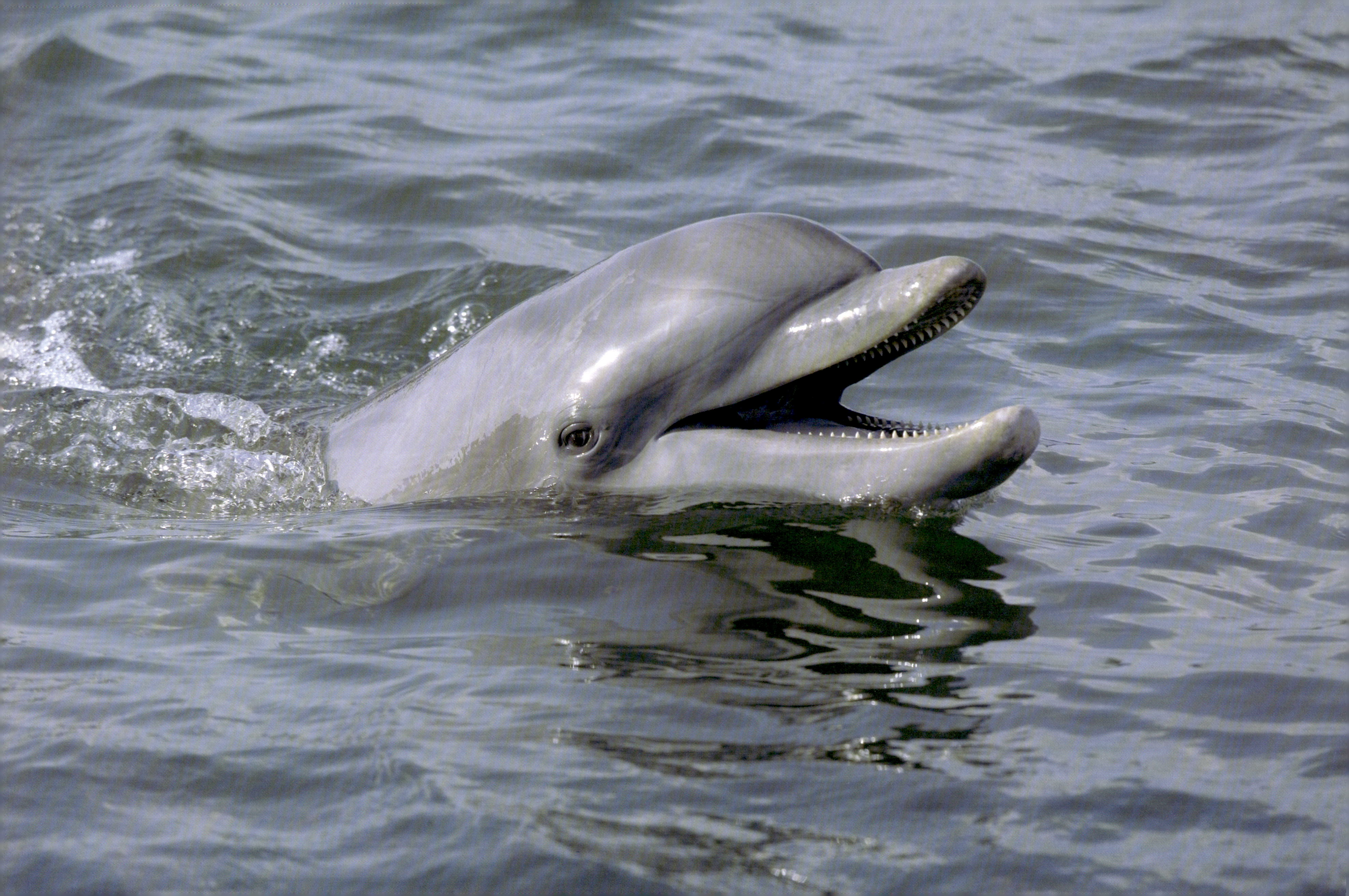

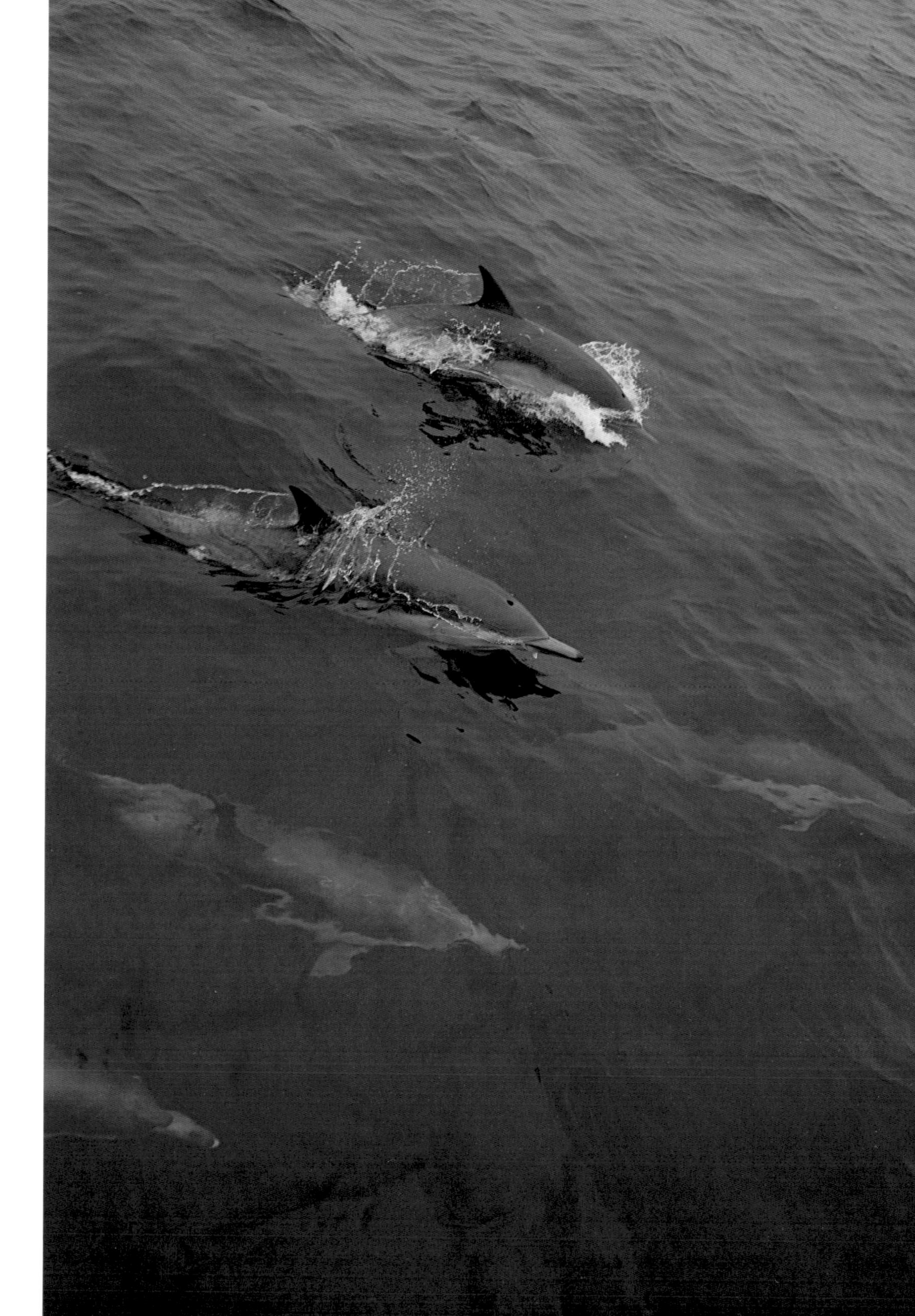

◄ dolphin celebration
► common dolphin surface

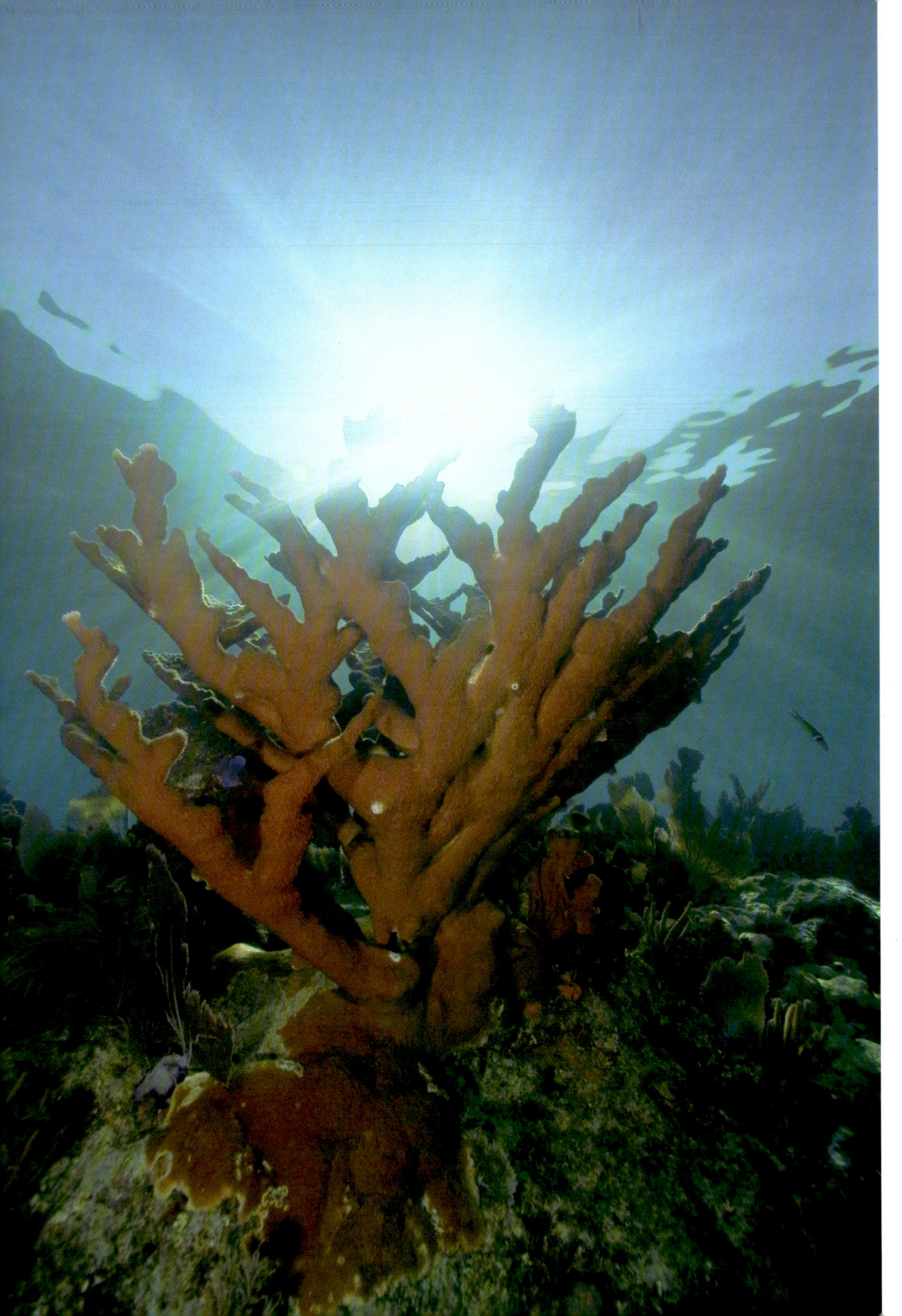

elkhorn light
warmth of the reef

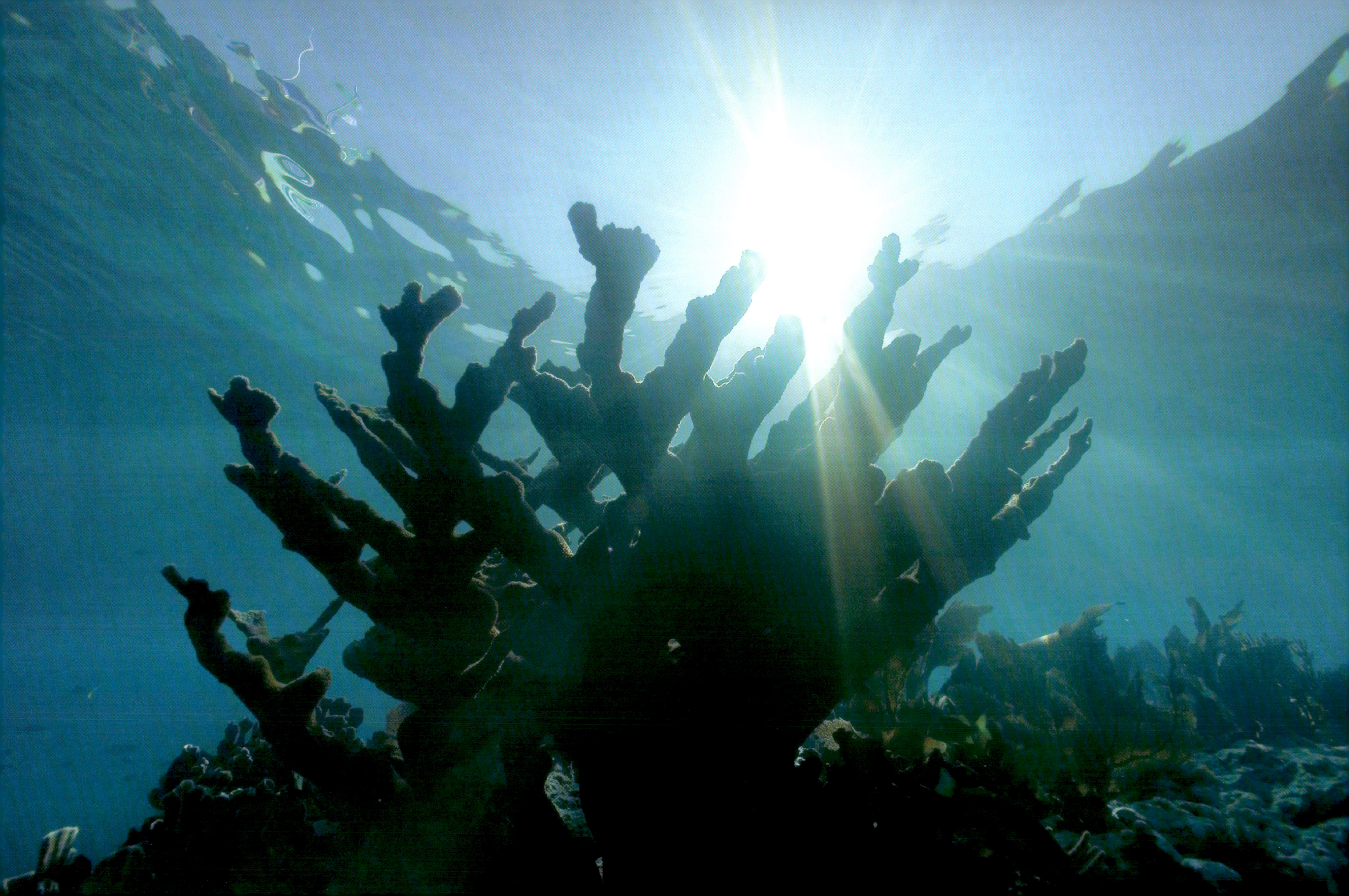

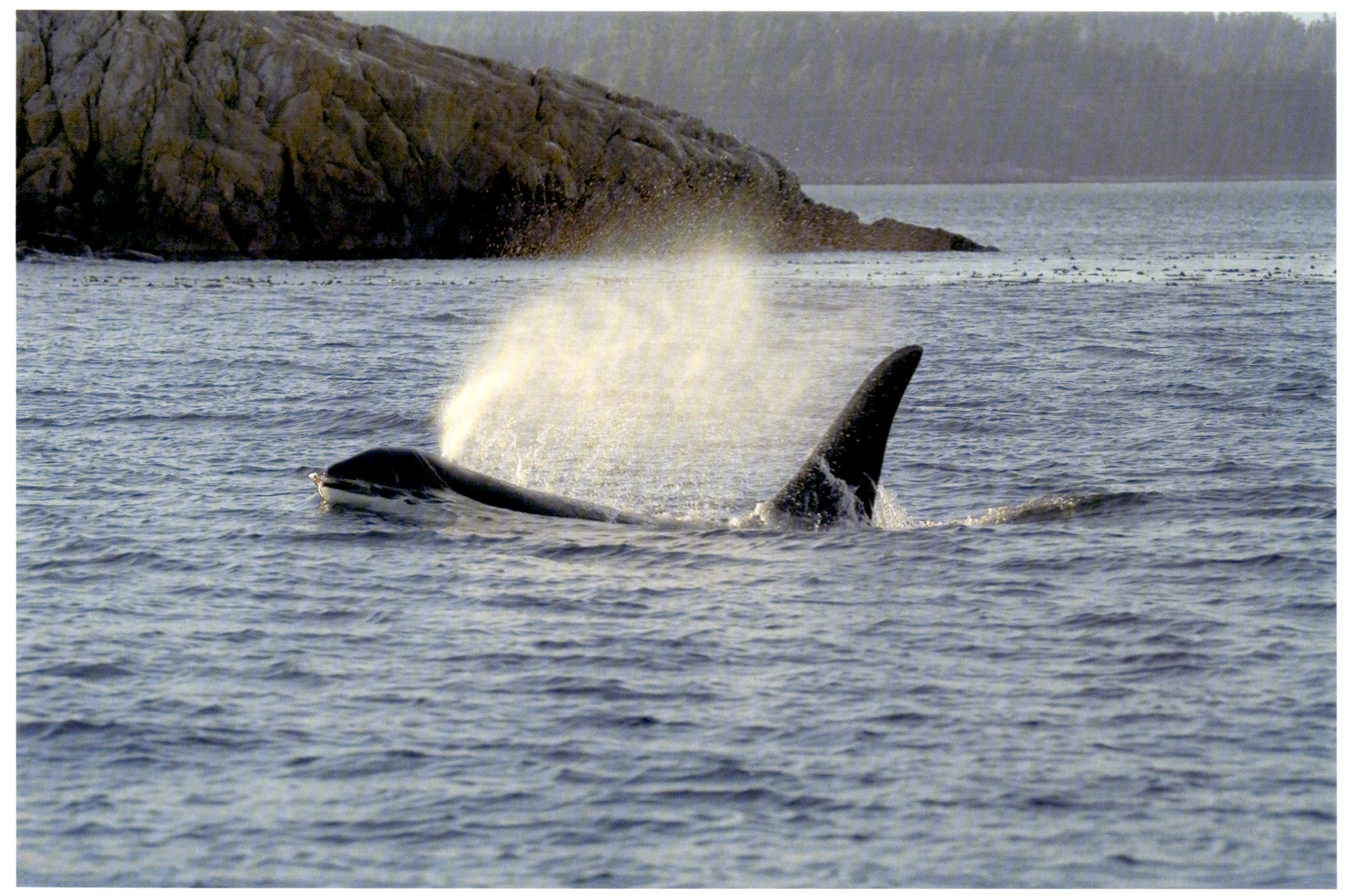

◄ orca spray
► orca breach

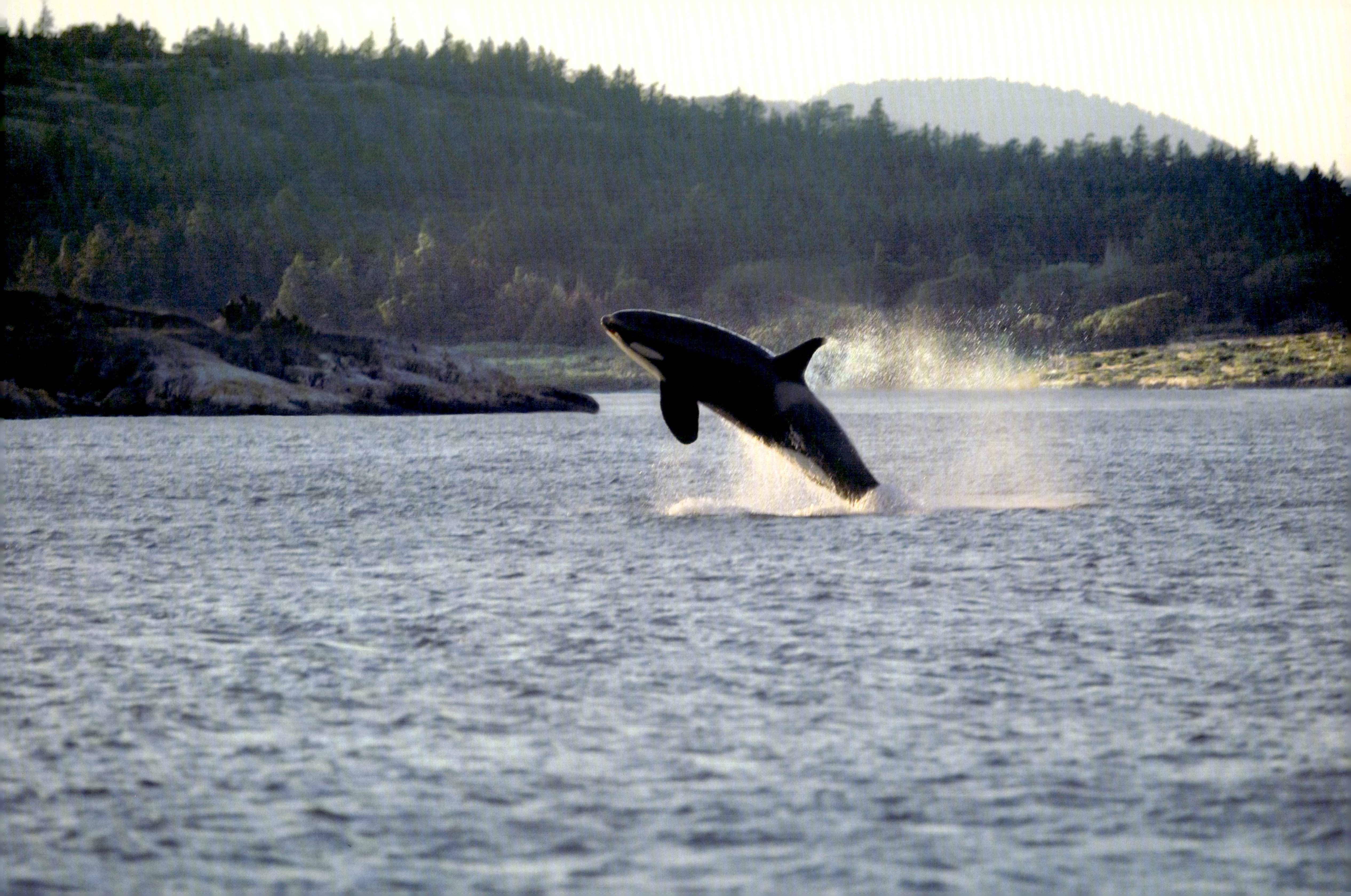

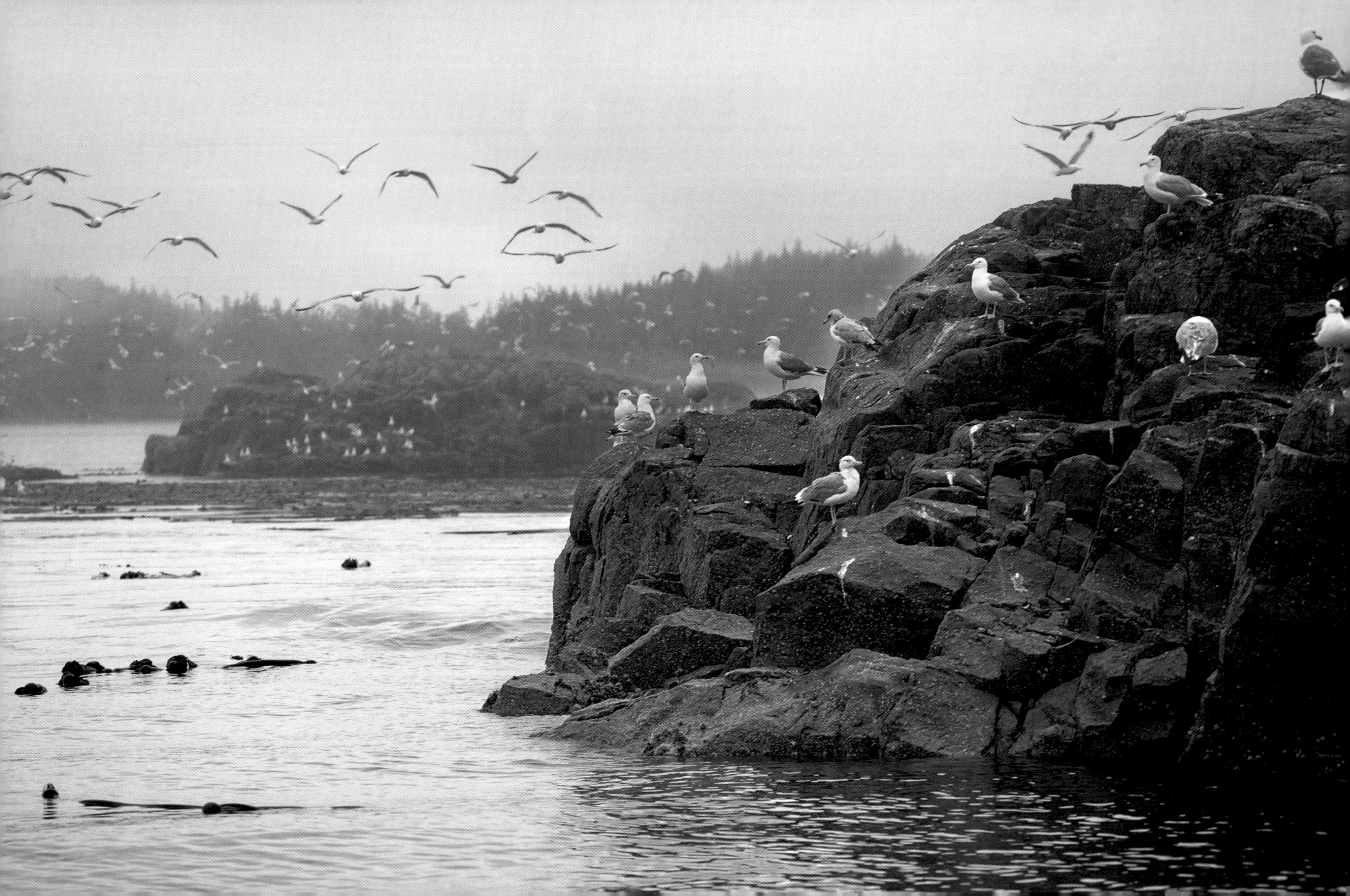

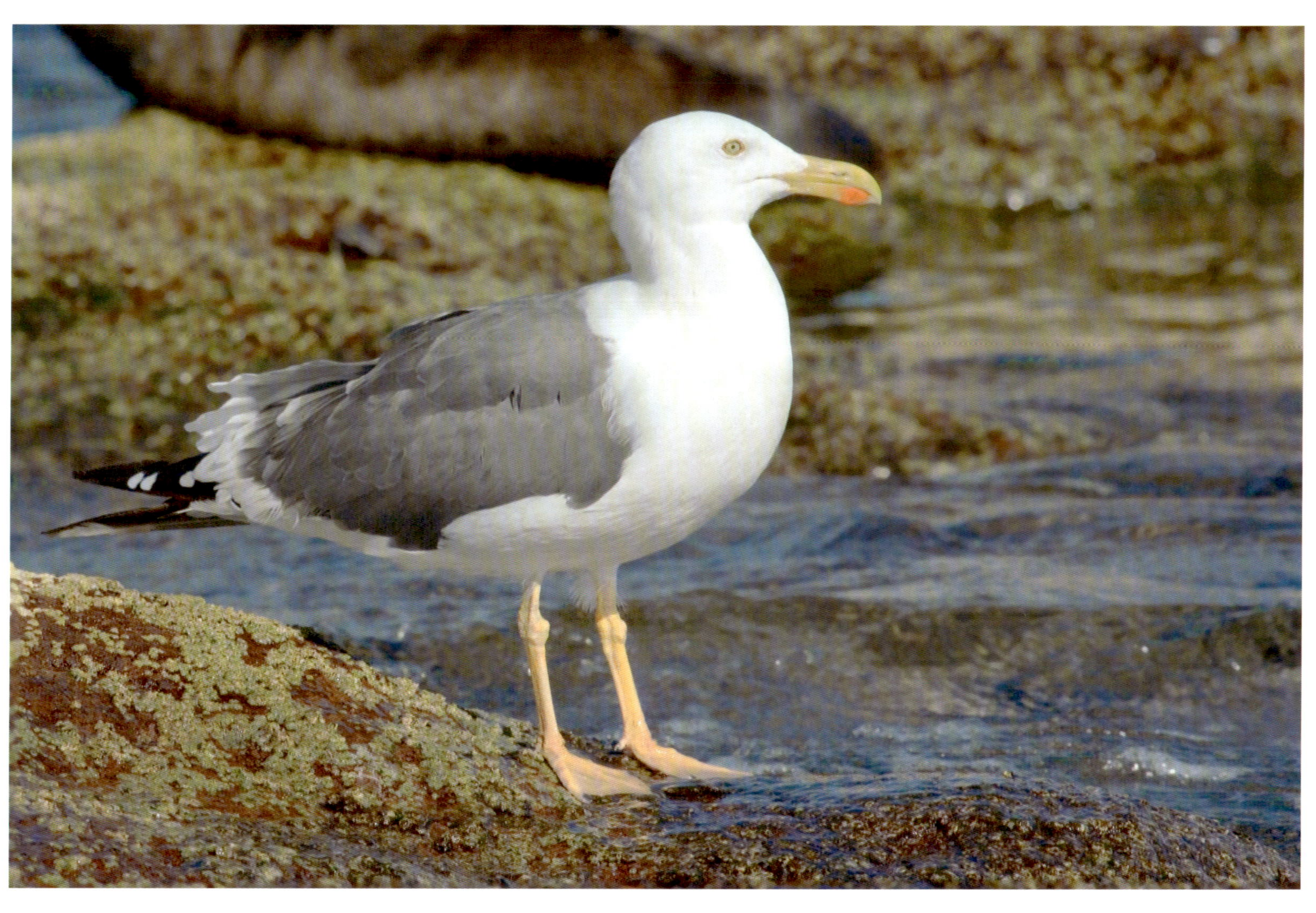

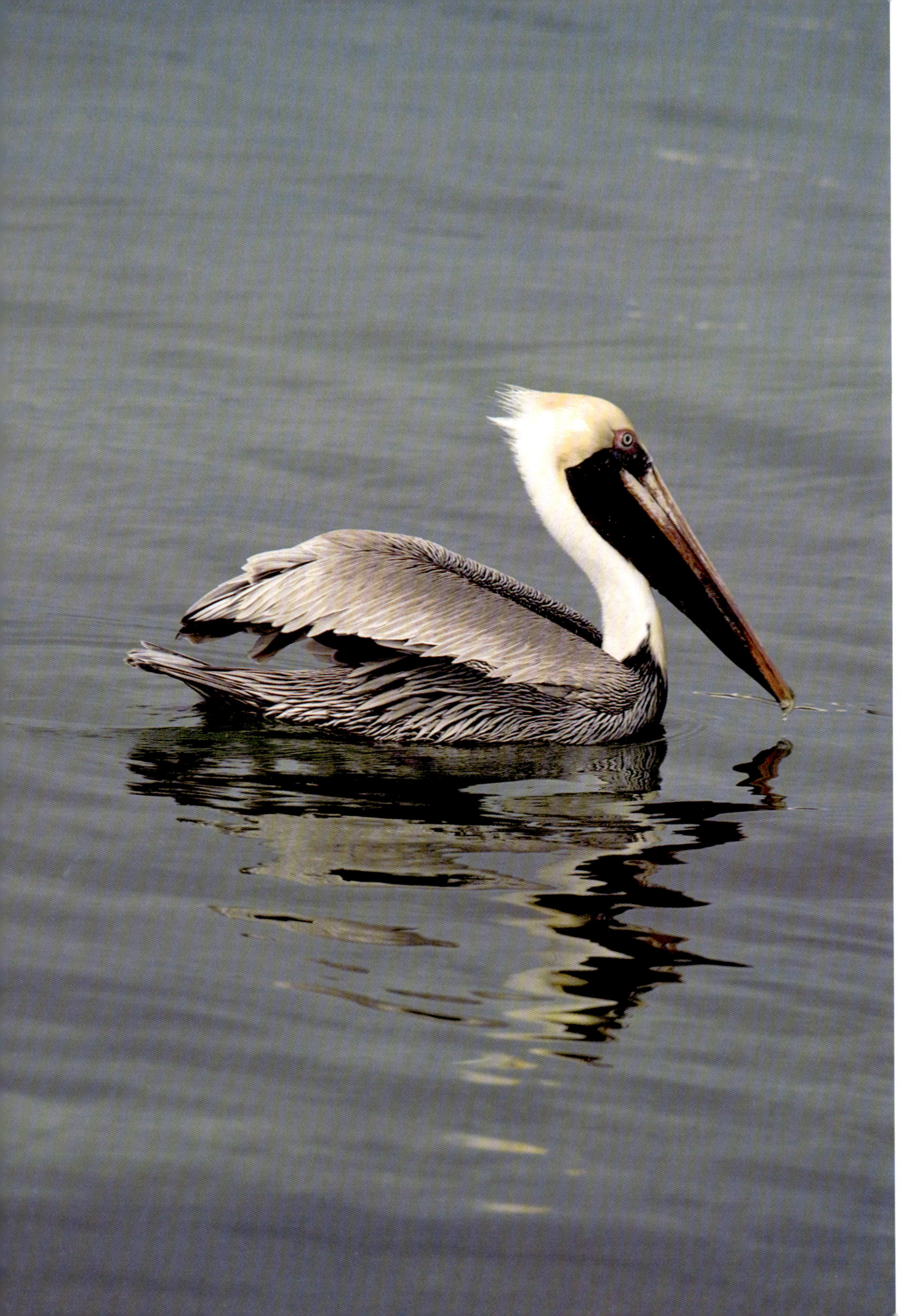

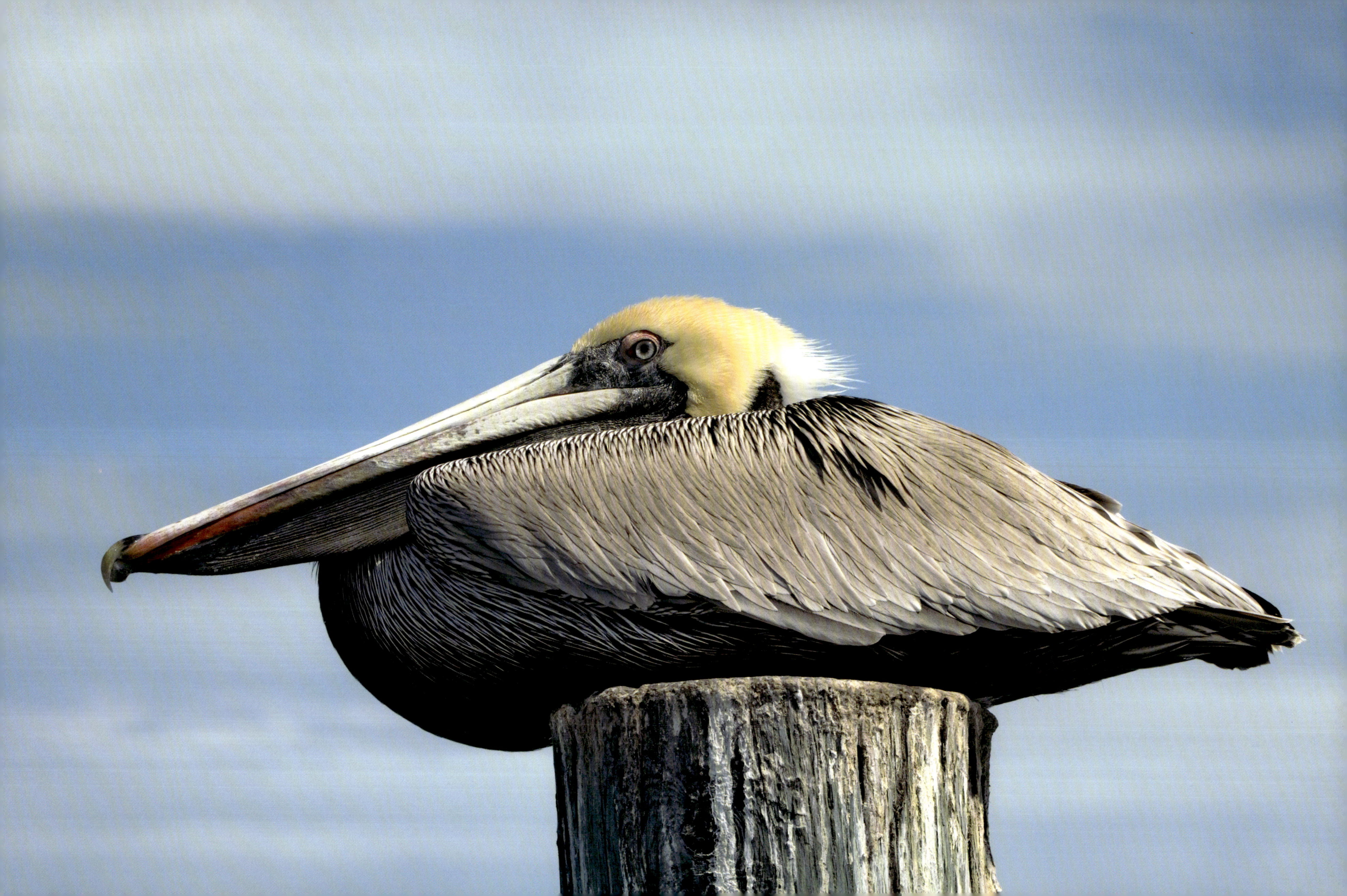

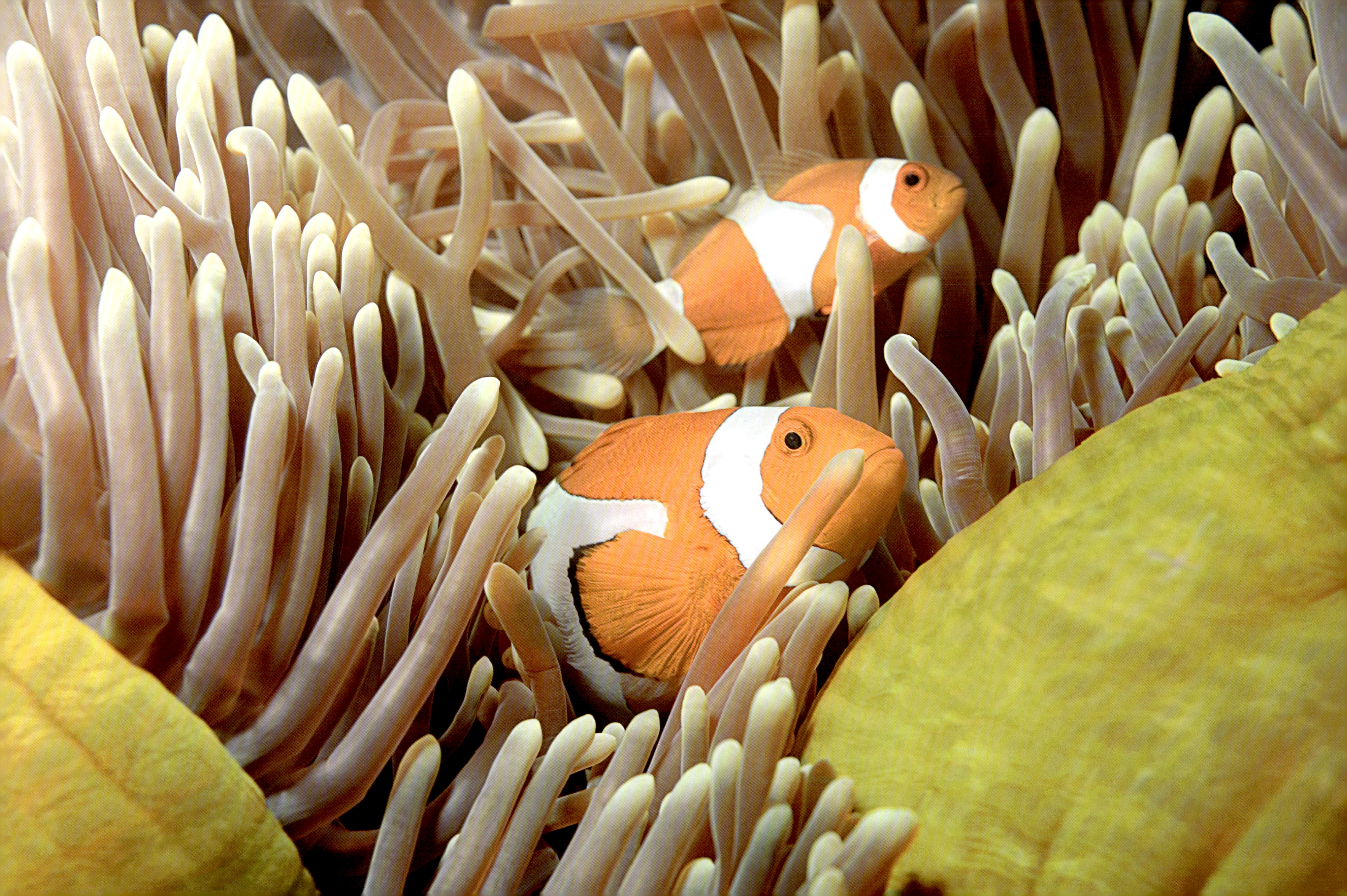

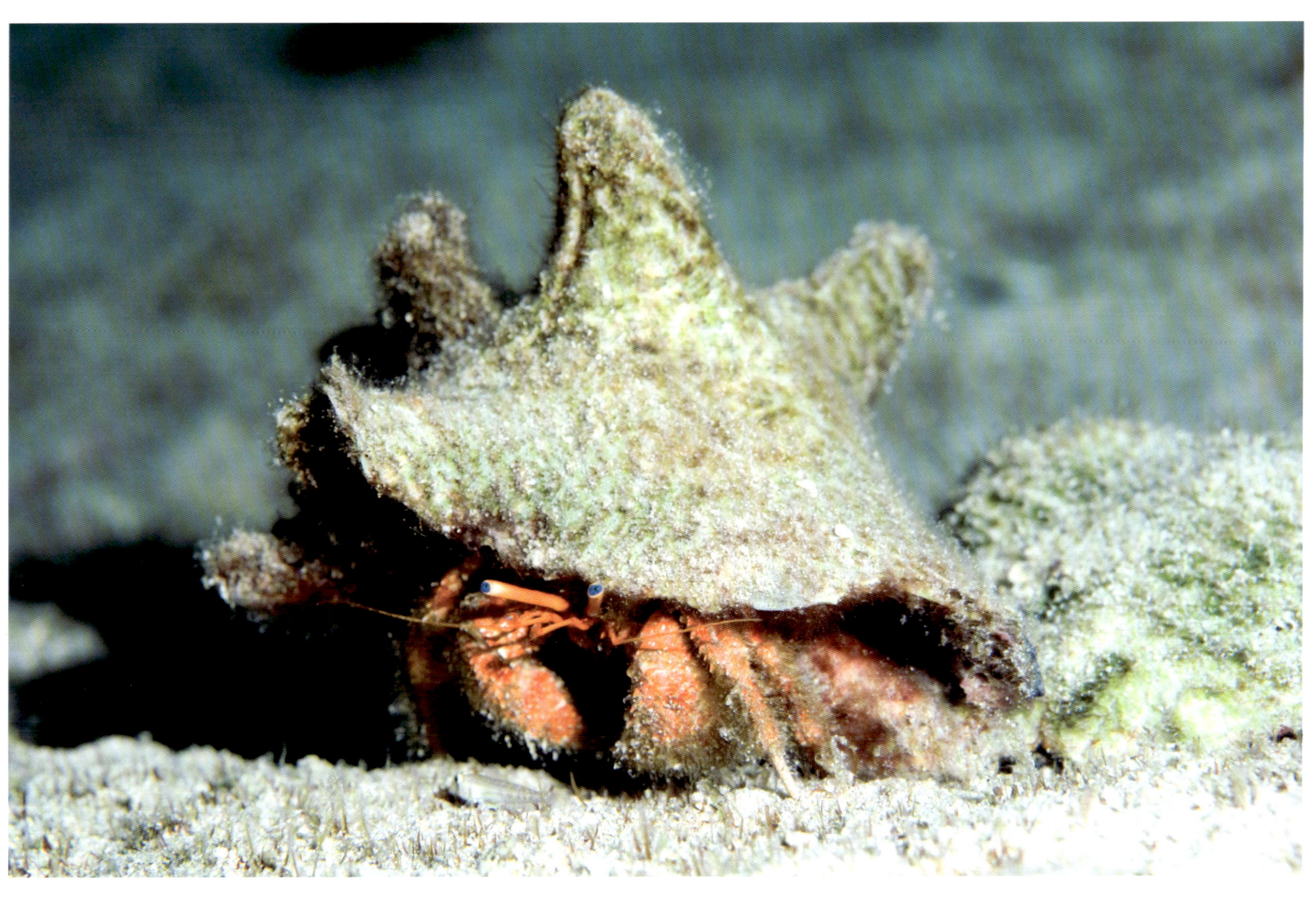

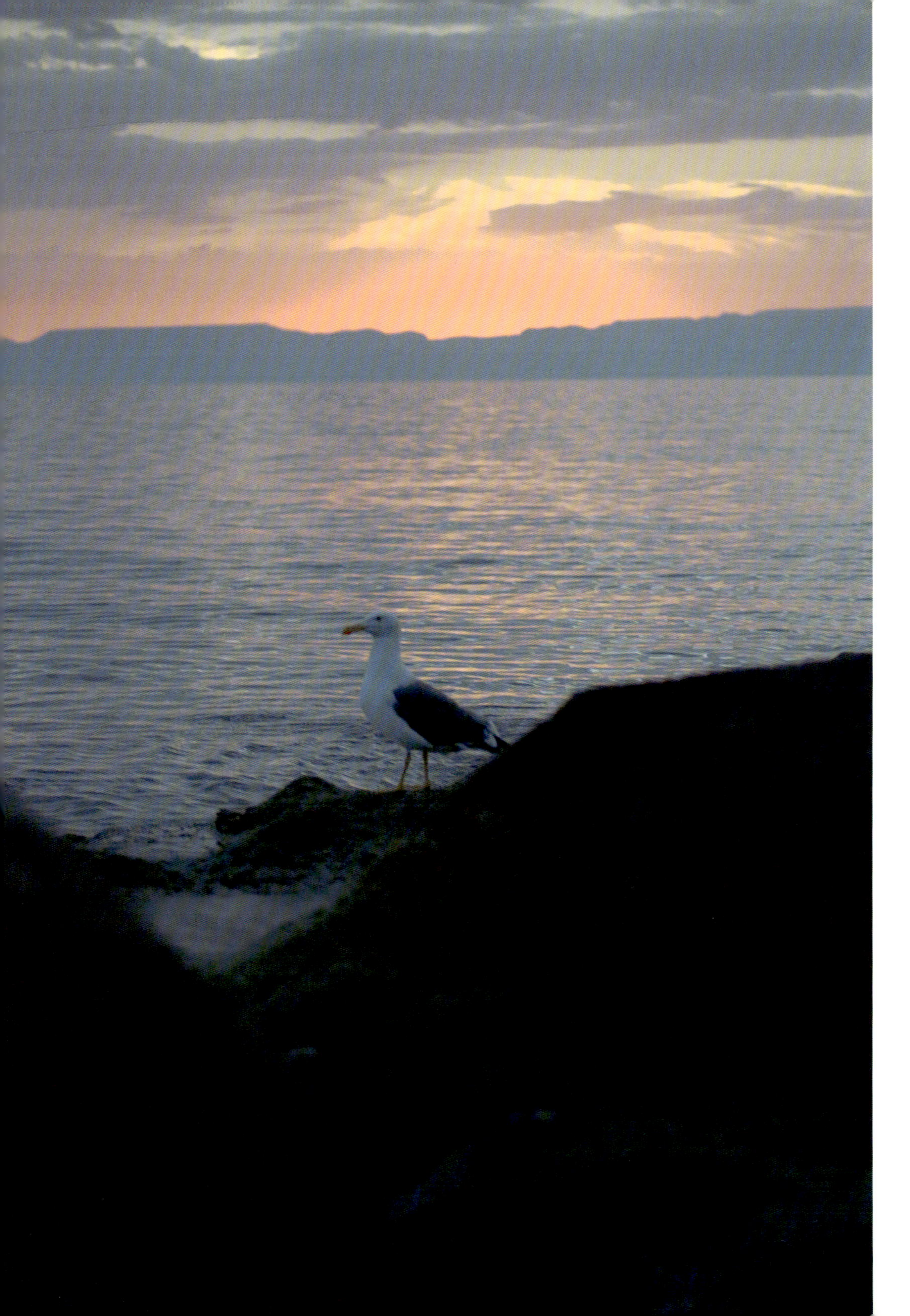

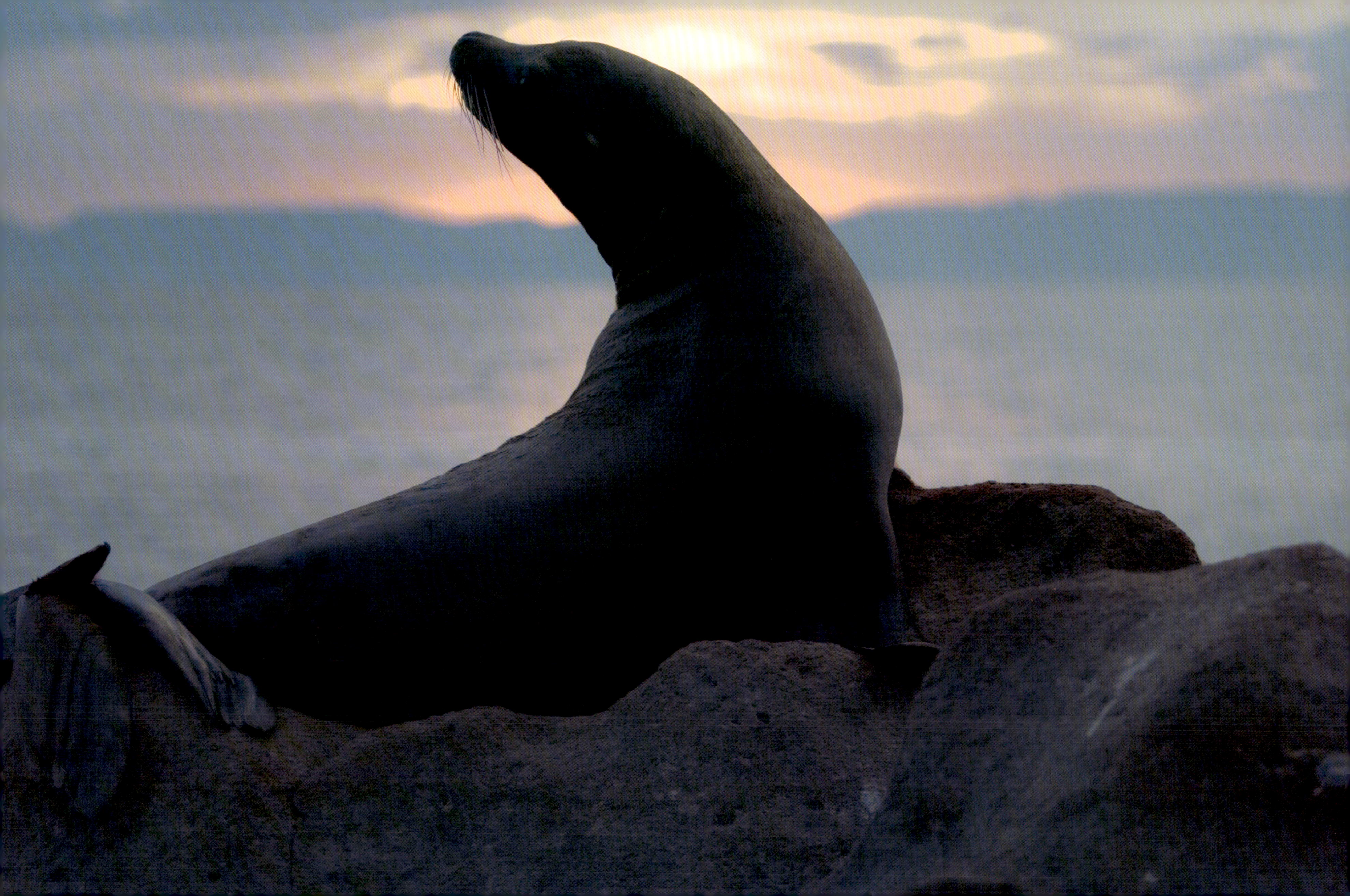

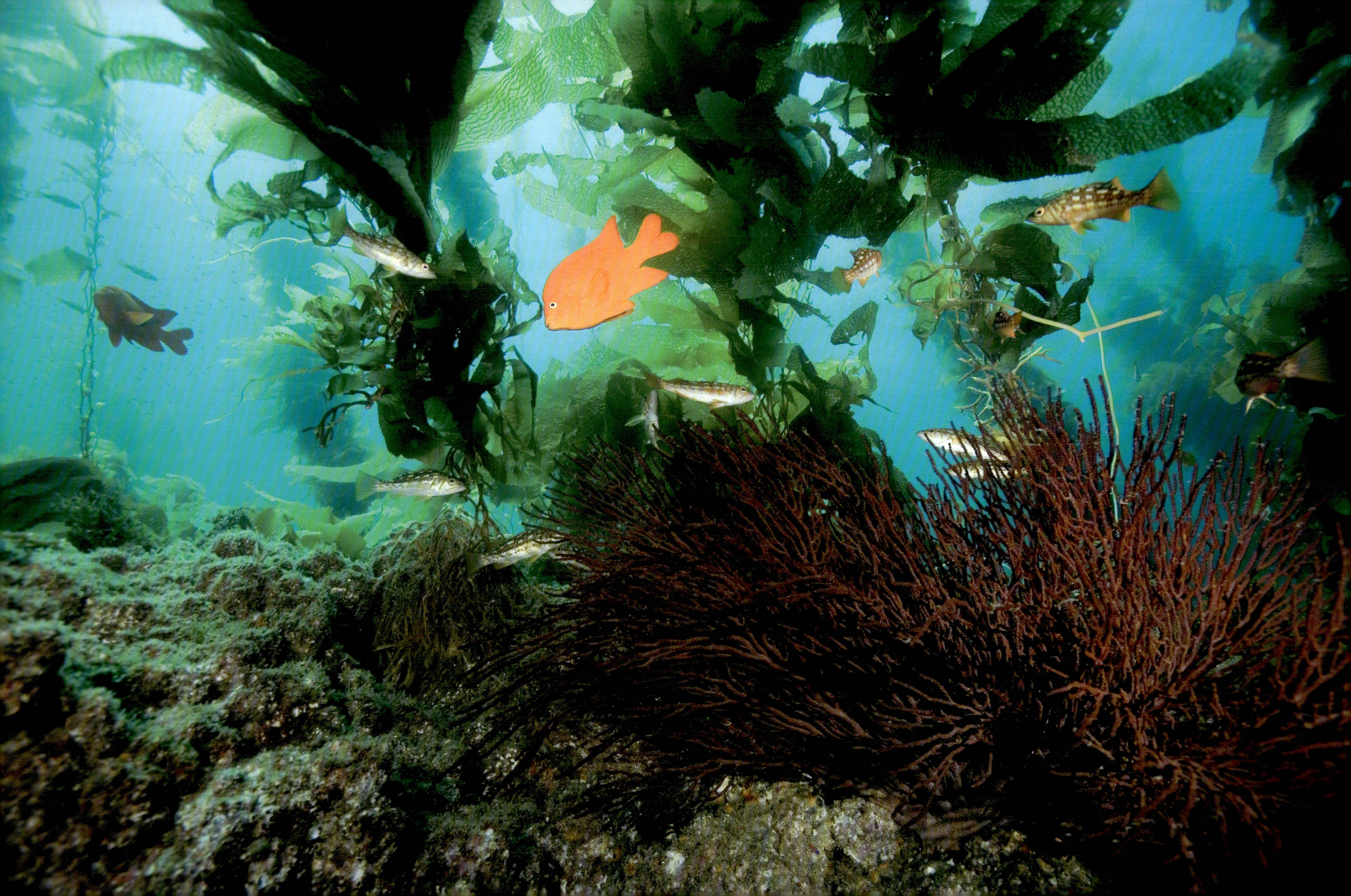

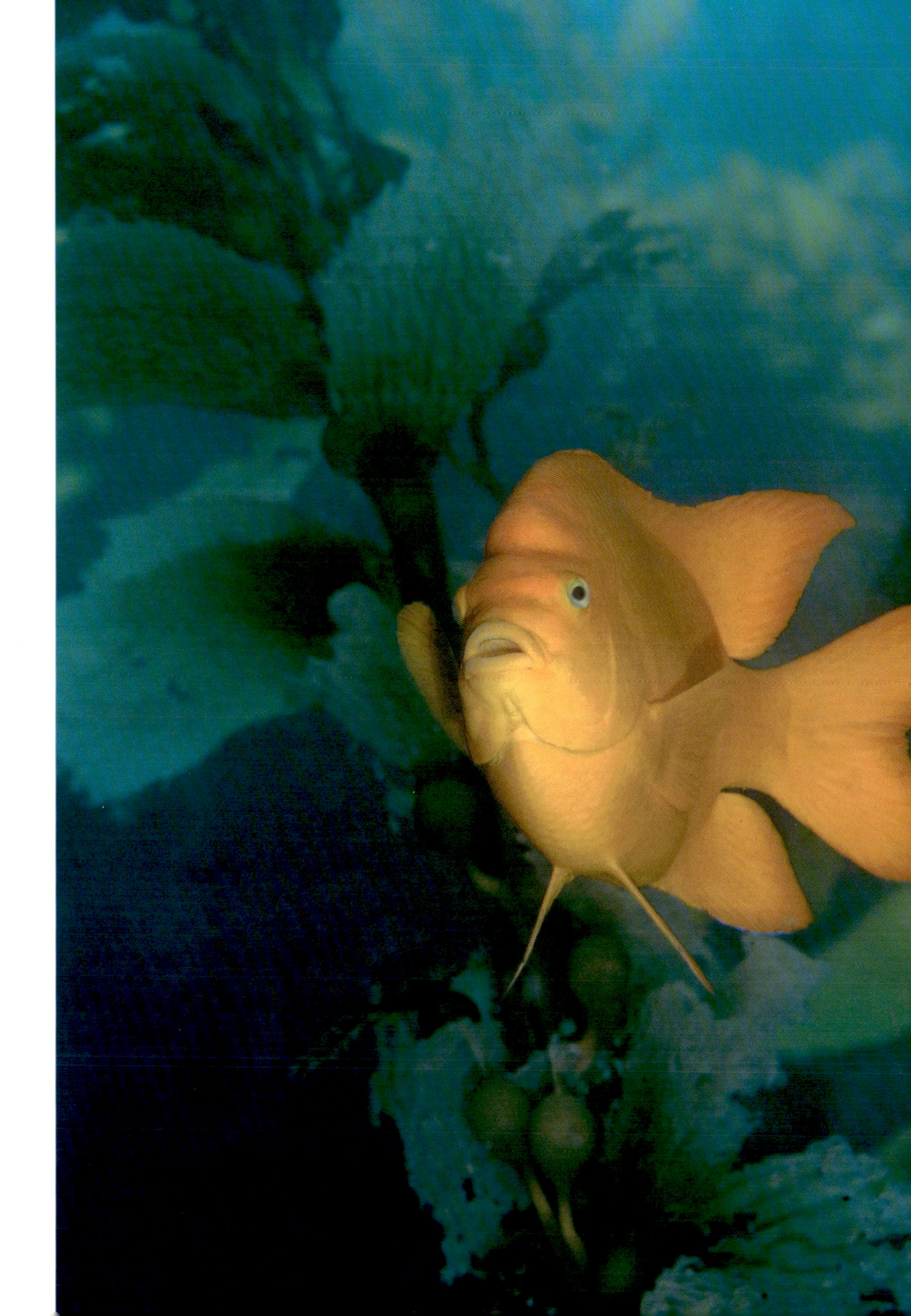

california kelp forest
friendly garibaldi

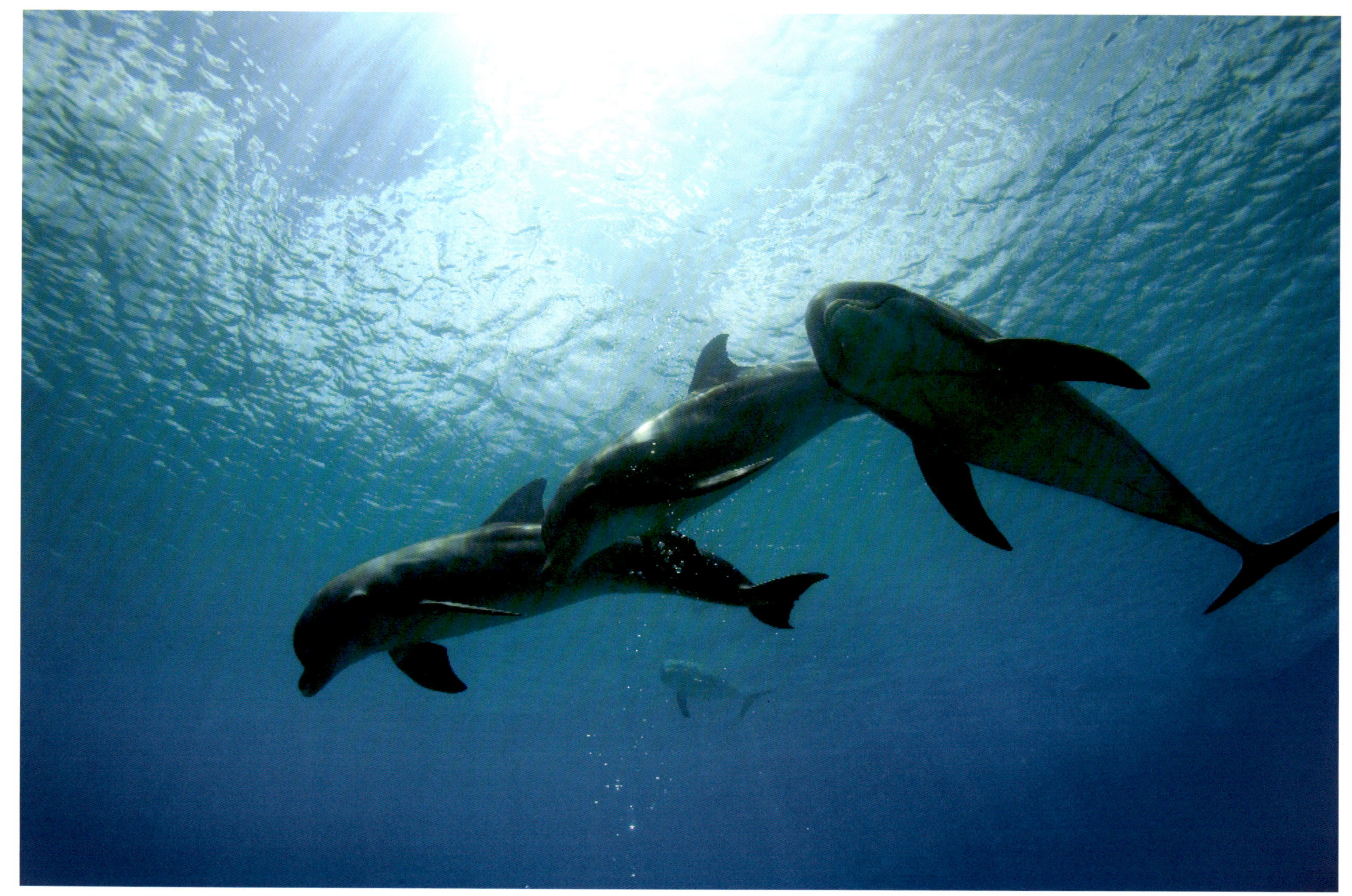

dolphin tribe
enter the sea

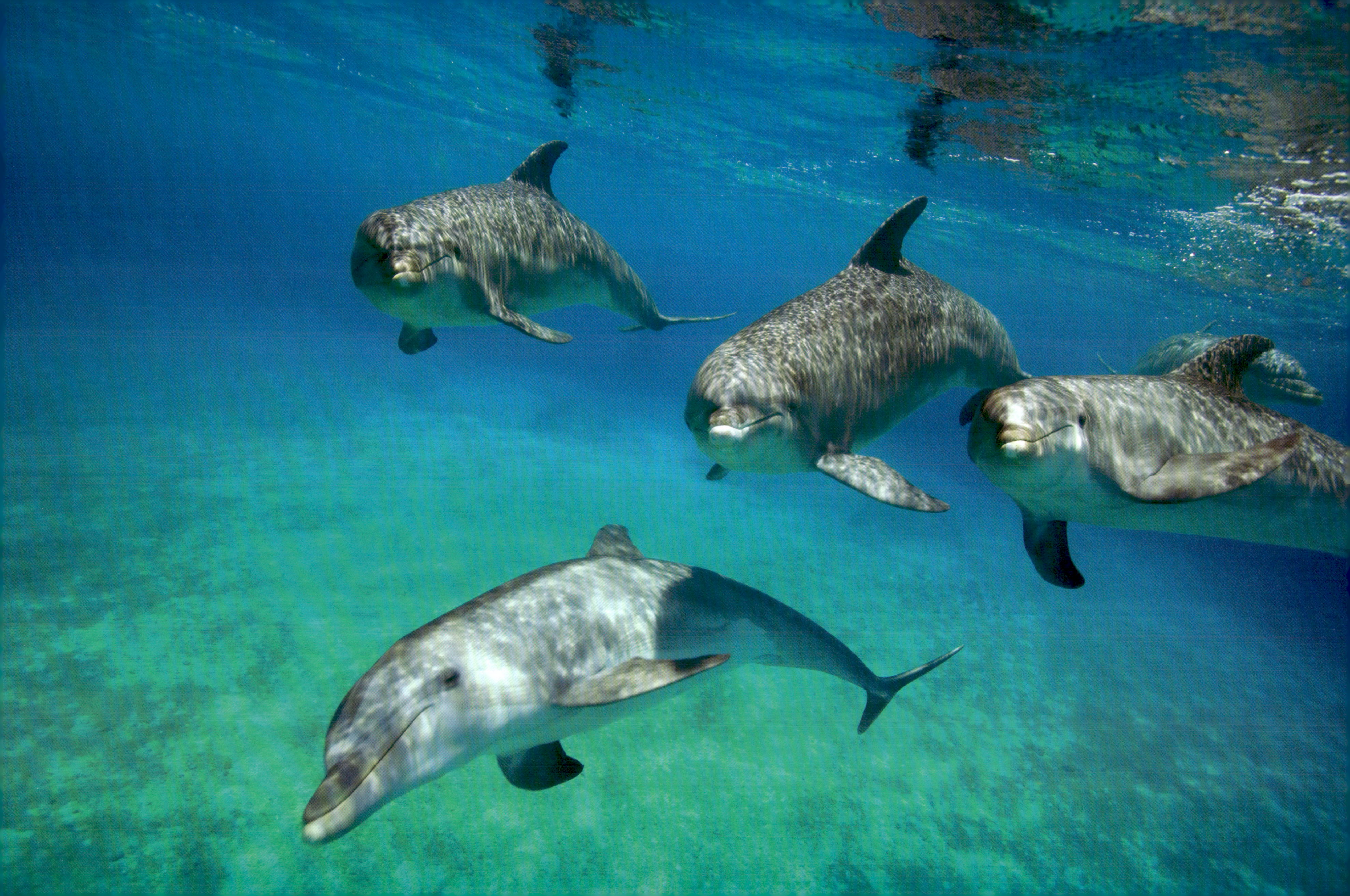

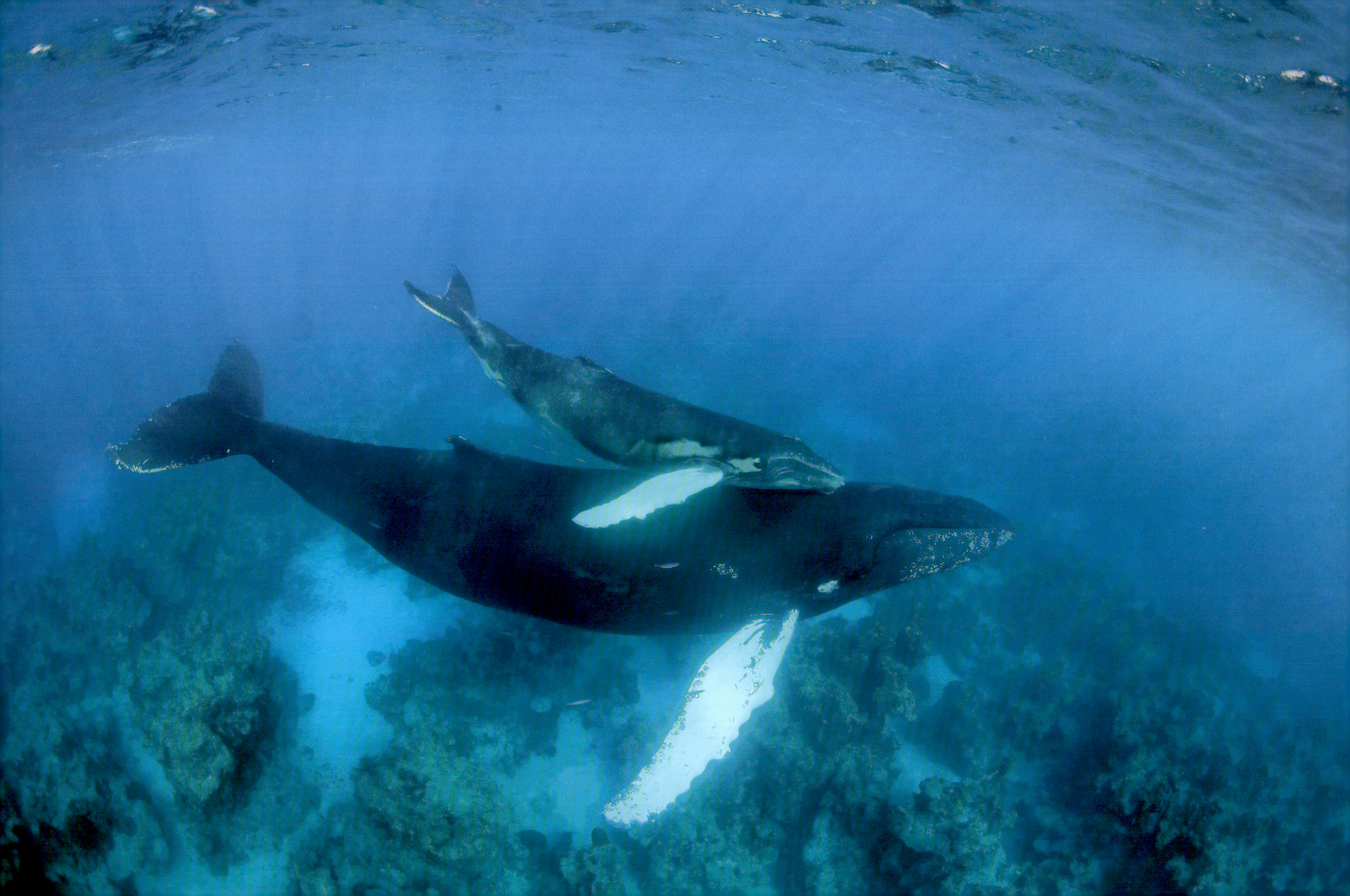

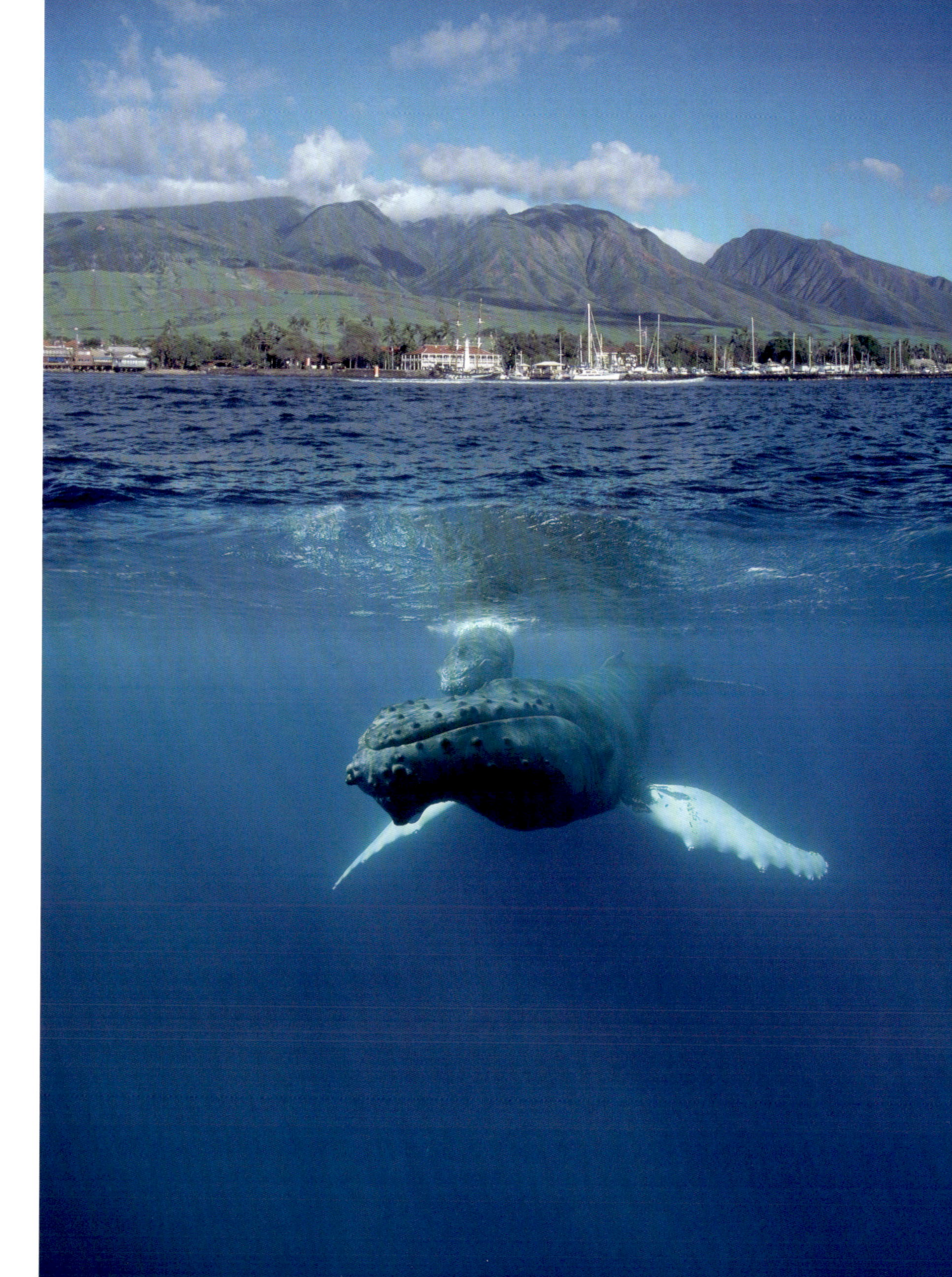

◀ ocean bond
▶ lahaina's humpback whales

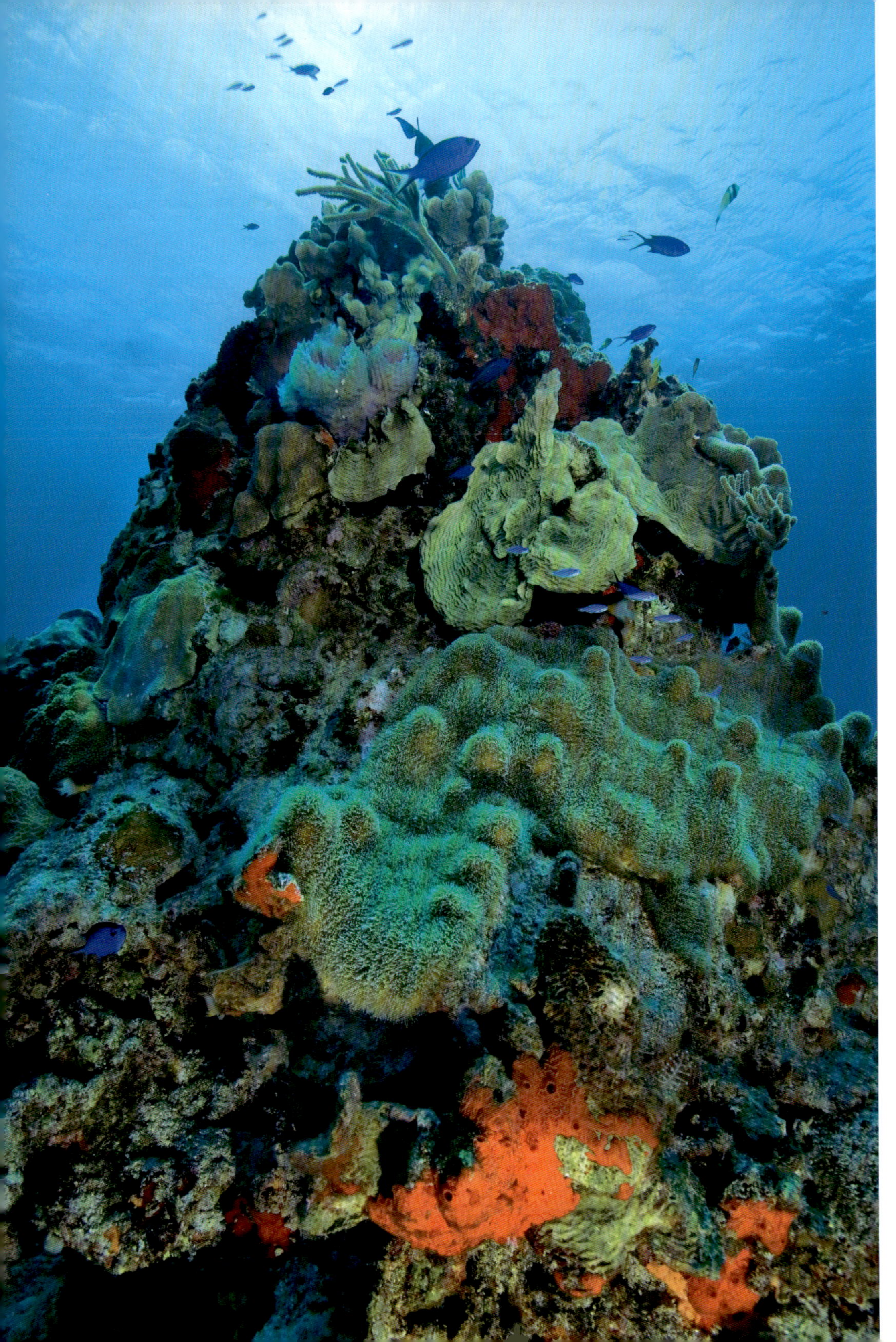

◀ christmas tree reef
▶ squid

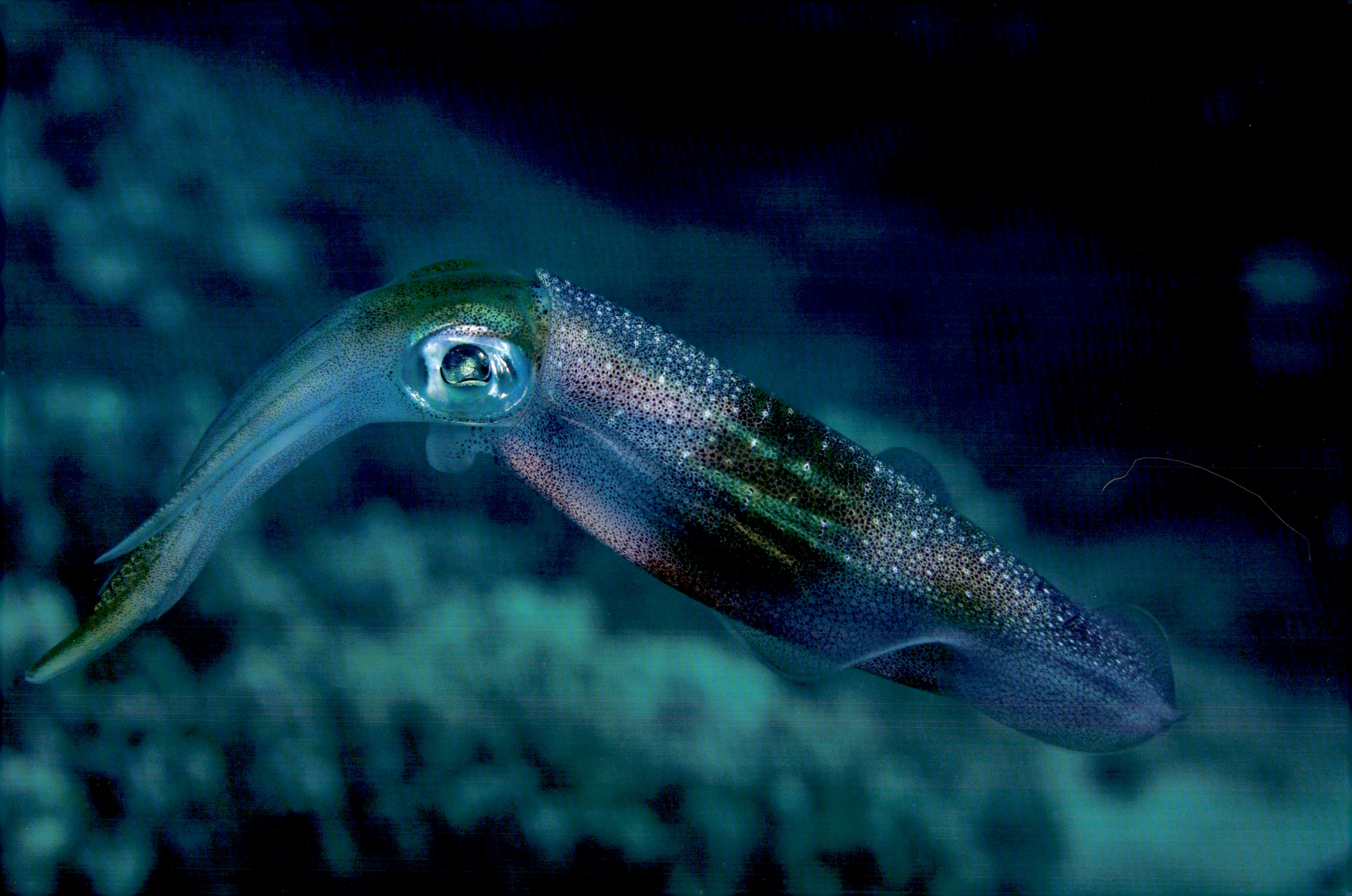

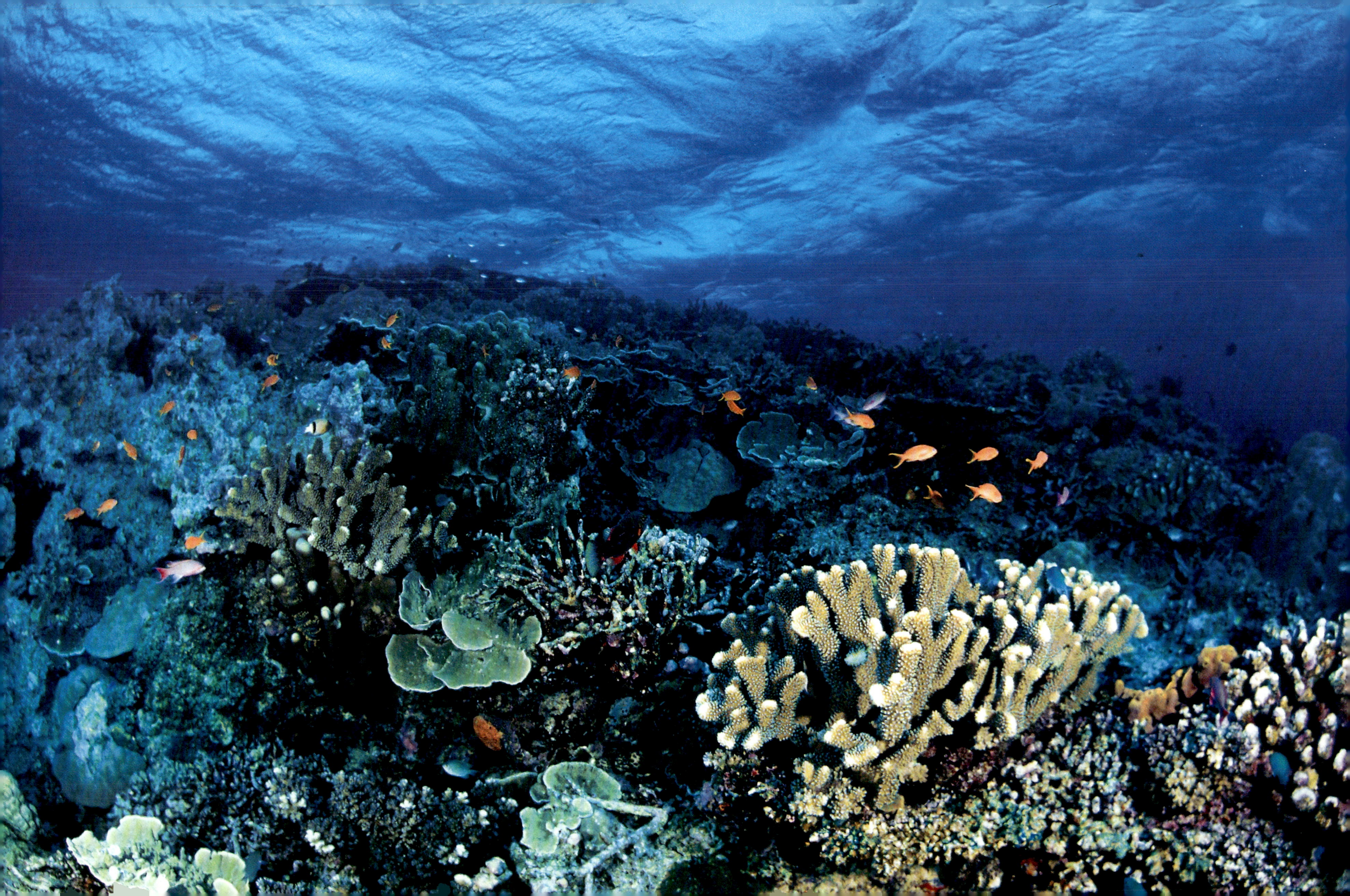

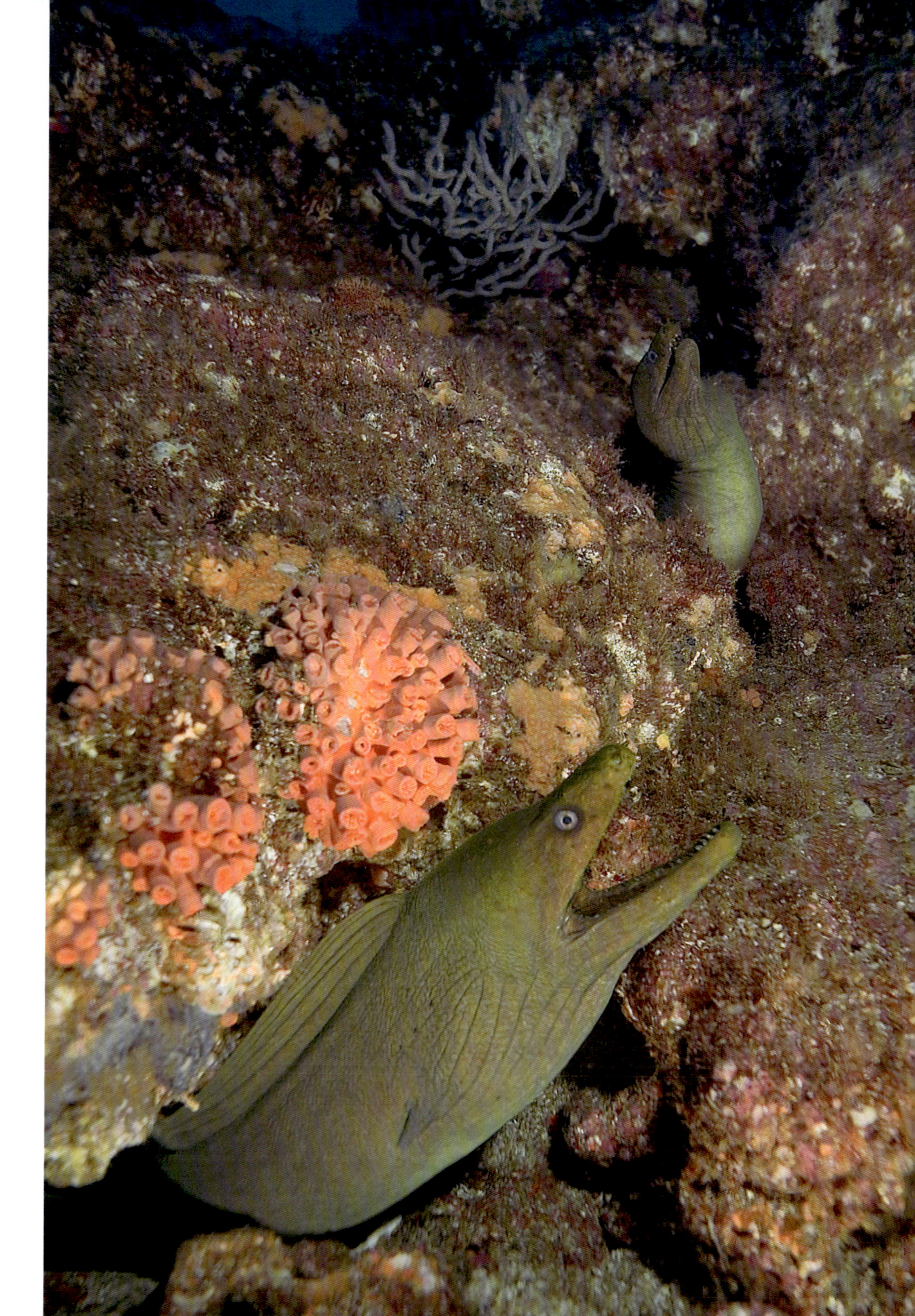

living reef below
green moray eels

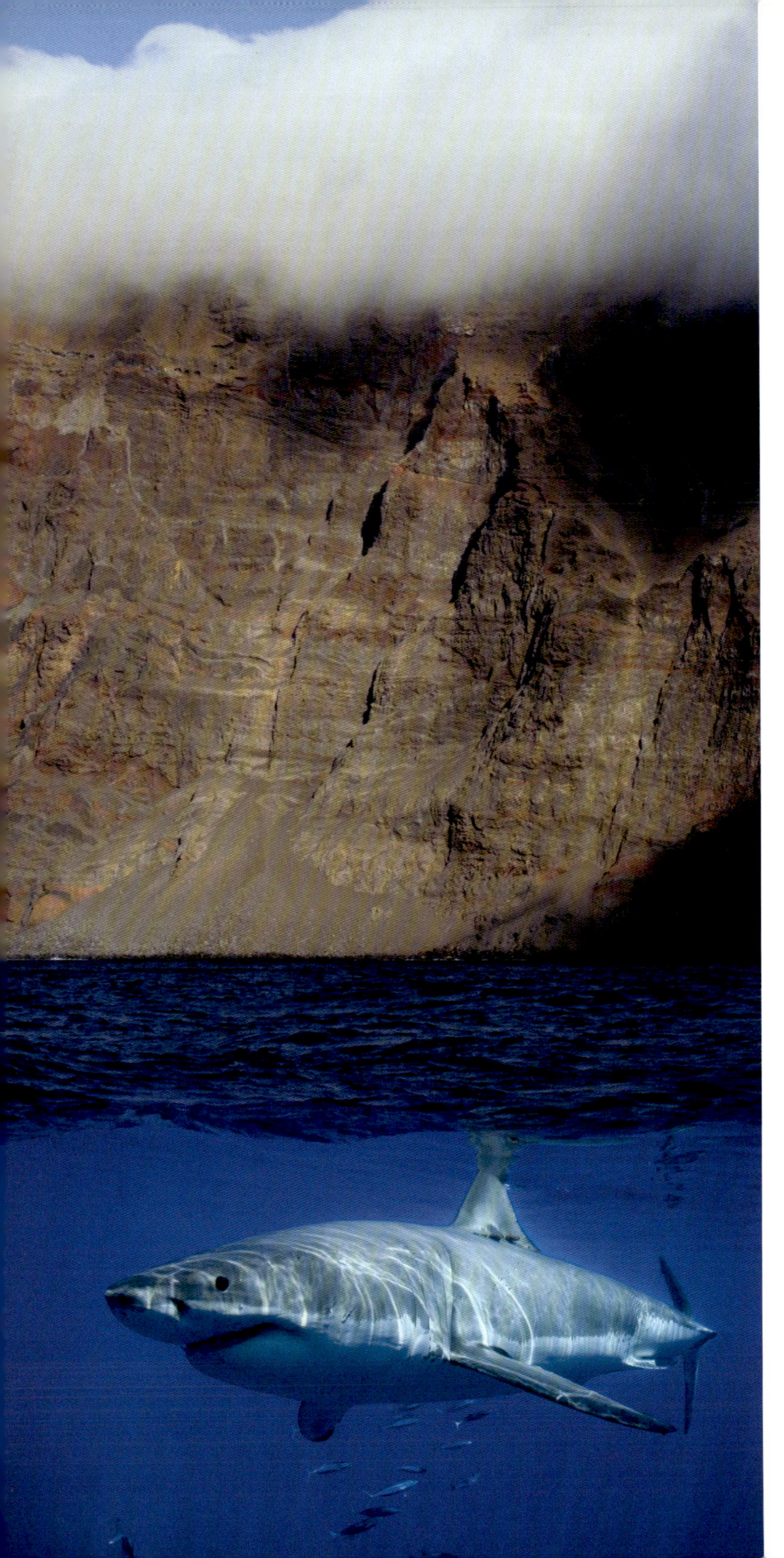

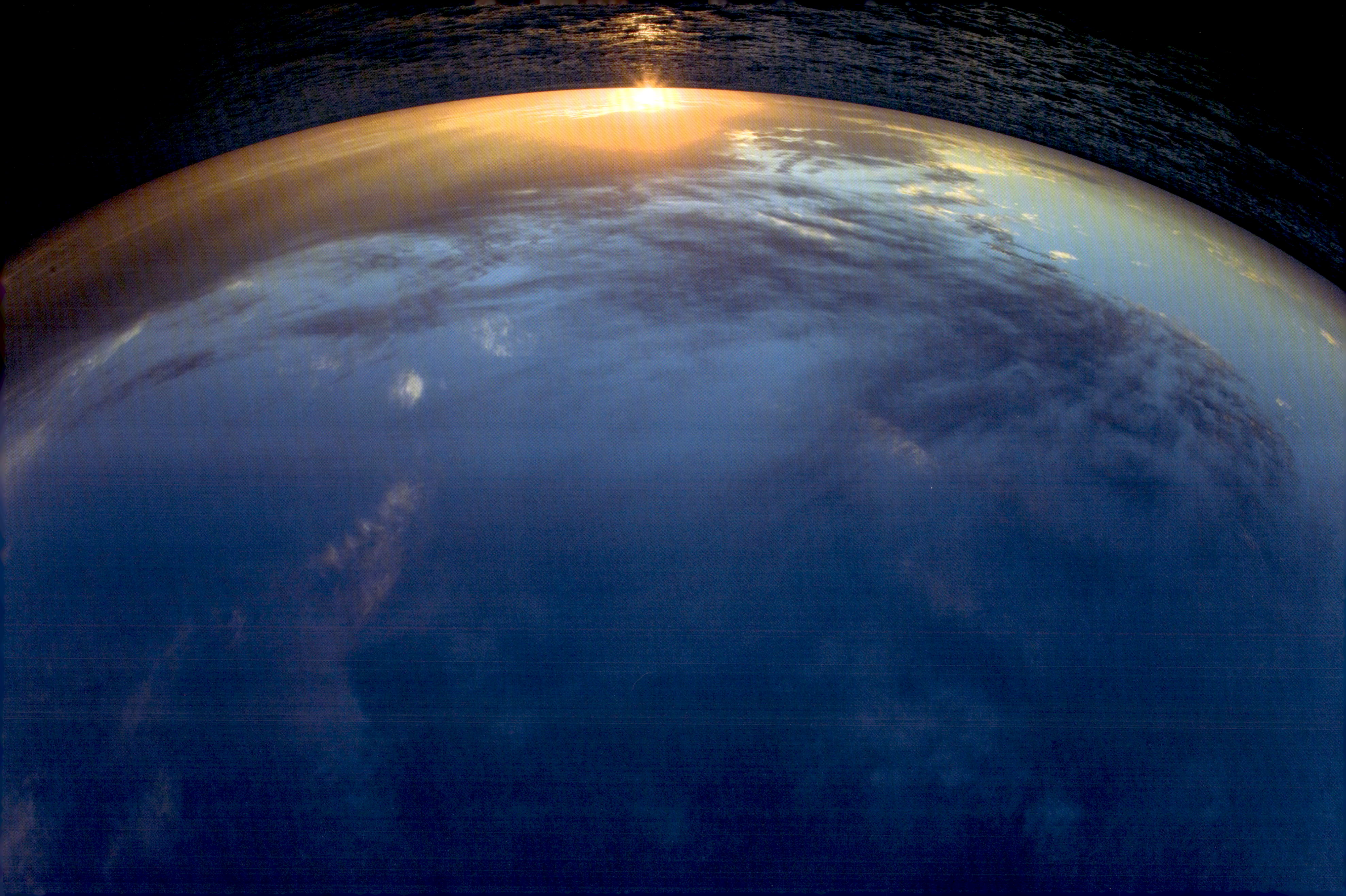

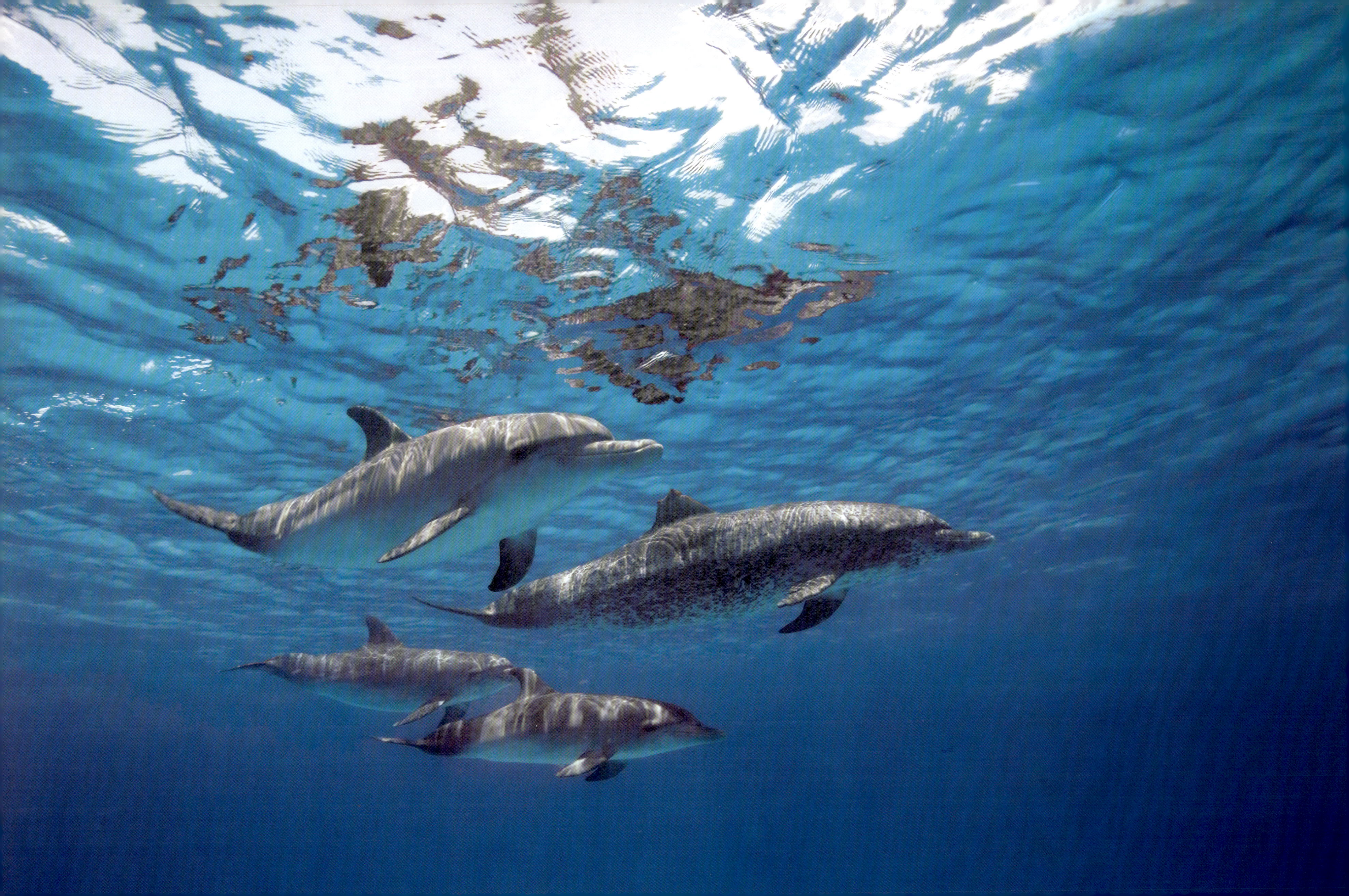

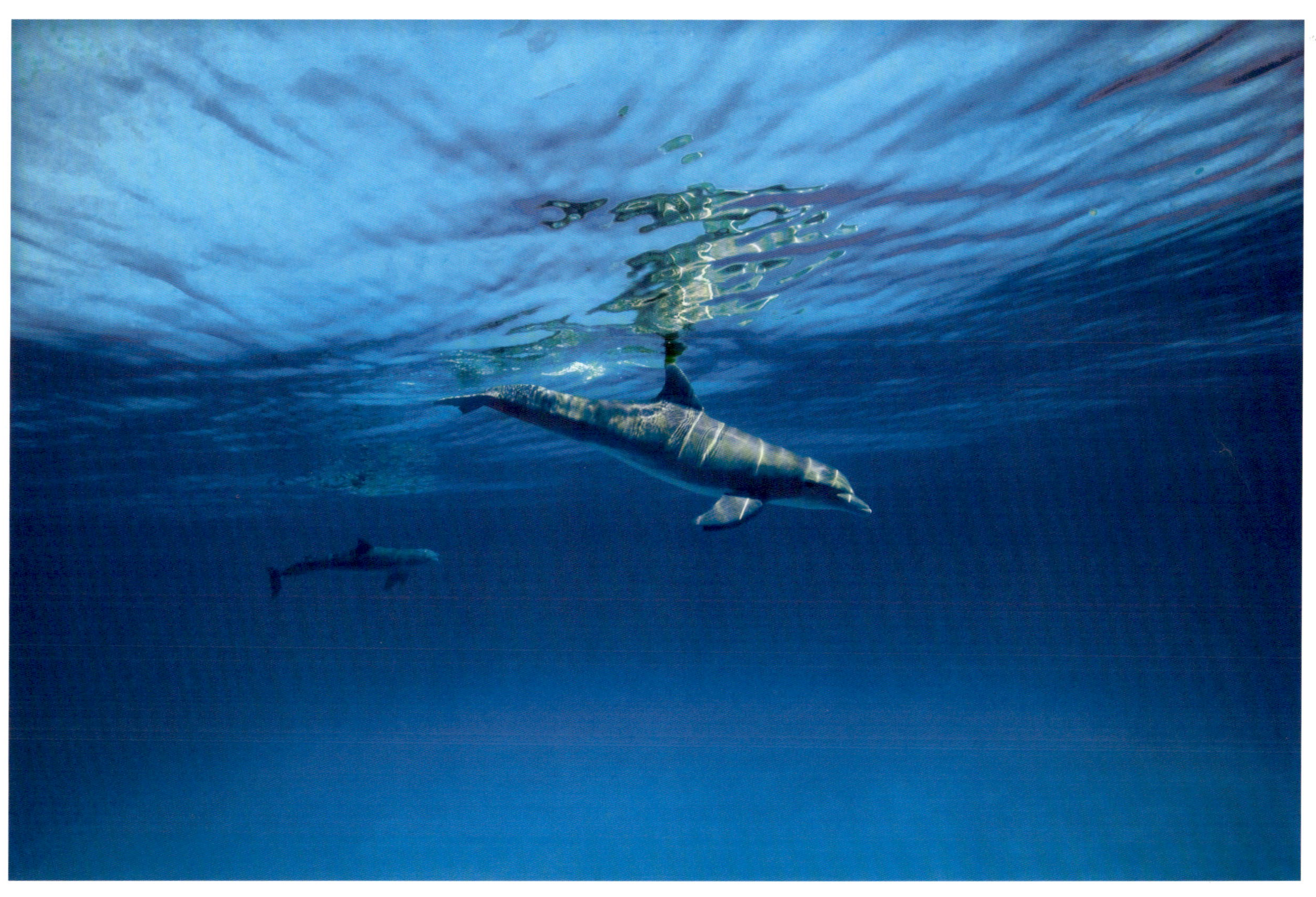

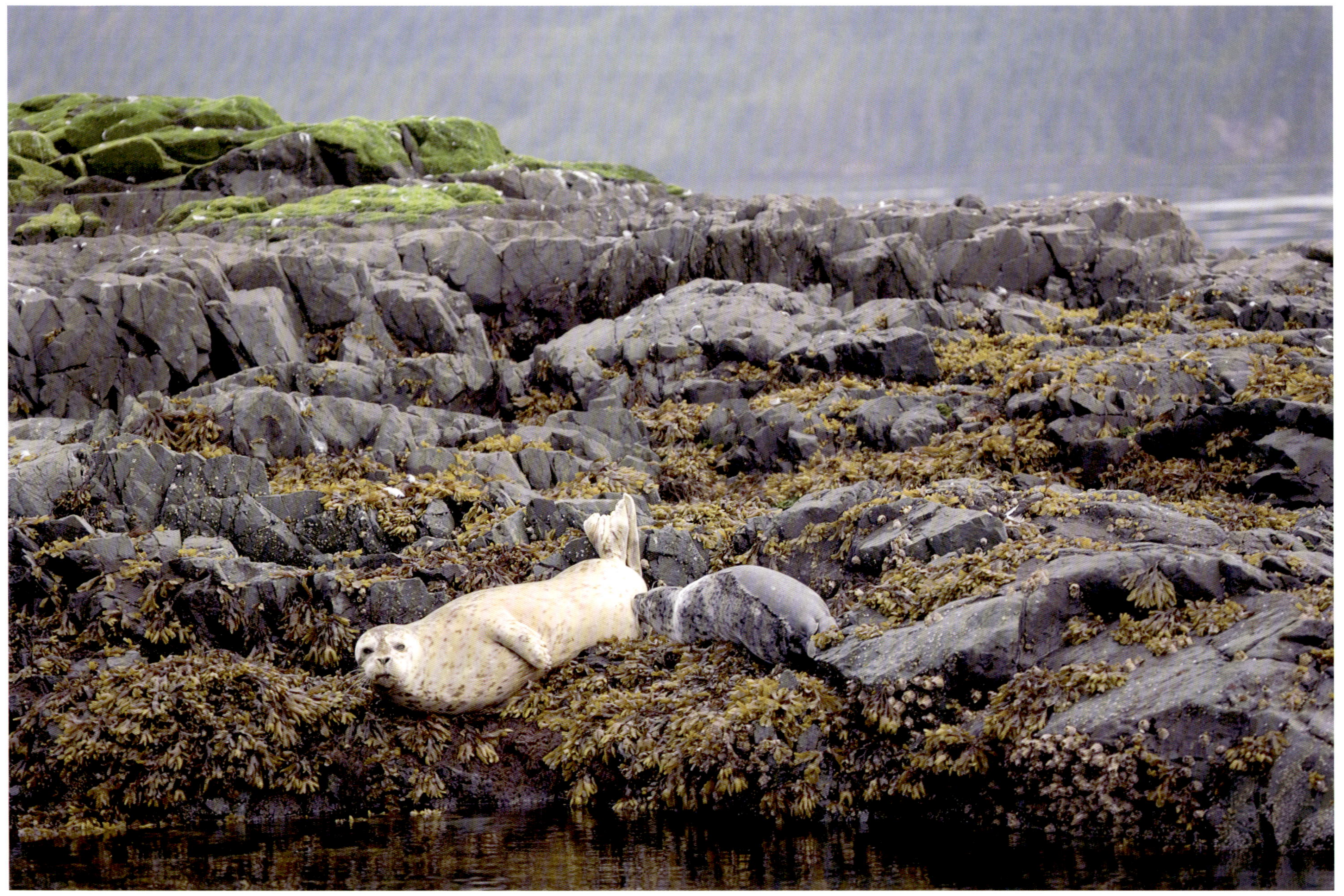

◄ feeding time
► harbor seal eyes

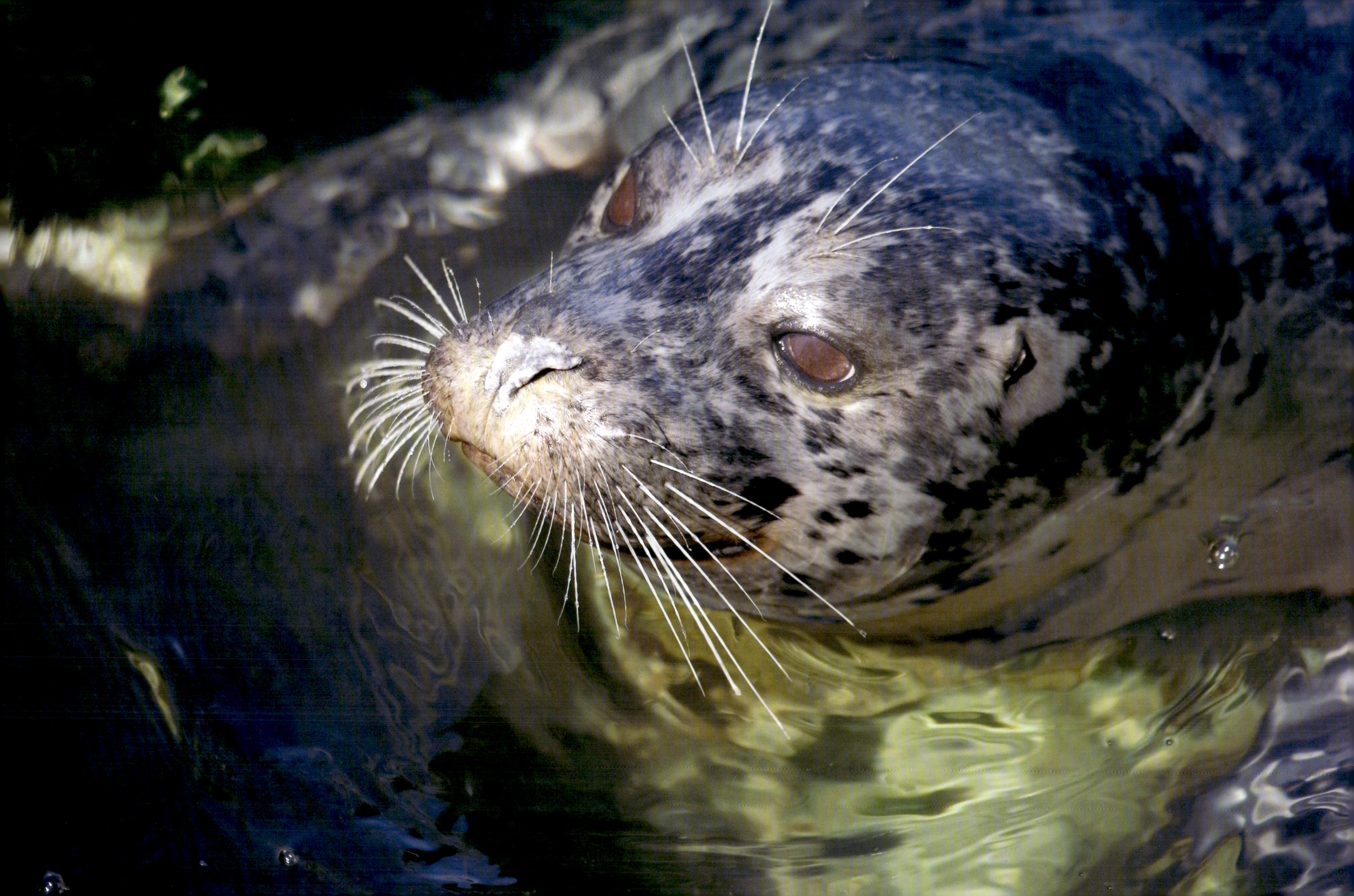

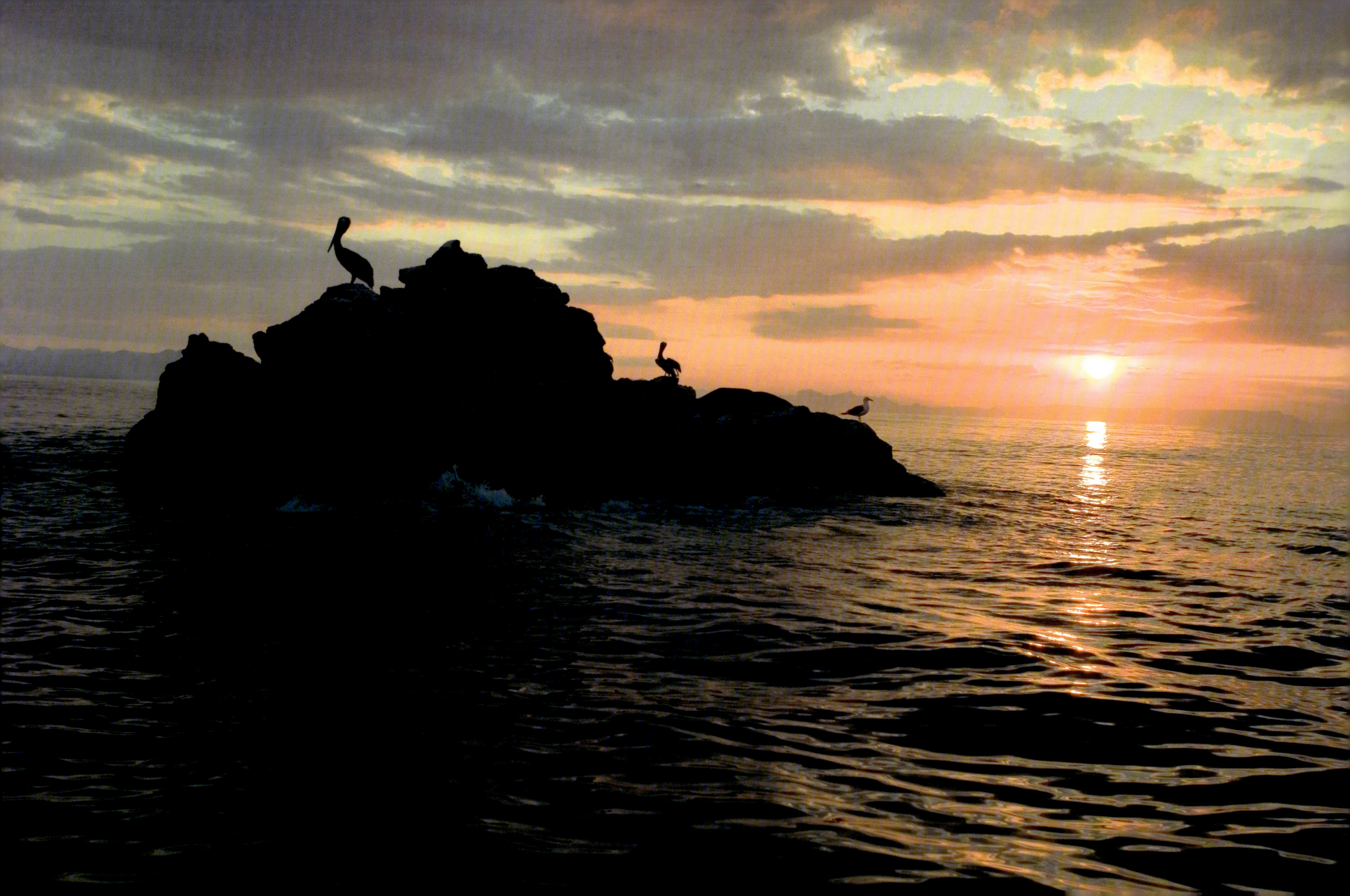

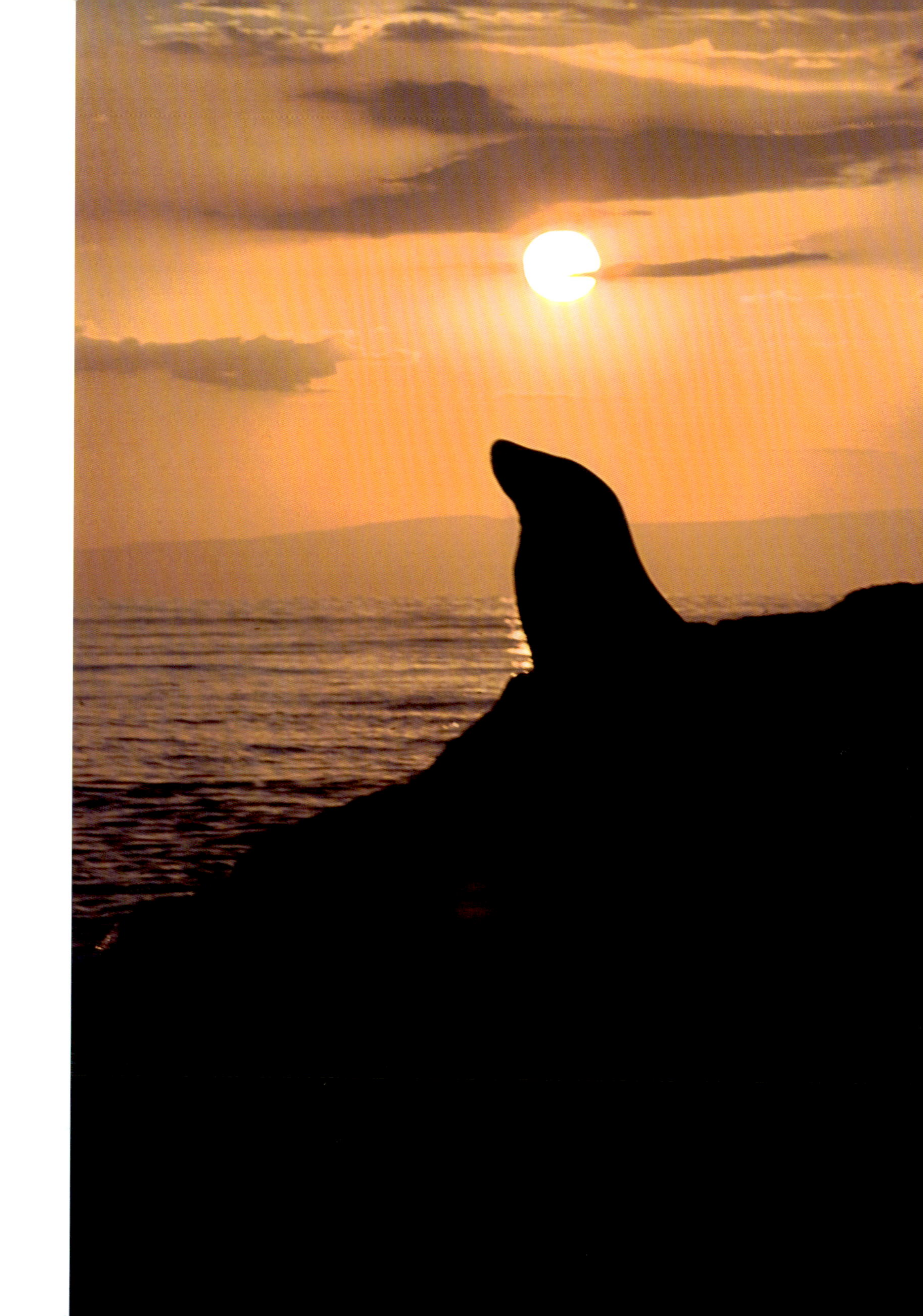

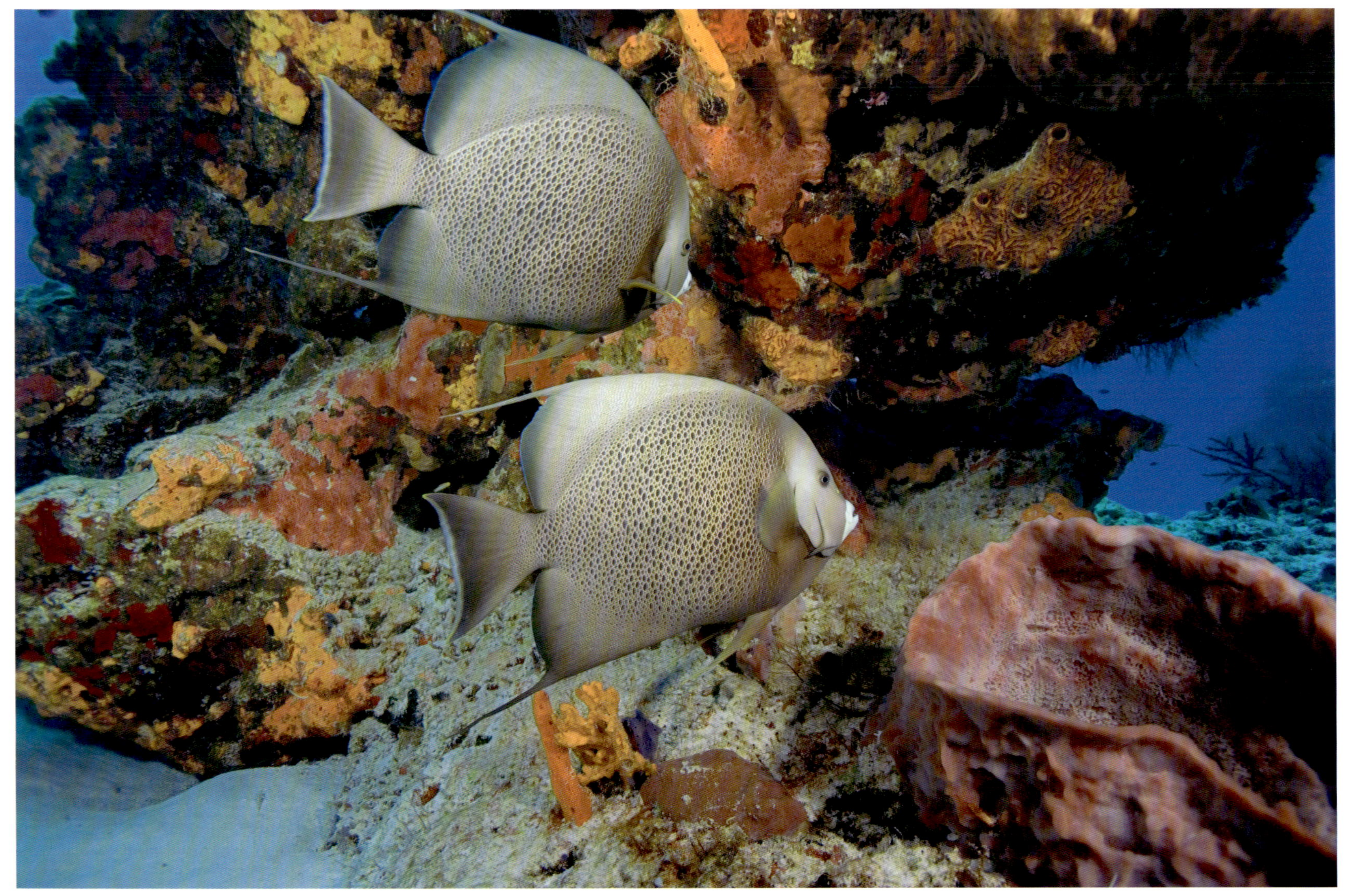

◀ gray angels reef
▶ sea turtle of the coral wall

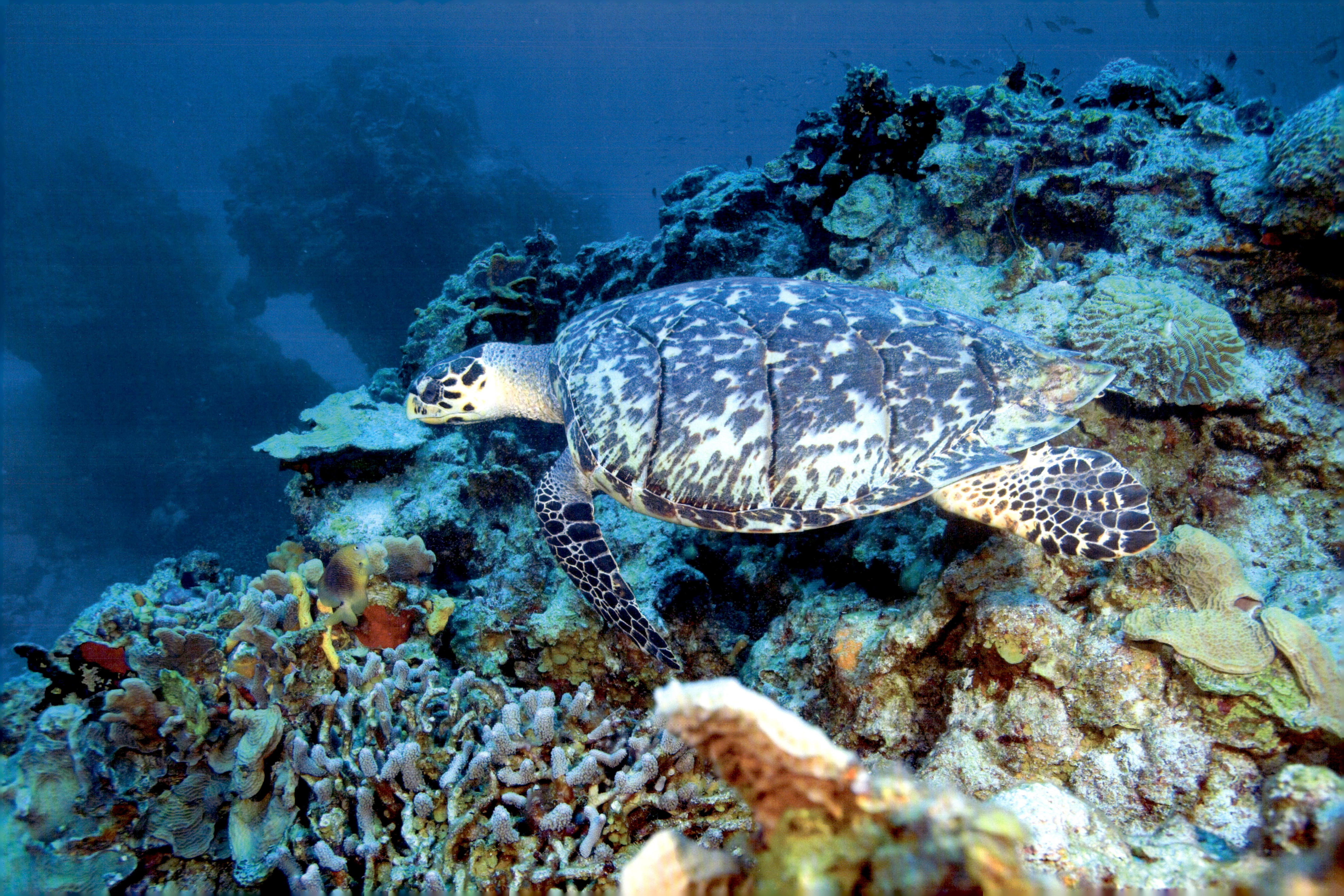

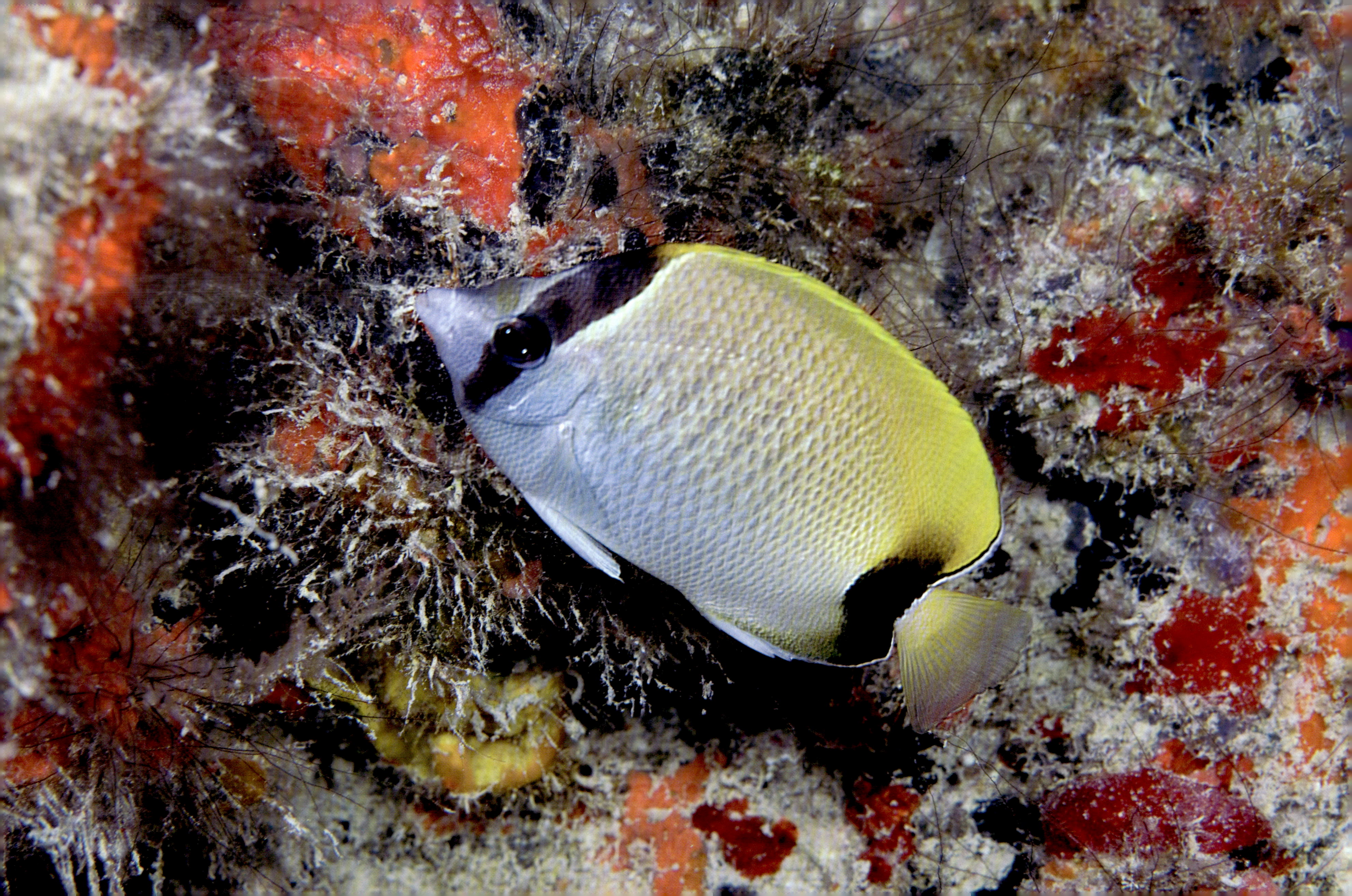

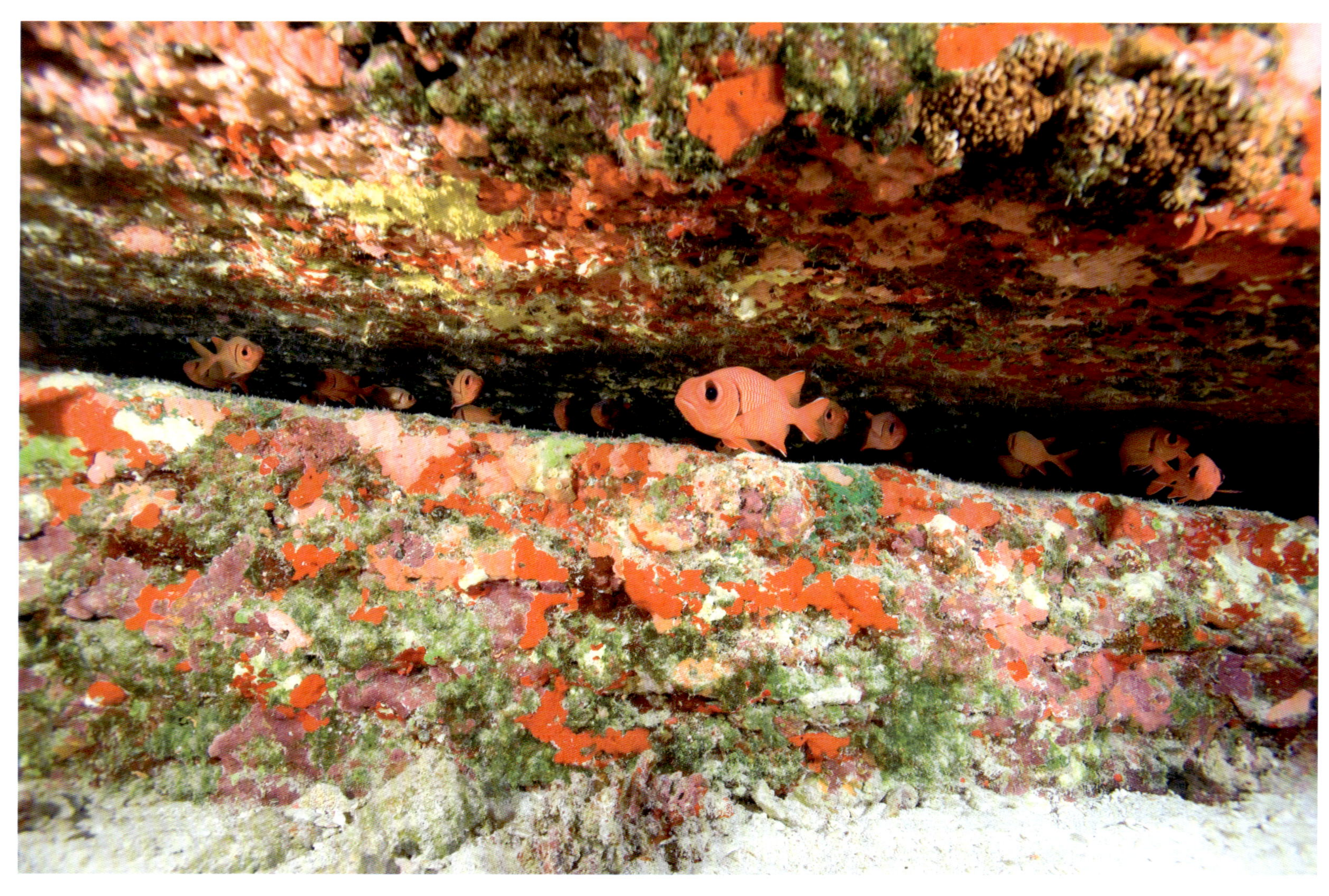

◀ butterfly reef
▶ soldier fish cave

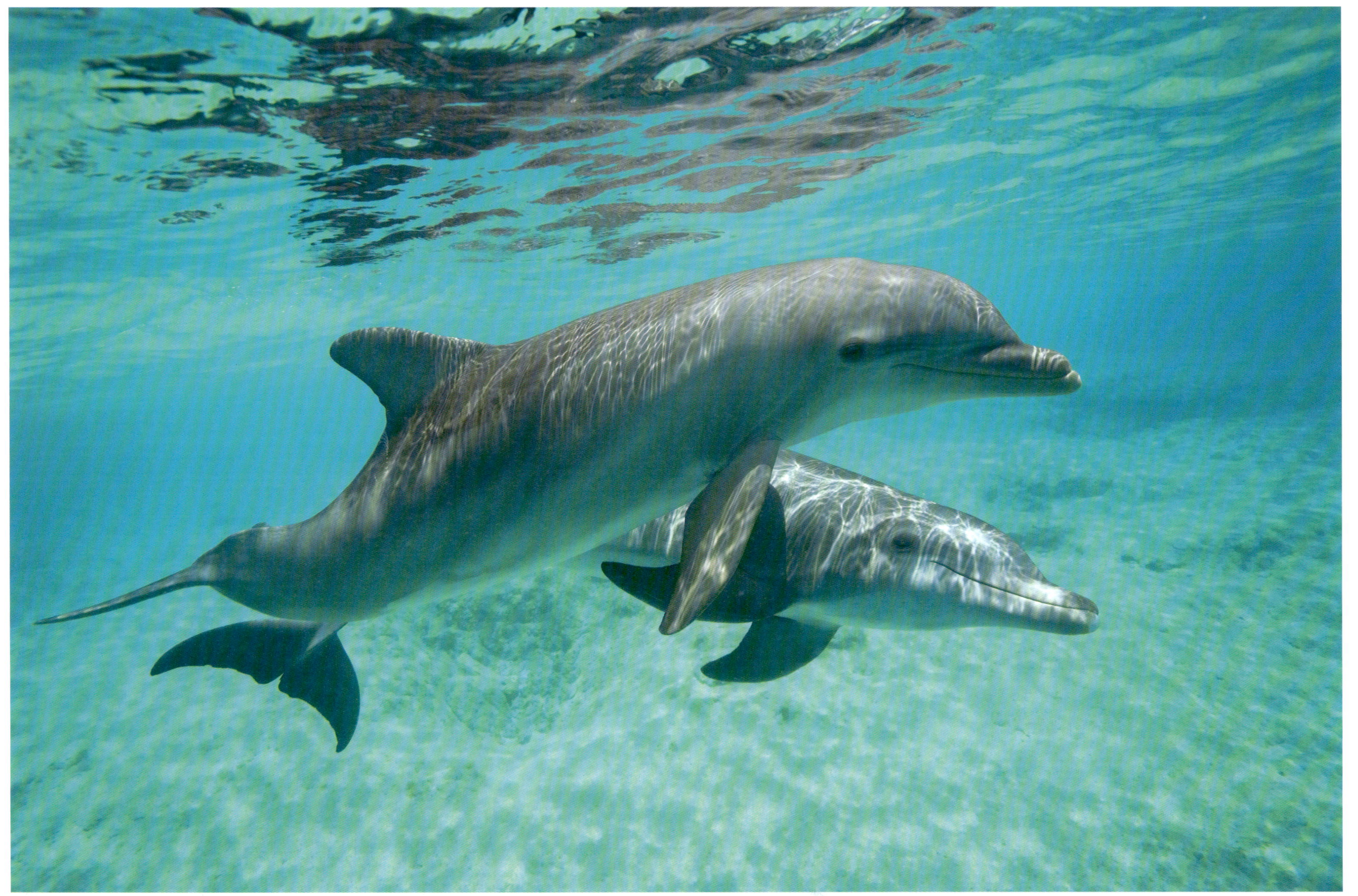

◄ dolphin duet
► dolphin reflection

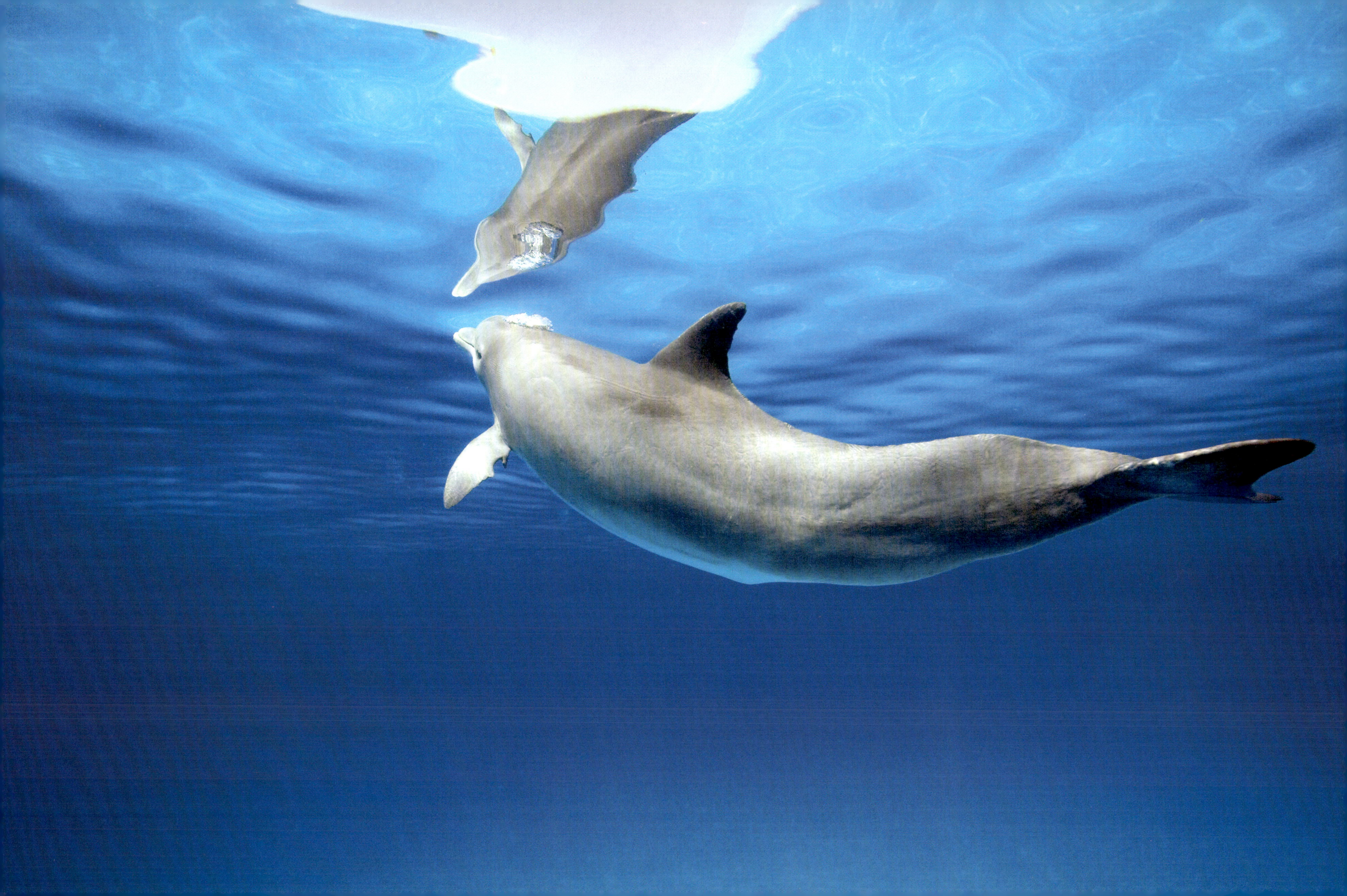

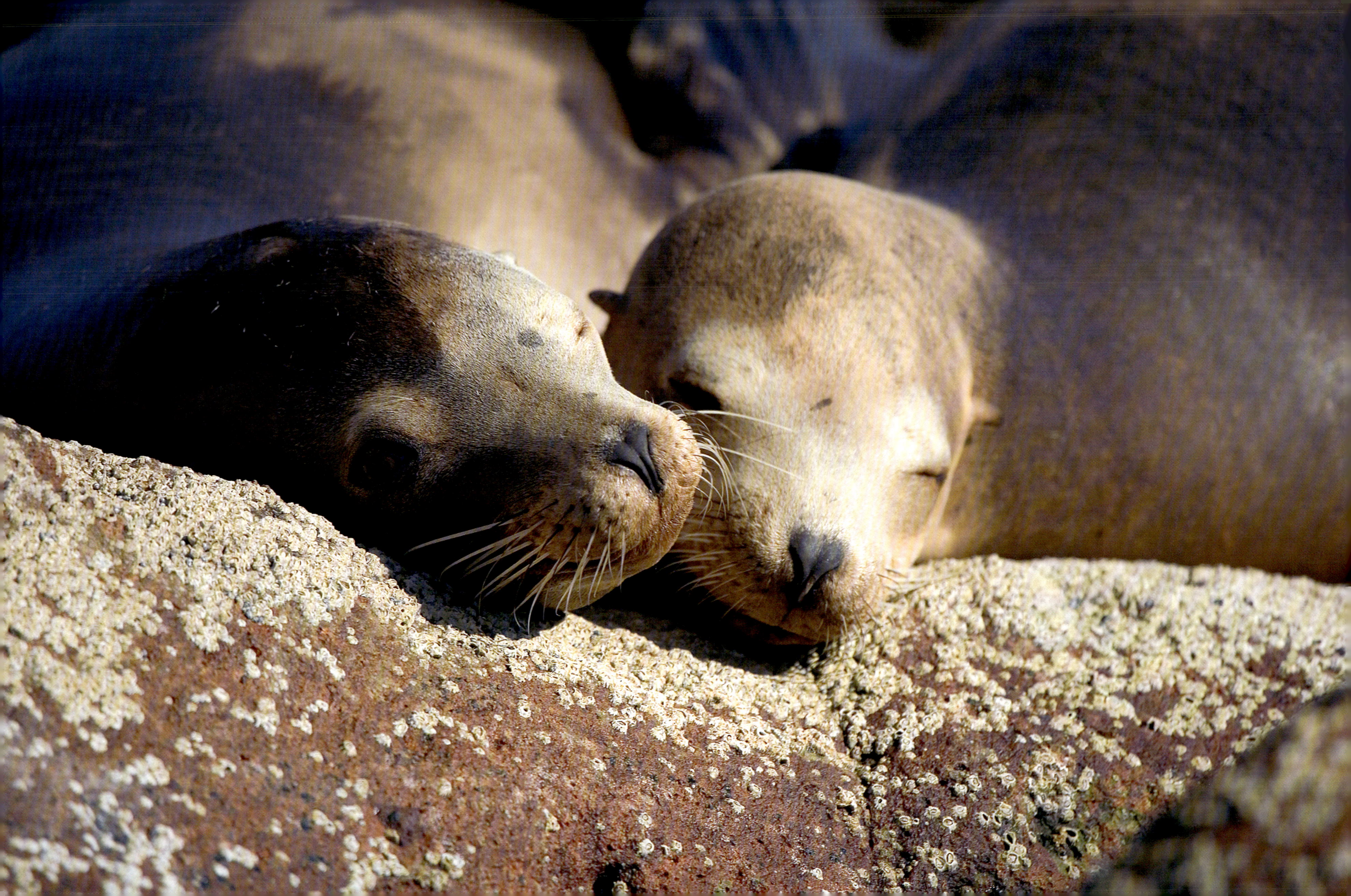

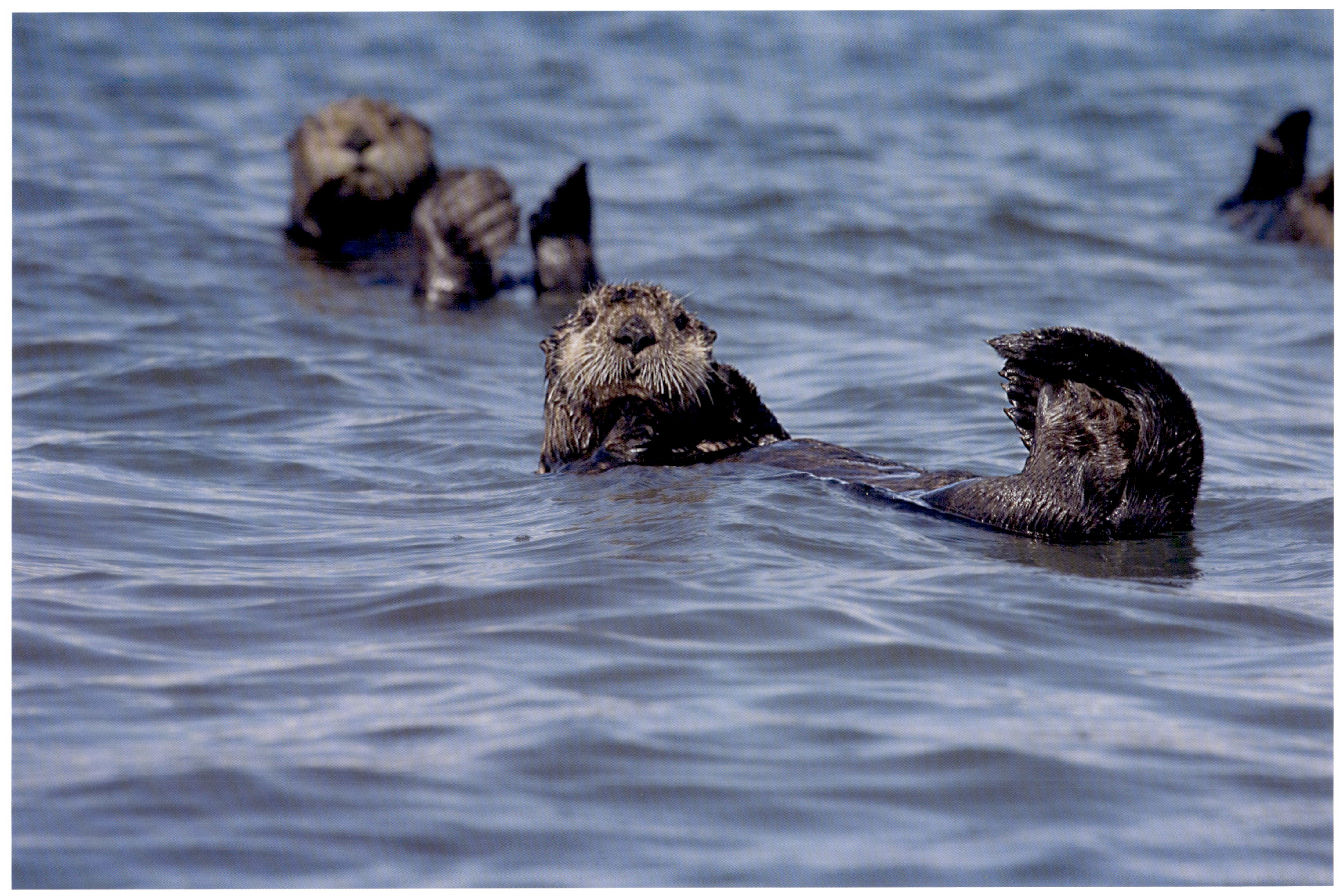

◄ seal love
▶ monterey sea otters

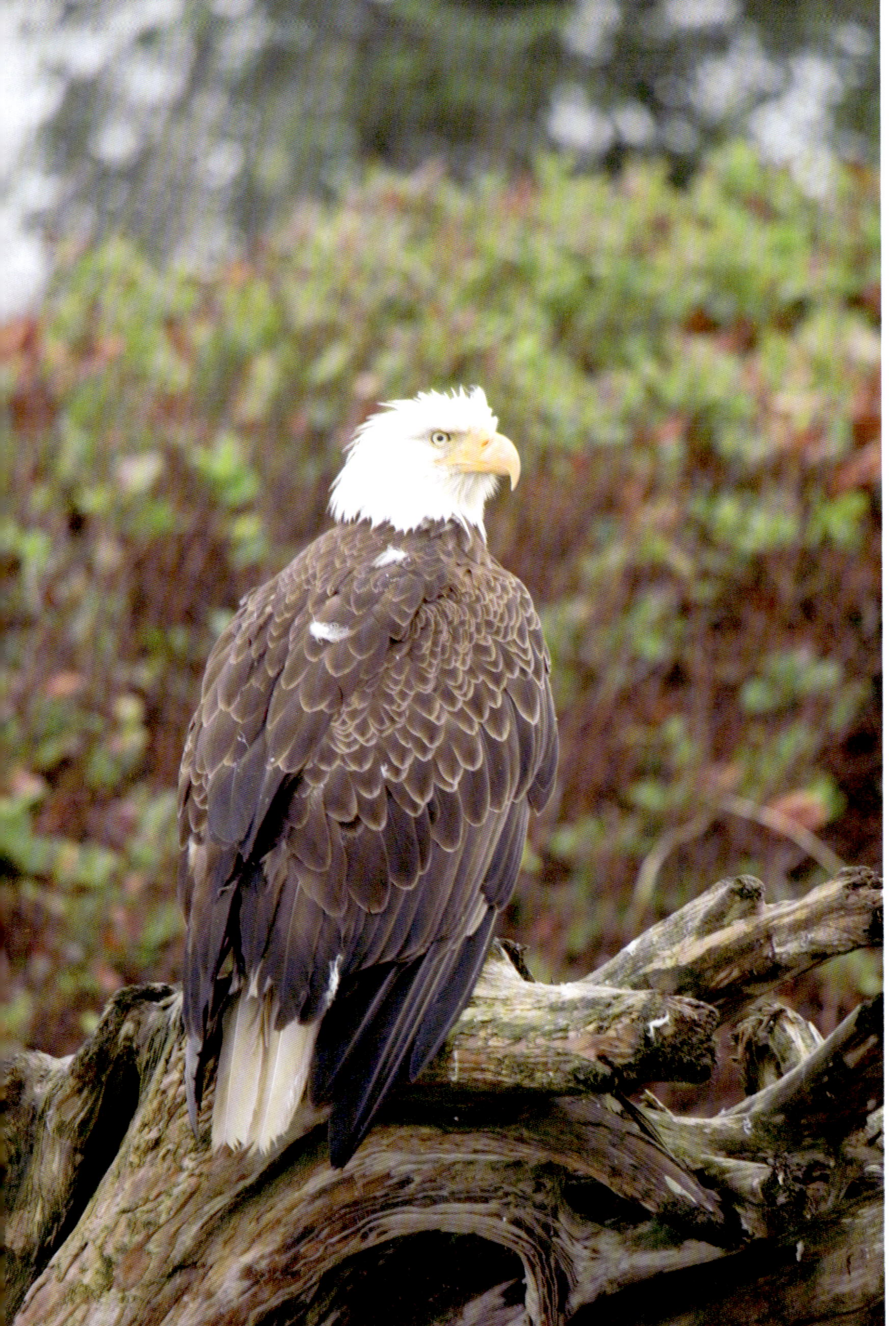

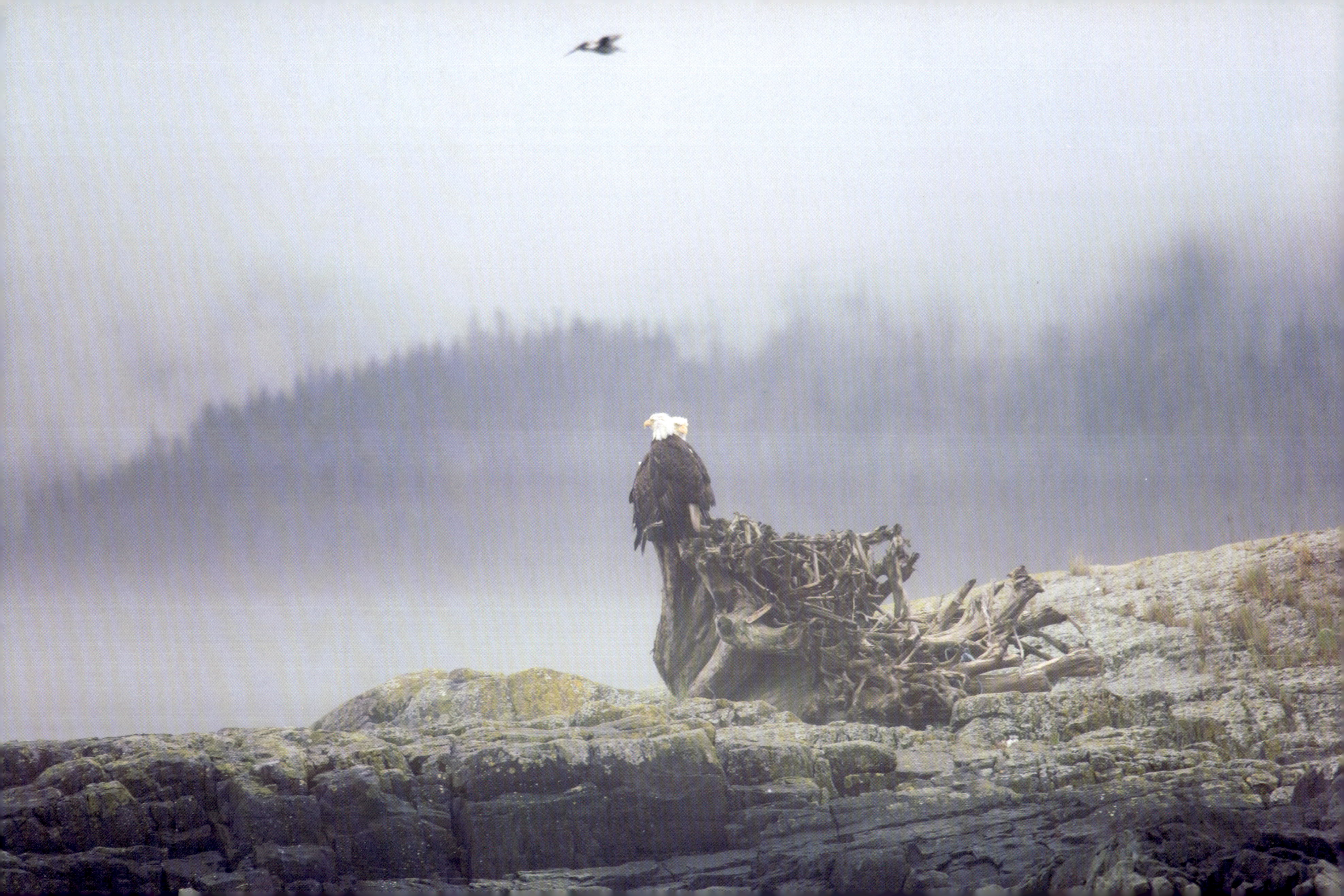

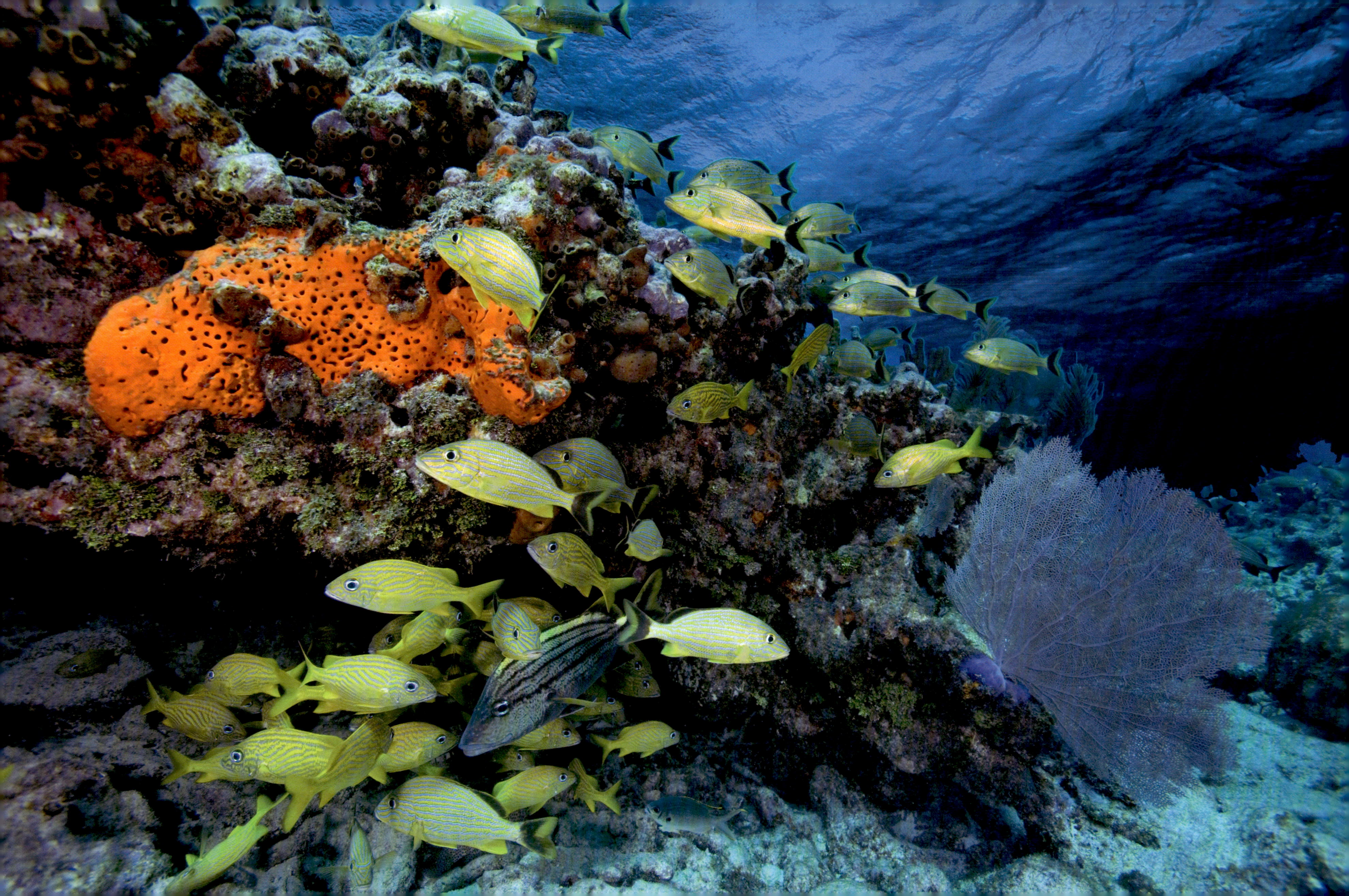

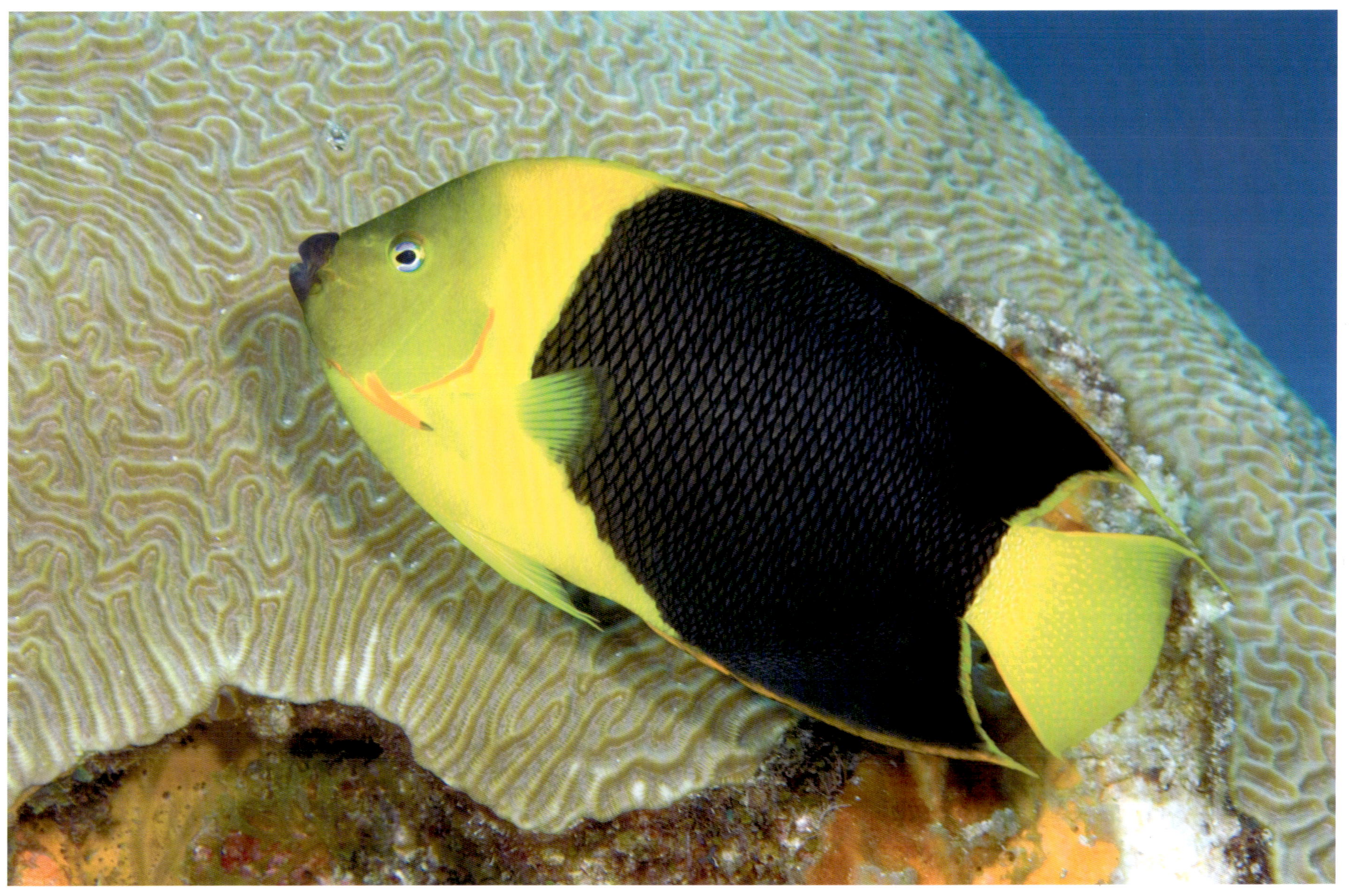

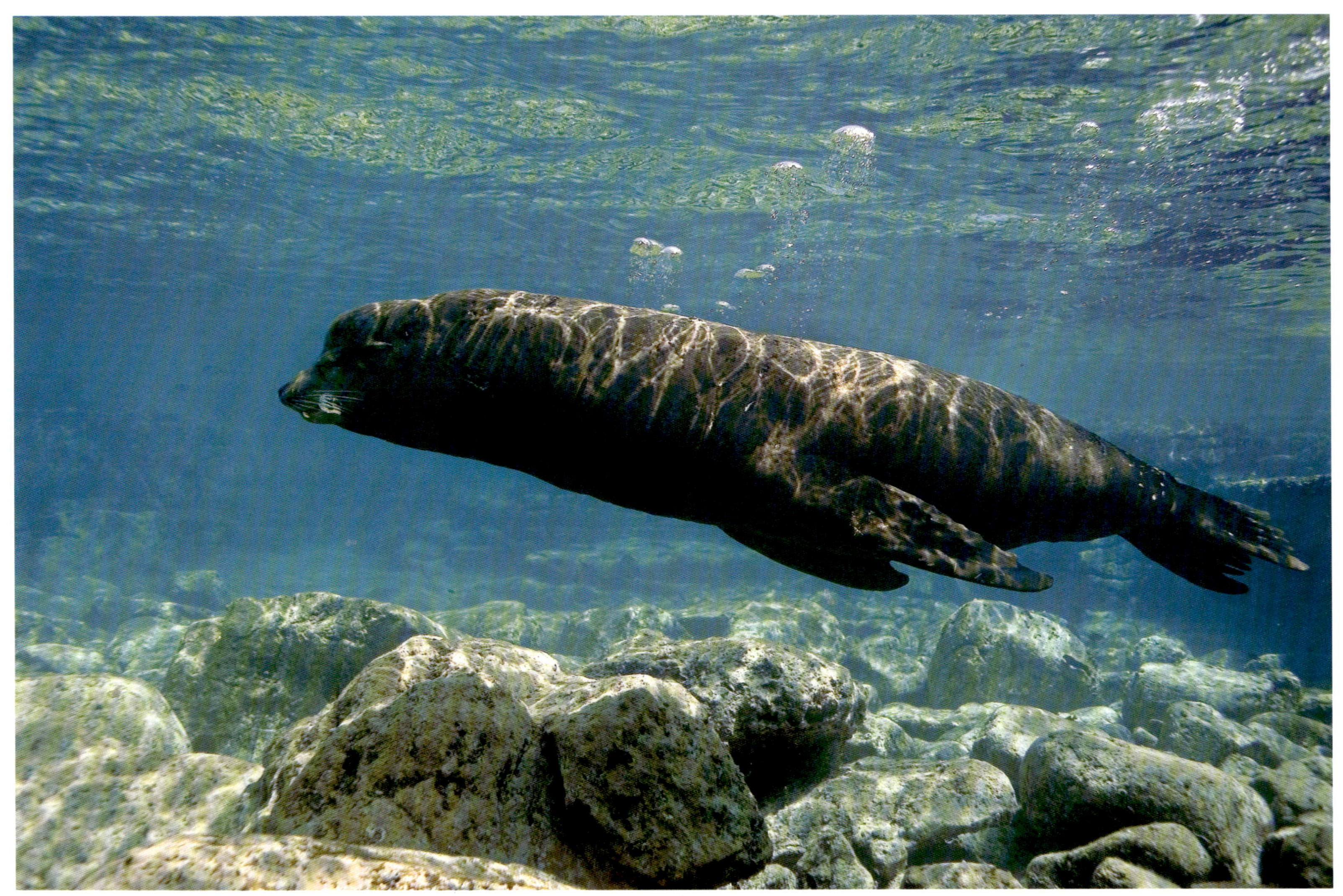

◀ sea lion bull
▶ lion bull encounter

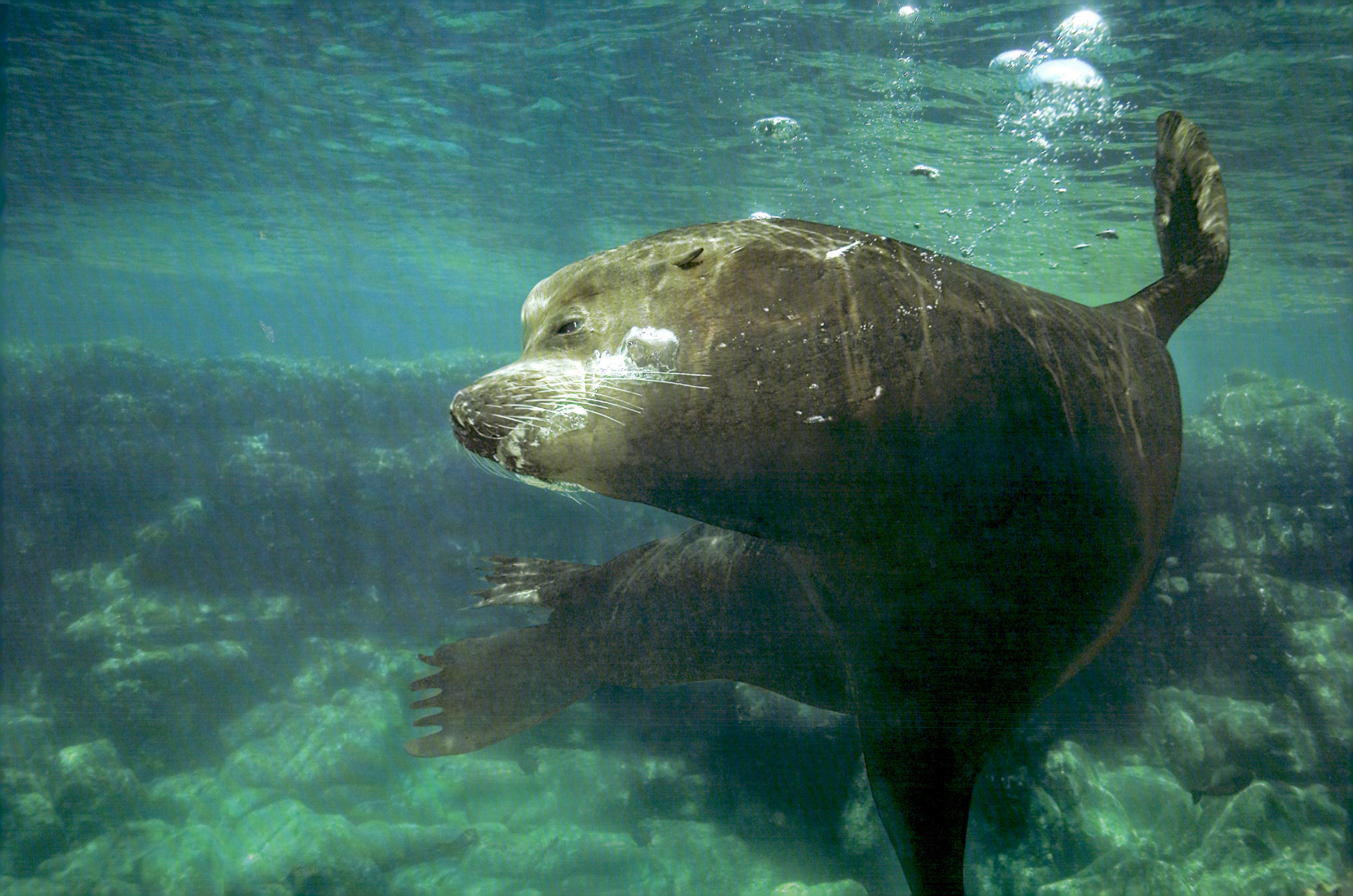

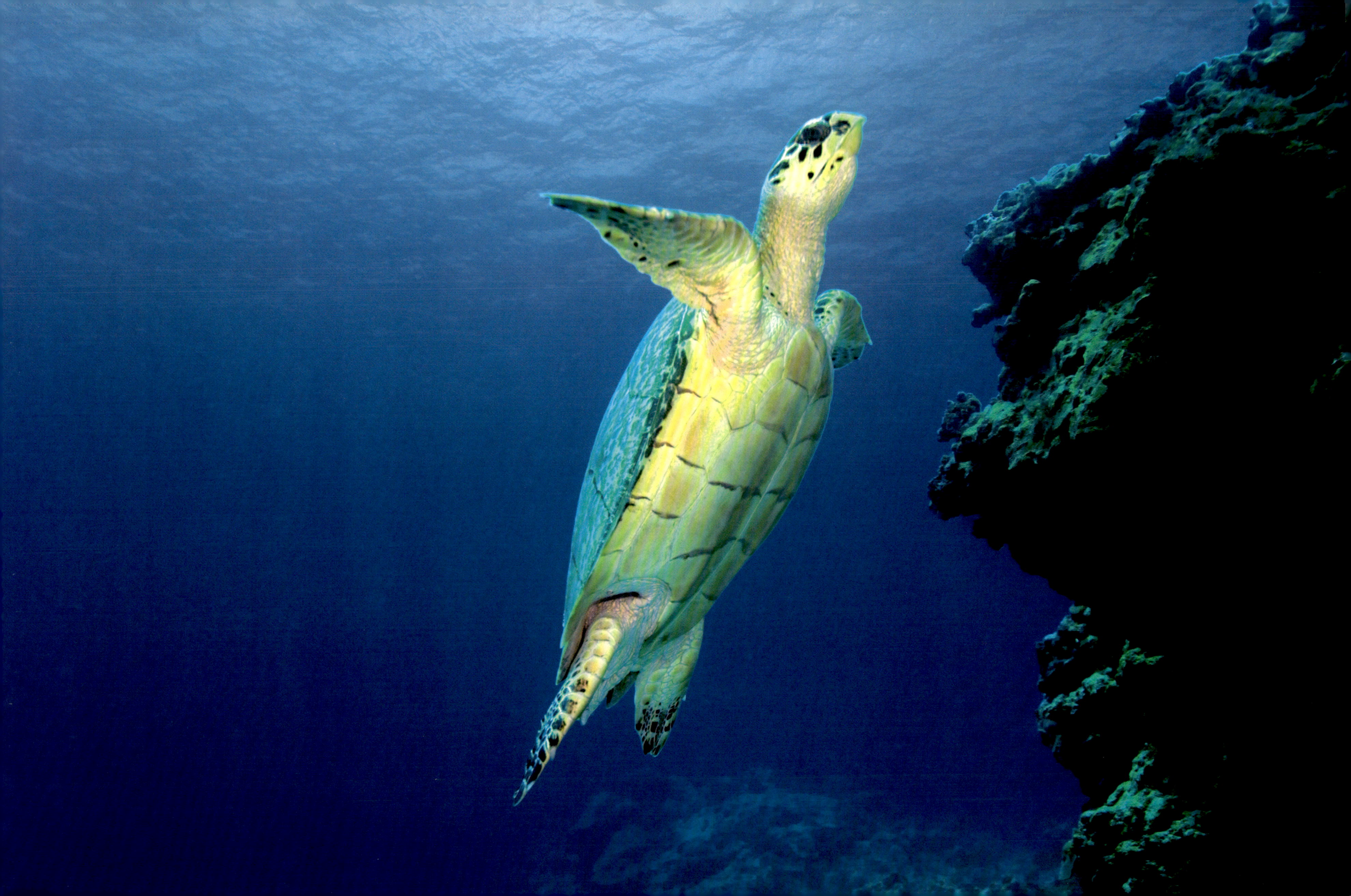

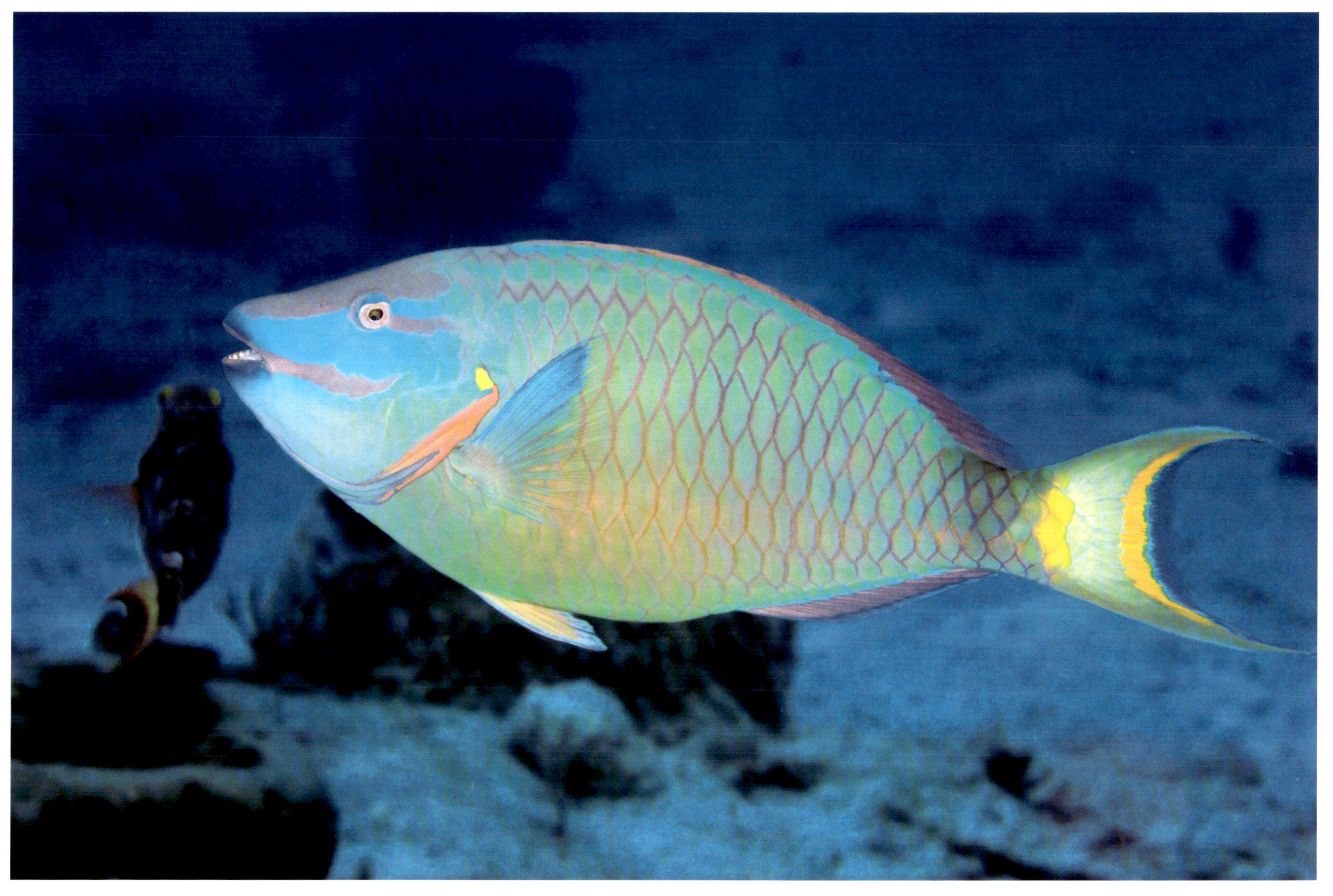

◀ hawksbill rising
▶ stoplight parrot fish

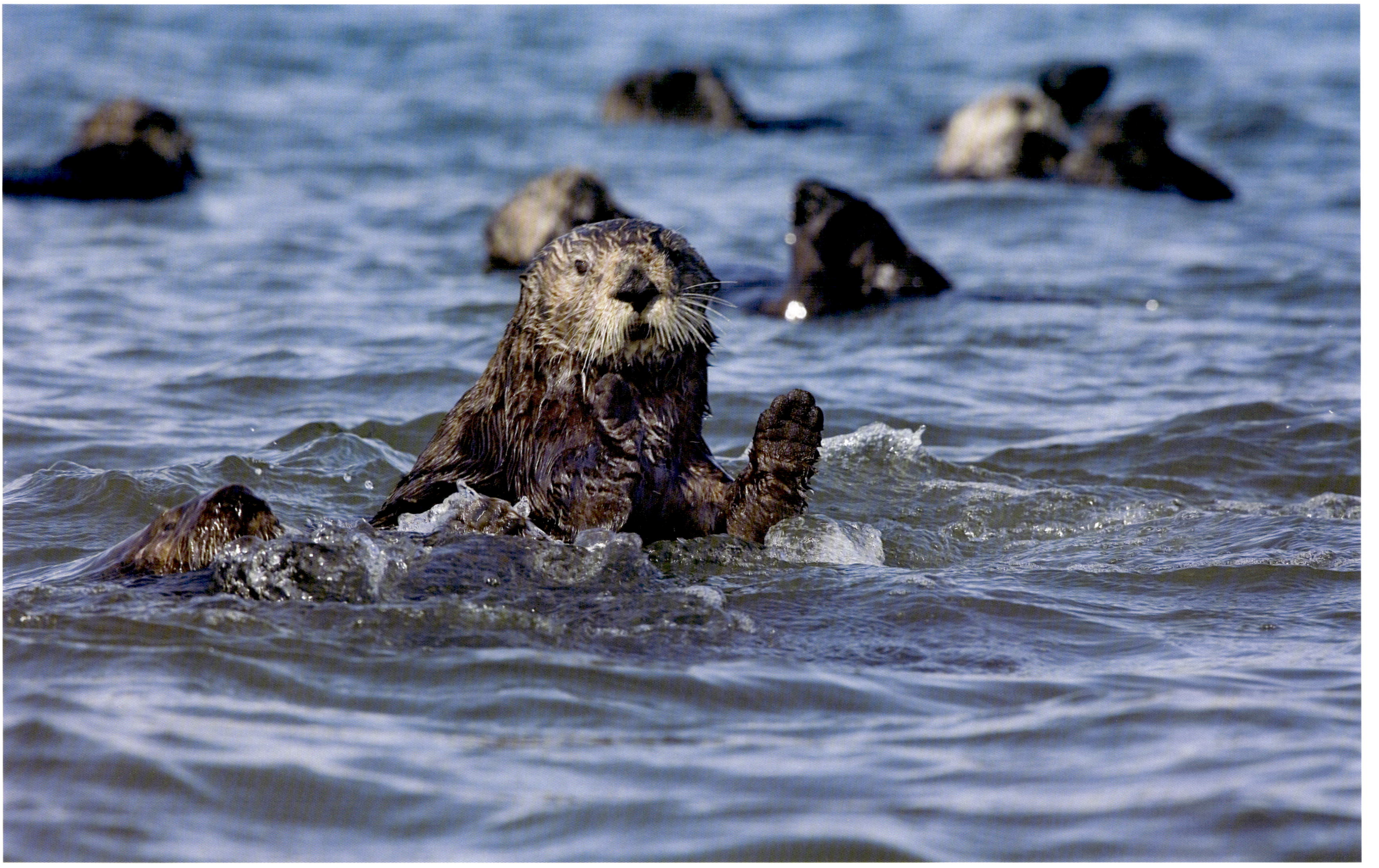

◄ sea otter wave
▶ sunset seals

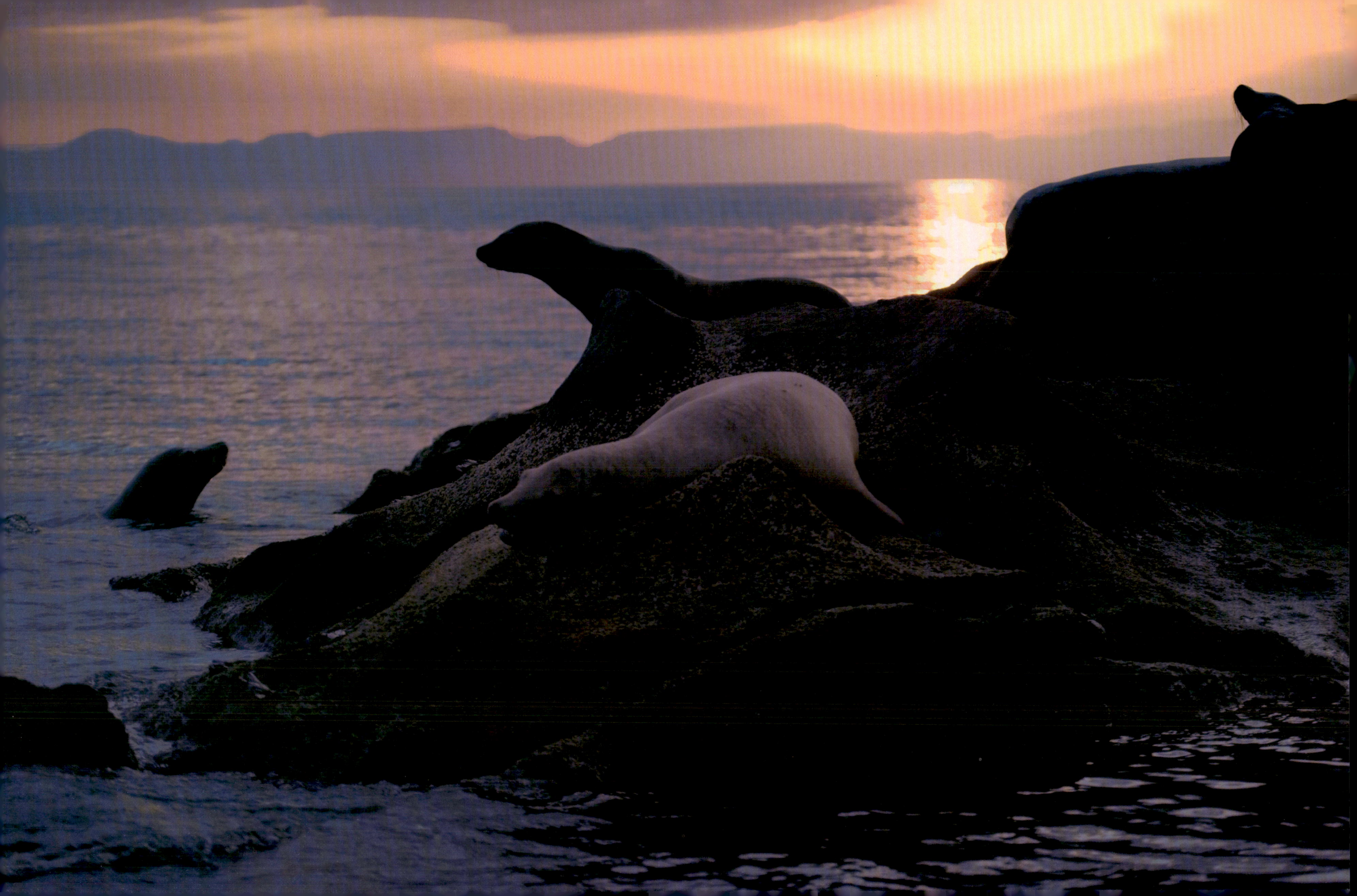

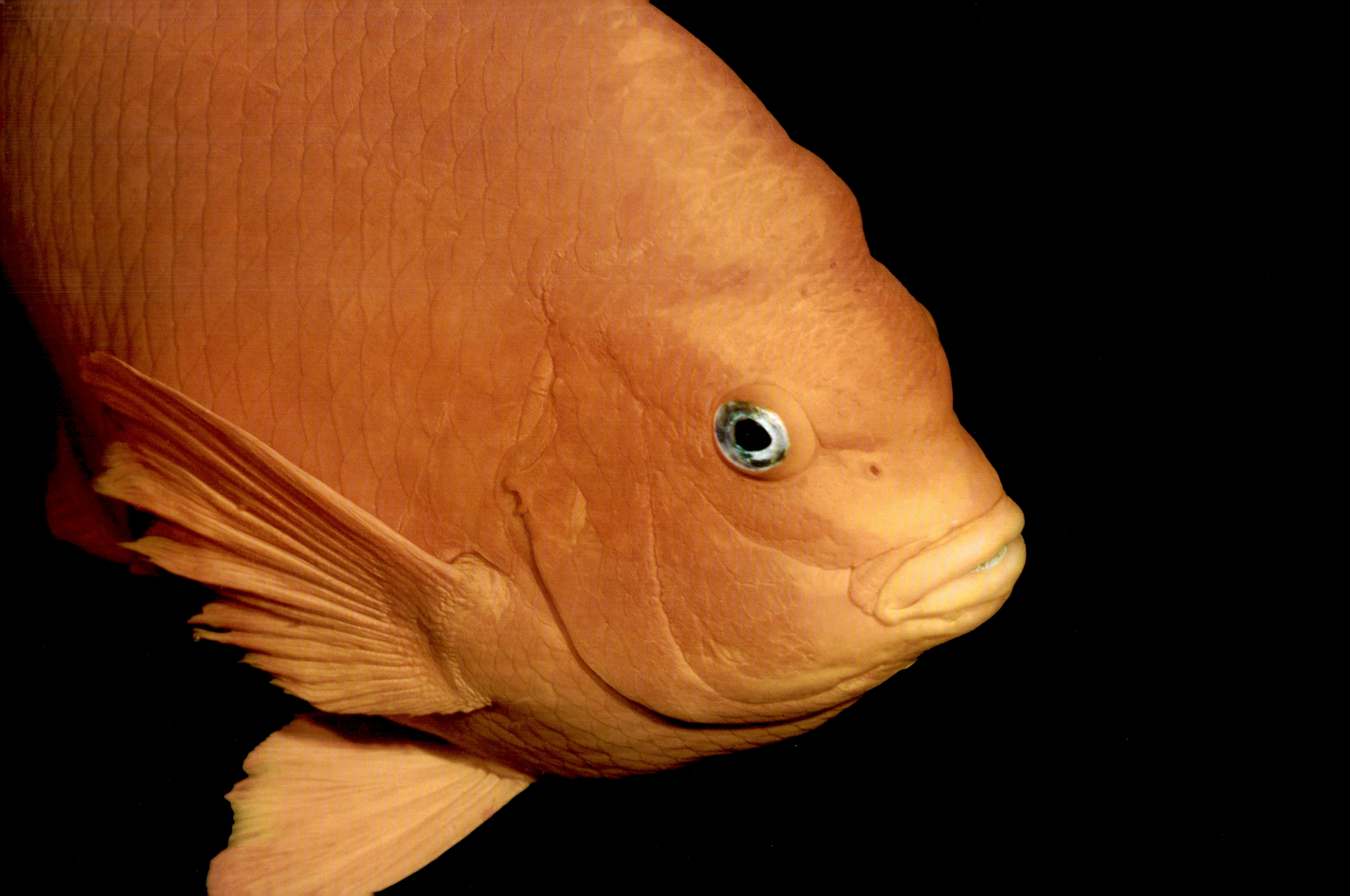

the ocean is fast becoming empty. we must now reverse the damage caused by the most dangerous predator on the planet —man ...

◀ portrait of a garibaldi

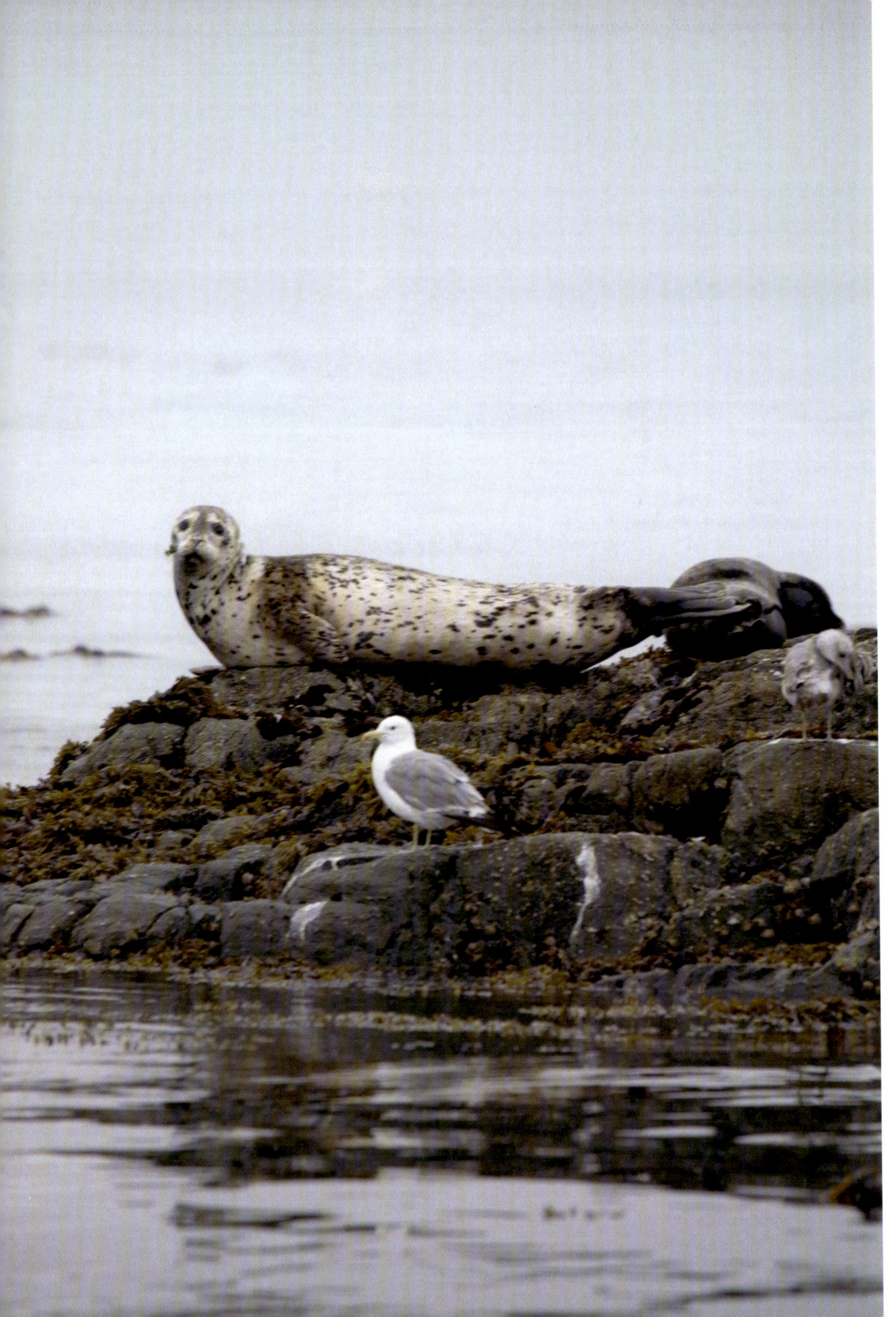

◄ harbor seal rock
► seal sanctuary

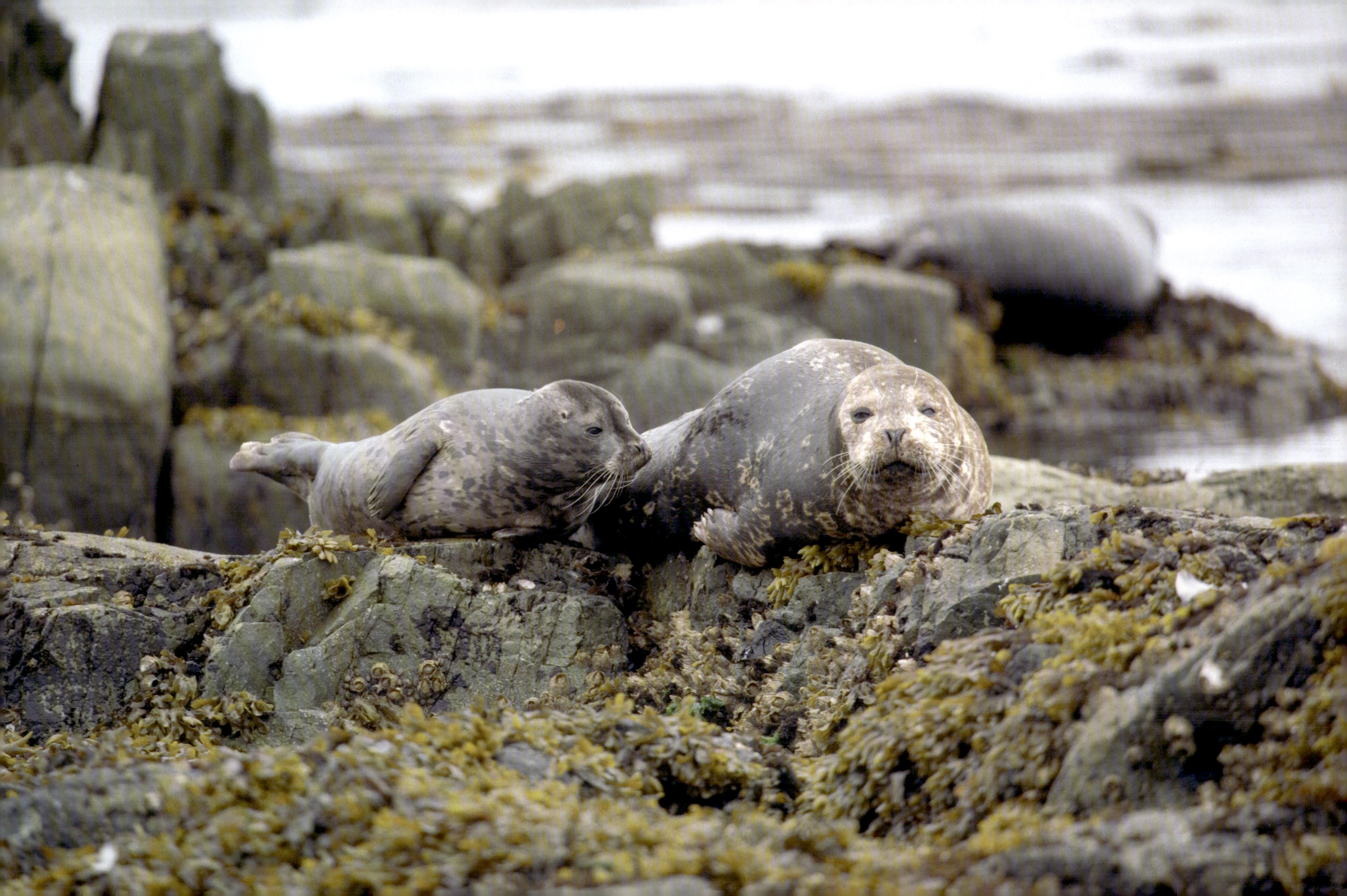

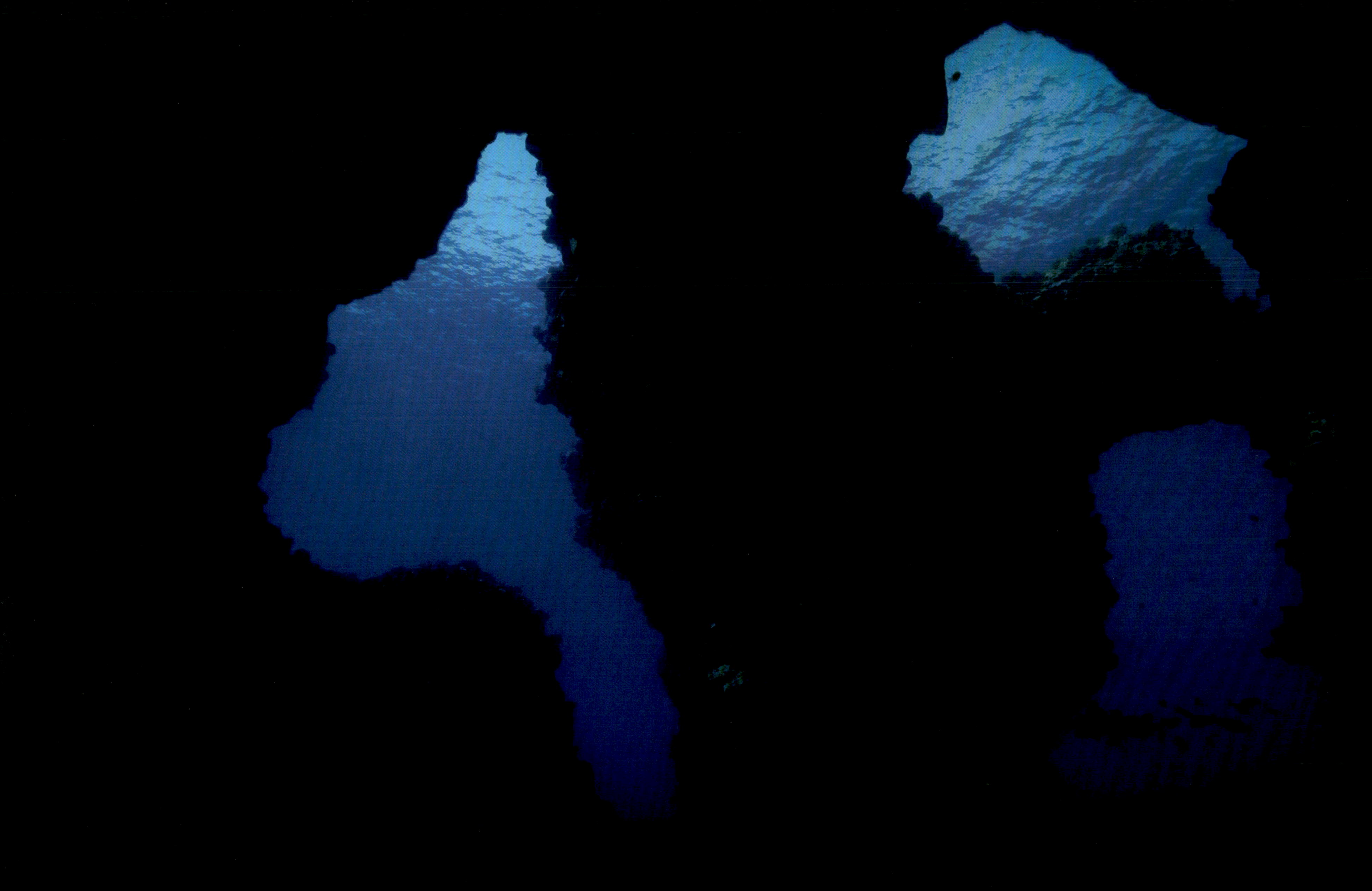

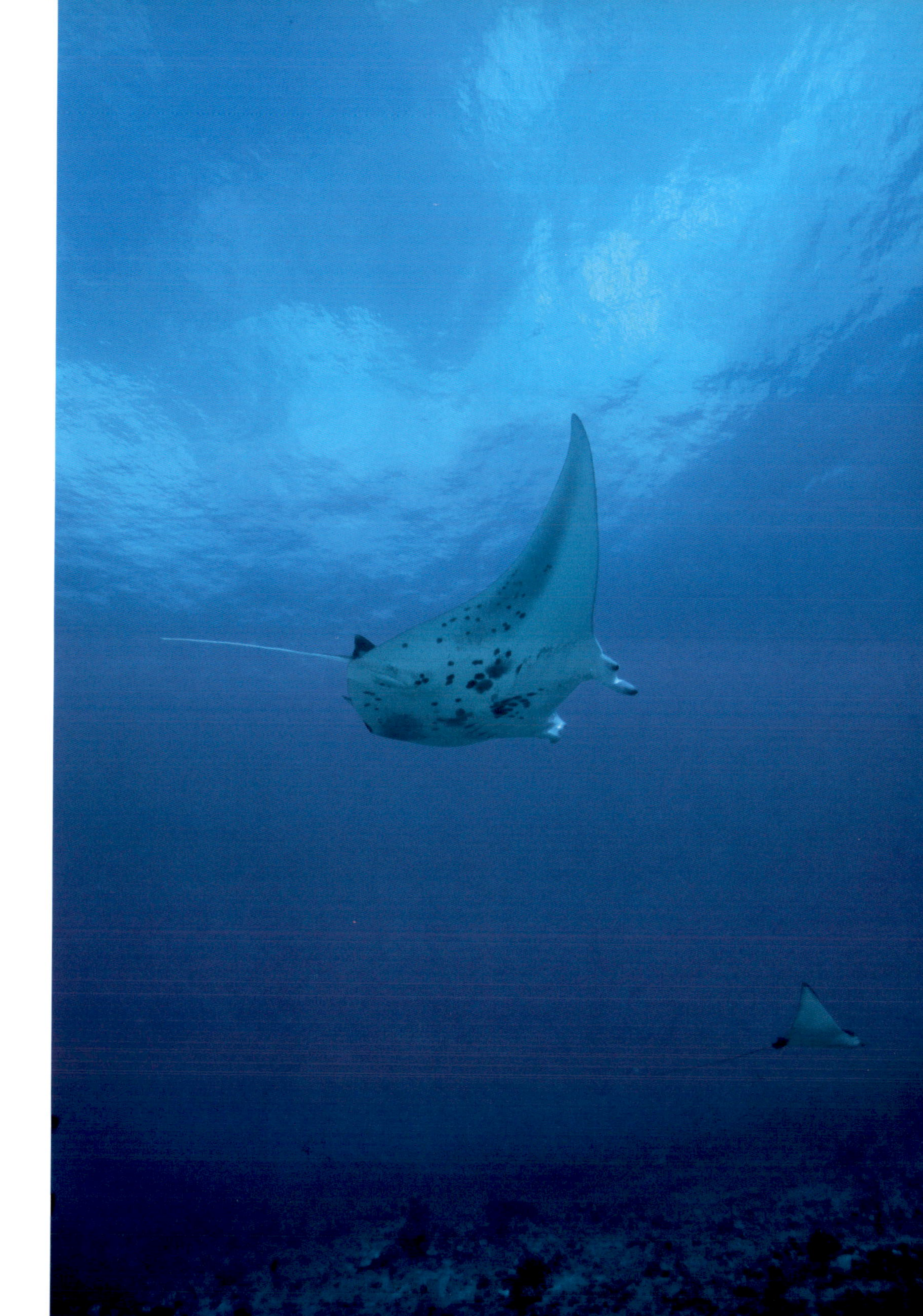

◀ lanai under sea cathedrals
▶ manta and spotted eagle ray

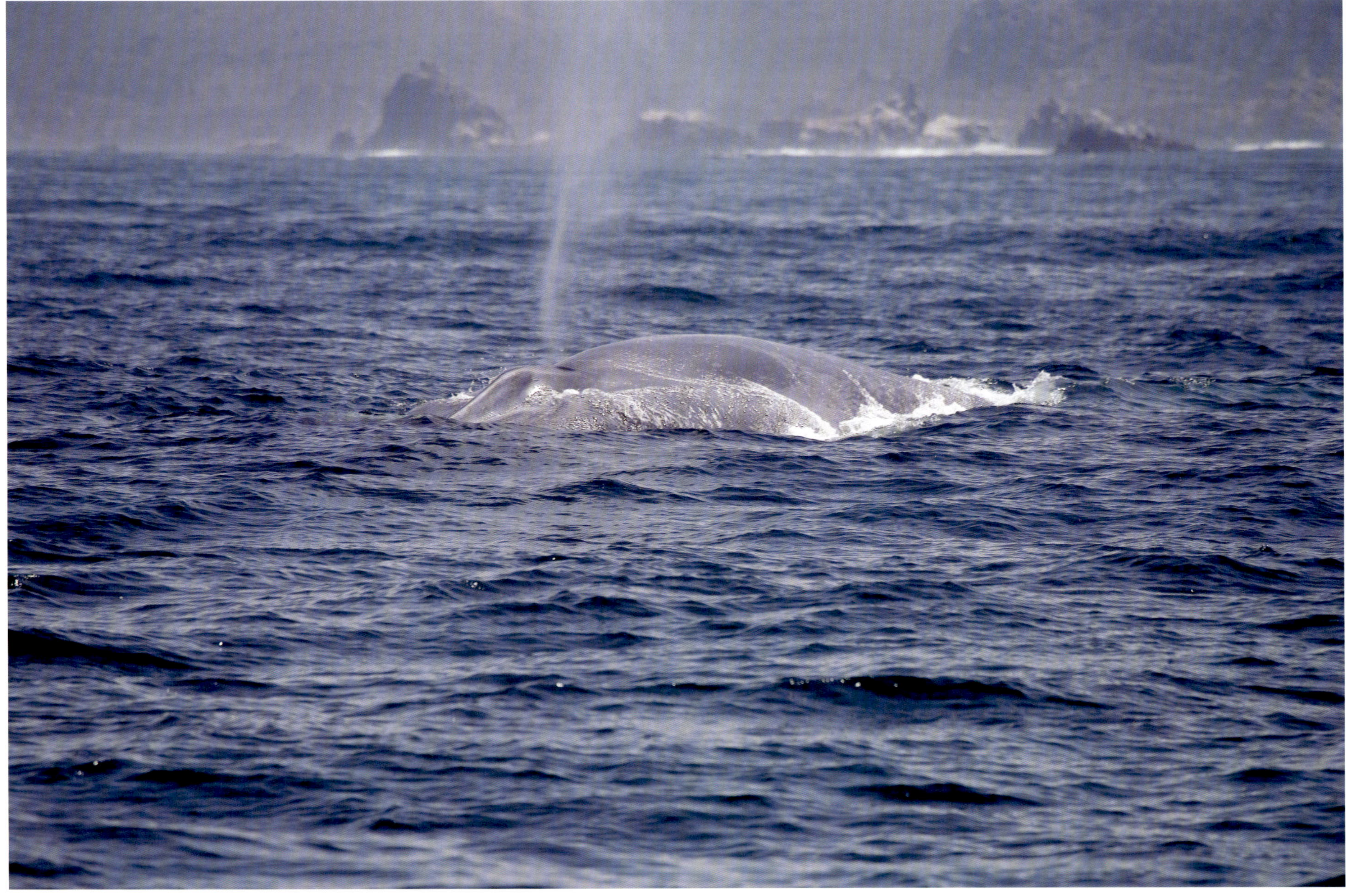

◄ blue whale spout
► blue whale sounding

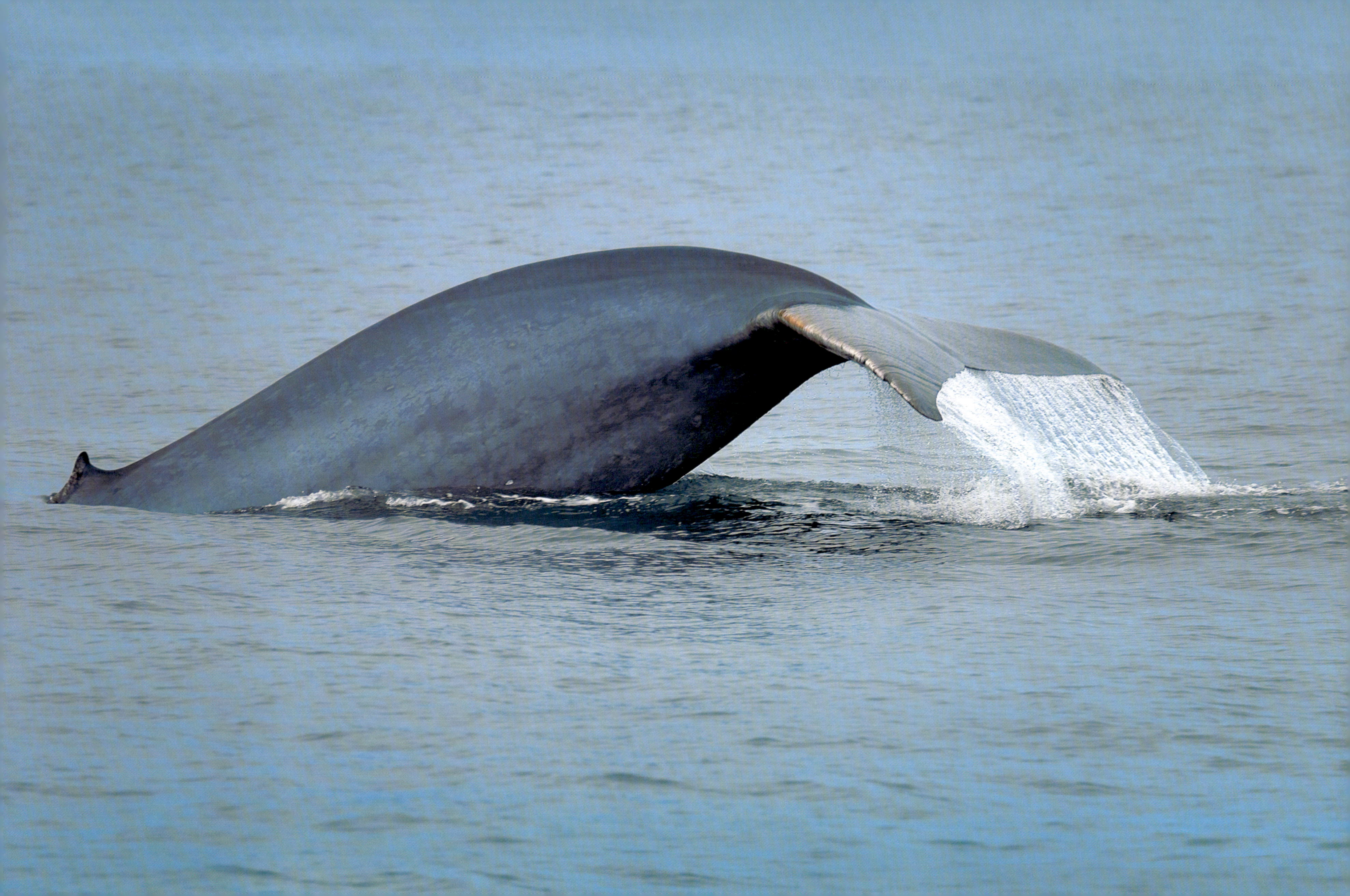

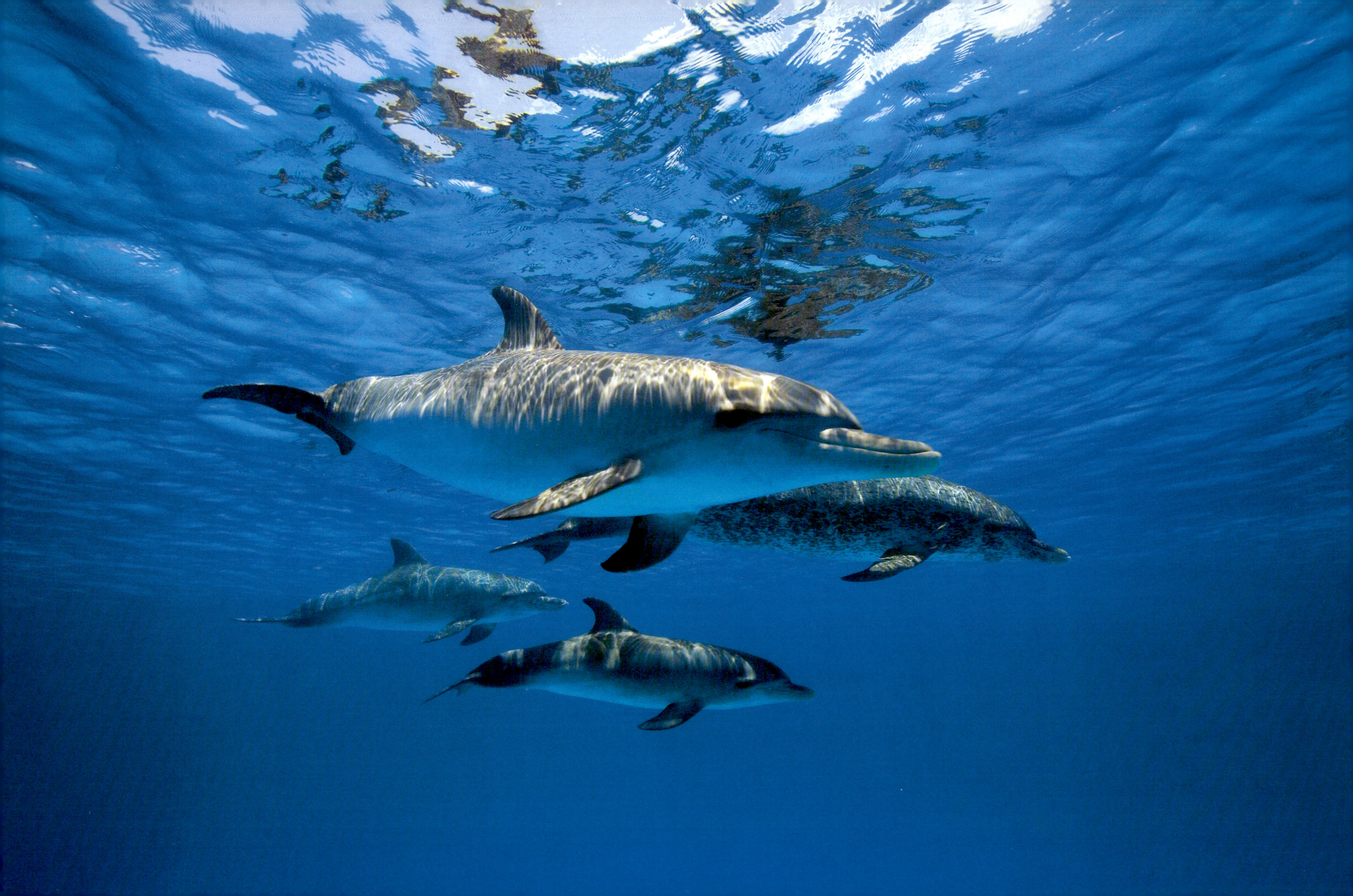

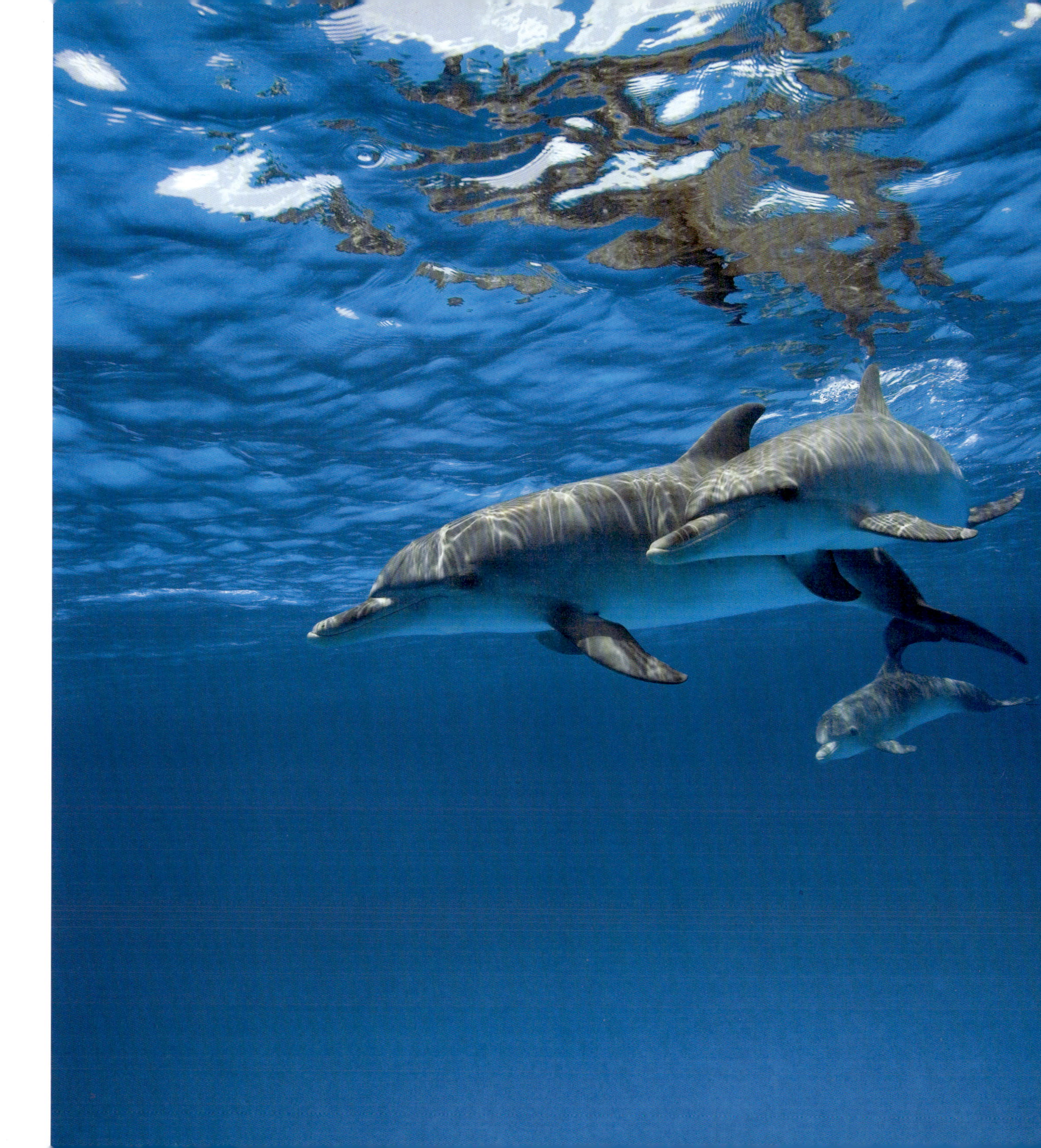

◀ spotted dolphin tribe
▶ spotted dolphin family

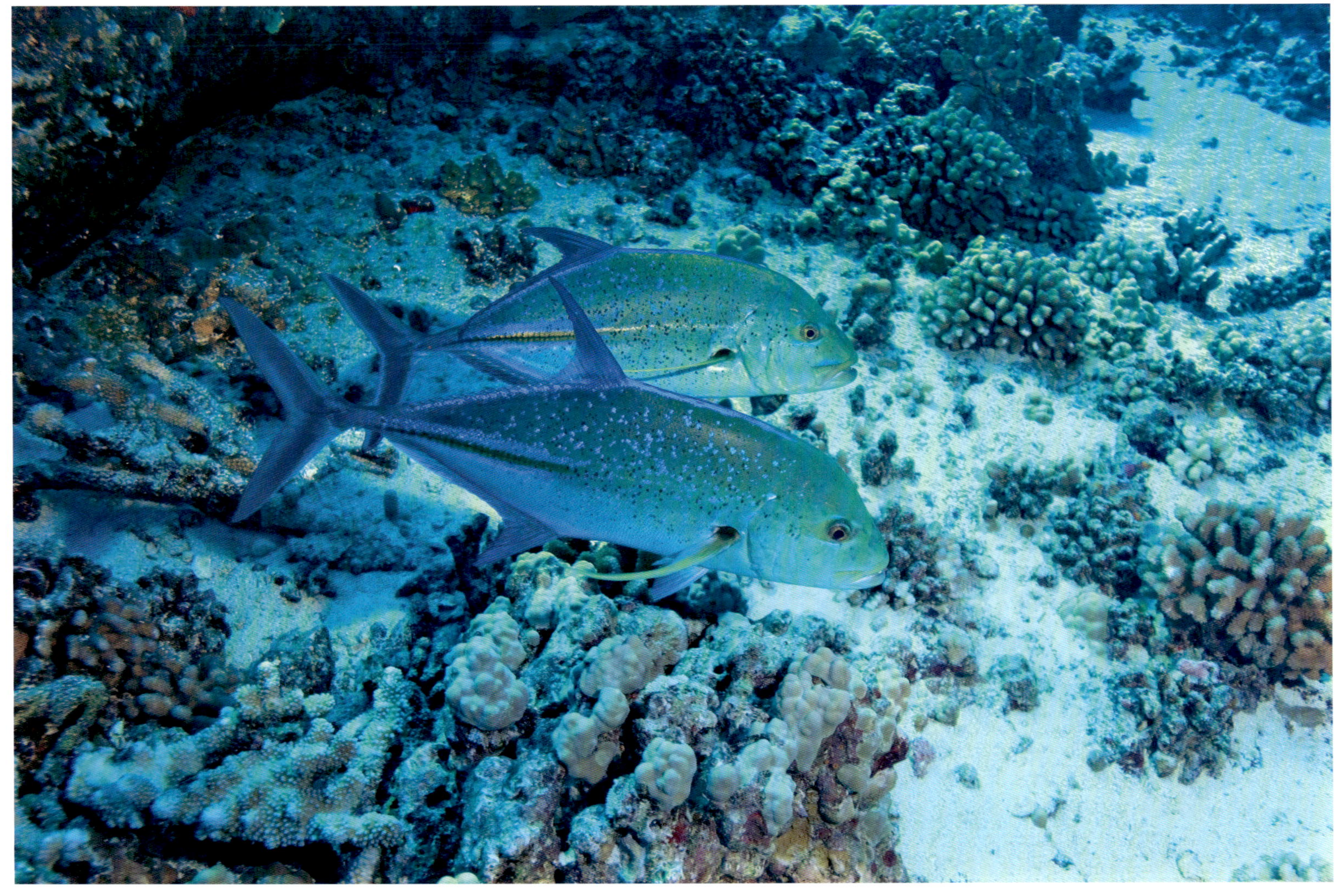

◀ ulua fish patrol
▶ french angel dance

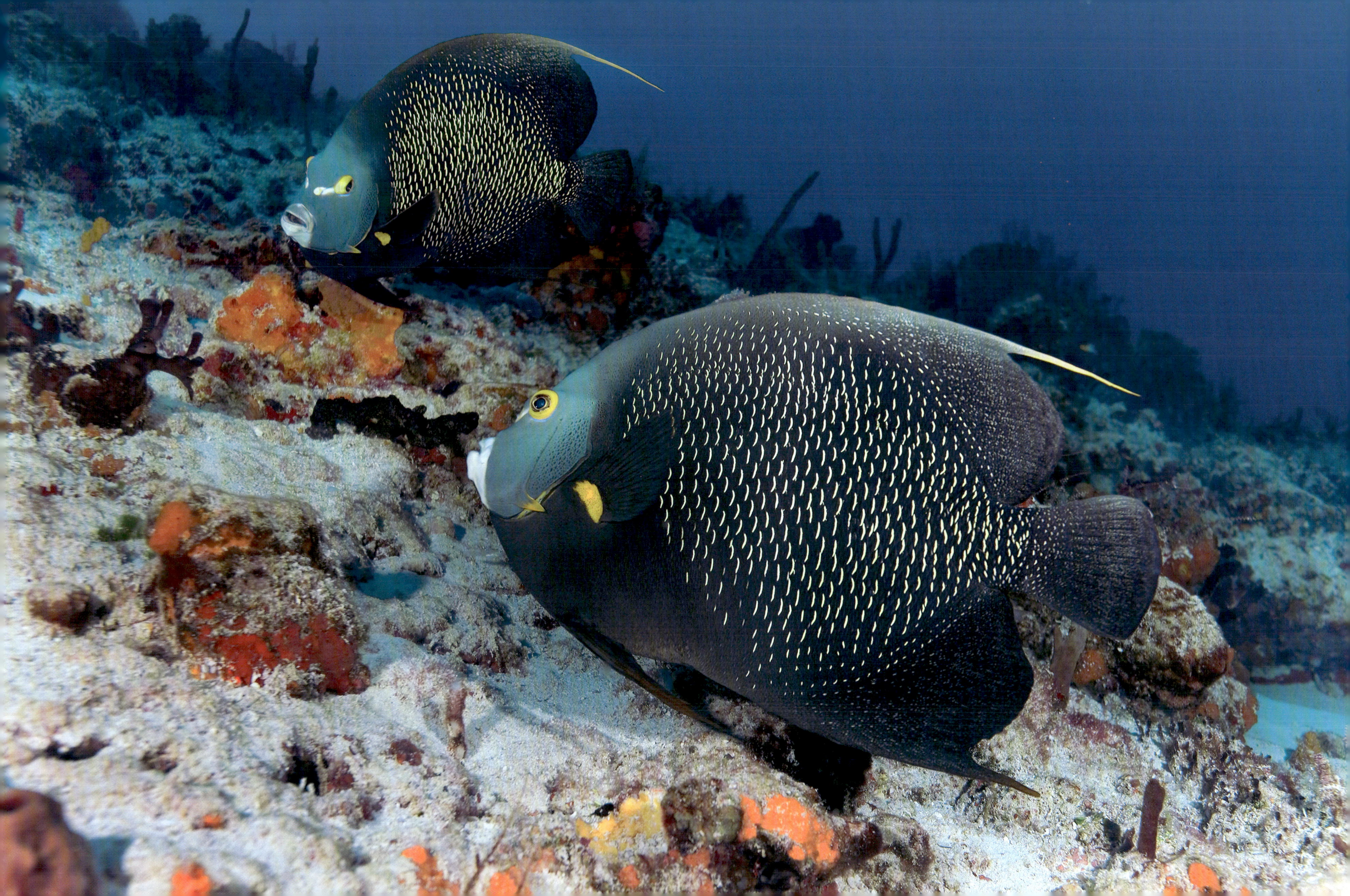

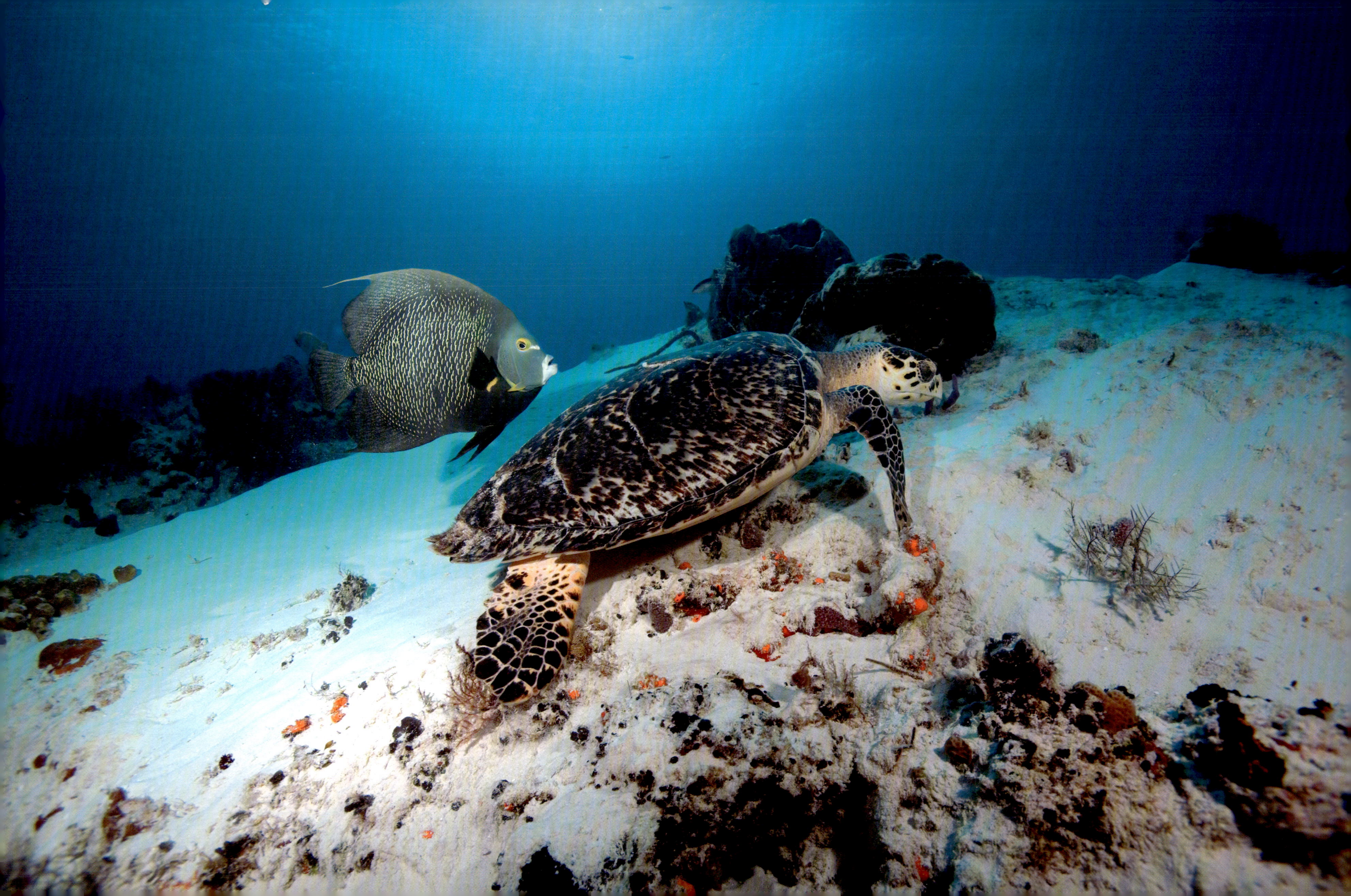

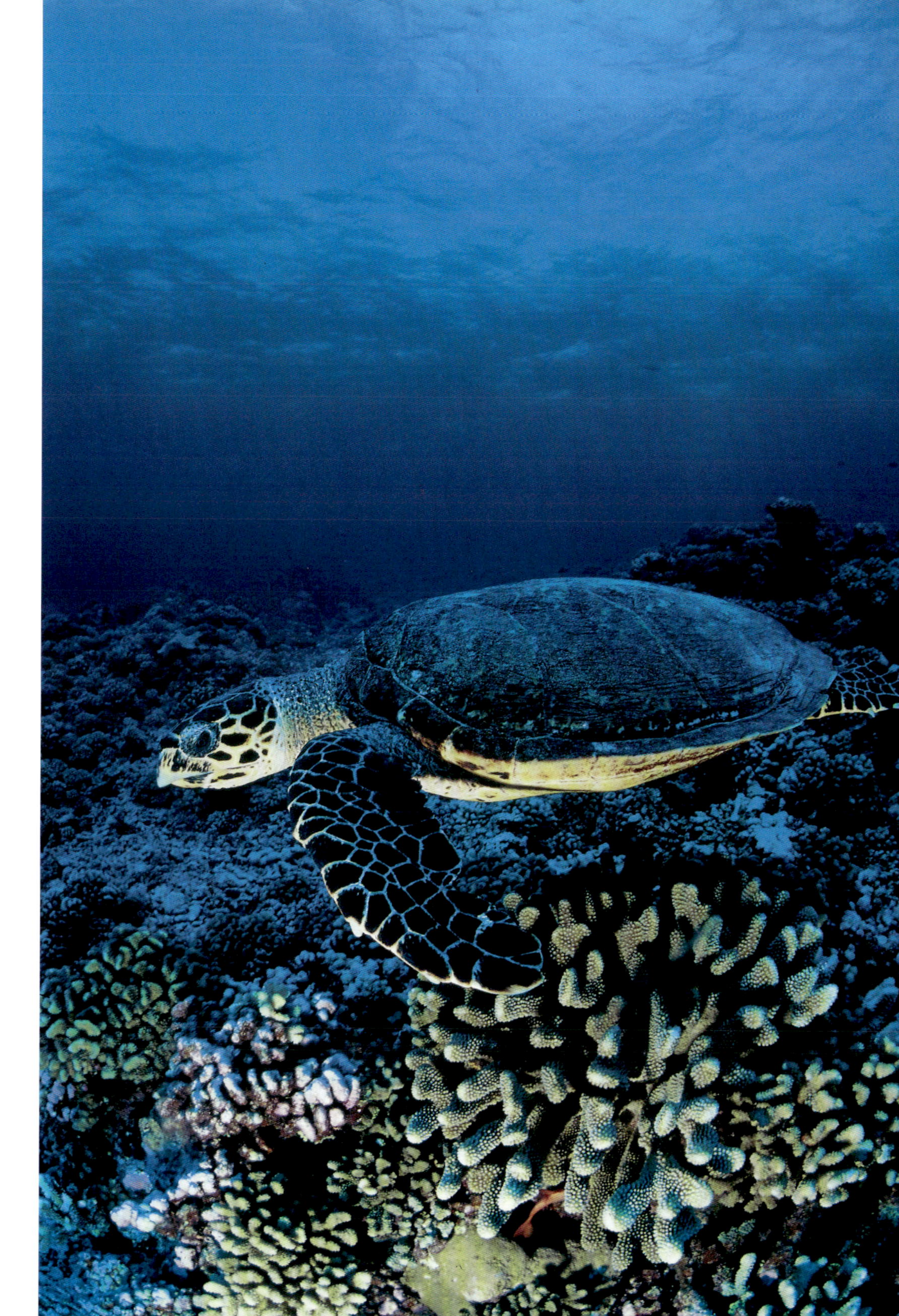

◀ hawksbill sandy reef
▶ hawksbill sea turtle reef

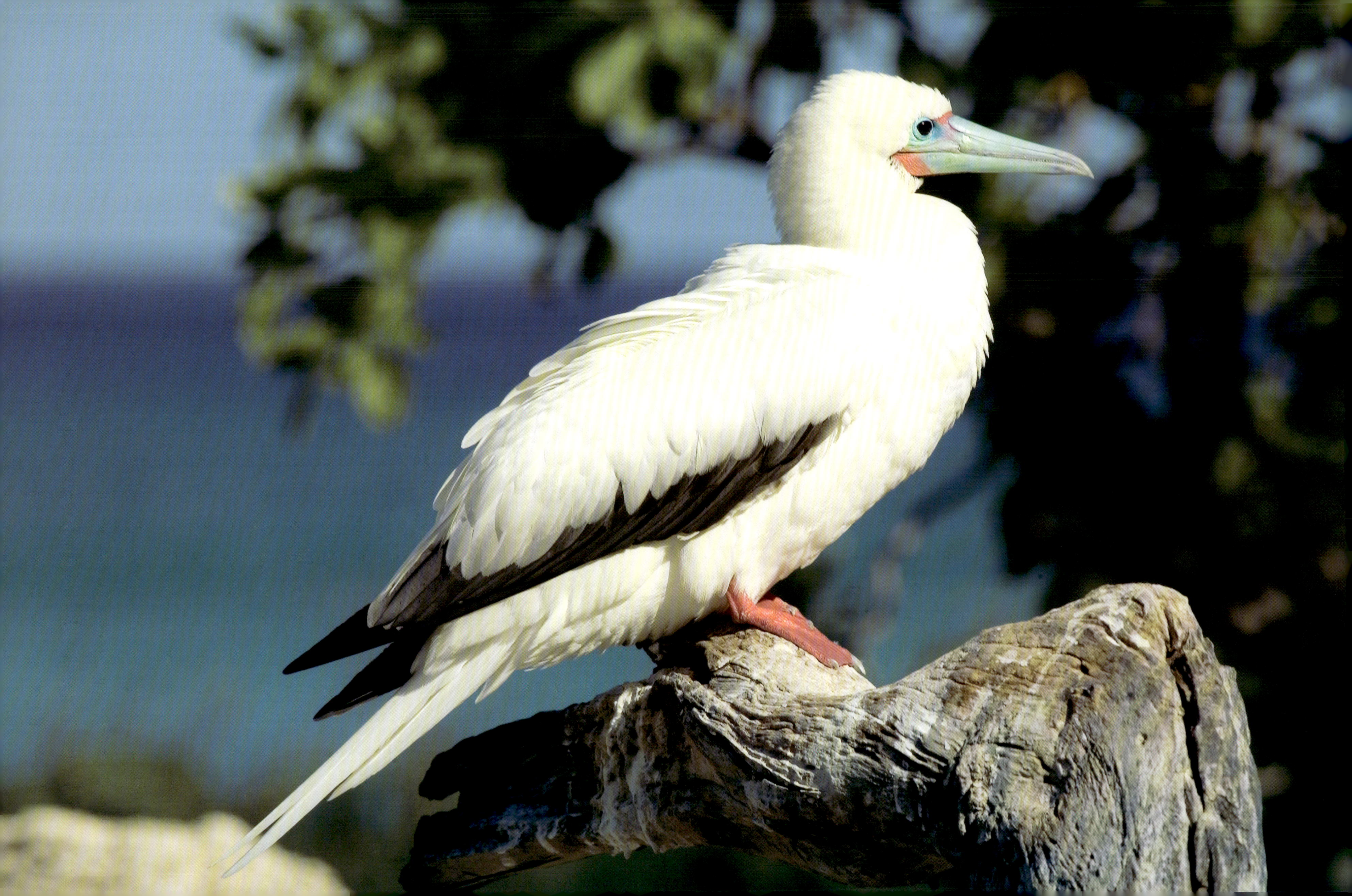

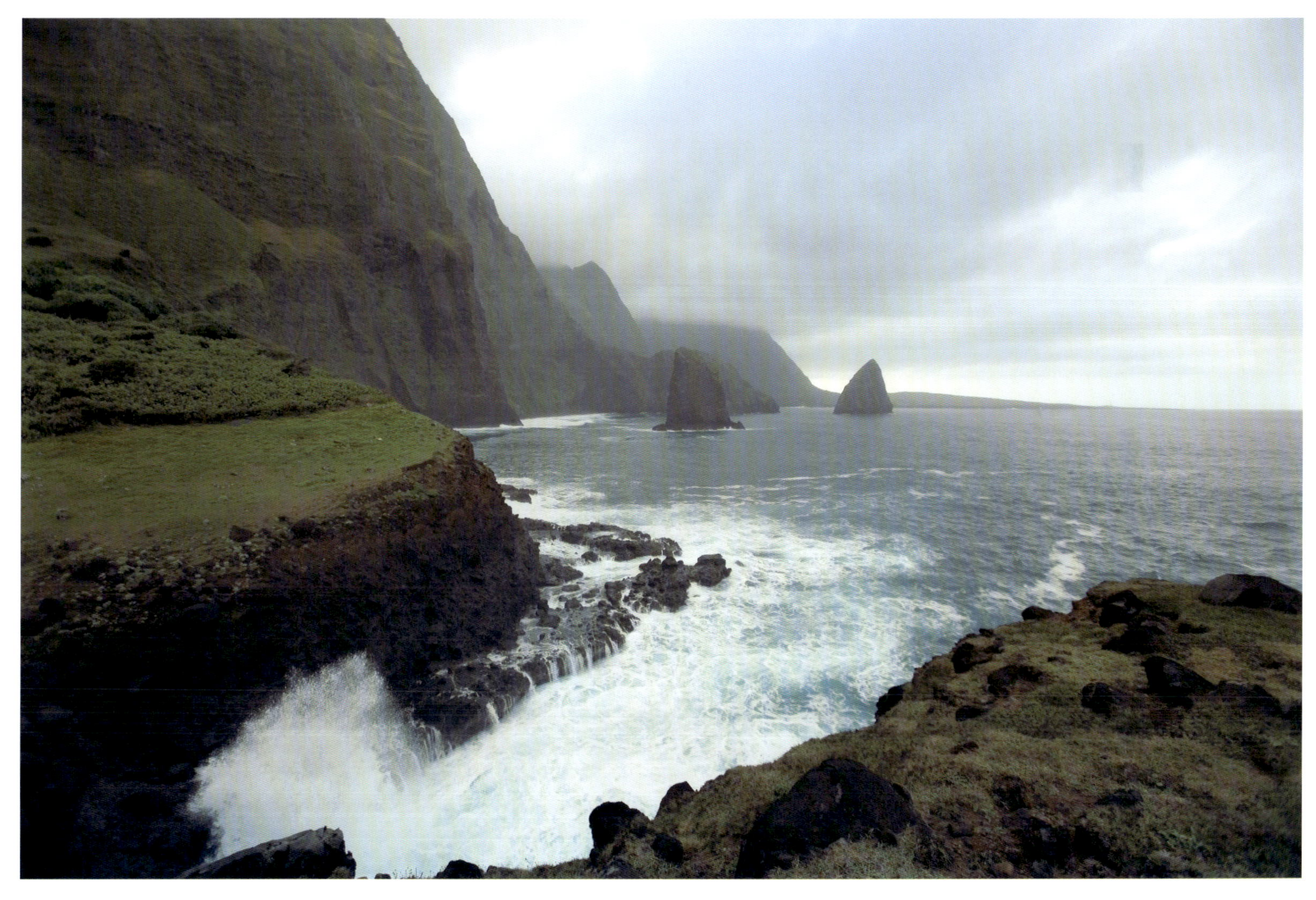

◄ island boobie
▶ molokai beach waves

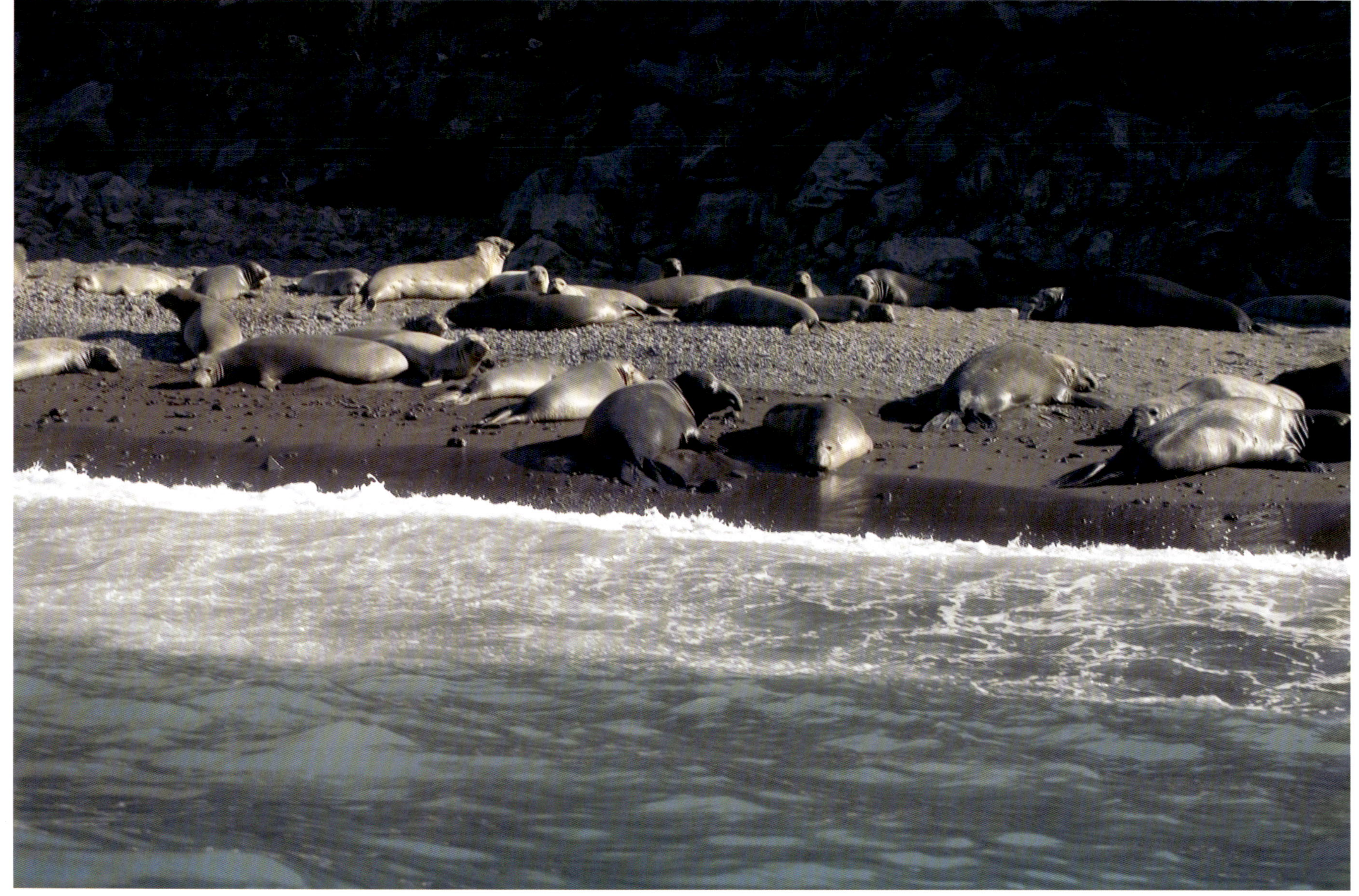

◄ elephant seal beach
► male elephant seals

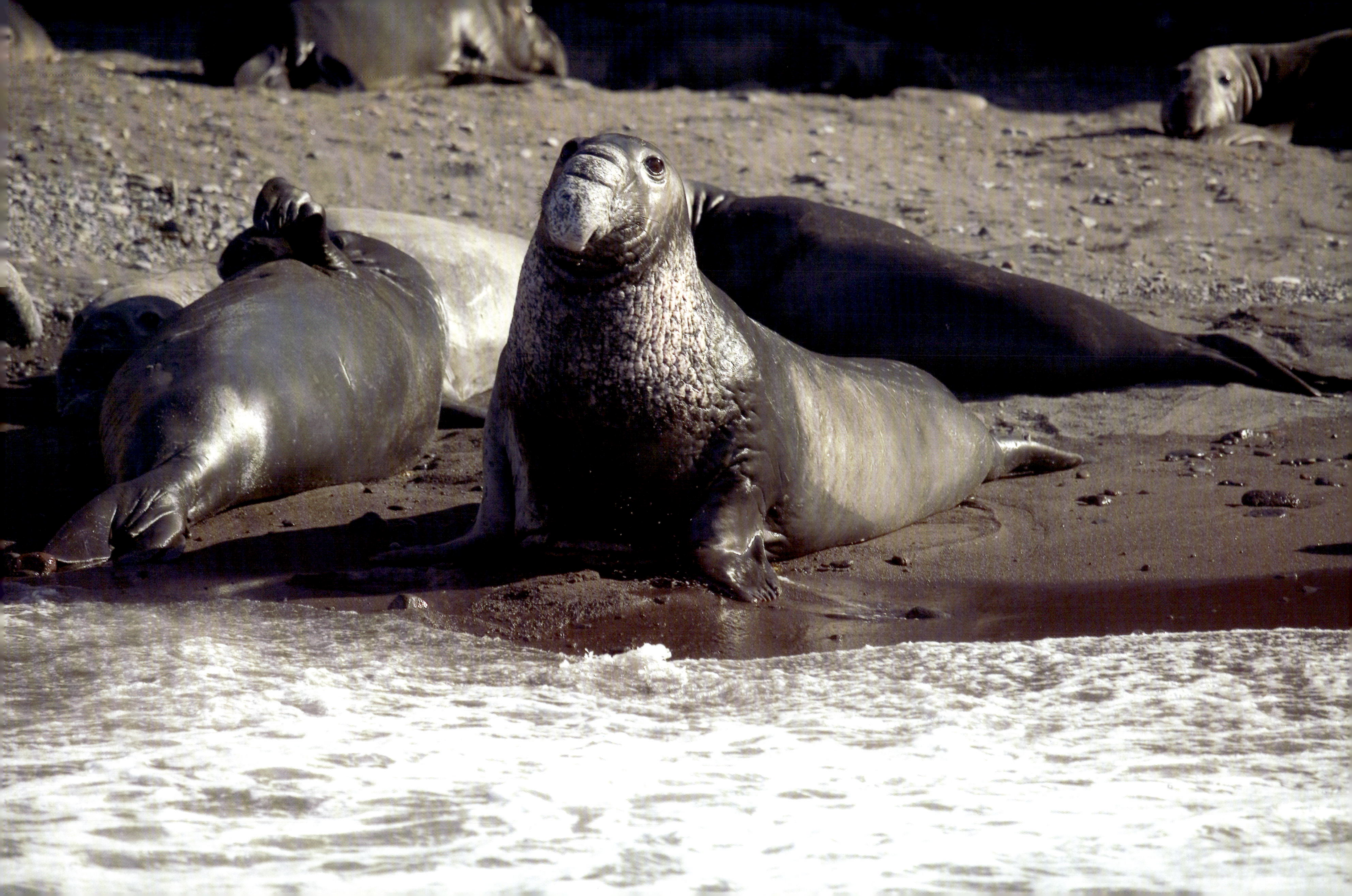

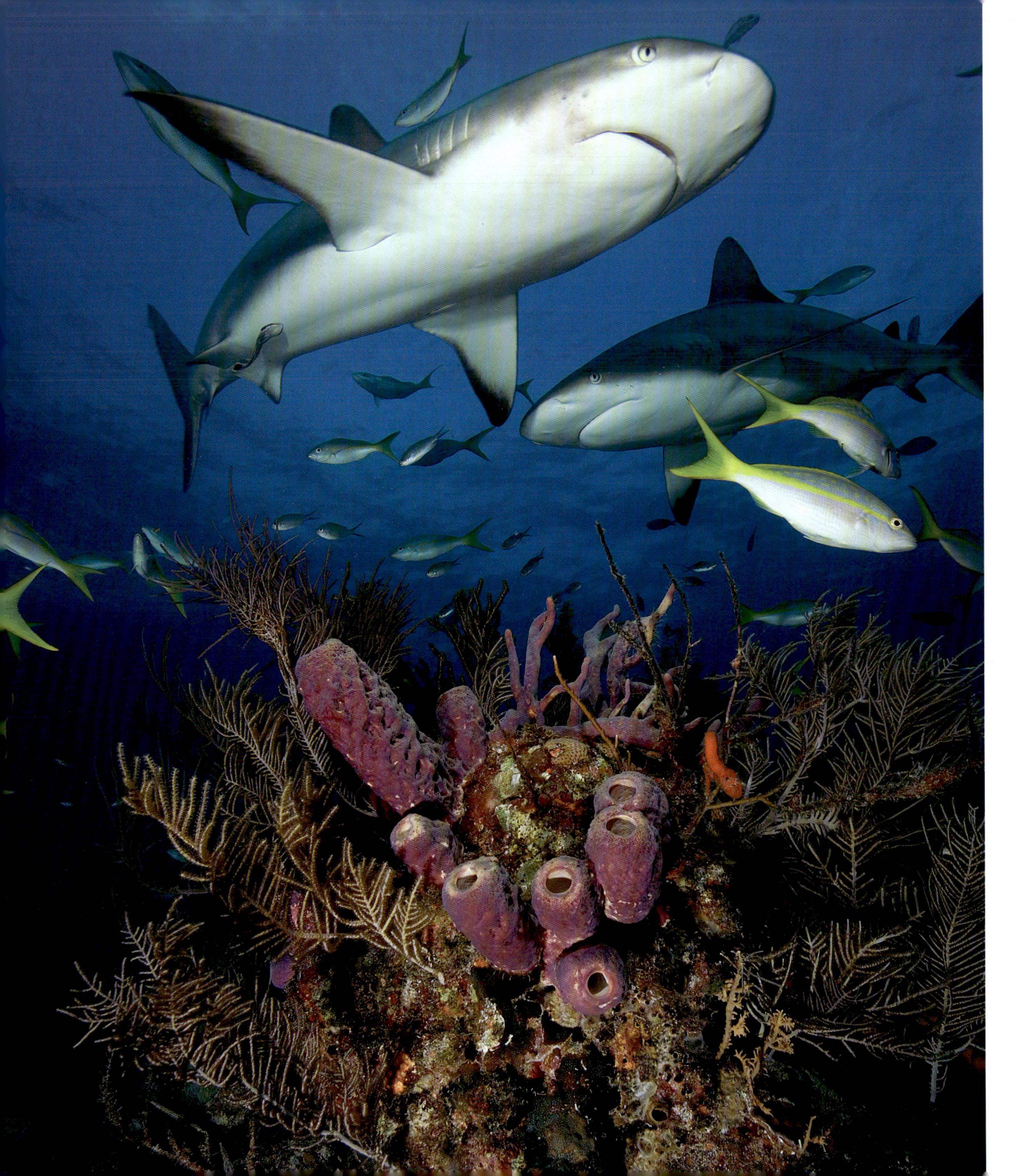

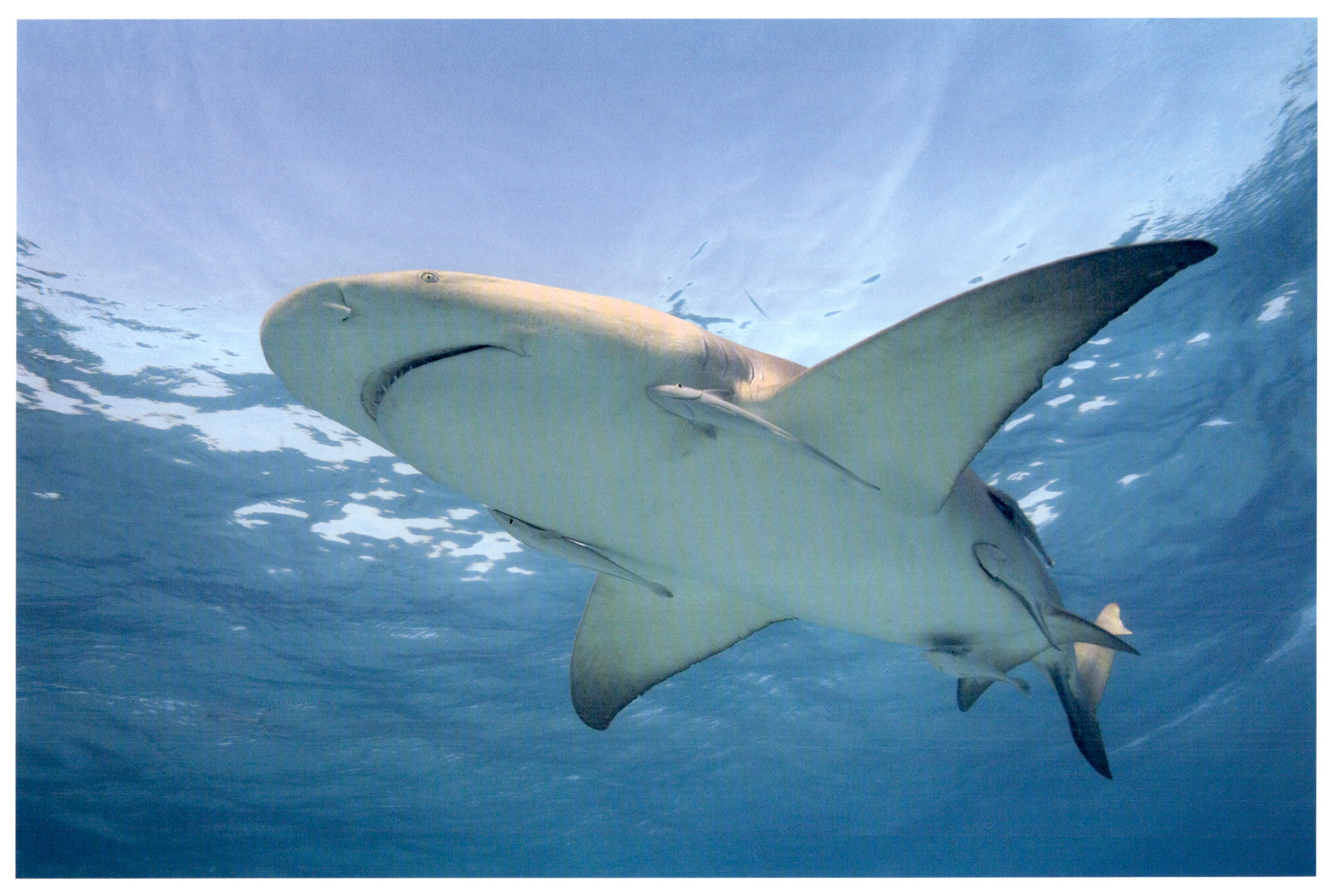

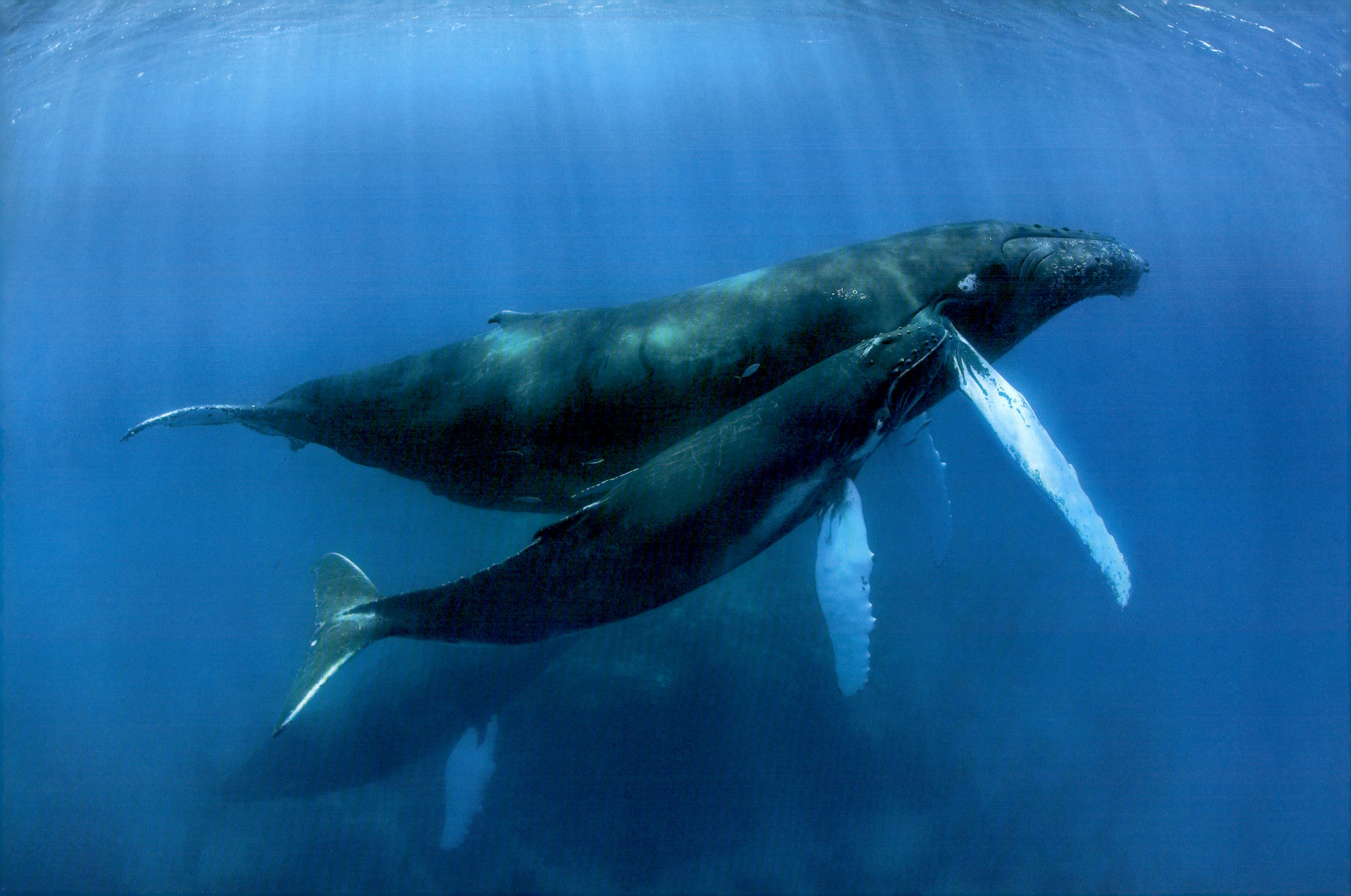

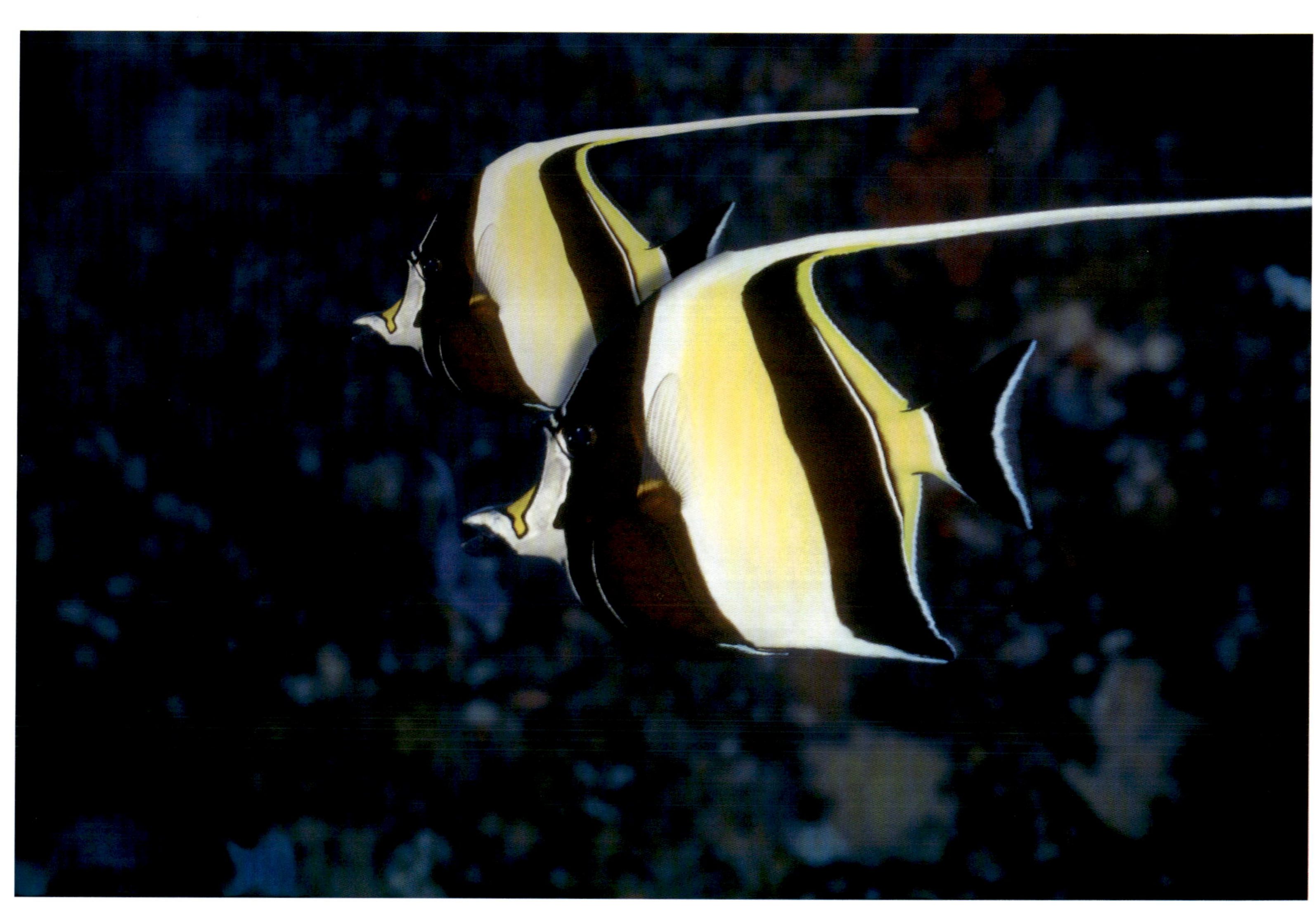

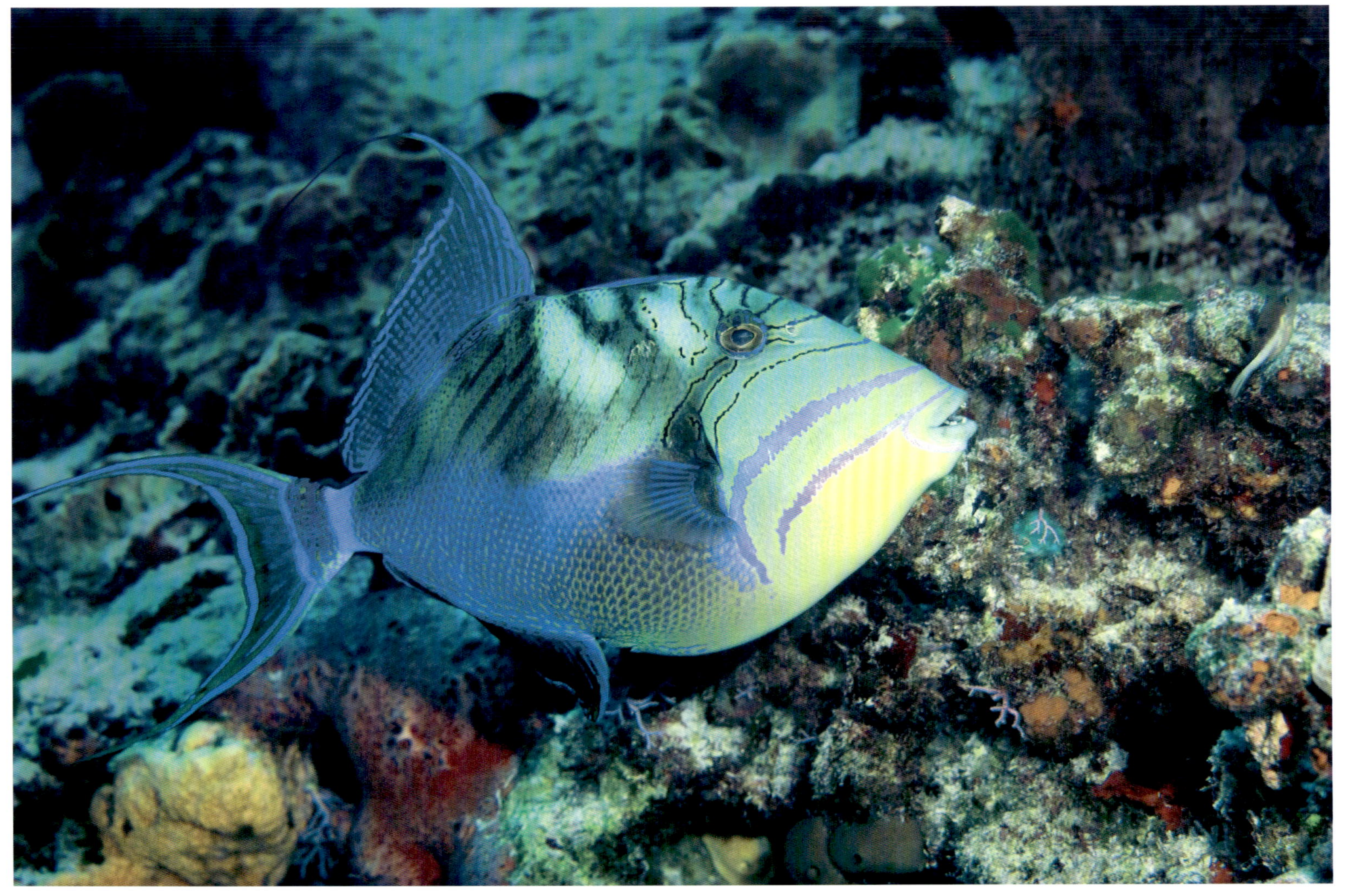

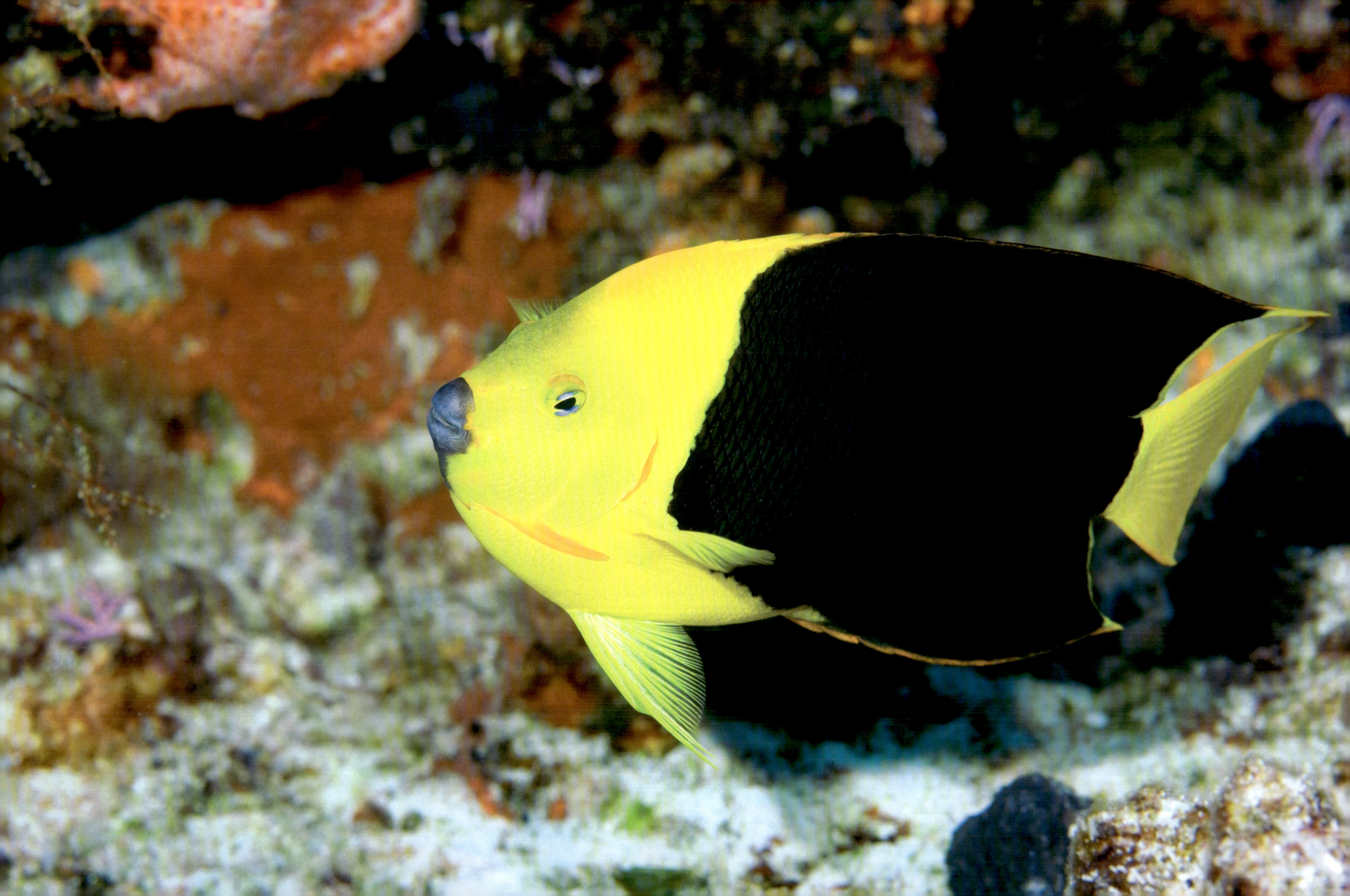

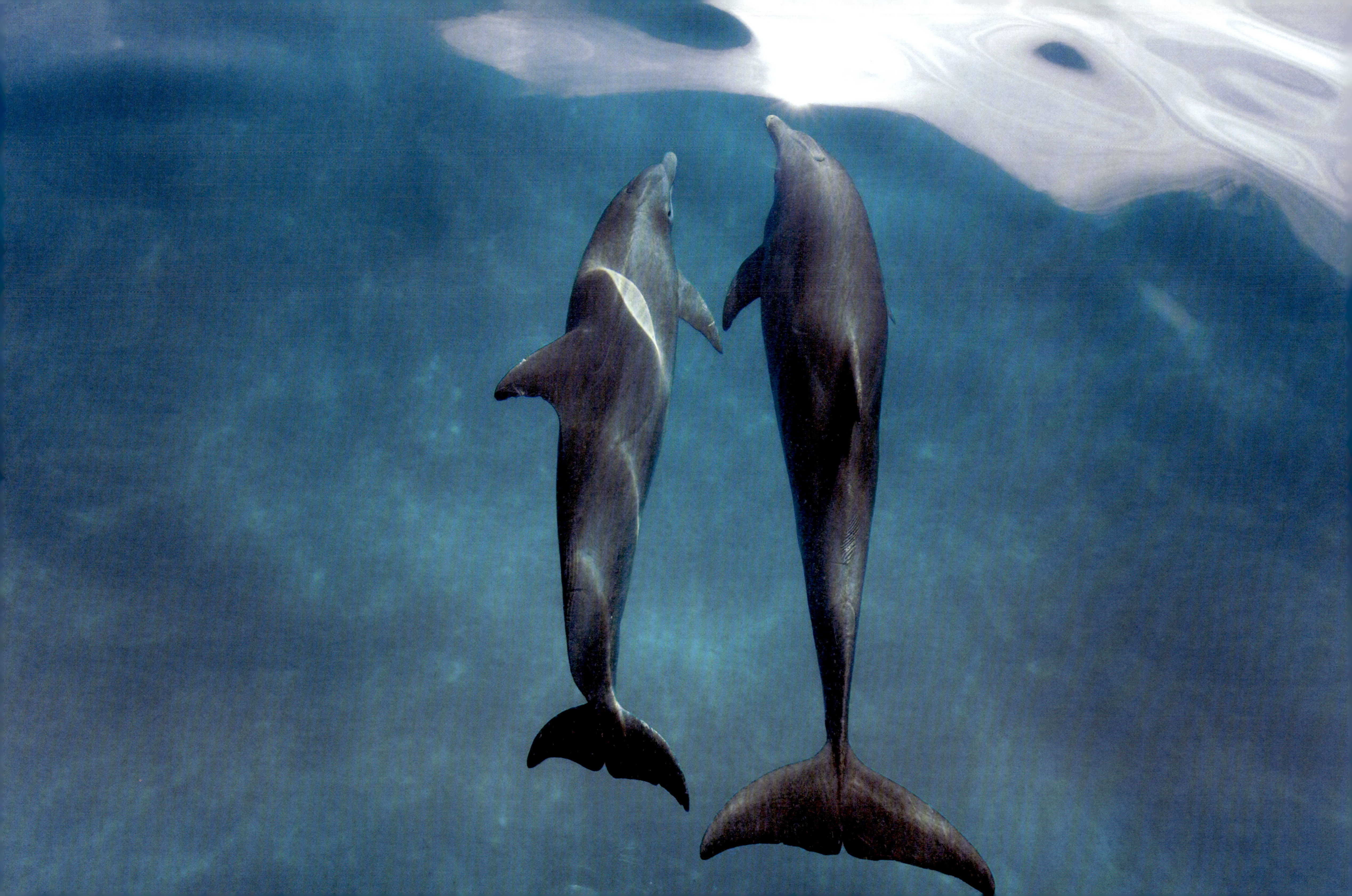

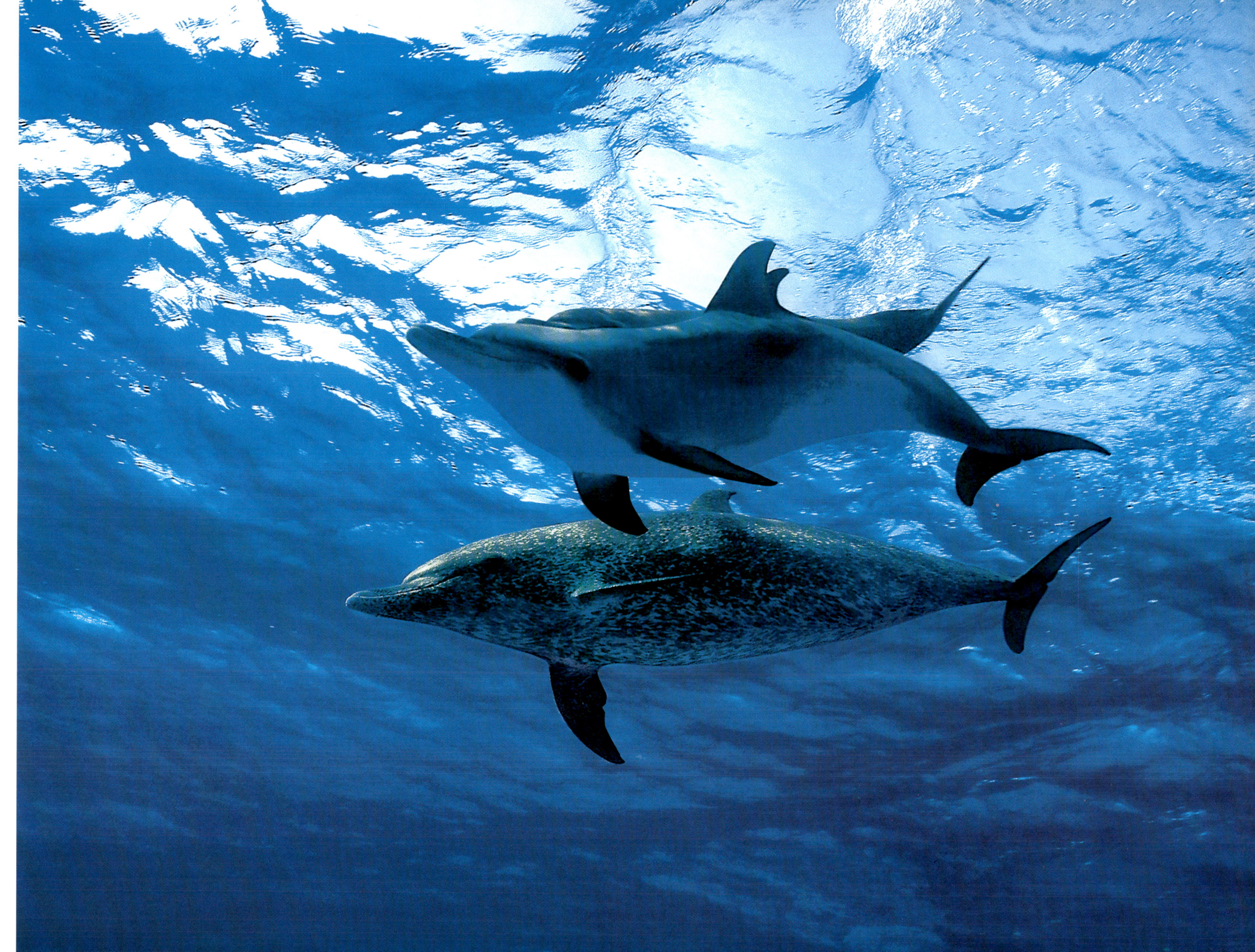

facing future seas
dolphin seas

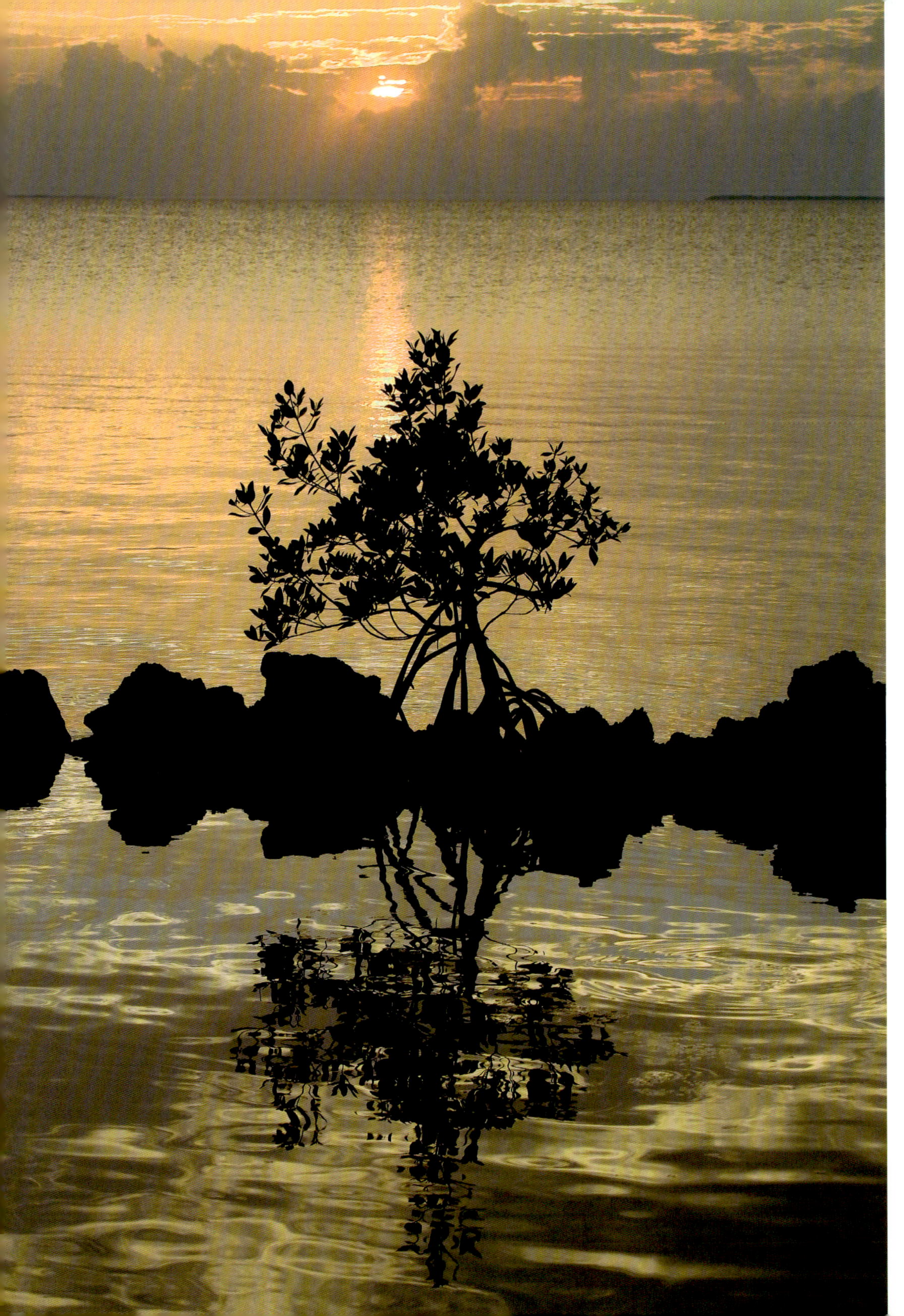

◀ mangrove sunset
▶ blue tang reef

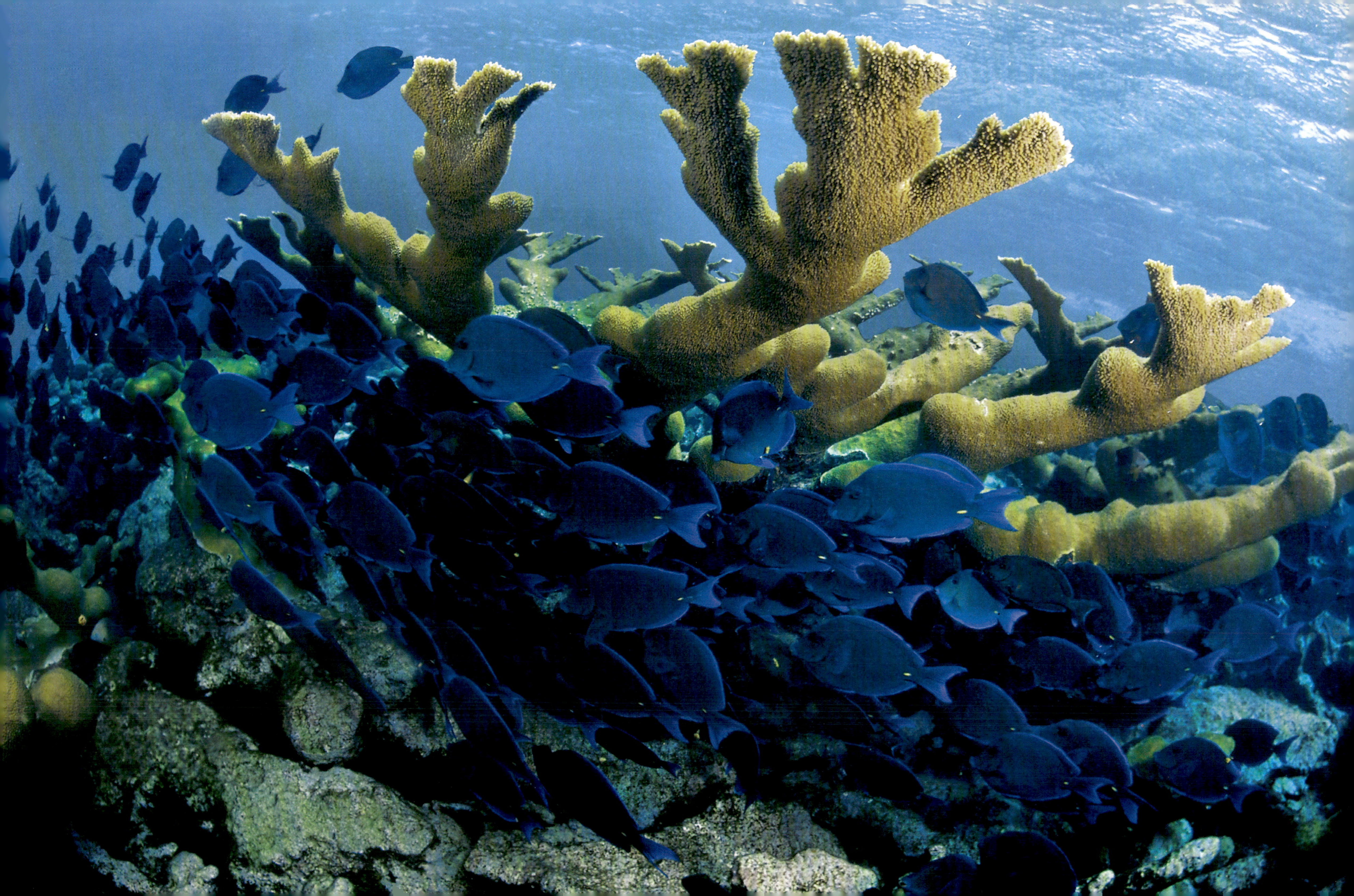

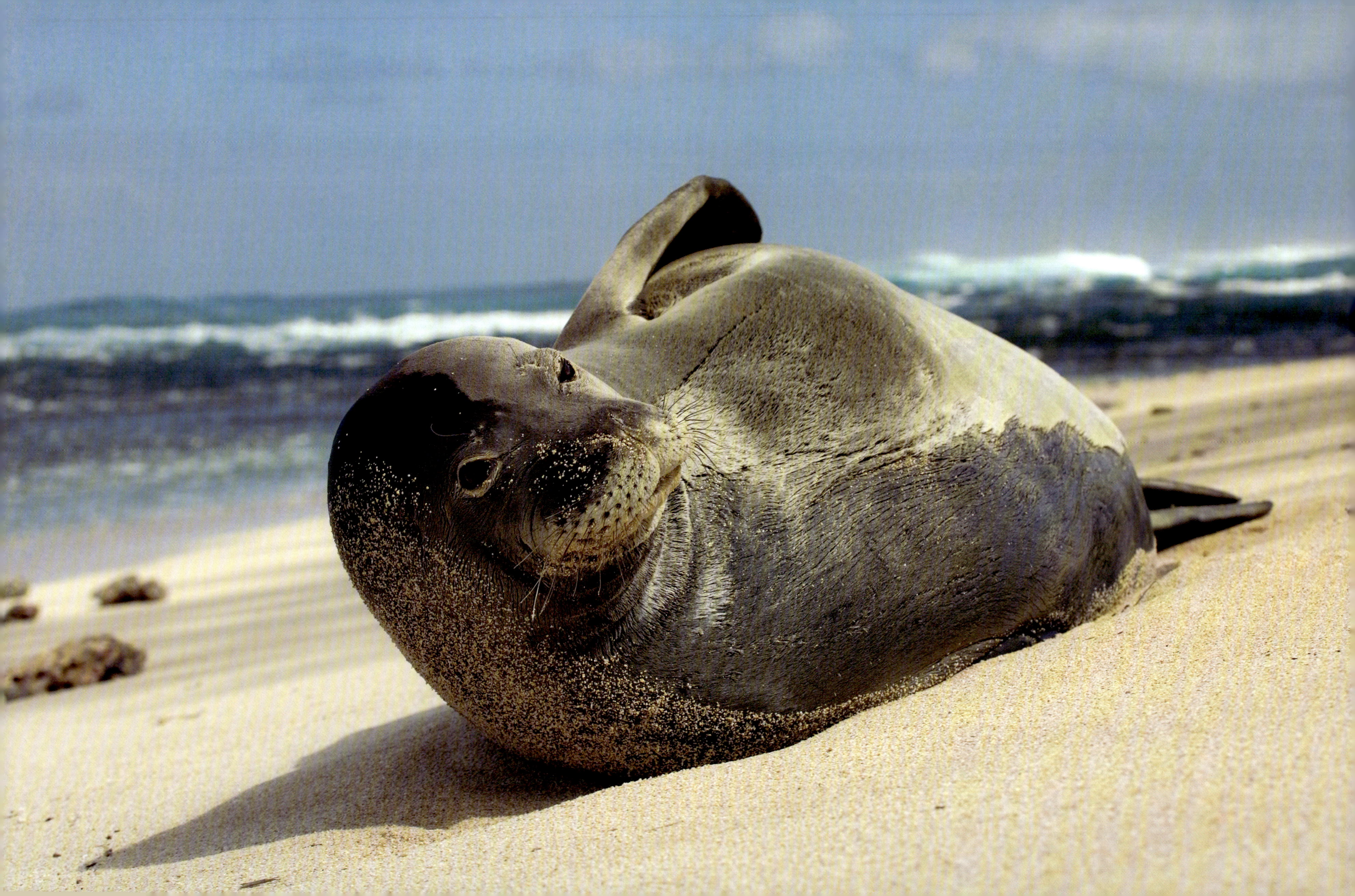

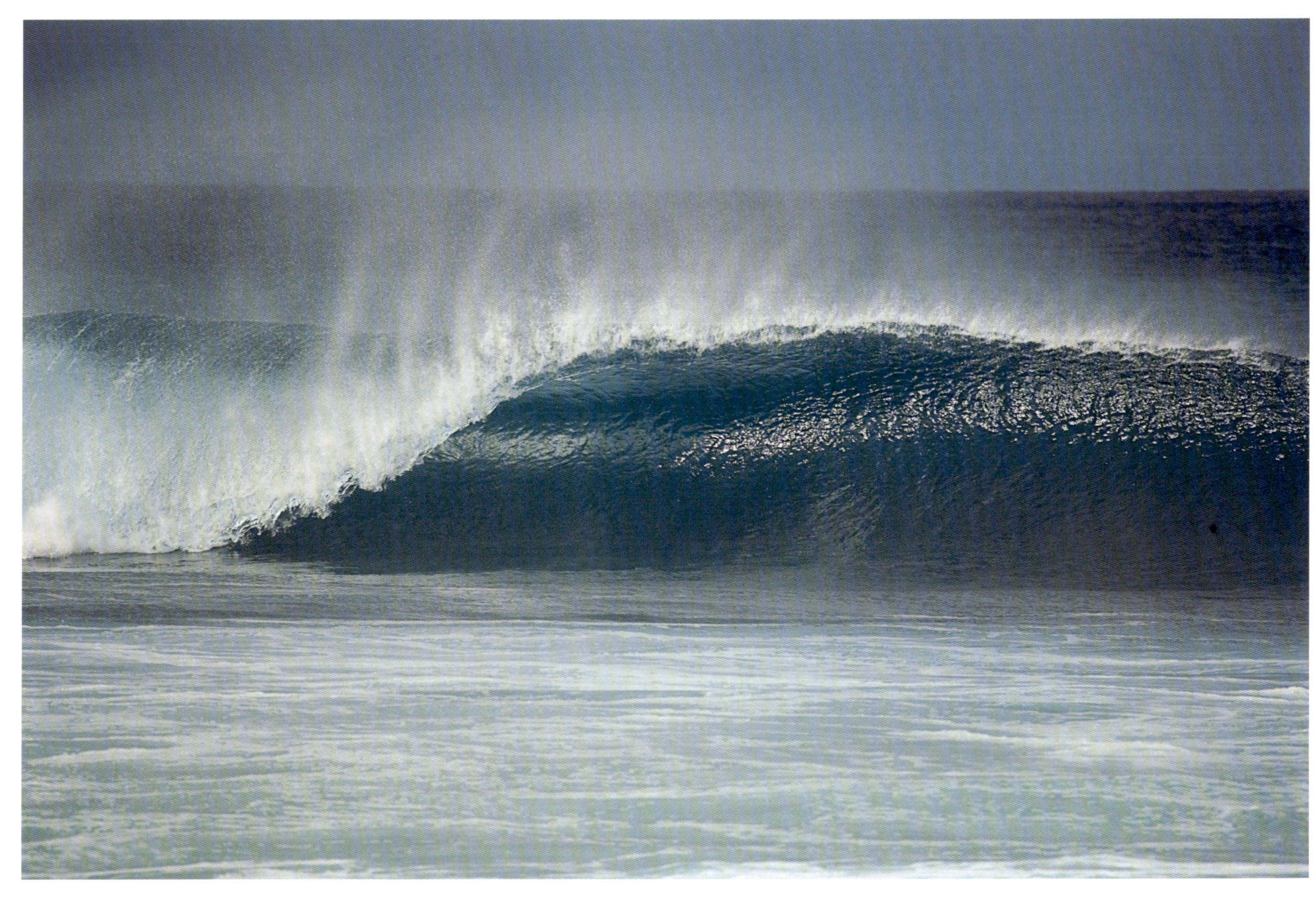

◀ hawaiian monk seal
▶ pipeline perfection

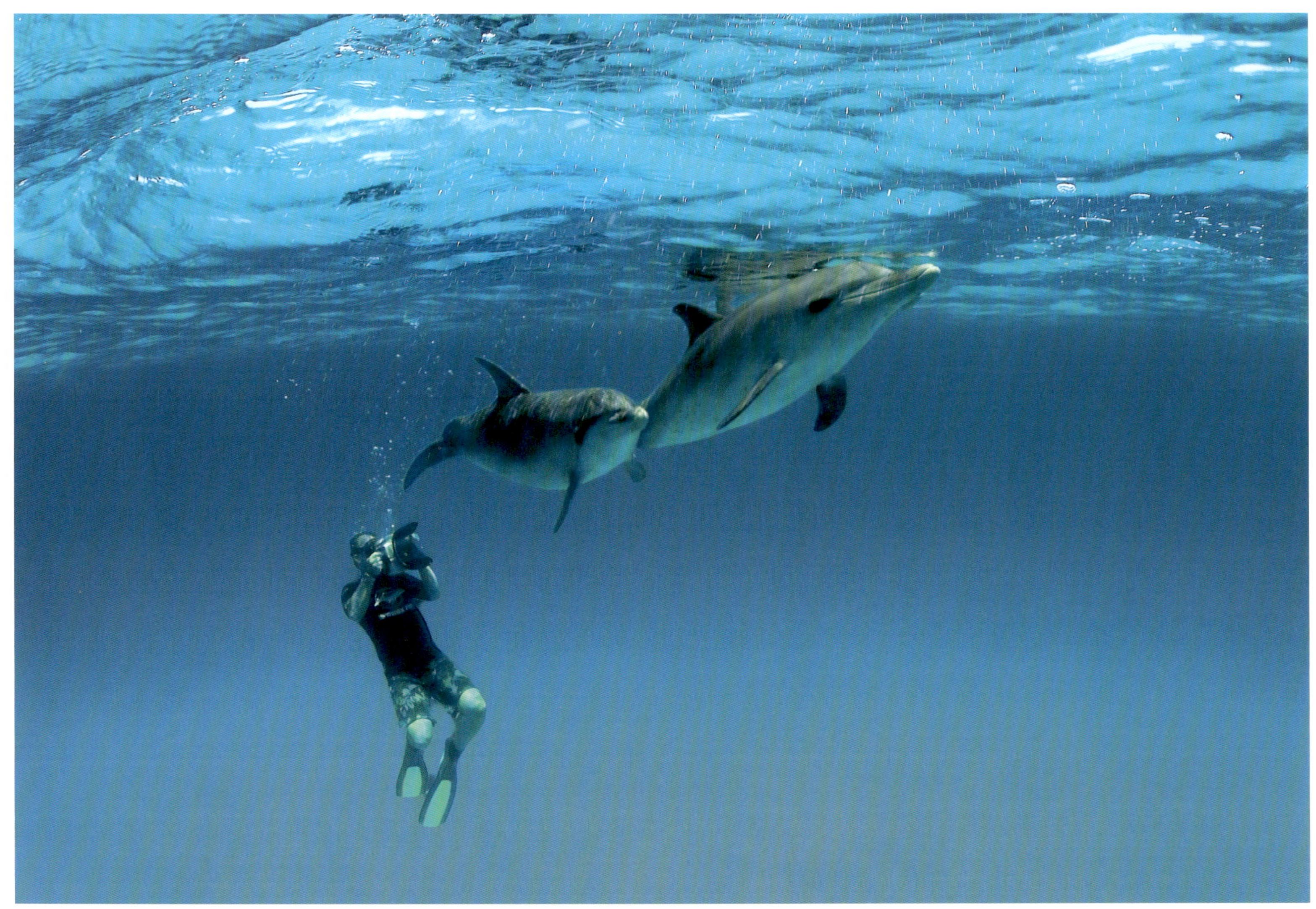

◀ wyland with spotted dolphin
▶ mother ocean

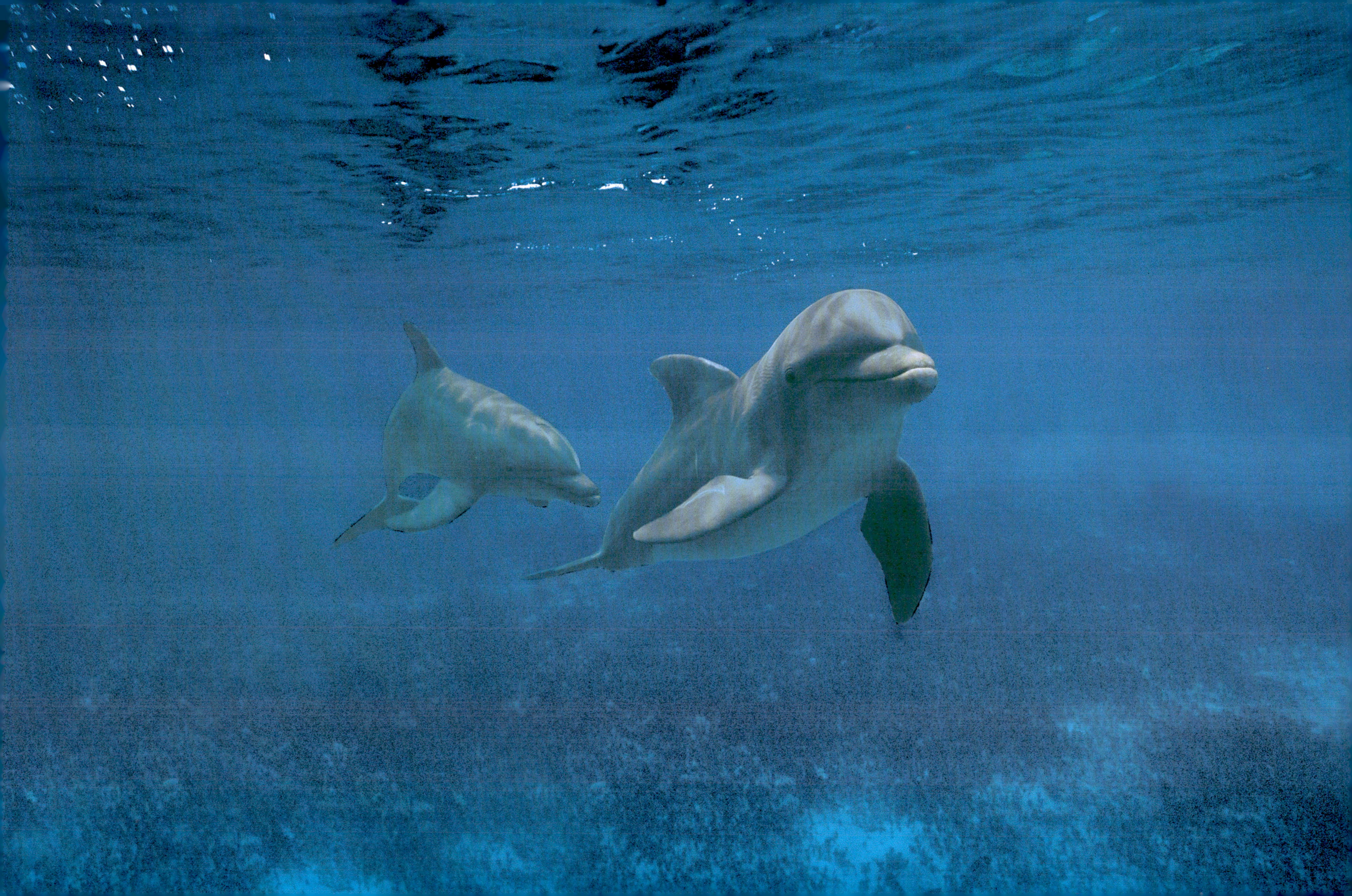

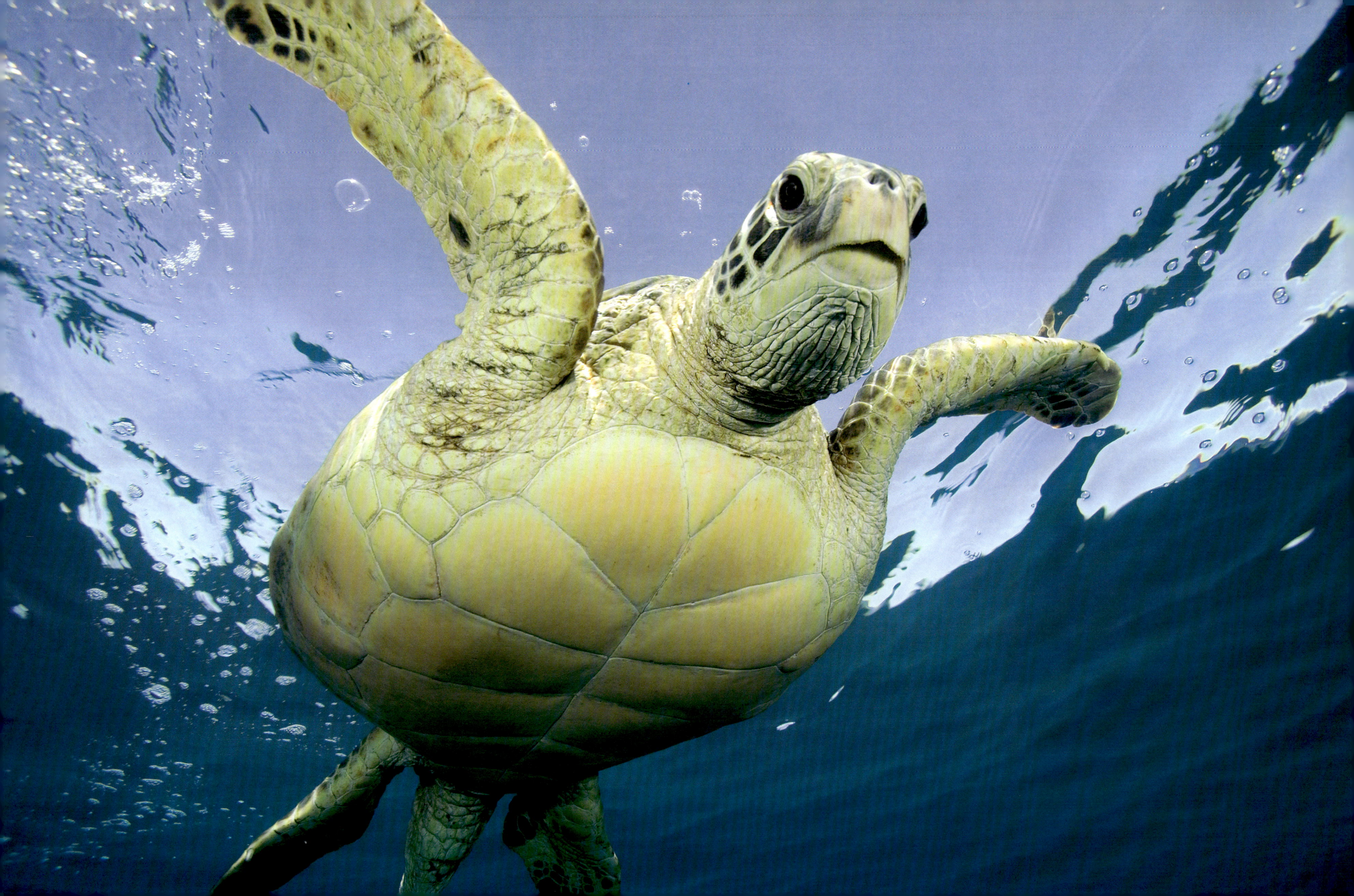

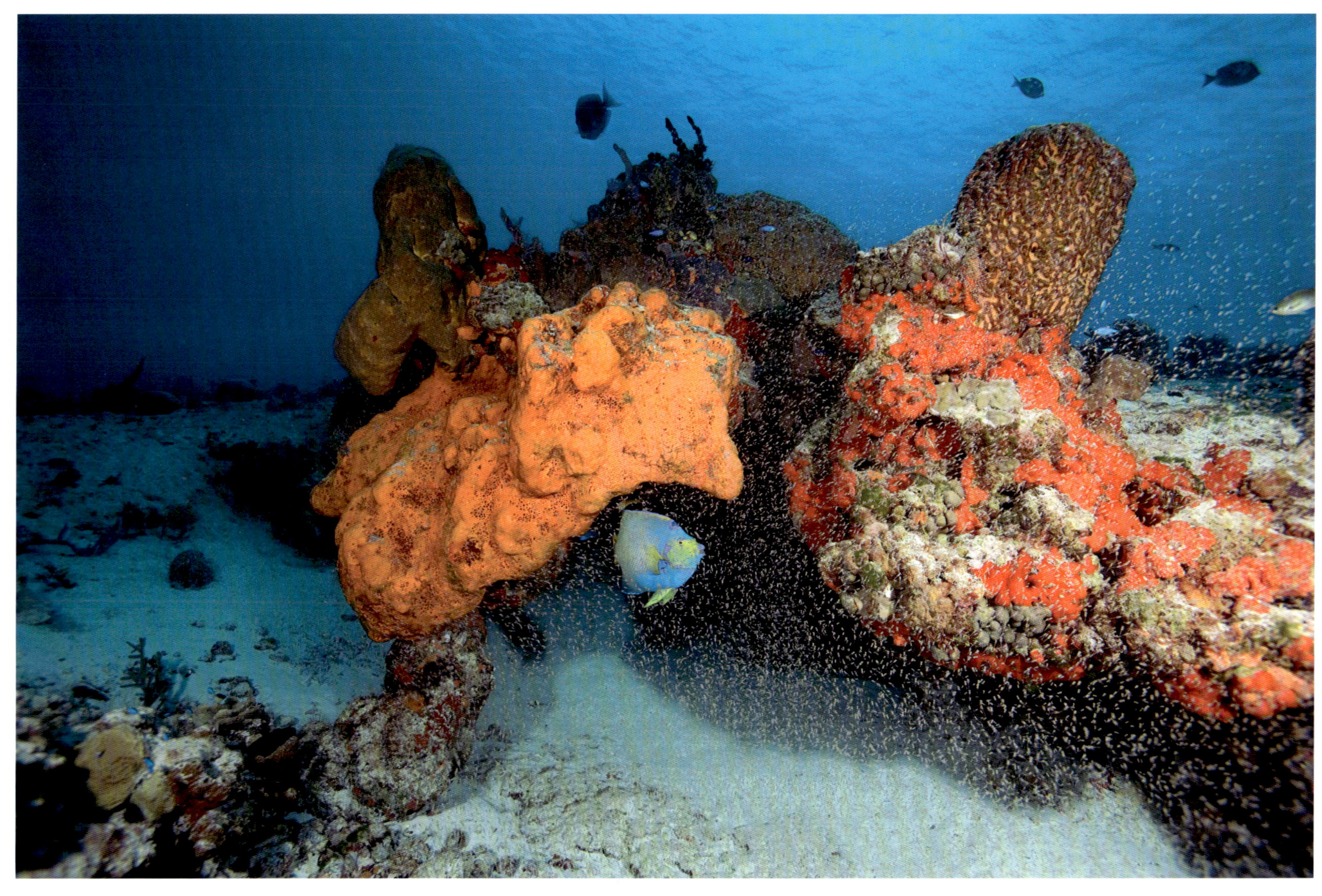

◀ friendly sea turtle
▶ queens coral reef home

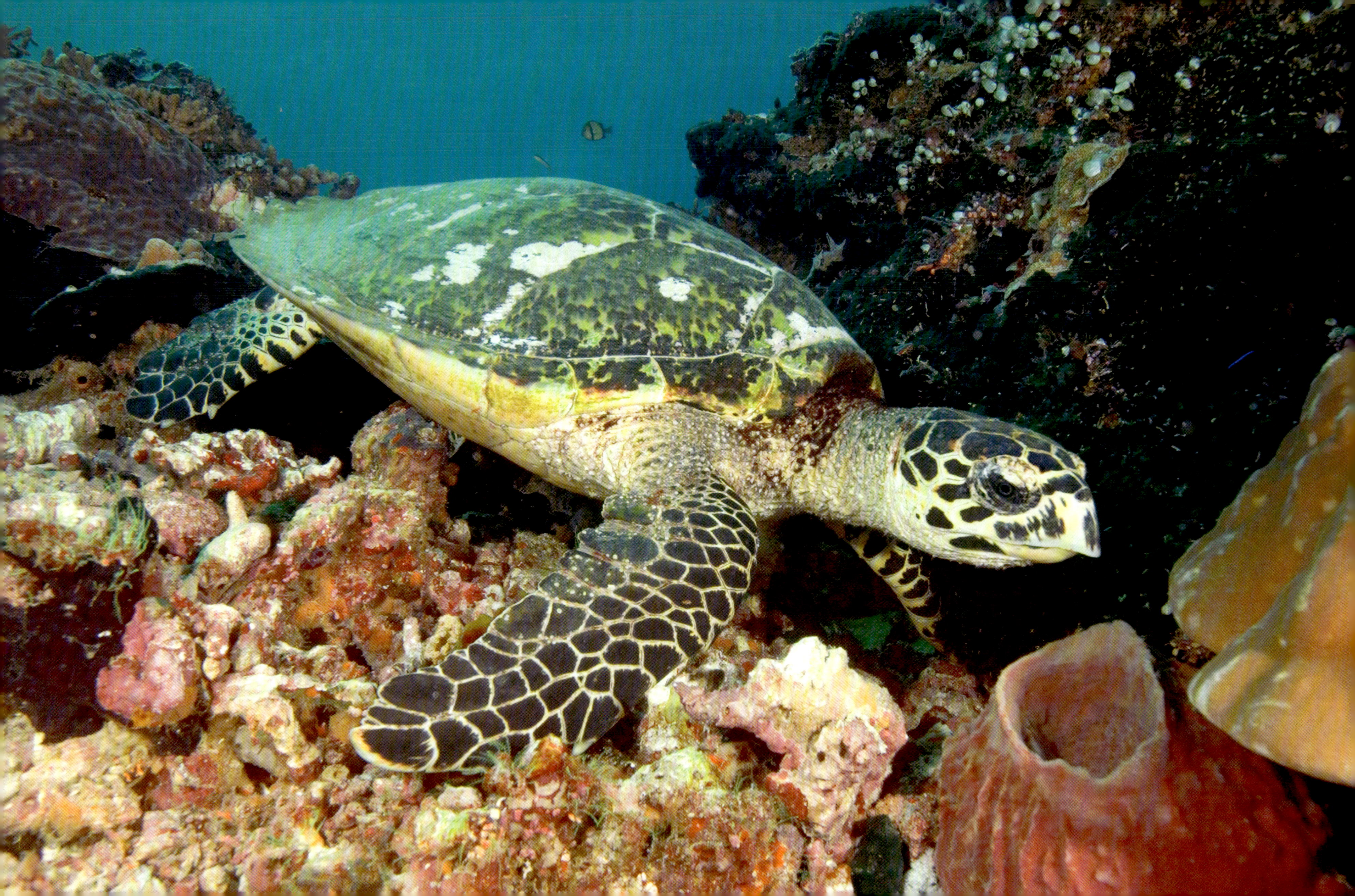

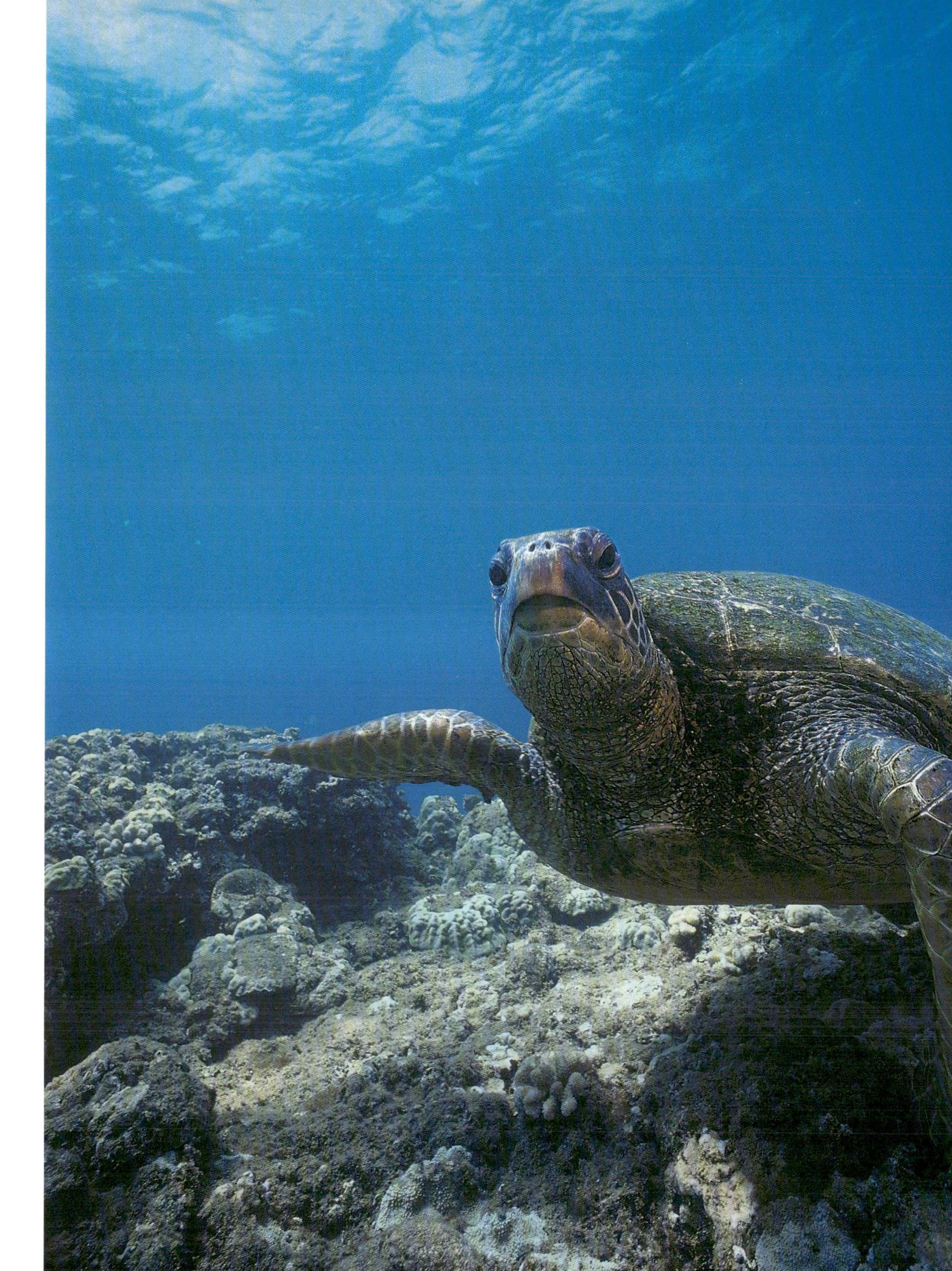

◀ hawksbill sea turtle reef II
▶ sea turtle encounter

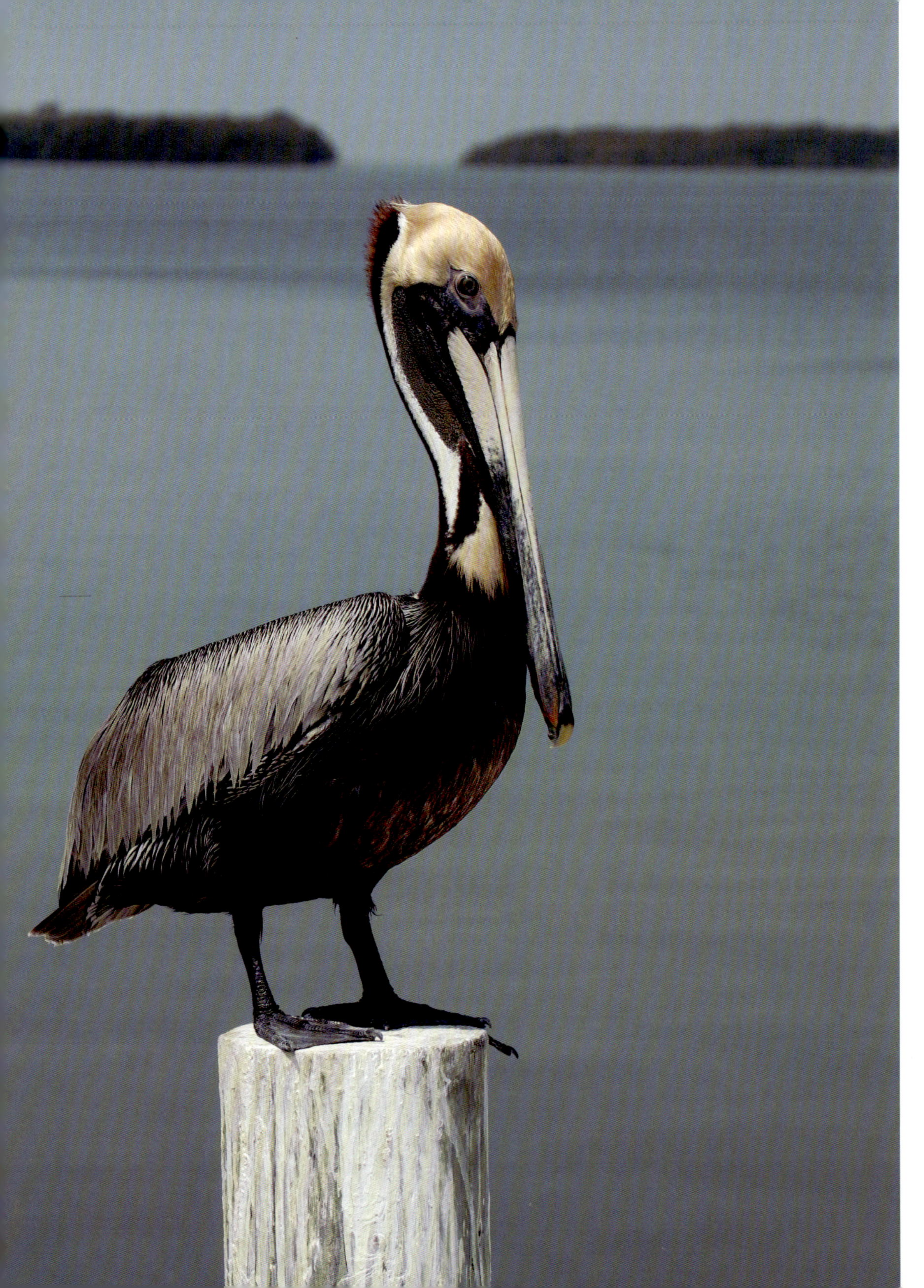

◀ pelican key
▶ three In the sea

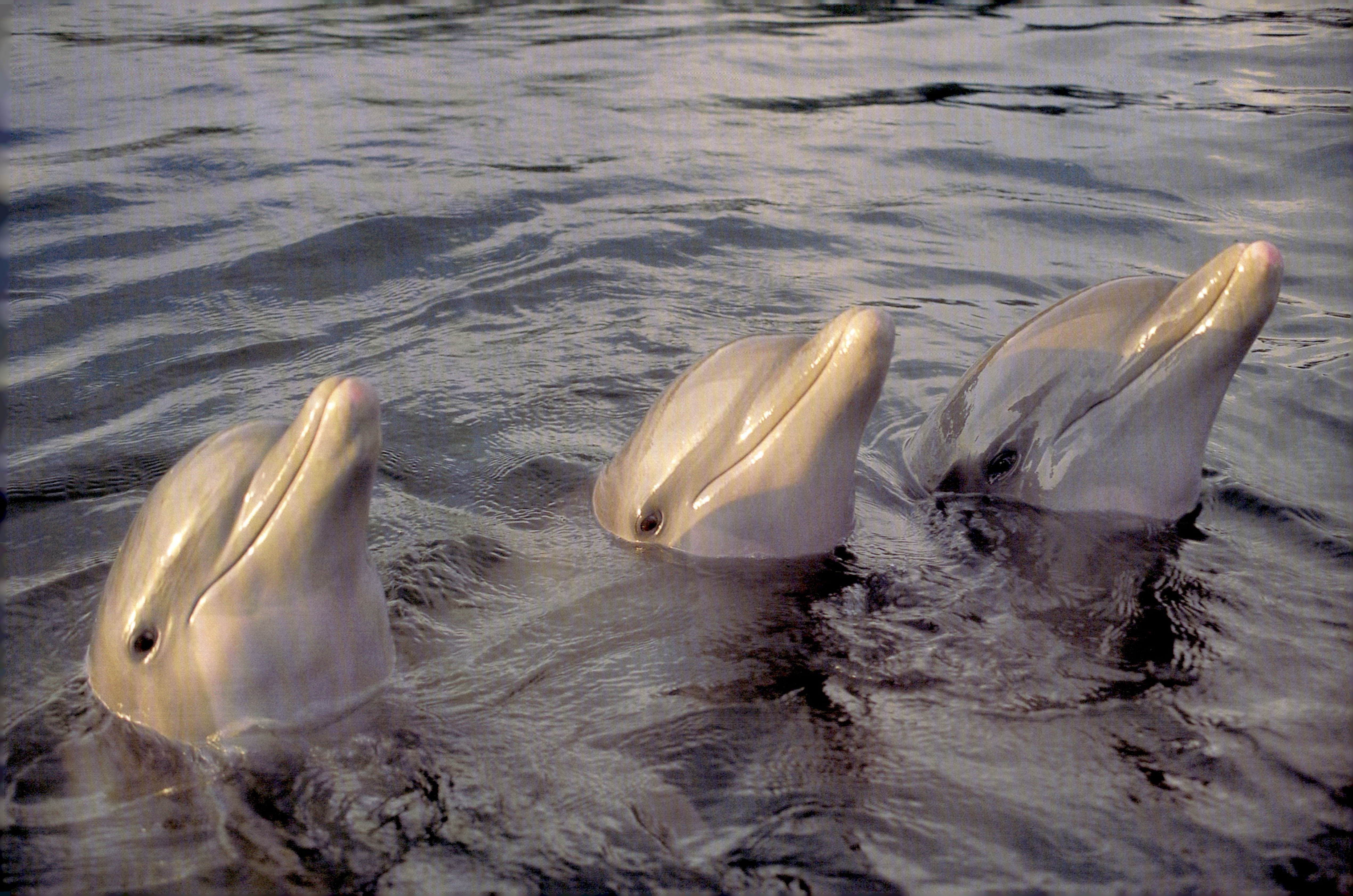

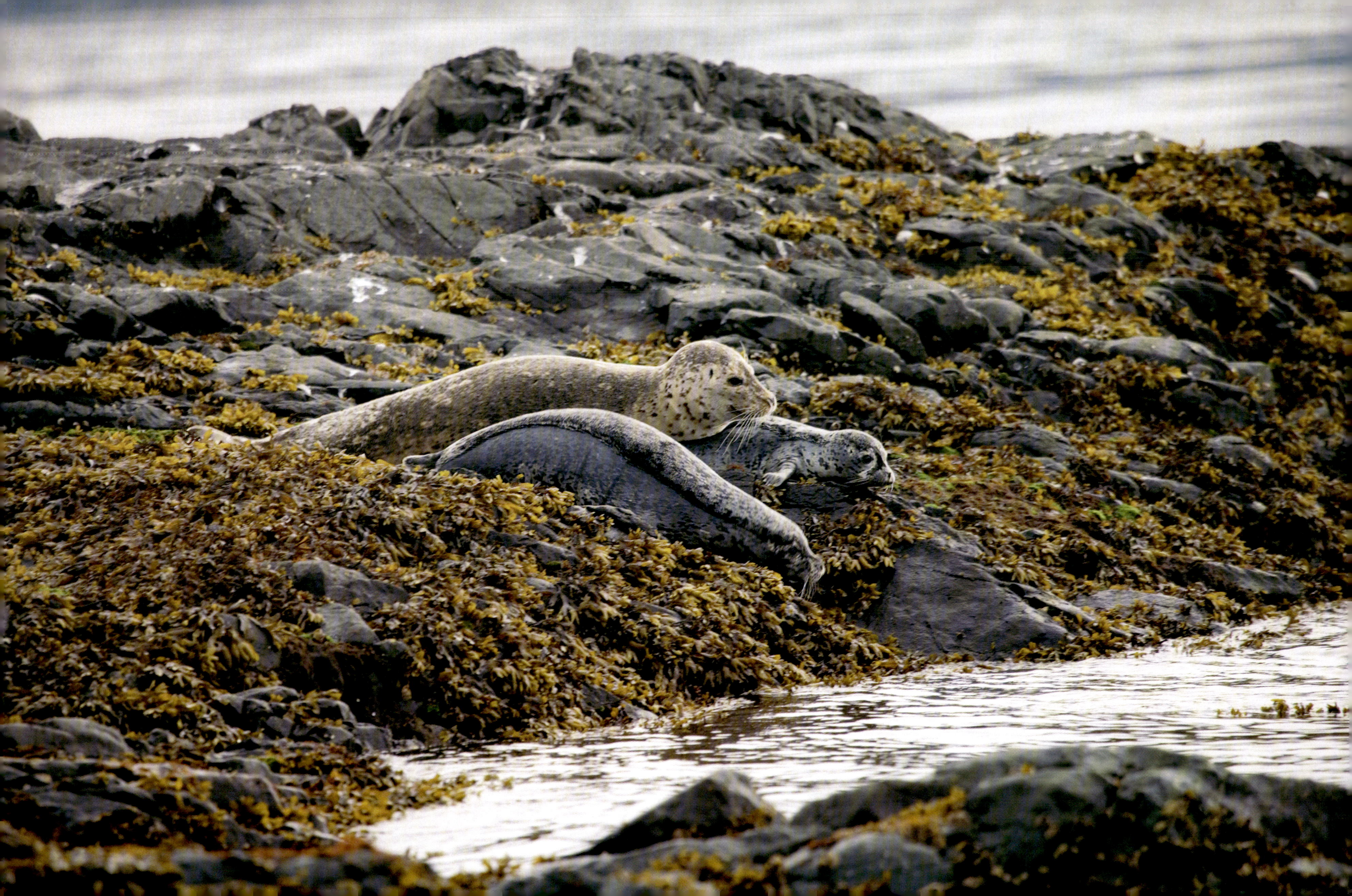

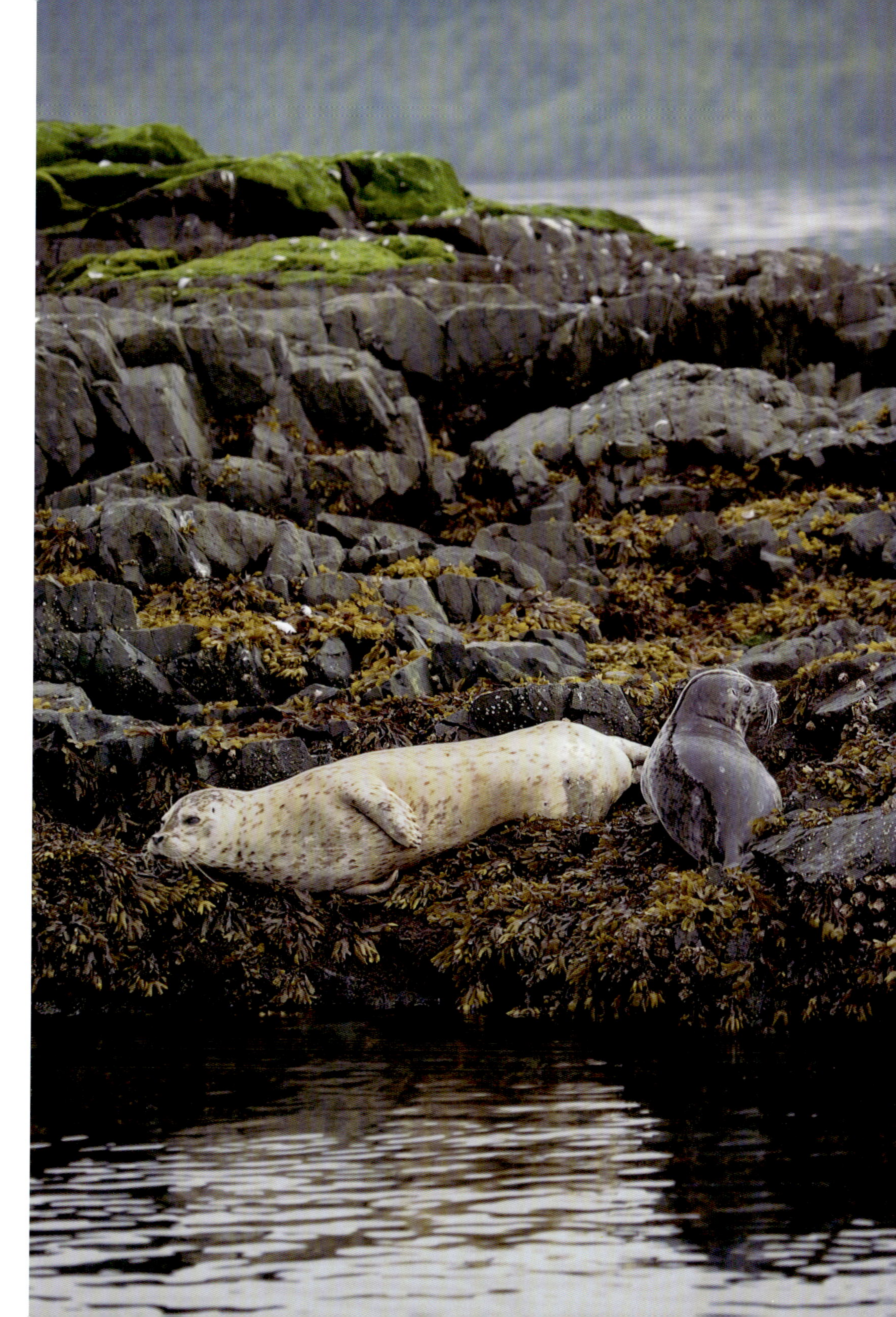

◀ two harbor seal pups
▶ harbor seal newborn

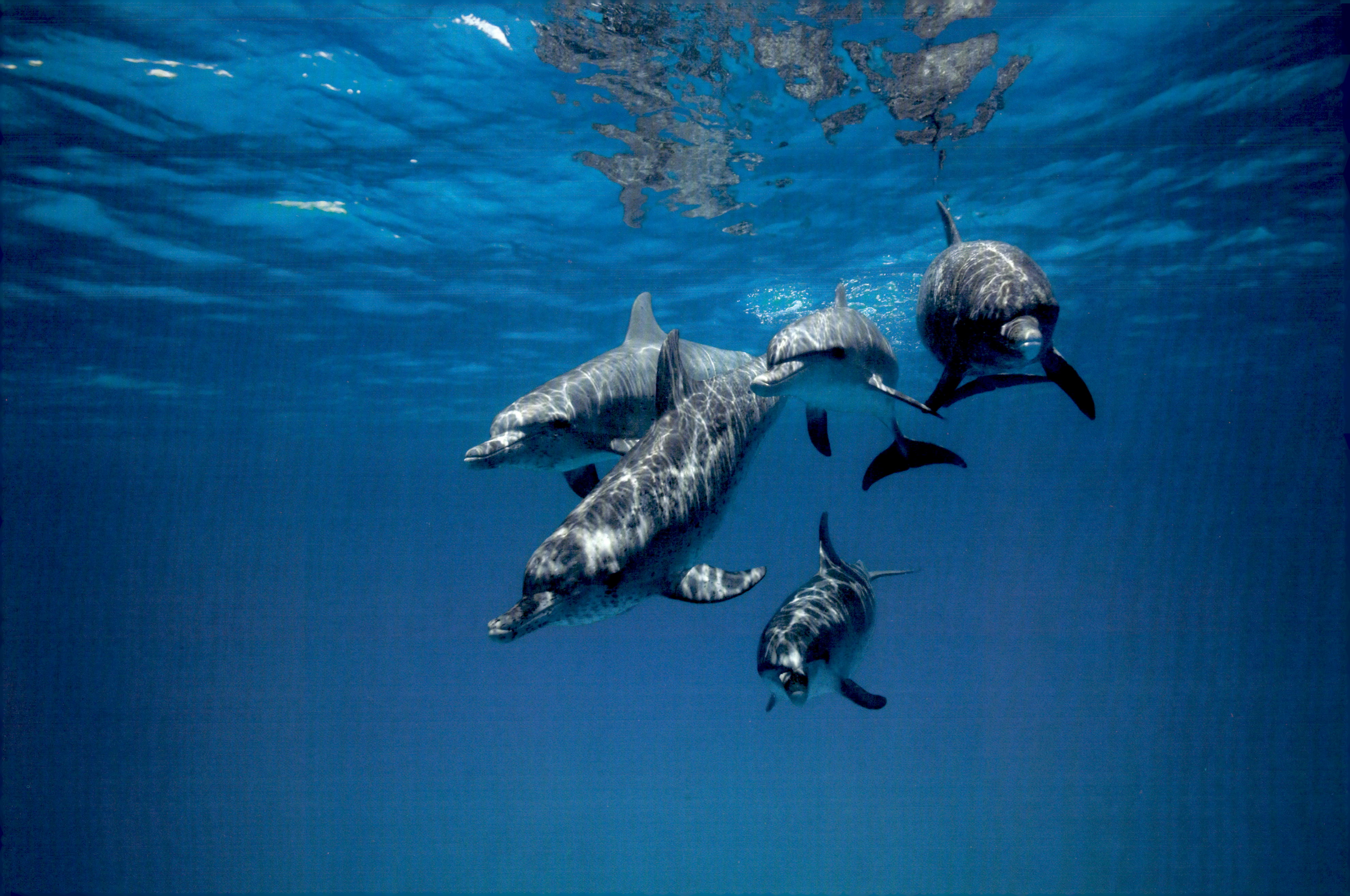

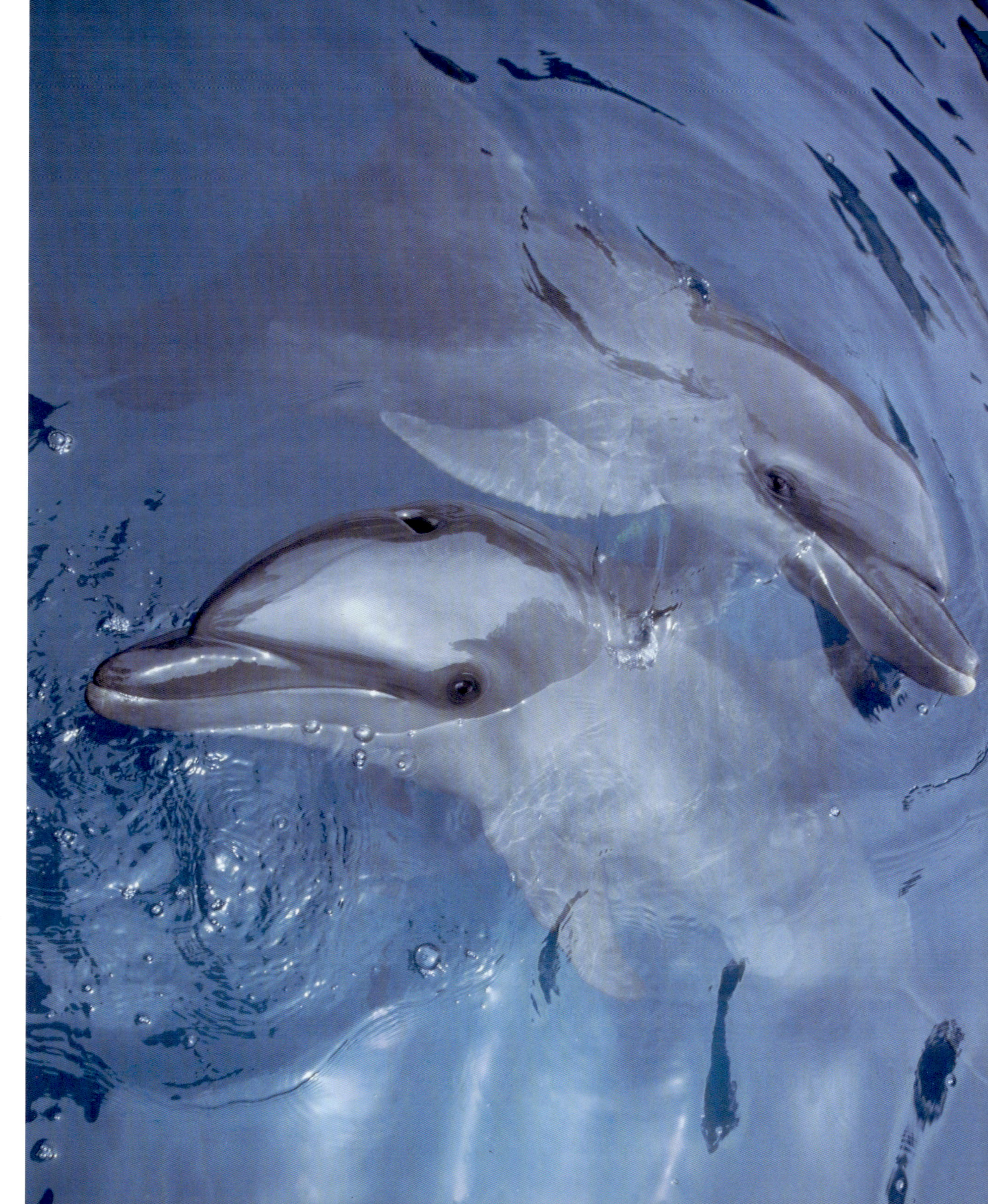

◀ spotted dolphin visit
▶ ocean of love

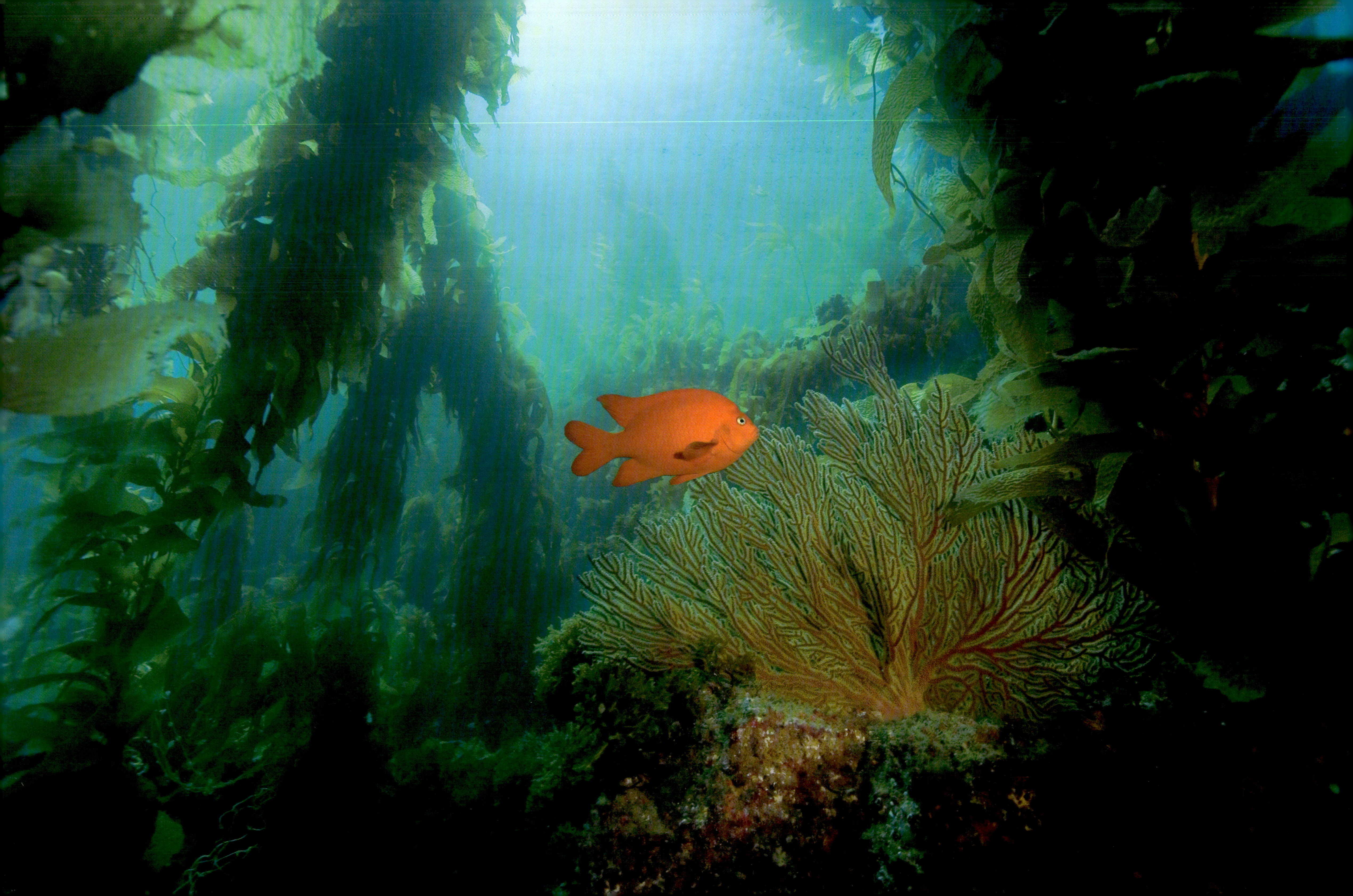

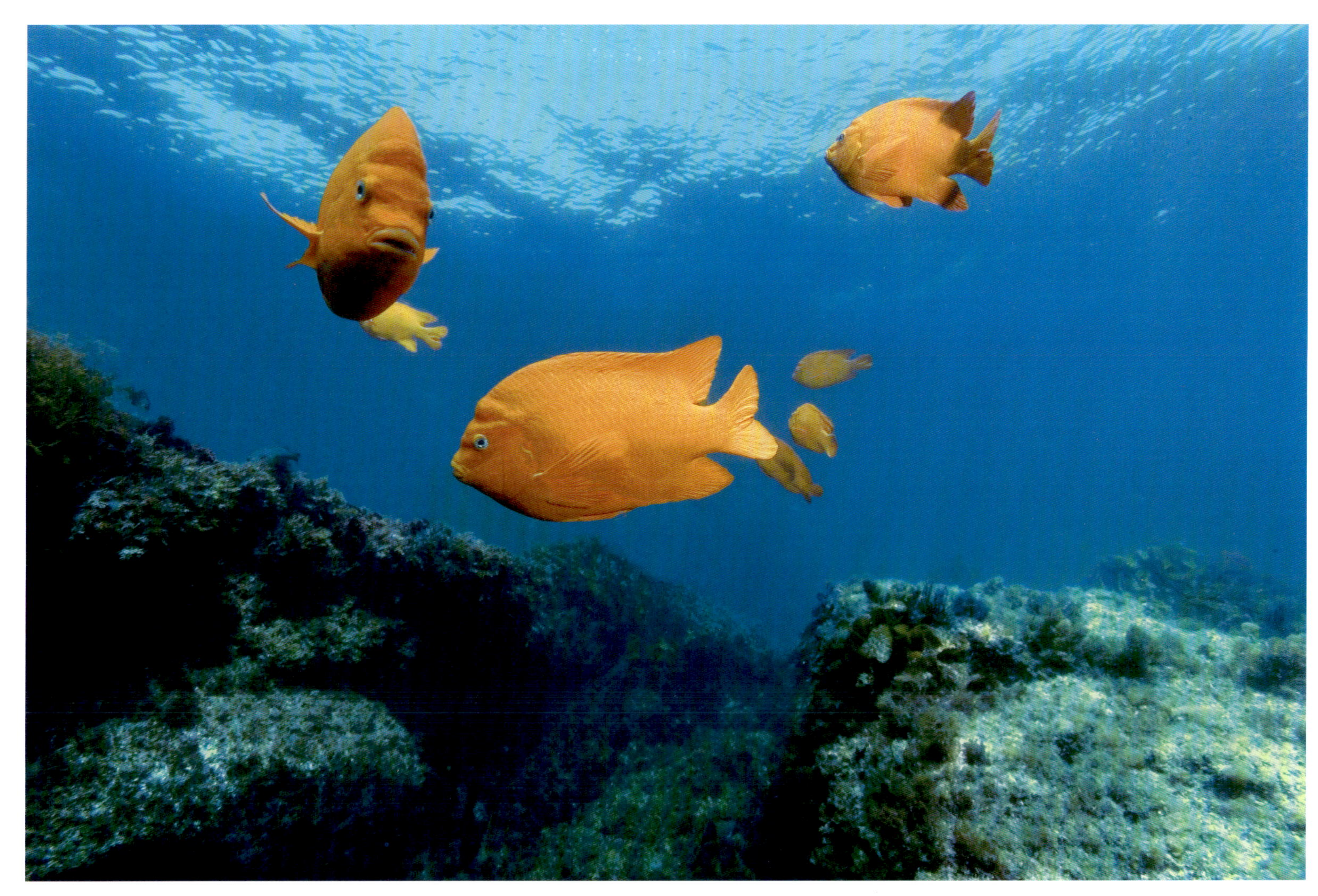

◄ healthy kelp forest
► garibaldi school

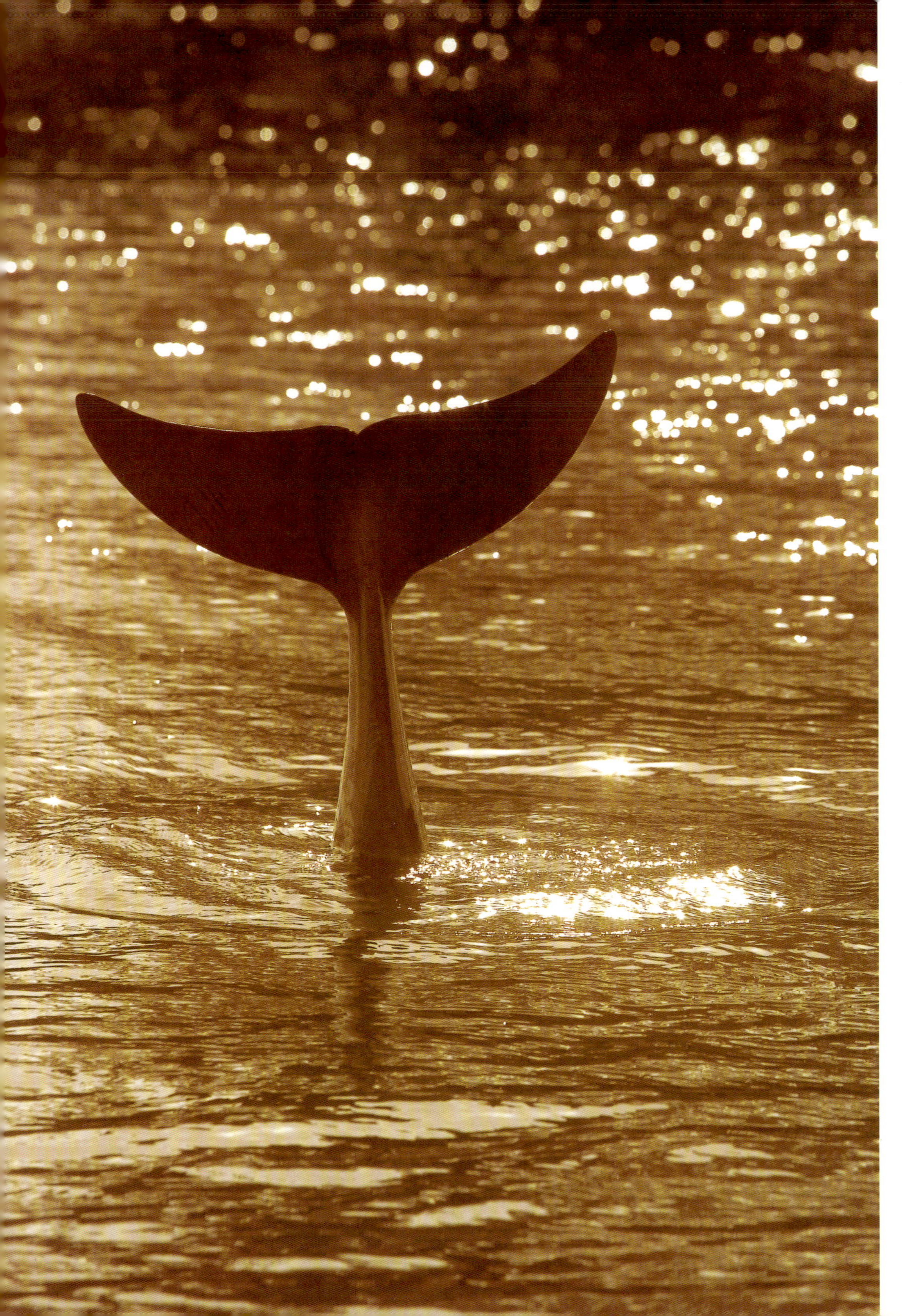

◄ dolphin tails
► the north shore surf

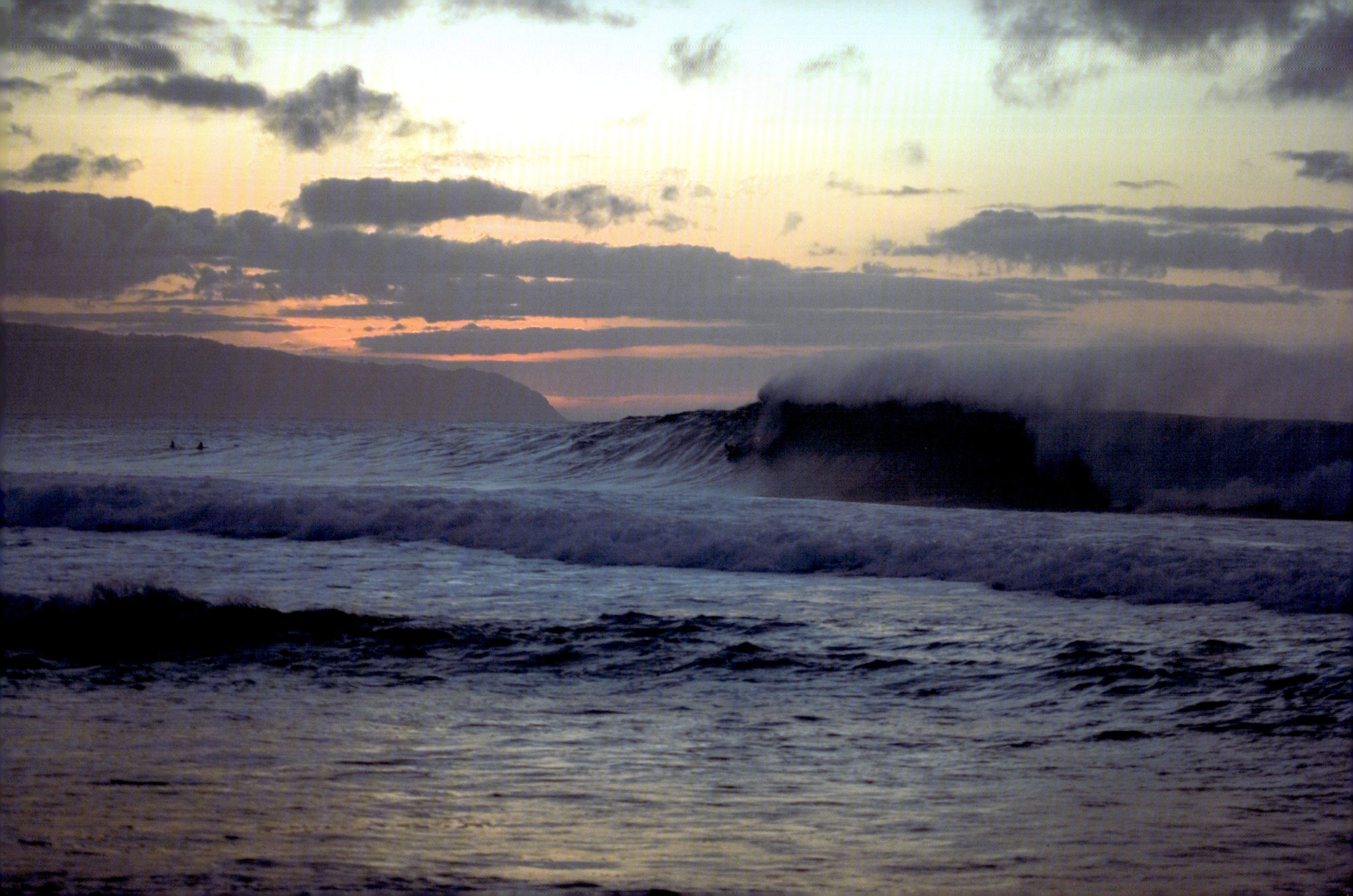

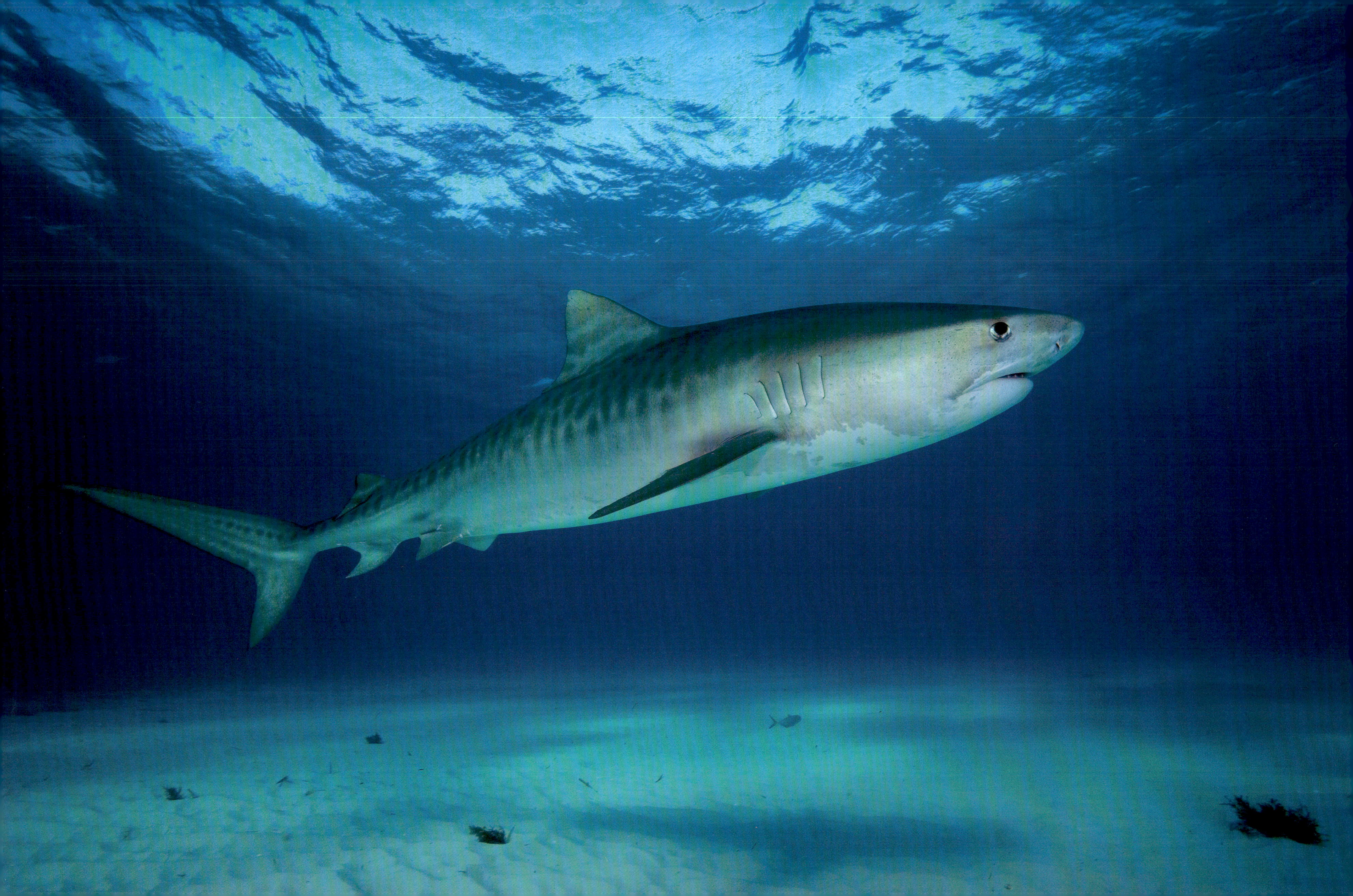

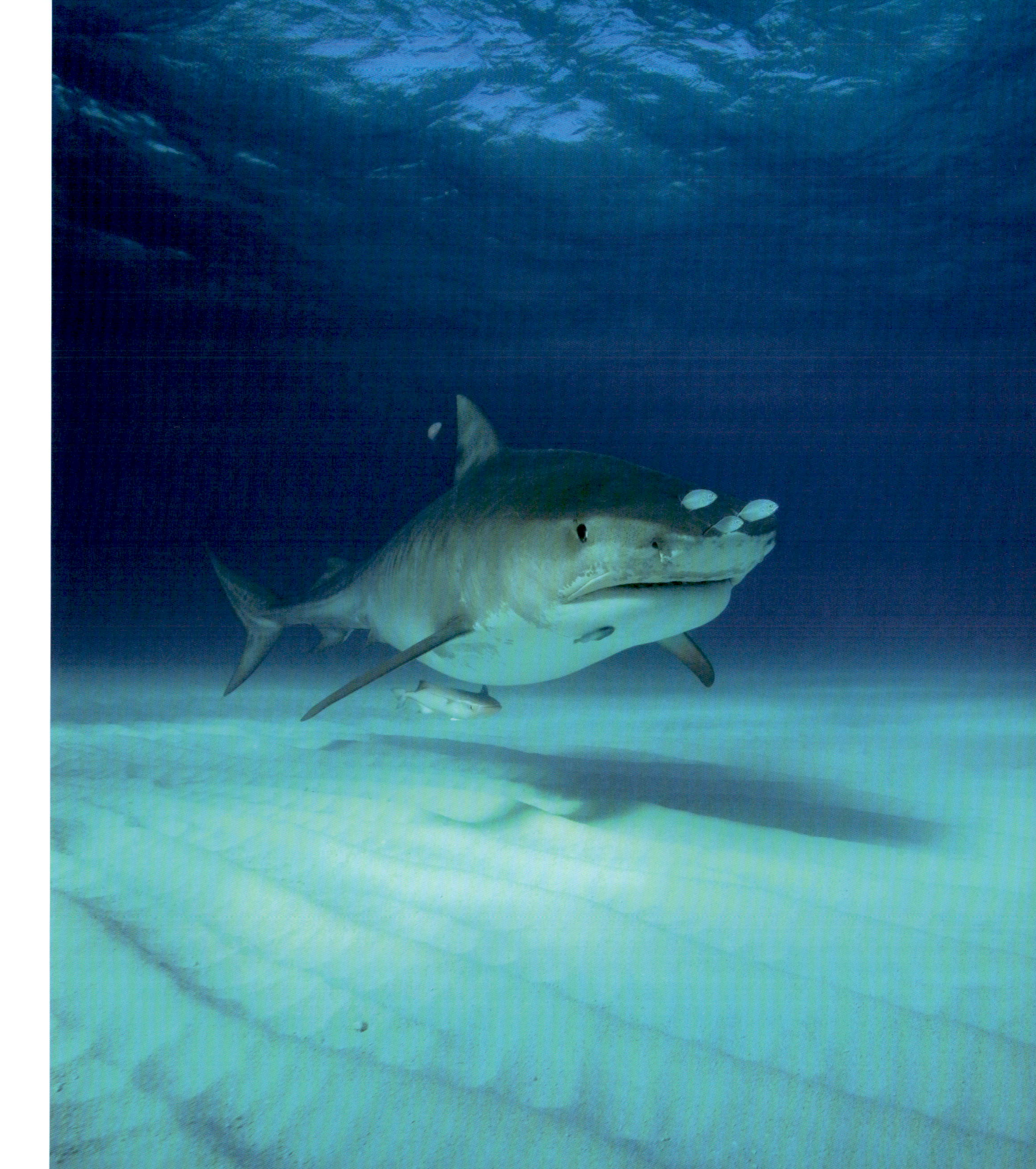

◀ tiger shark sea
▶ tiger beach

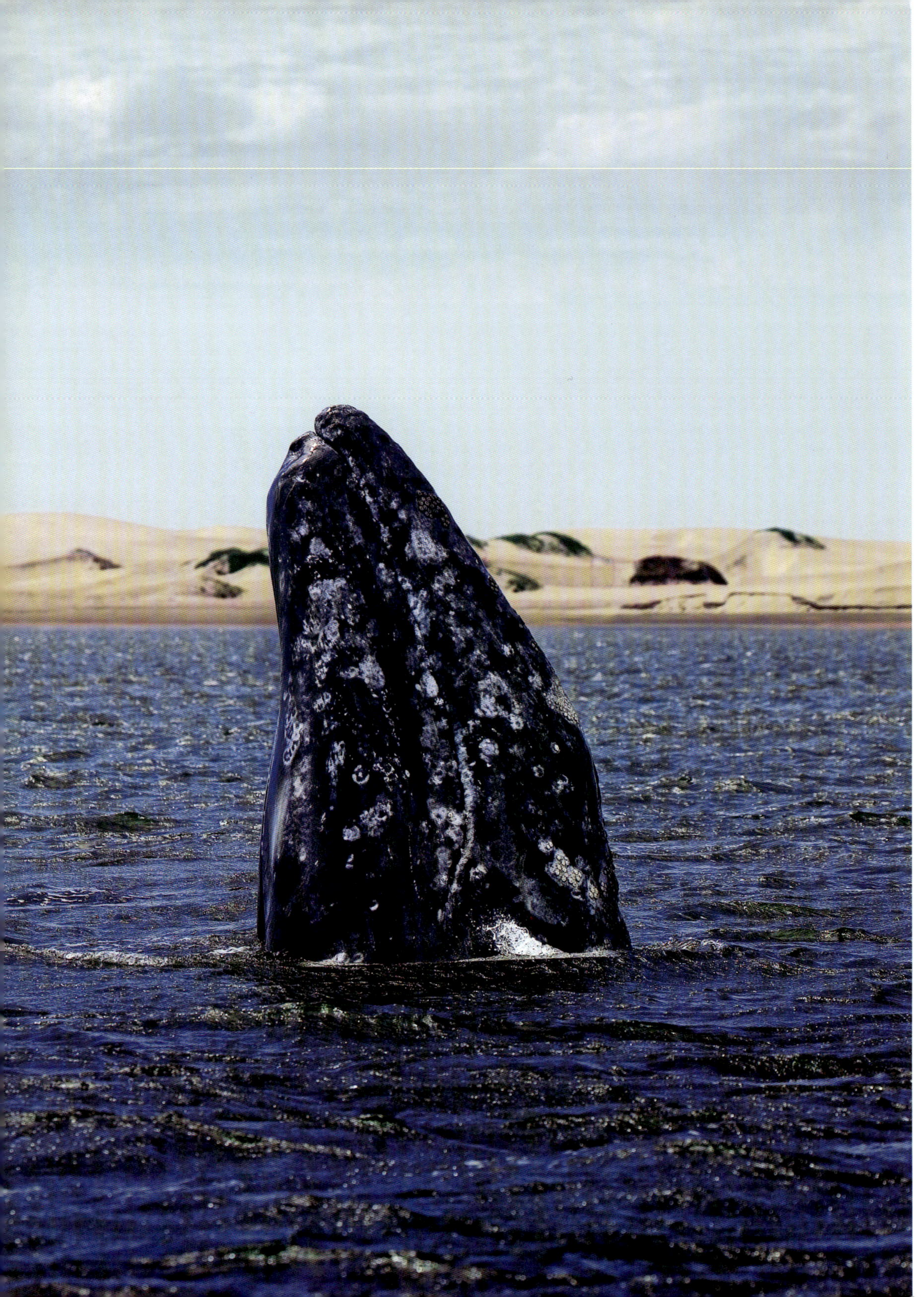

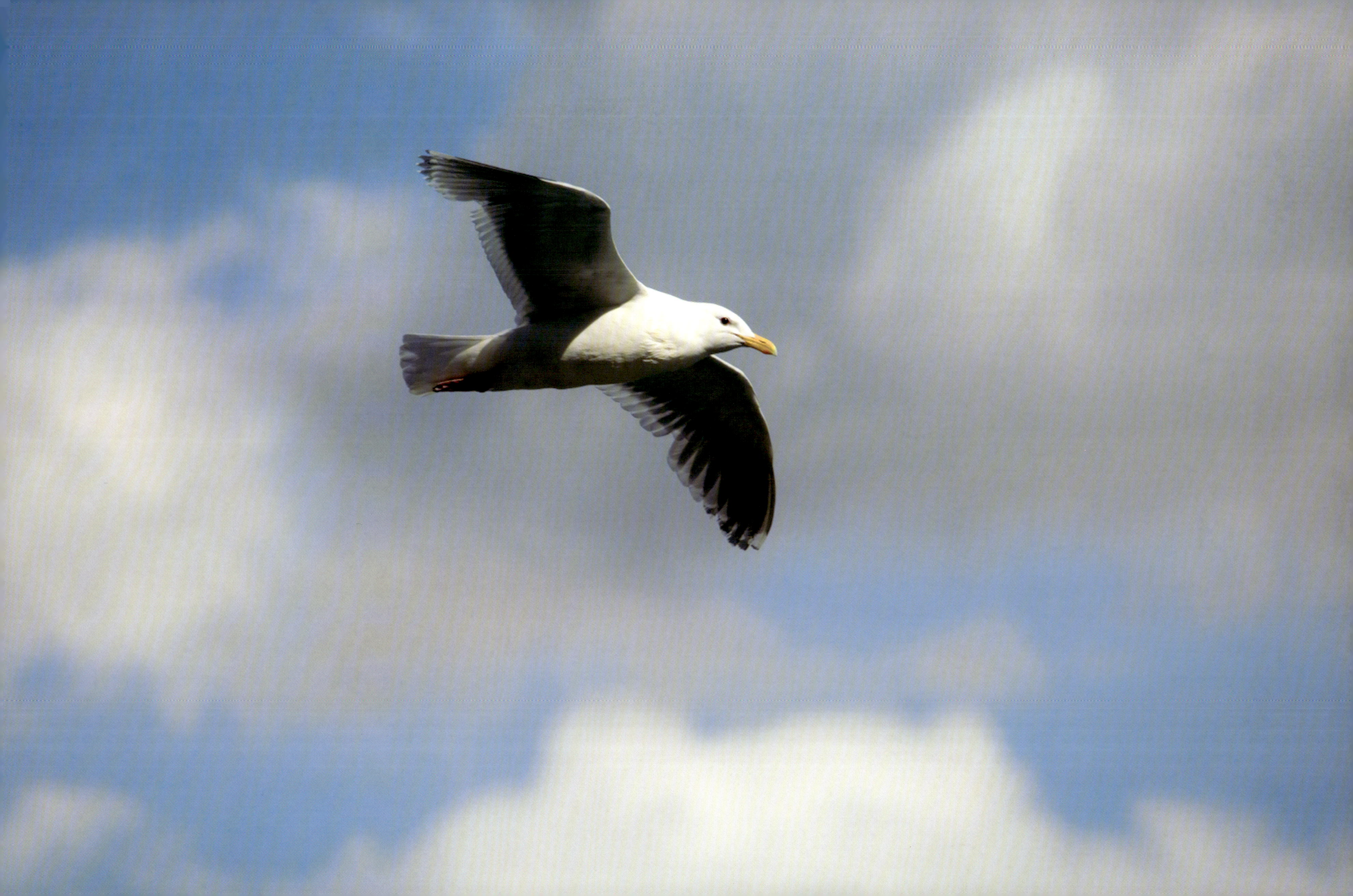

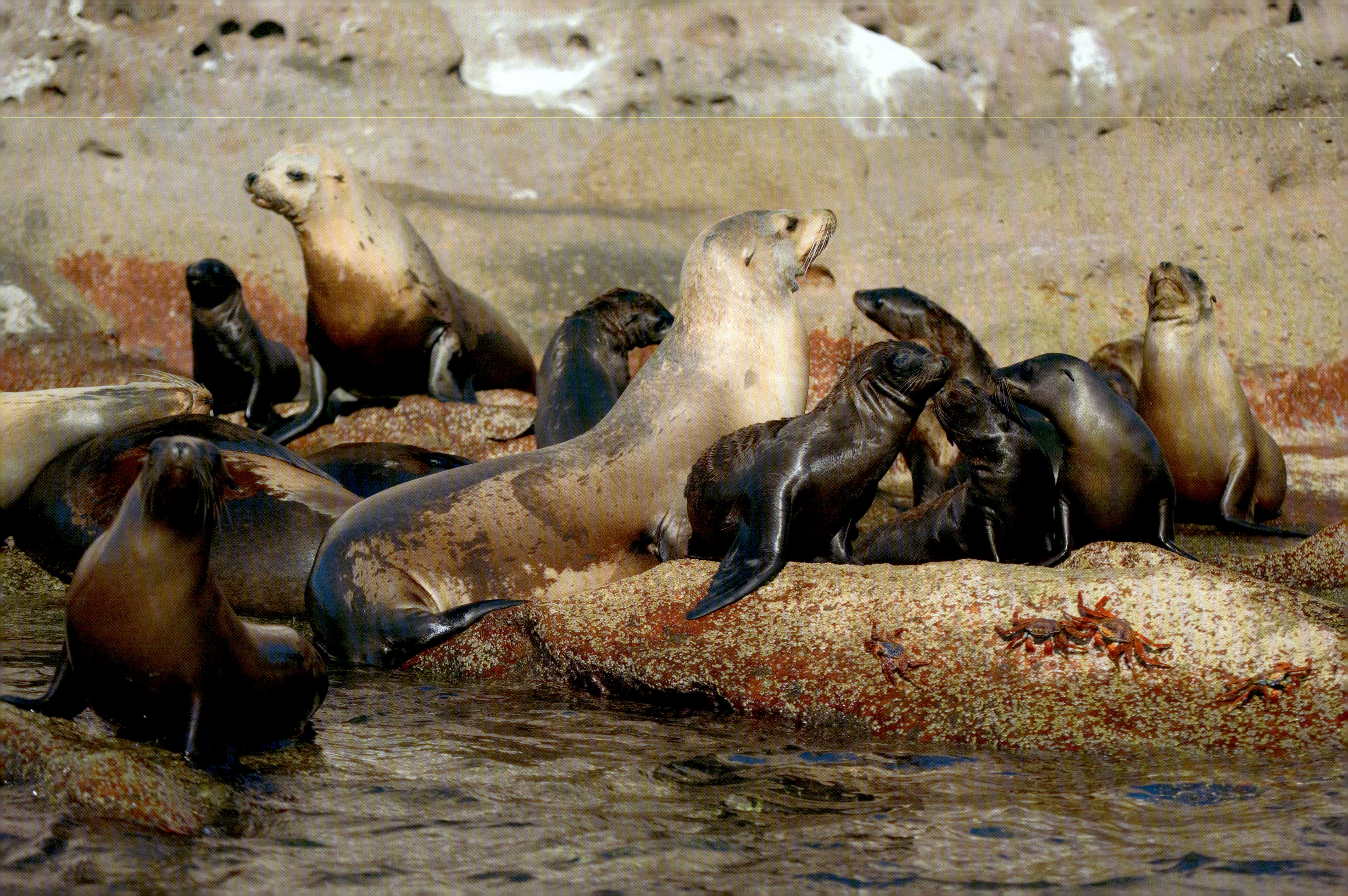

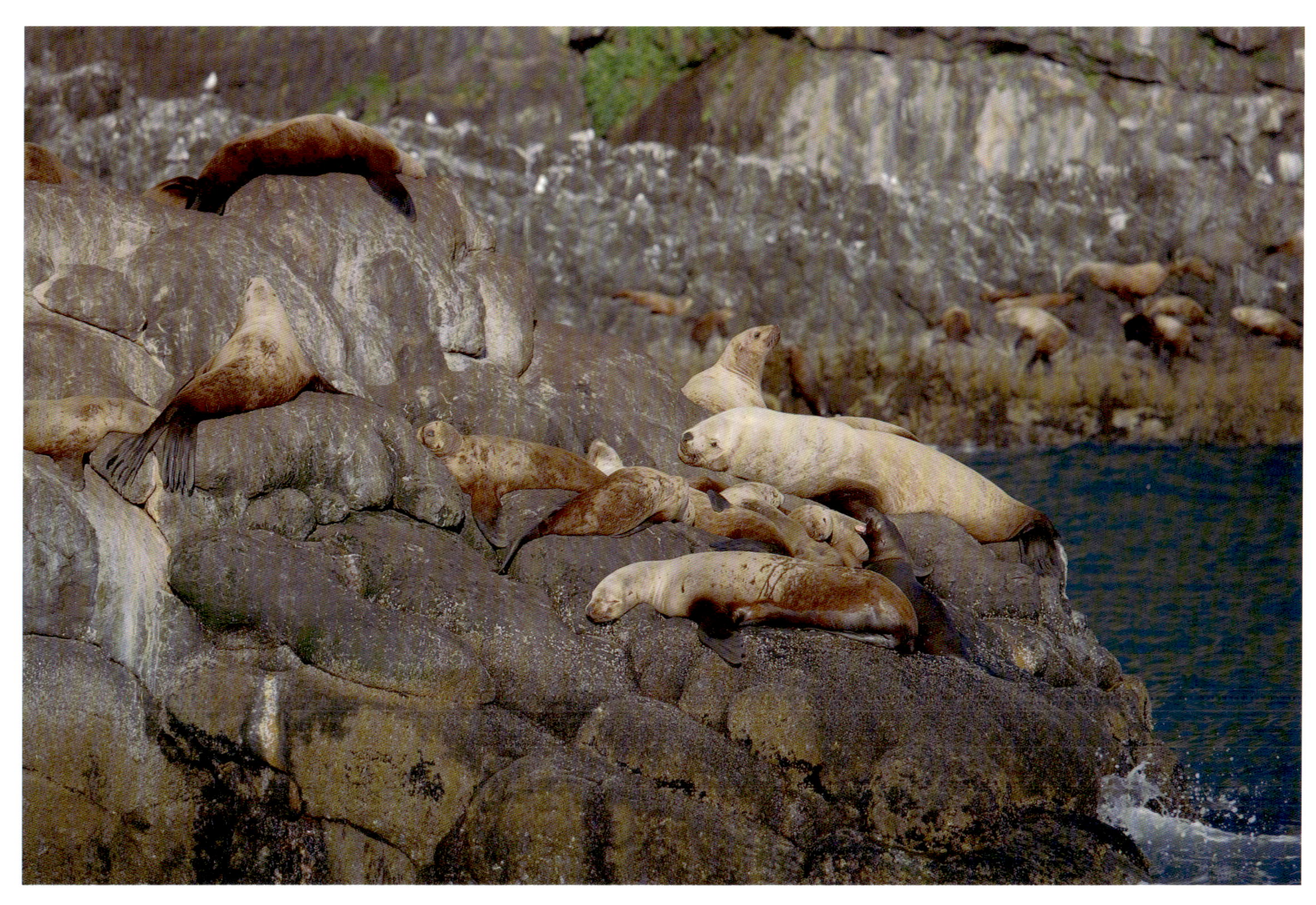

sea lion nursery
stellar sea lion rock

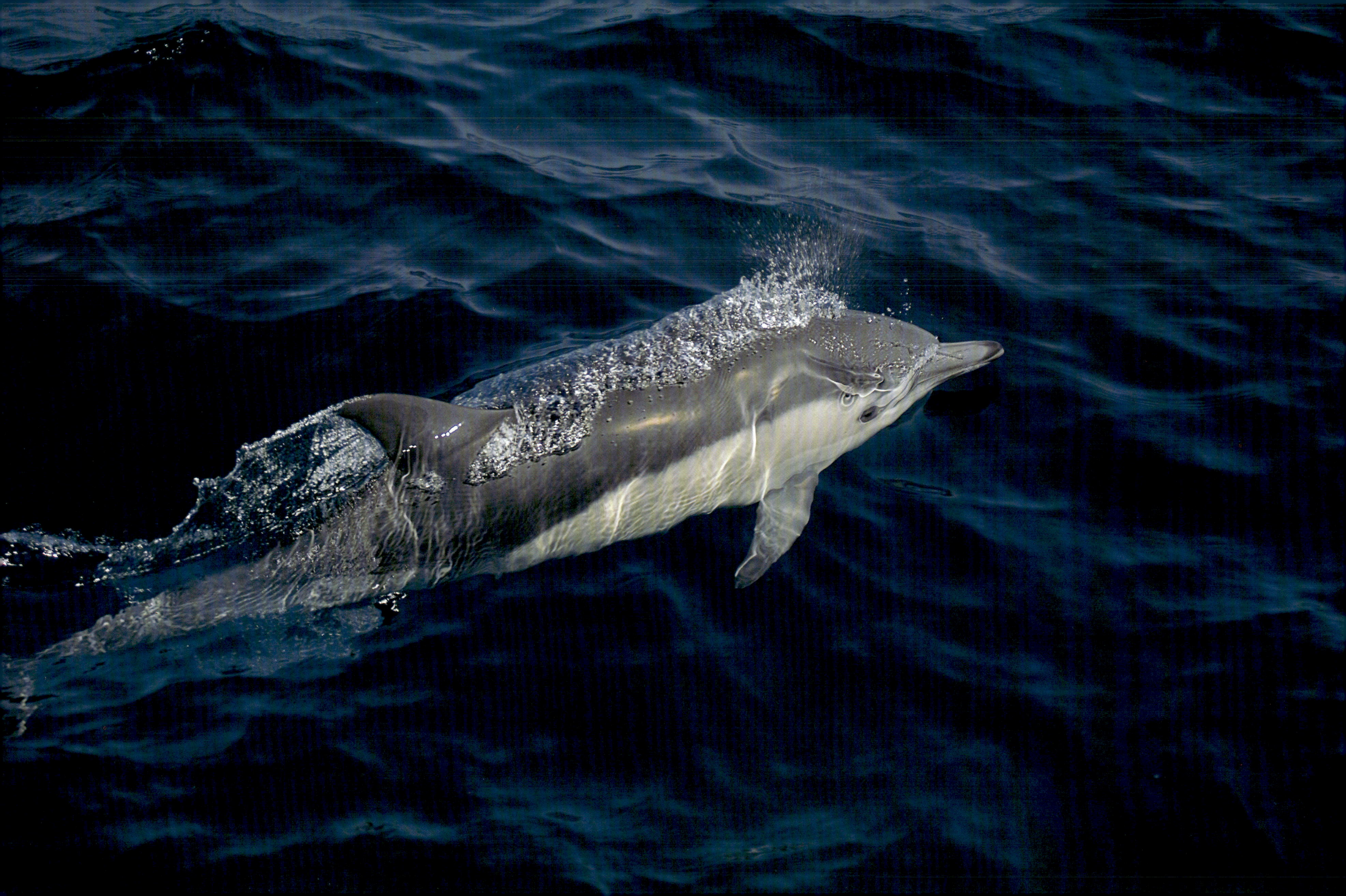

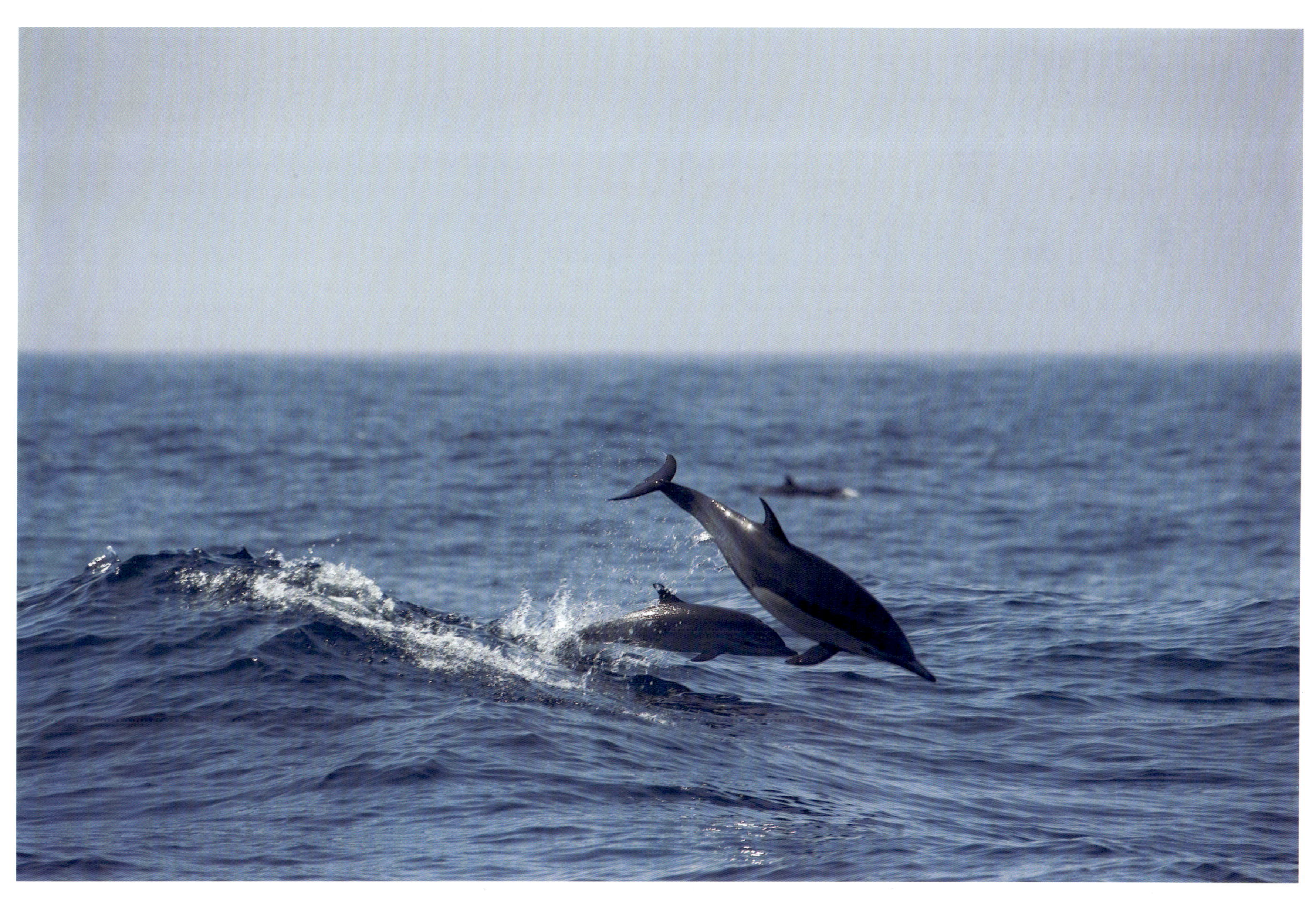

◀ common dolphin
▶ common dolphin sea

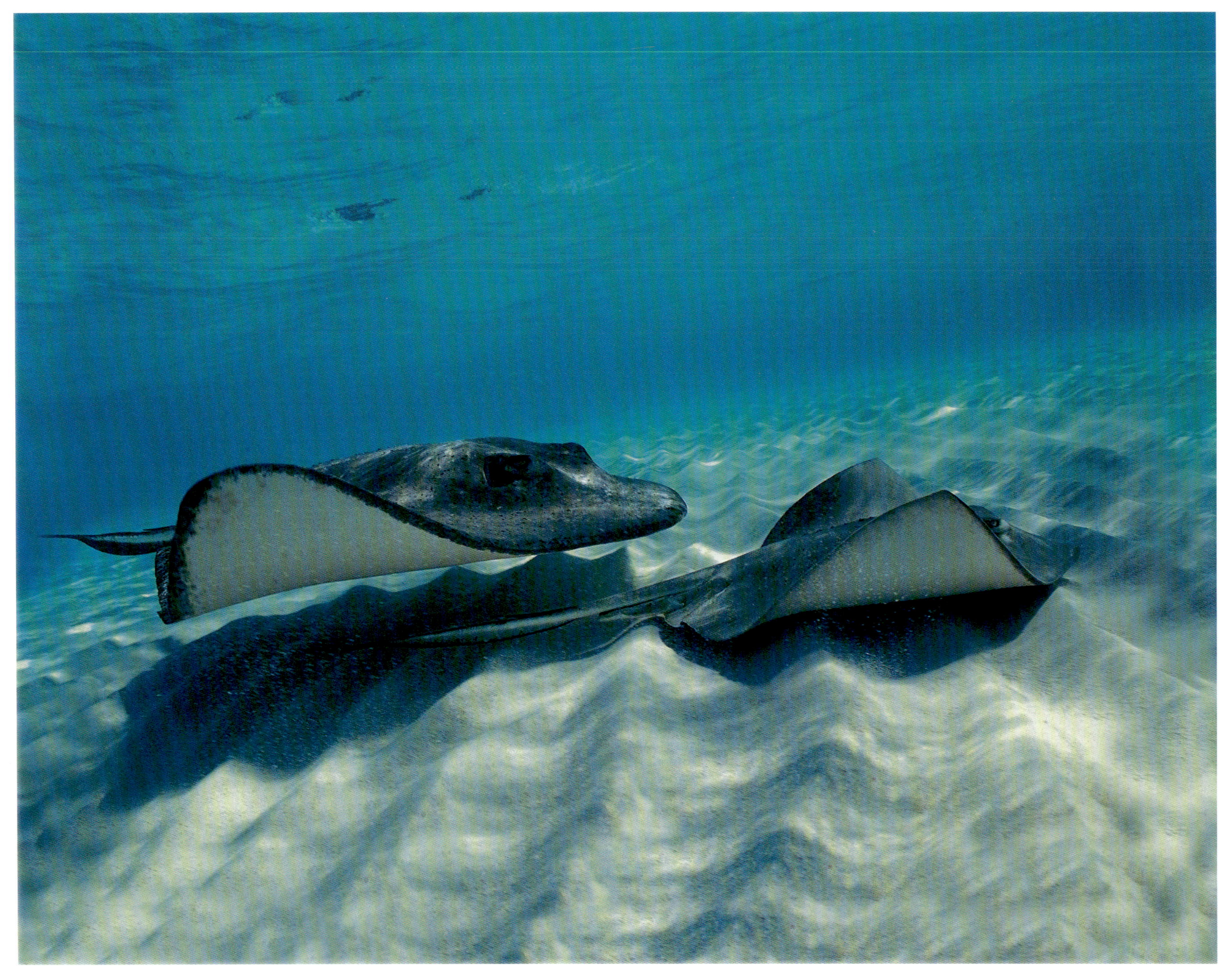

◀ sting rays
▶ friendly sting rays

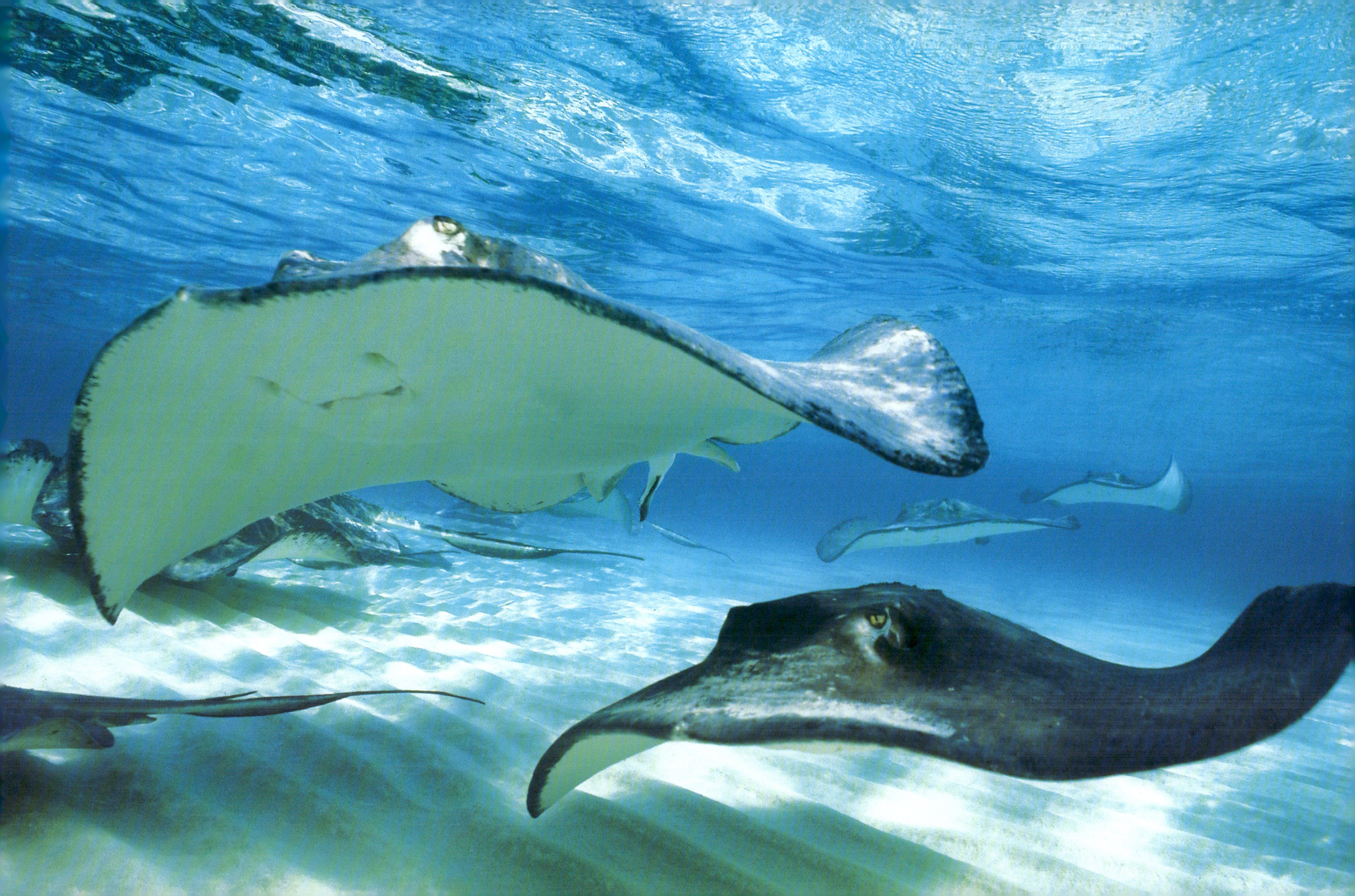

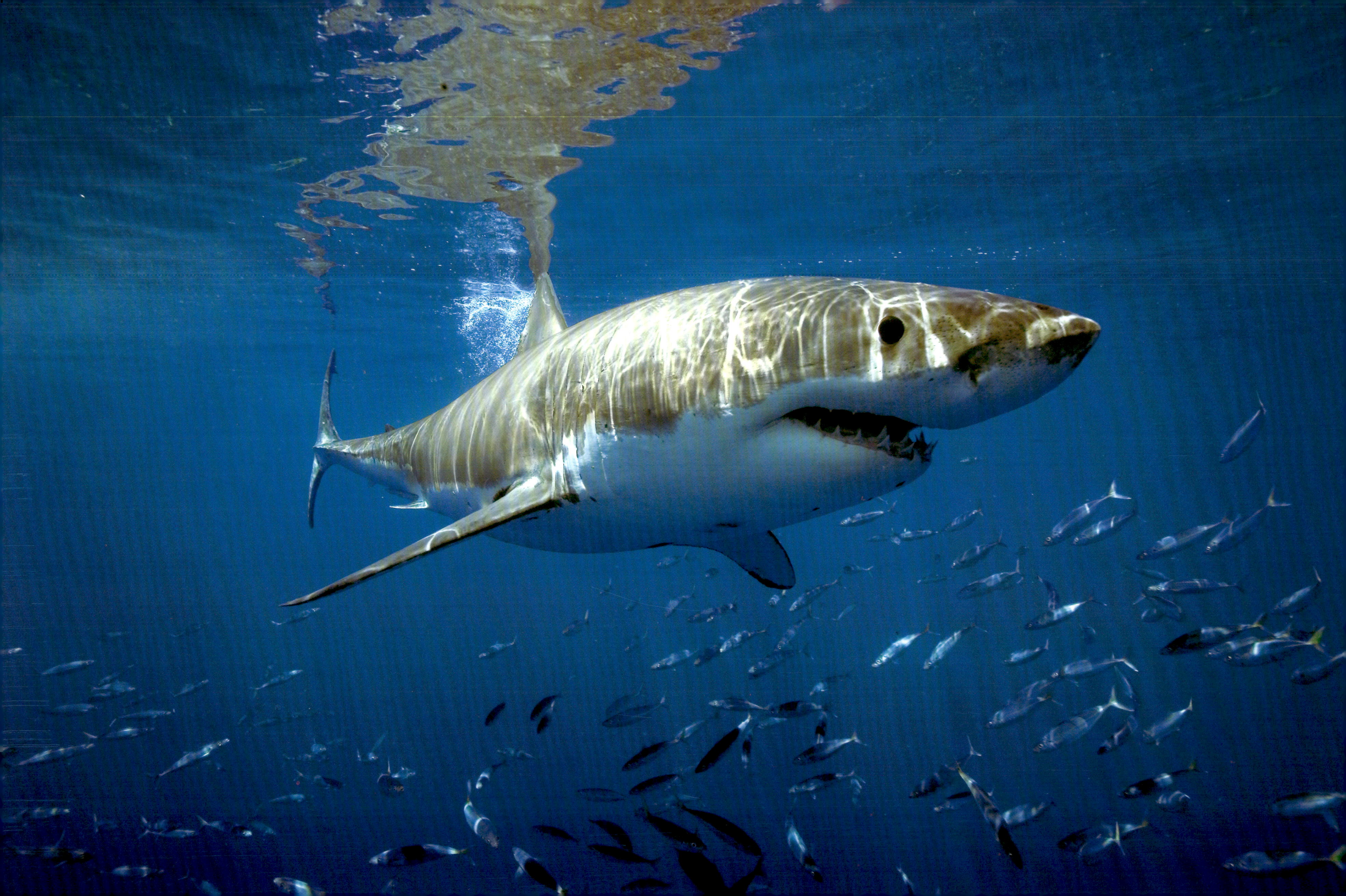

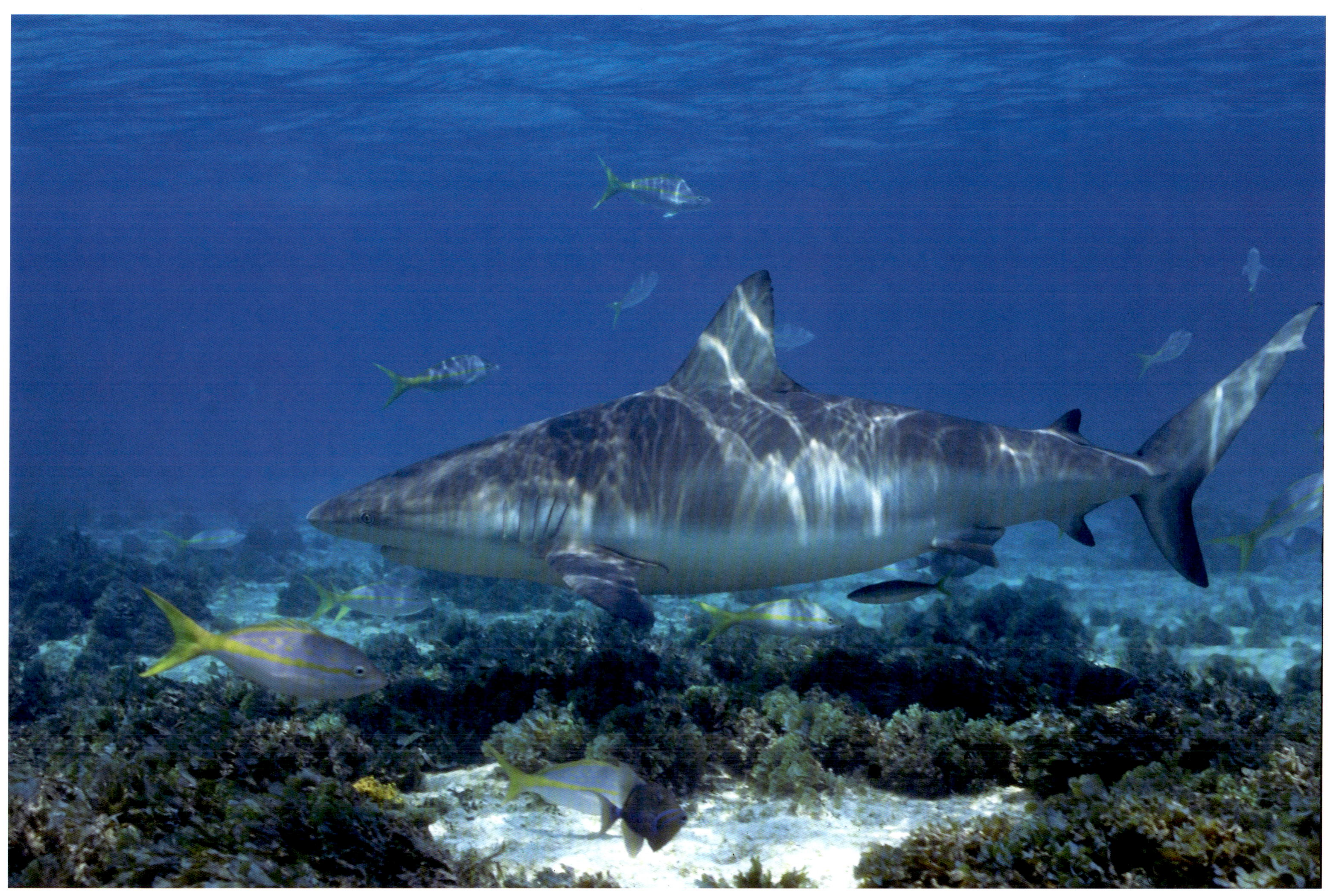

◀ great white reflection
▶ bull of the sea

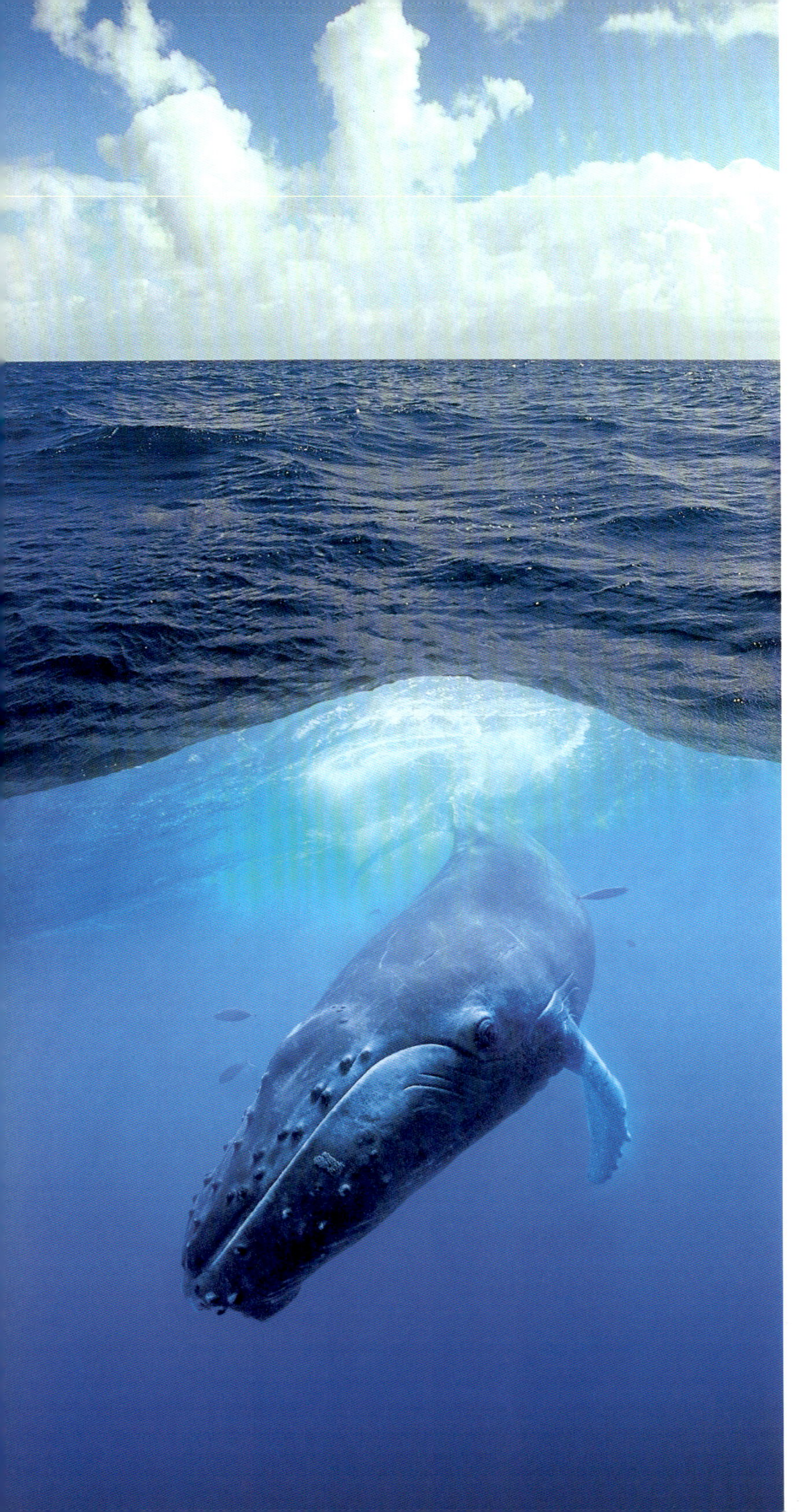

◄ blue sounding
► hang time

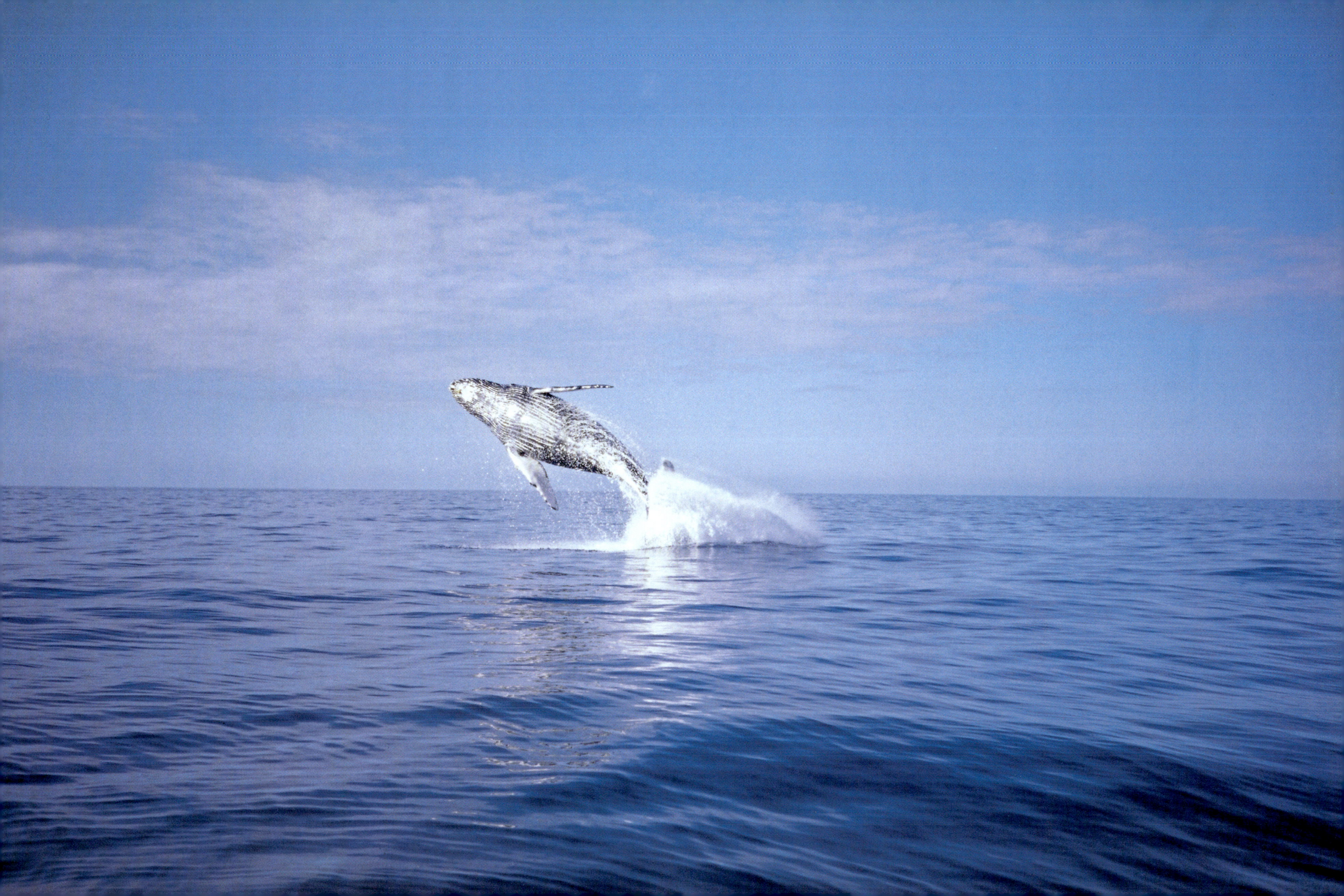

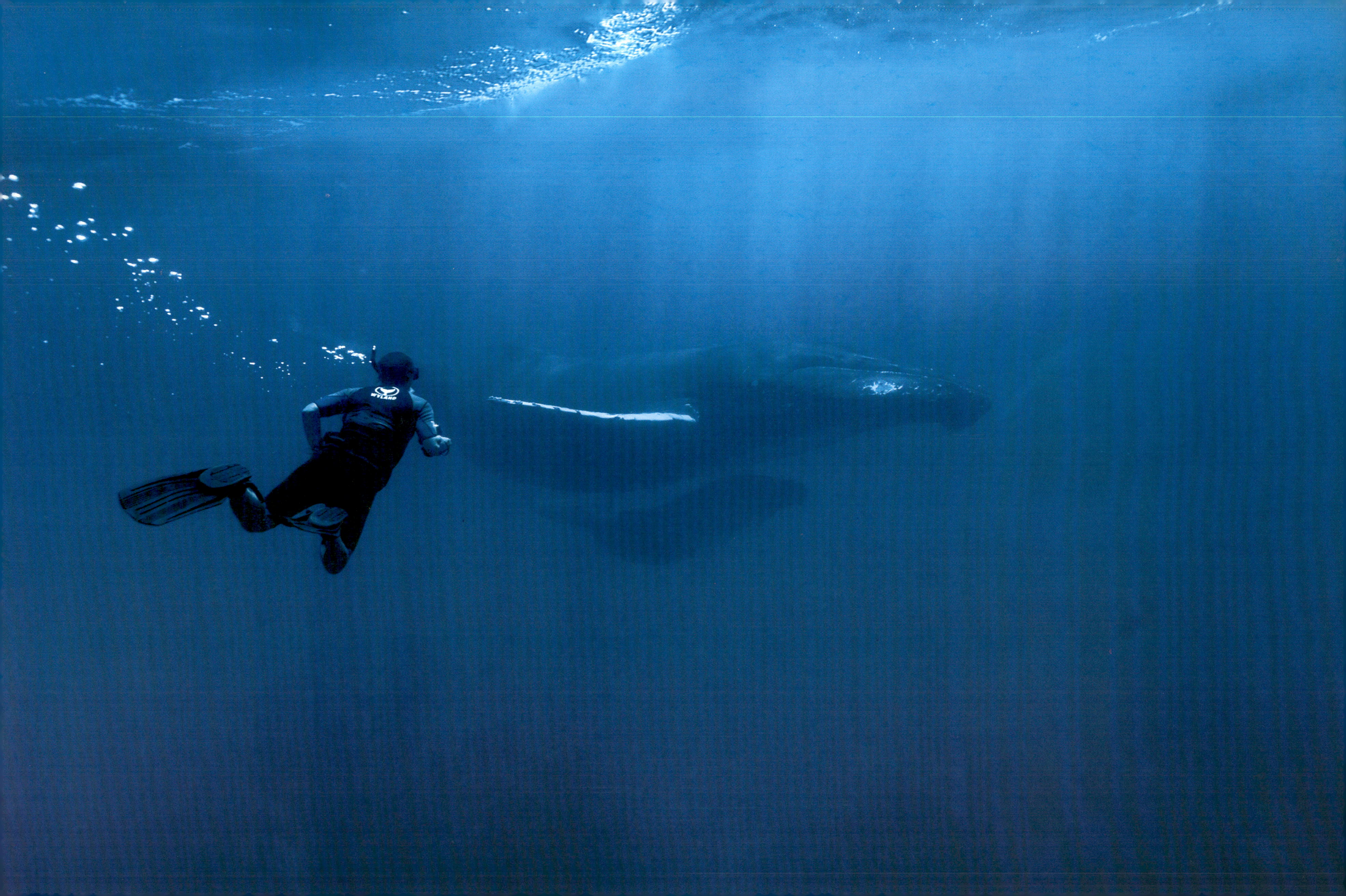

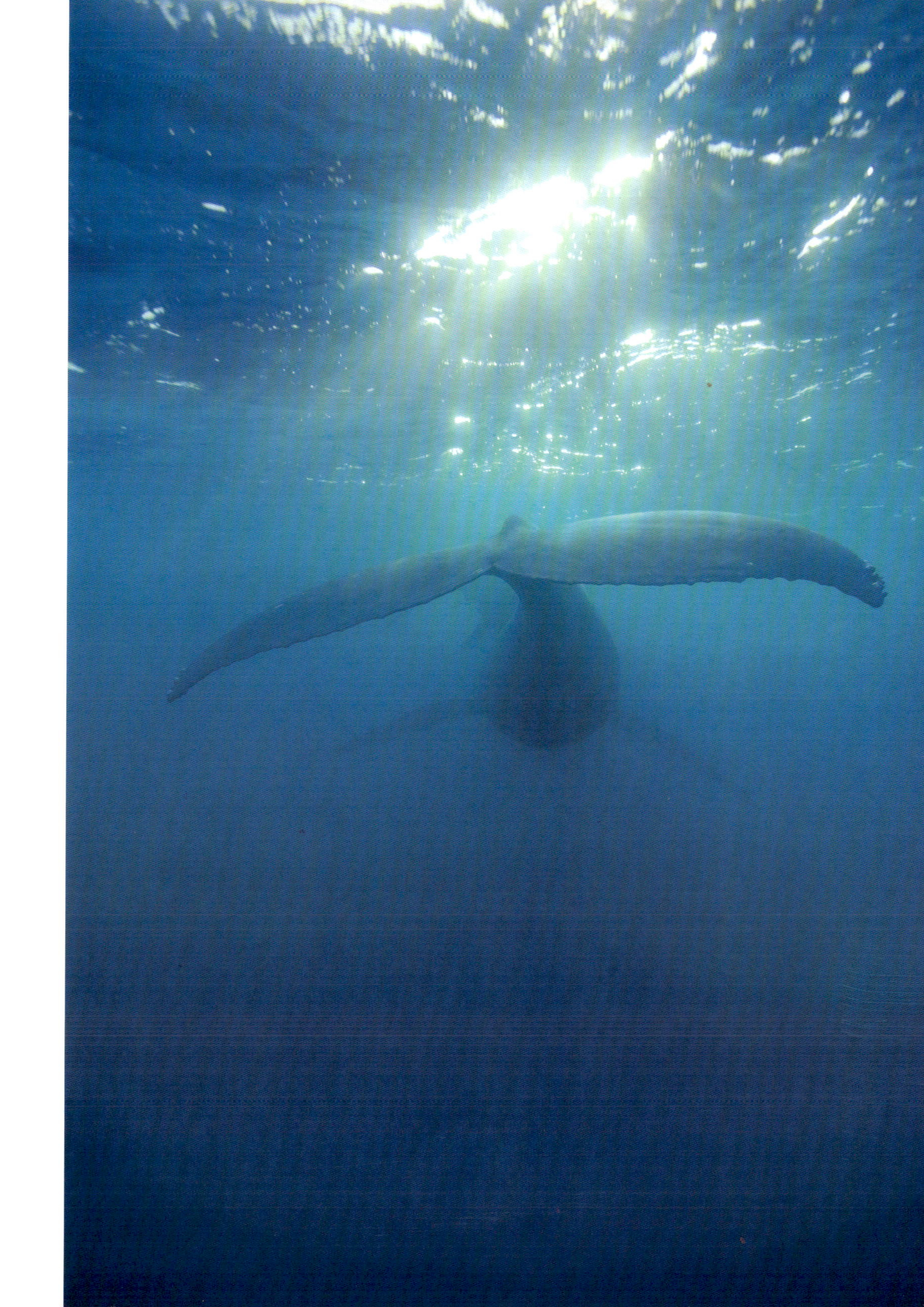

◄ wyland humpback encounter
▶ the great whale

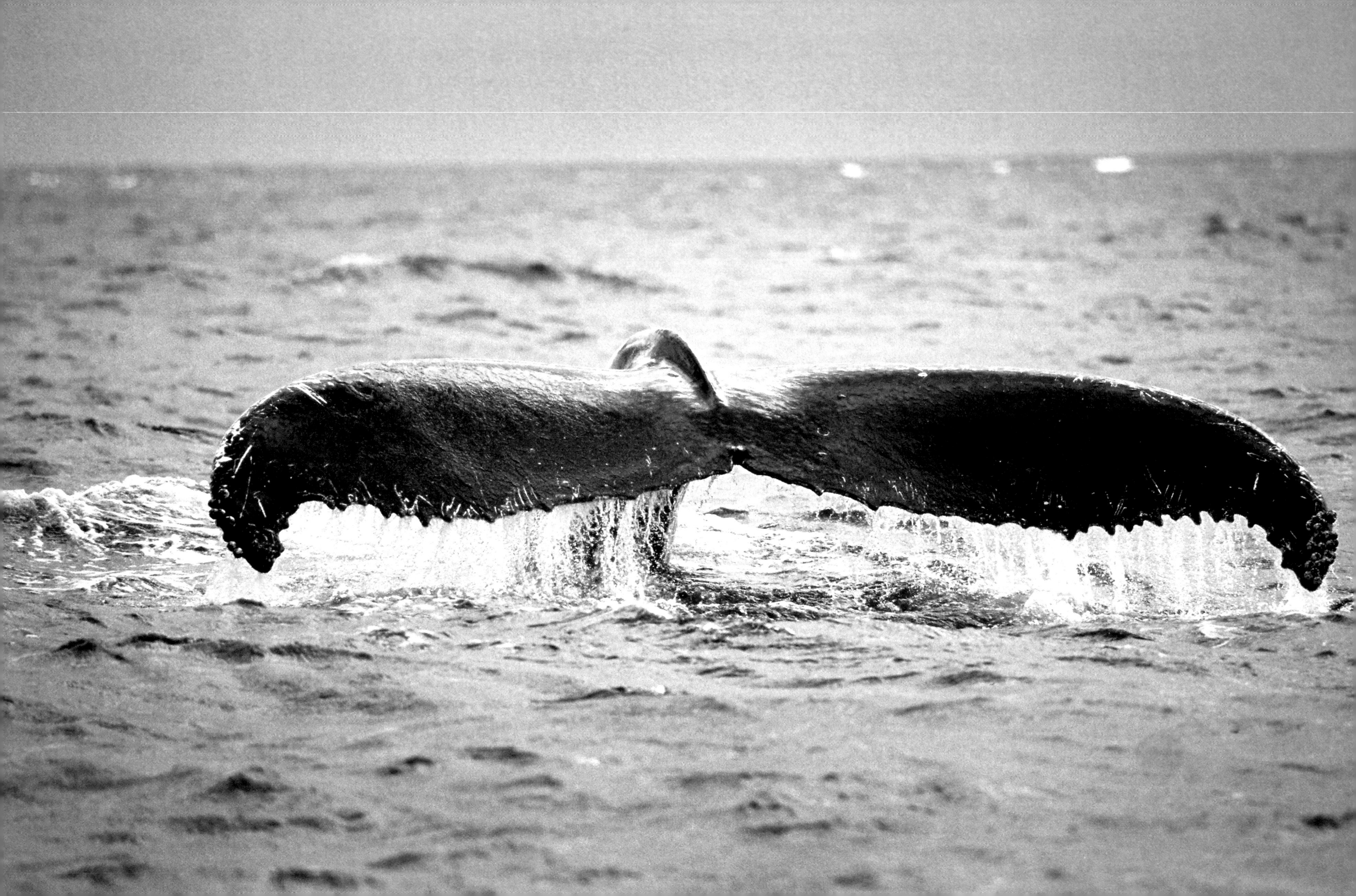

black and light
by wyland

Renowned photographer Ansel Adams pioneered black and white photography in the 20th century. Today, Ernie Brooks and a few others have continued to create black and white images that inspire us. I, too, have been inspired to paint black and white images with my camera. To me, black and white is raw. It is the "less is more" approach to photographing nature. Everything is revealed. I call mine black and light. The challenge is always looking for the light to illuminate the scene and that magic moment when you see it in your mind and capture it forever with one pull of the trigger. When you get it, it is exciting beyond belief. You just hope you had the right settings. It has always been easy for me to position myself in the ocean to capture the image. For artists, our strongest resource is our ability to compose, but there are a lot of variables when you are floating in deep blue sea, waiting for animals to reveal themselves. This is when the magic happens, when an animal decides that it will share its world with you even for a fleeting moment. You may never see it again. Yes, I can paint it. Even in black and white. But there is something unique about photography, even more so about black and white photography. It reaches us on an emotional level and may very well be the most pure art form there is. One image can change the way we see the natural world. It certainly has changed the way I see the water planet.

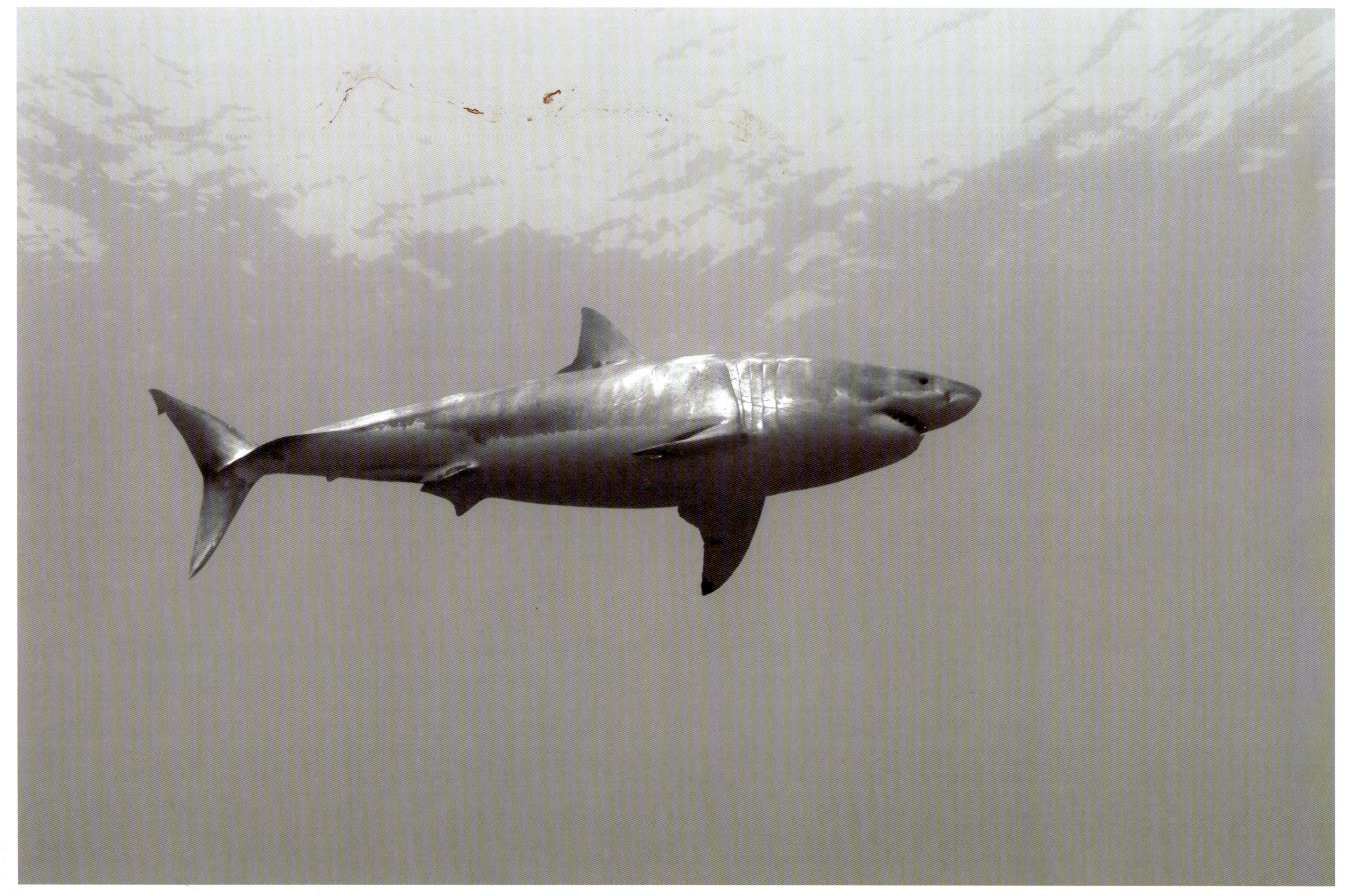

◄ great white above
► white death

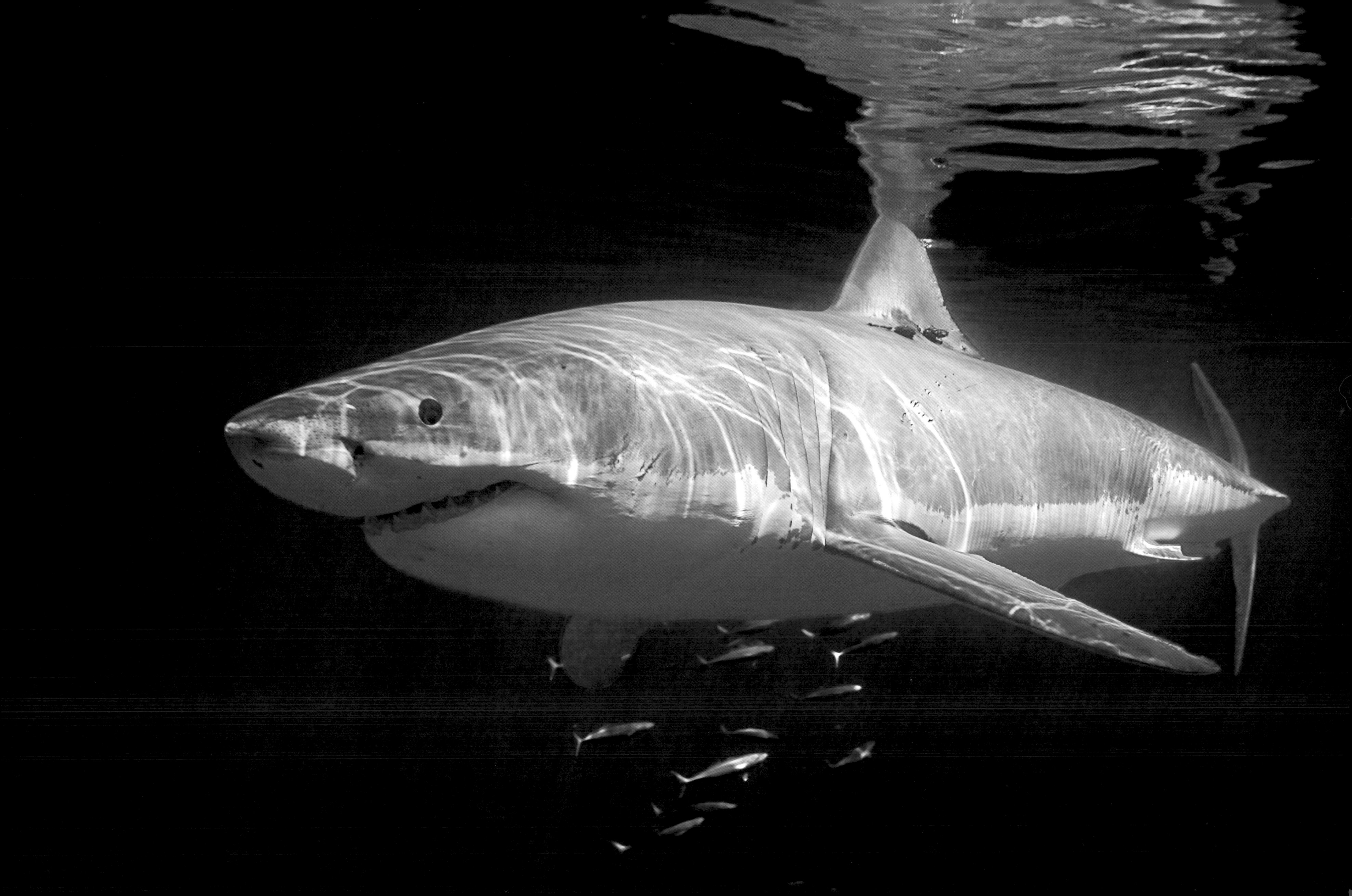

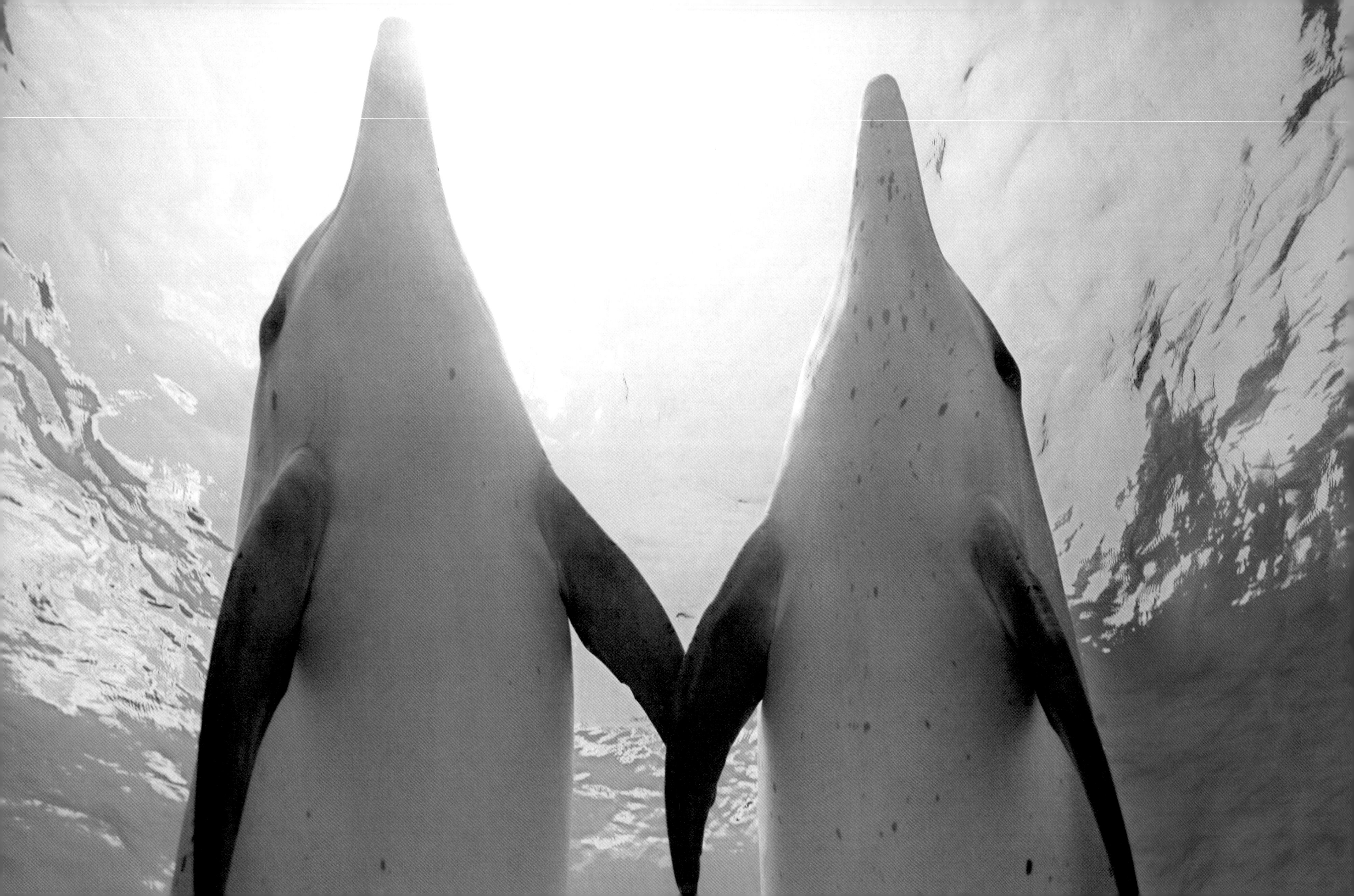

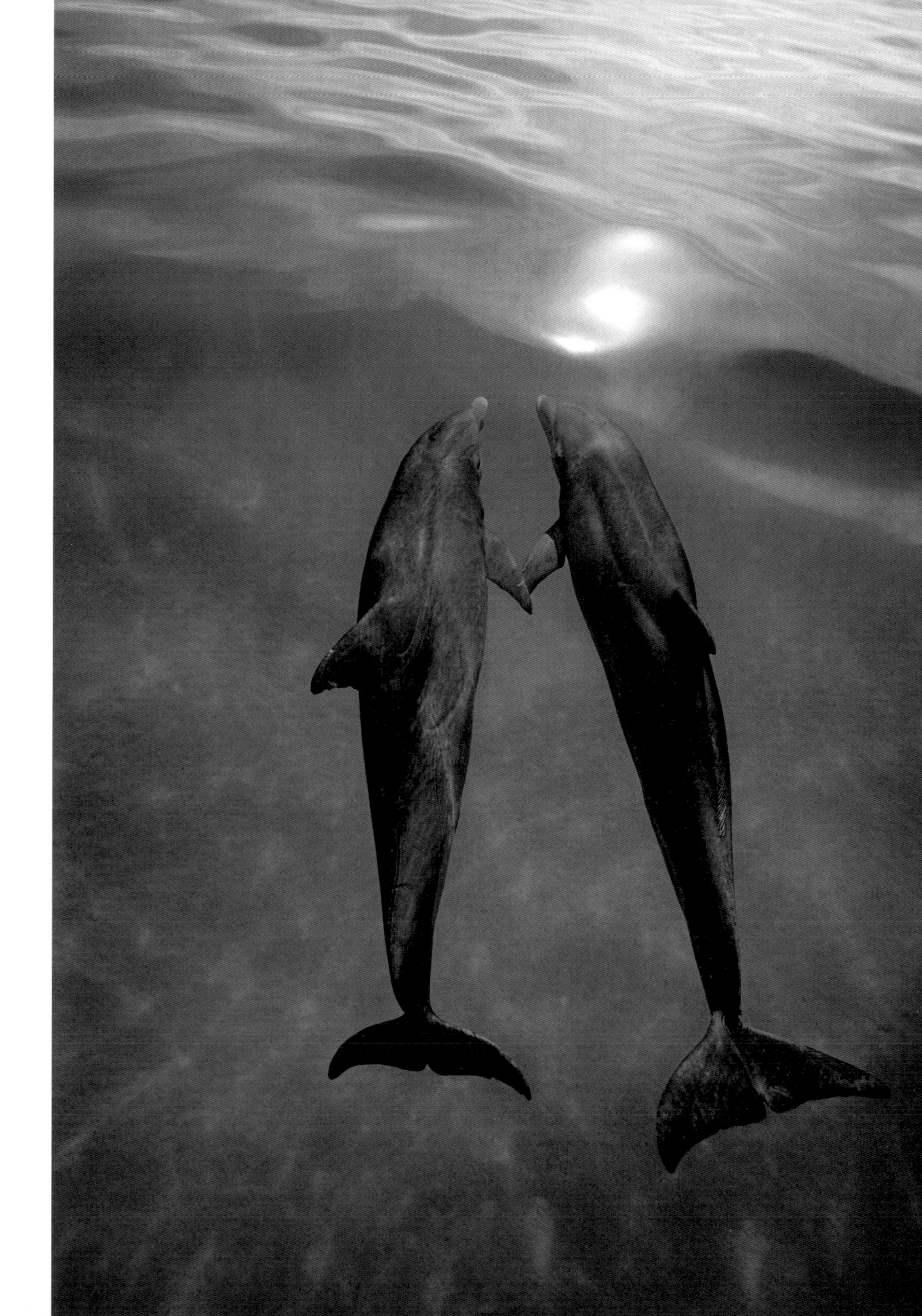

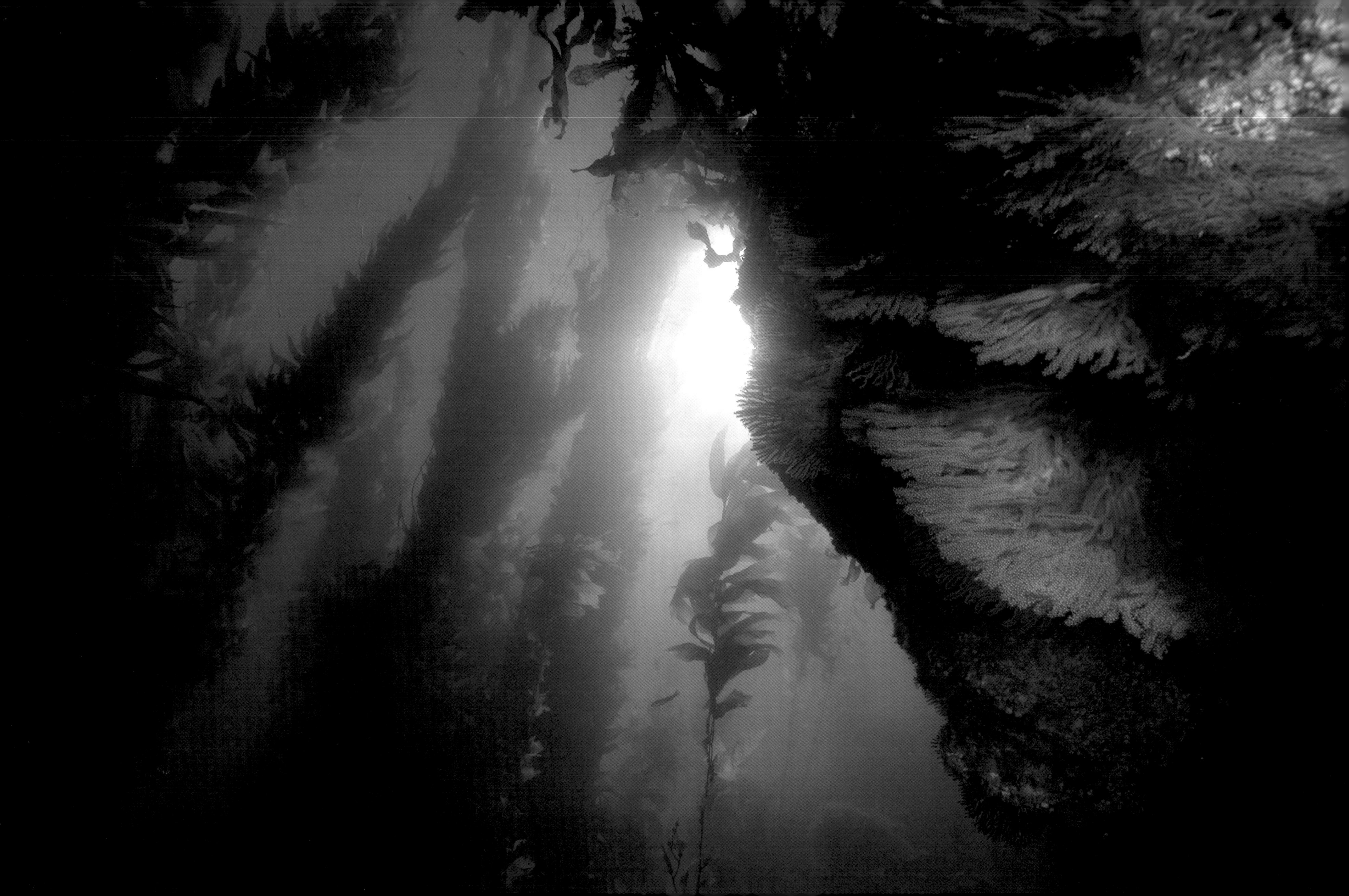

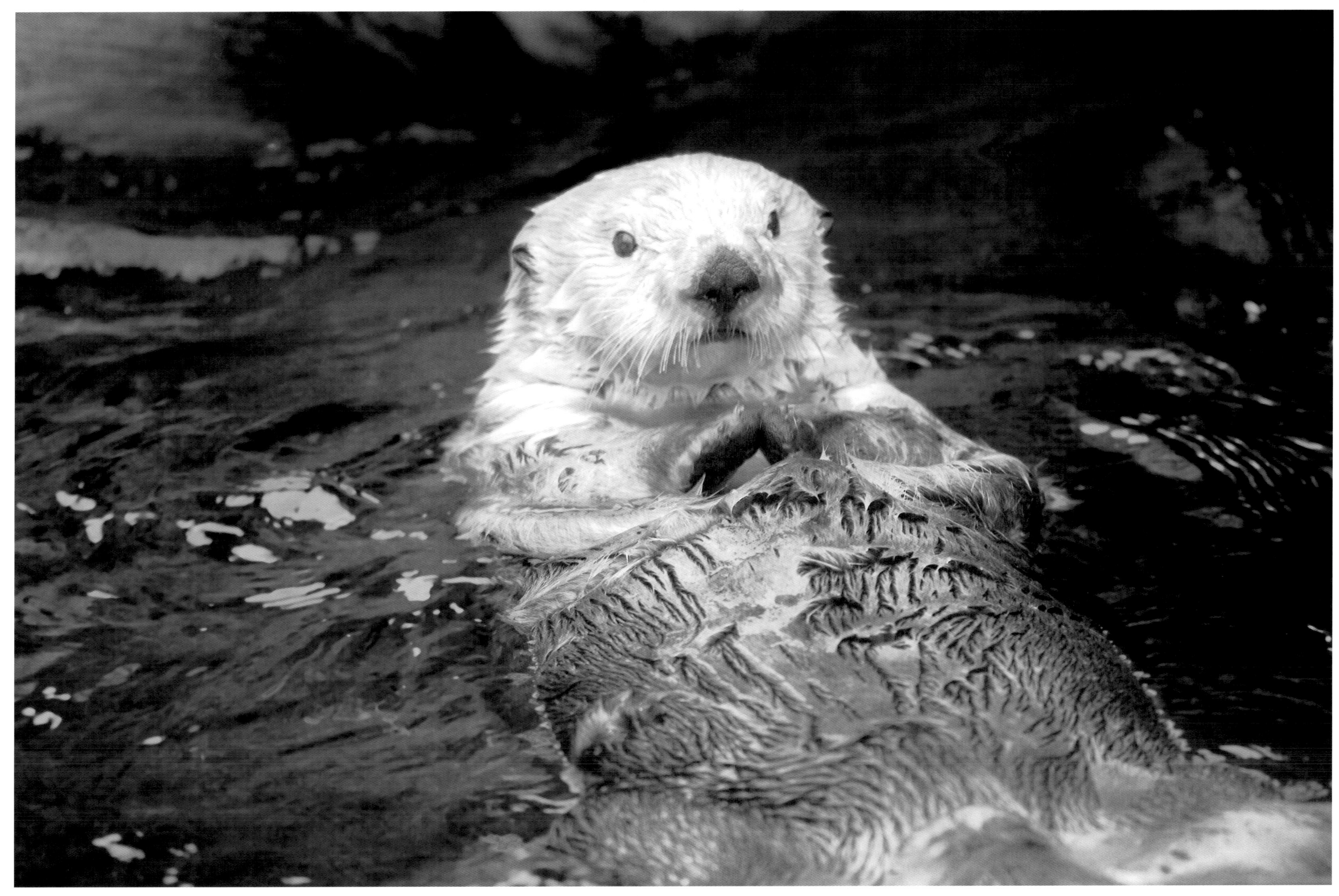

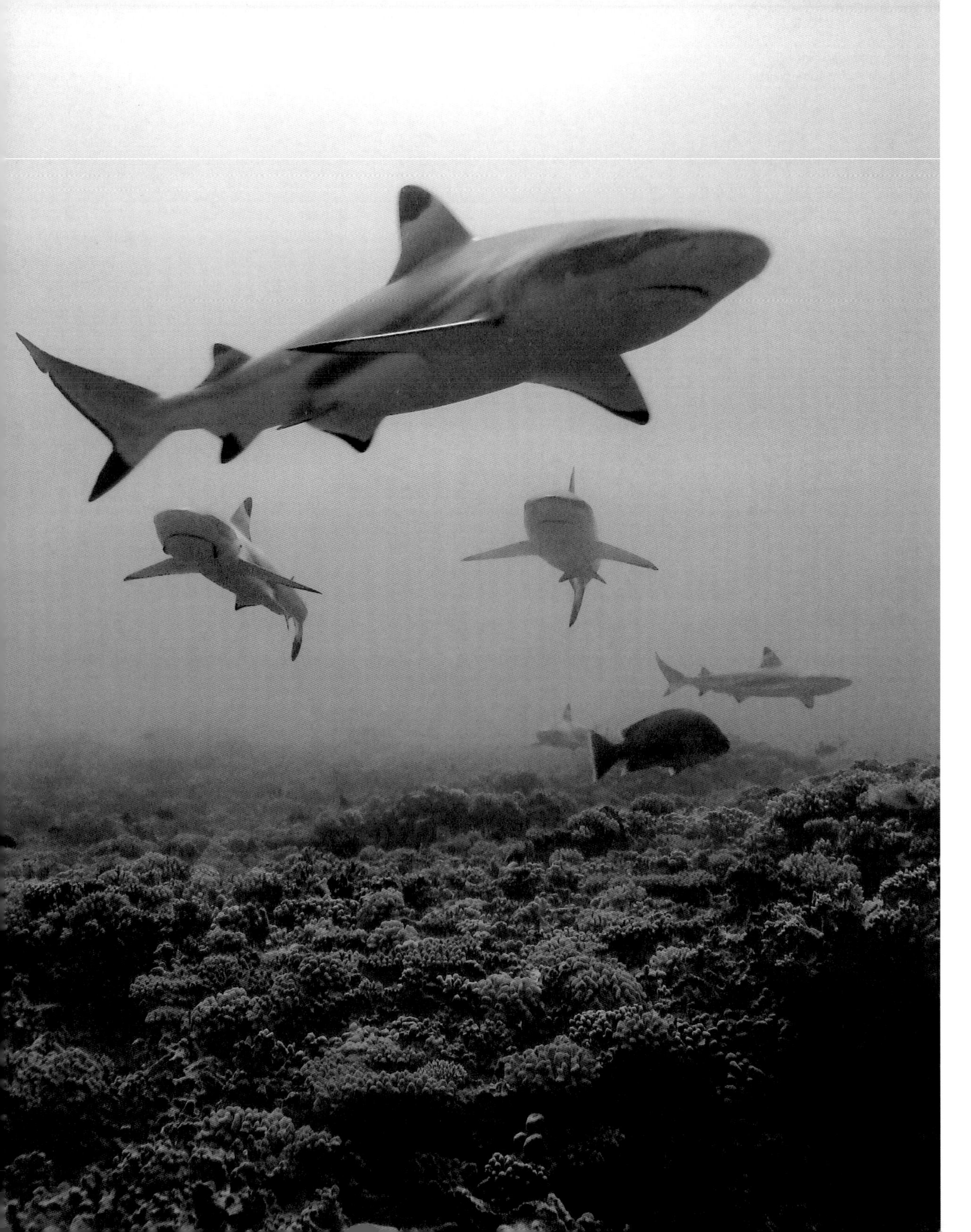

◄ tahiti reef sharks
► free swimming nurse shark

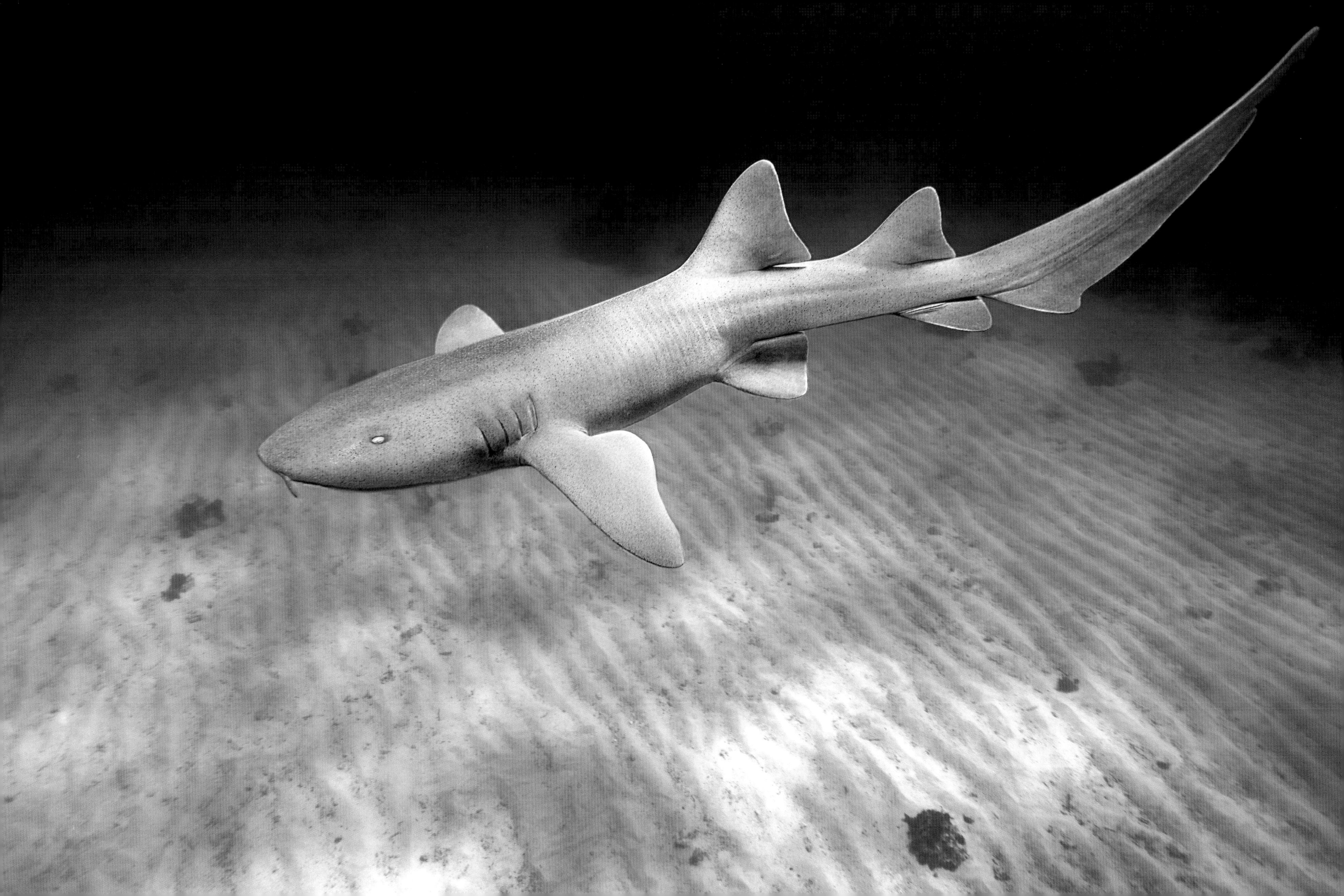

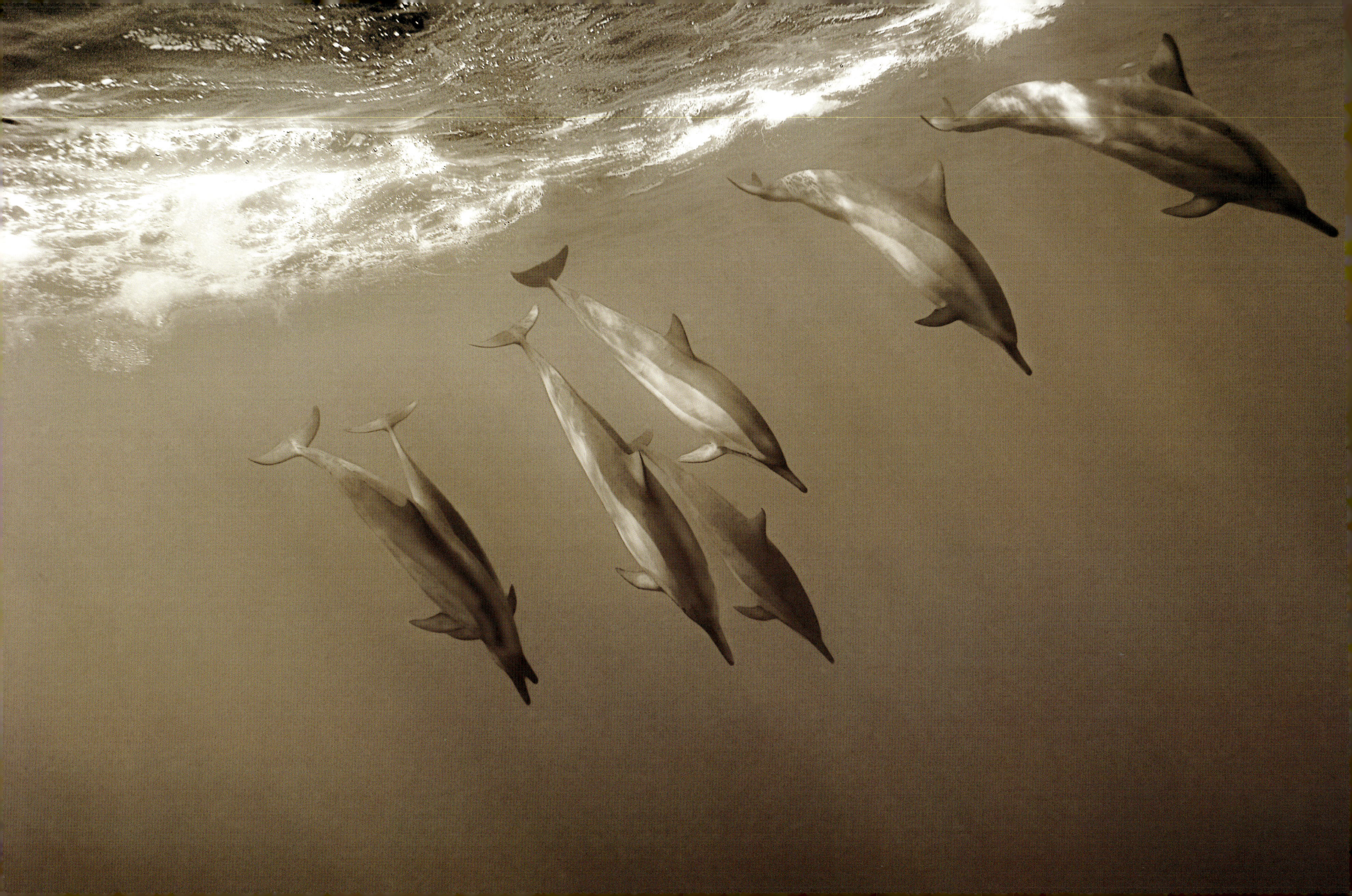

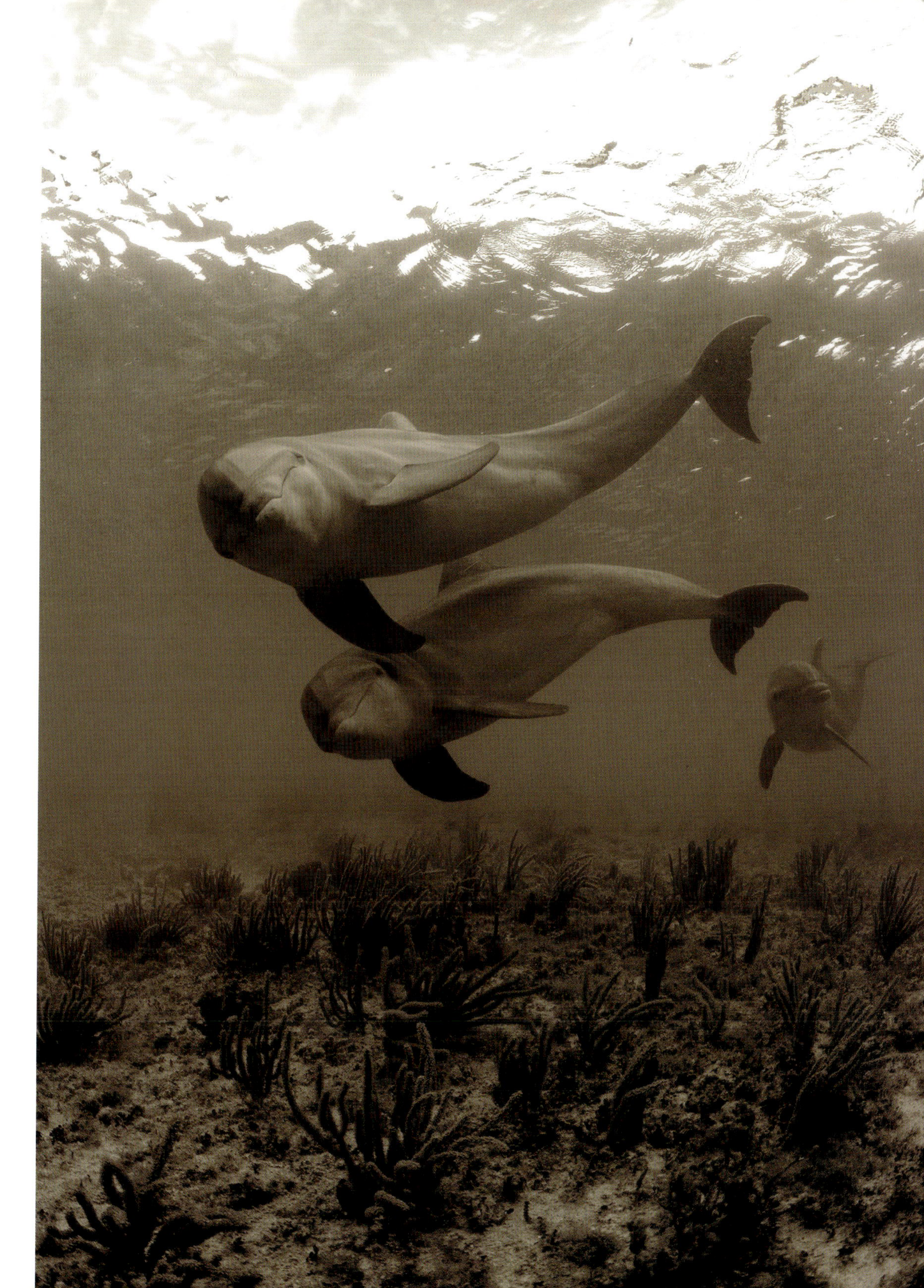

◀ spinners below
▶ planet dolphin

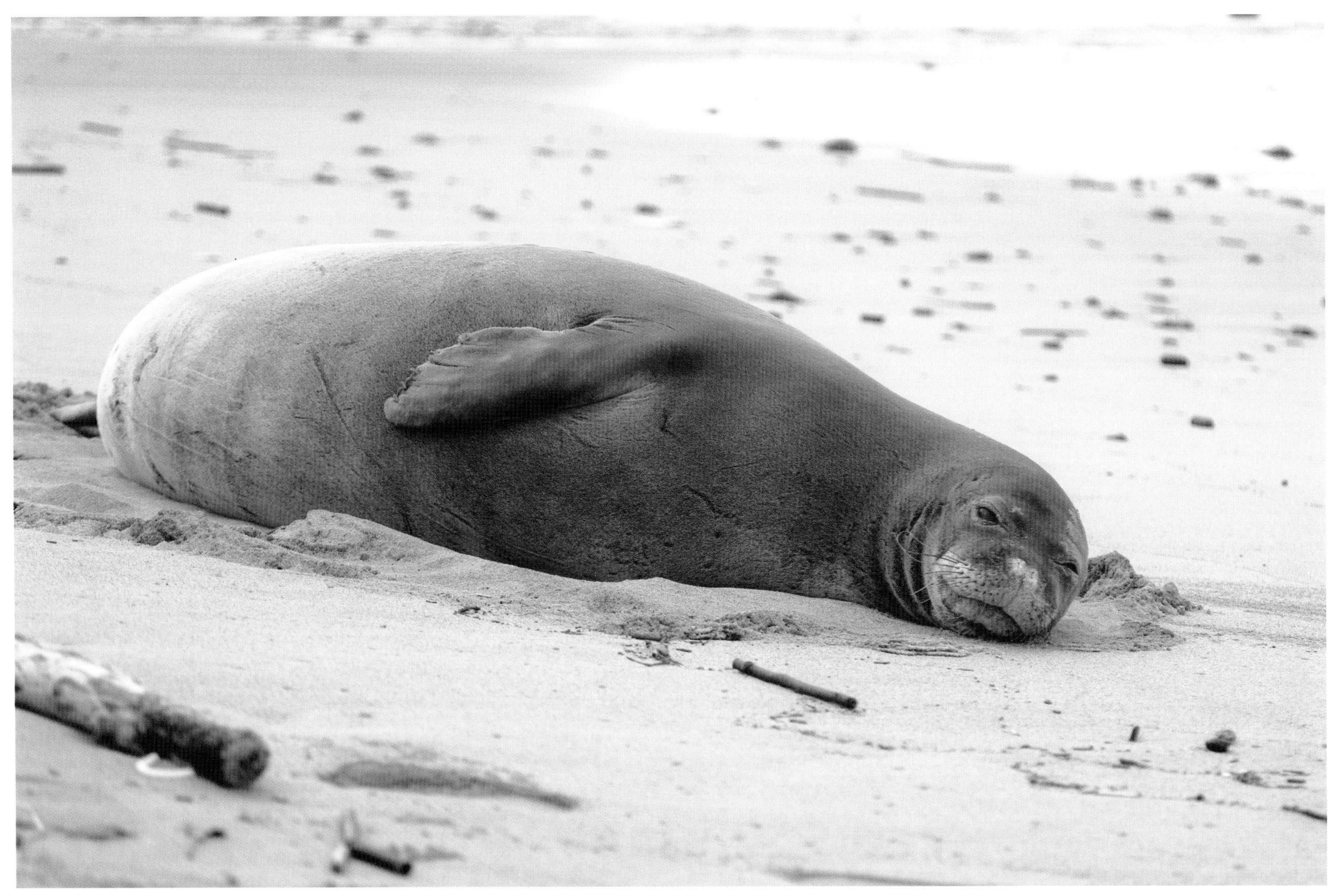

◀ monk seal rest
▶ monk seal surf

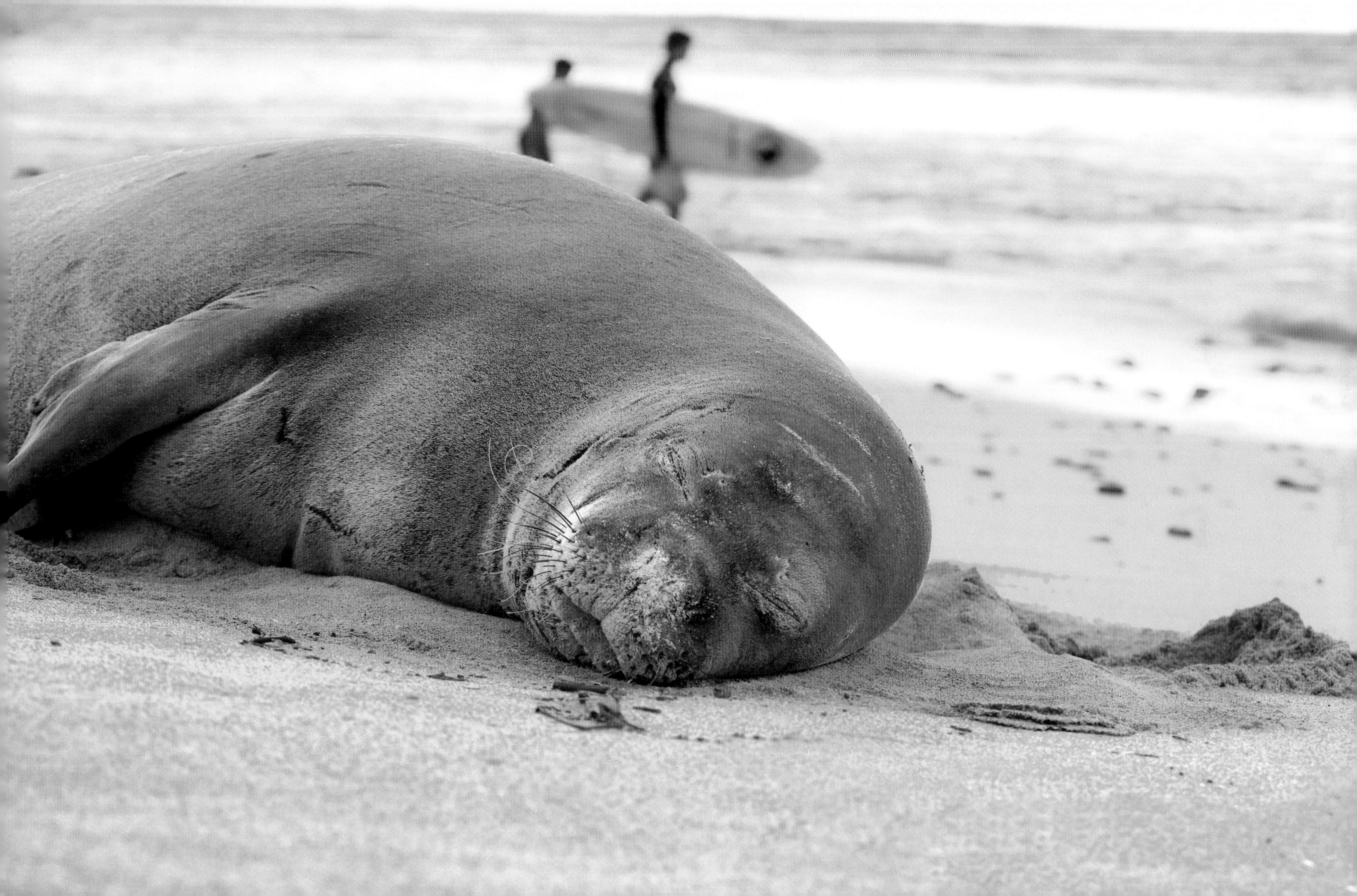

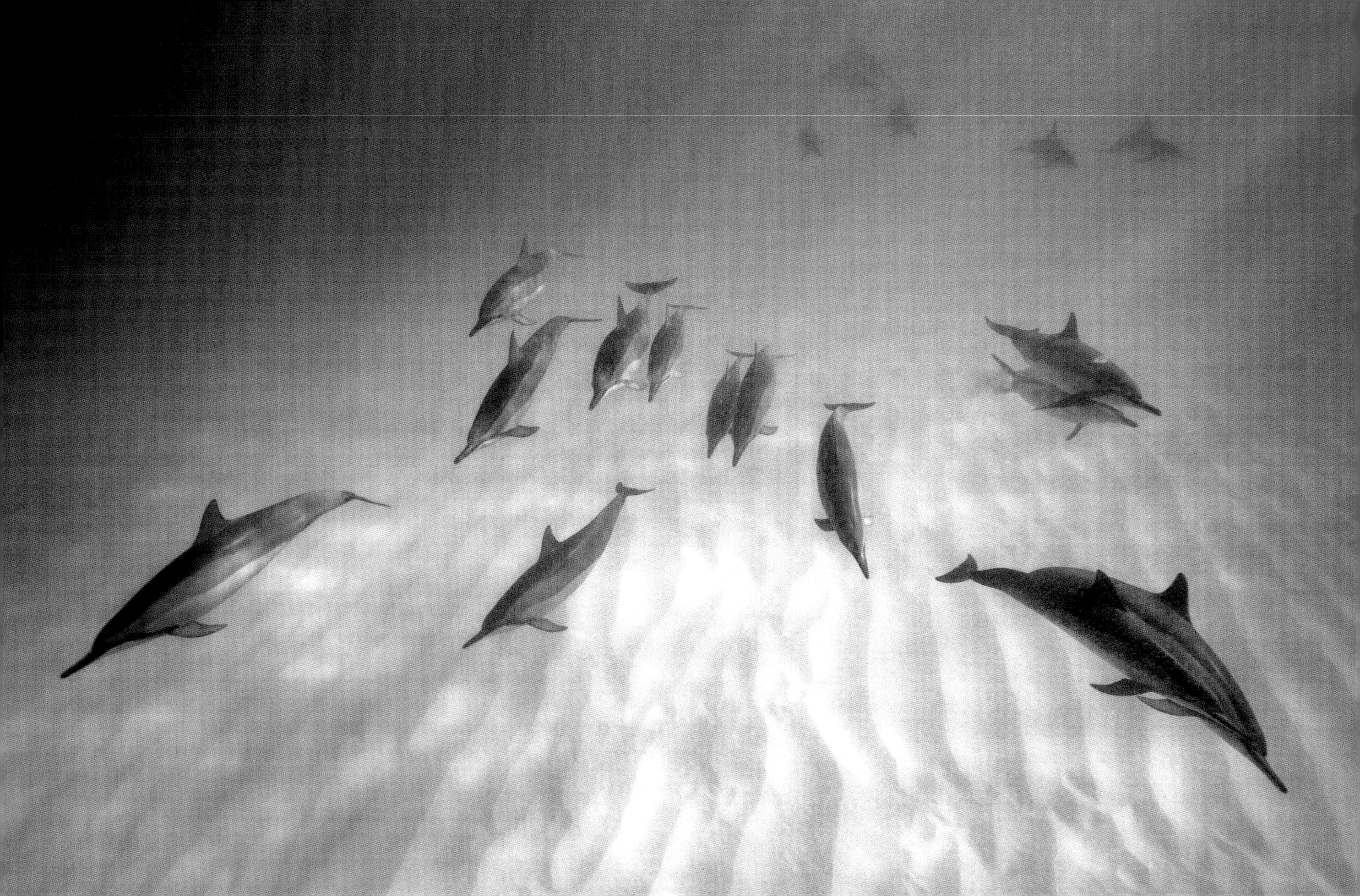

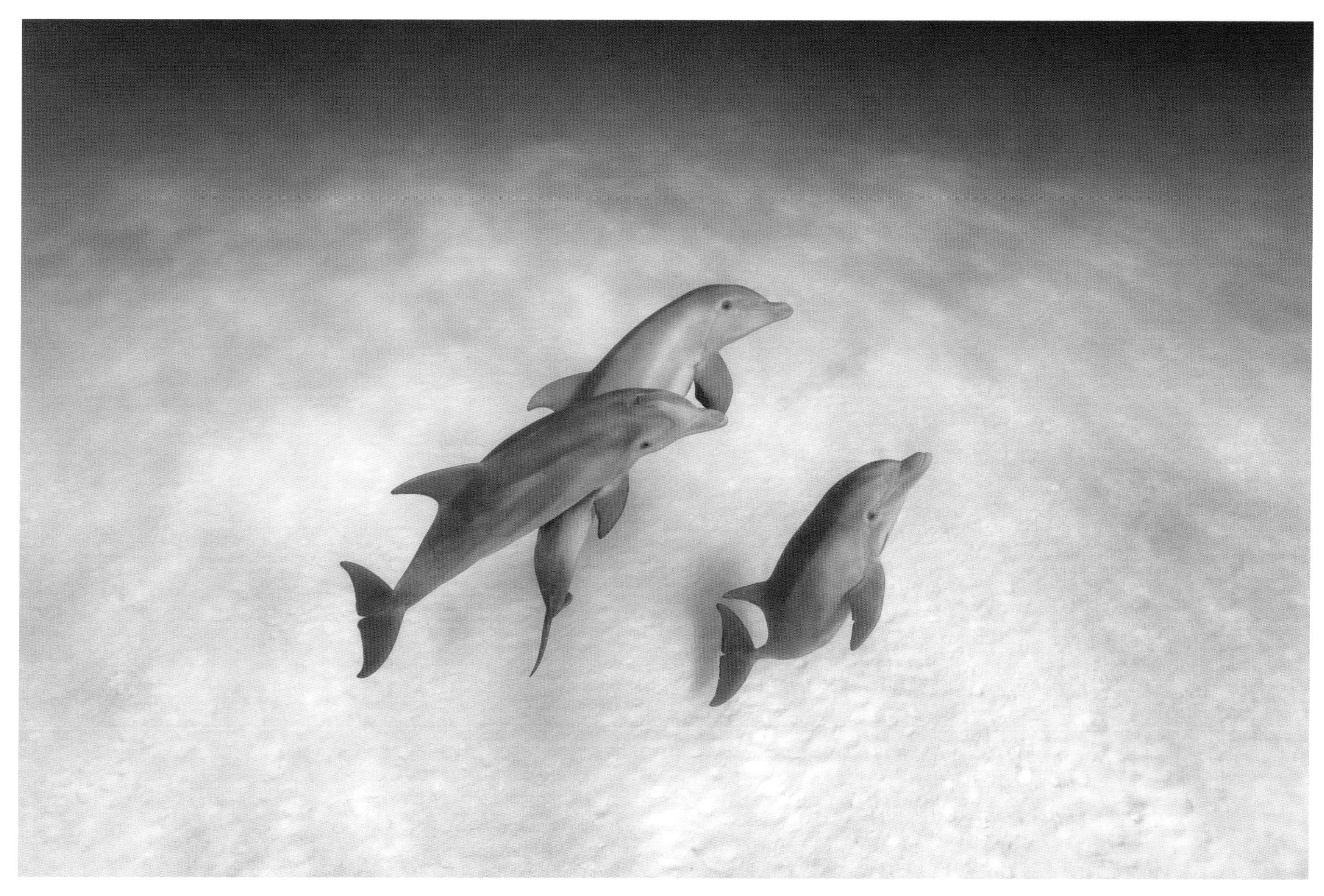

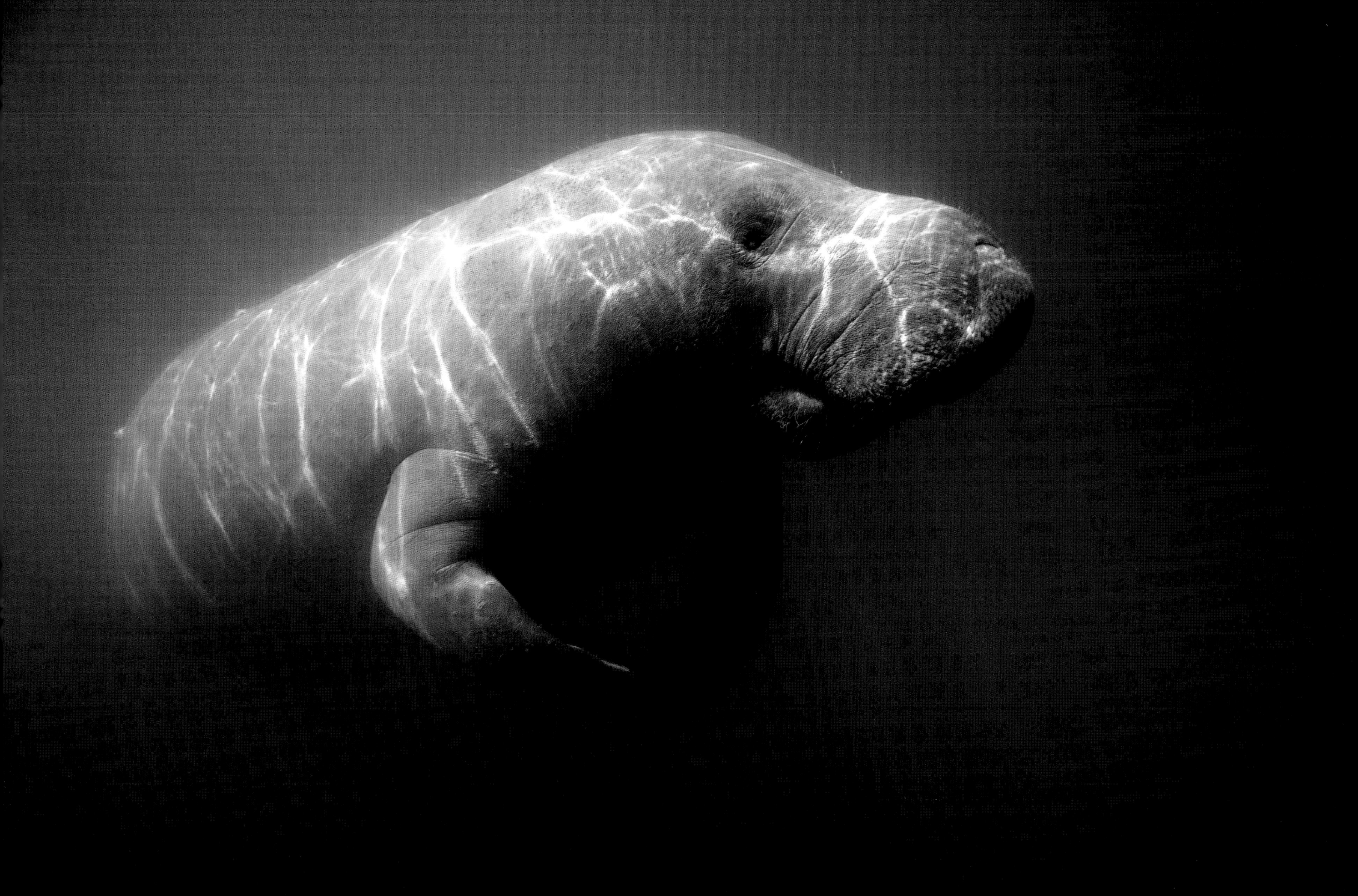

freedom lies in the weightless world below...

WYLAND

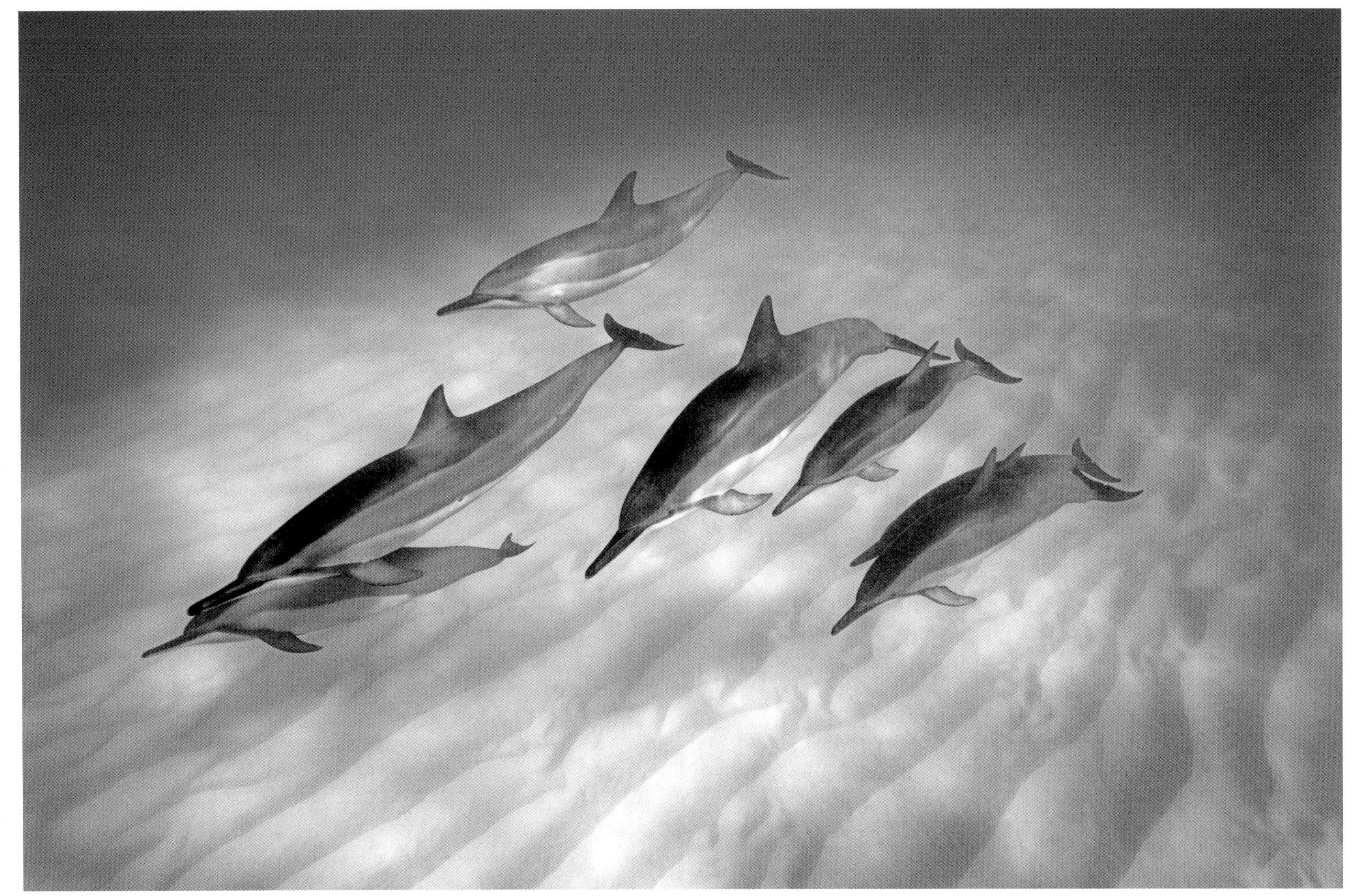

◀ spinner sandy bottom
▶ spinner school

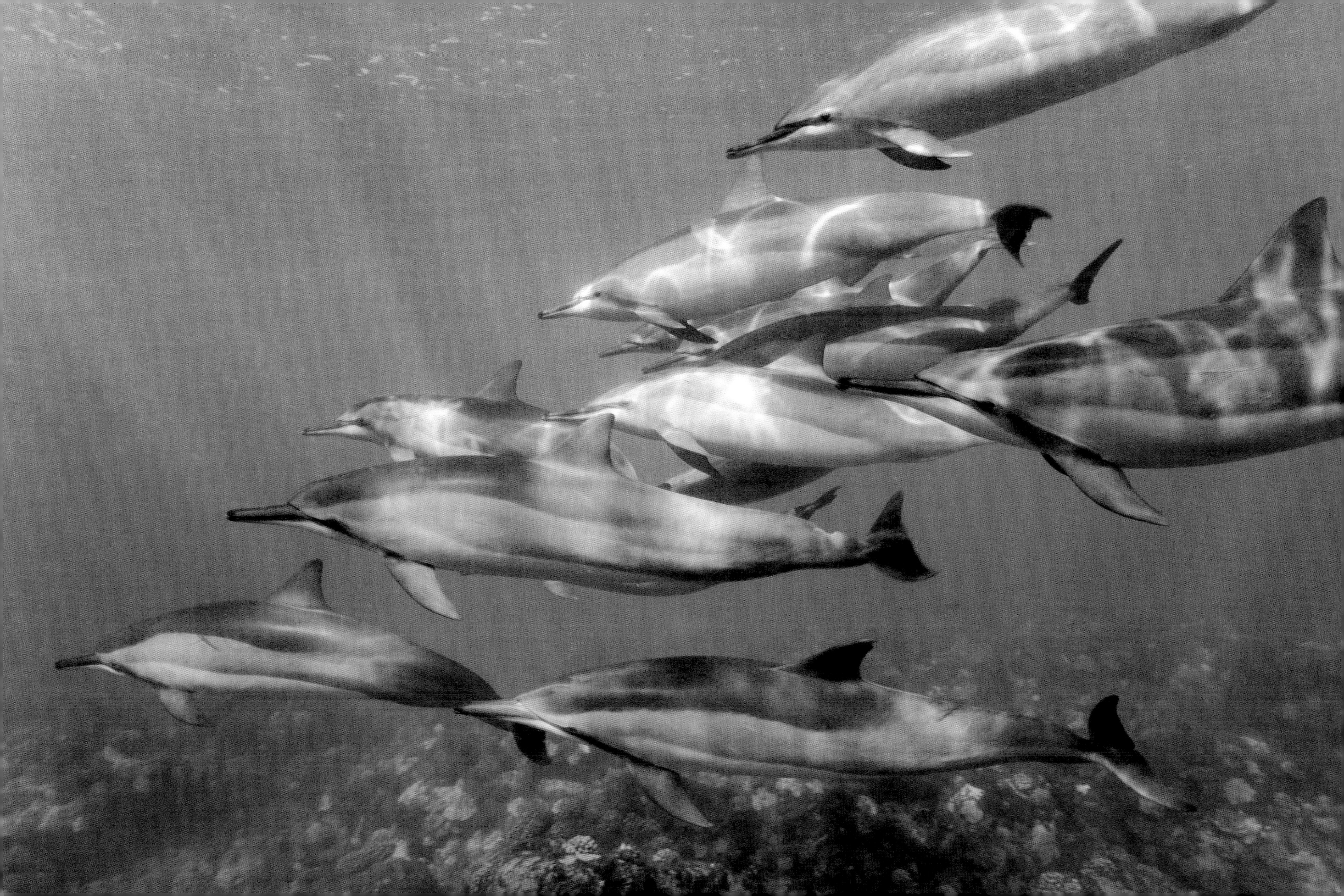

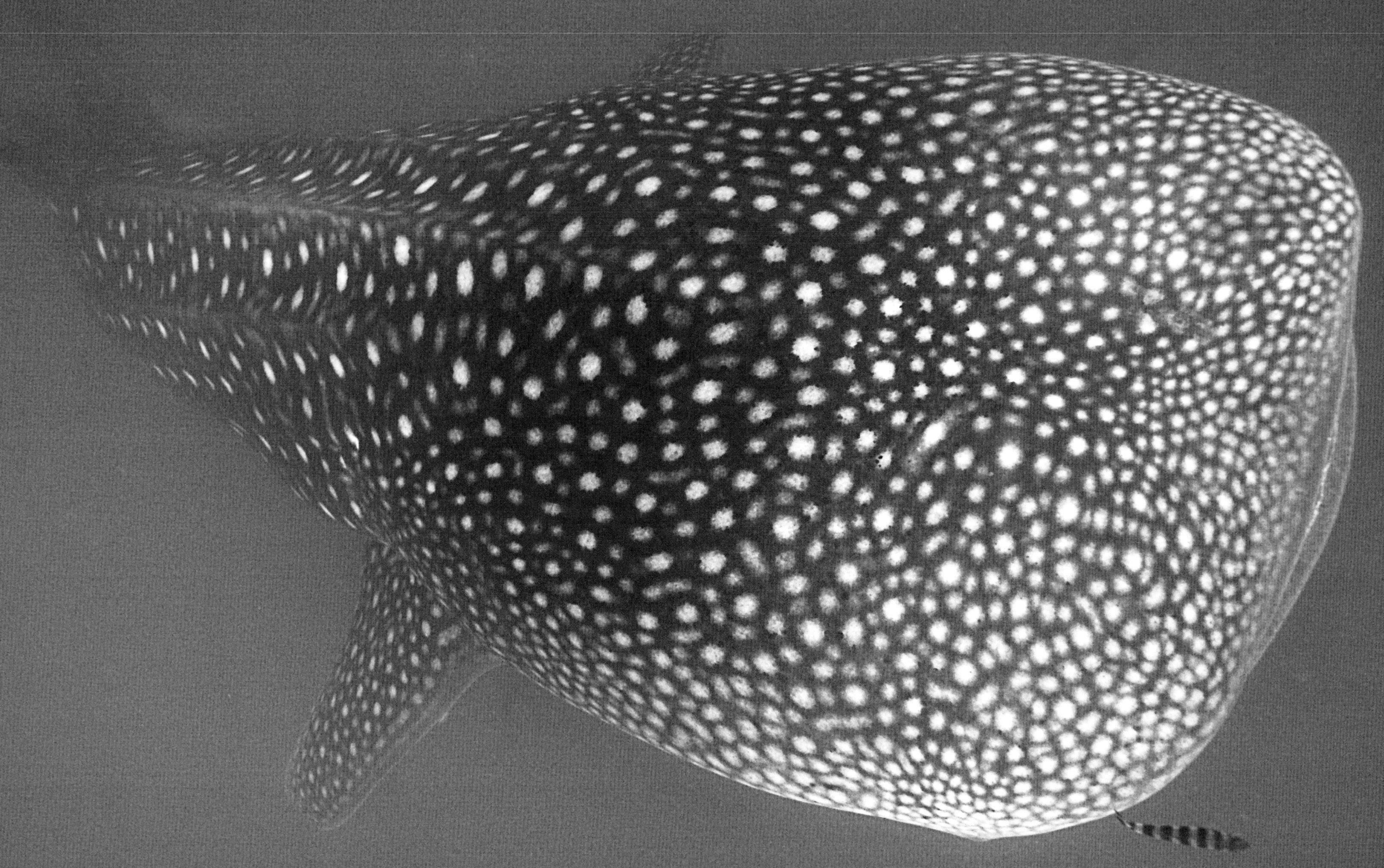

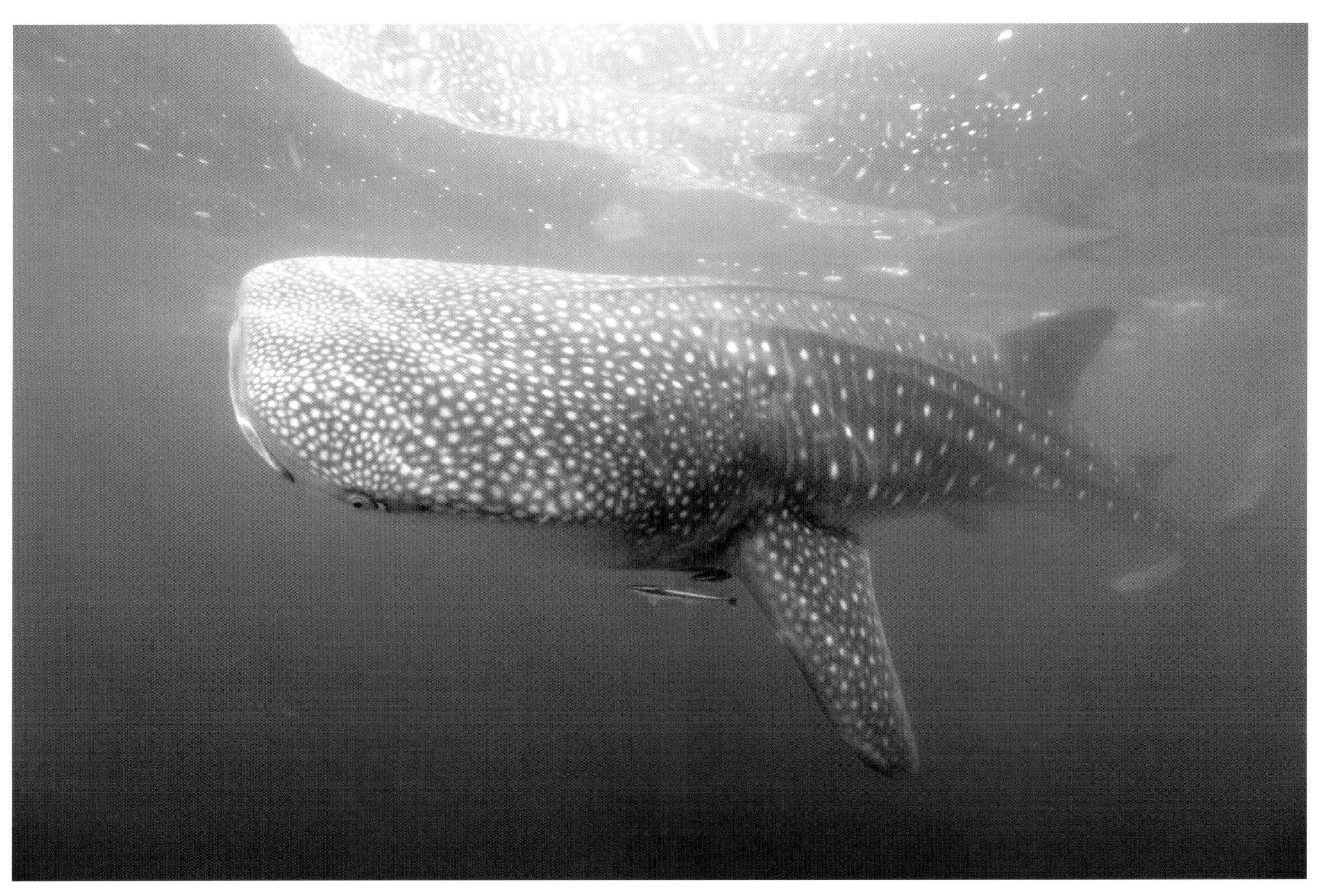

the pilot and the whale shark
gentle shark giant

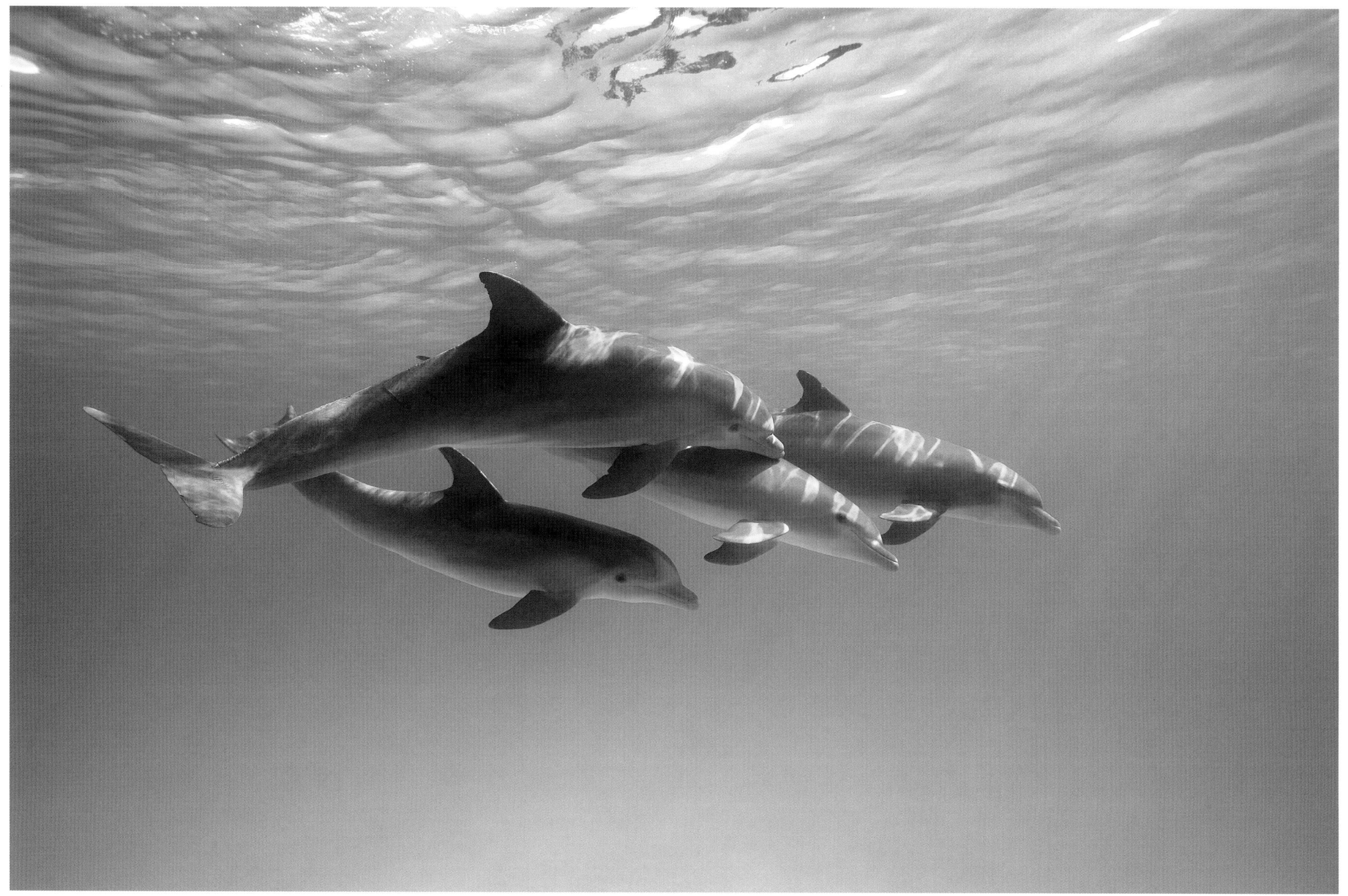

◄ dolphin friends
► playful bottlenose dolphins

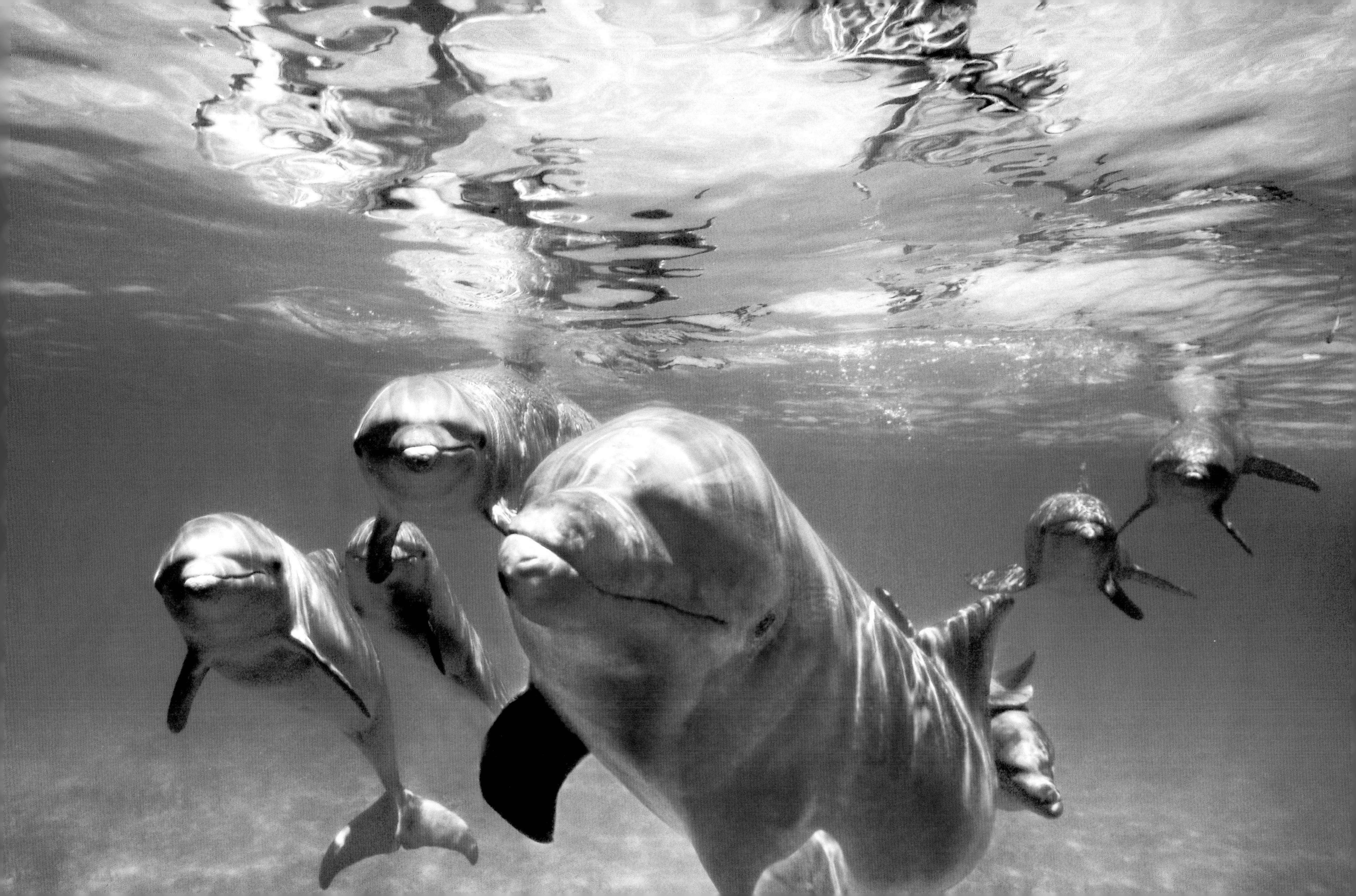

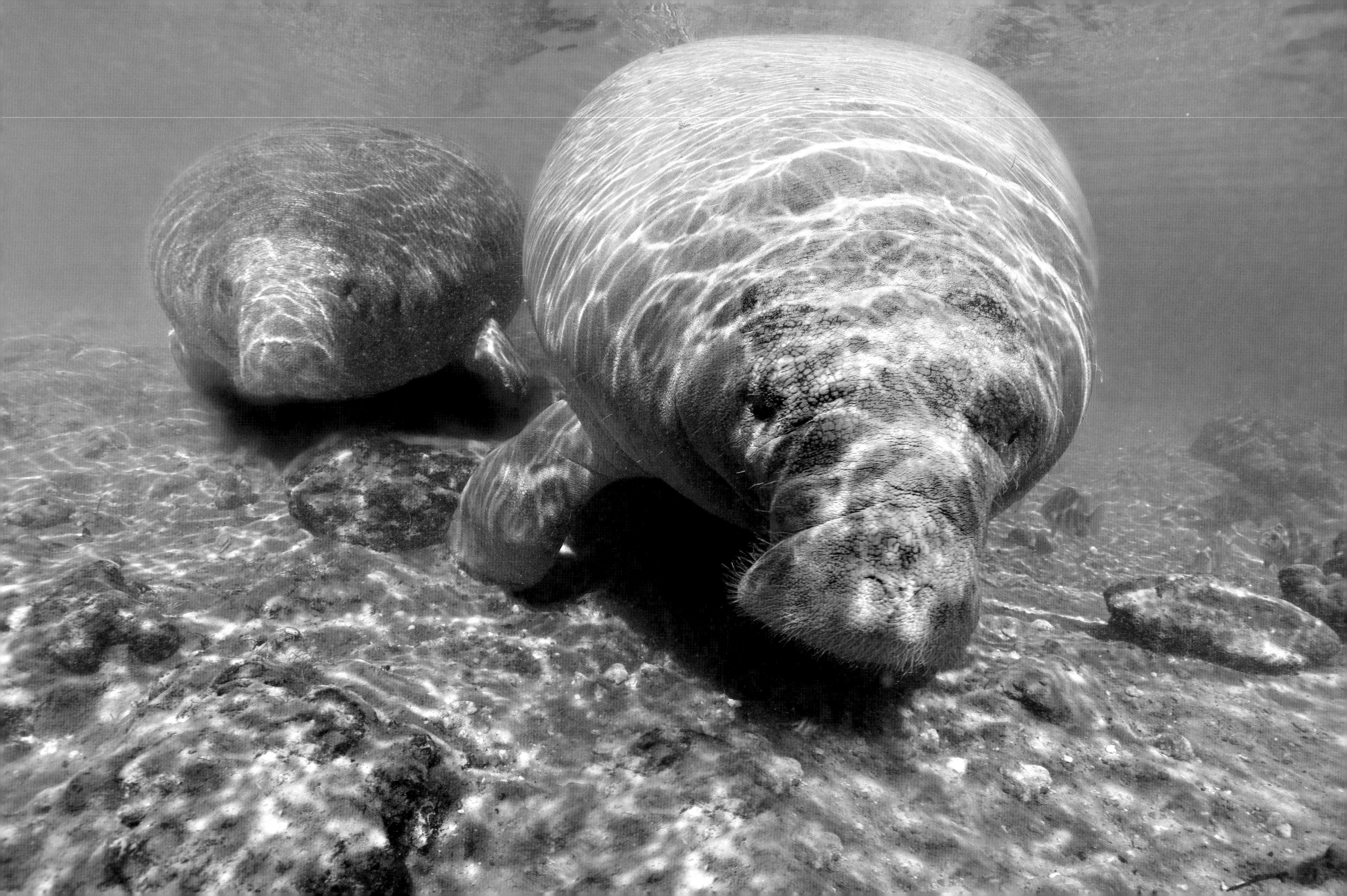

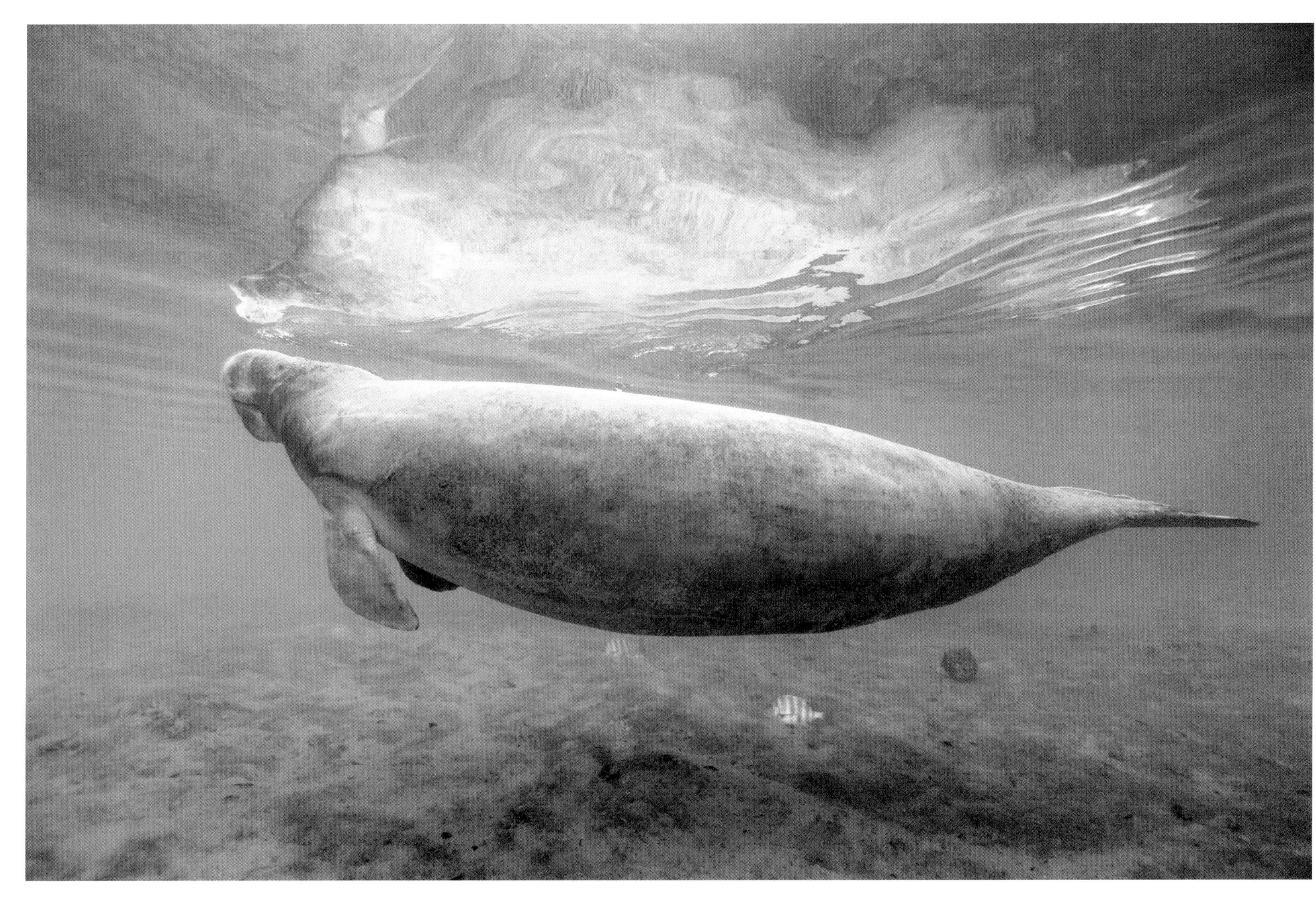

◀ mother manatee
▶ manatee at the surface

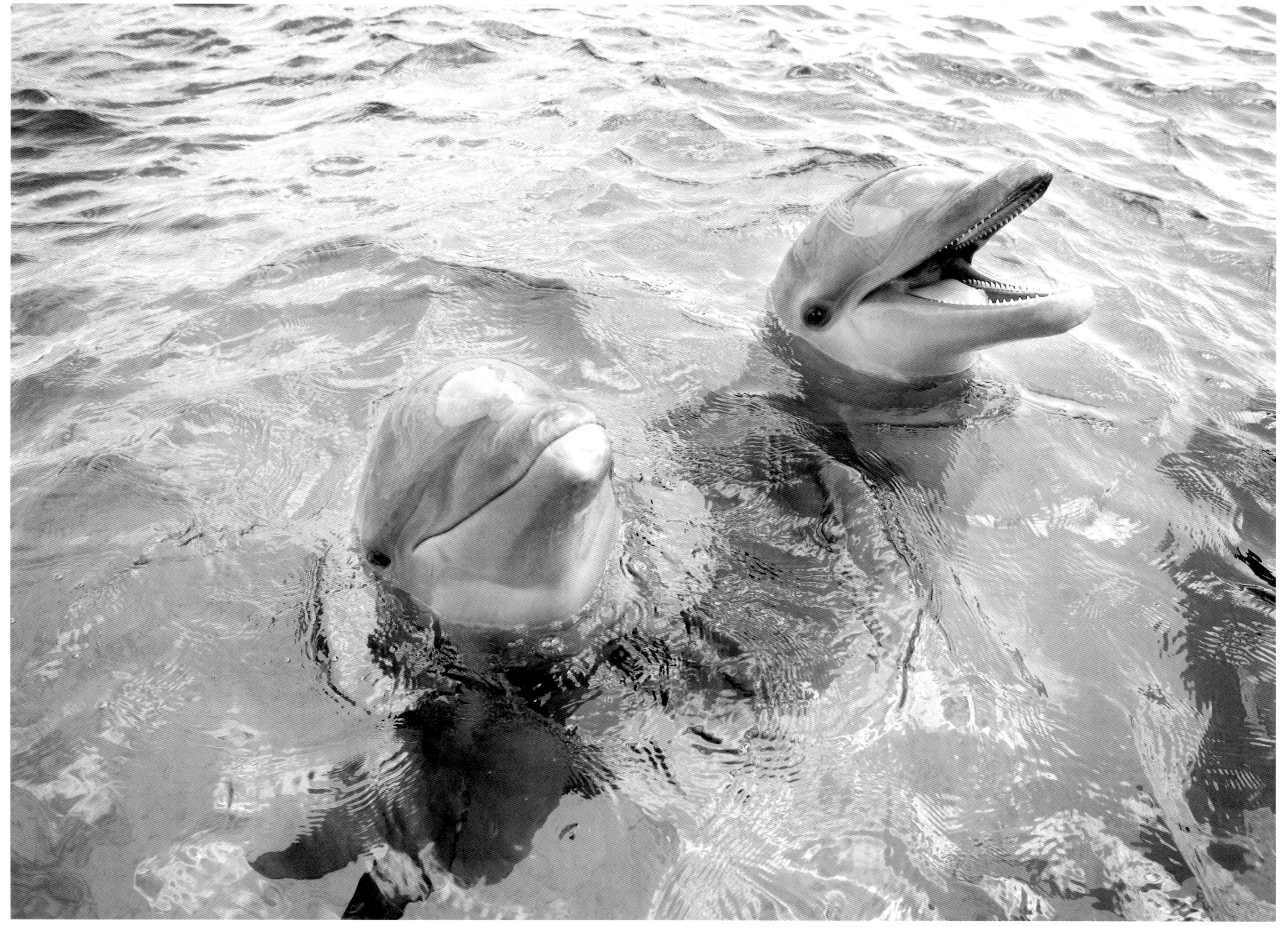

◄ dolphin play
► happy dolphin

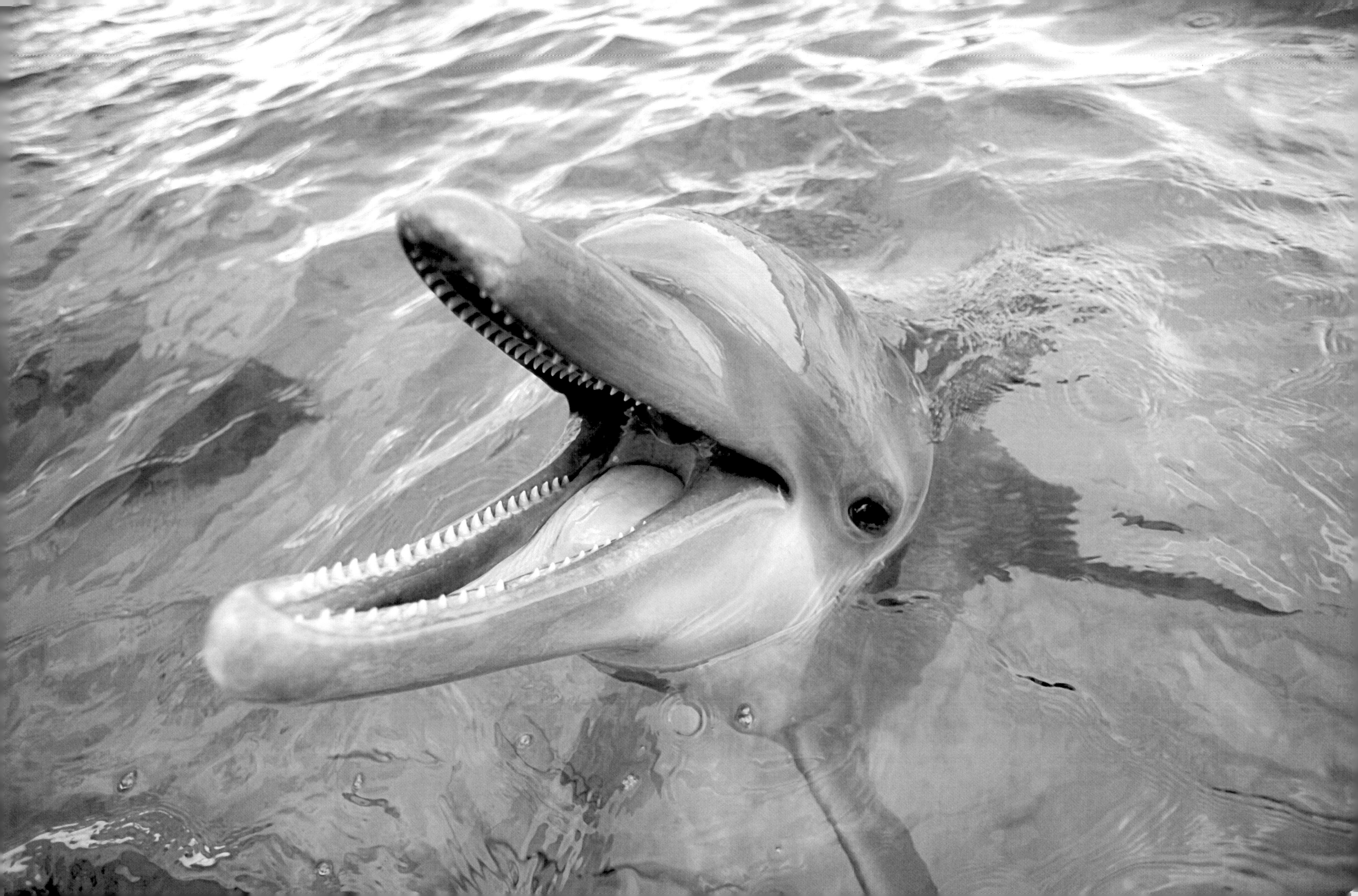

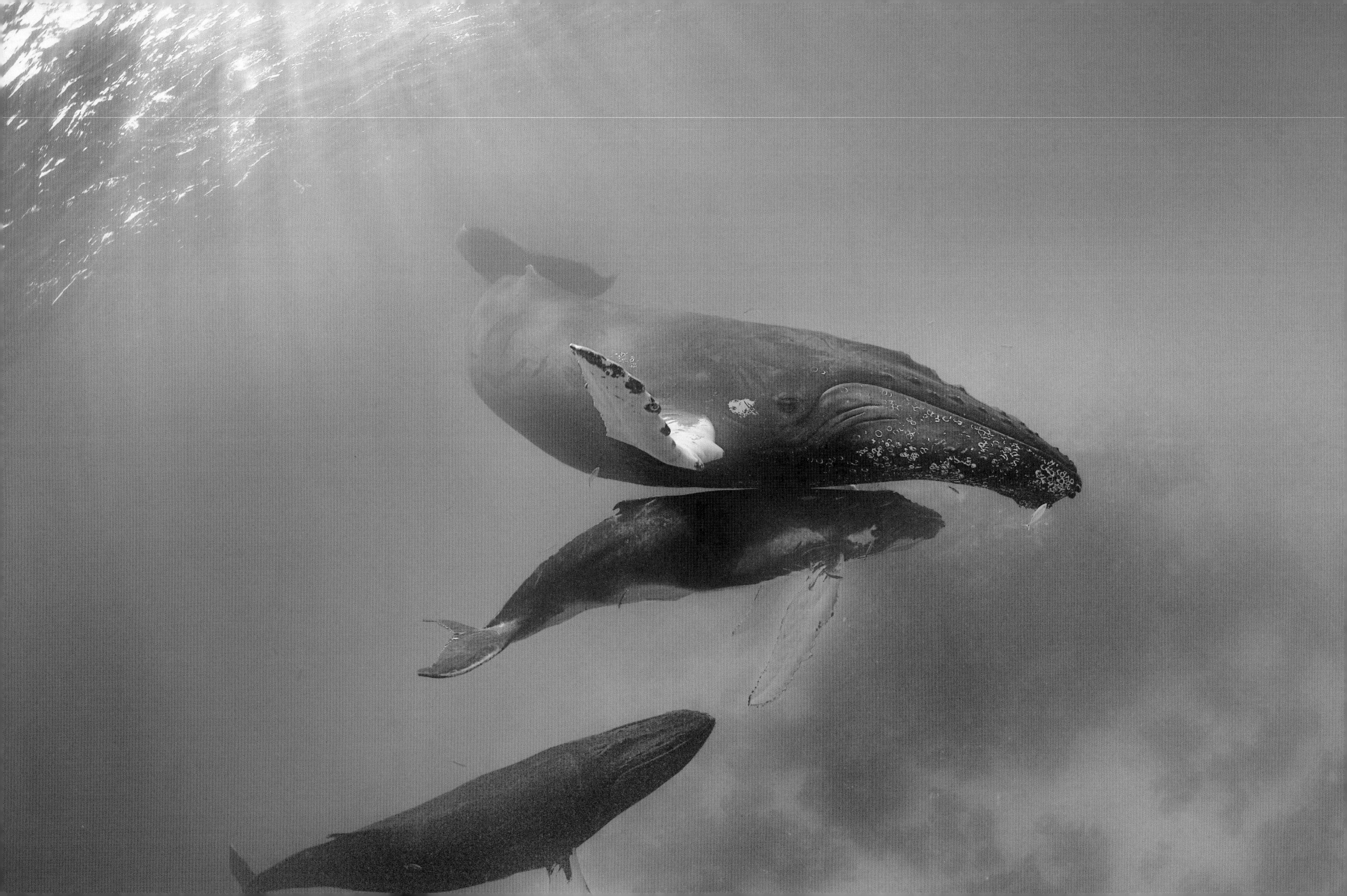

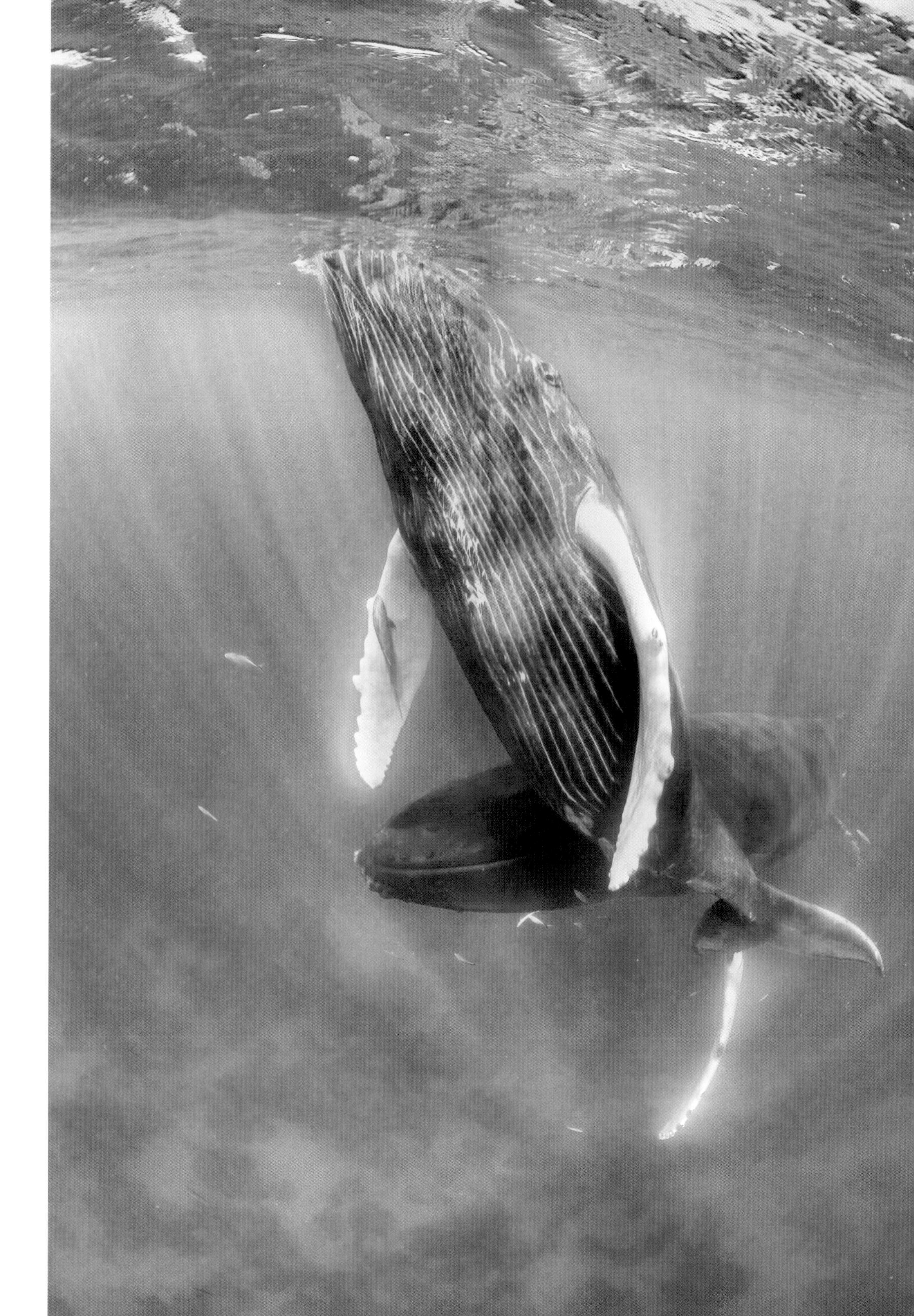

◄ born in the sea
► new calf below

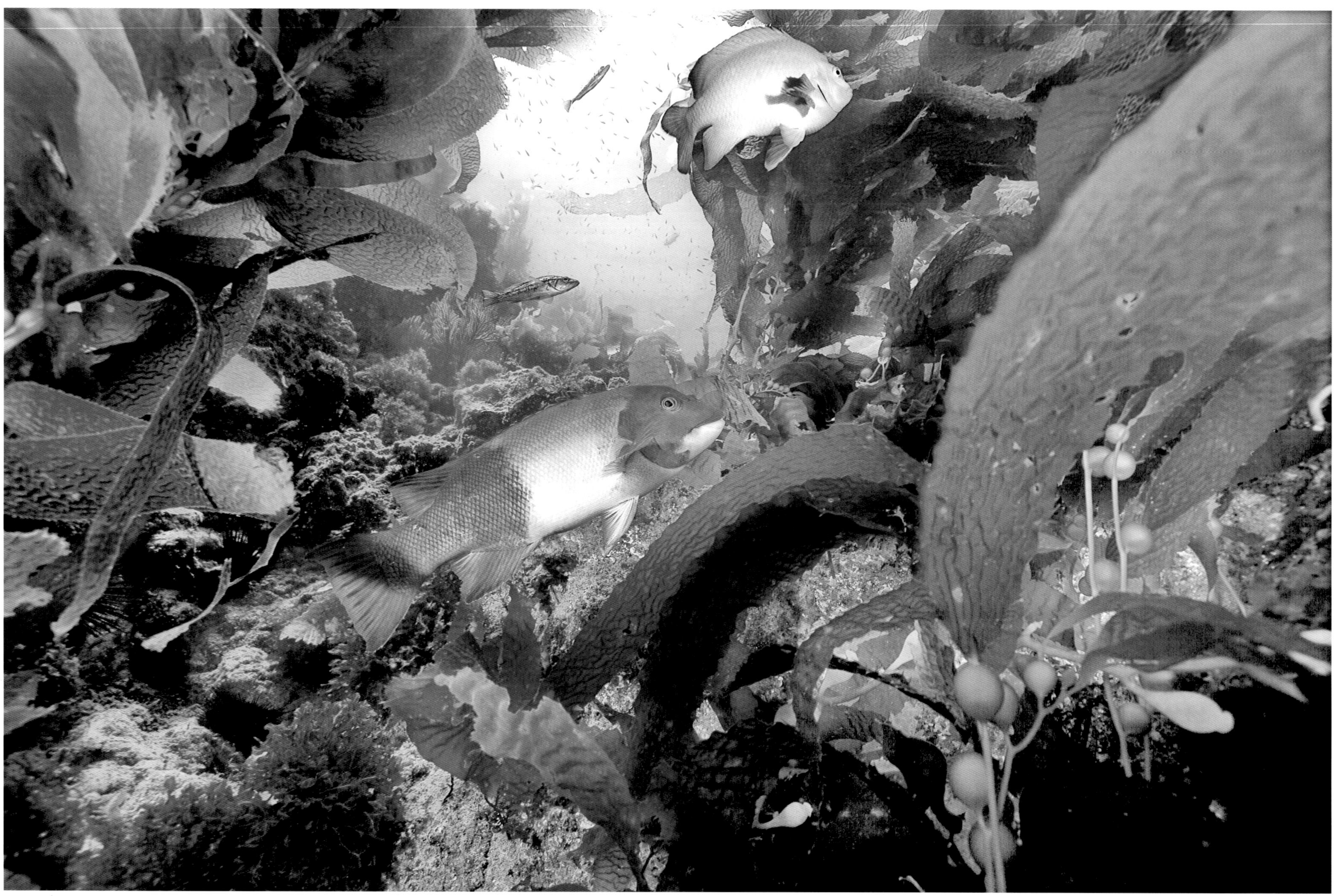

◄ sheepshead kelp forest
► peaceful seas

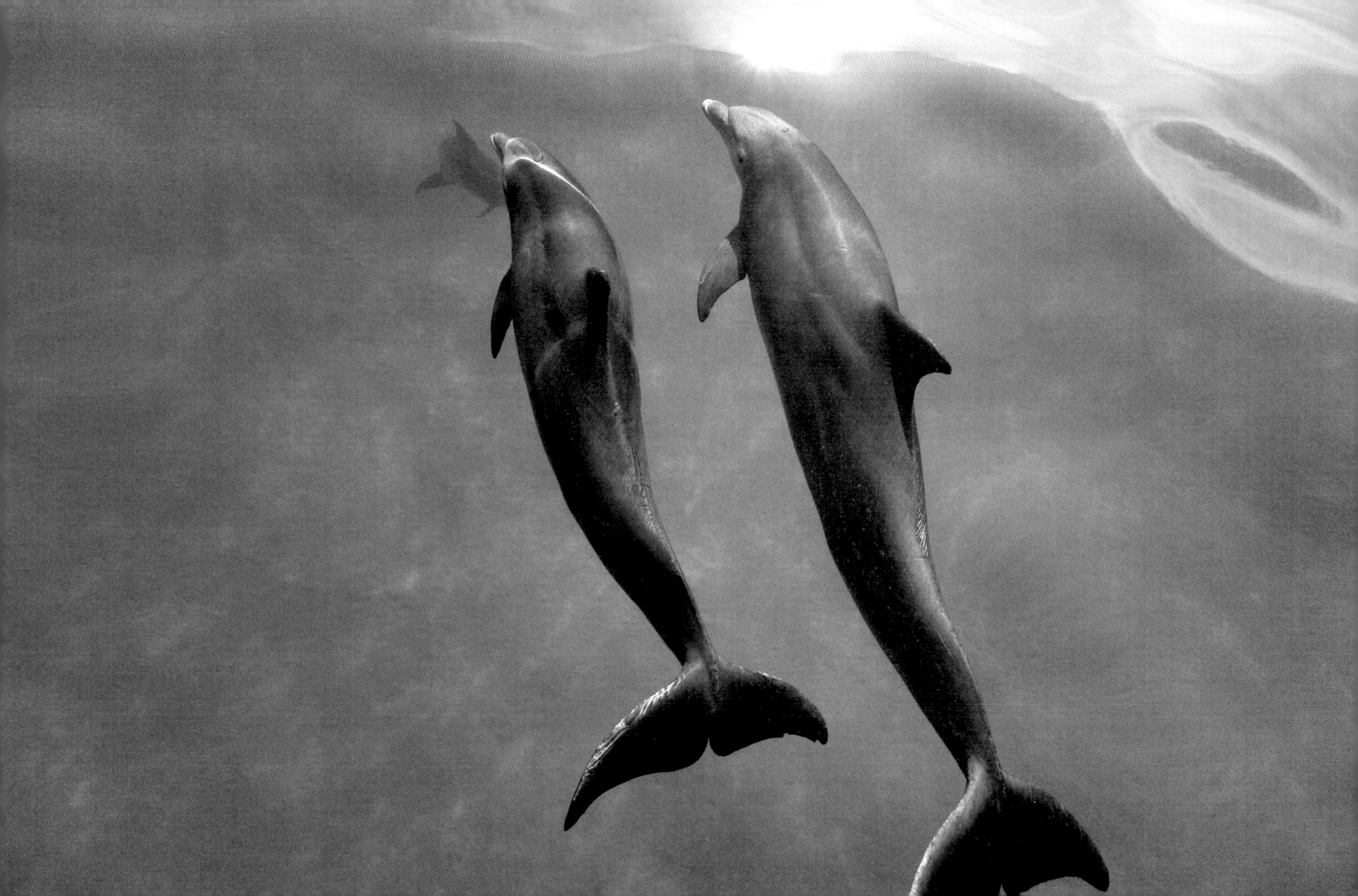

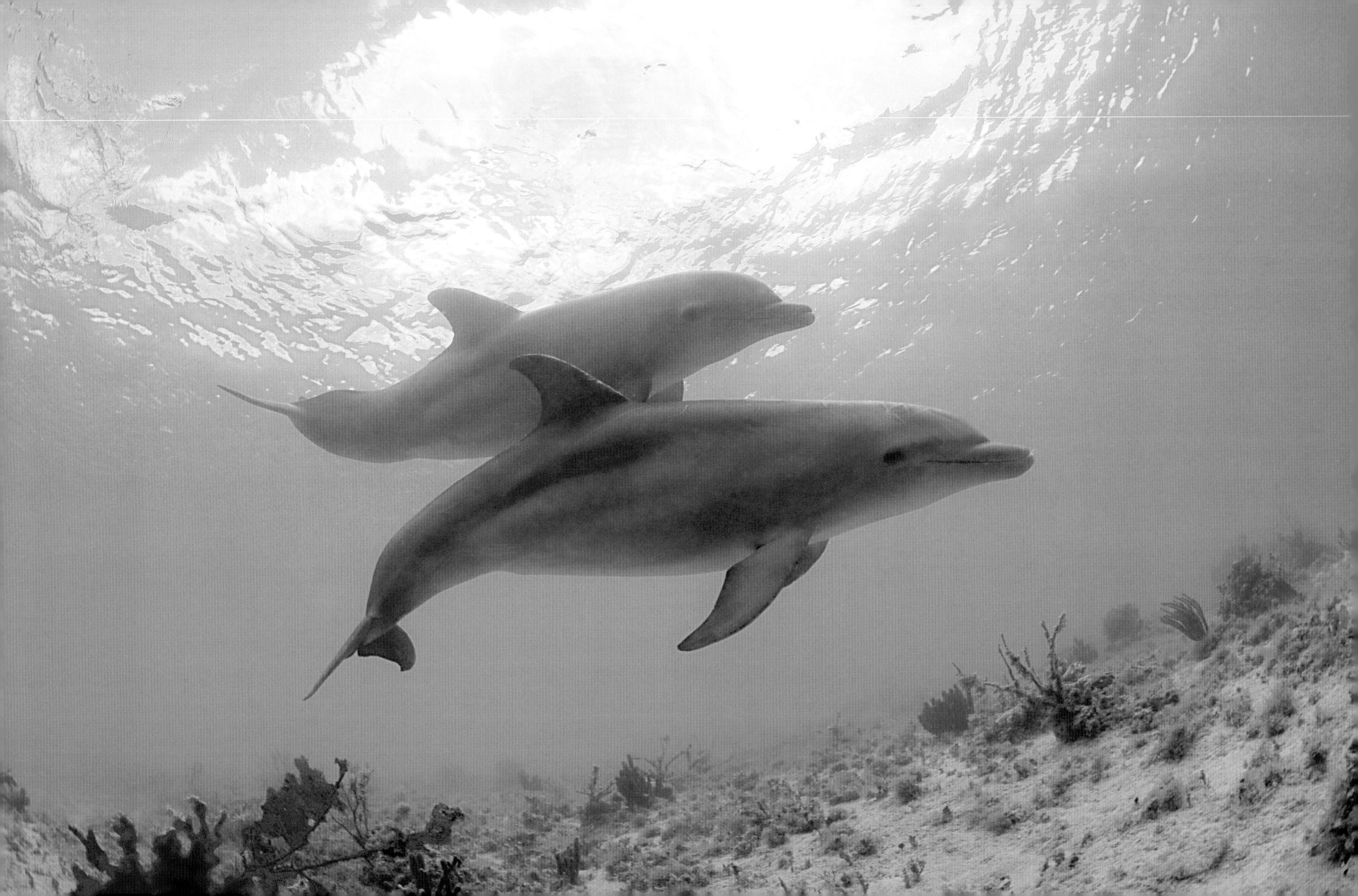

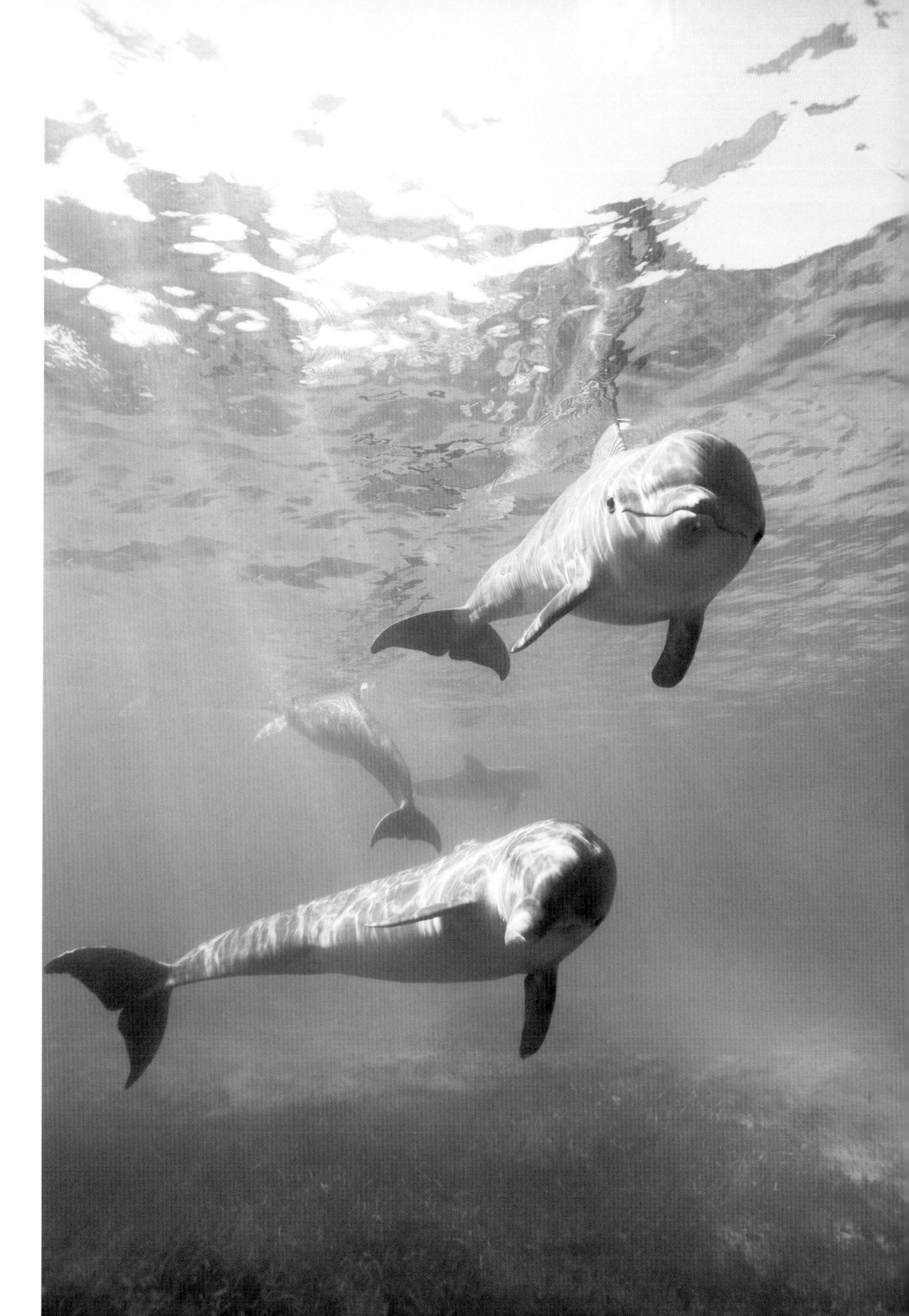

◀ dolphins below
▶ dolphin welcome

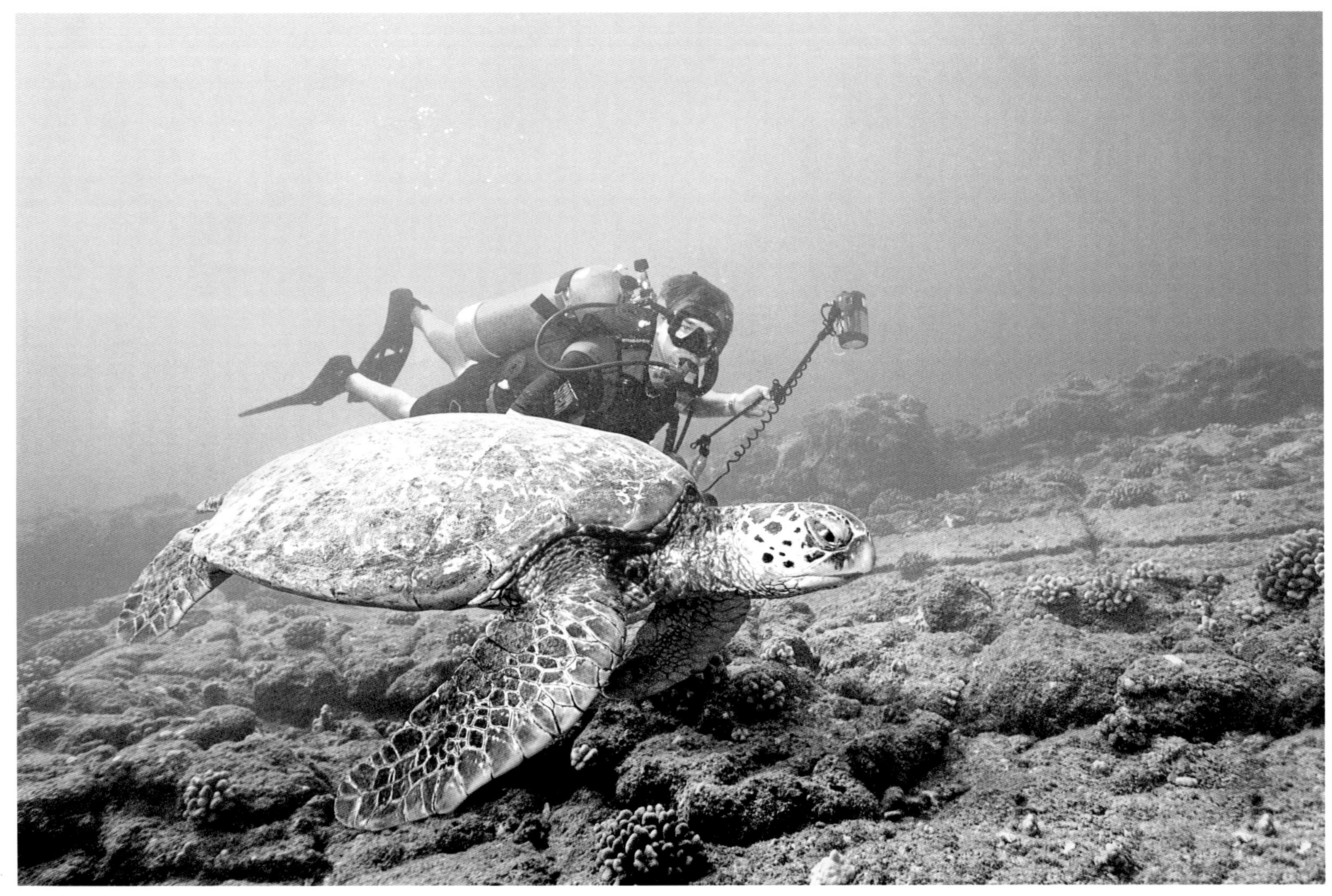

◄ wyland sea turtle dive
► sea turtle beach

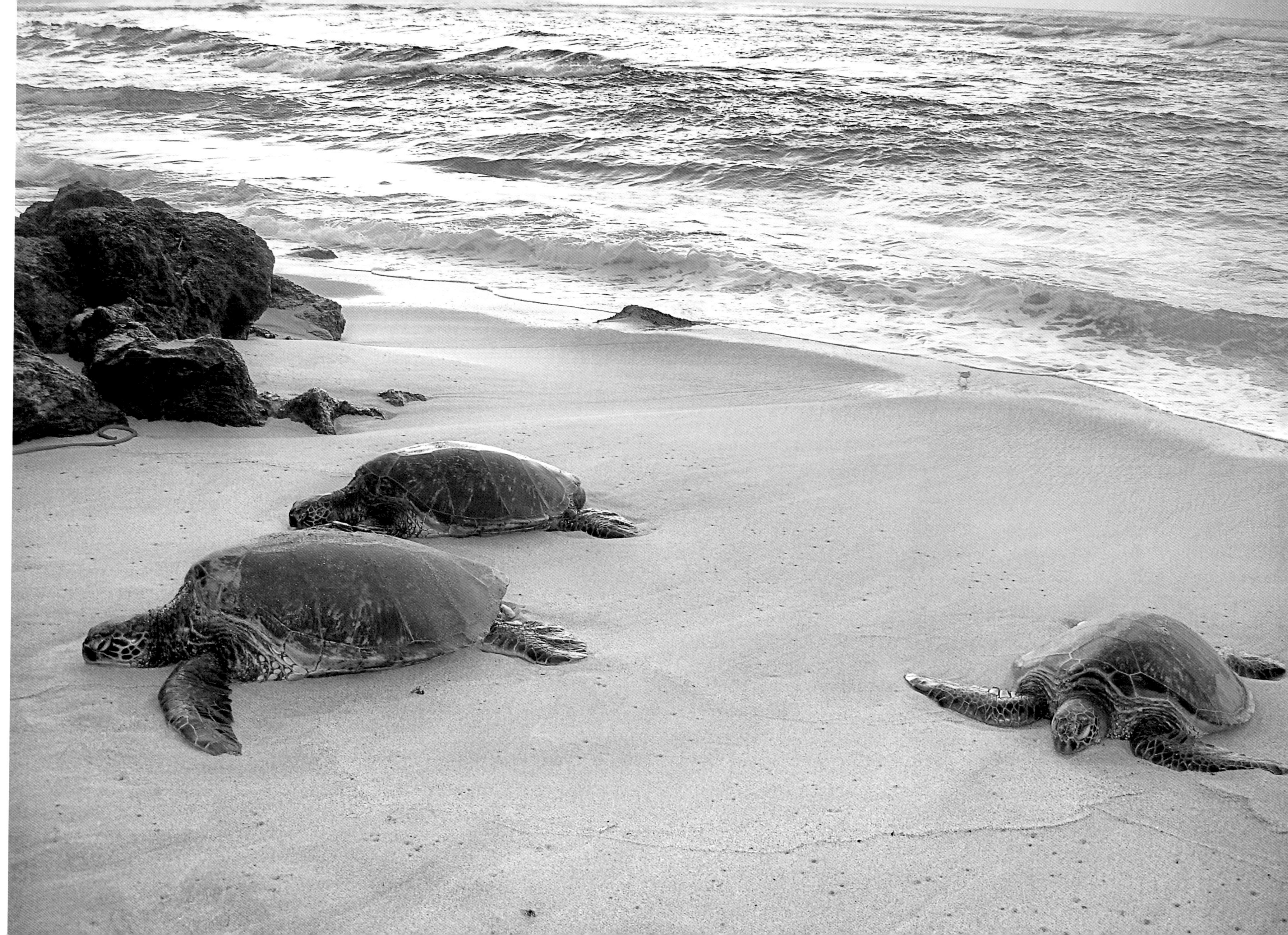

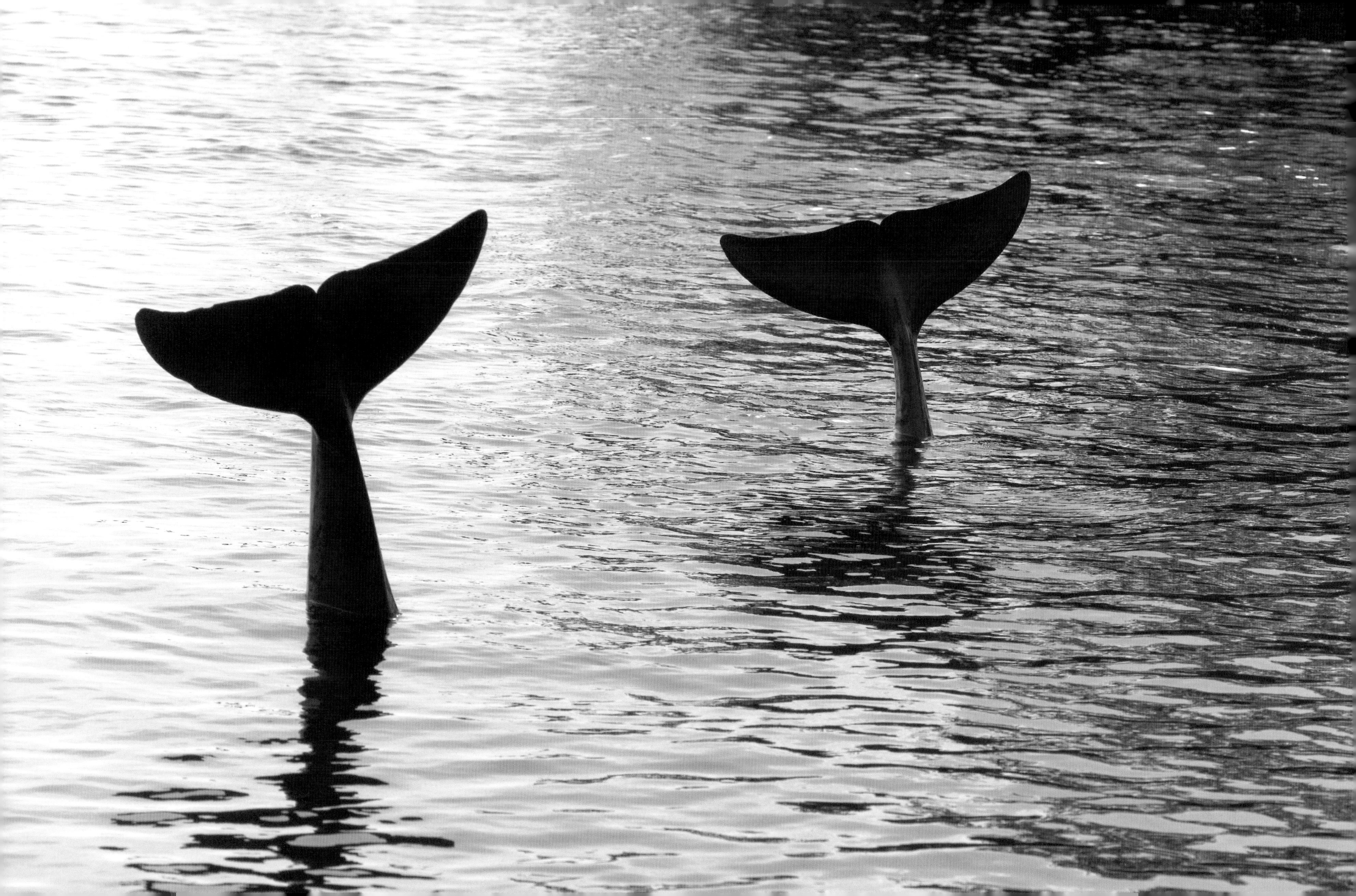

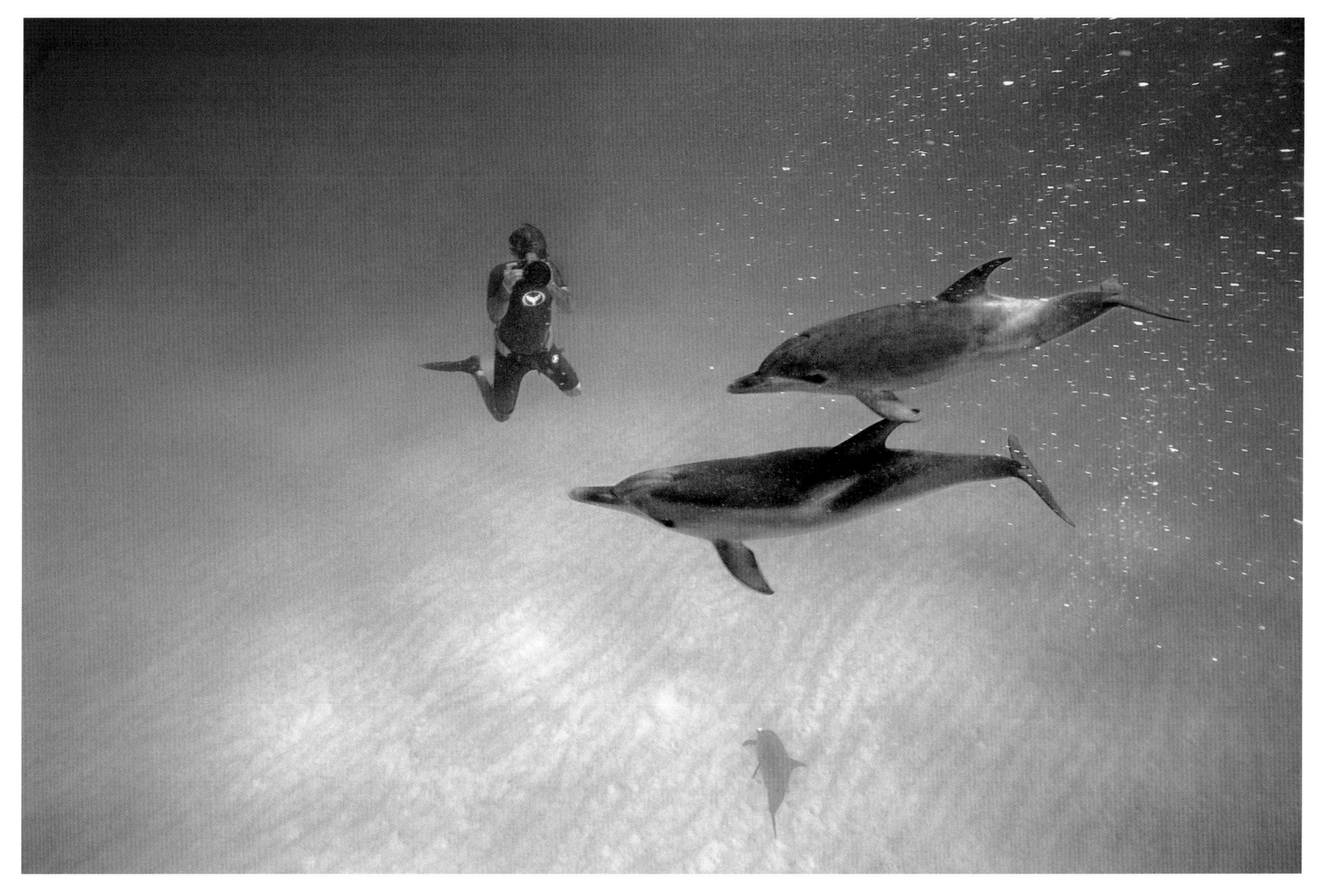

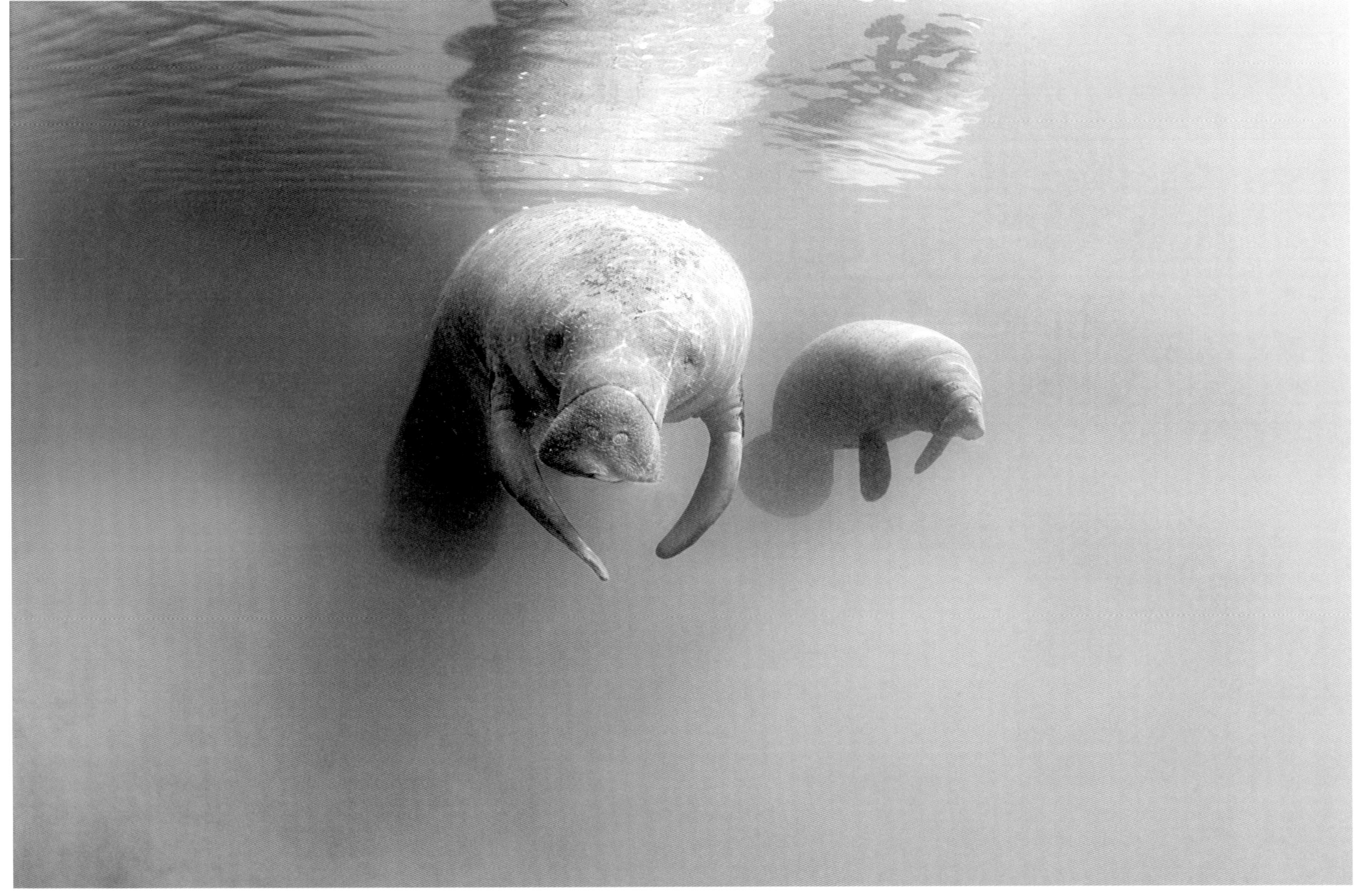

◄ manatee newborn
▶ manatee in the sea grass

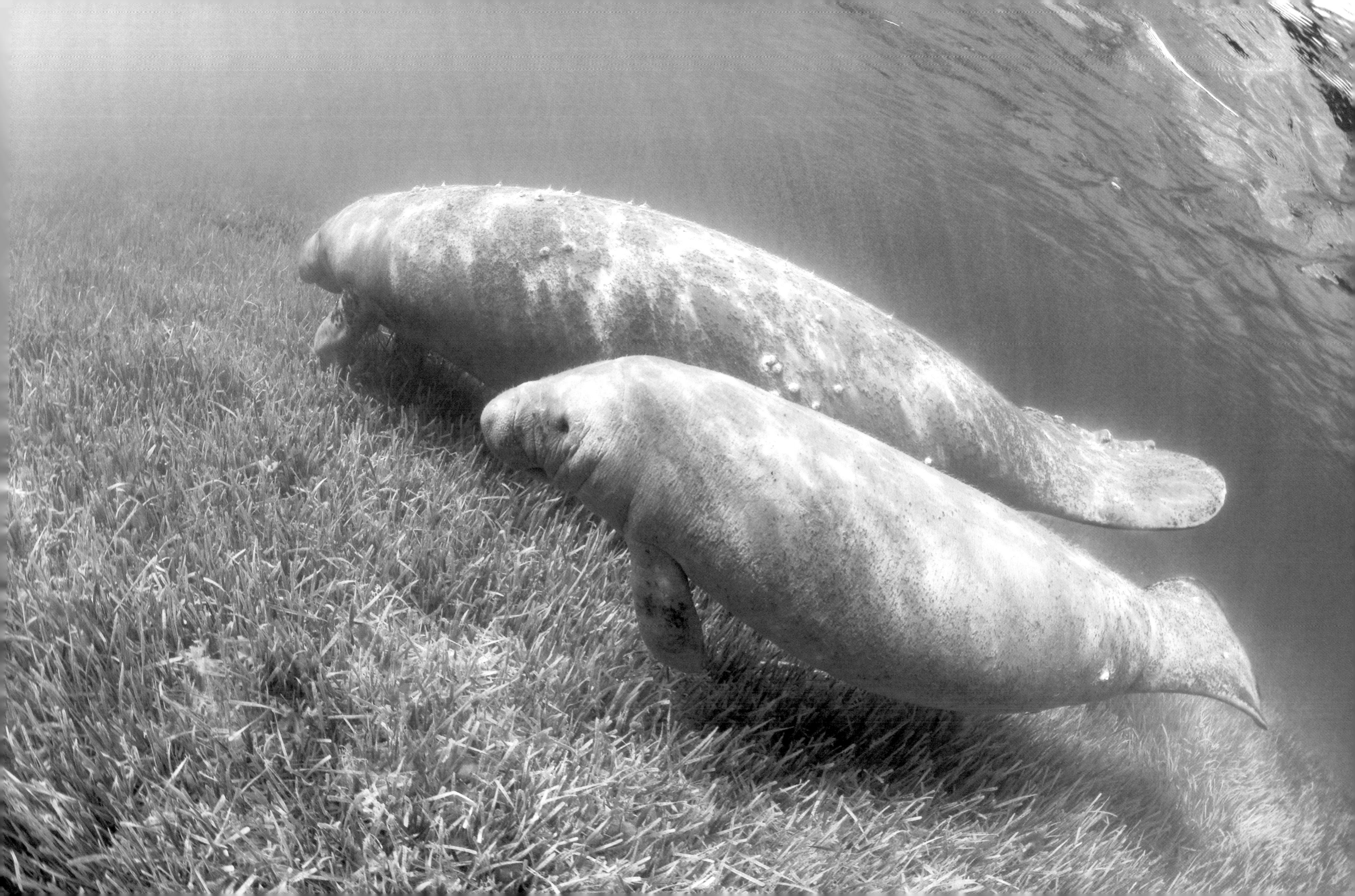

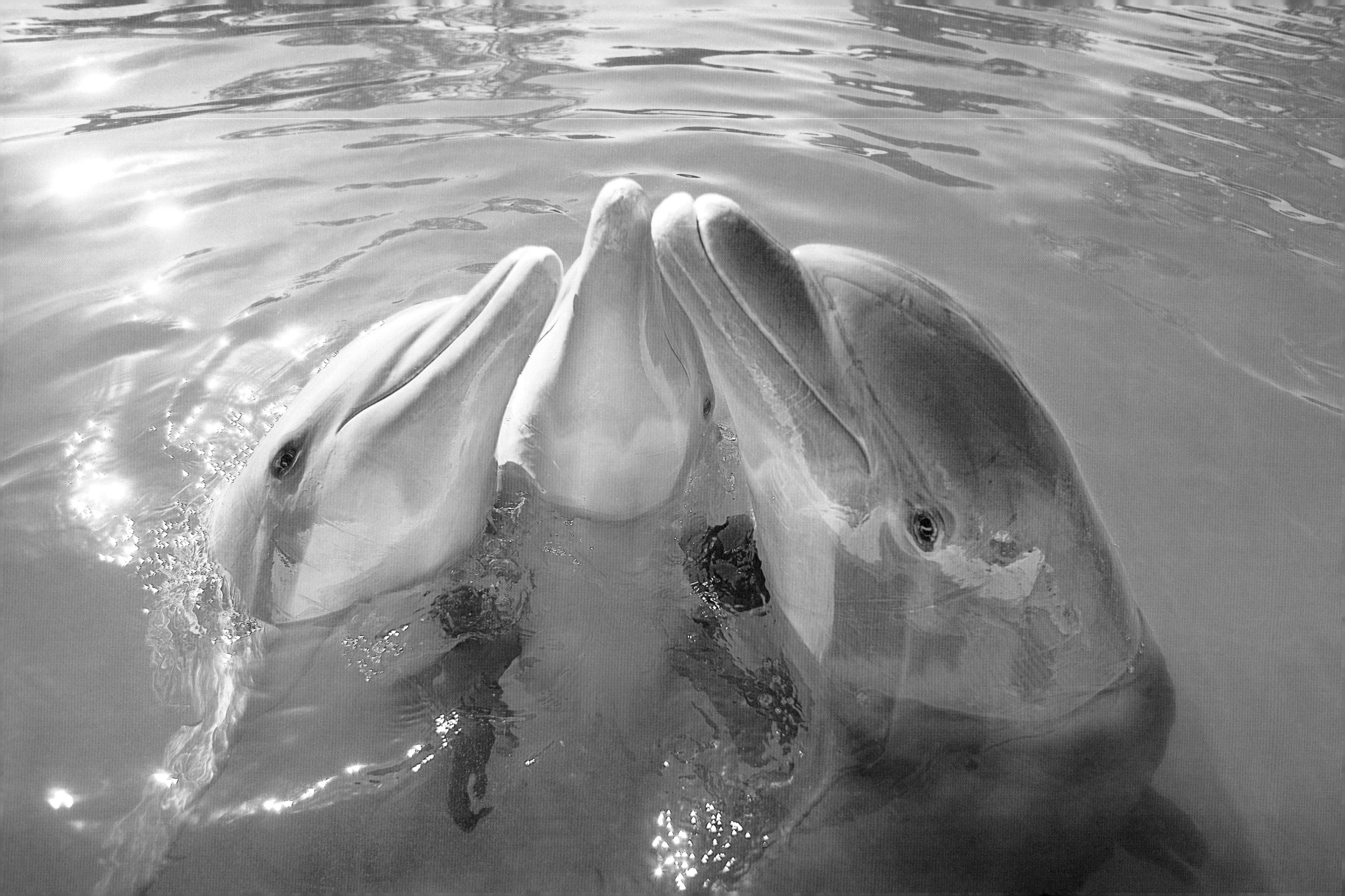

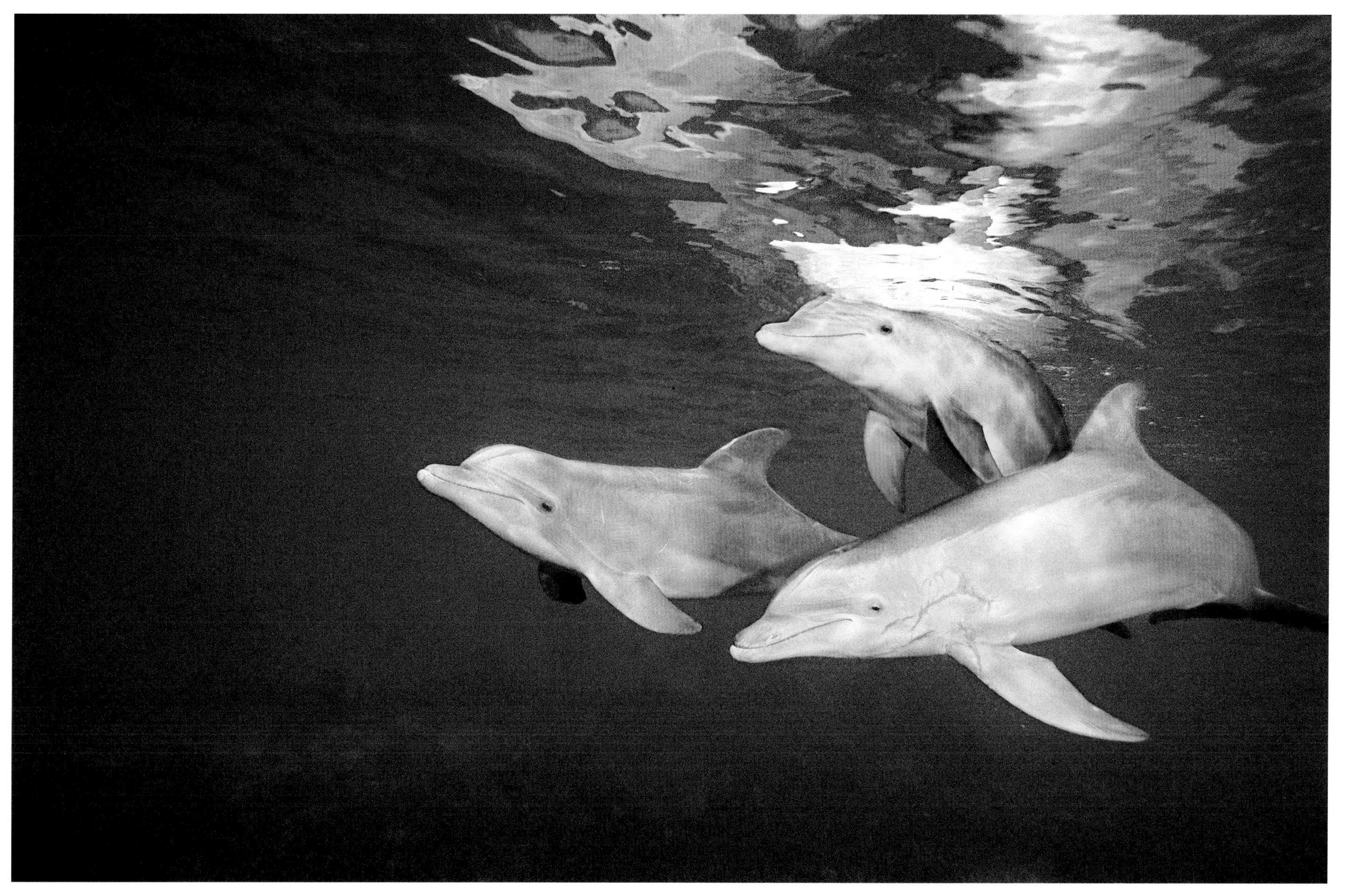

dolphins surface
dolphin reflection

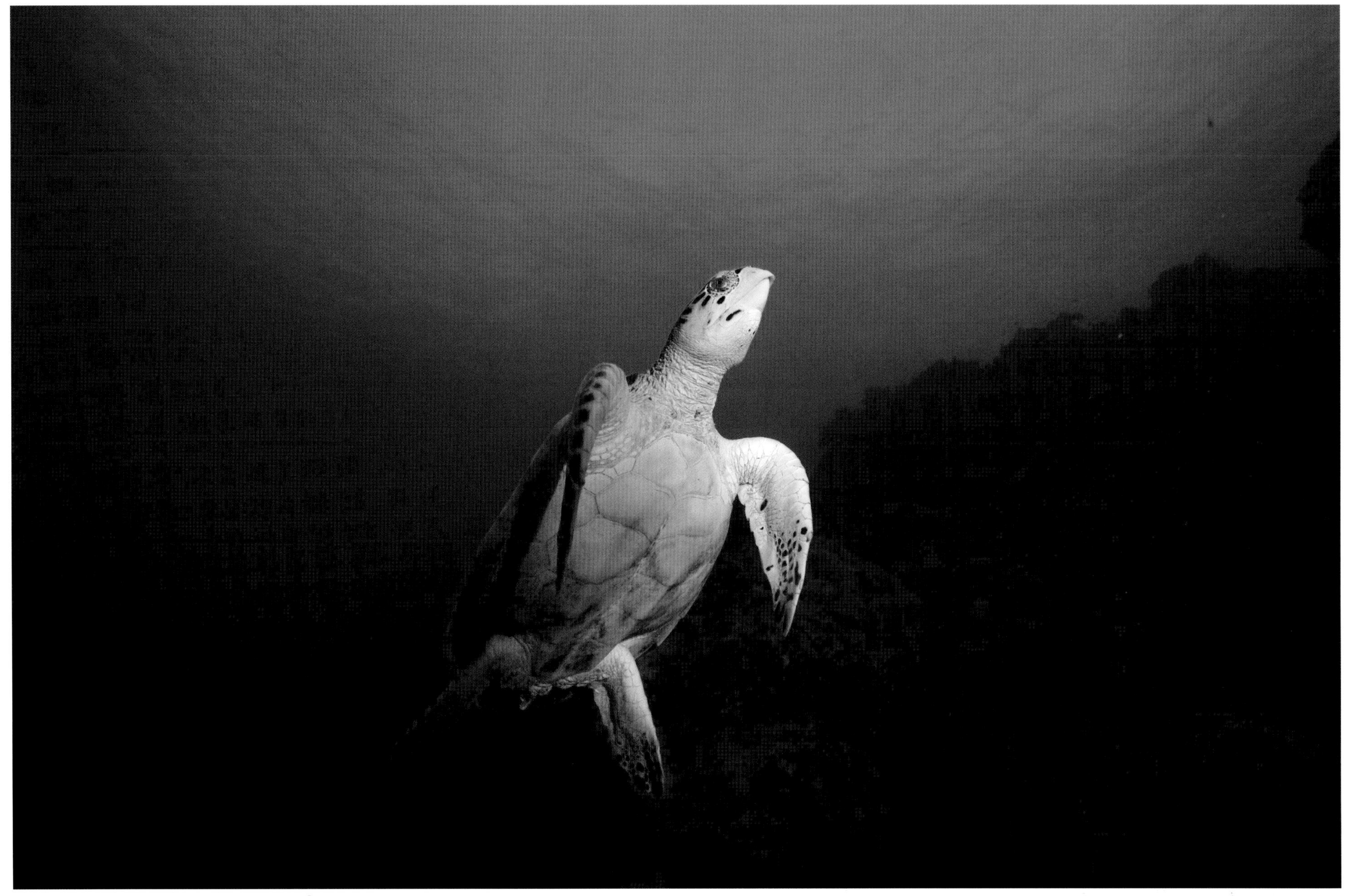

◀ sea turtle rising
▶ turtle ship wreck

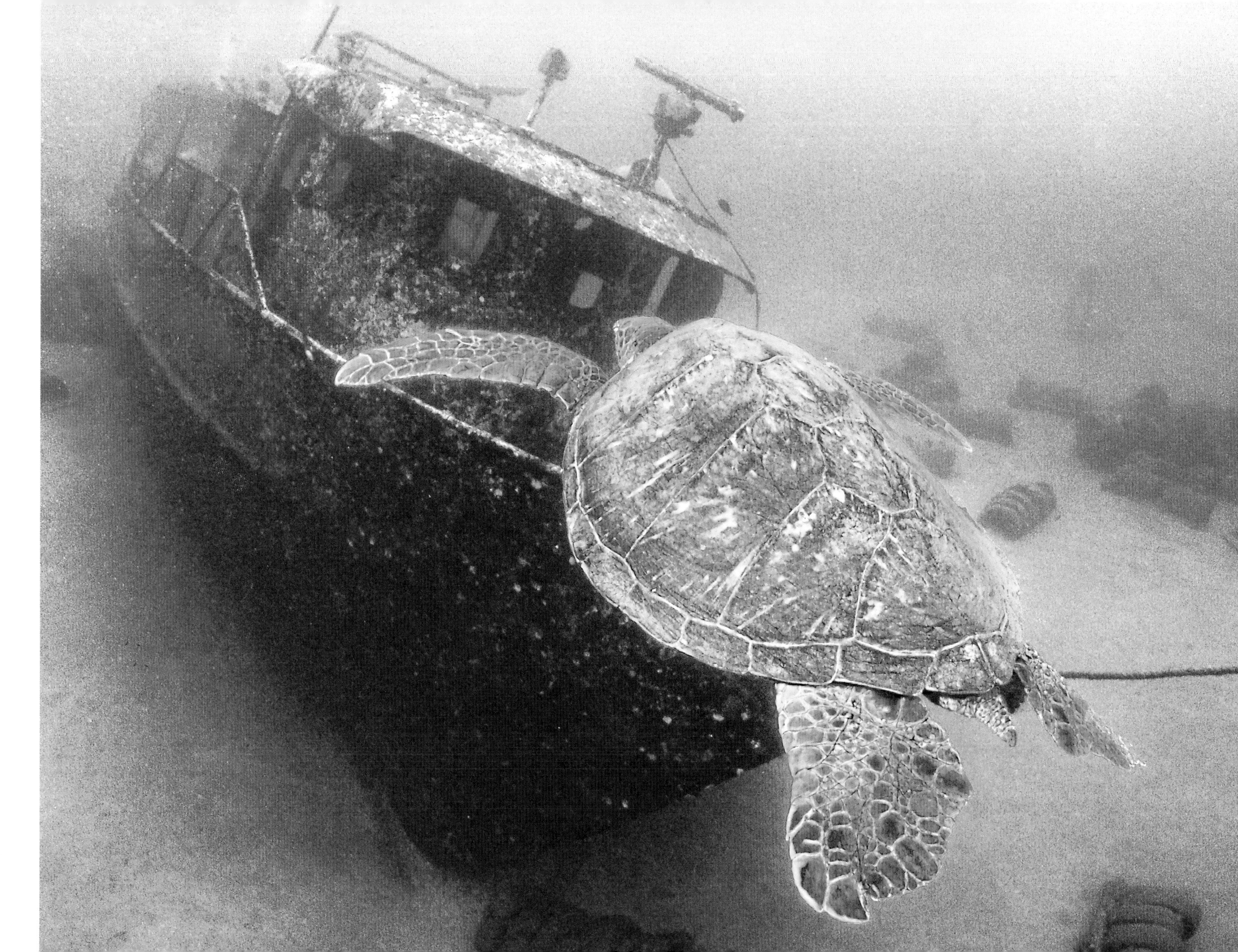

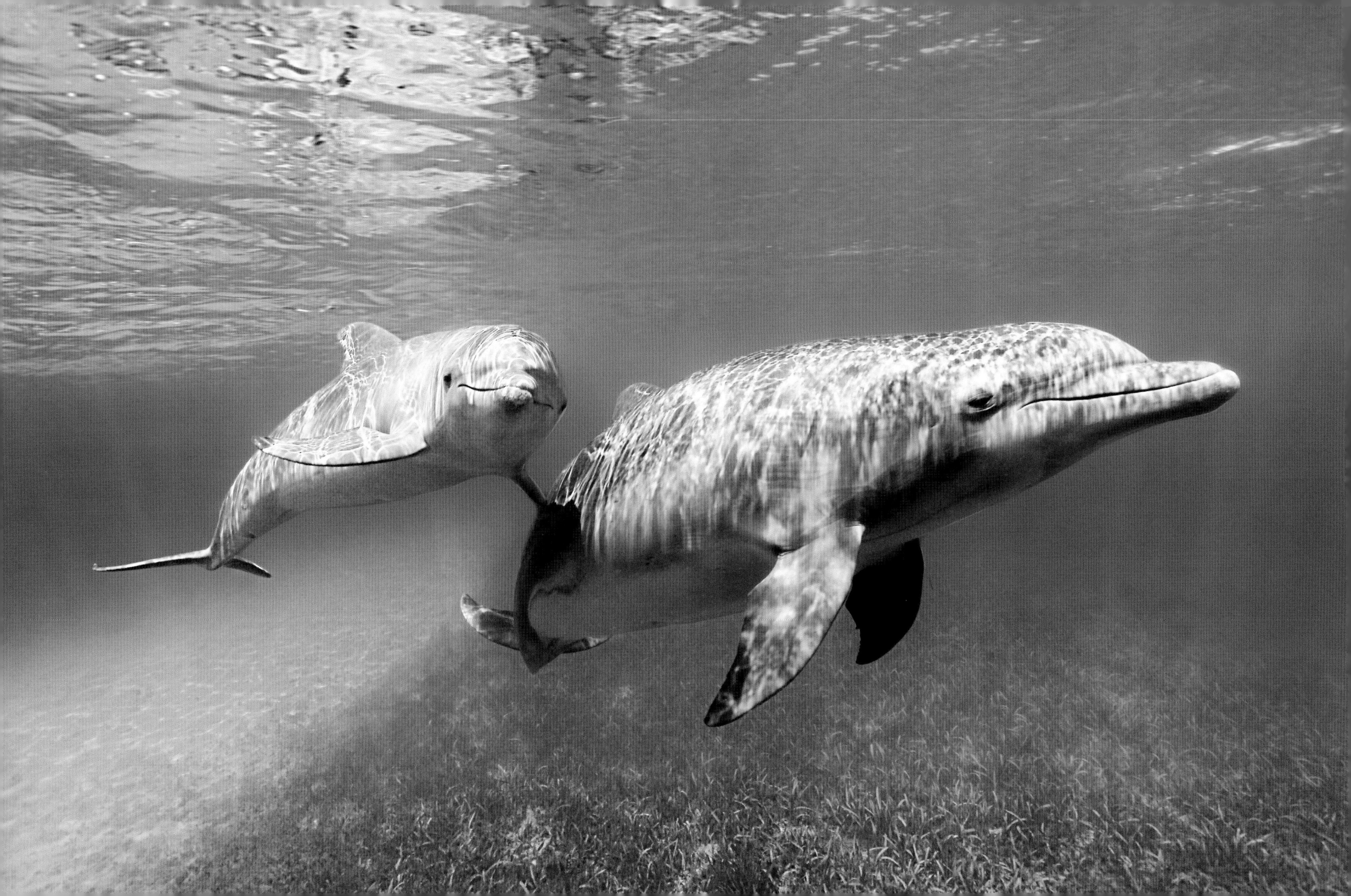

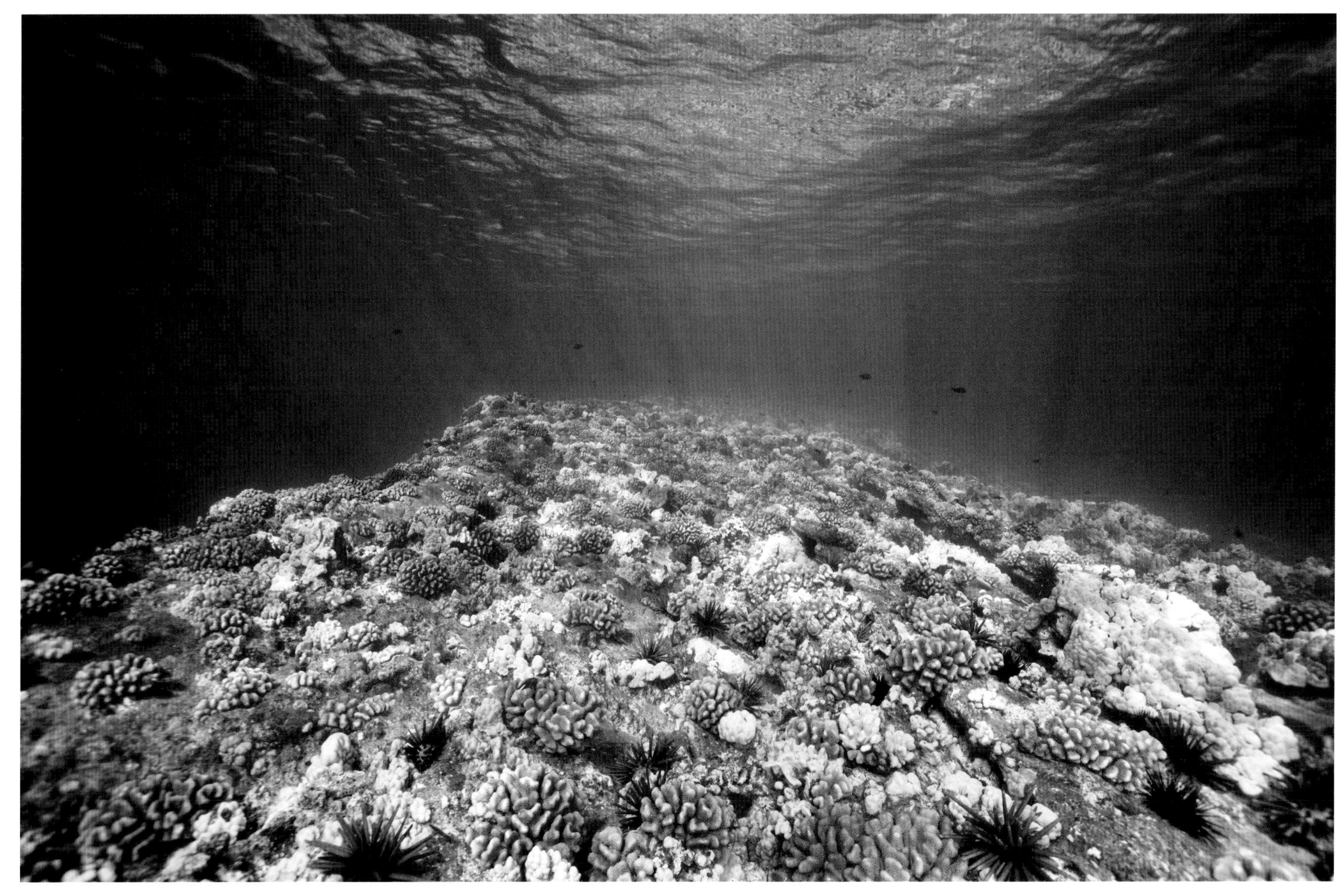

◀ dolphin and baby below
▶ living coral

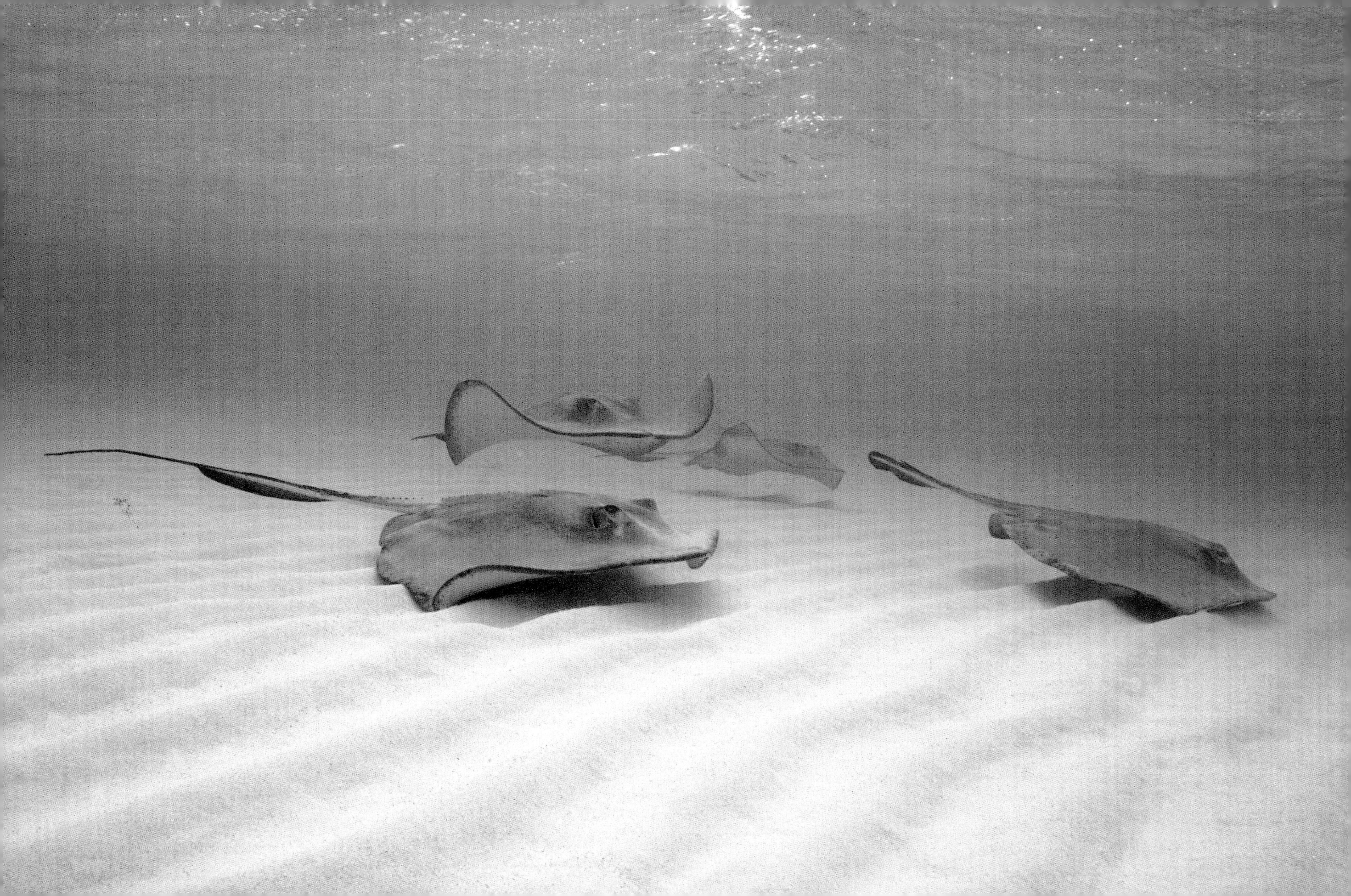

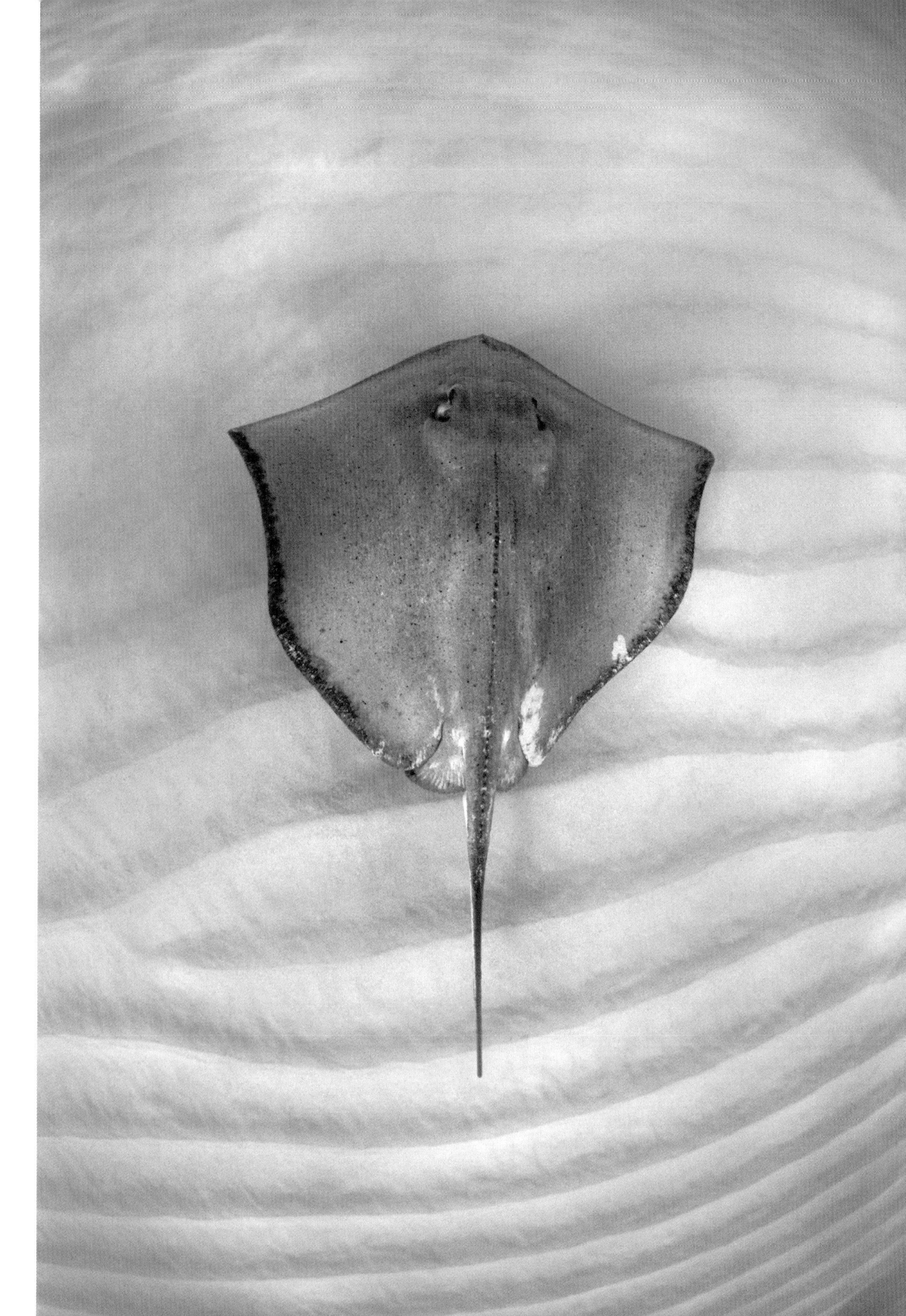

cayman rays
sting ray below

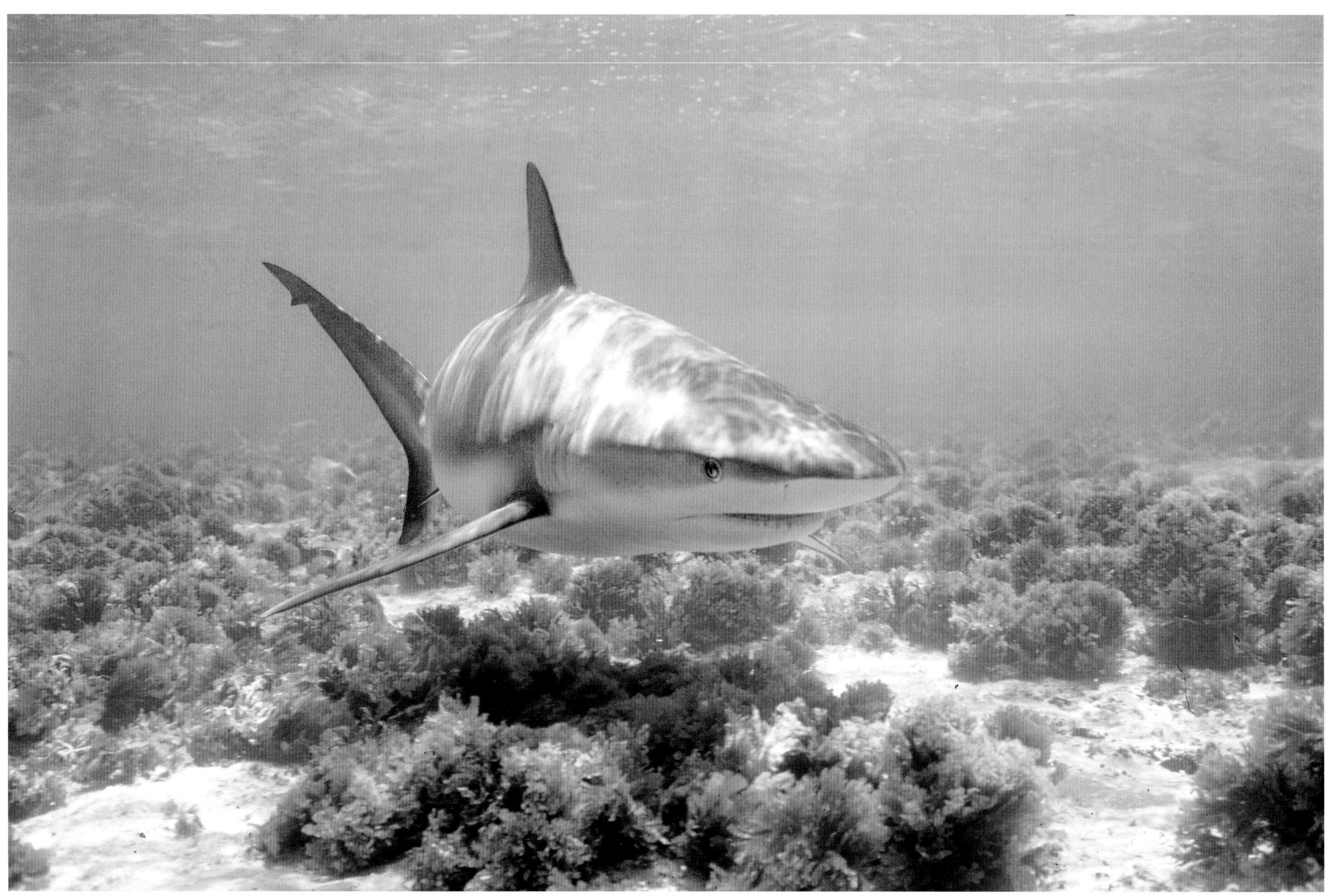

◄ bull shark encounter
► kiss the sea

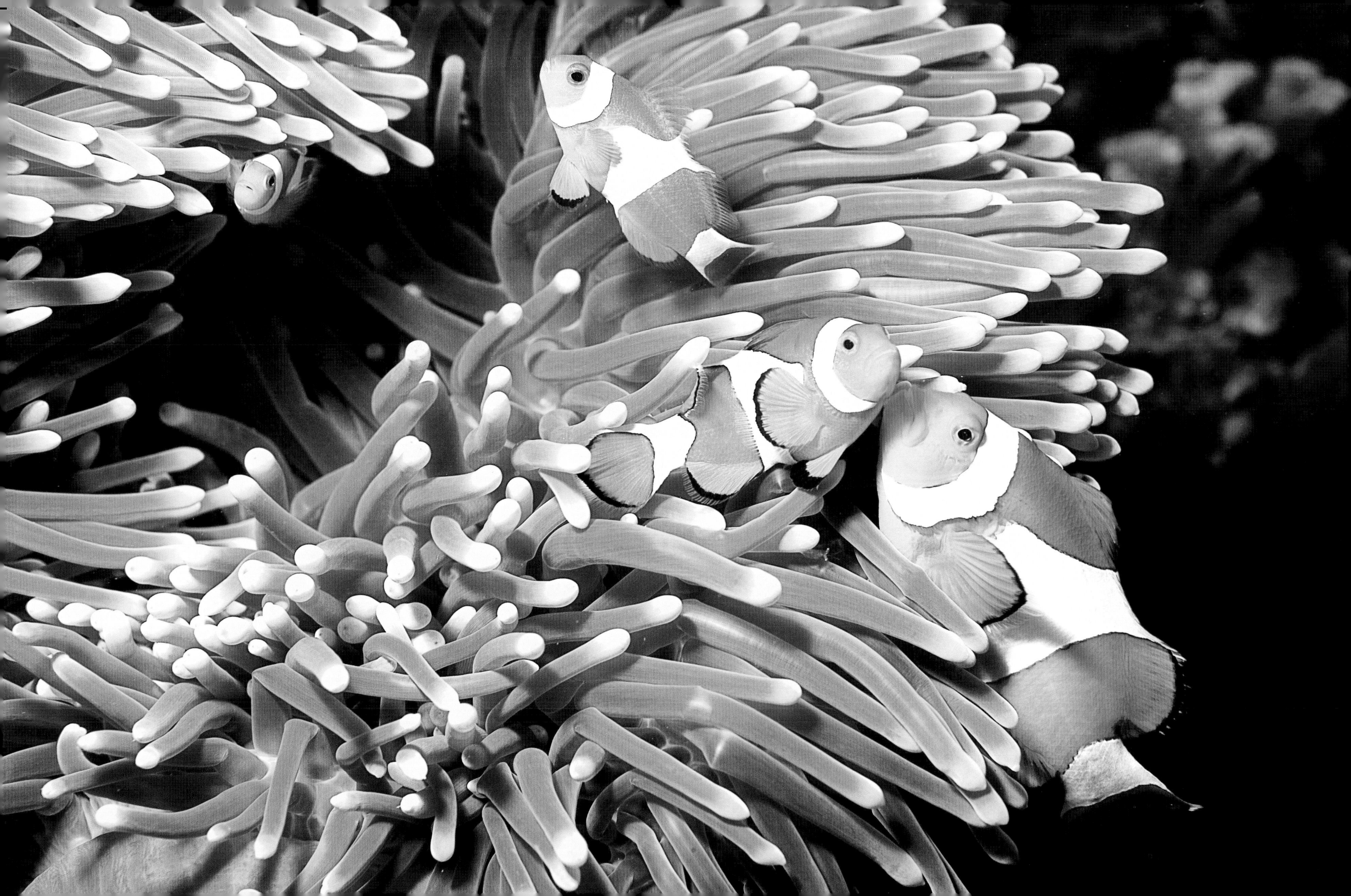

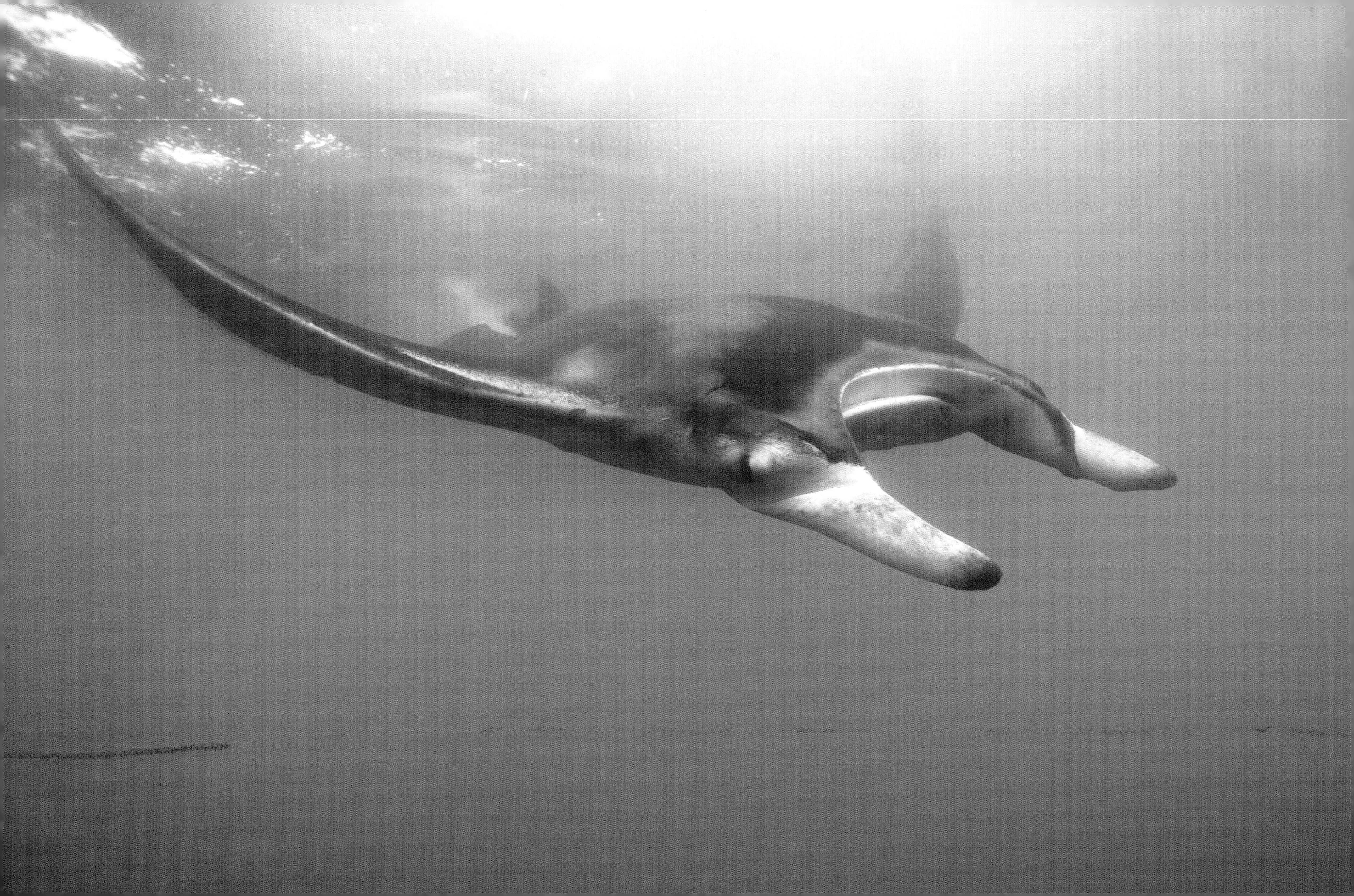

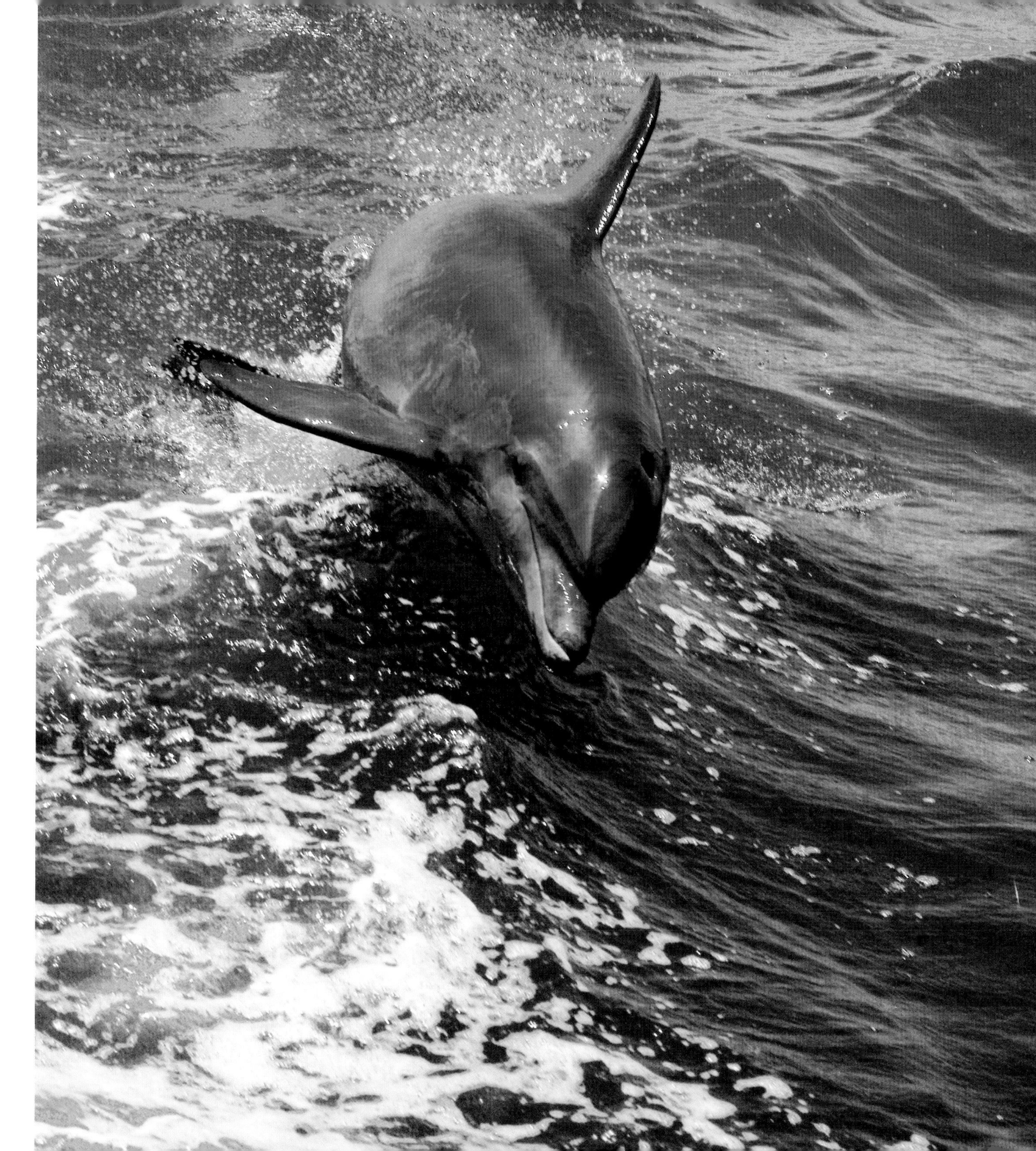

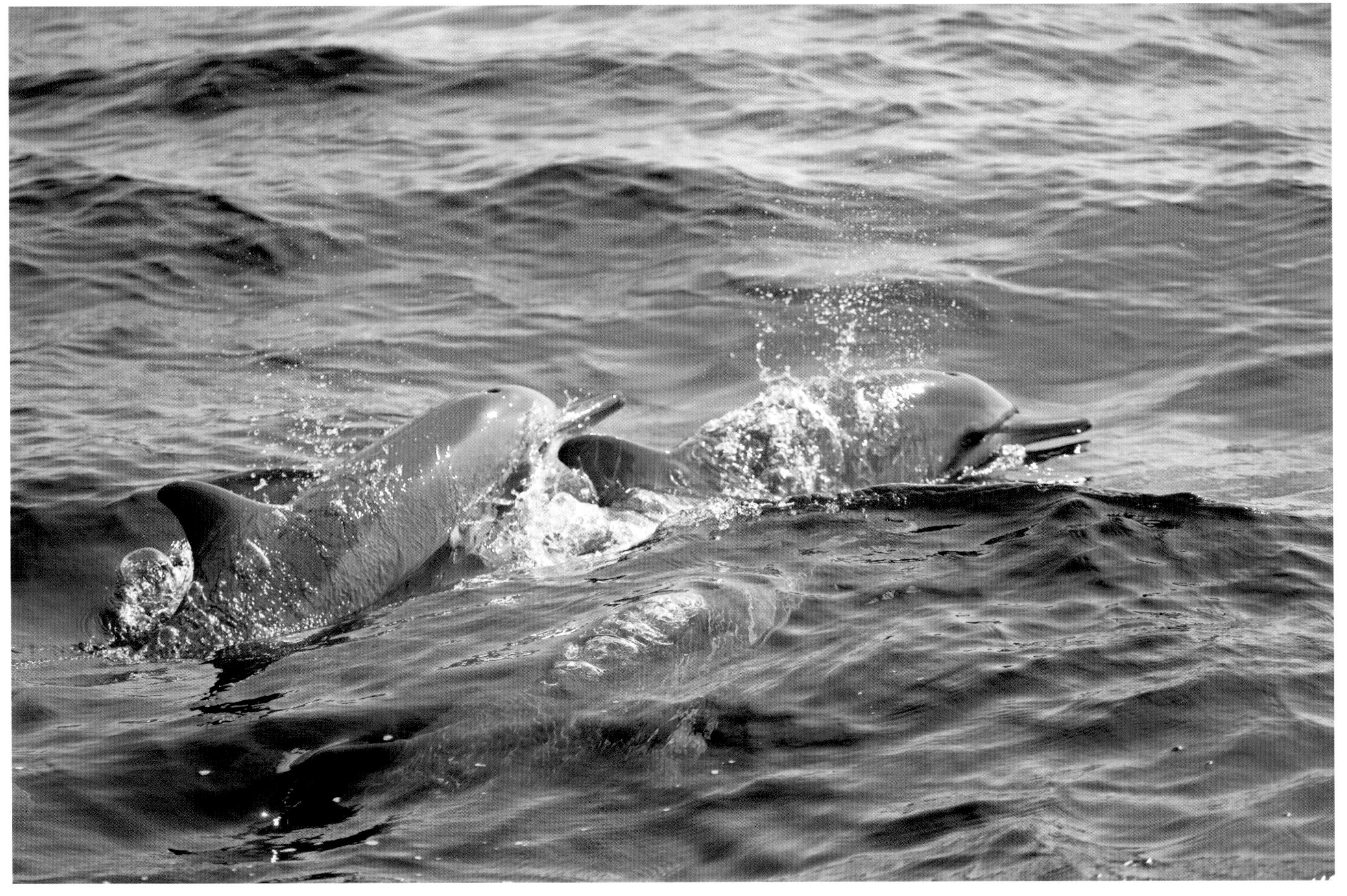

◀ spinner surface
▶ dolphin flight

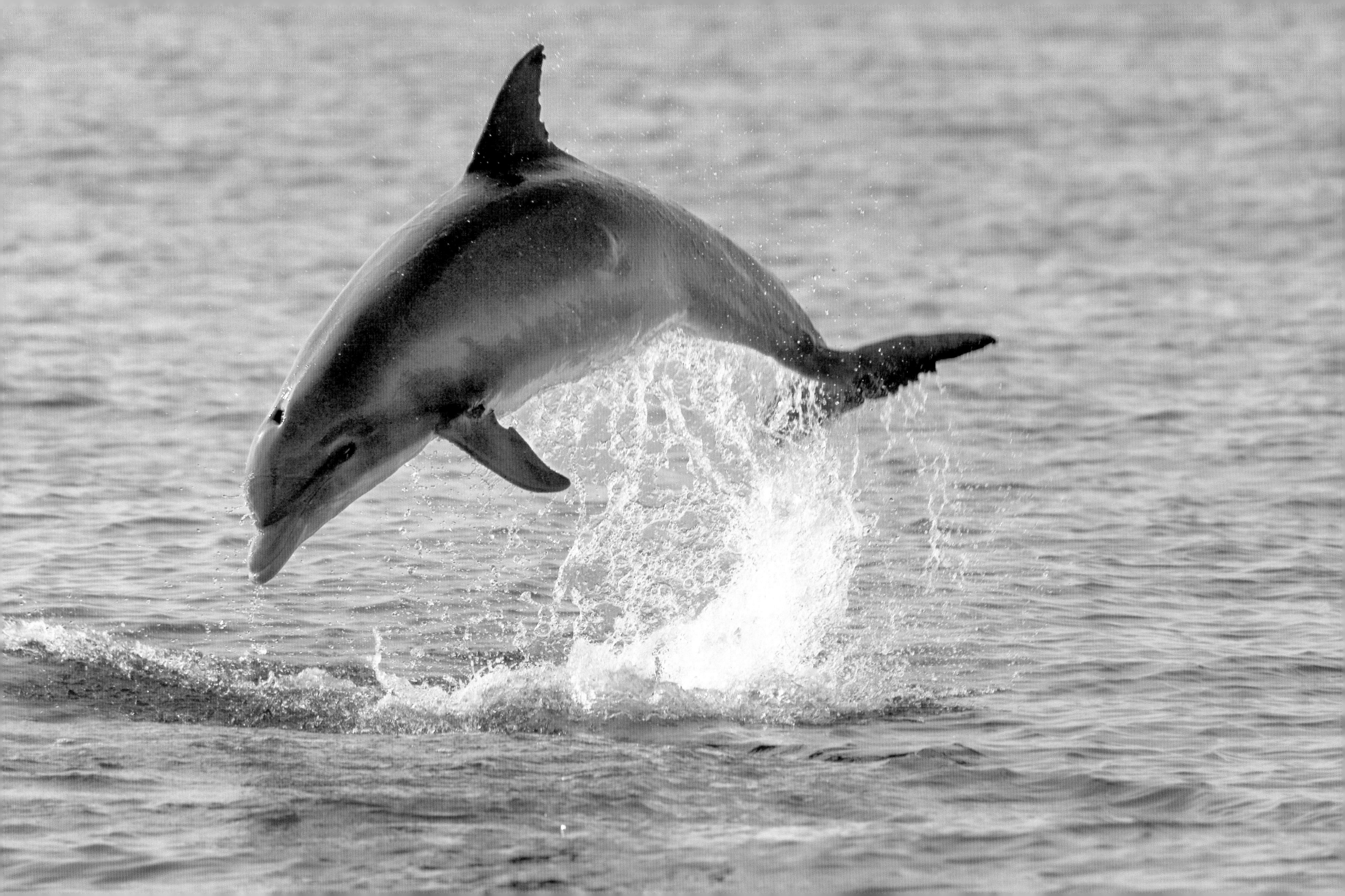

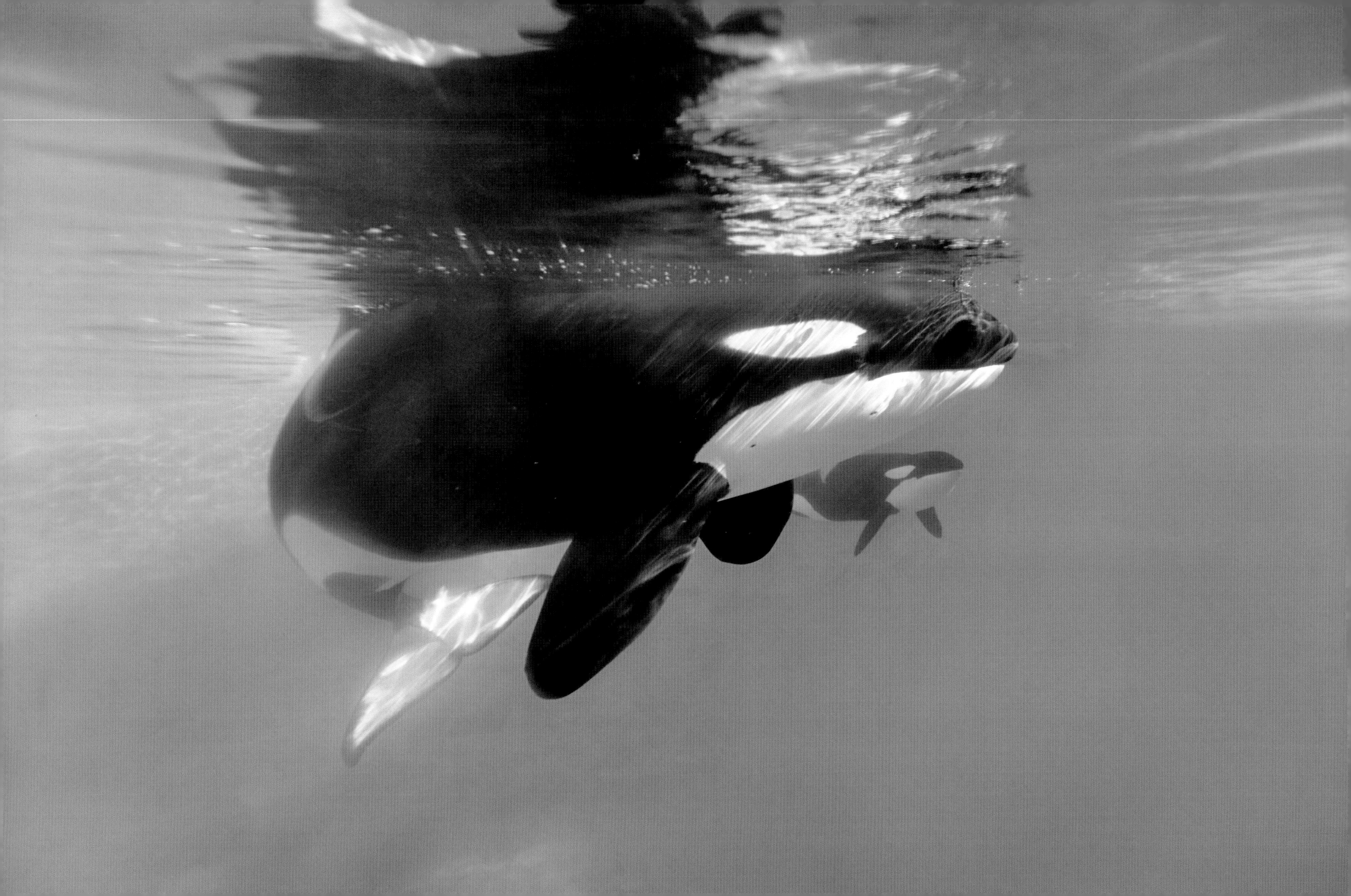

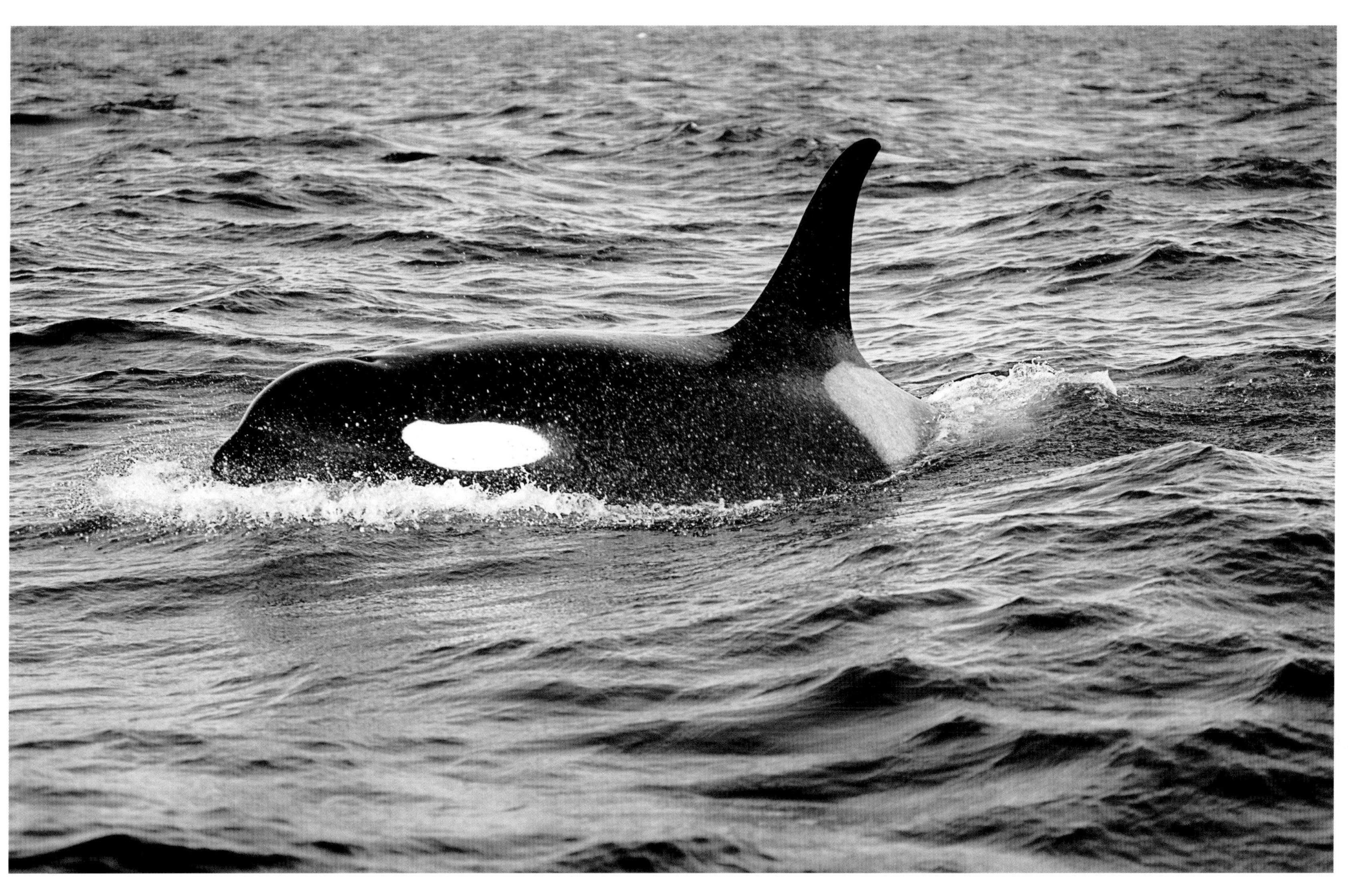

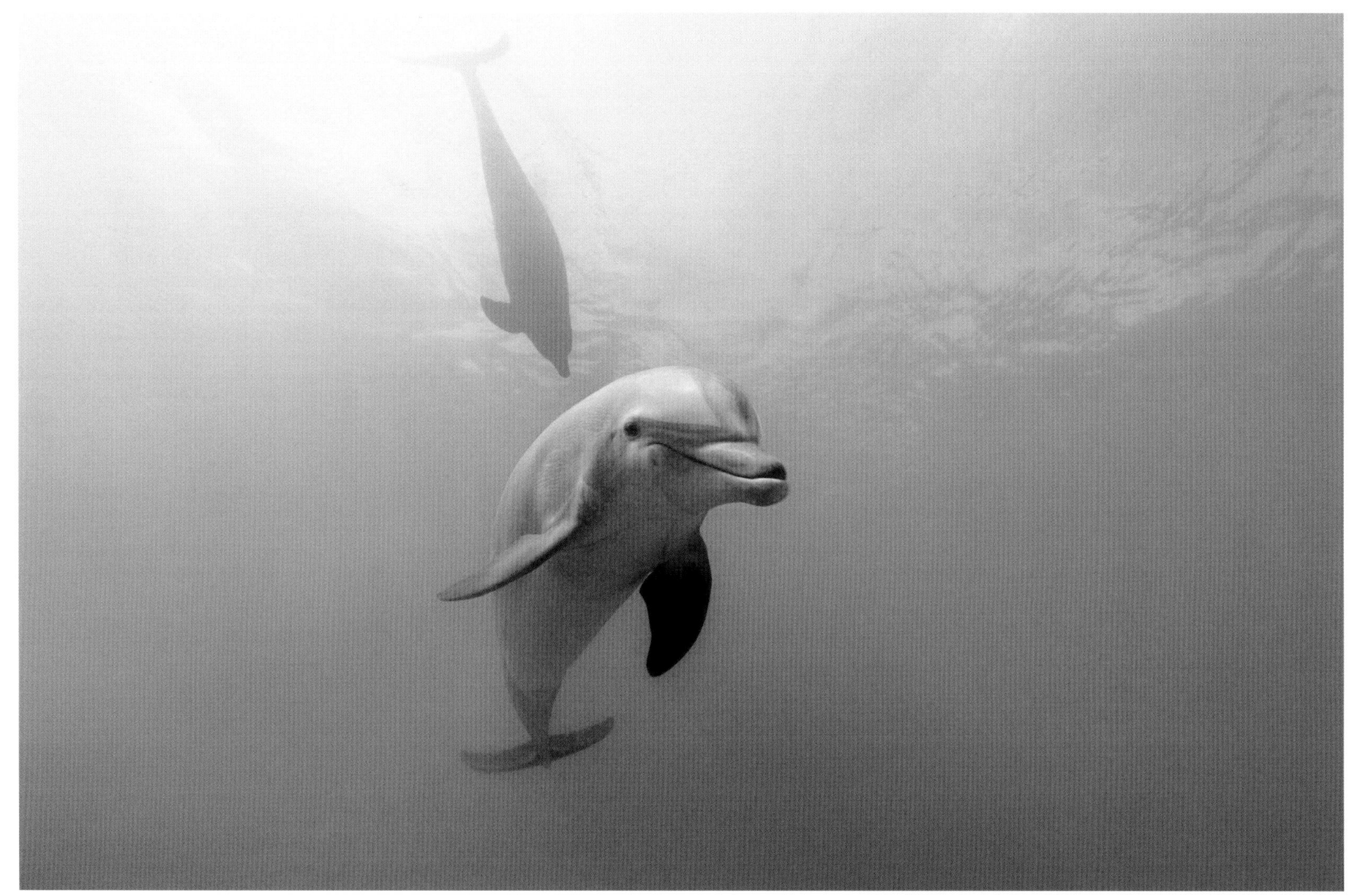

◀ a dolphin life
▶ sea floor light

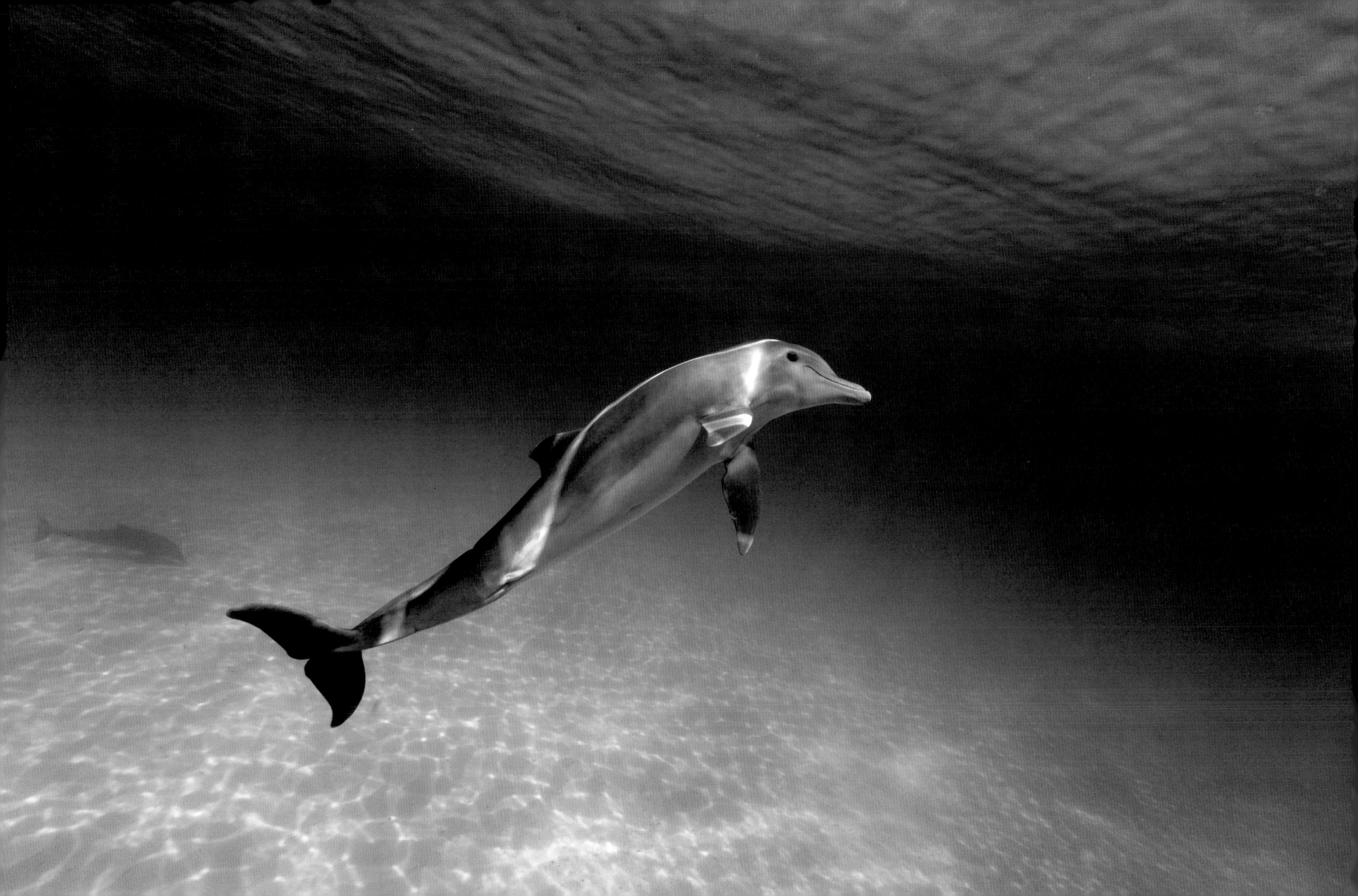

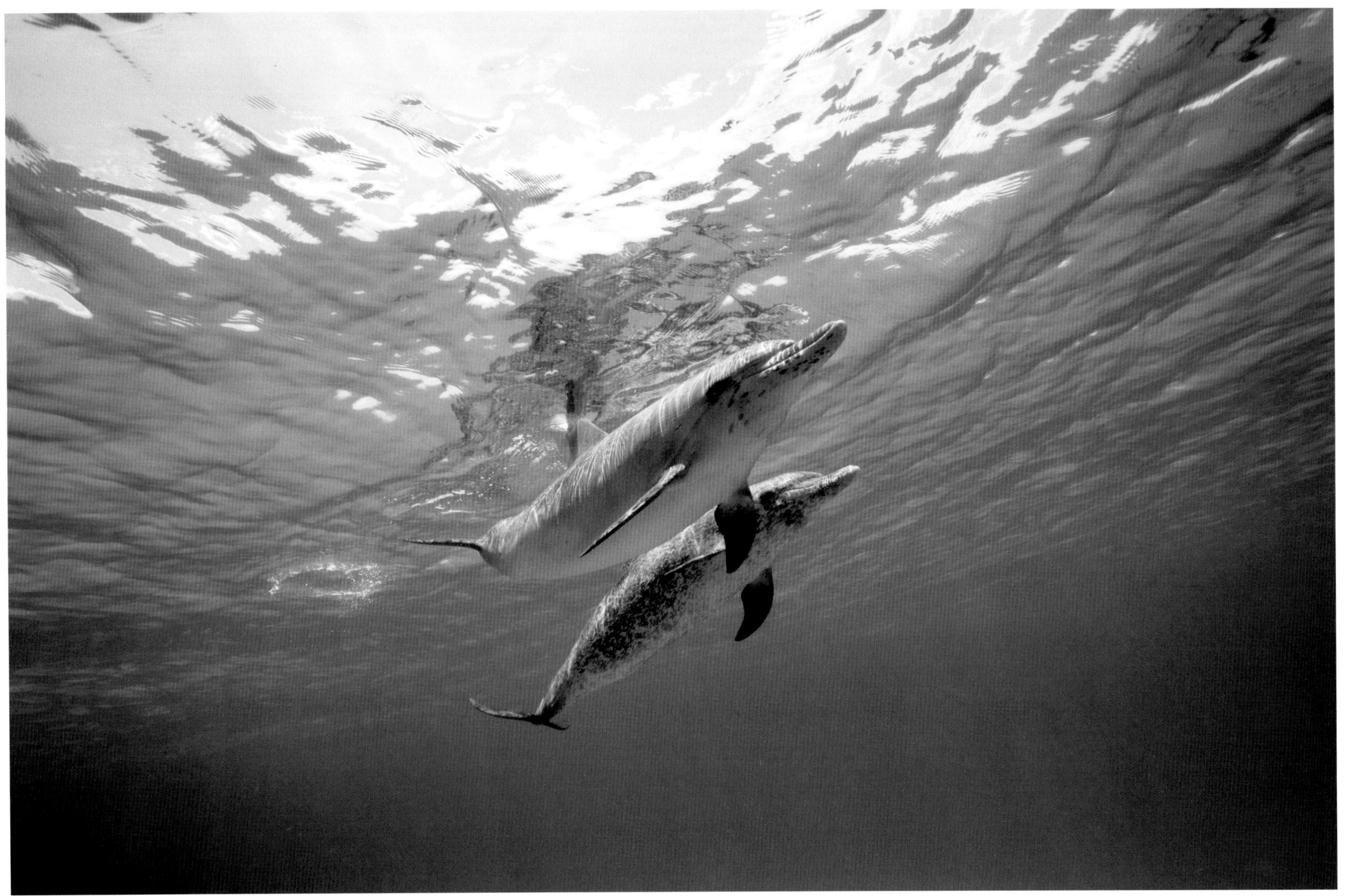

◀ spotted seas
▶ bottlenose tribe

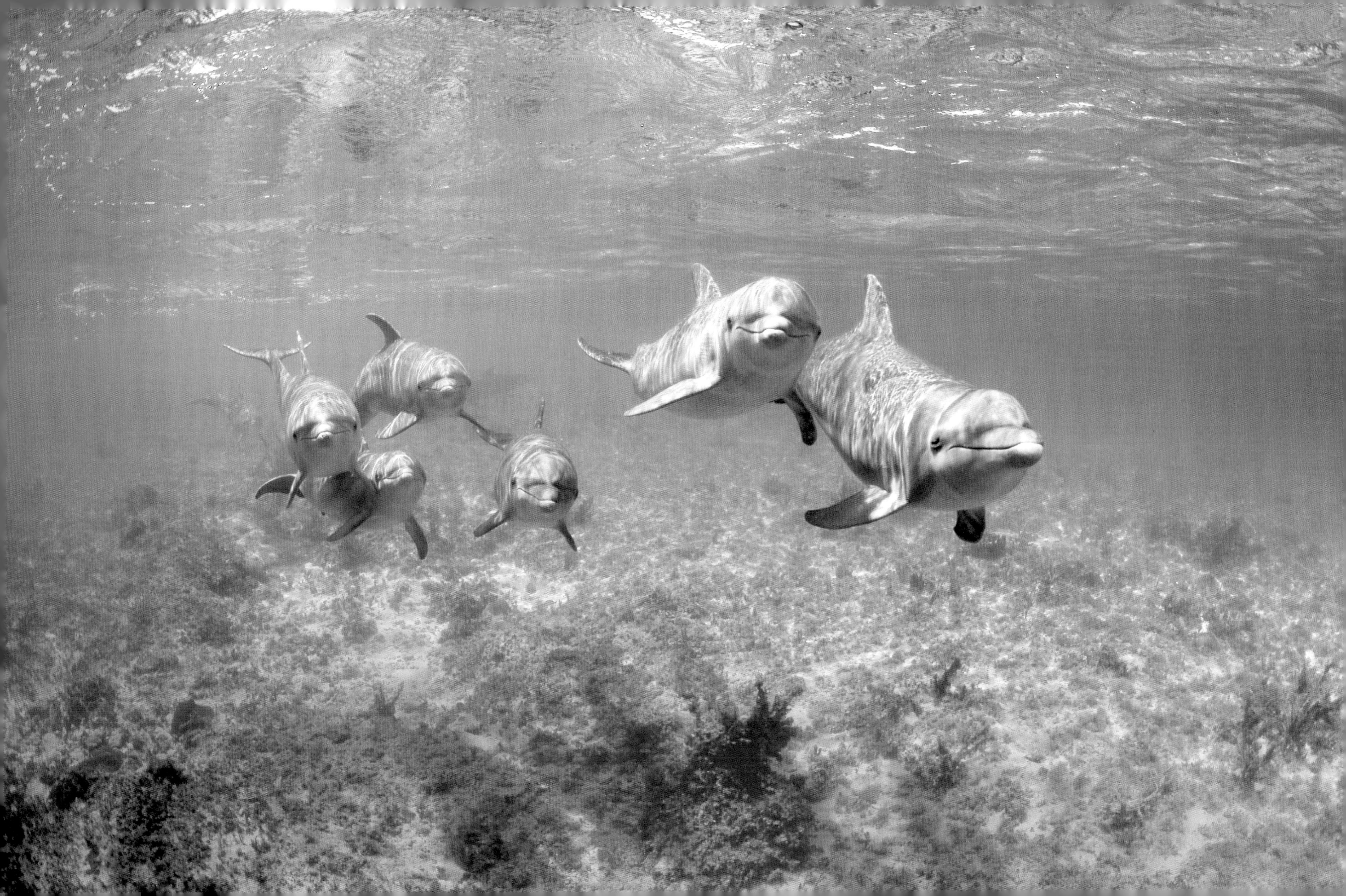

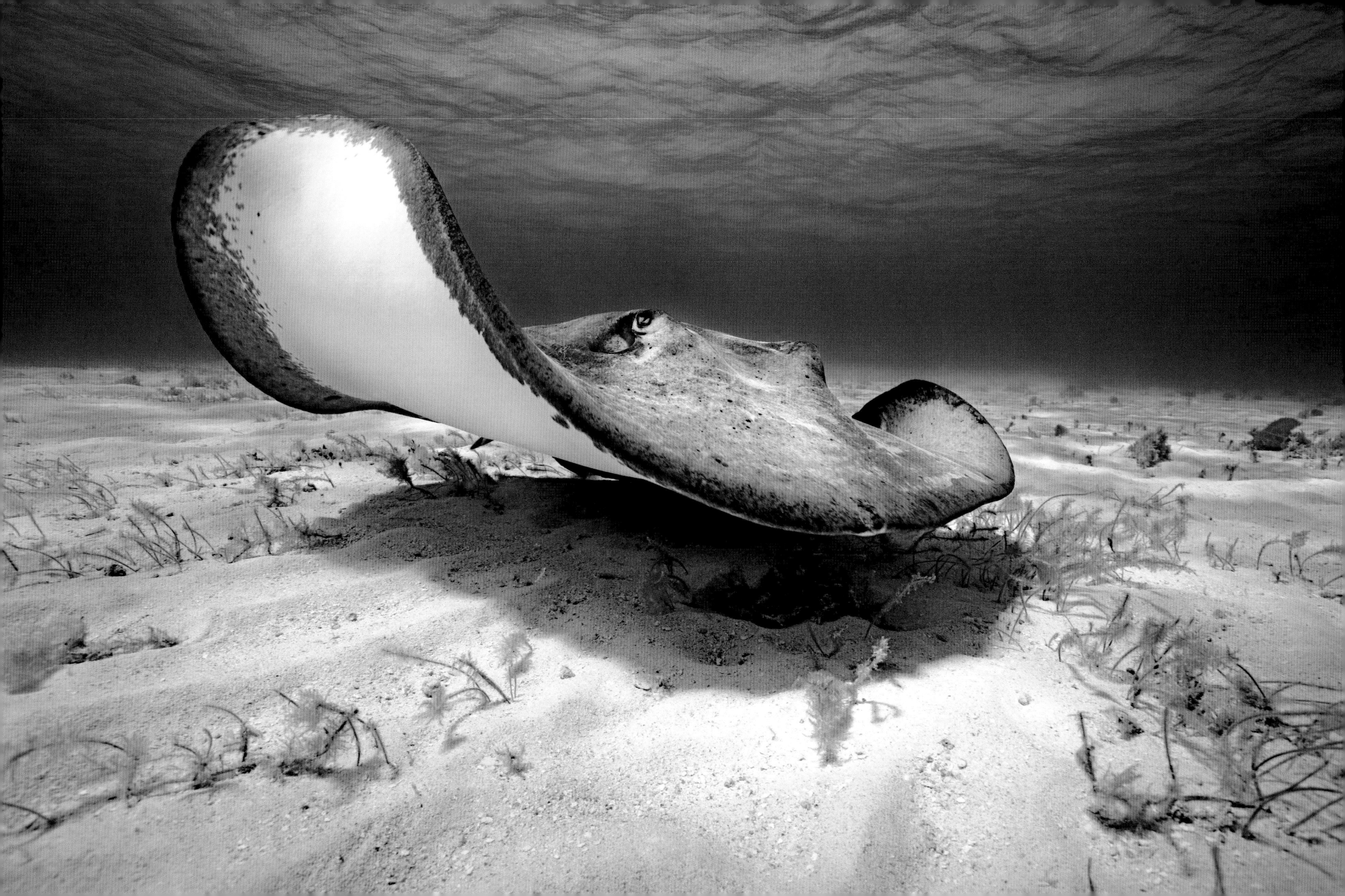

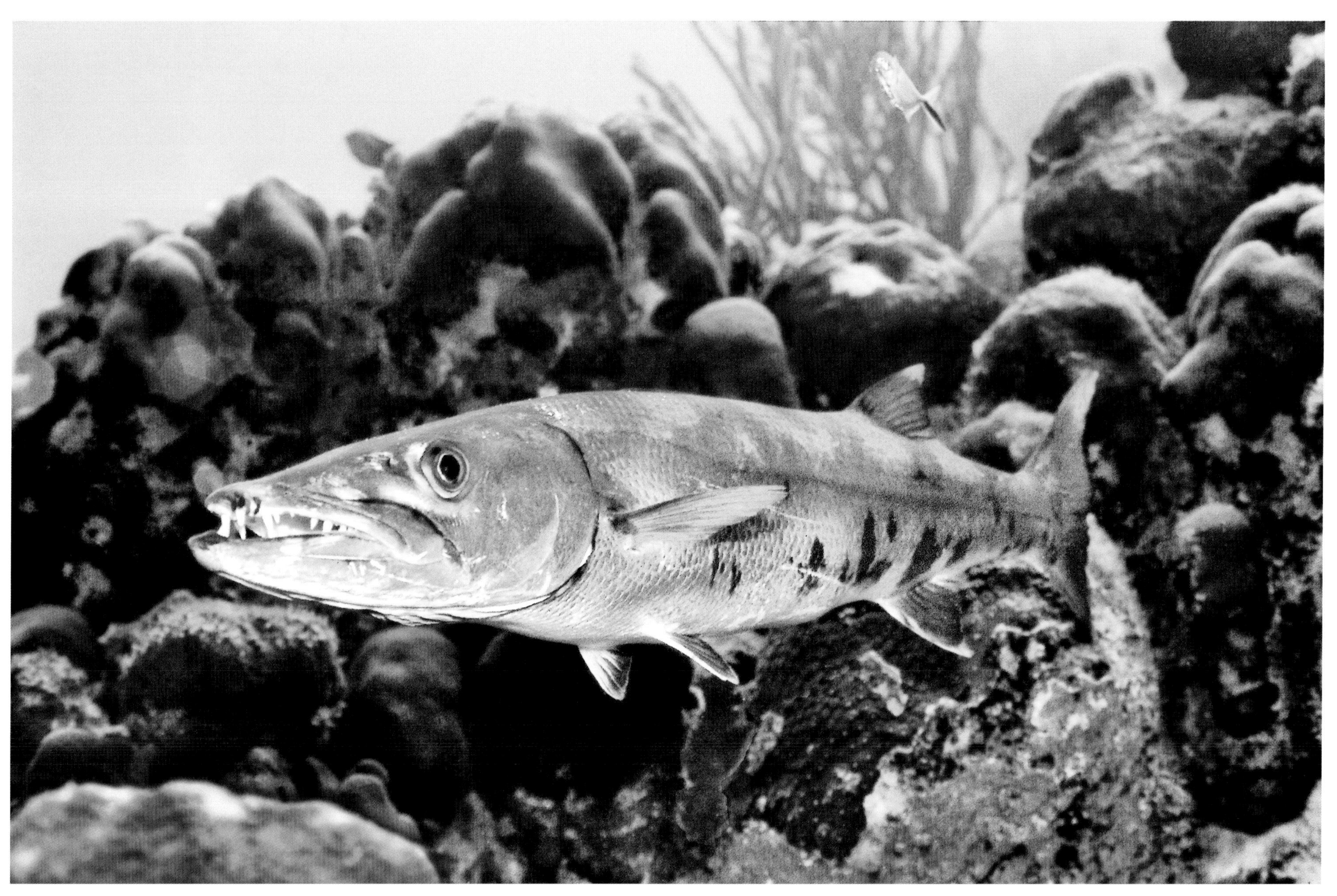

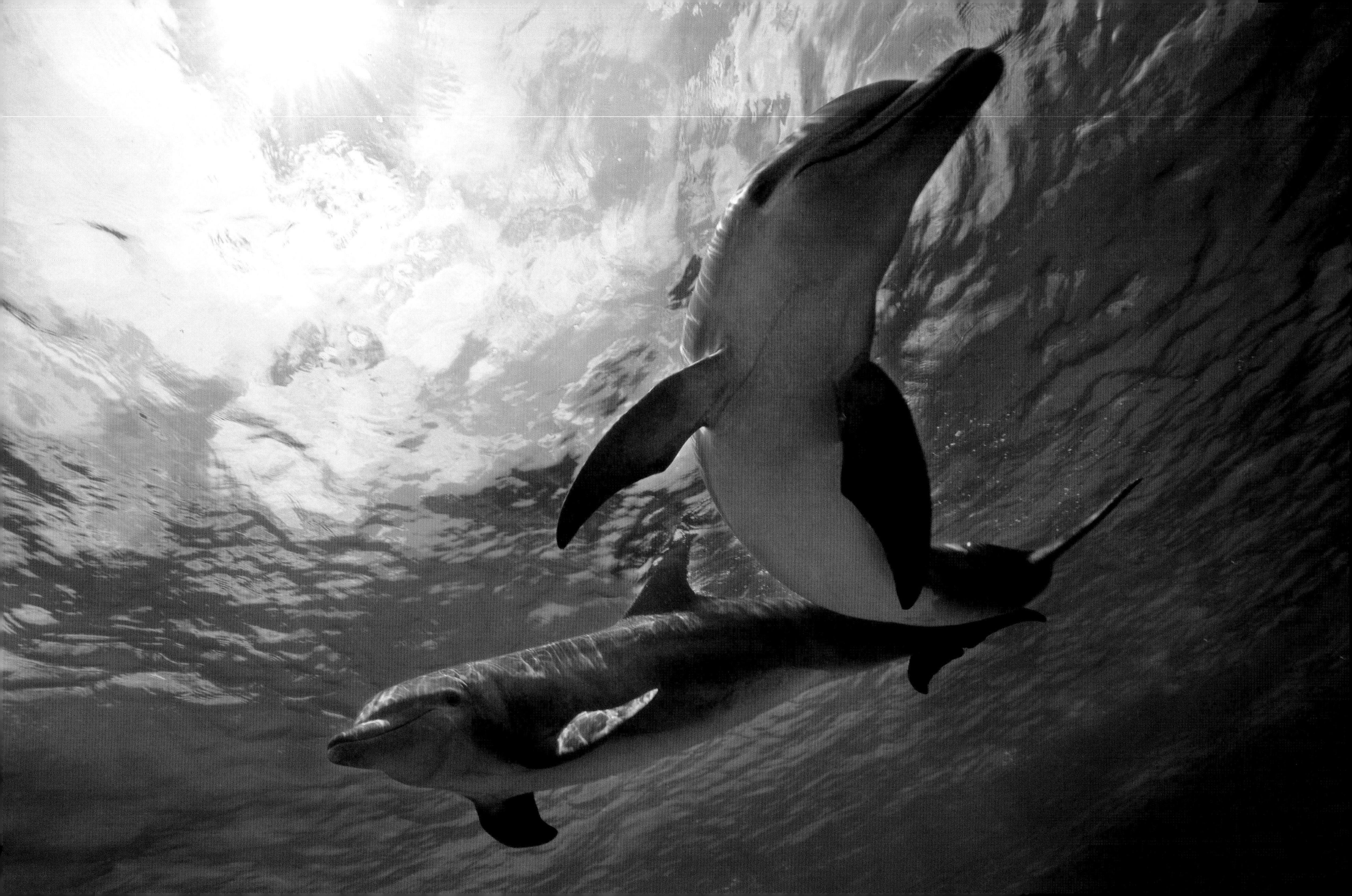

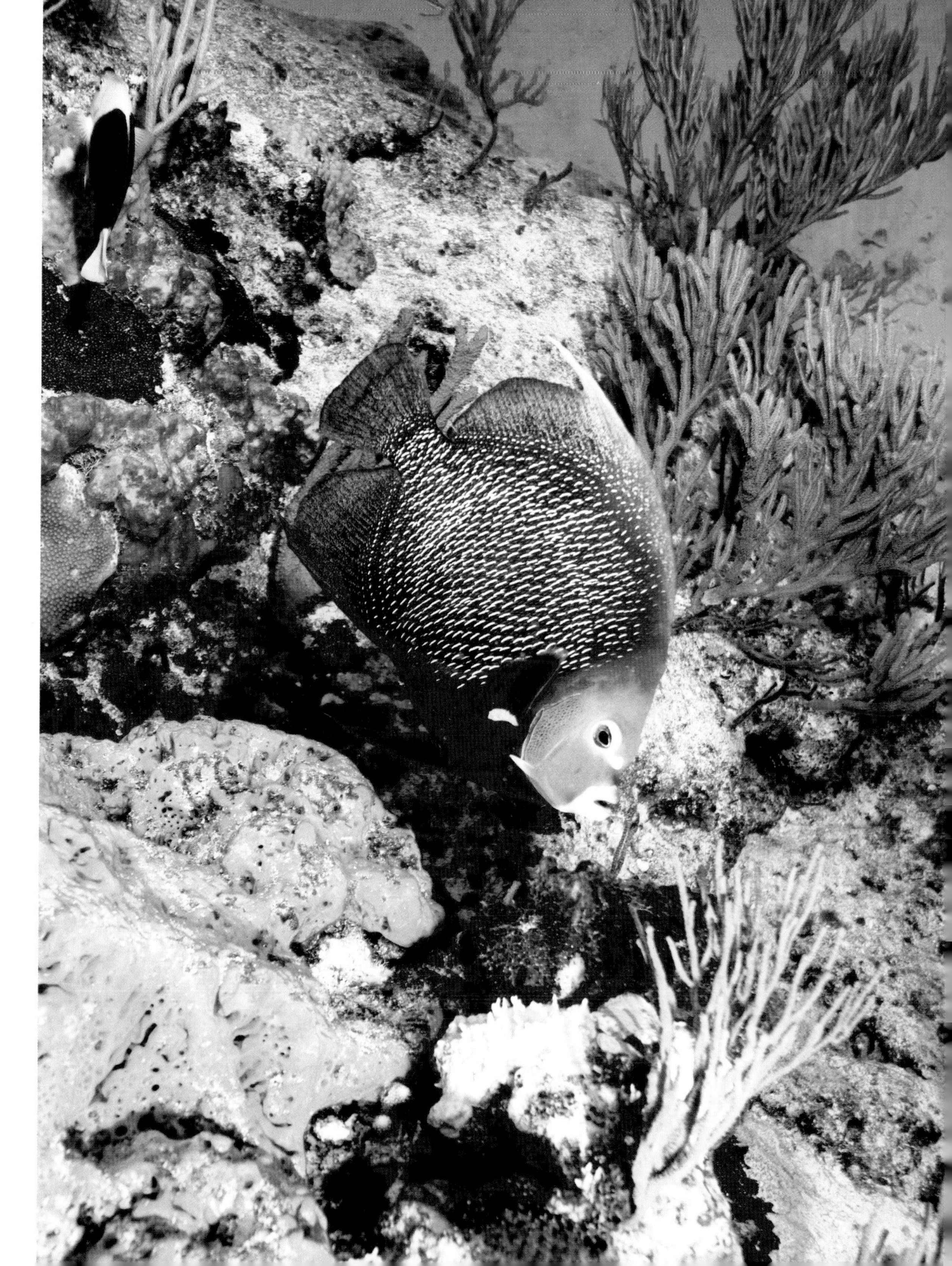

the dolphin realm
french angel reef

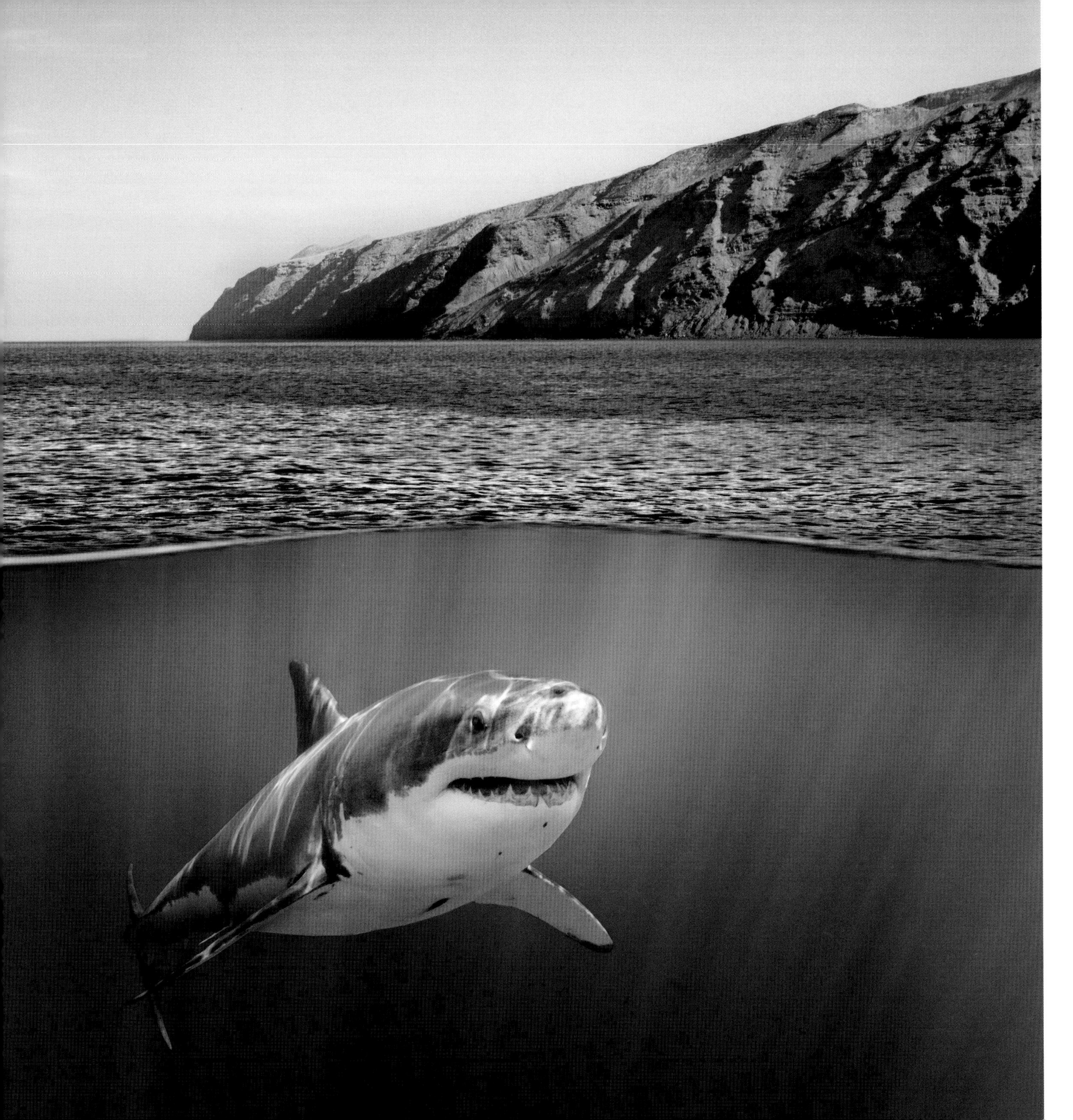

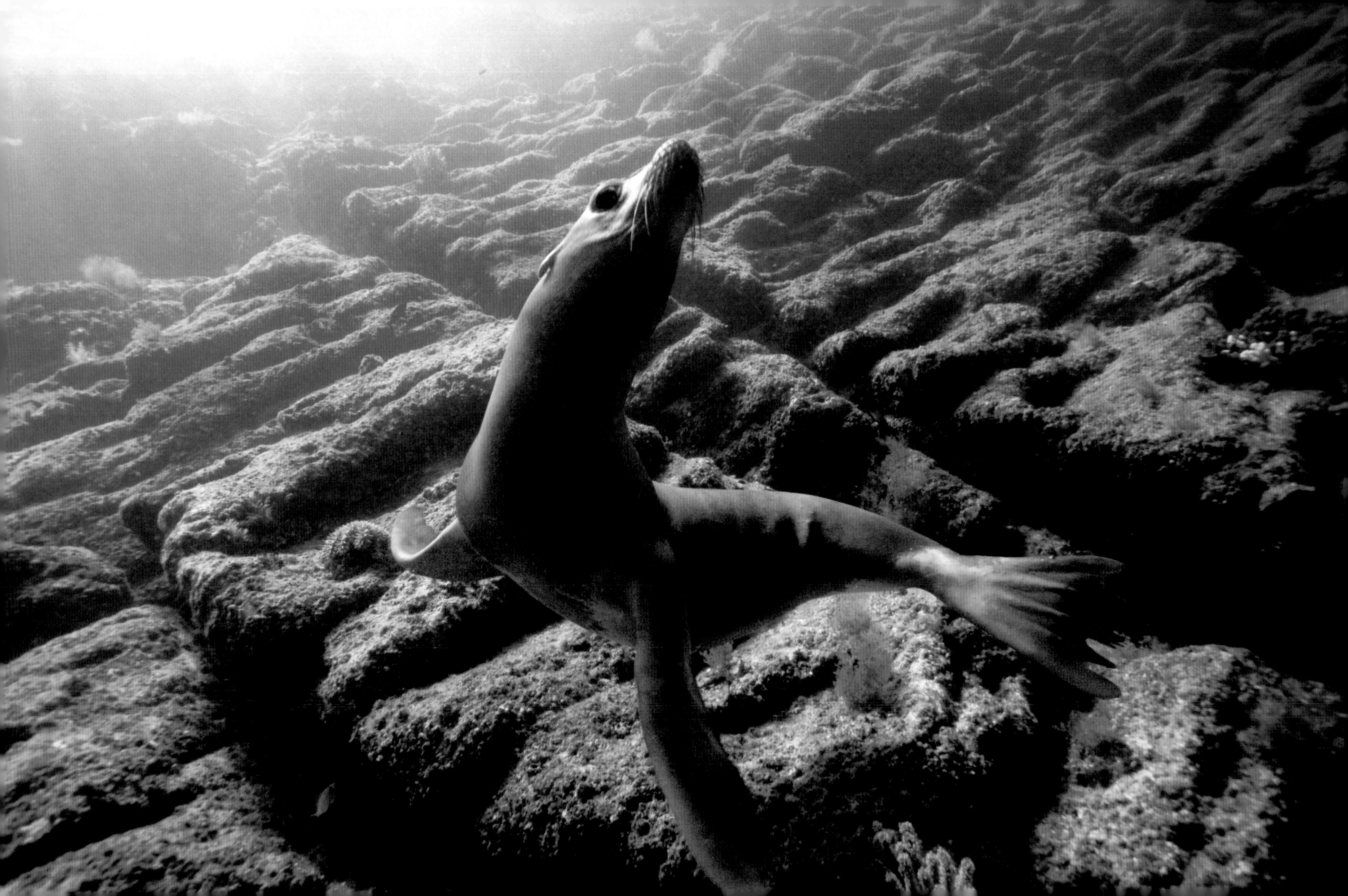

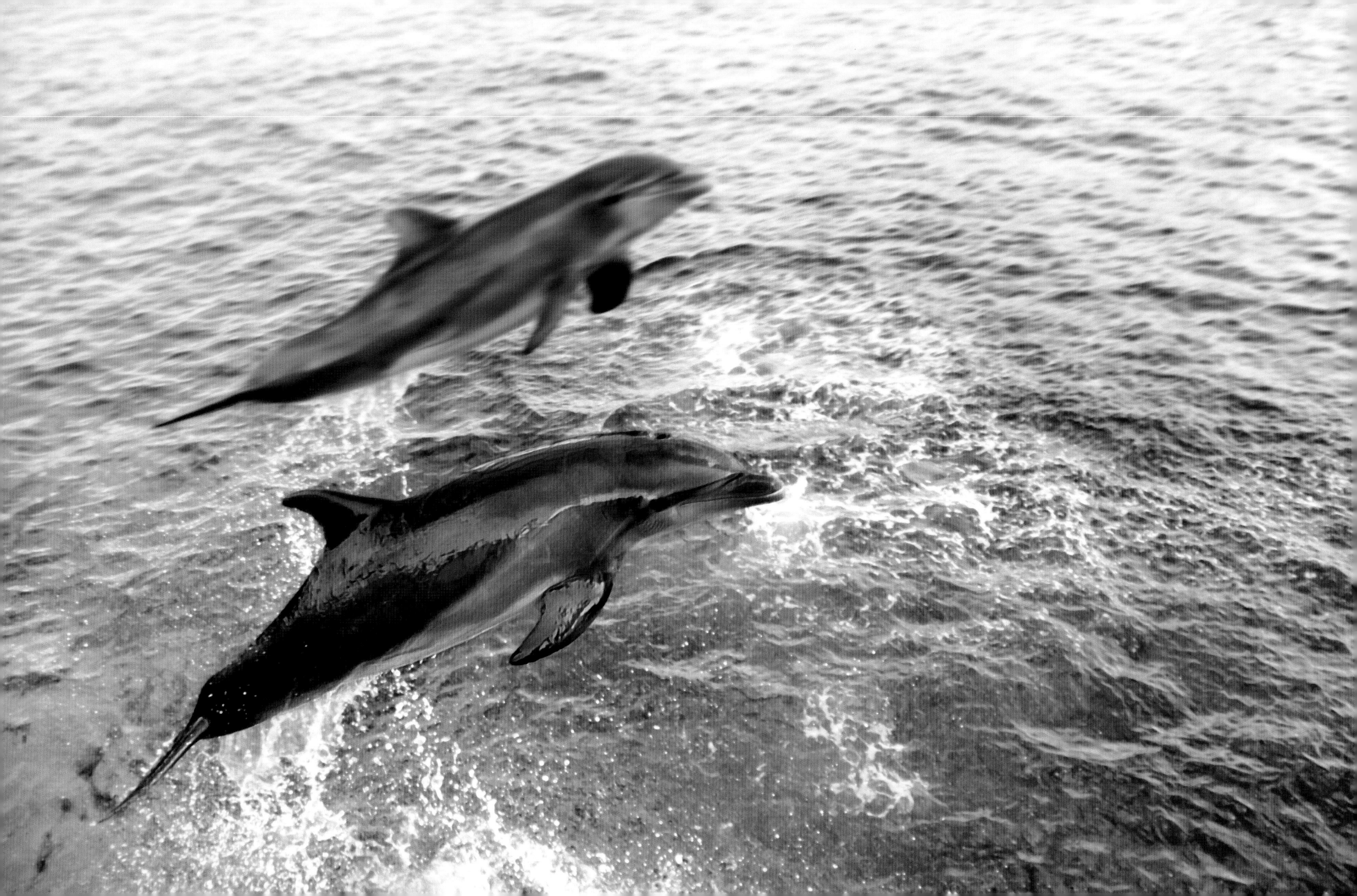

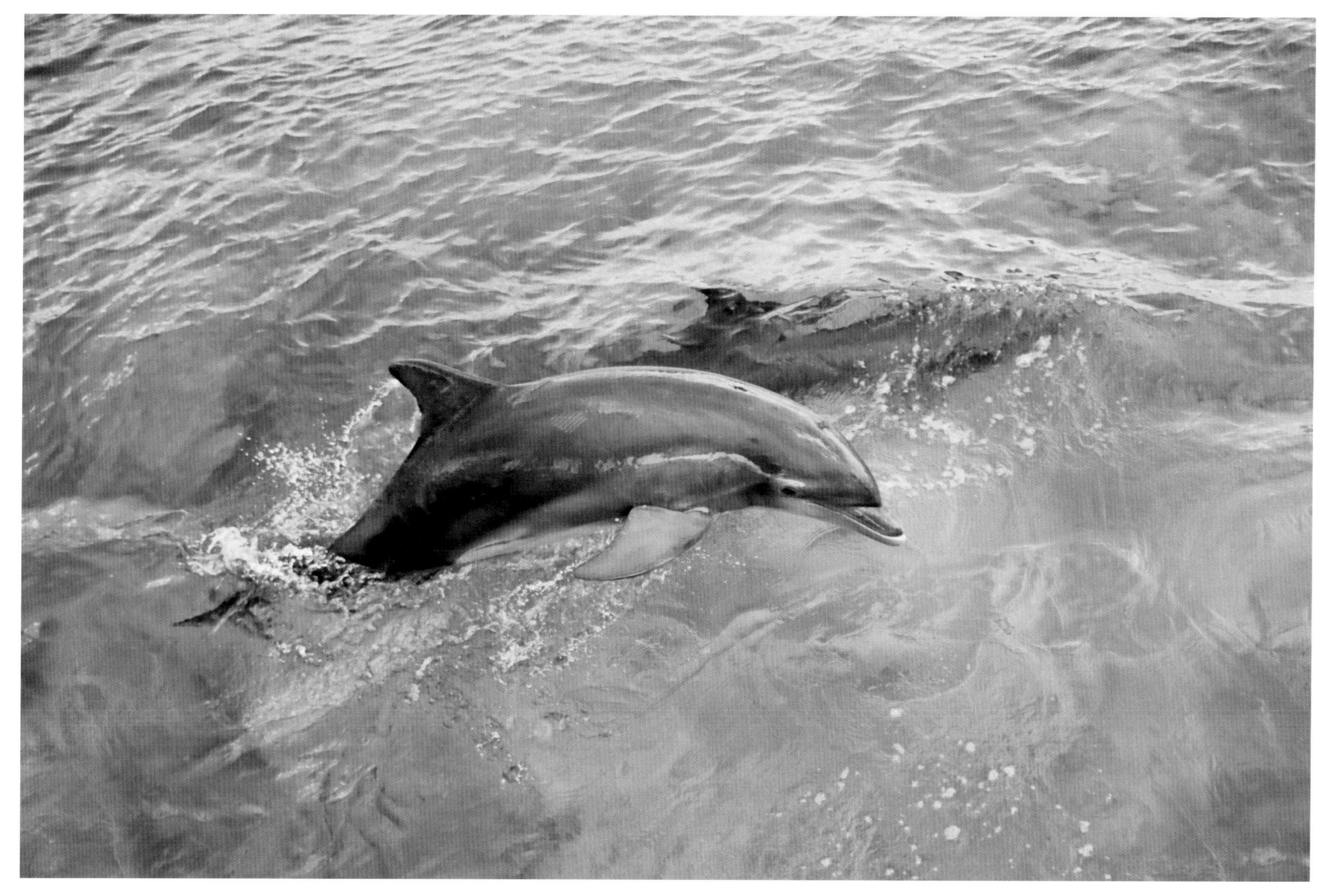

◄ rise from the sea
▶ dolphin traveler

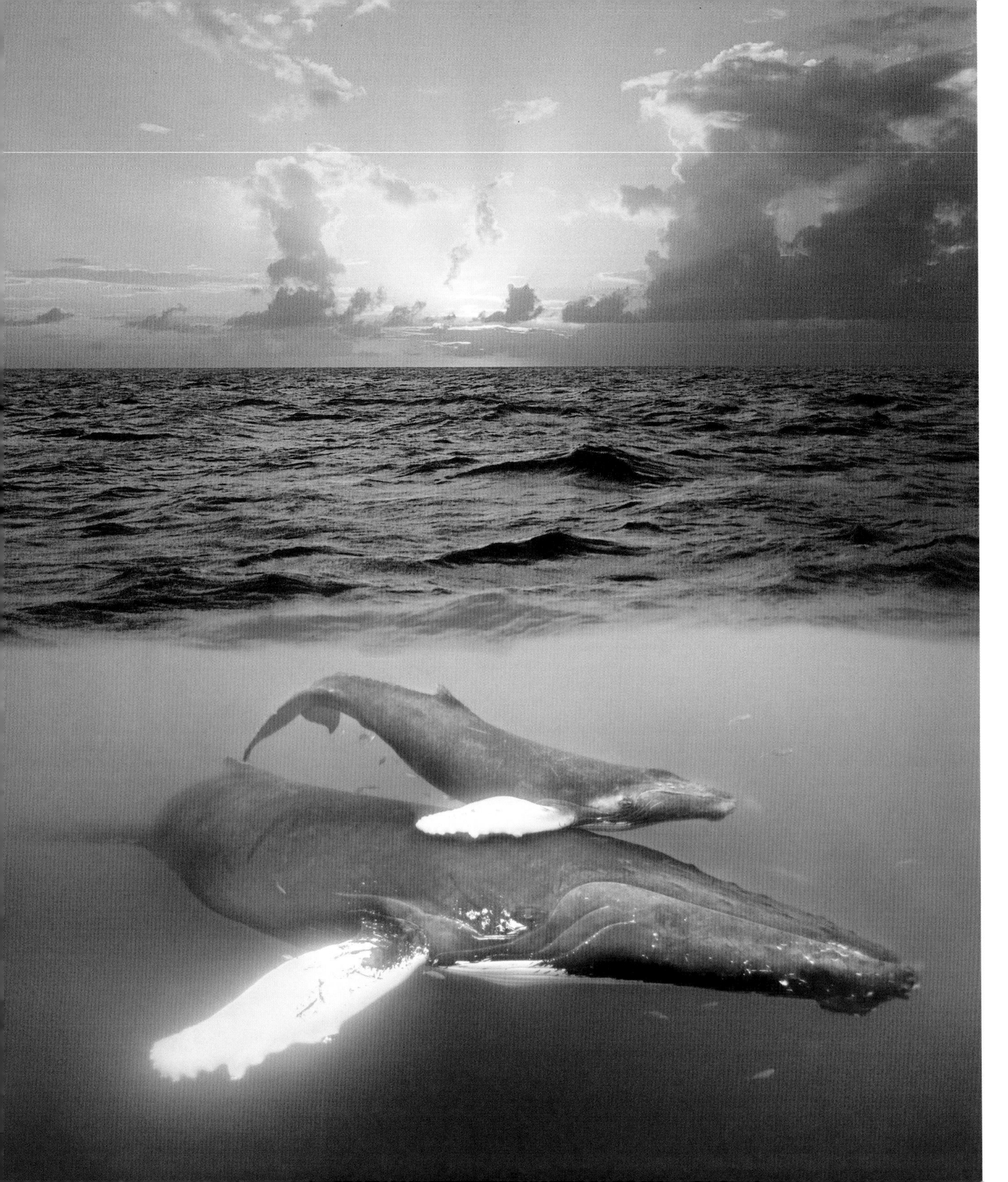

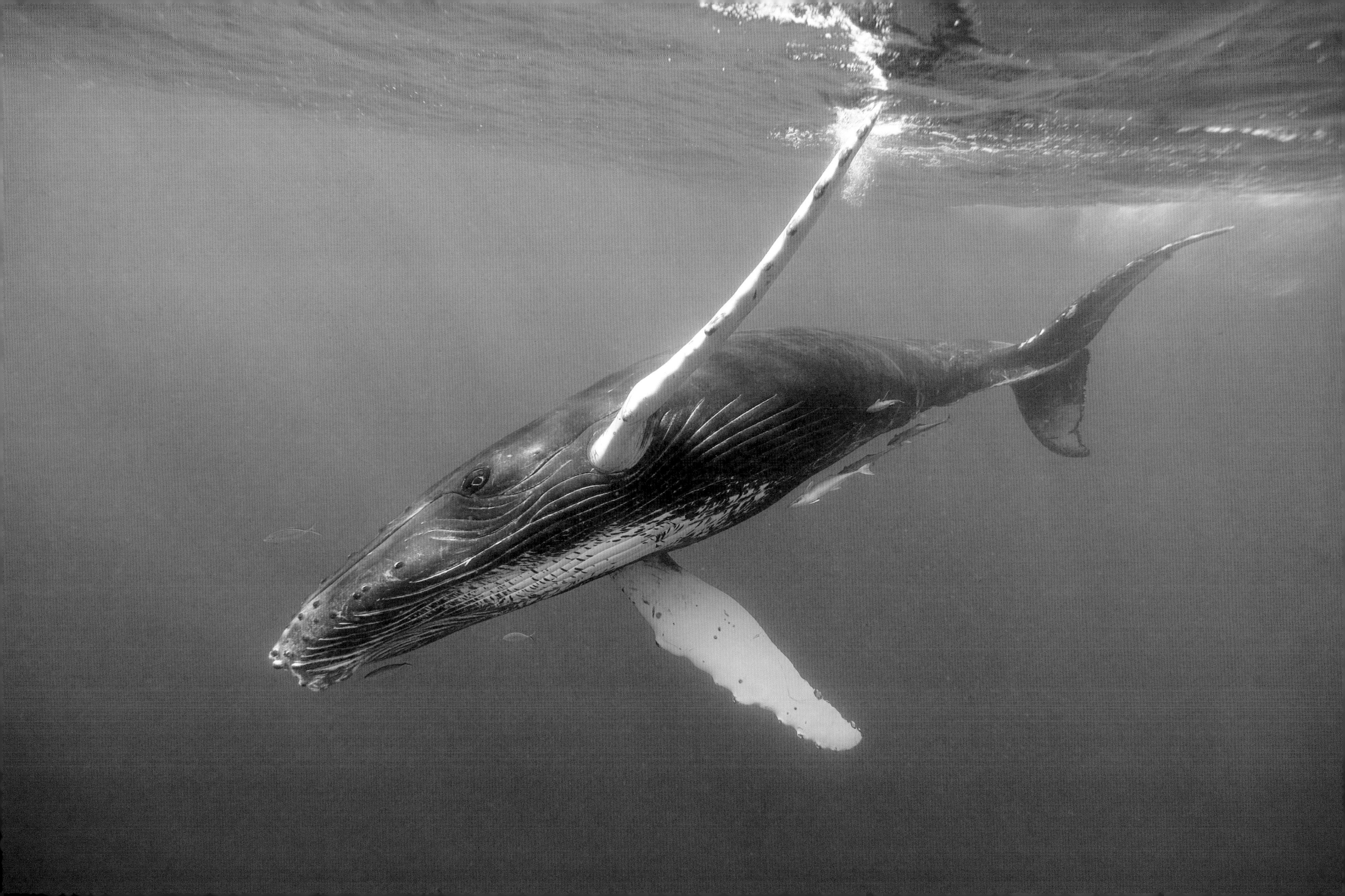

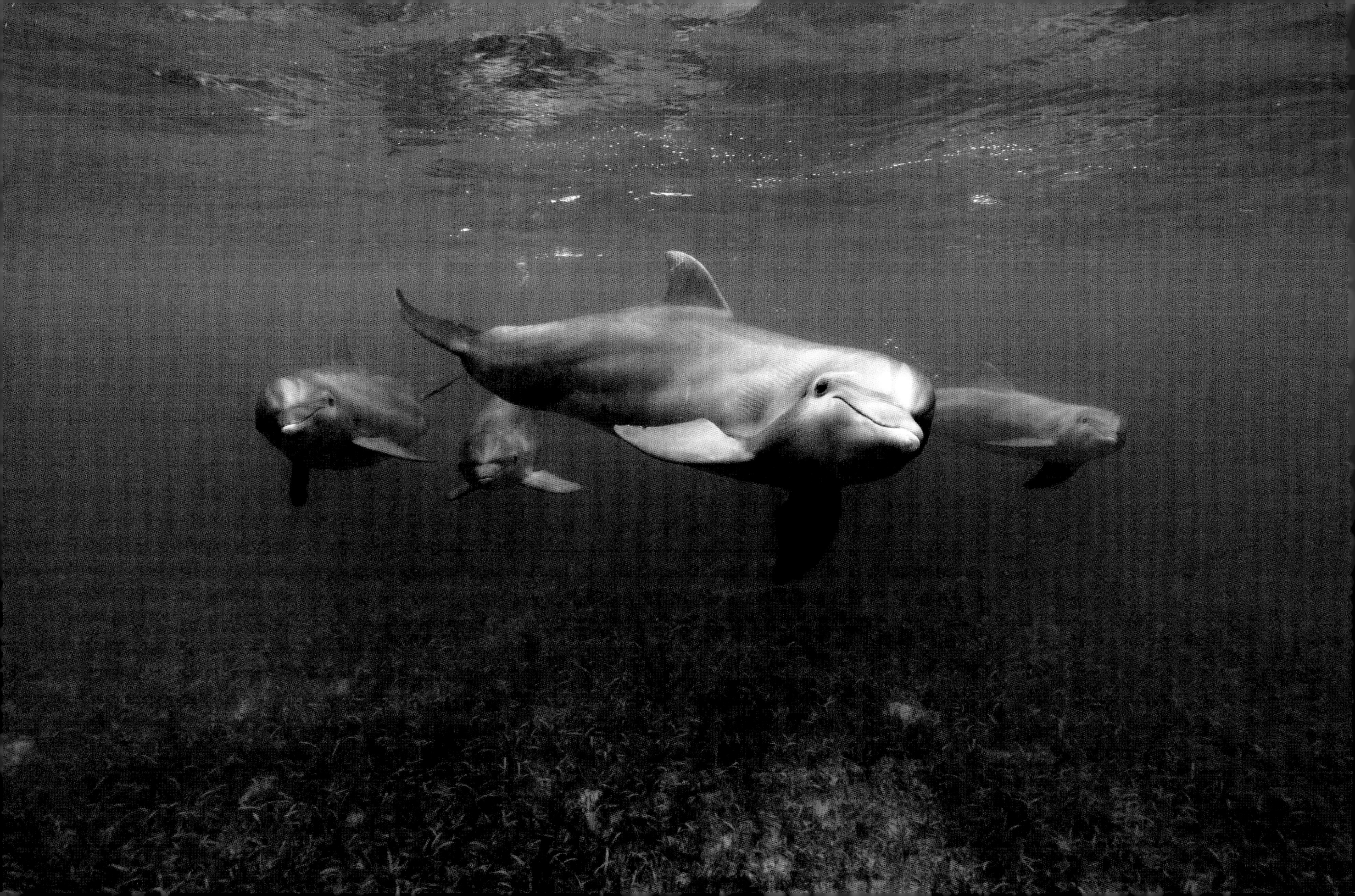

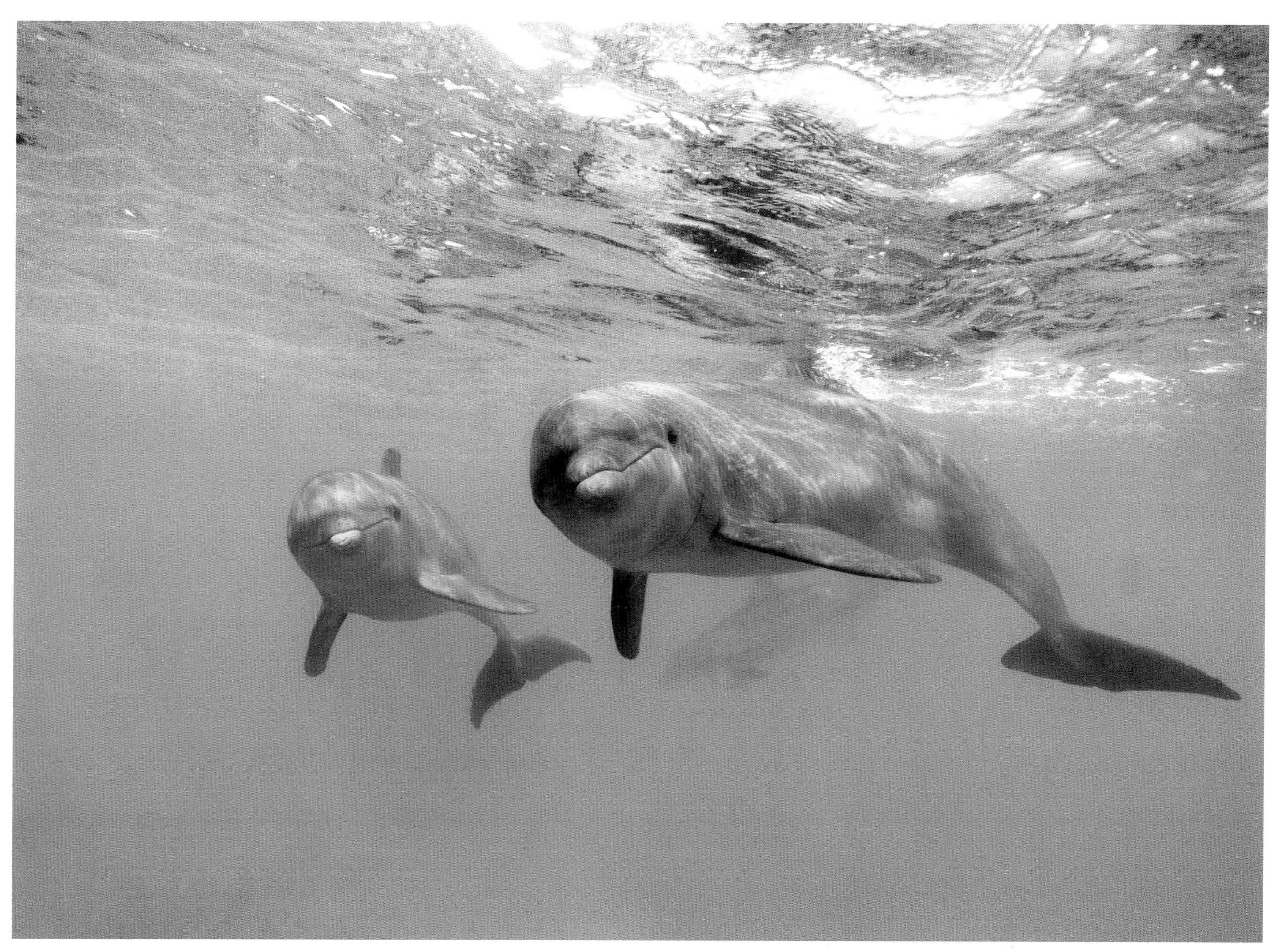

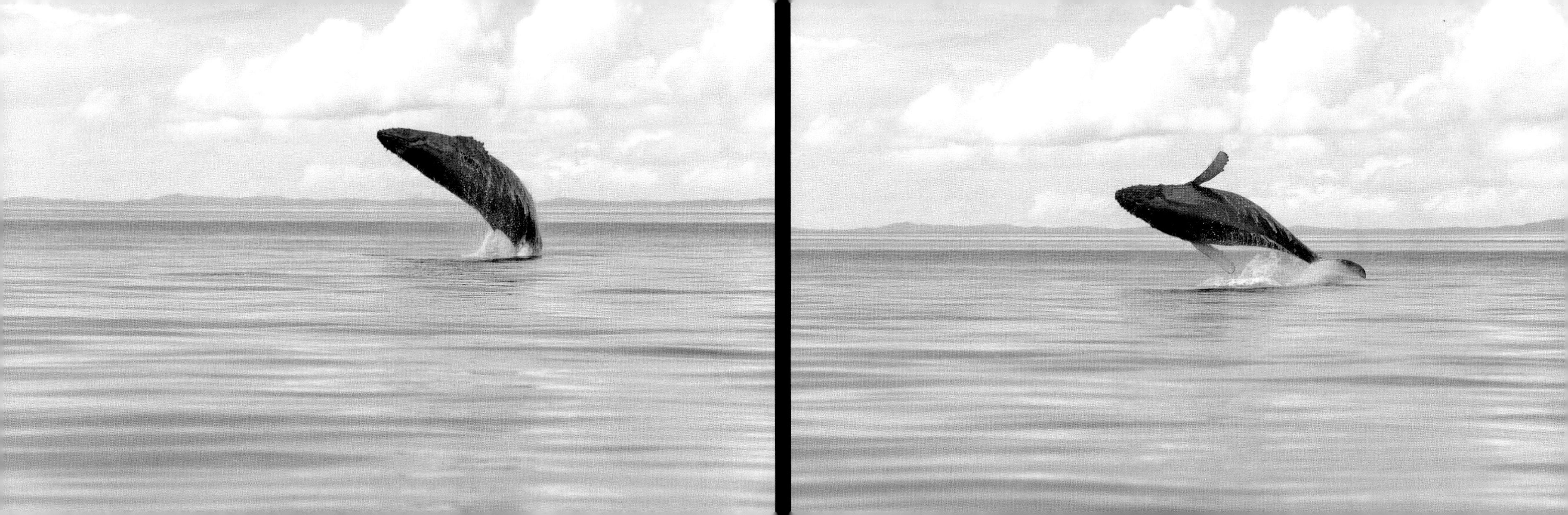

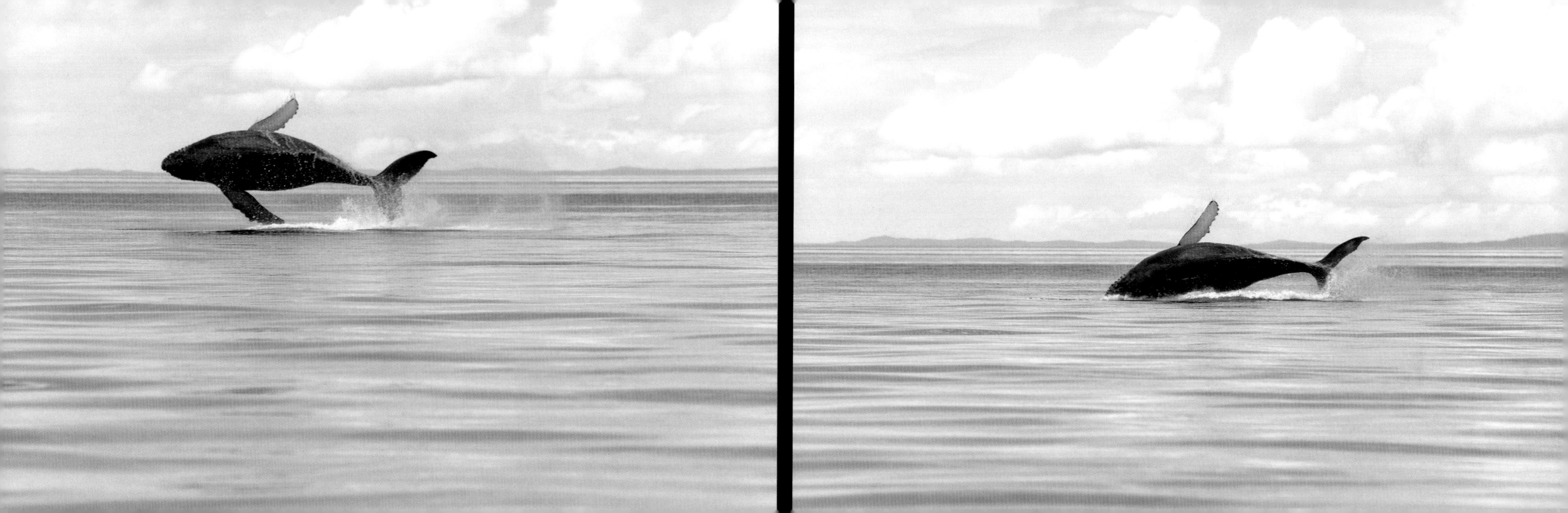

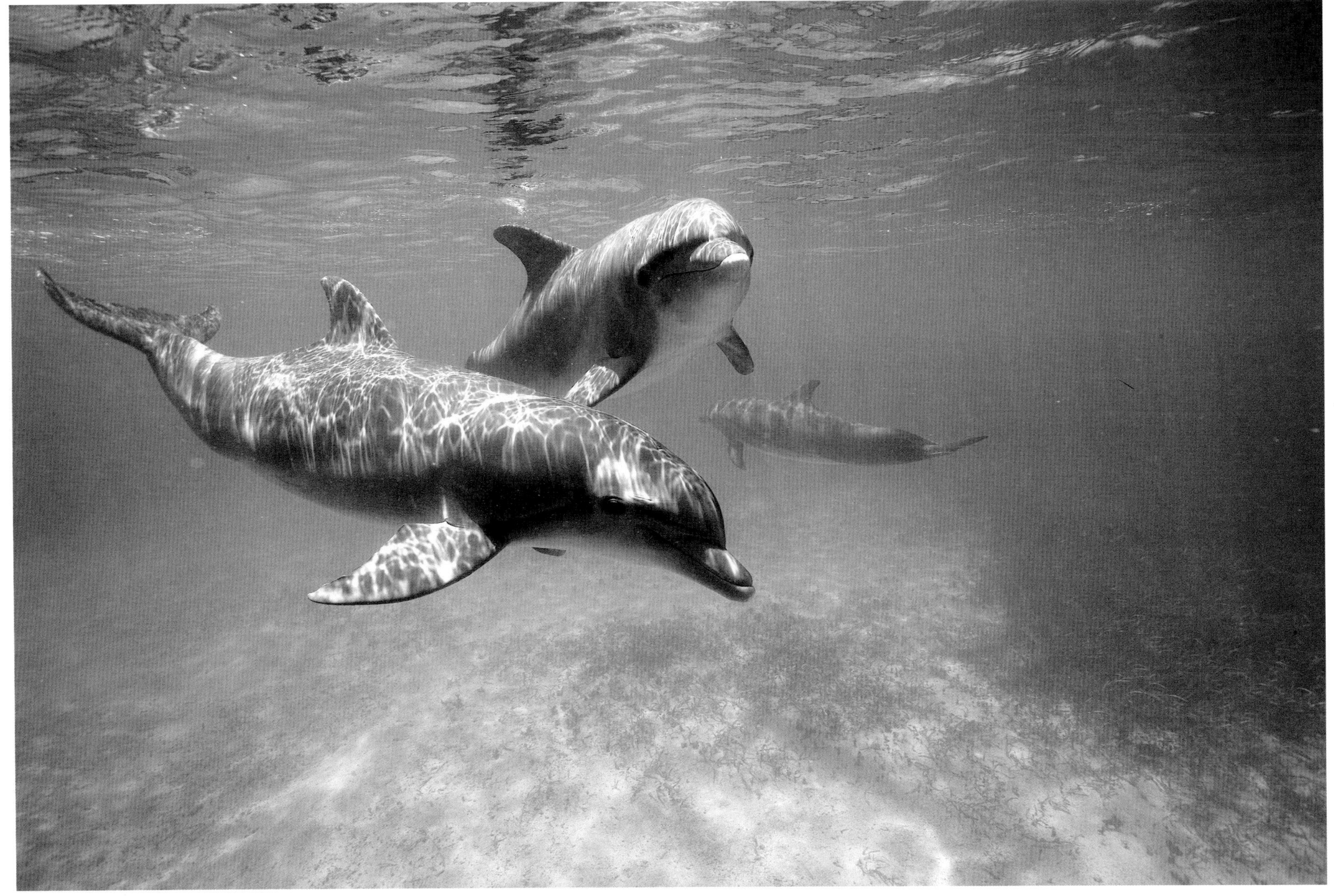

◄ seeing dolphins
▶ beautiful bottlenose

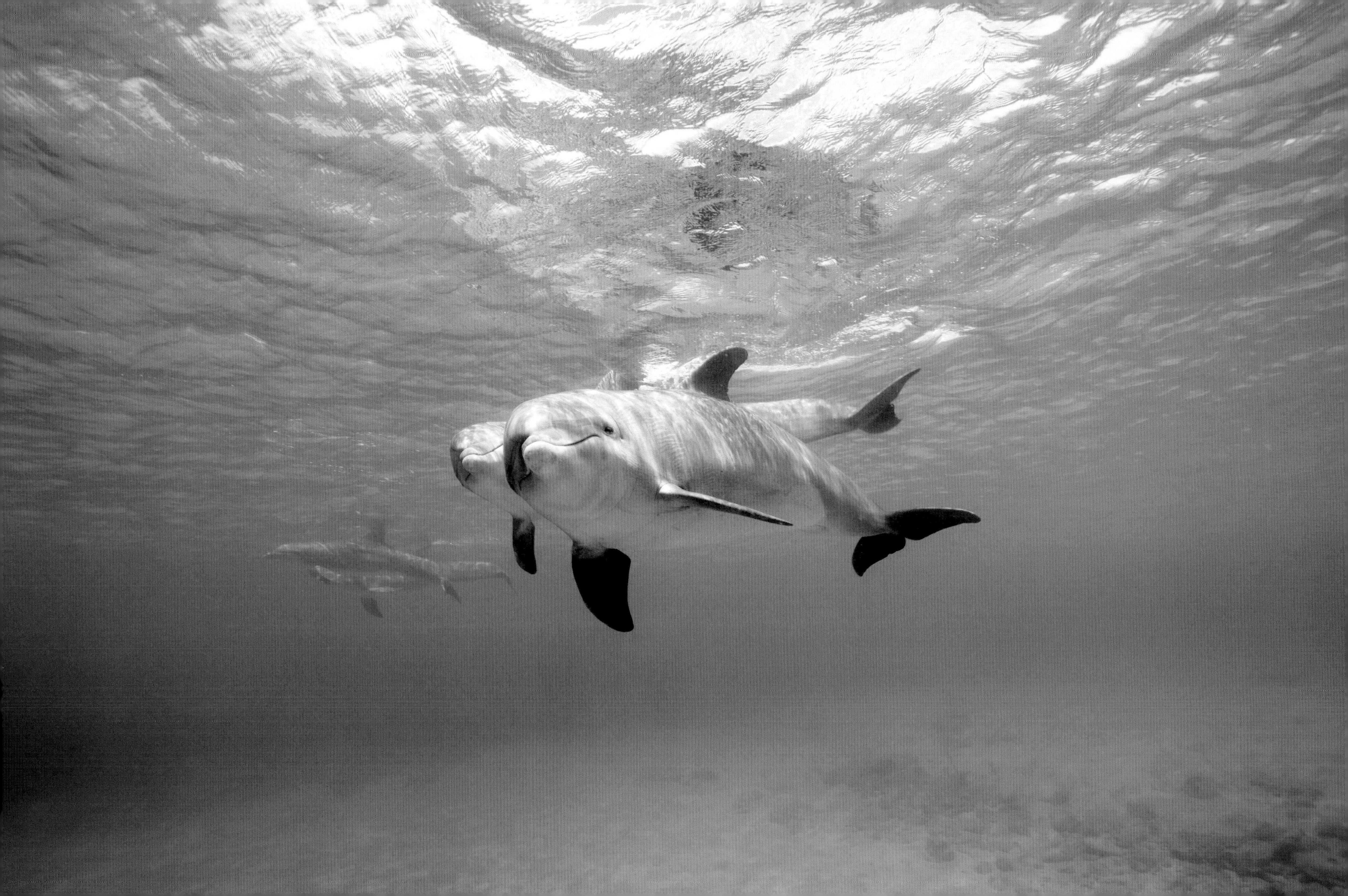

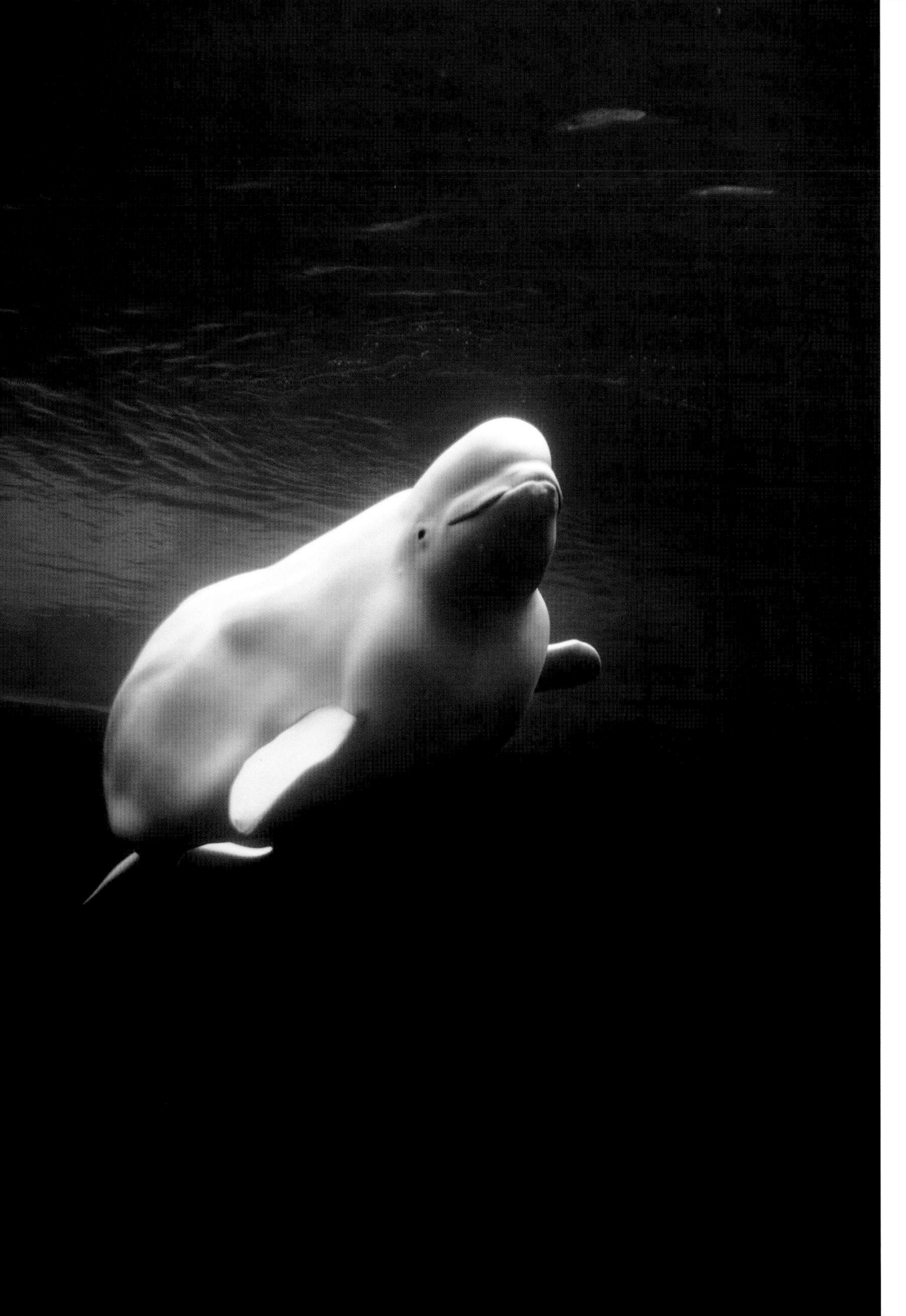

◄ beluga
► white whale

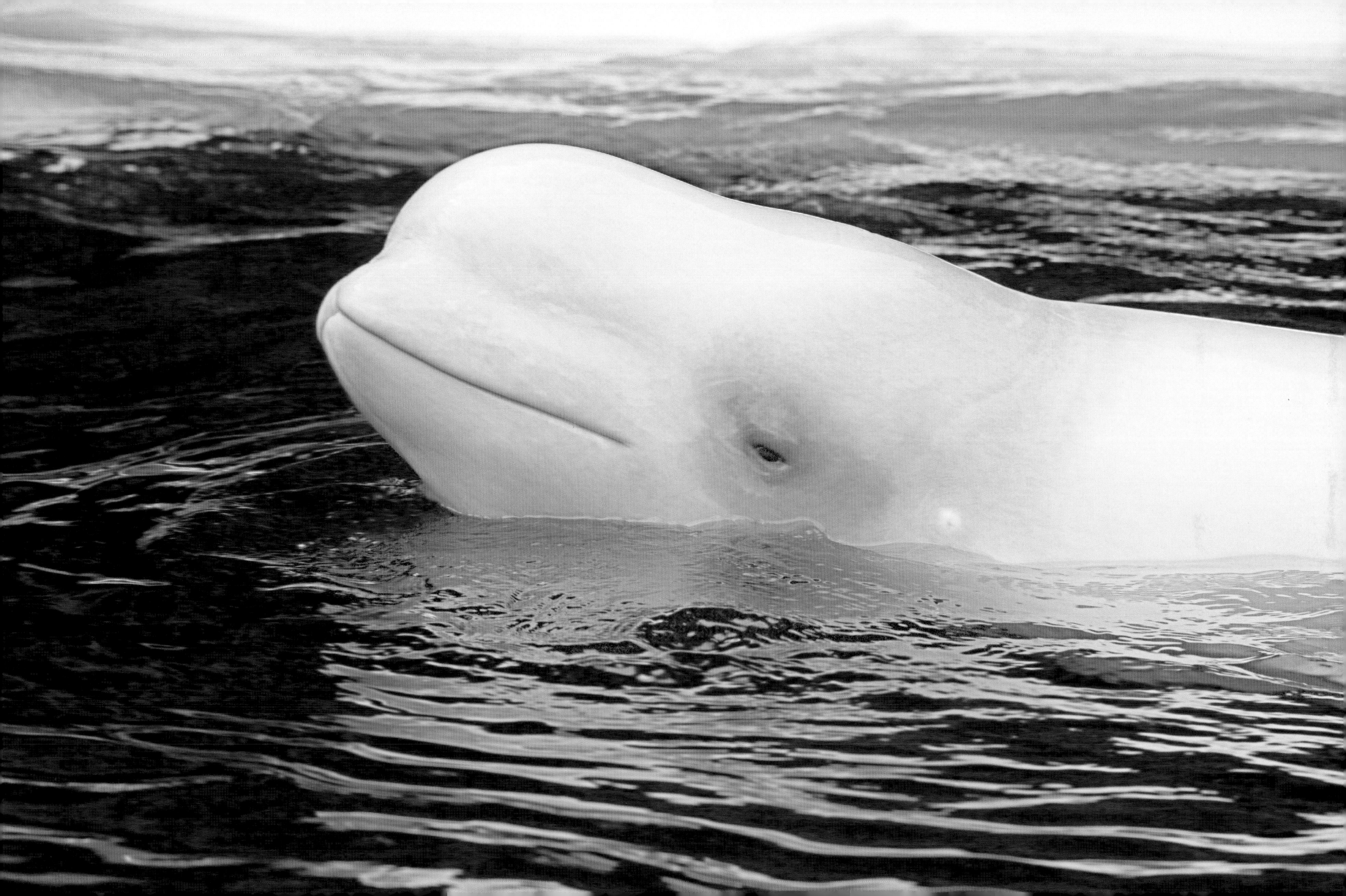

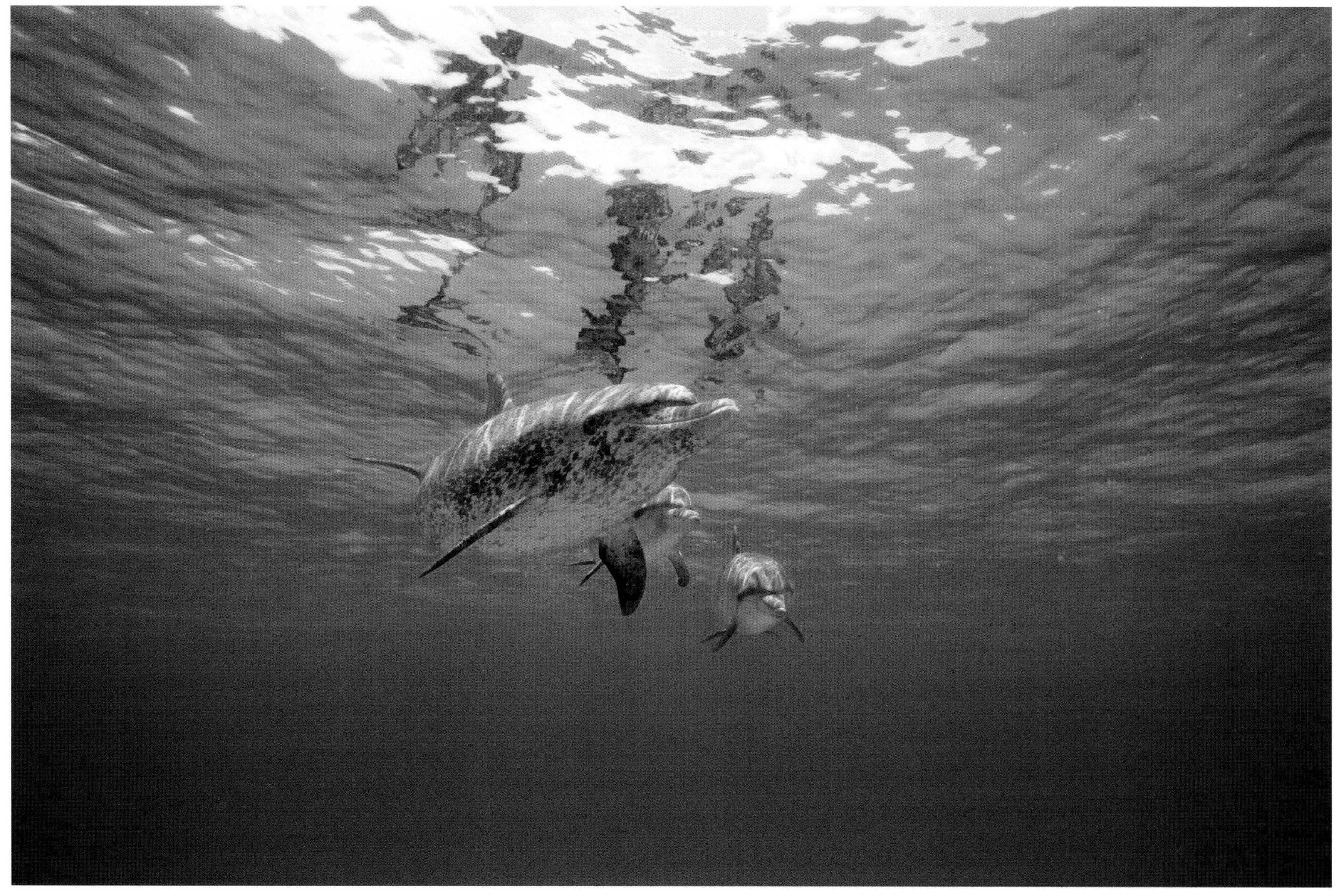

◀ meet the spotted dolphins
▶ new born sea life

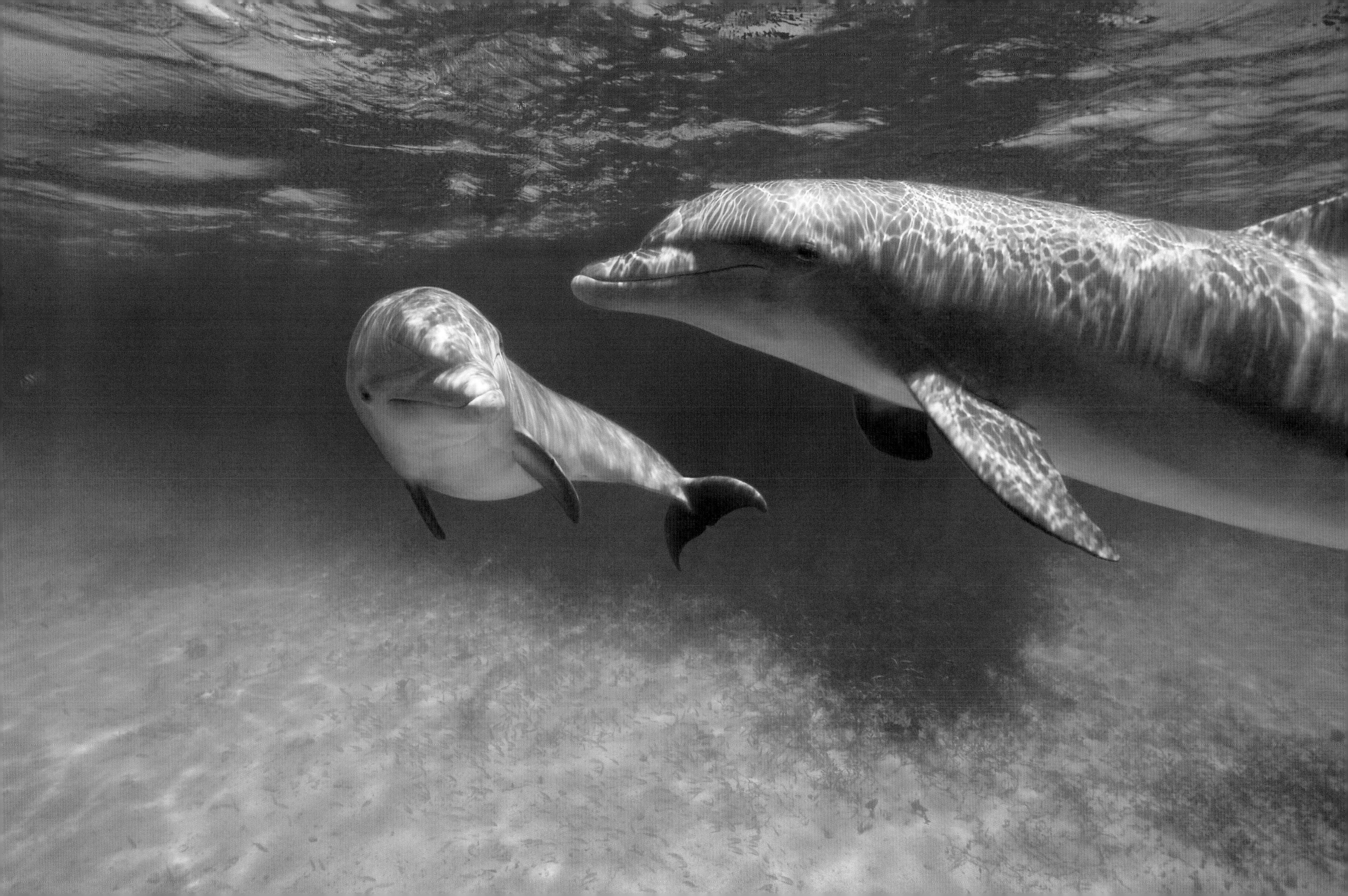

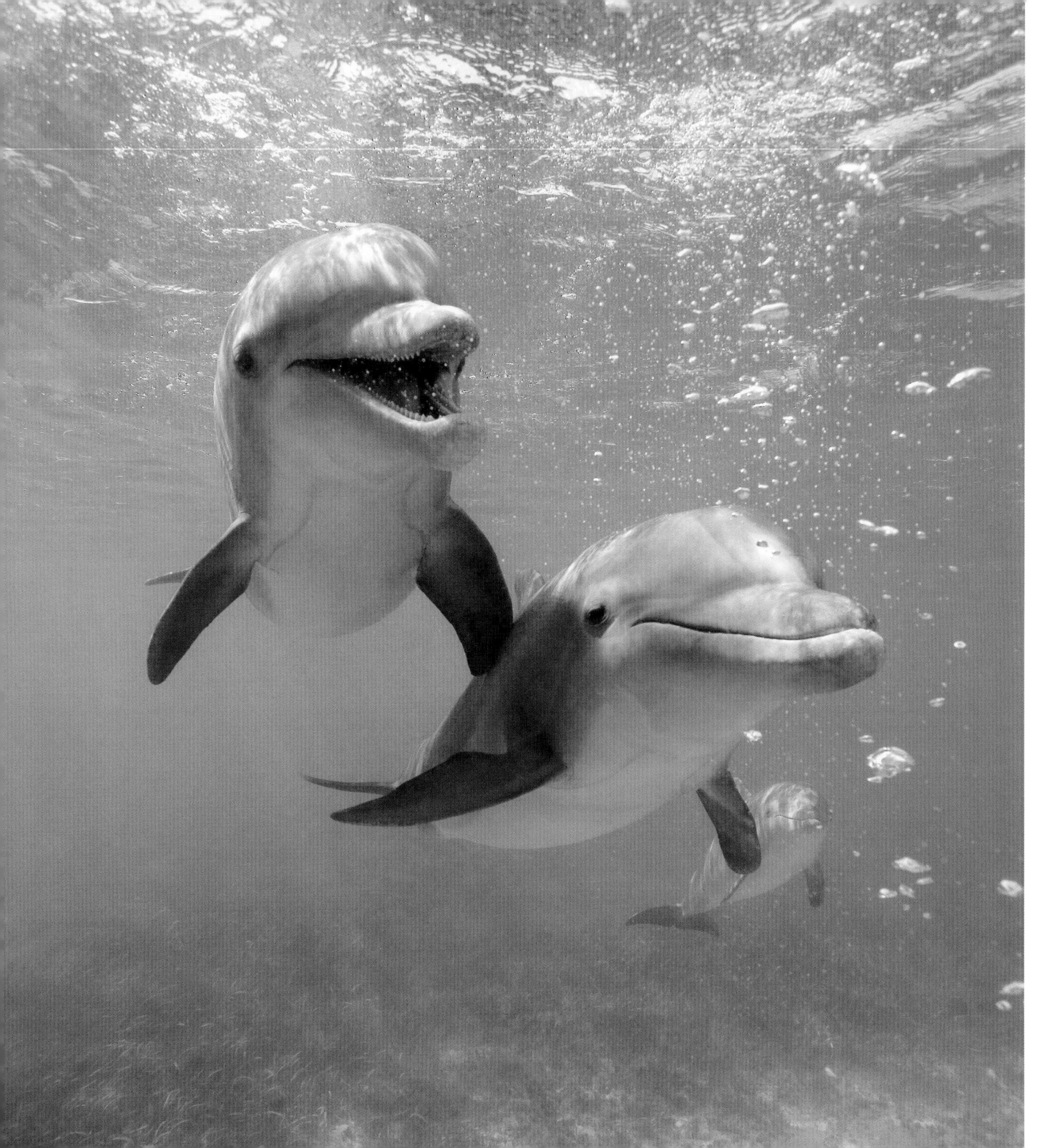

◄ dolphin speak
► splash

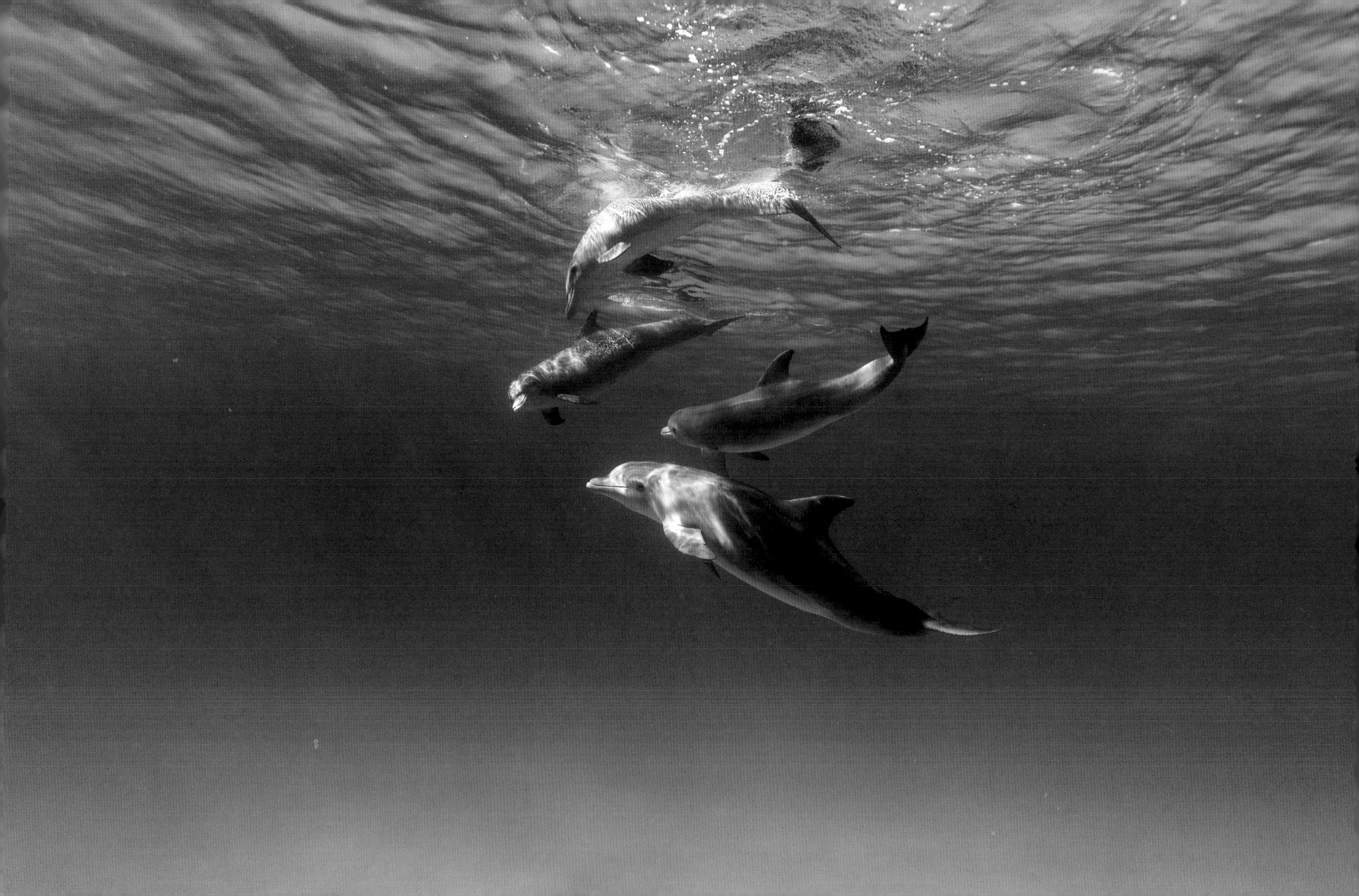

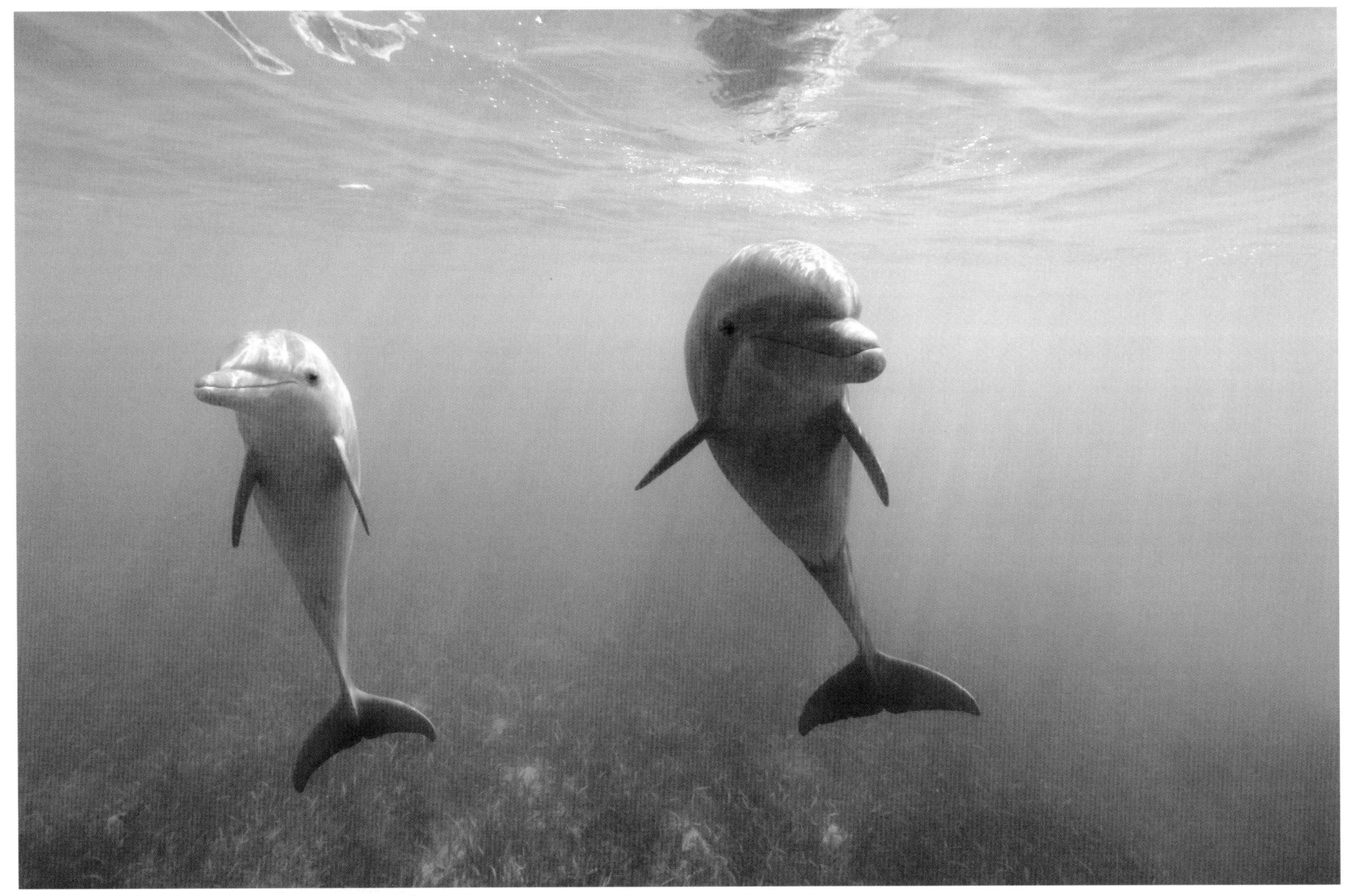

◀ buoyant sea
▶ new dolphin calf

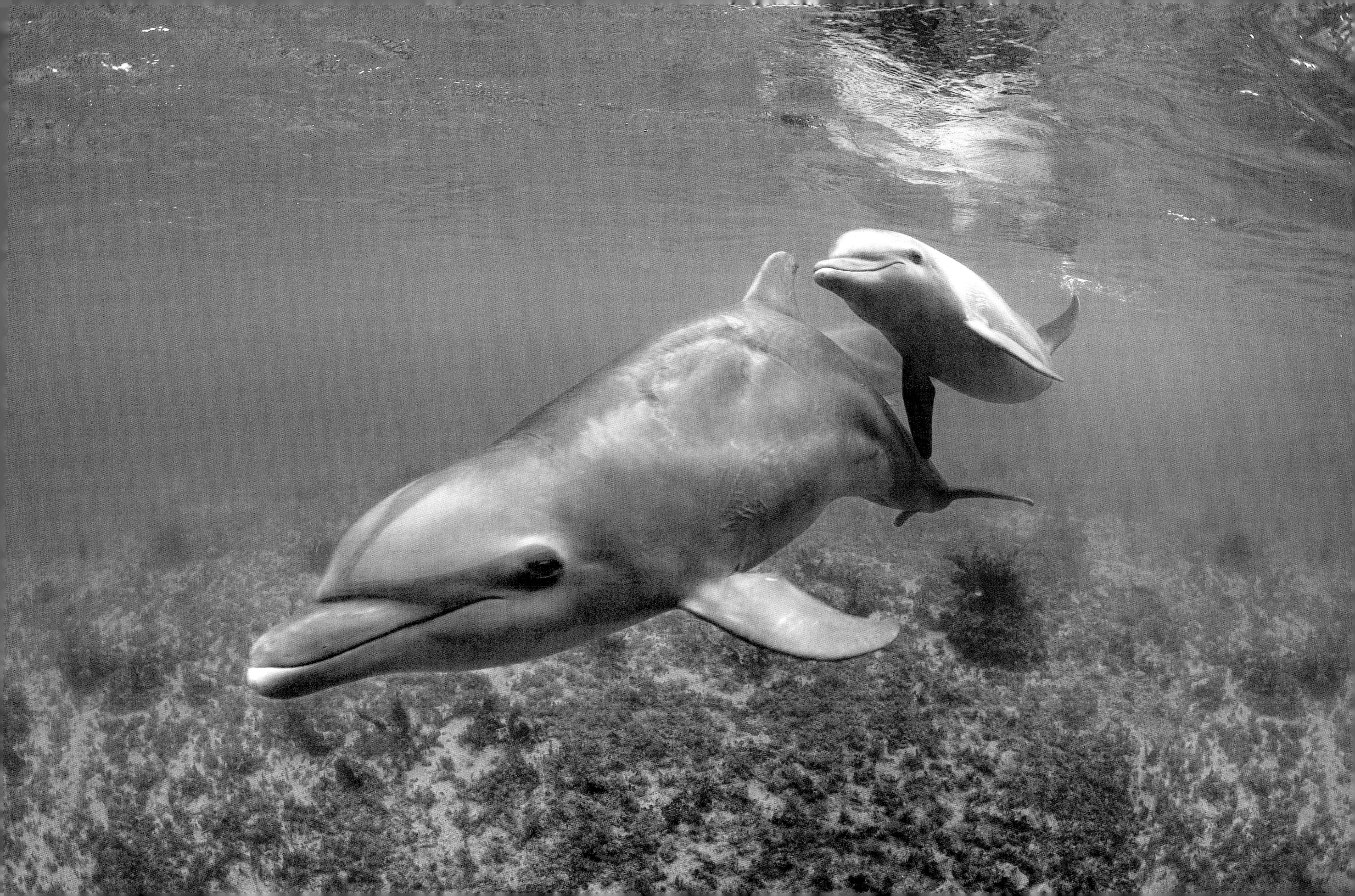

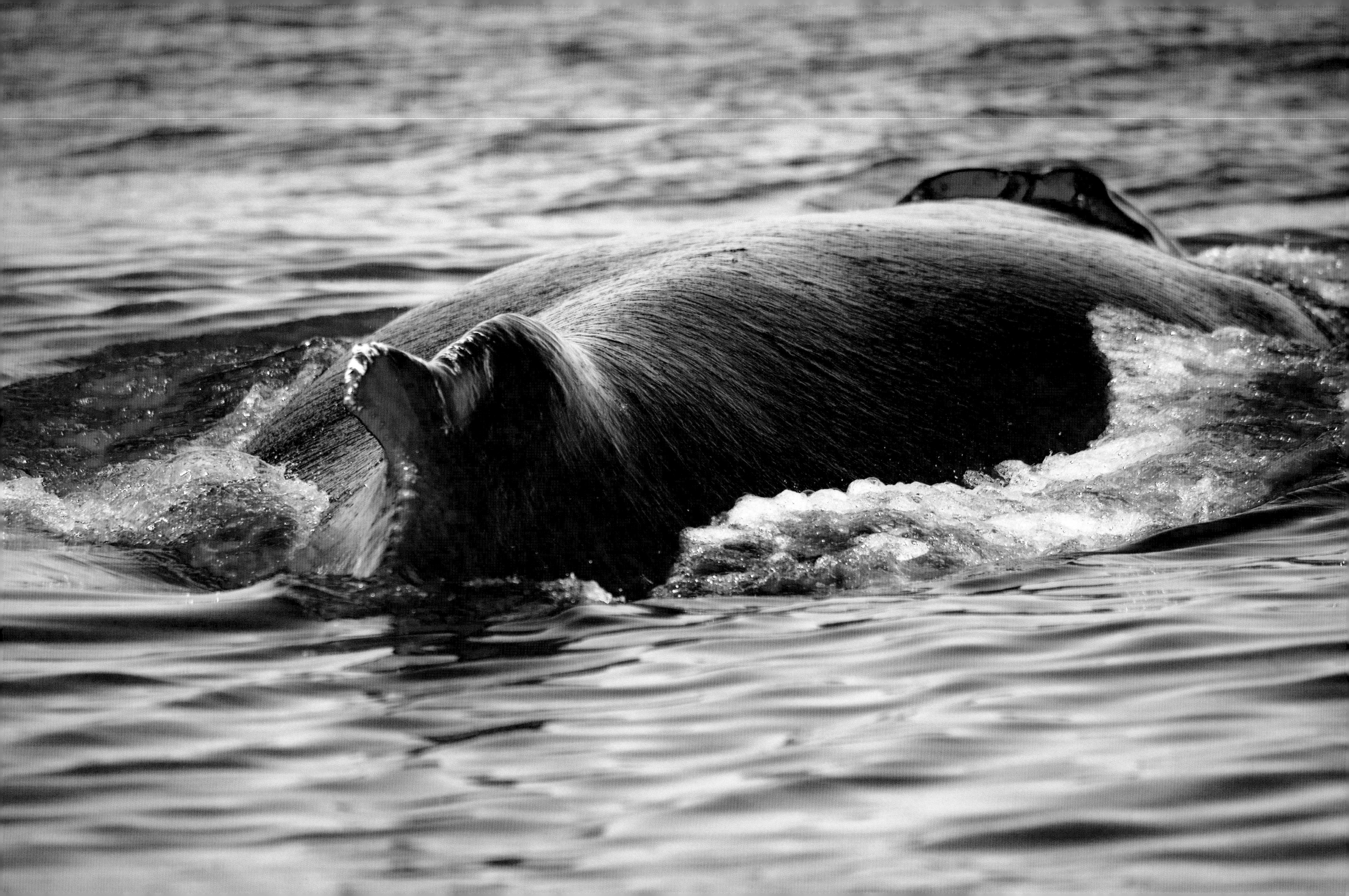

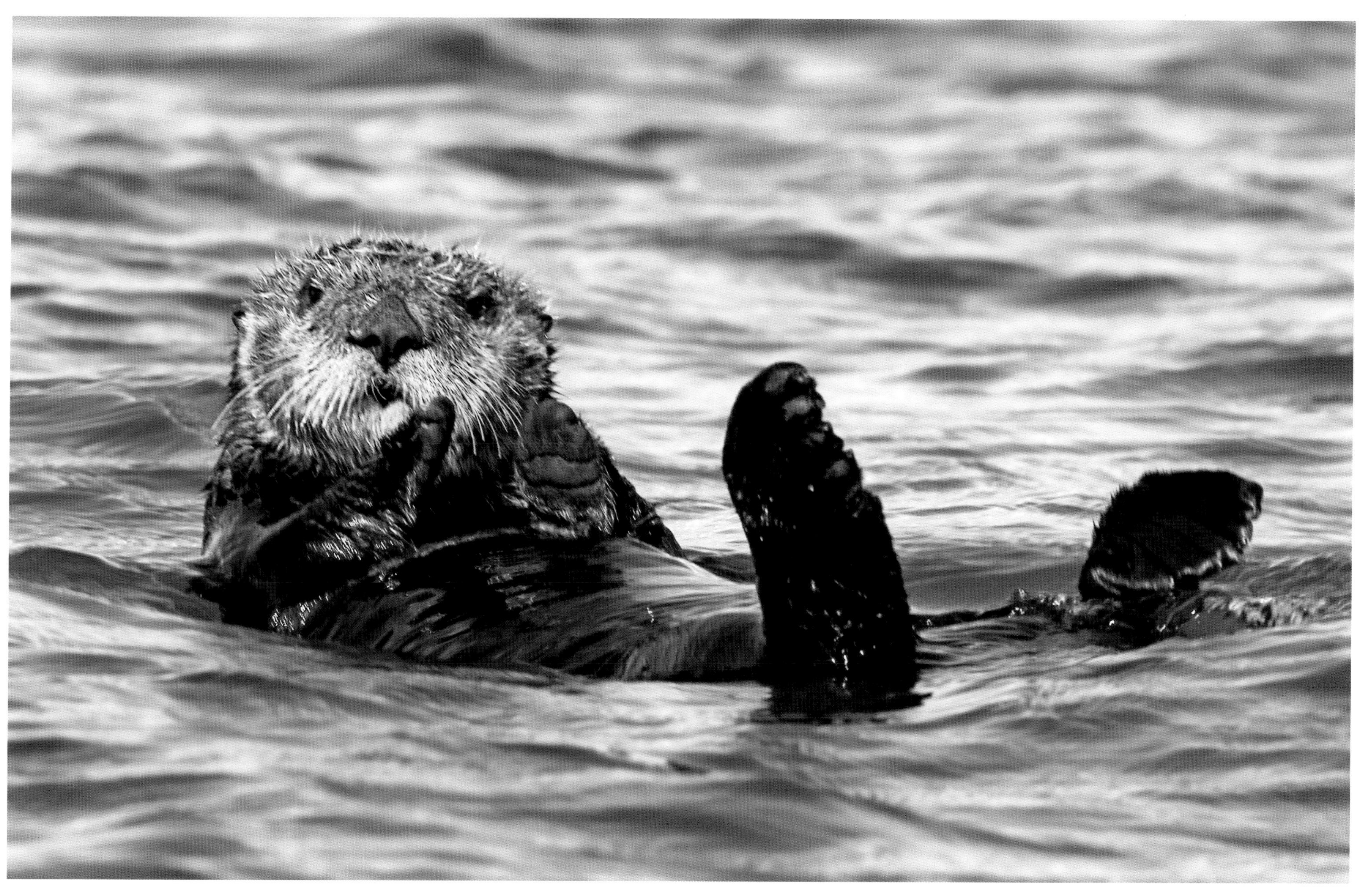

◄ humpback surface
▶ sea otter play

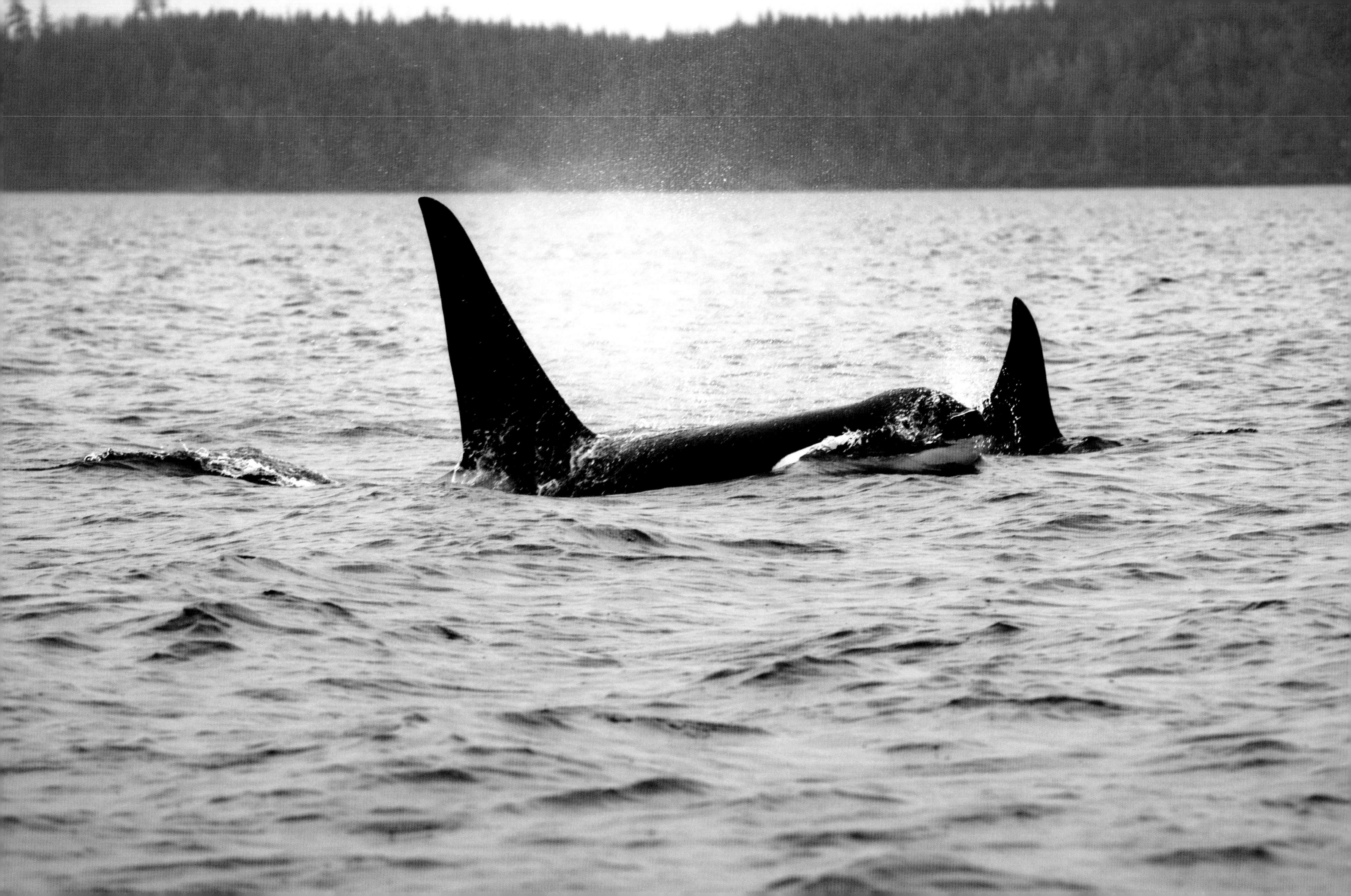

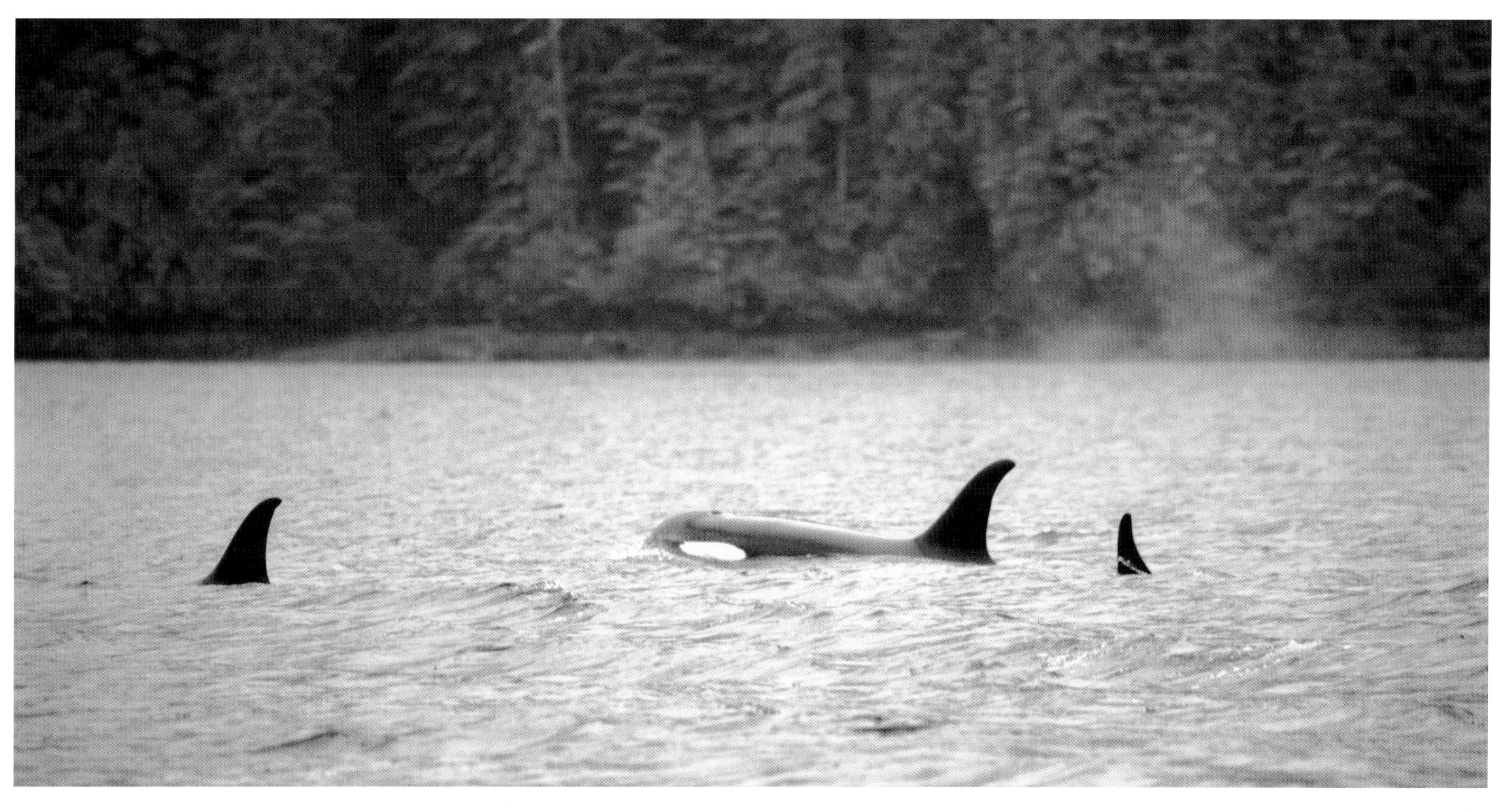

◀ orca pair
▶ orca pod

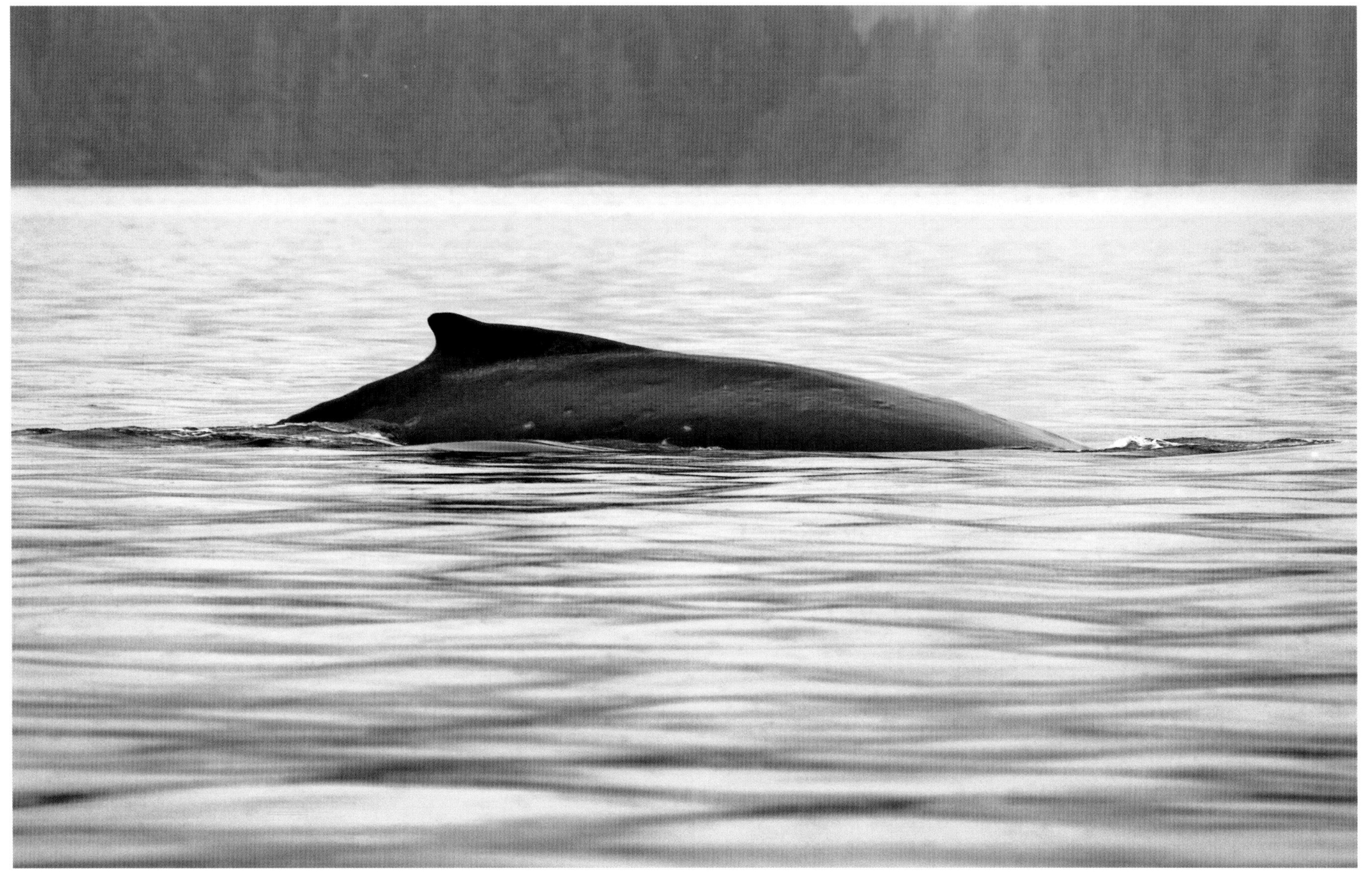

◀ humpback sighting
▶ deep sounding

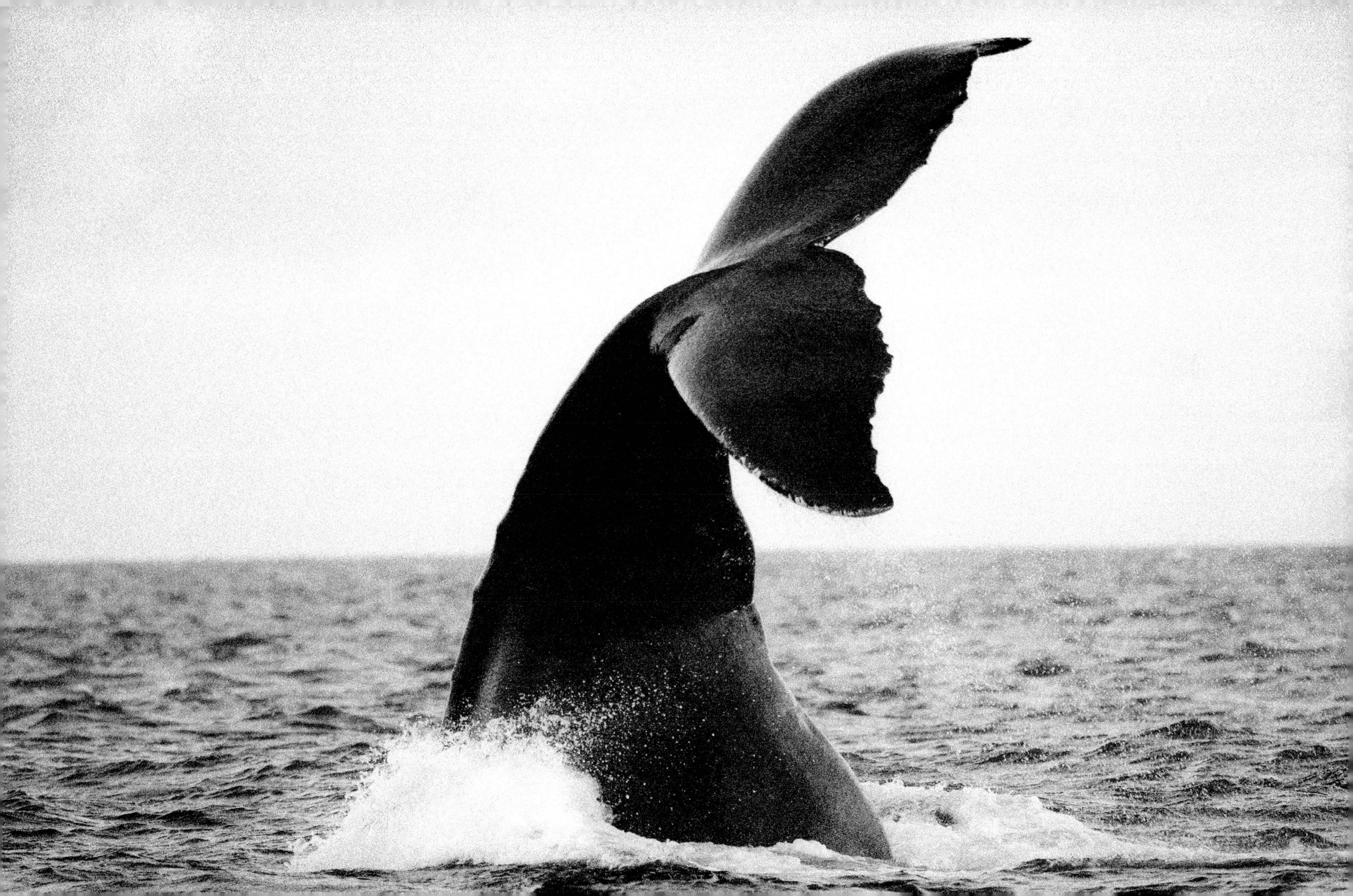

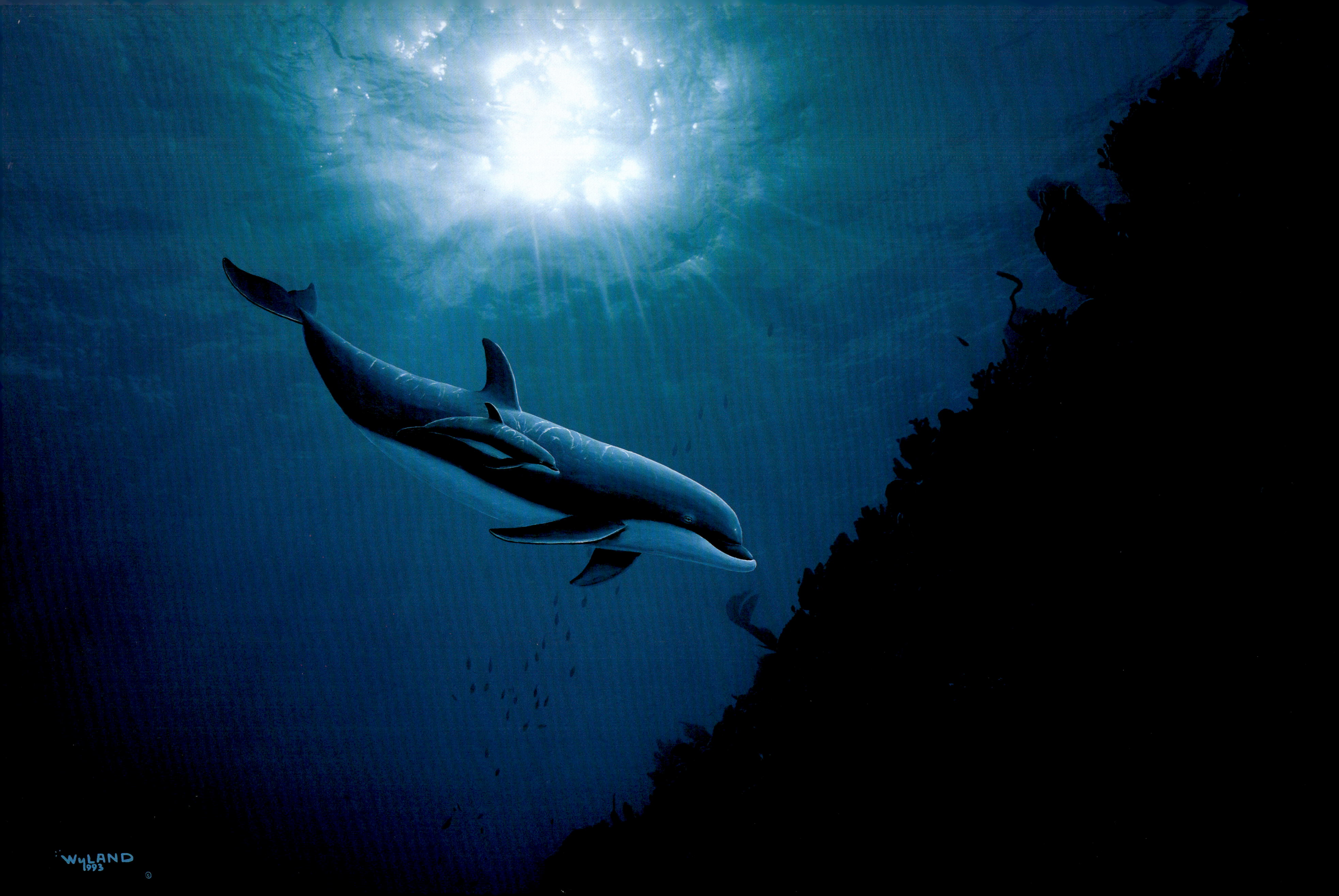

WYLAND
1993

I remember the first time I dived in St. Lucia, a beautiful little island in the Caribbean. I had just purchased one of the most expensive underwater cameras in the world at the time, the Nikon Nikonos RS. My goal was to create incredible underwater photography that I could sell in Wyland Galleries to pay for this new camera. On the very first dive over a giant coral reef wall, the sun burst out sending light deep into the water. At seventy feet, I looked through the wide-angle lens, shut off the strobe lights and photographed the ocean against the black, silhouetted reef. A funny thing happened moments after I took the photographs. I imagined dolphins swimming in front of the camera and when I returned to my studio and got the slides back, I decided to blow up the image to a large forty inch by sixty inch Cibachrome. I mounted the Cibachrome on archival board and placed it on my easel, as if I had painted the ocean background. Indeed, I did paint it, but with a camera. I decided to experiment and painted directly over the photograph in oil. To my surprise it worked perfectly, and I completed a portrait of an Atlantic bottlenose dolphin and calf directly on the photograph. I had this composite image digitally scanned and released a Cibachrome with the new underwater photography painting. It didn't look like a photograph or a painting. It looked like something different. It was my first artistic image and it captured the imagination of my collectors and the entire edition sold out in months.

Today, I believe having the opportunity to draw, paint, photograph, and use many mediums to create an image is a wonderful gift. For artists, we are meant to break the rules, and artistic imaging allows me to forward the medium and create paintings that are unlike any before. In the future, I'm sure more technology will allow more creativity, but in the end, it's still the artist who puts everything together, and shares his personal vision.

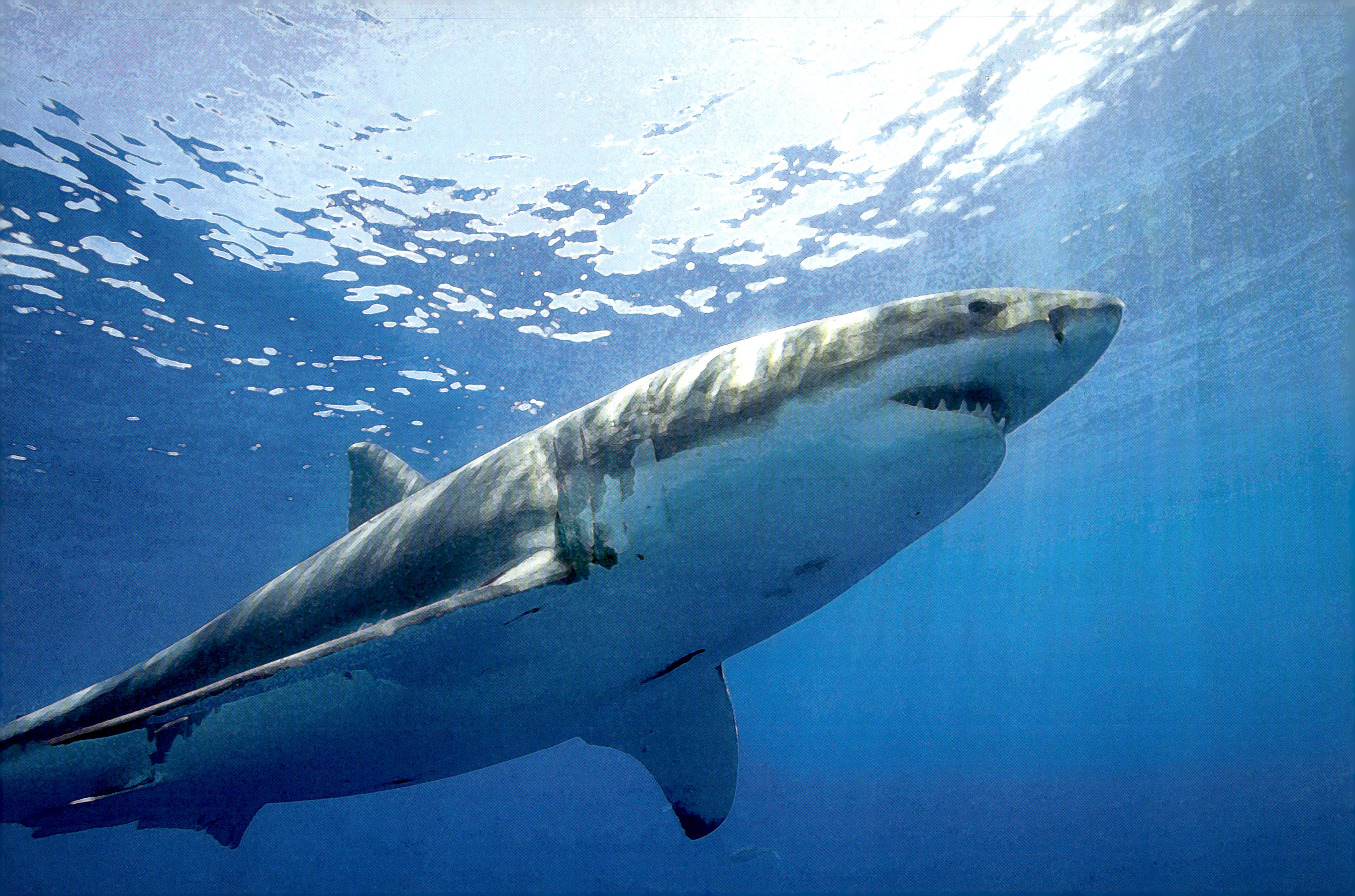

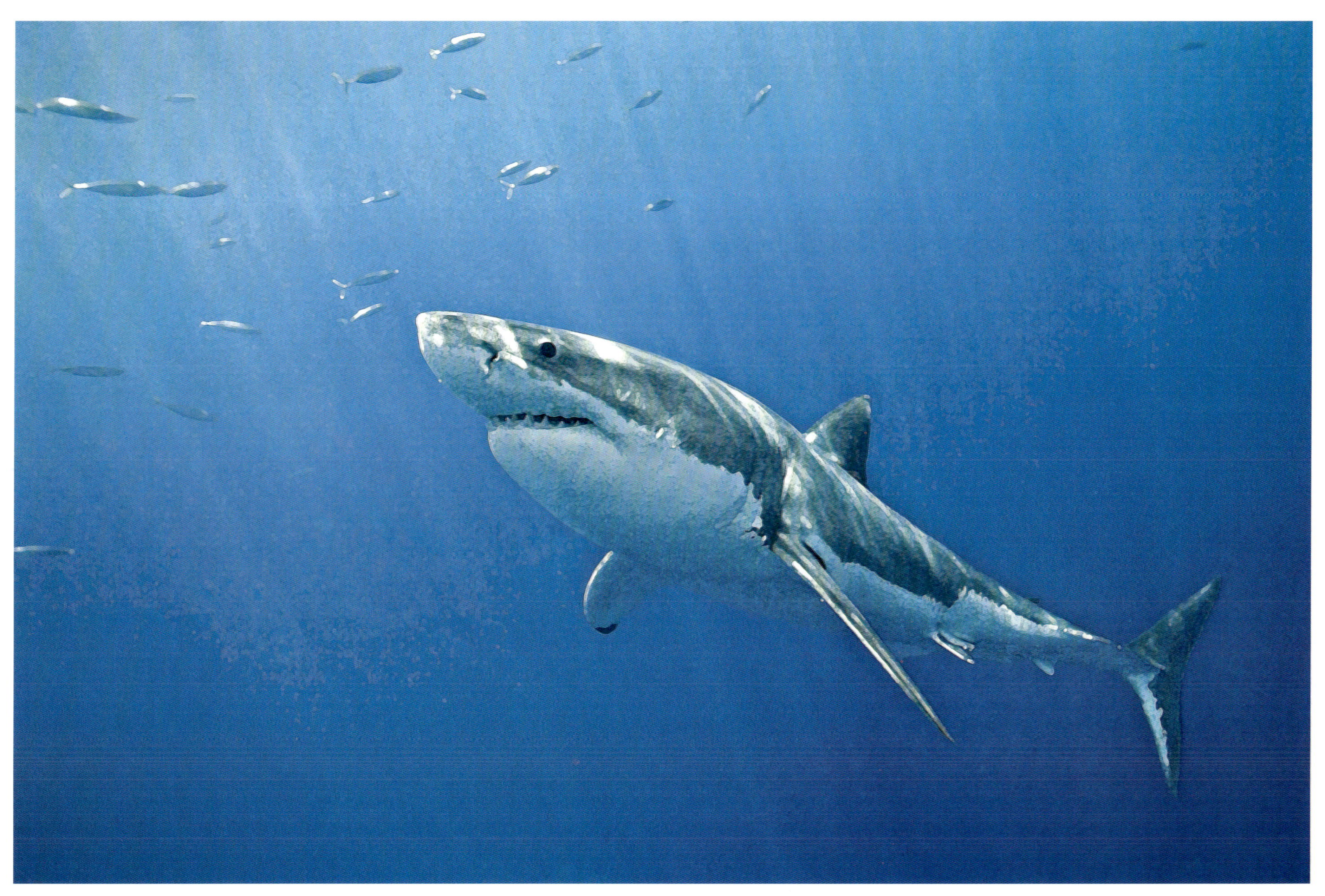

◄ great white shark waters
► white shark sea

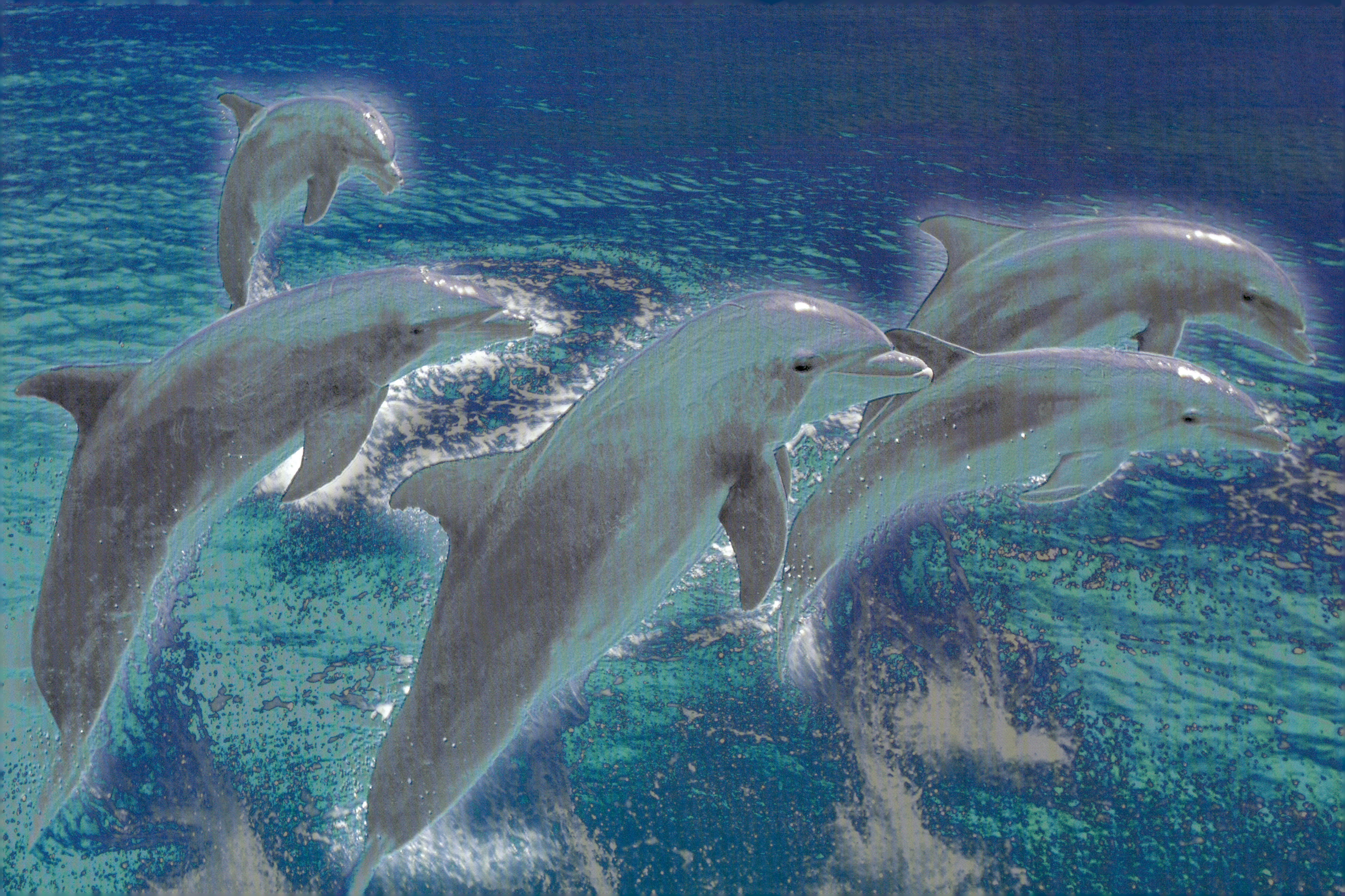

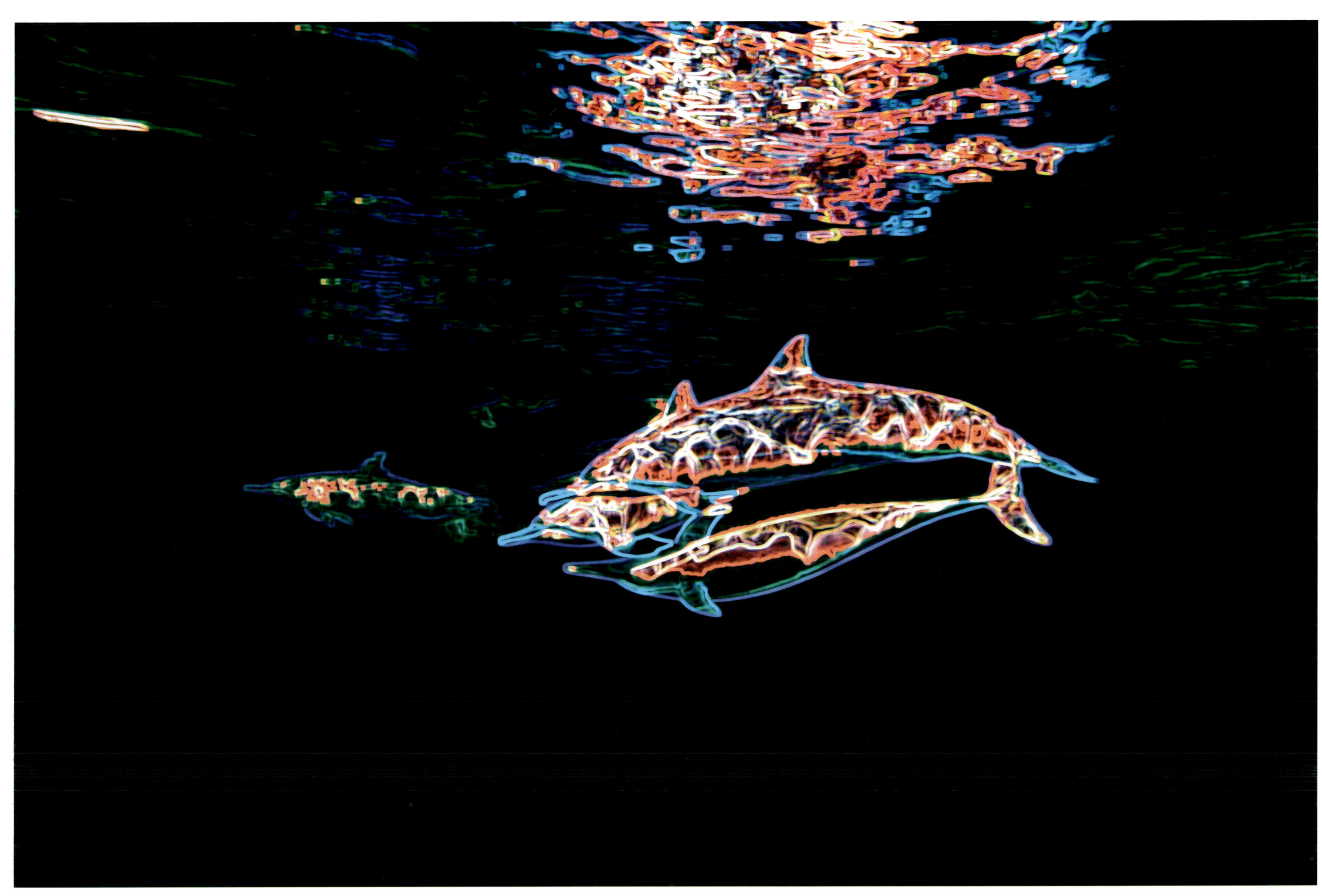

in the end the sea will survive, It is man who may well be endangered...

Wyland

▶ whale vision

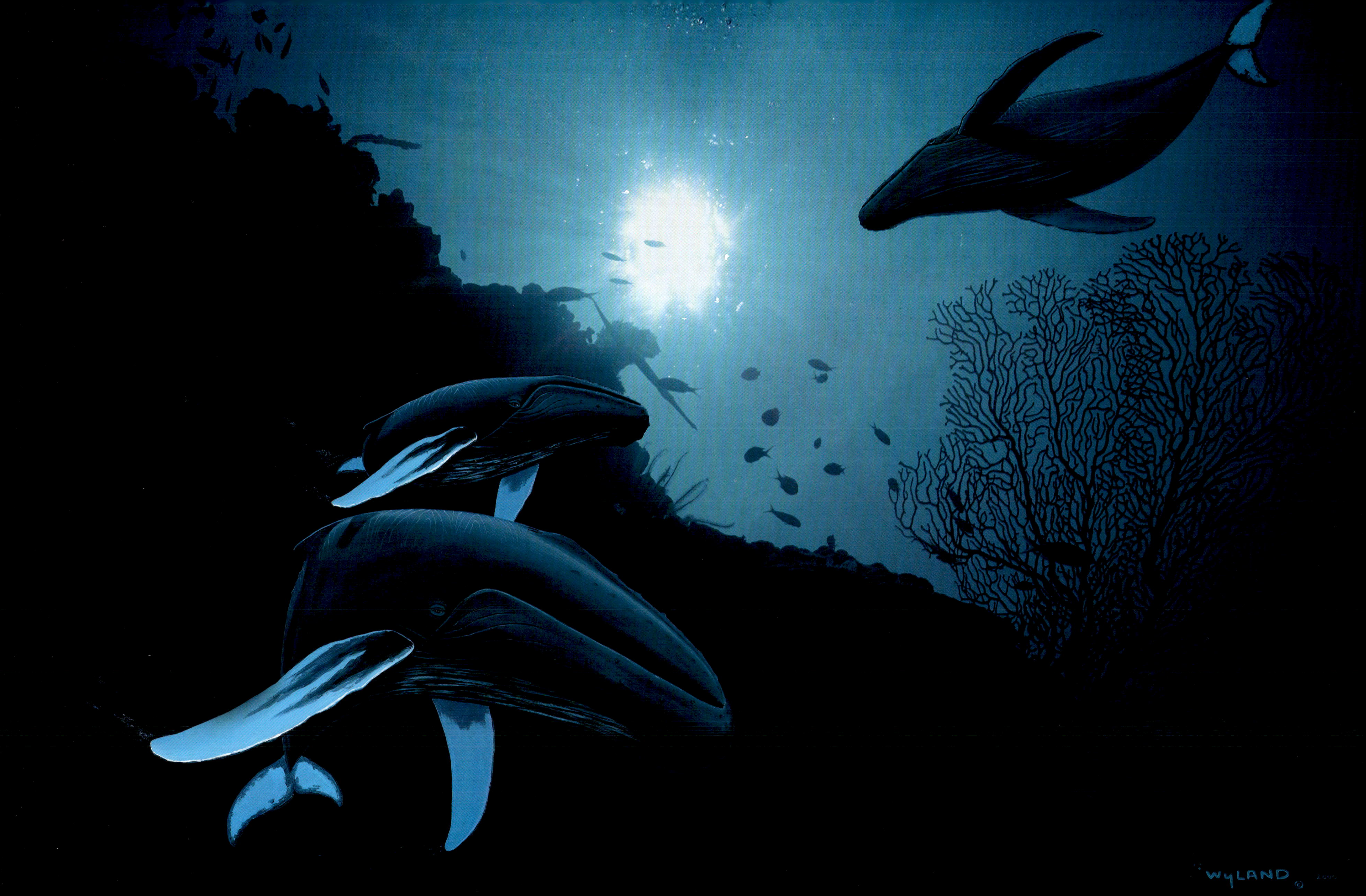

WYLAND

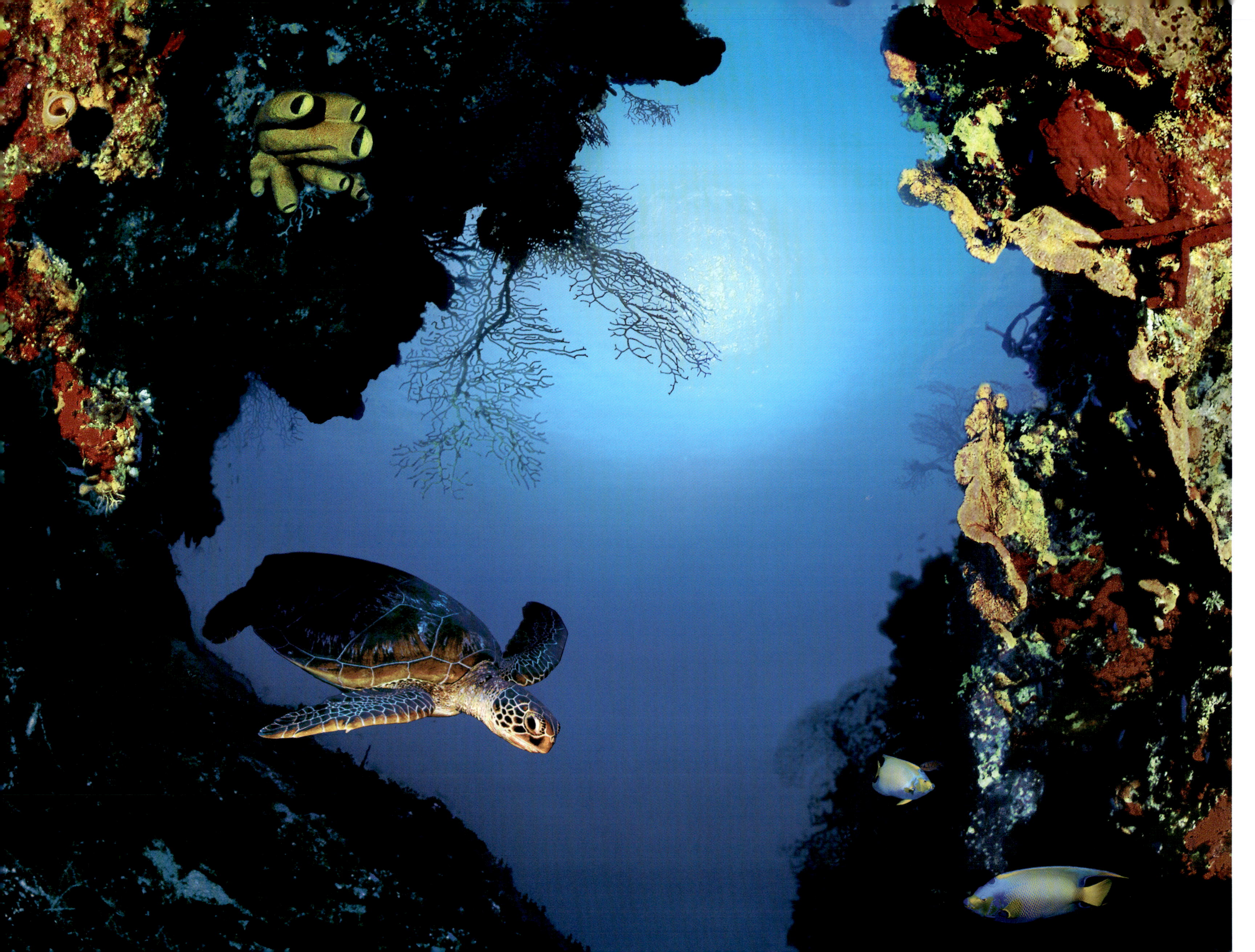

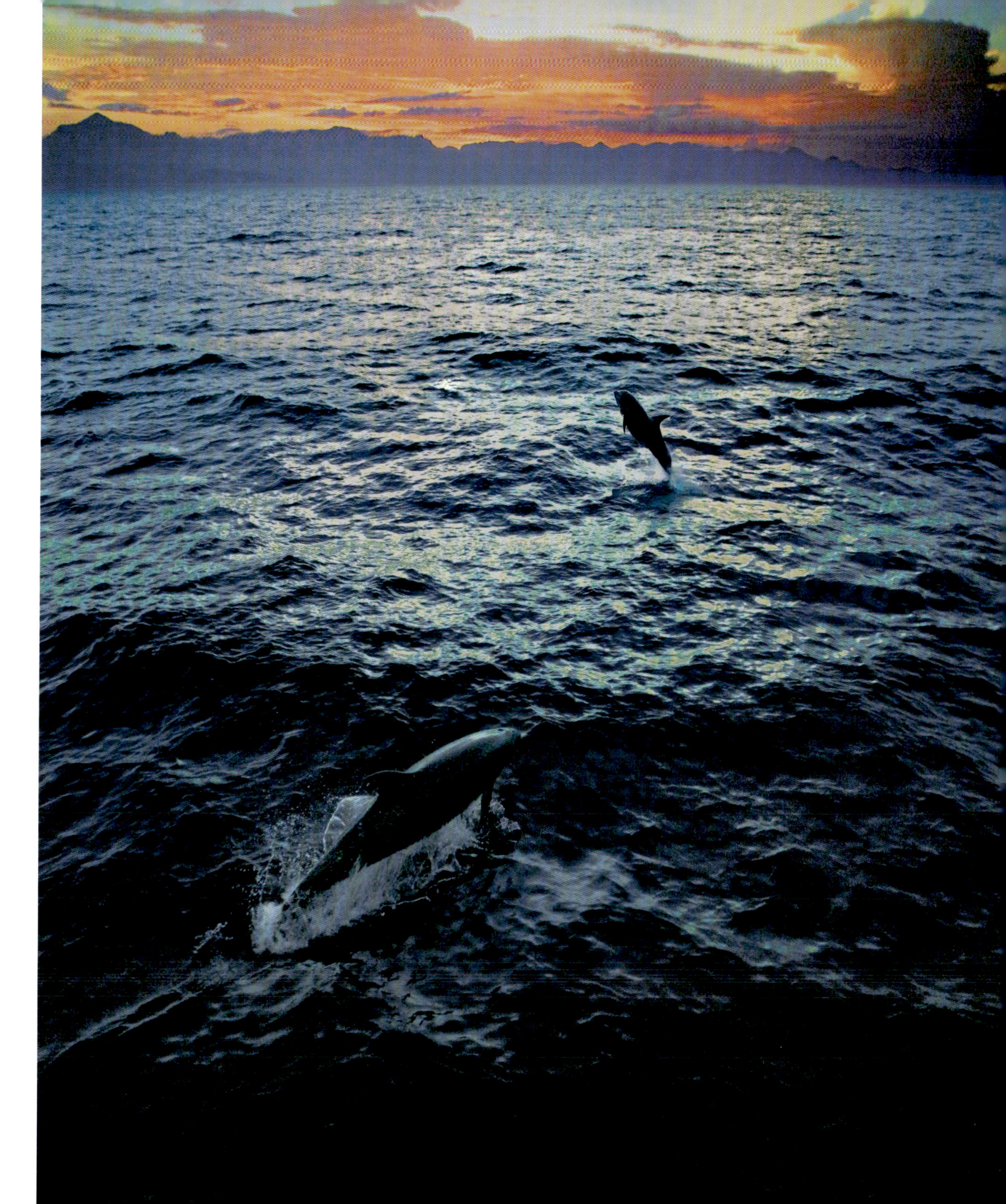

ocean portal
sea of cortez

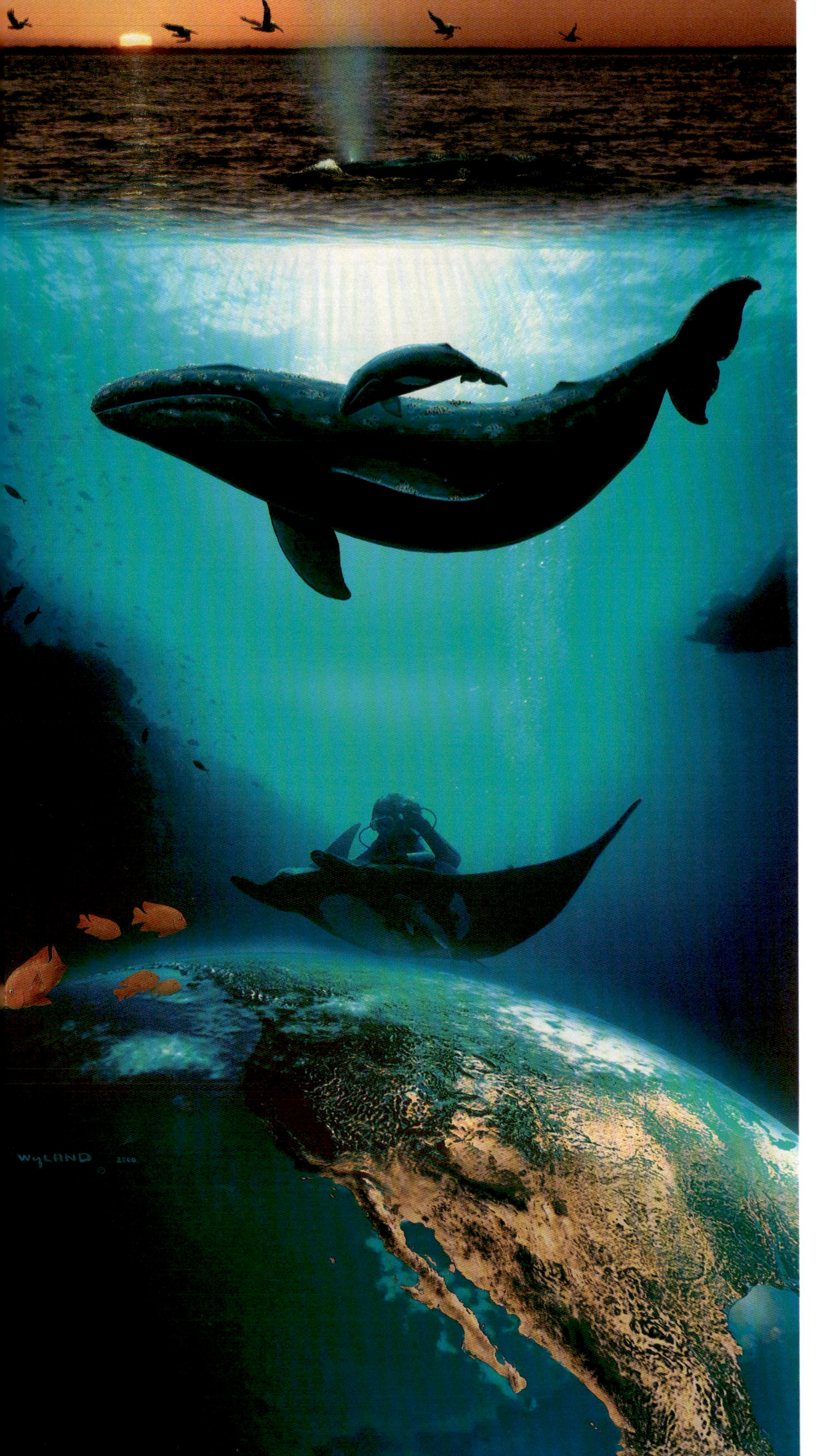

mankind is at an environmental crossroads. it's time to save our planet

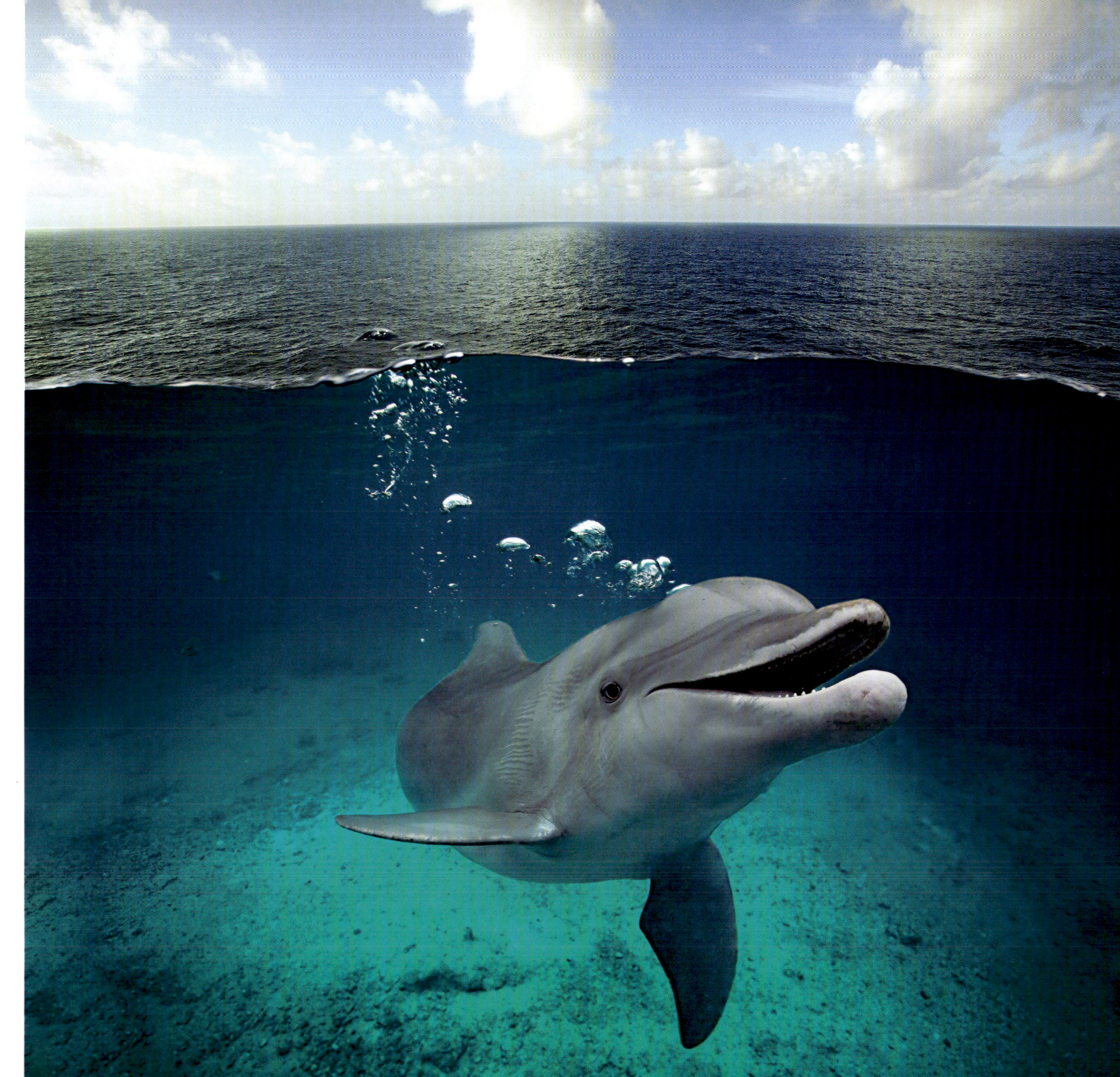

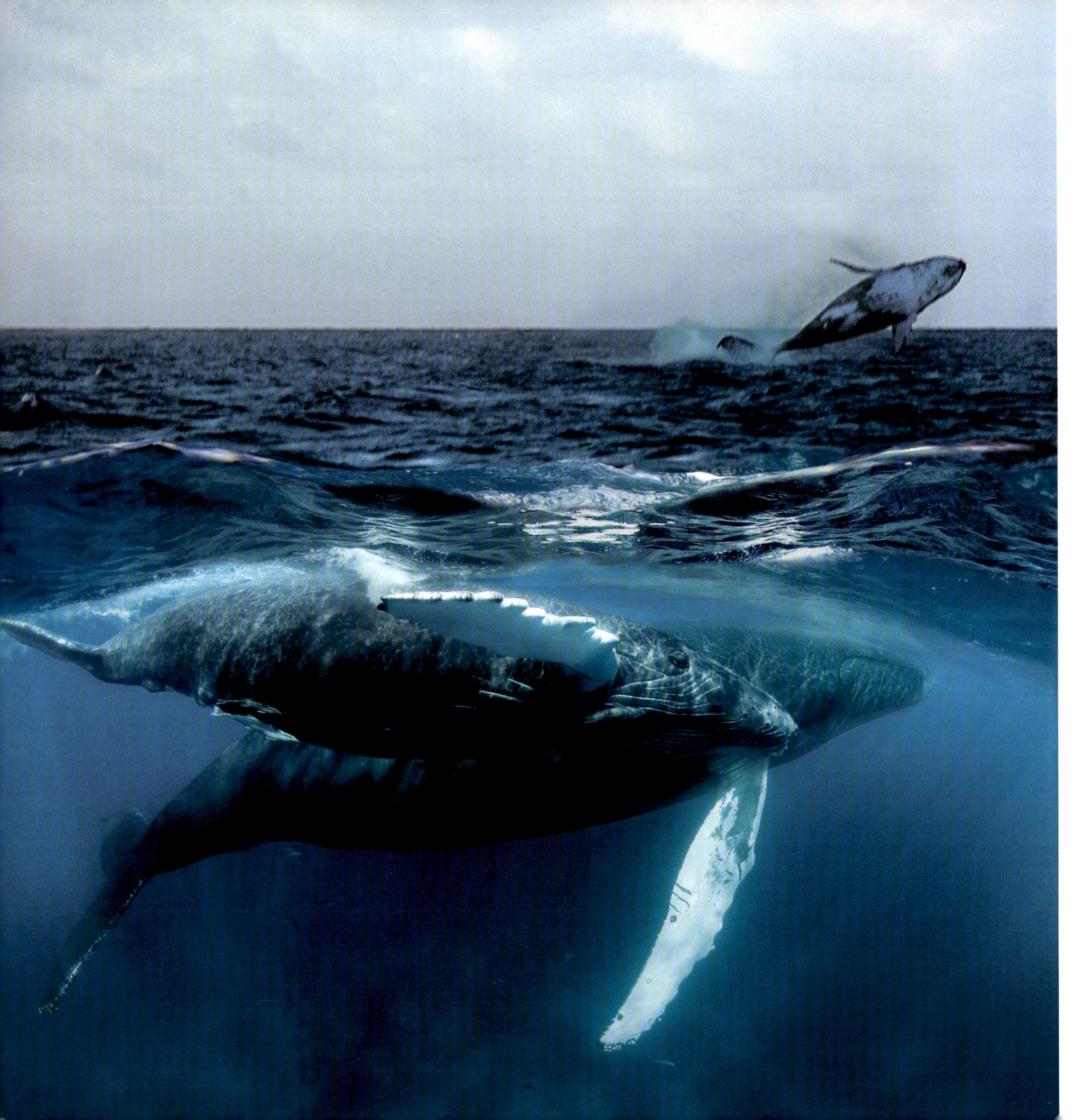

◀ two worlds of whales
▶ humpback encounter

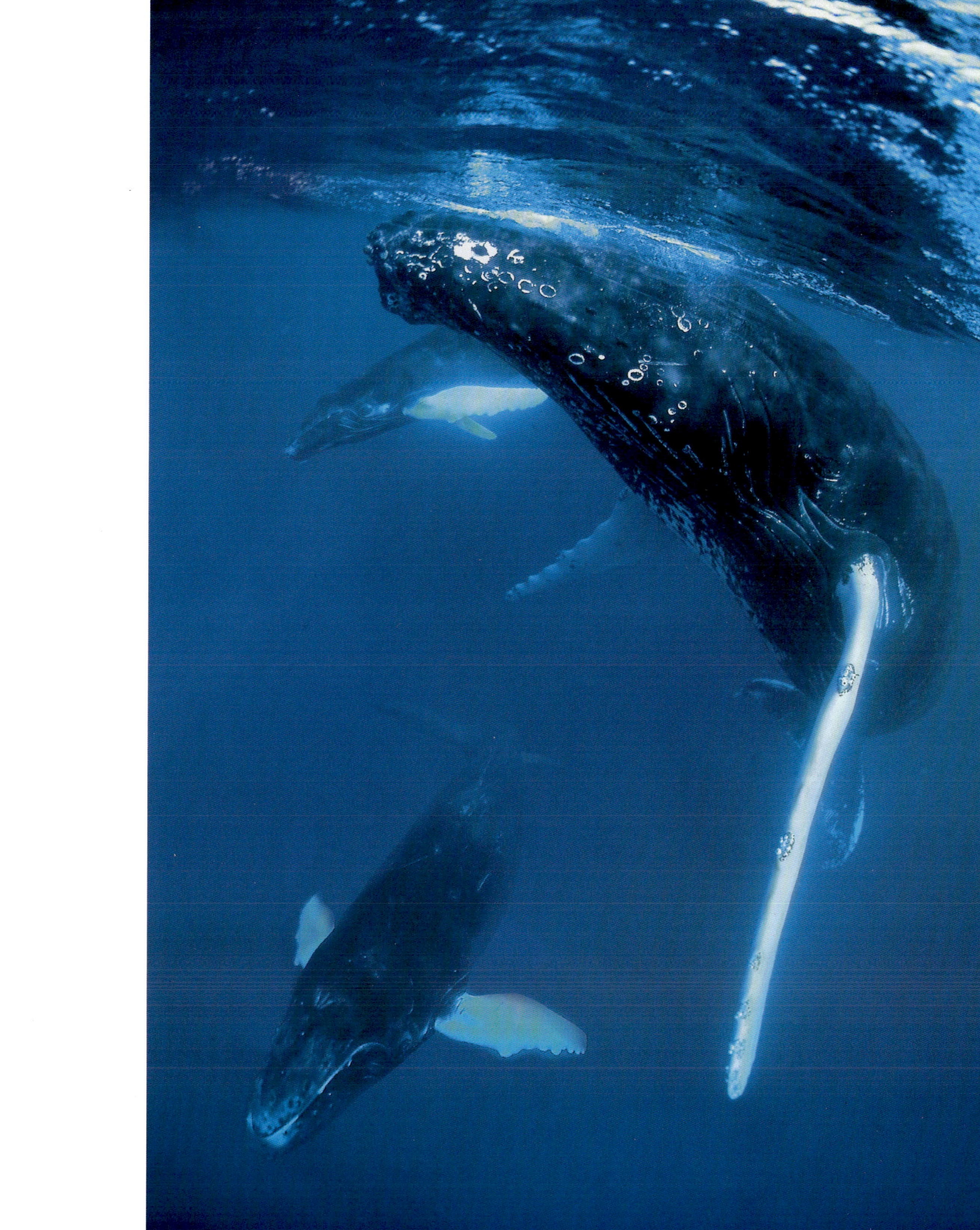

we must not only see the world of whales with our eyes, but with our hearts...

Wyland

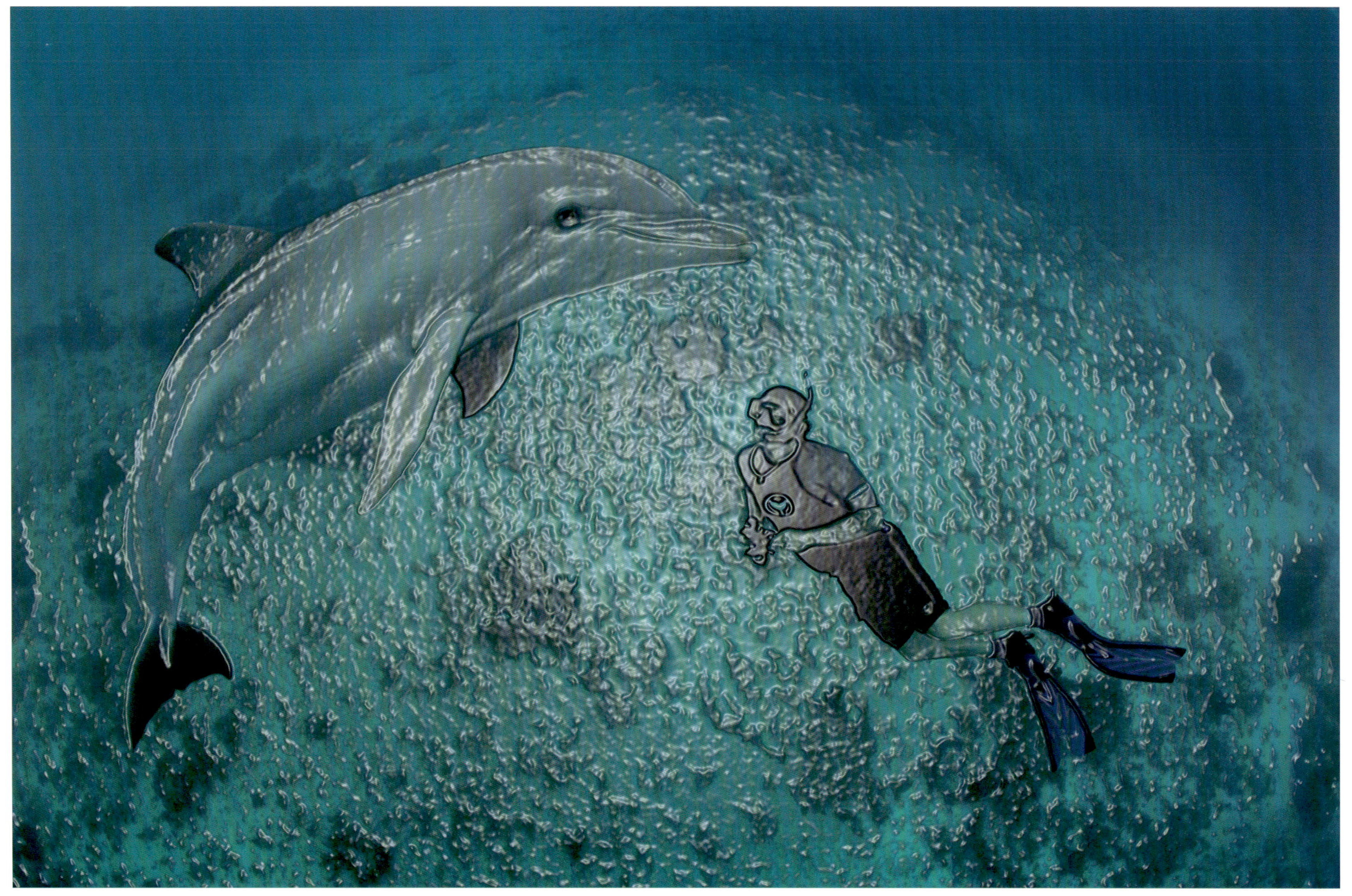

◀ artist underwater dolphin view
▶ dolphin sketch

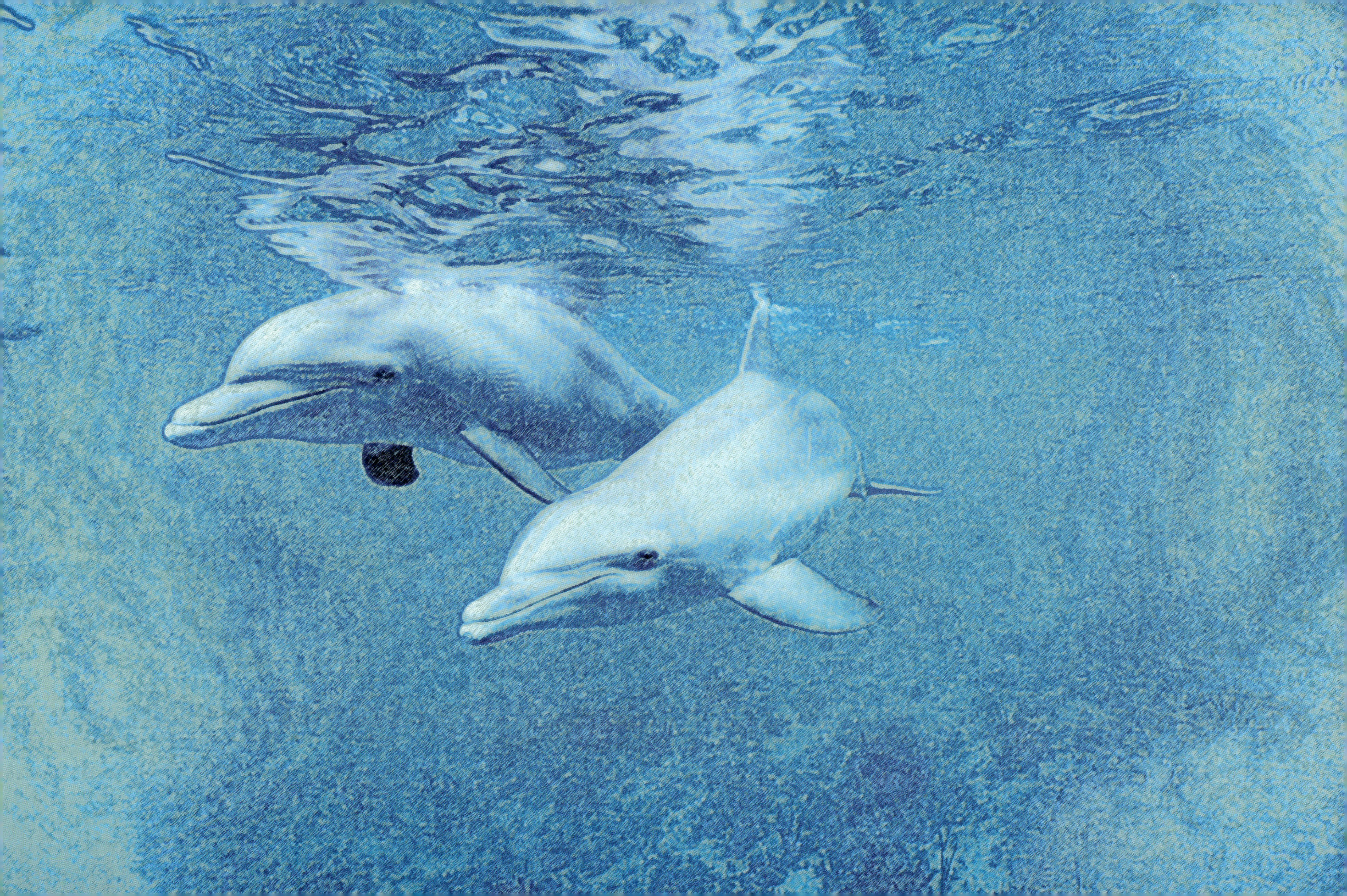

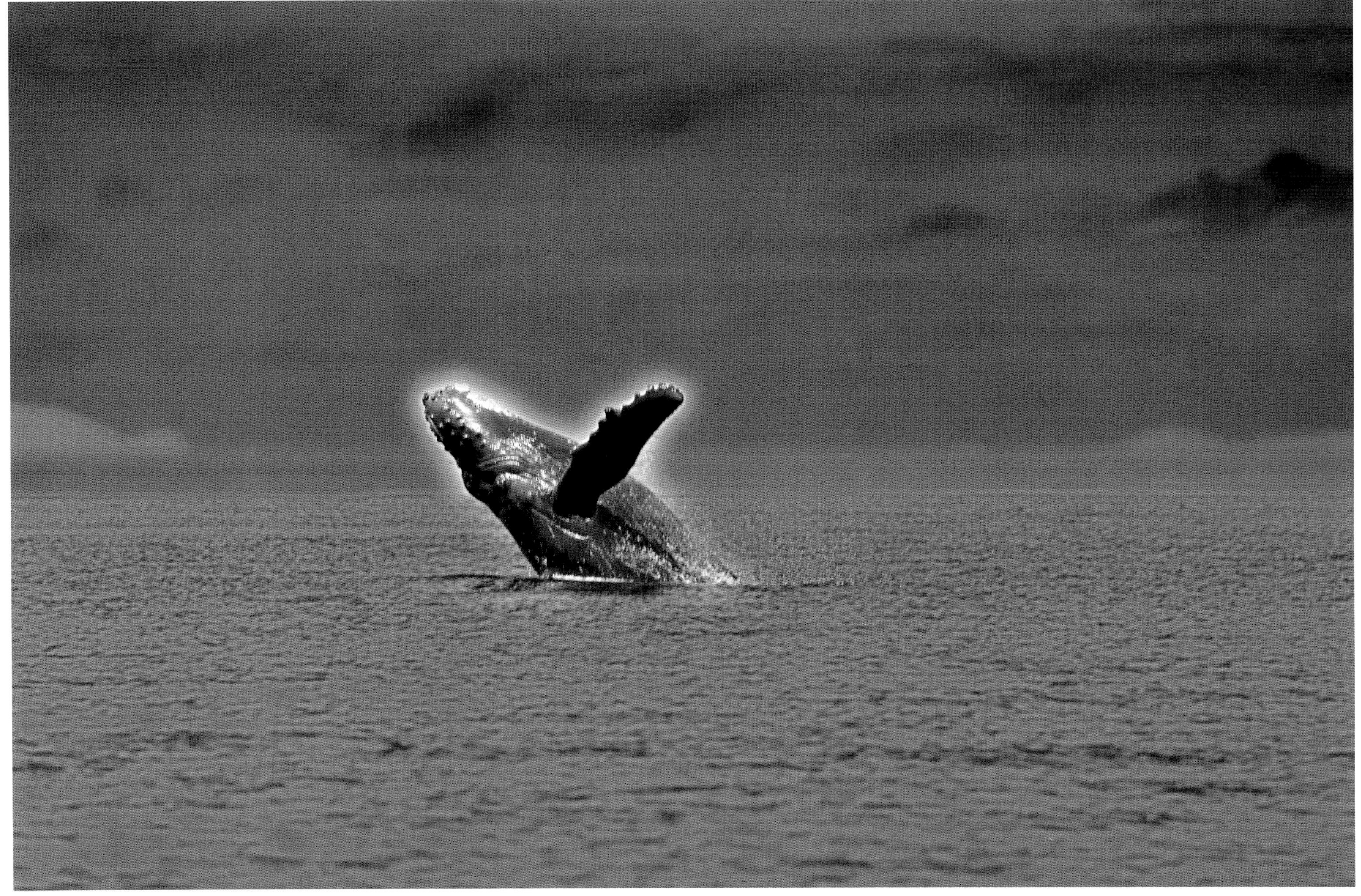

◀ humpback rising

▶ endangered hawaiian monk seal

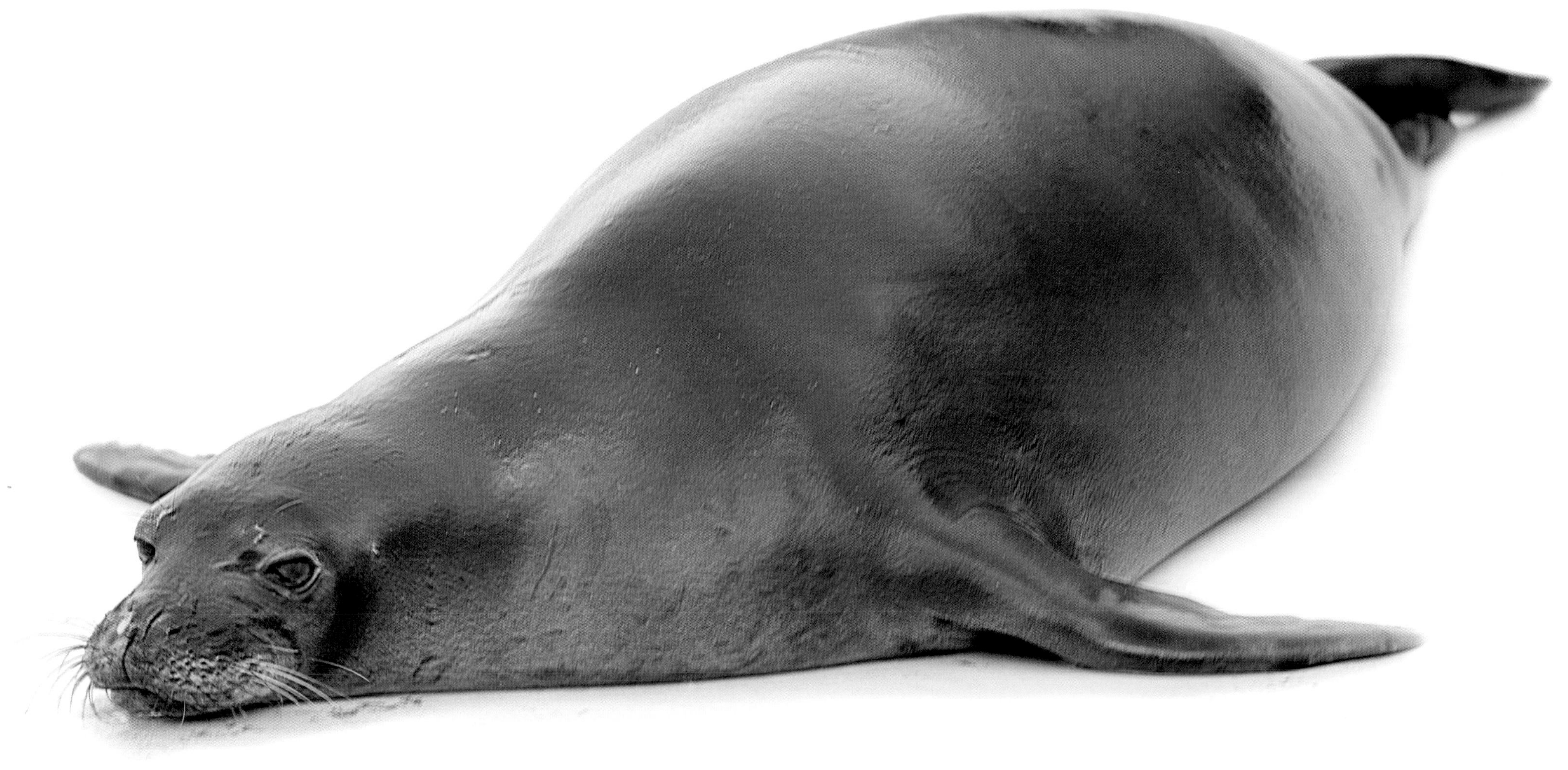

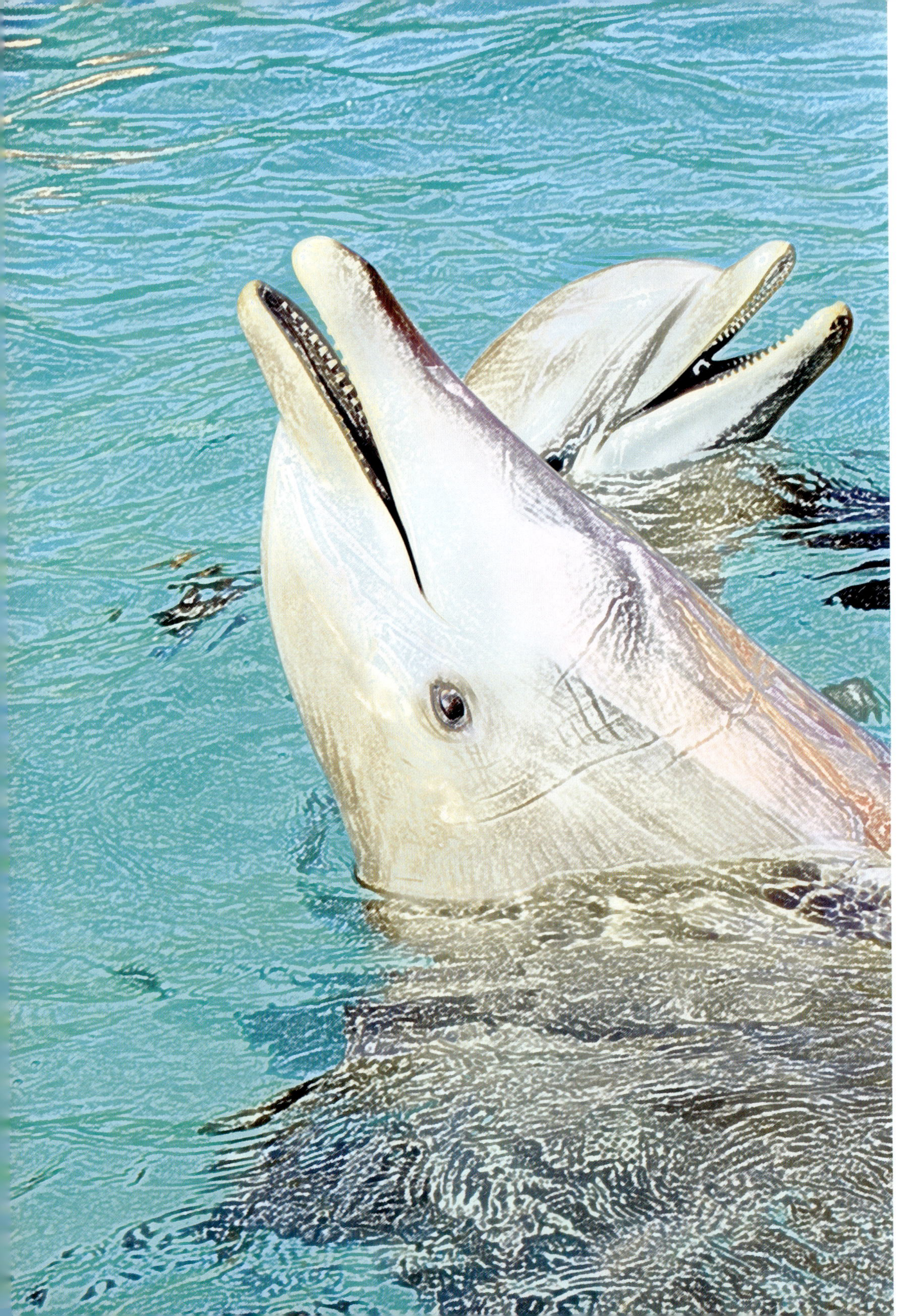

clean water and a healthy ocean are not only important to the animals of the sea,

they are the source of our very future ...

Wyland

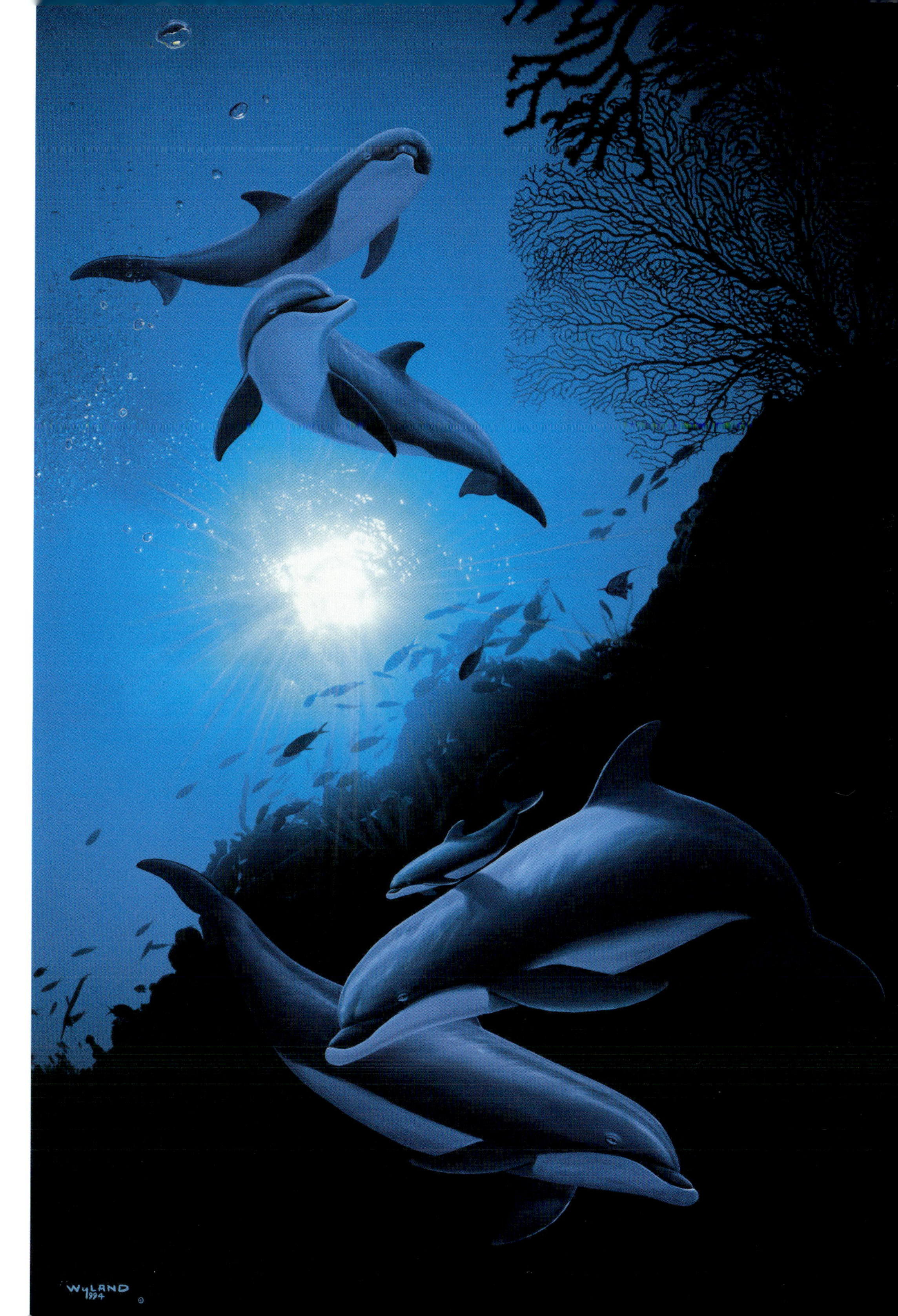

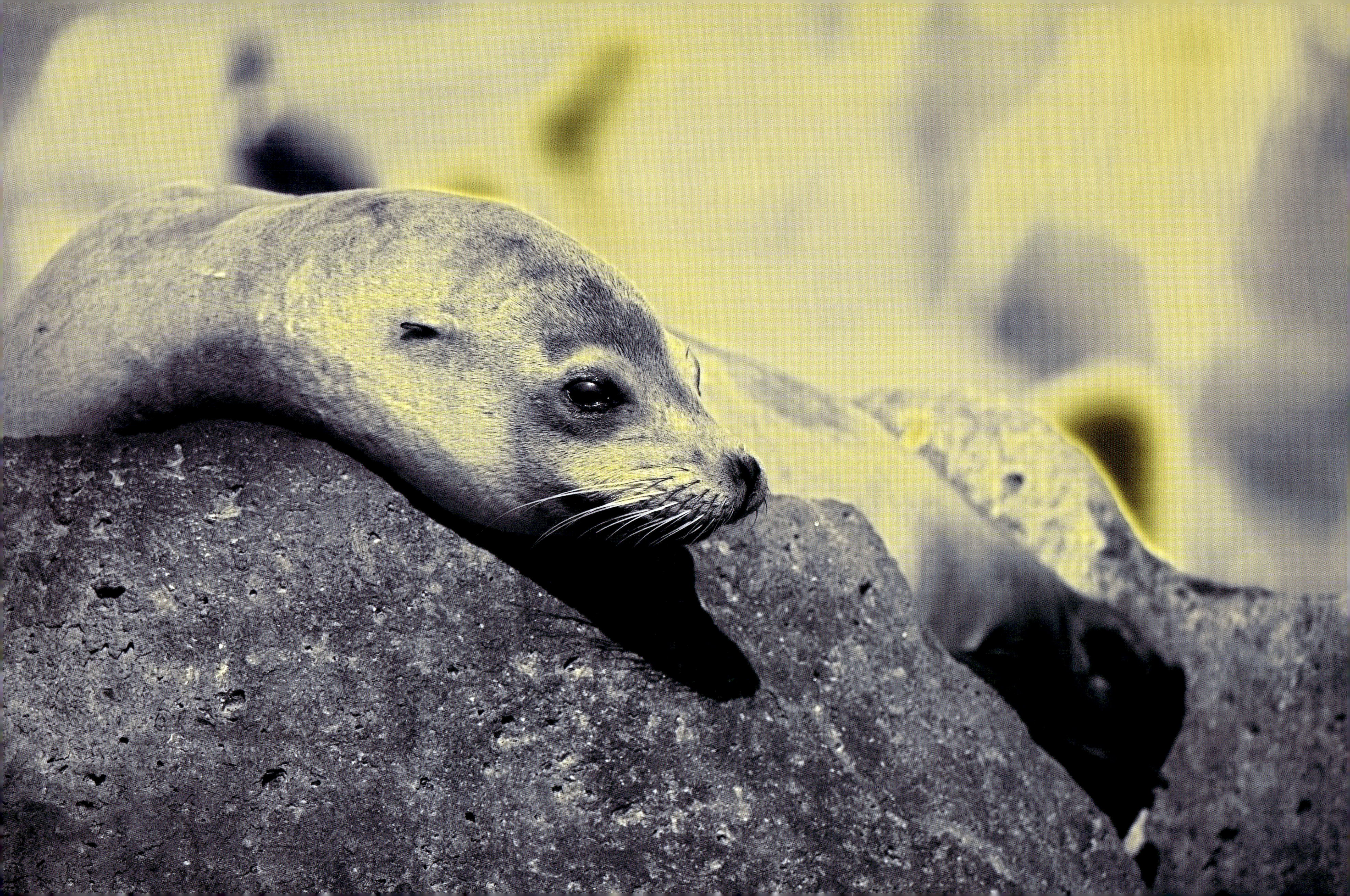

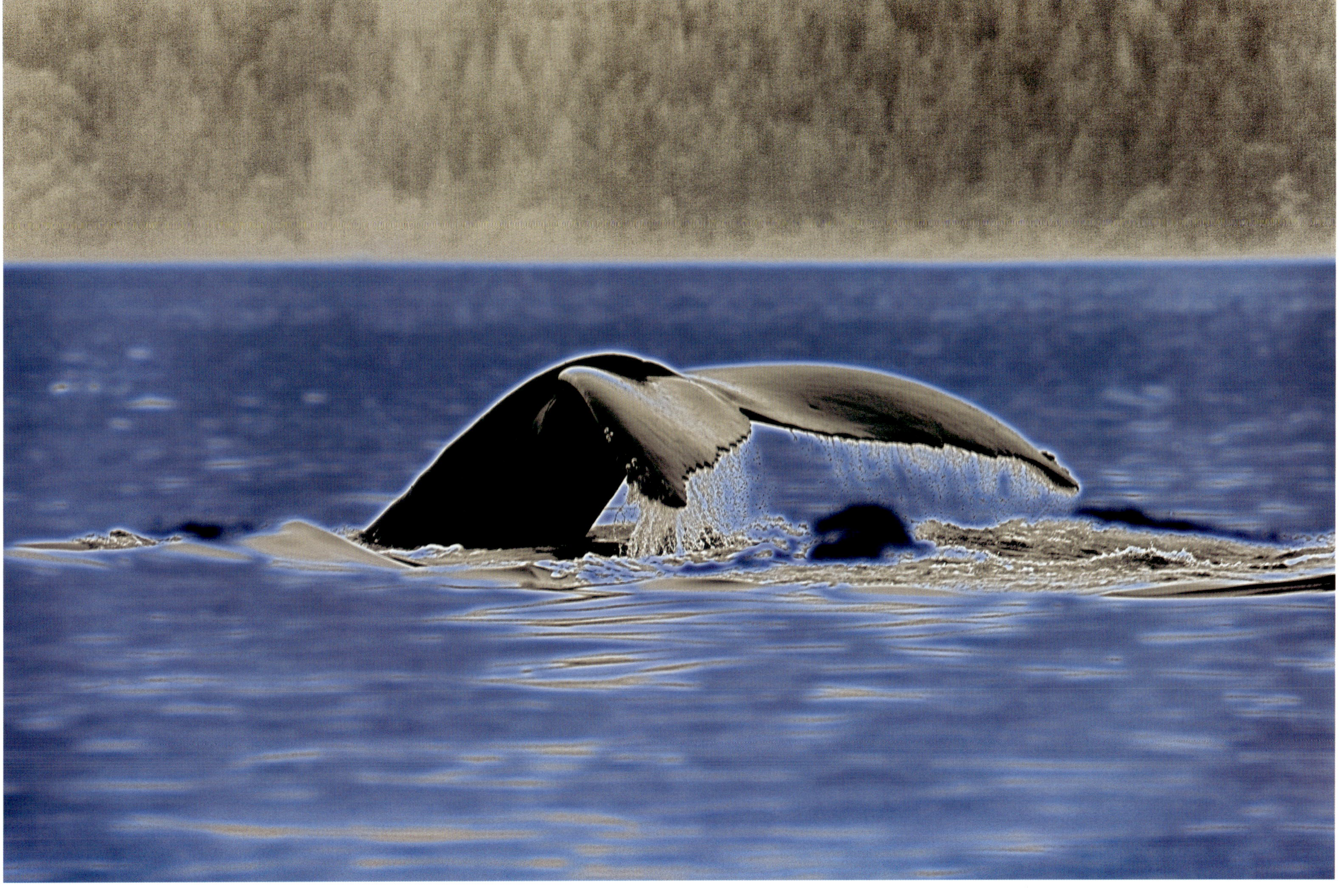

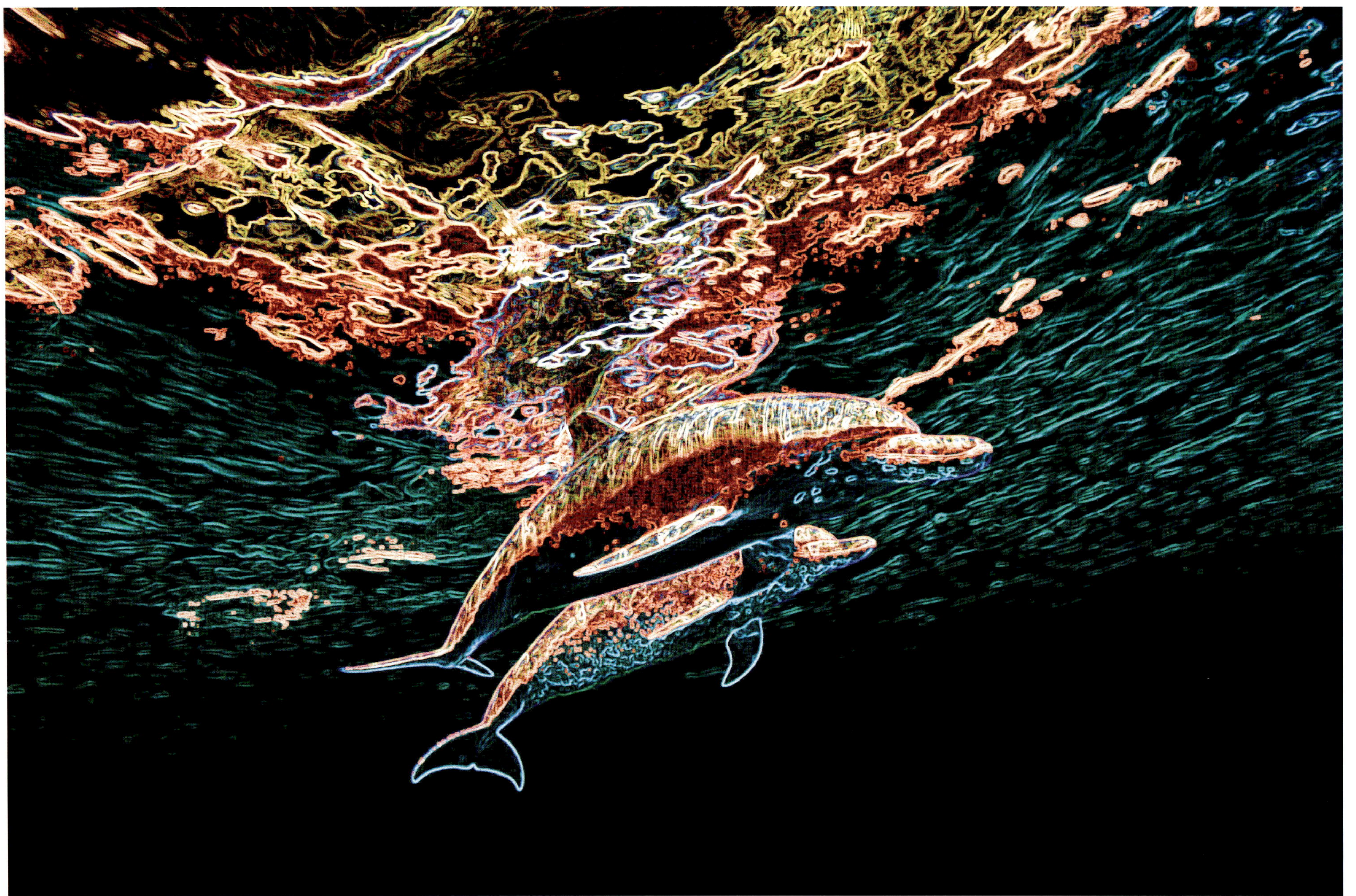

◄ neon color dolphins
► dolphin tail walk

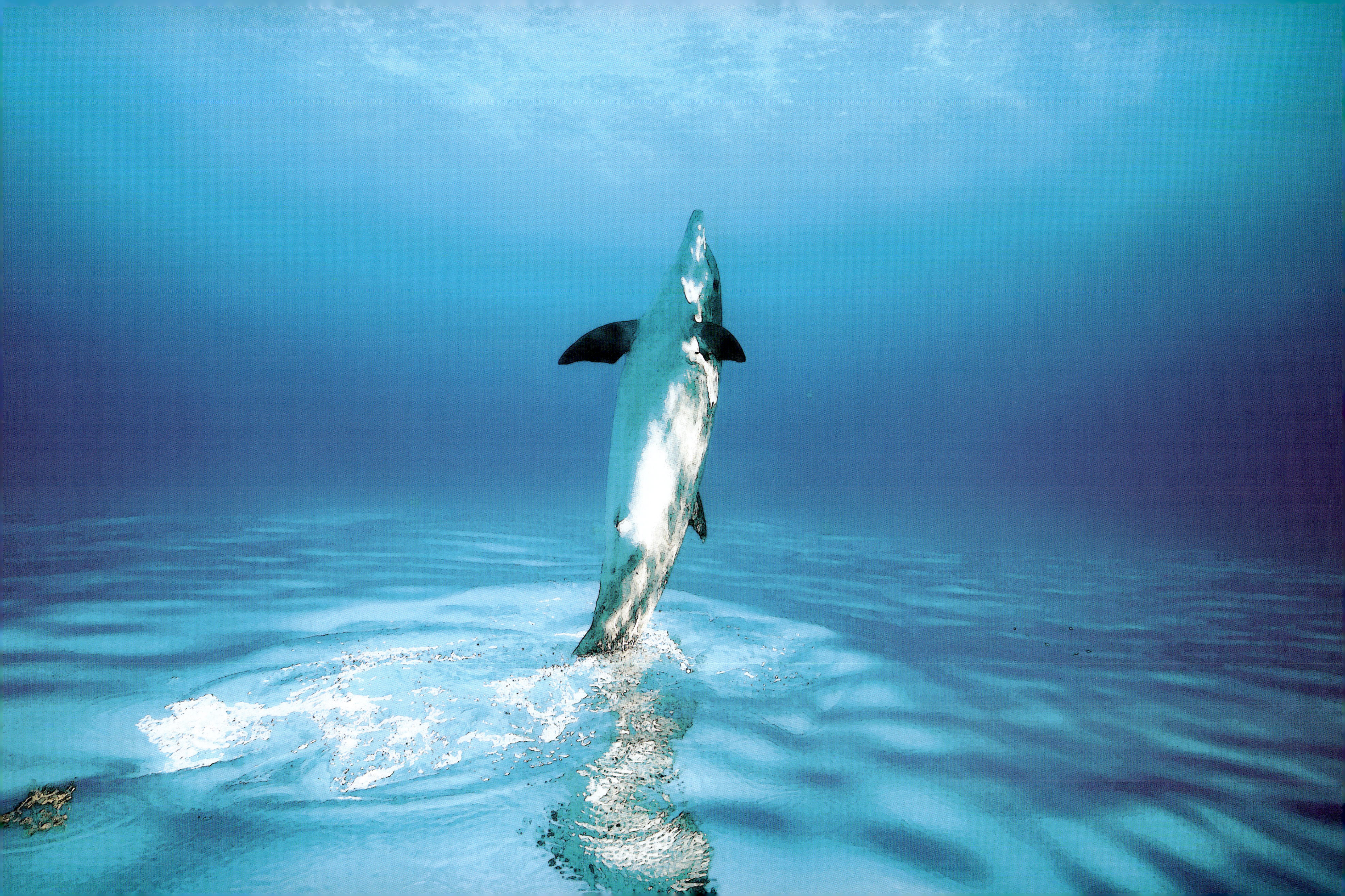

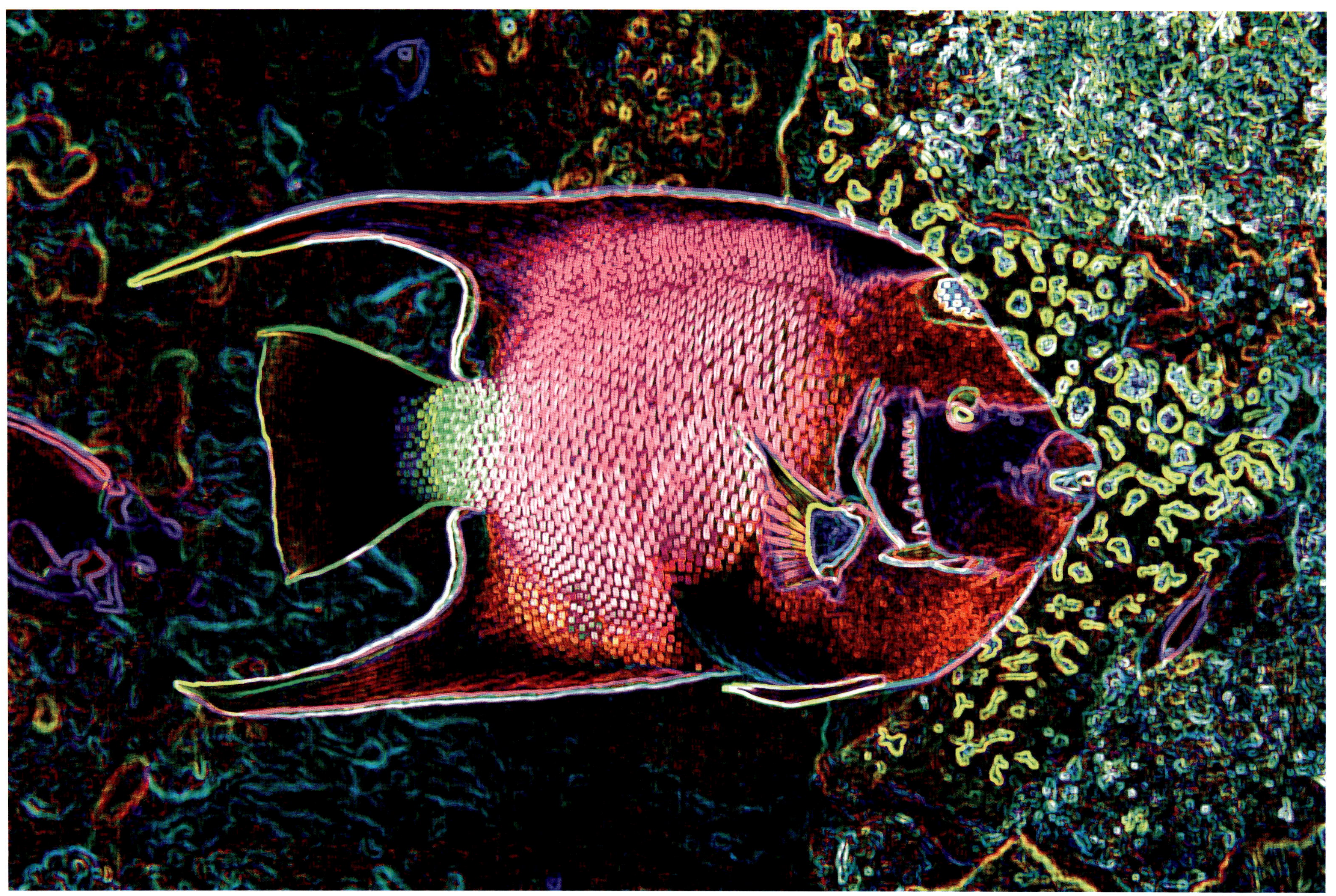

◄ neon queen of the sea
► neon reef colors

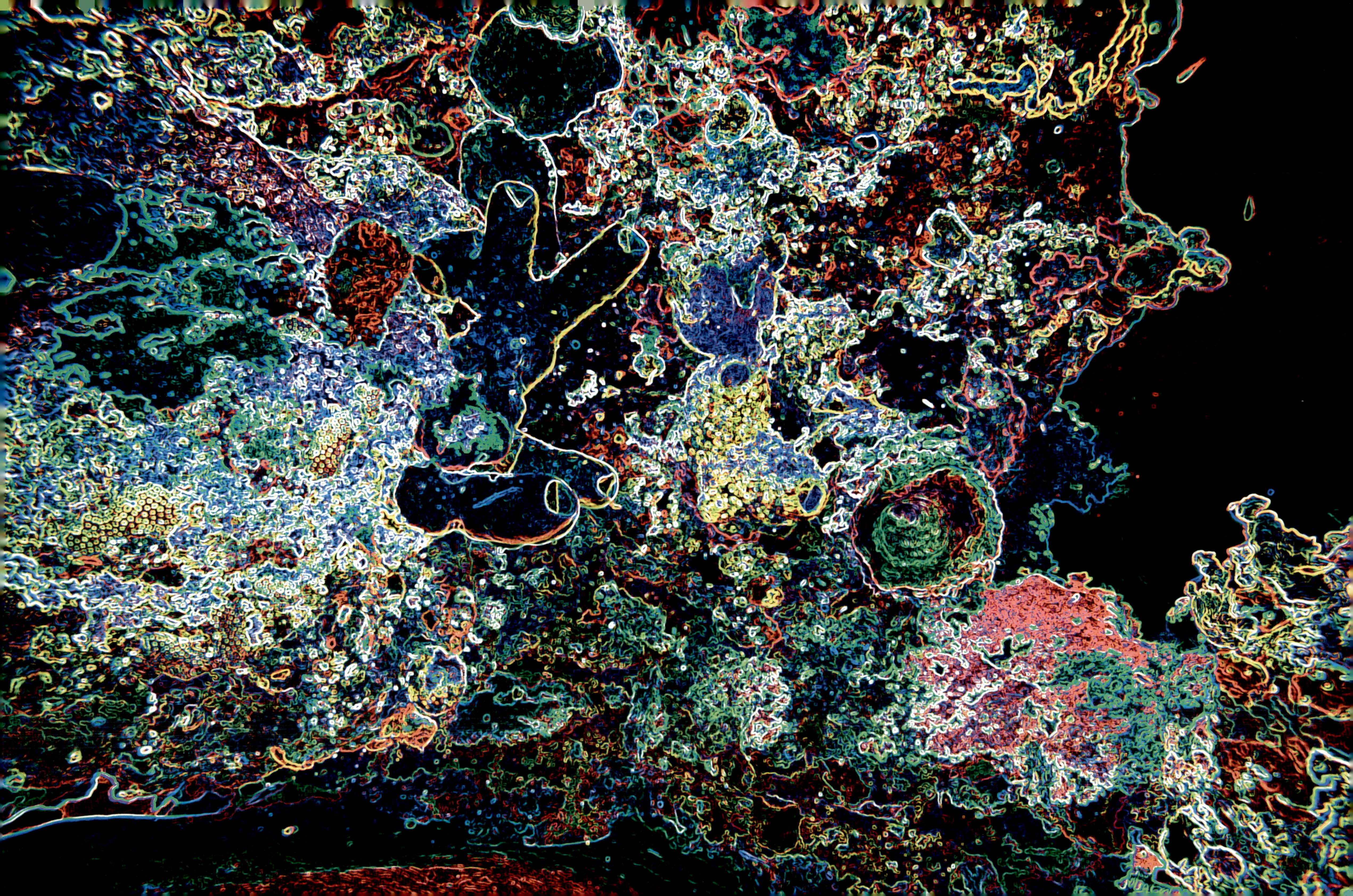

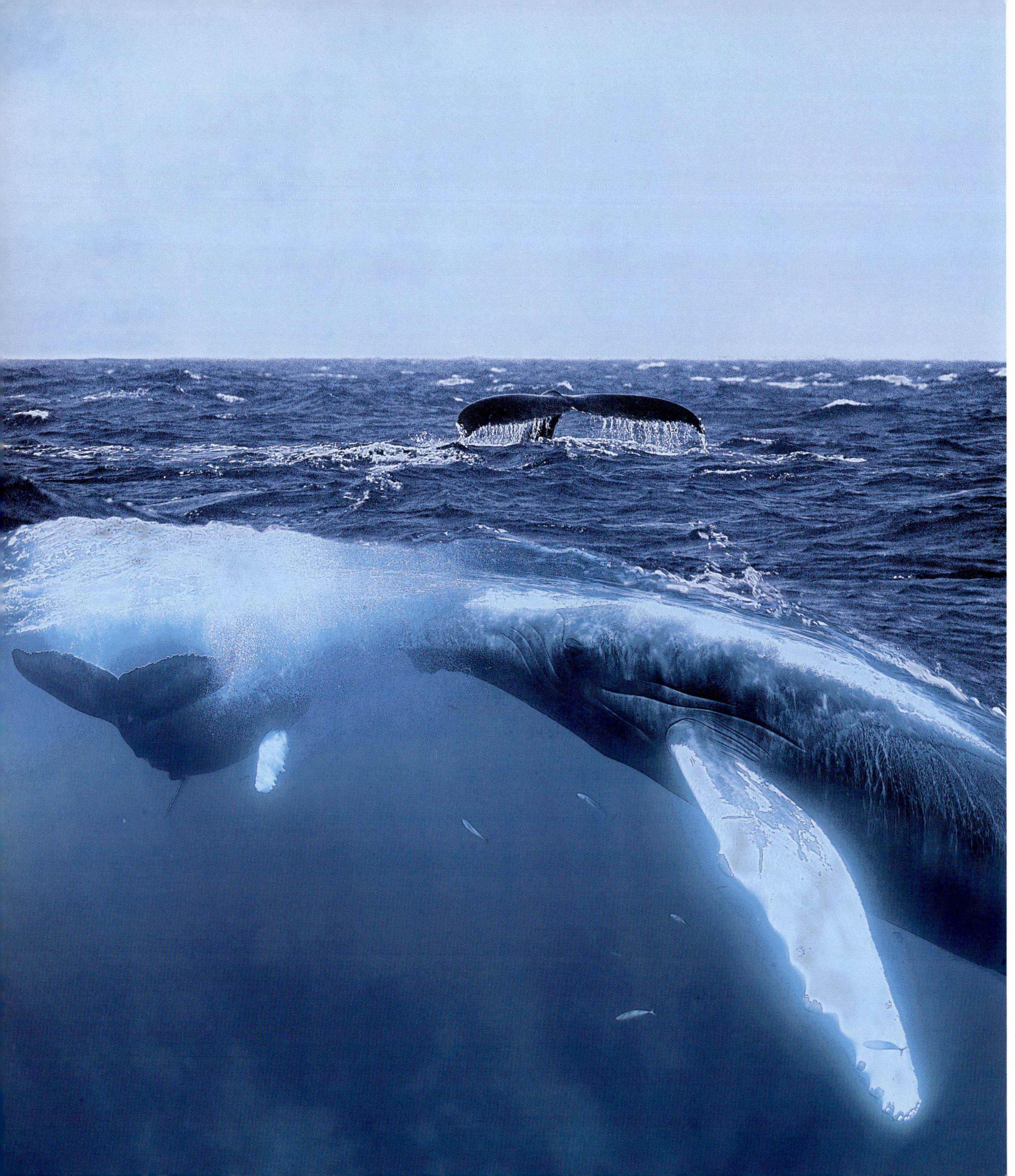

◄ humpback two world view
► dolphin touch

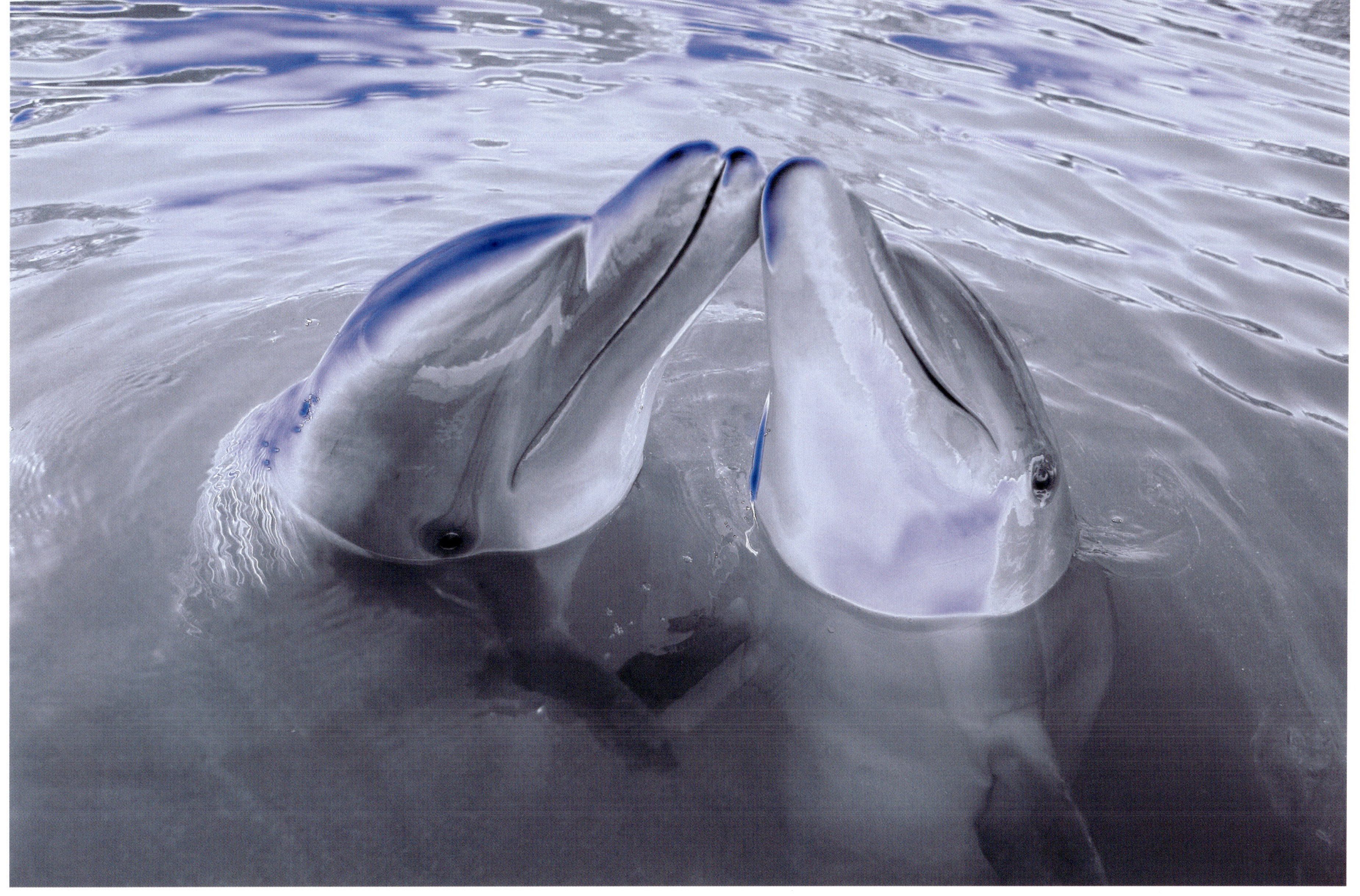

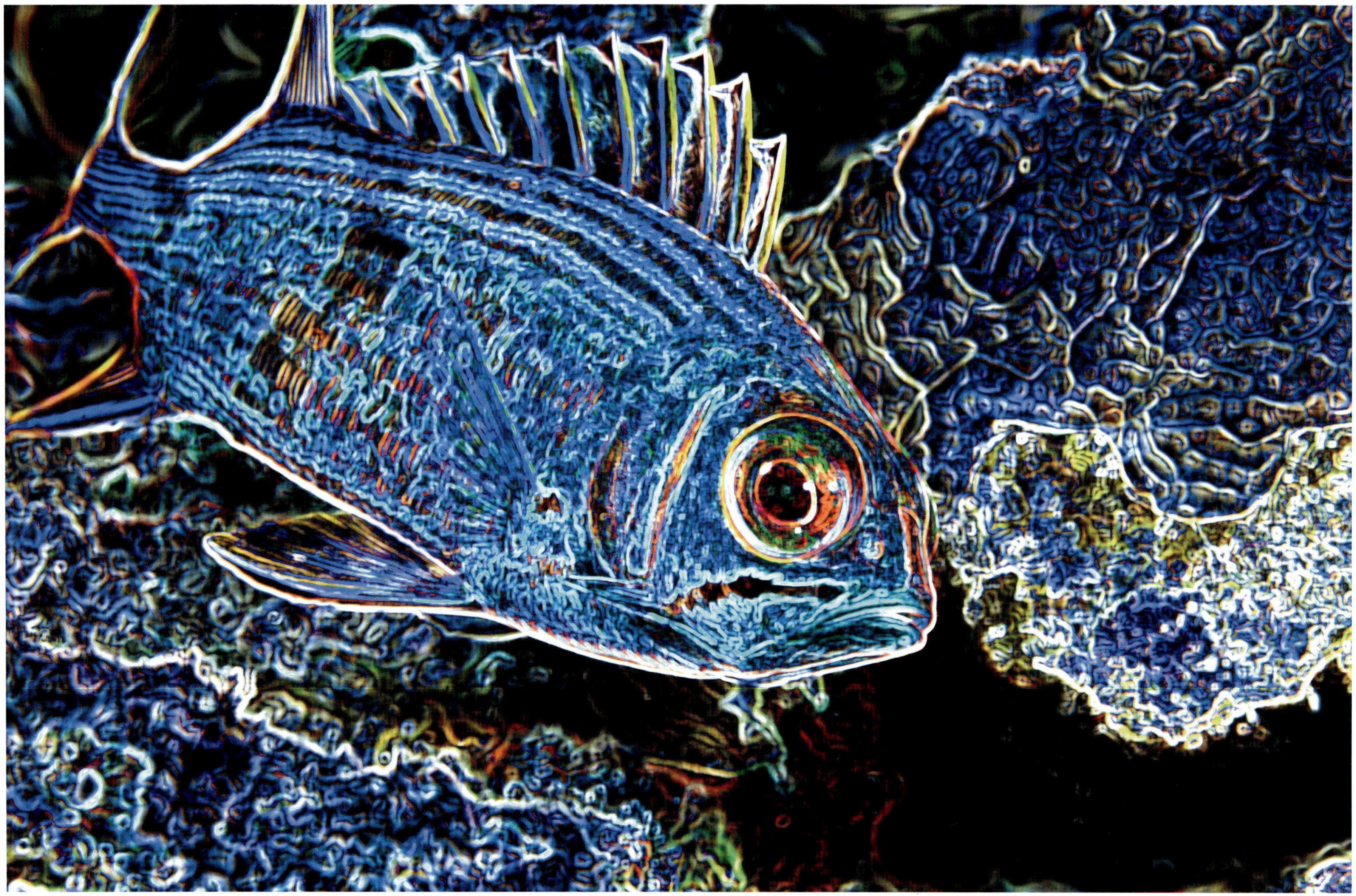

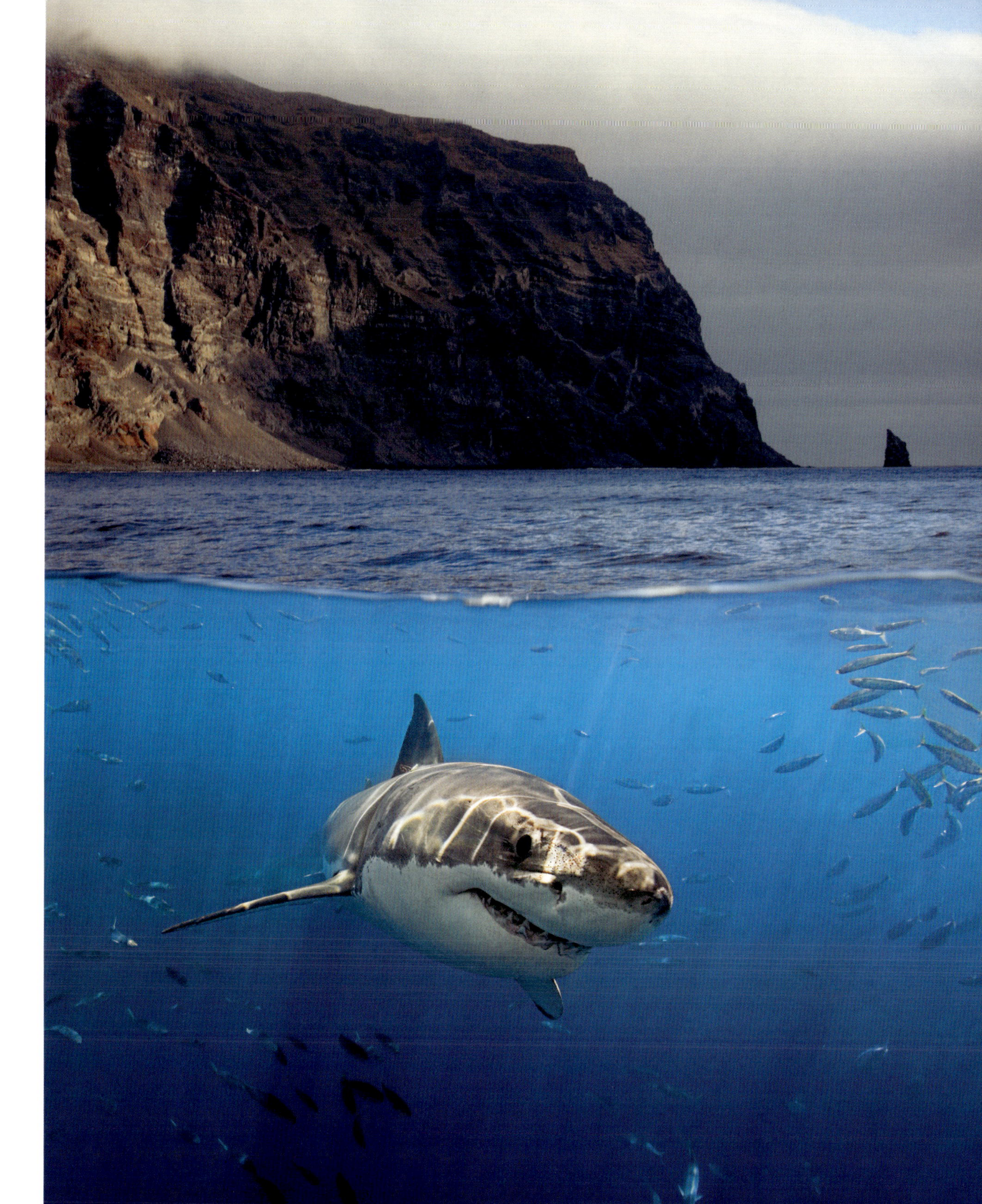

◄ neon squirrel fish
▶ shark waters

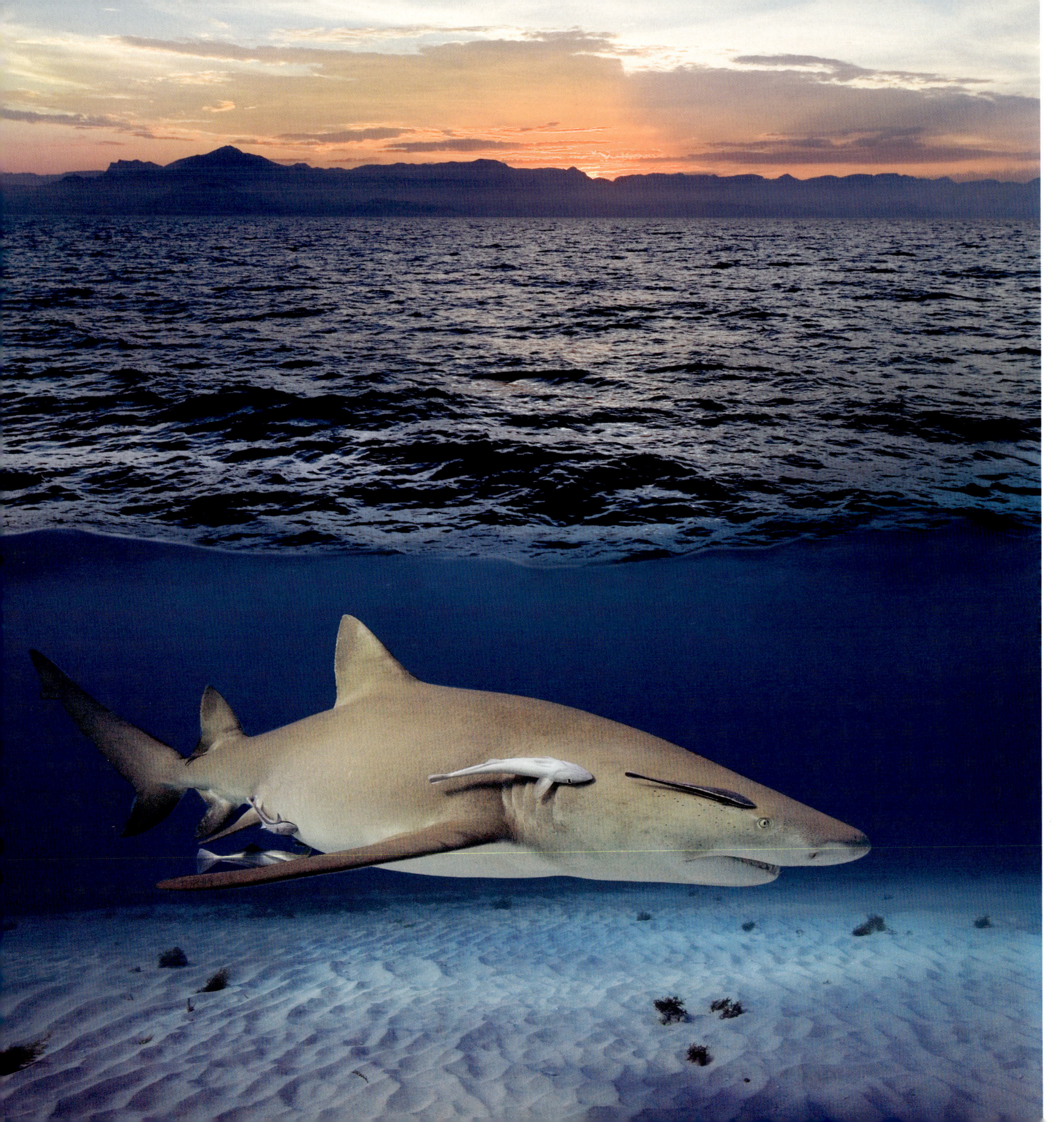

◄ lemon below the sea
► painted spinner dolphins

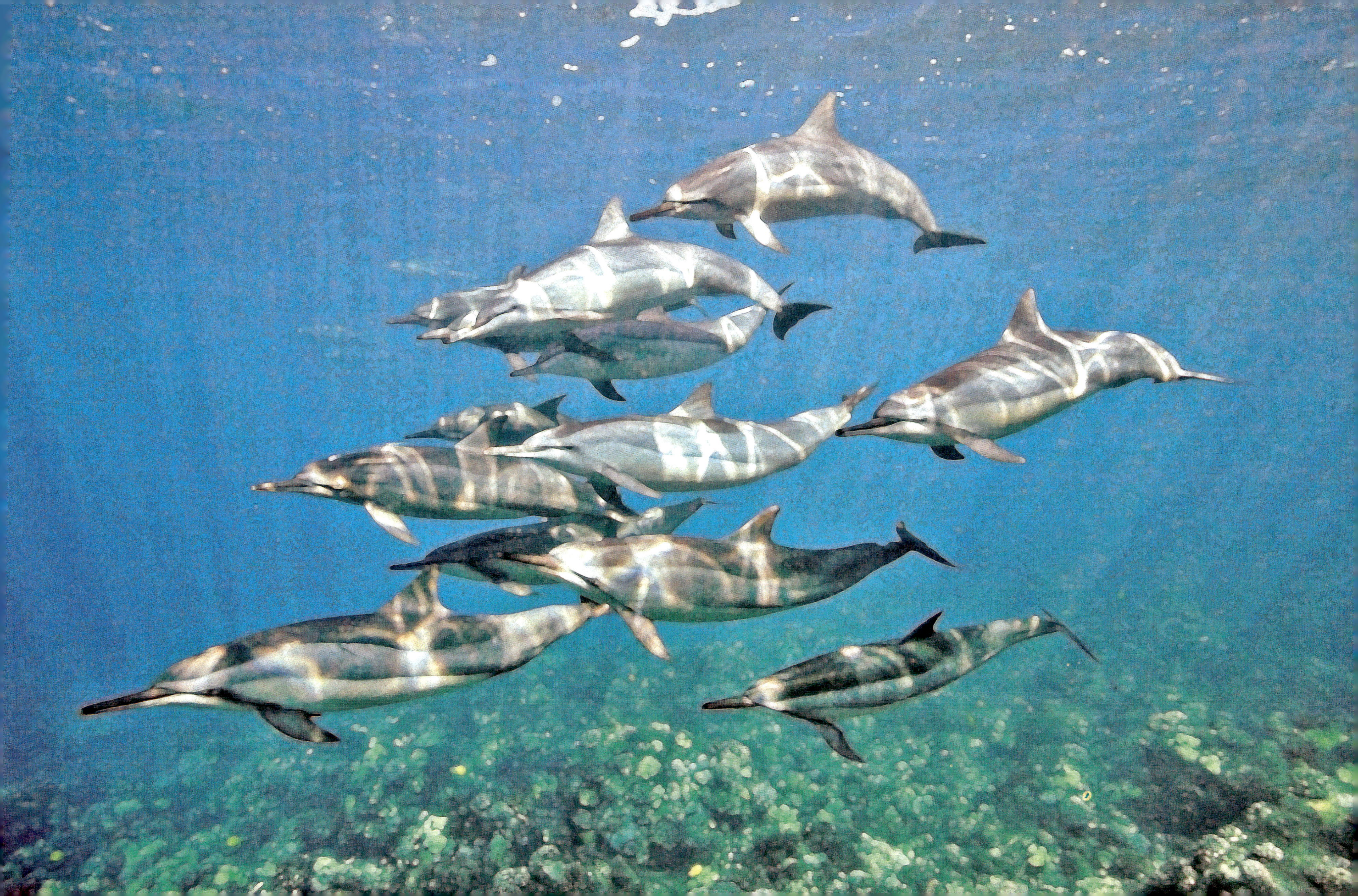

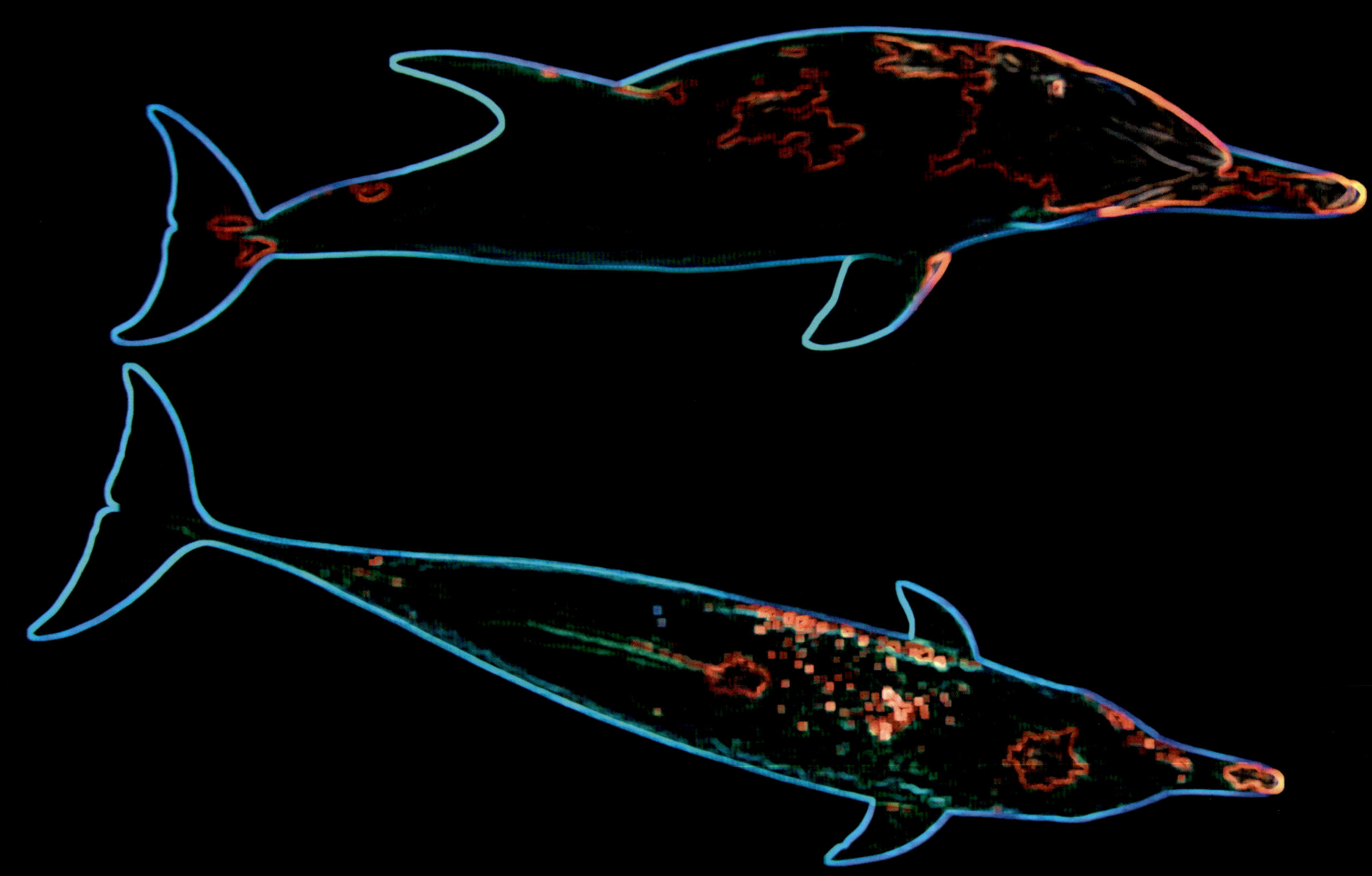

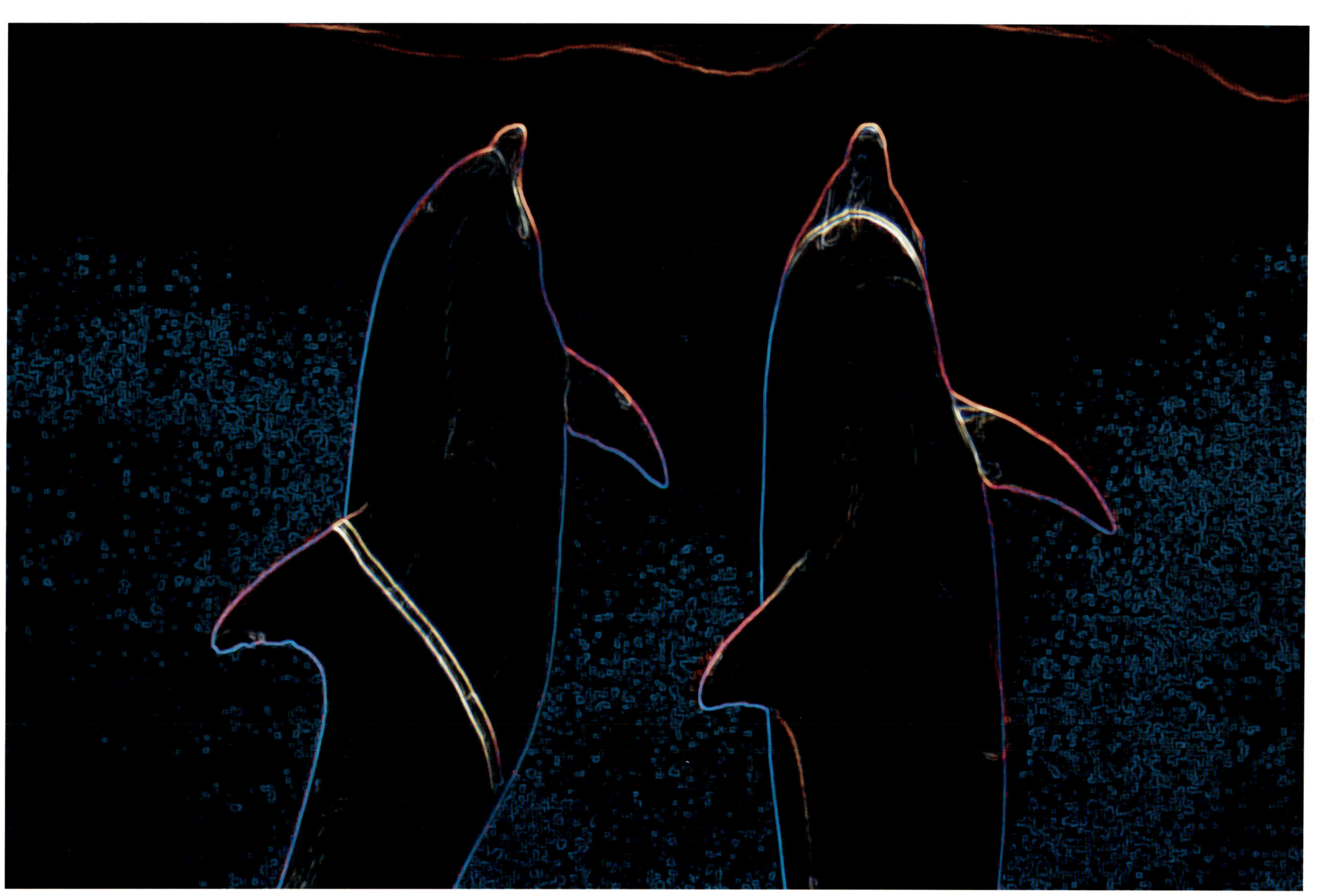

◄ dolphin aura
► dolphin color lines

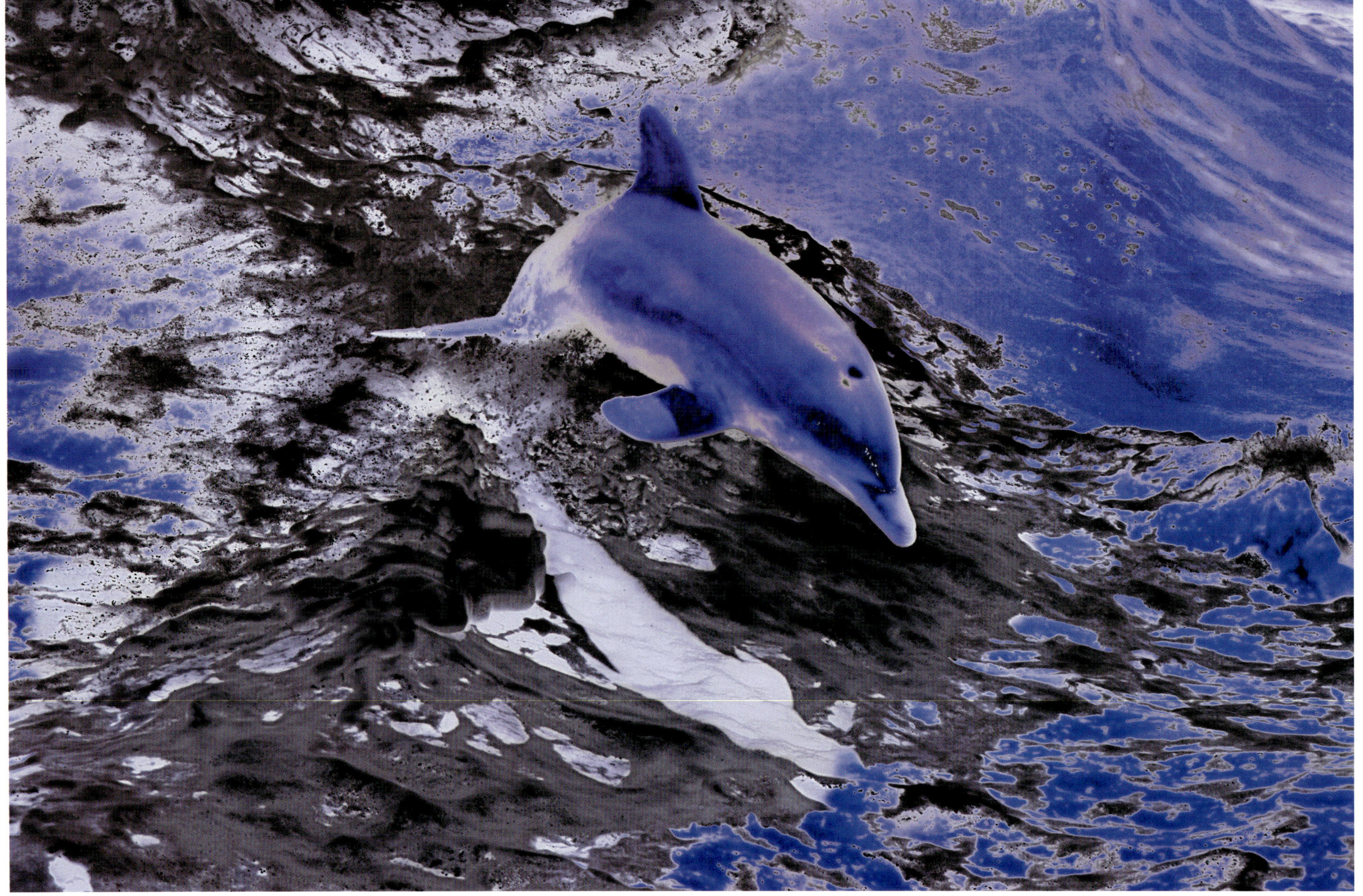

◄ liquid blue
► painted bottlenose

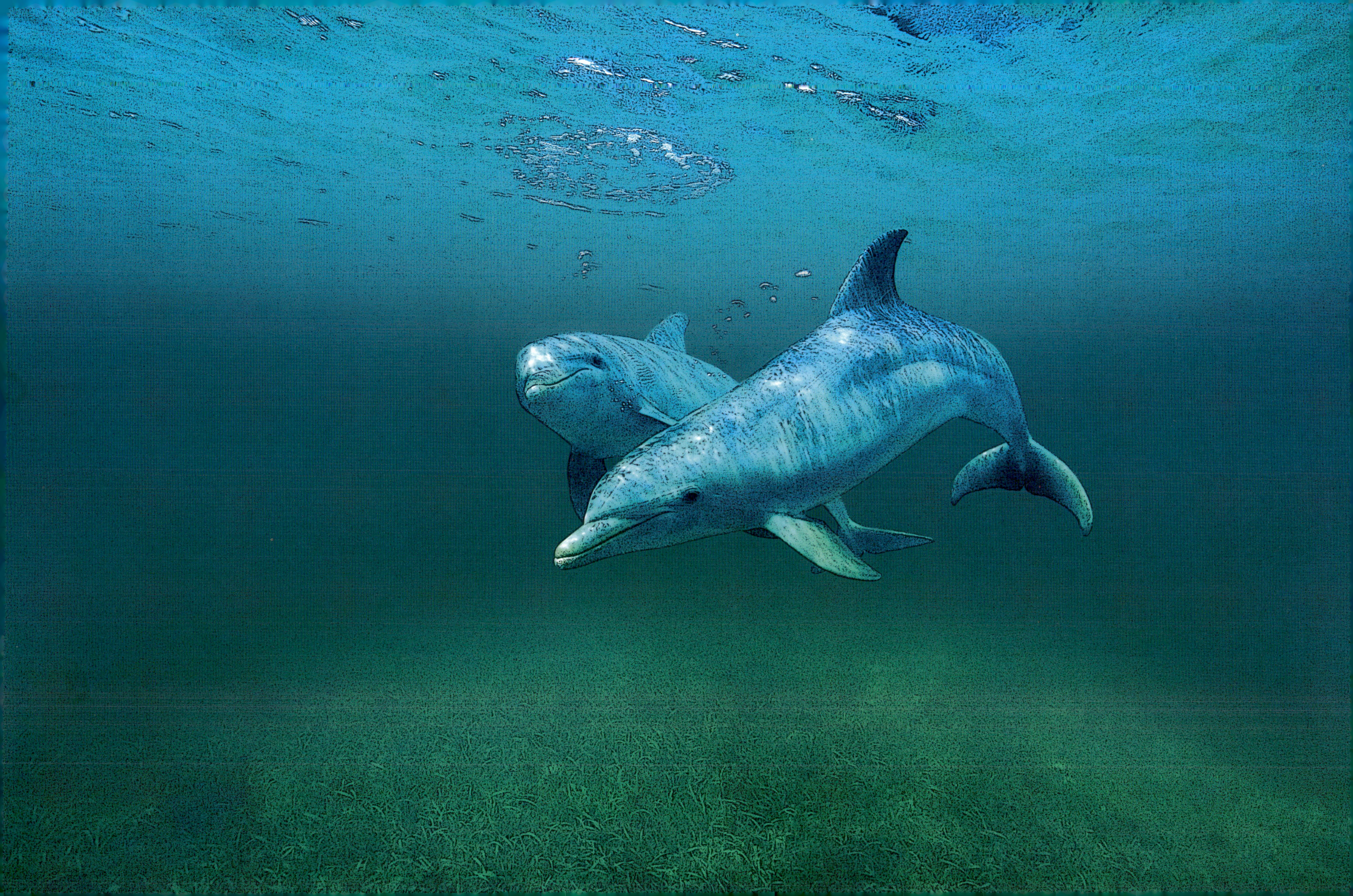

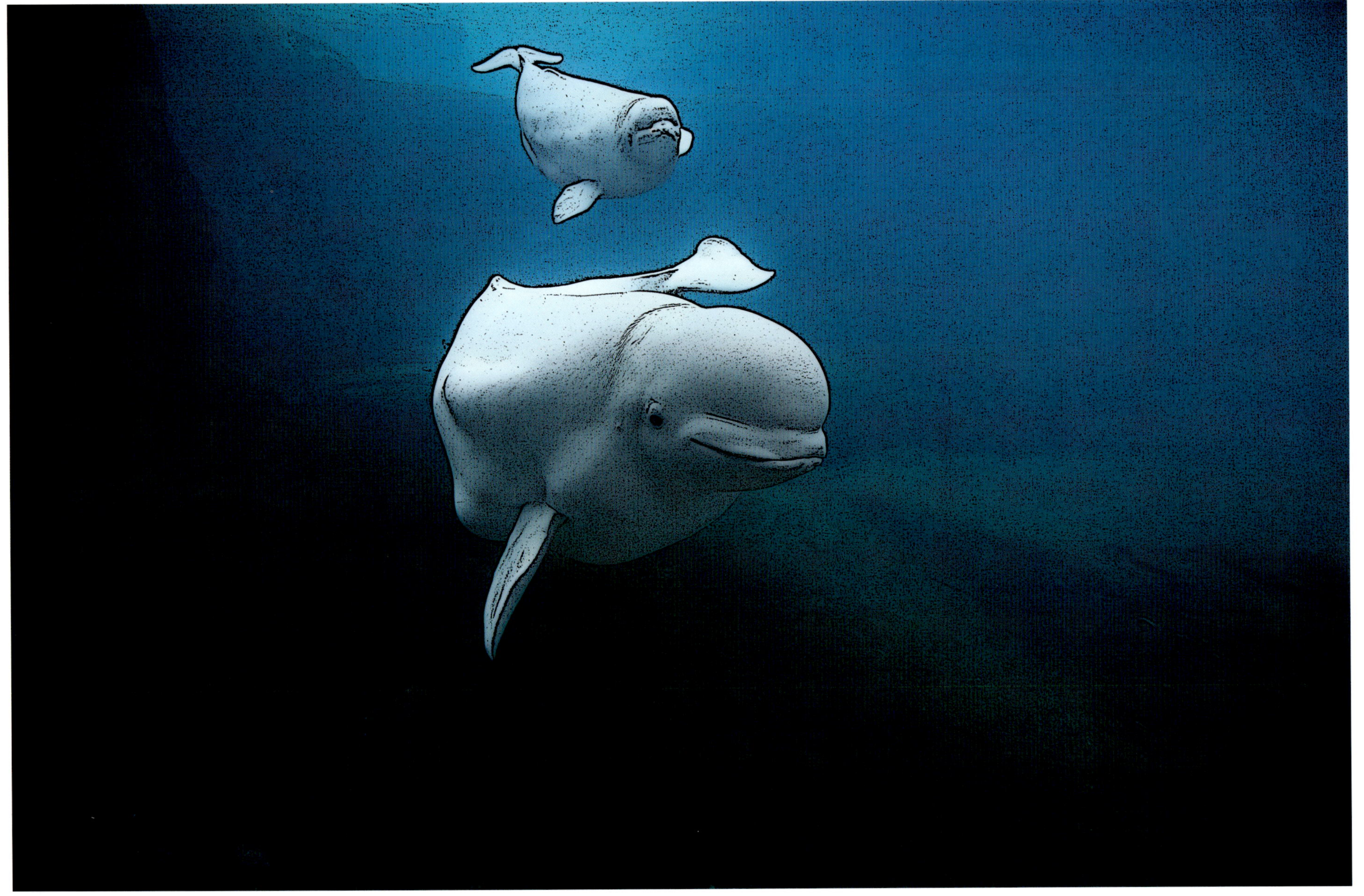

◀ painted beluga and calf
▶ beluga love

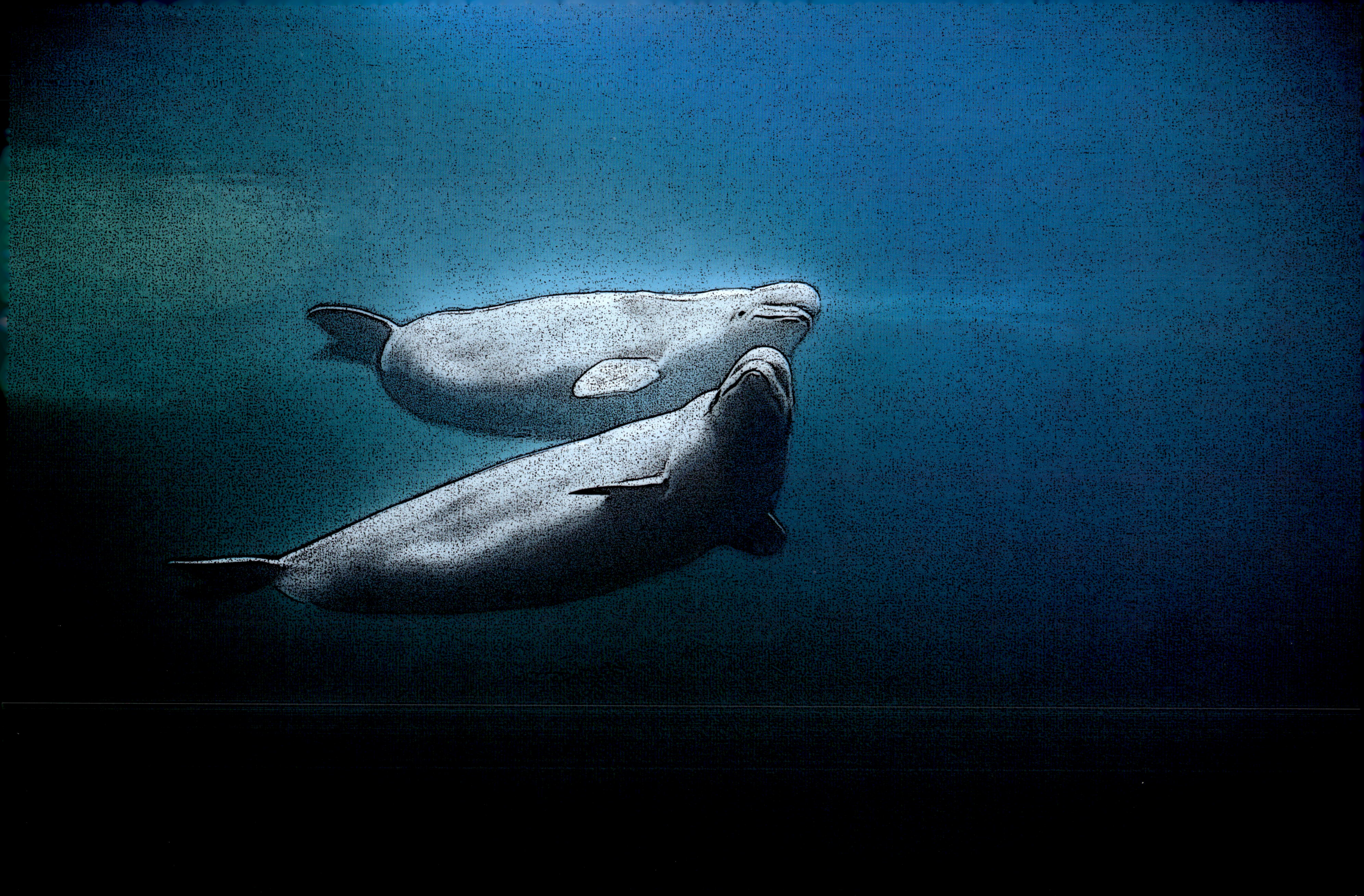

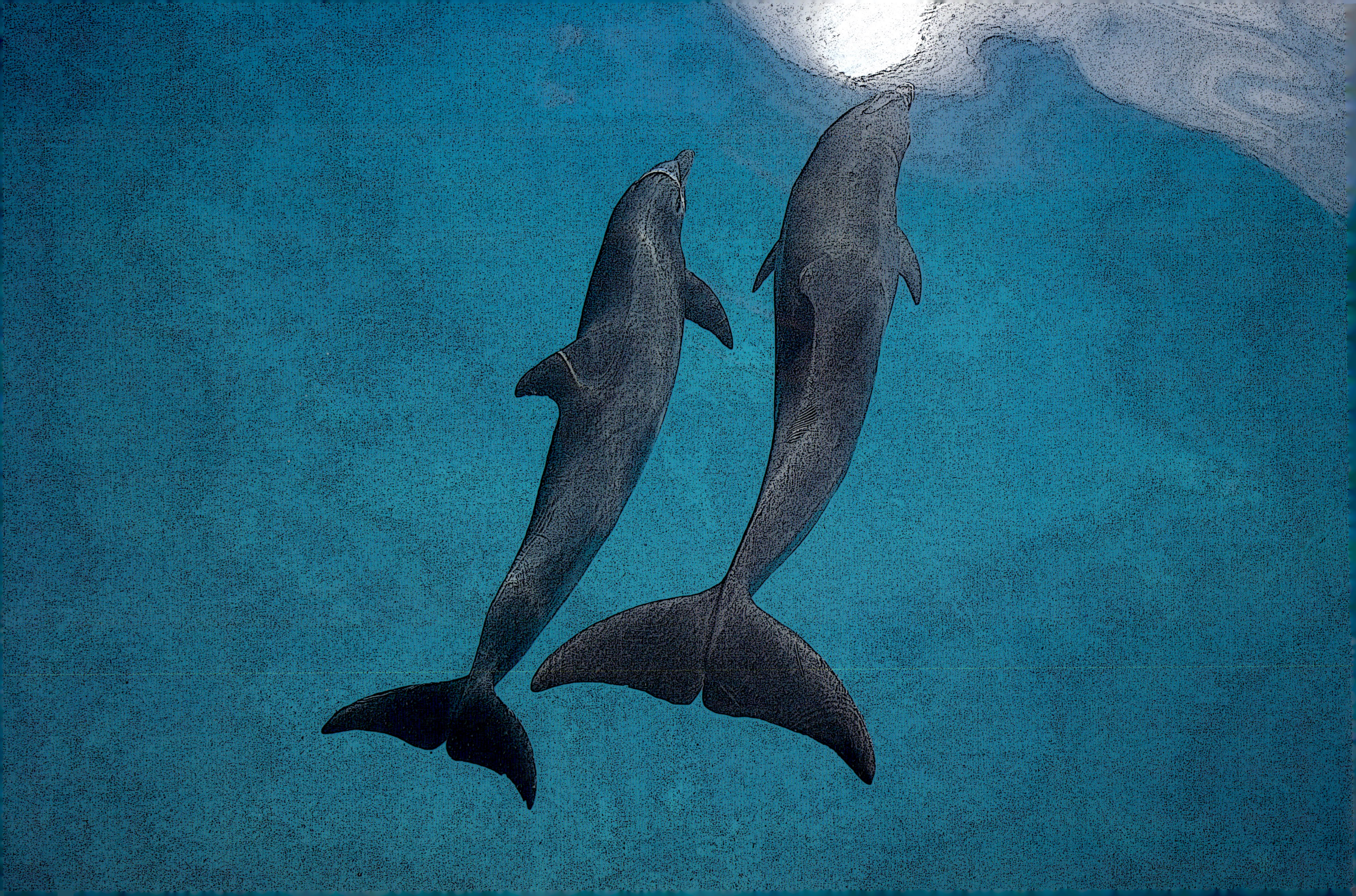

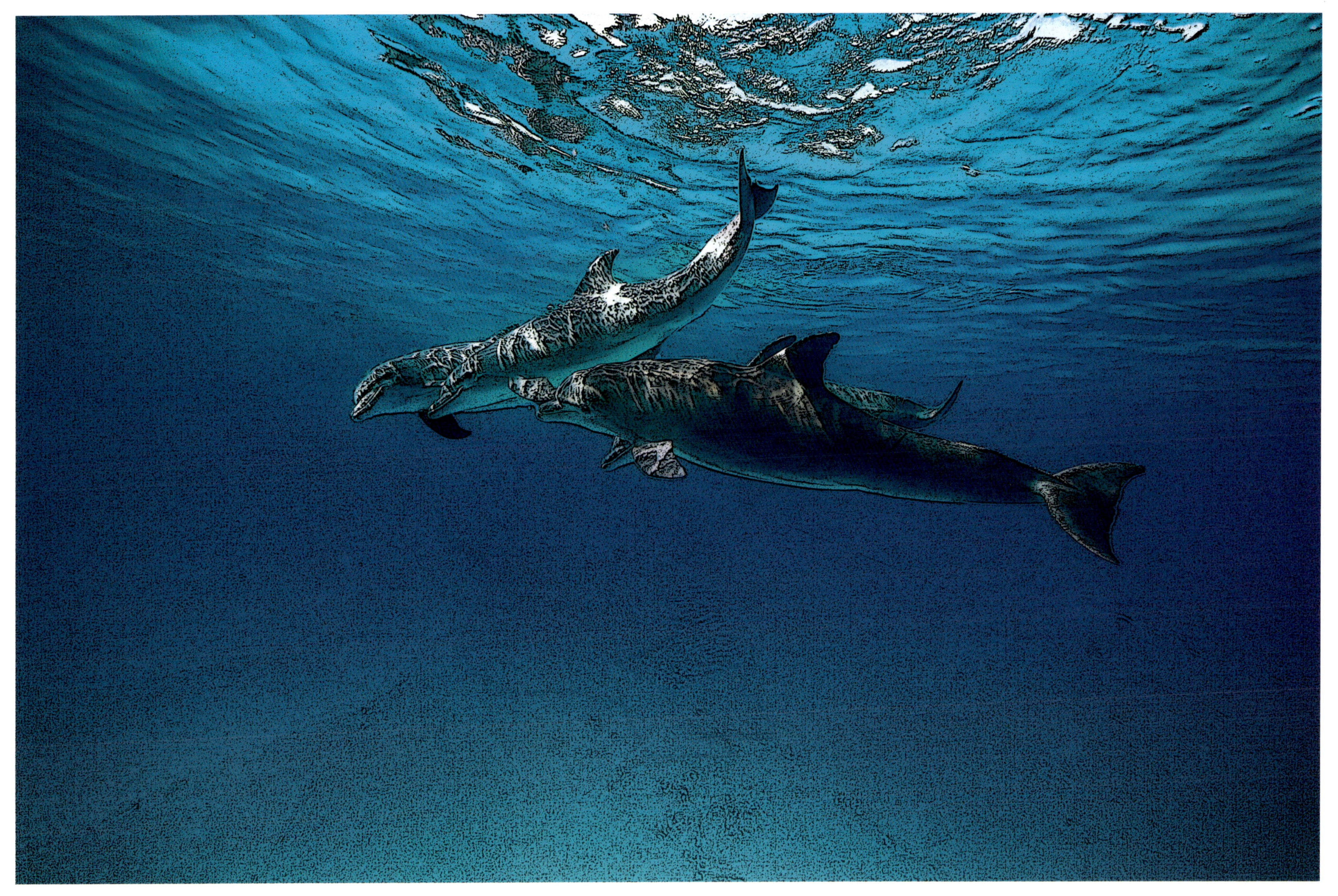

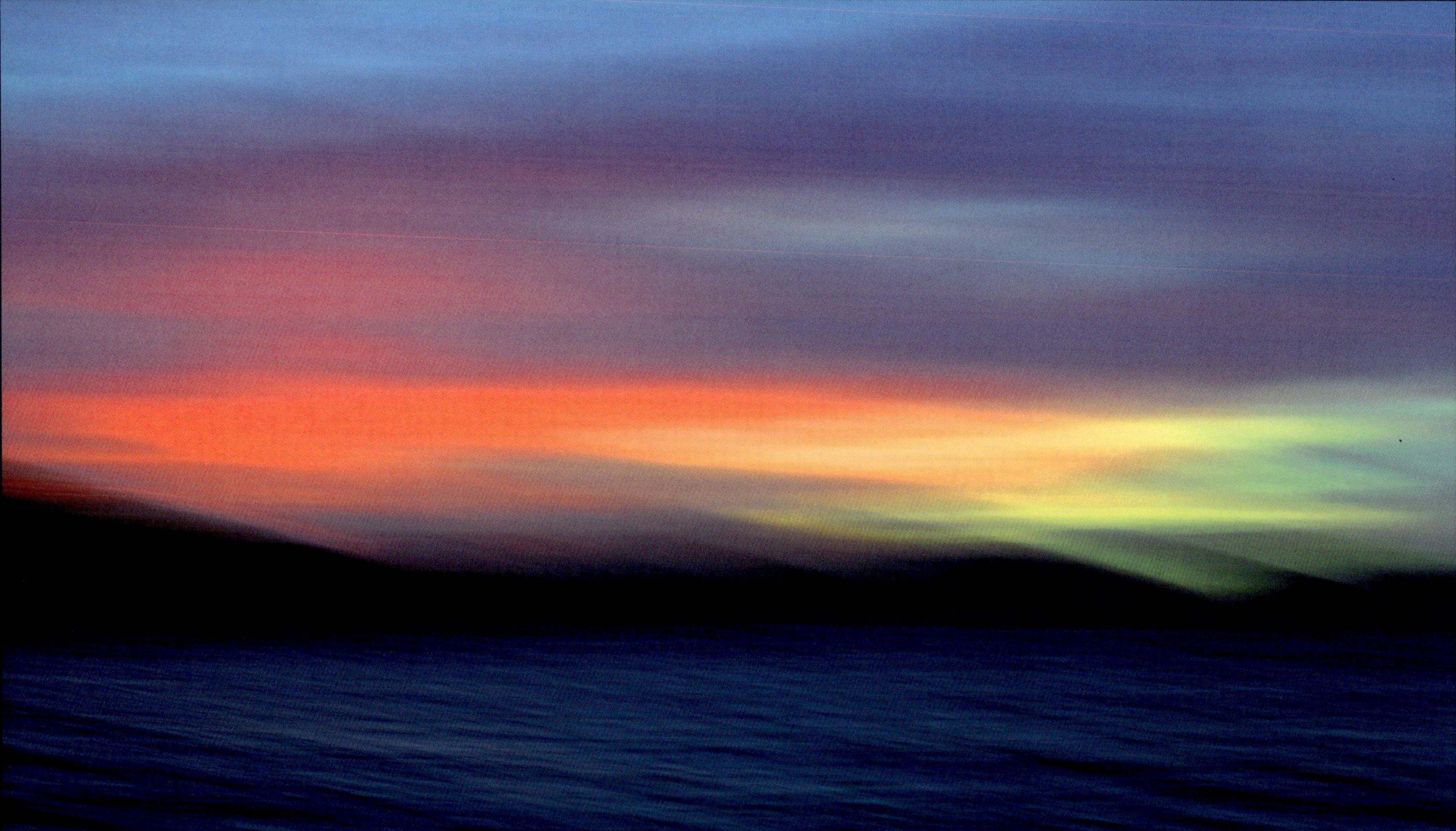

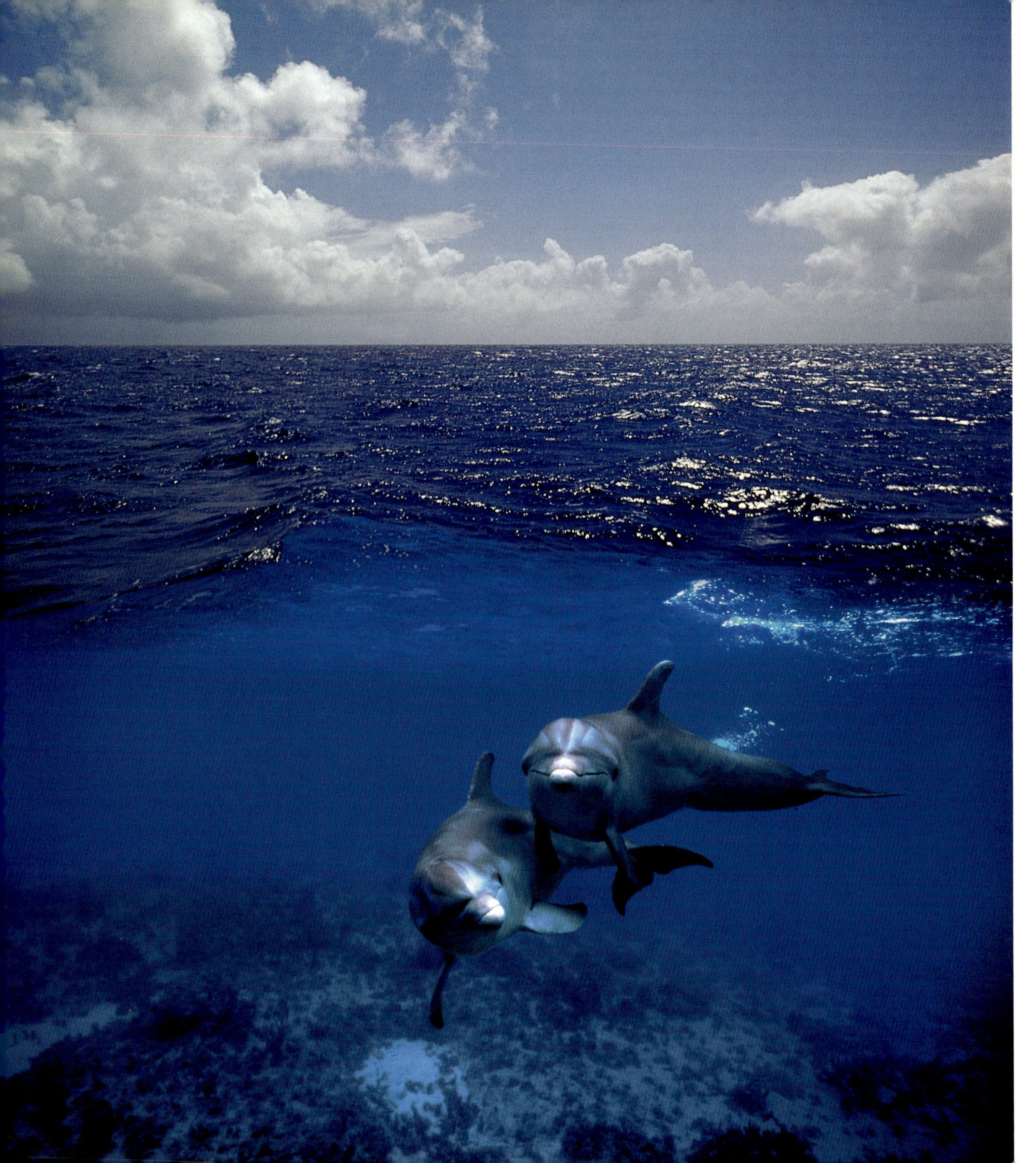

◄ a dolphin world below
▶ painted sea otter

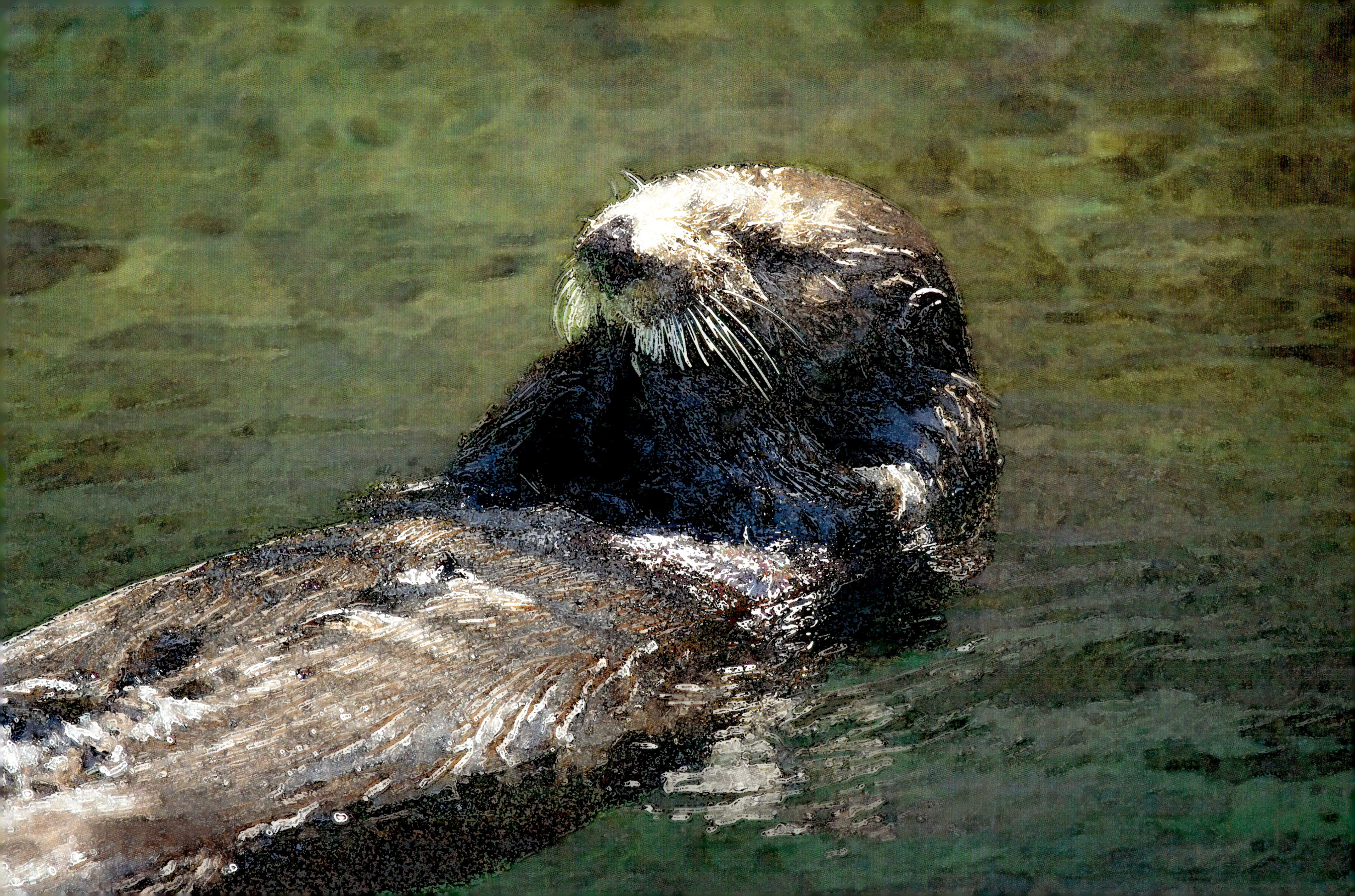

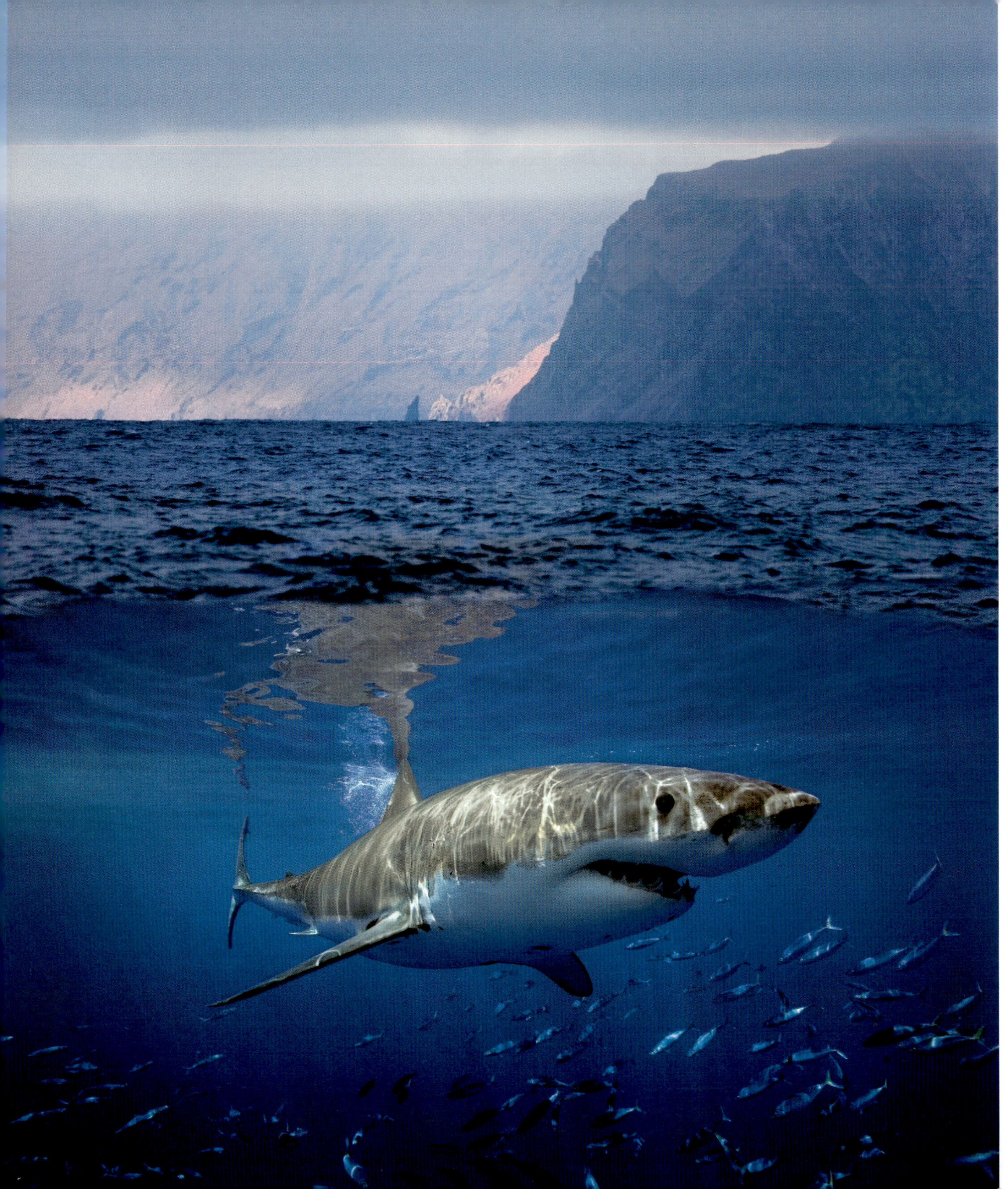

◀ great white shark world
▶ sperm whale below

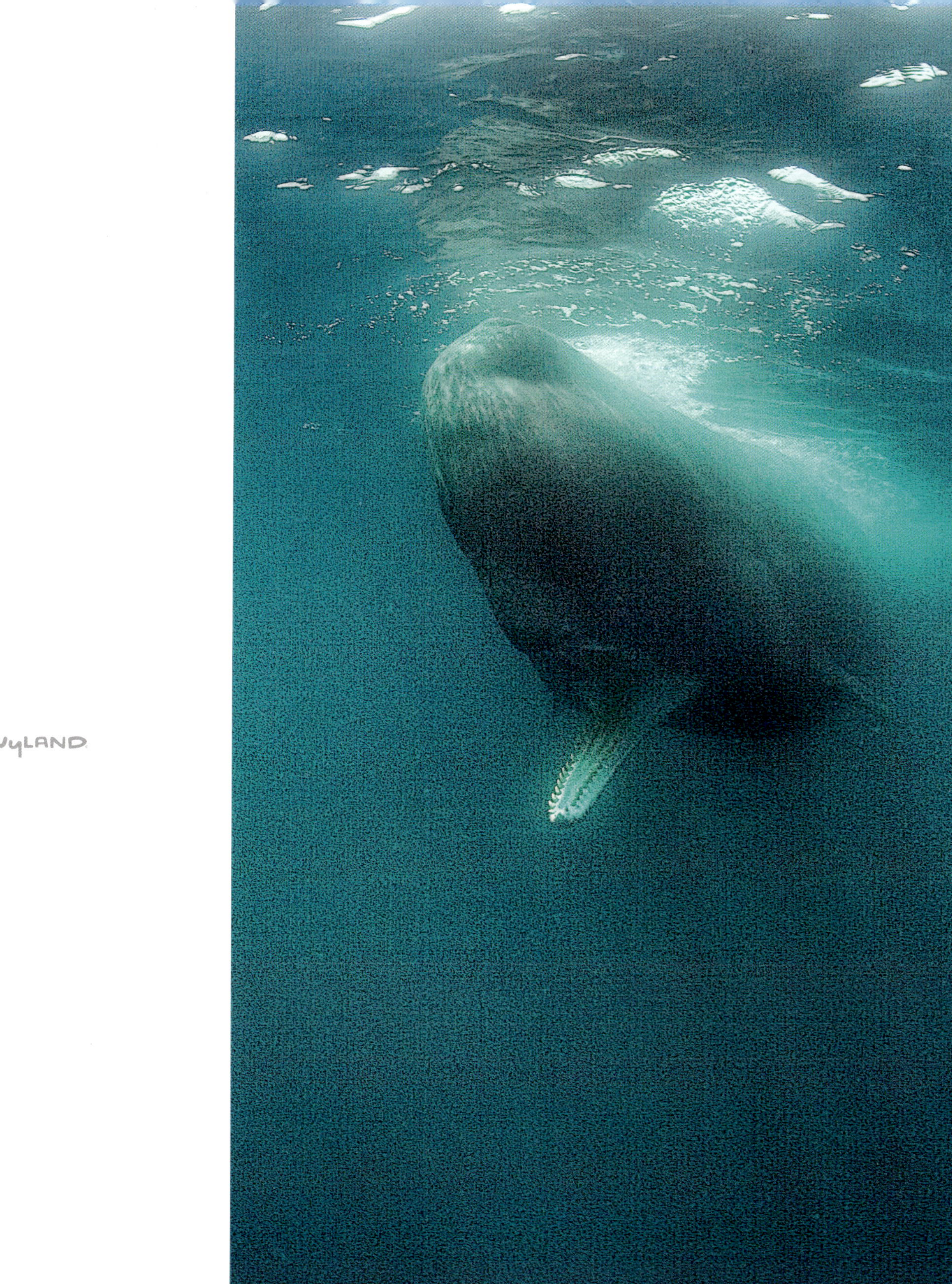

the sperm whale has the largest brain on the planet, but we continue to threaten its survival...

WYLAND

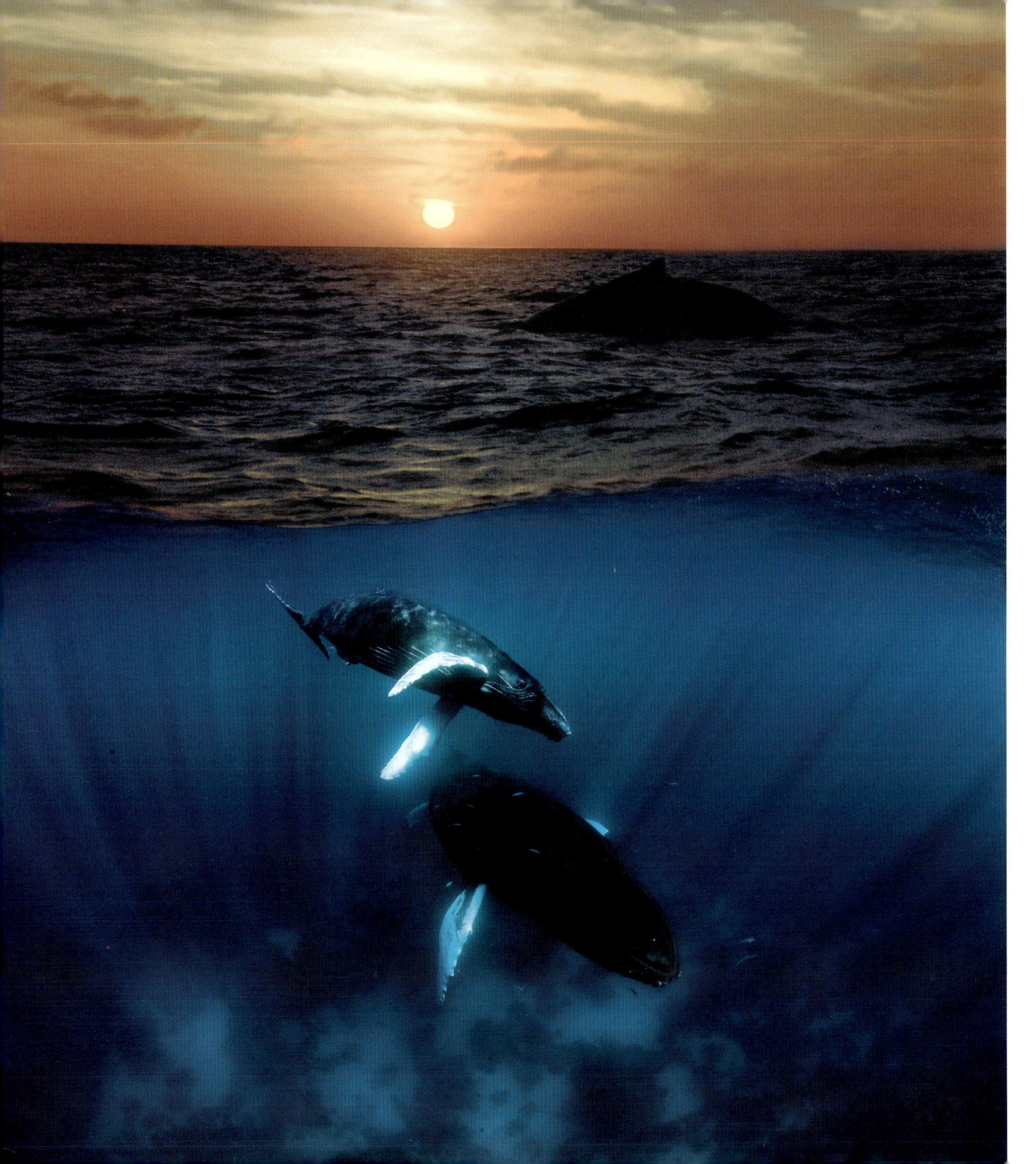

warm cool humpback sea
maui humpback magic

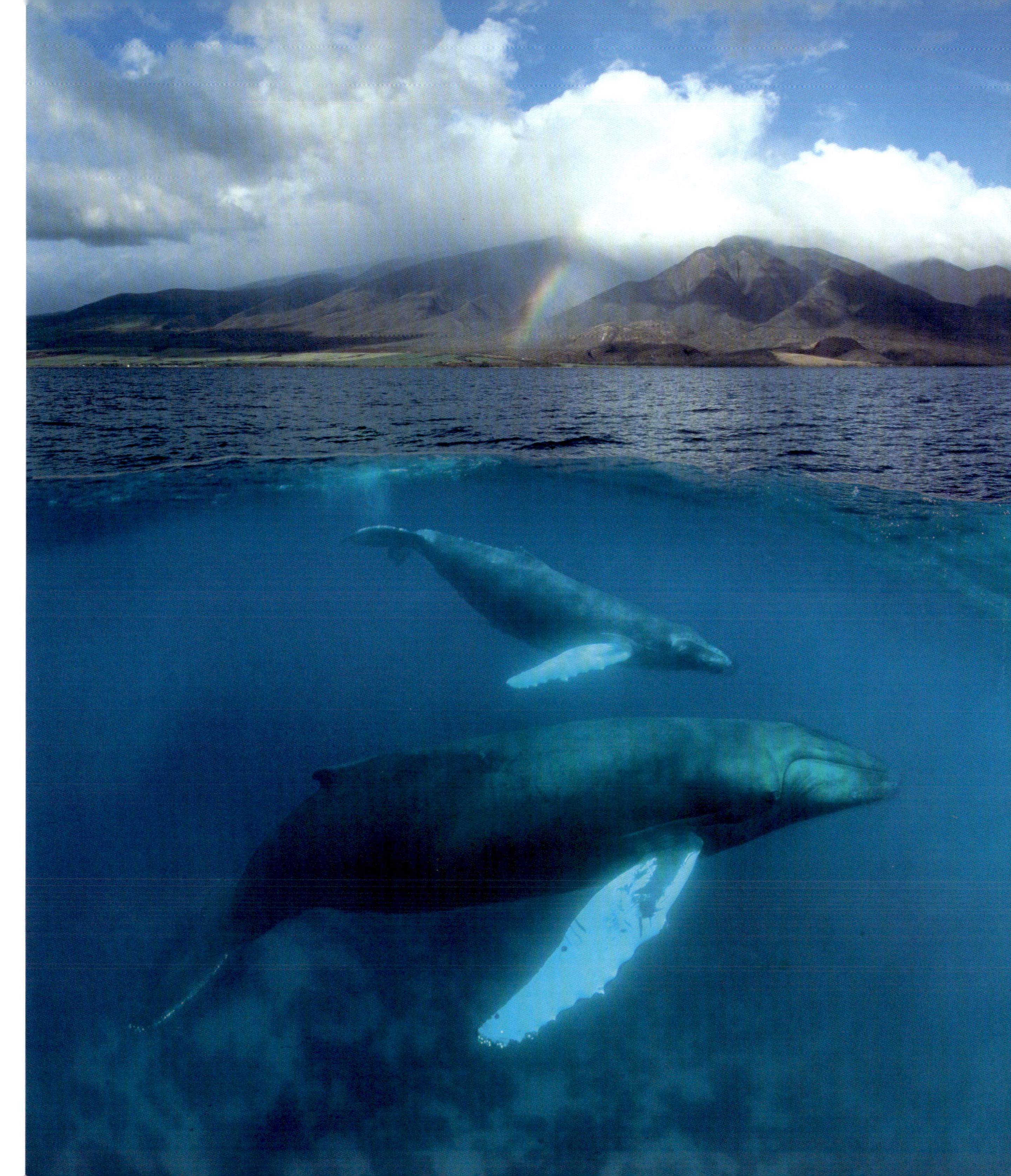

the land and sea are connected. like every drop of water,
you can't protect one without protecting the other...

WYLAND

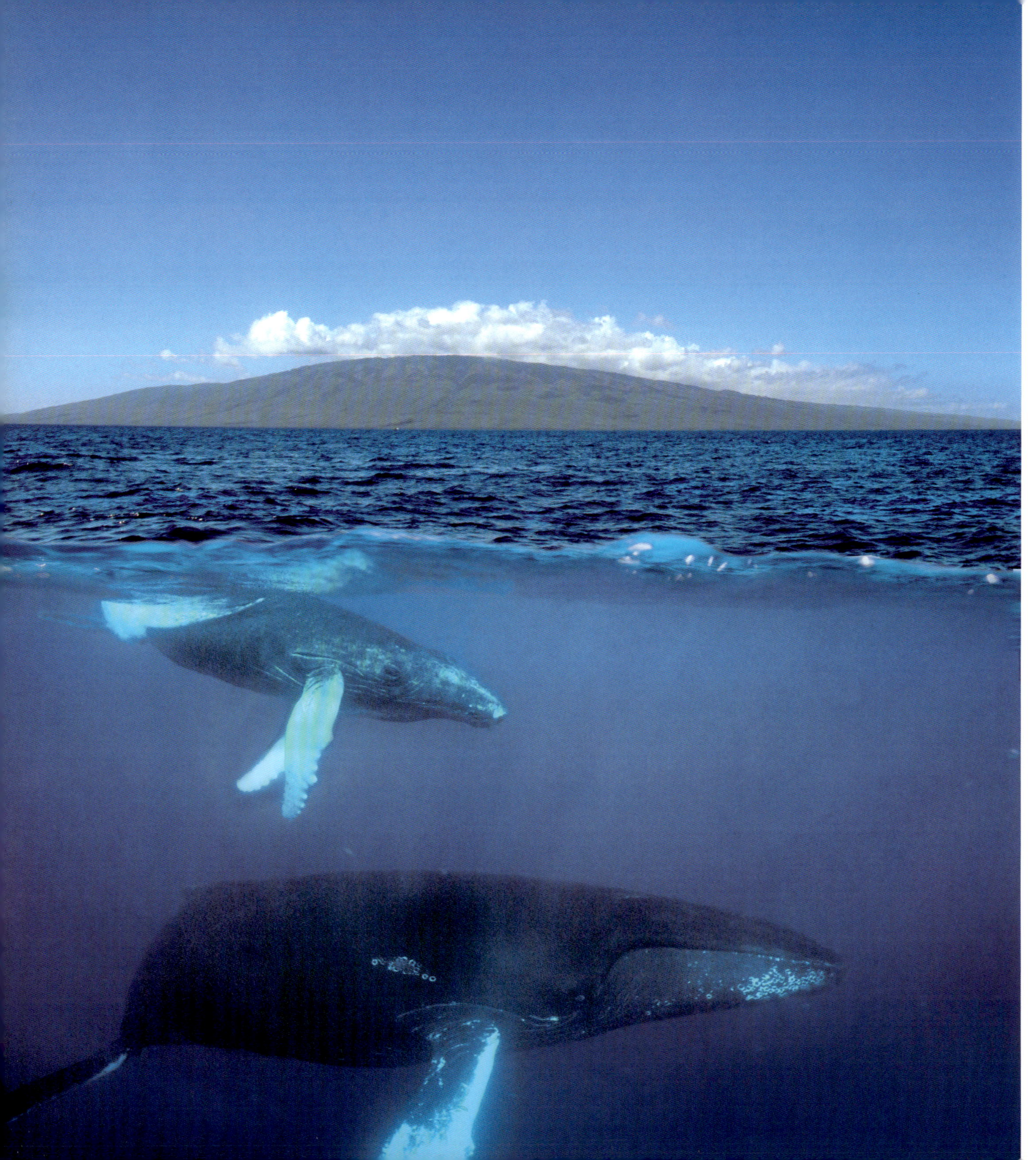

humpback off lanai
humpback warmth

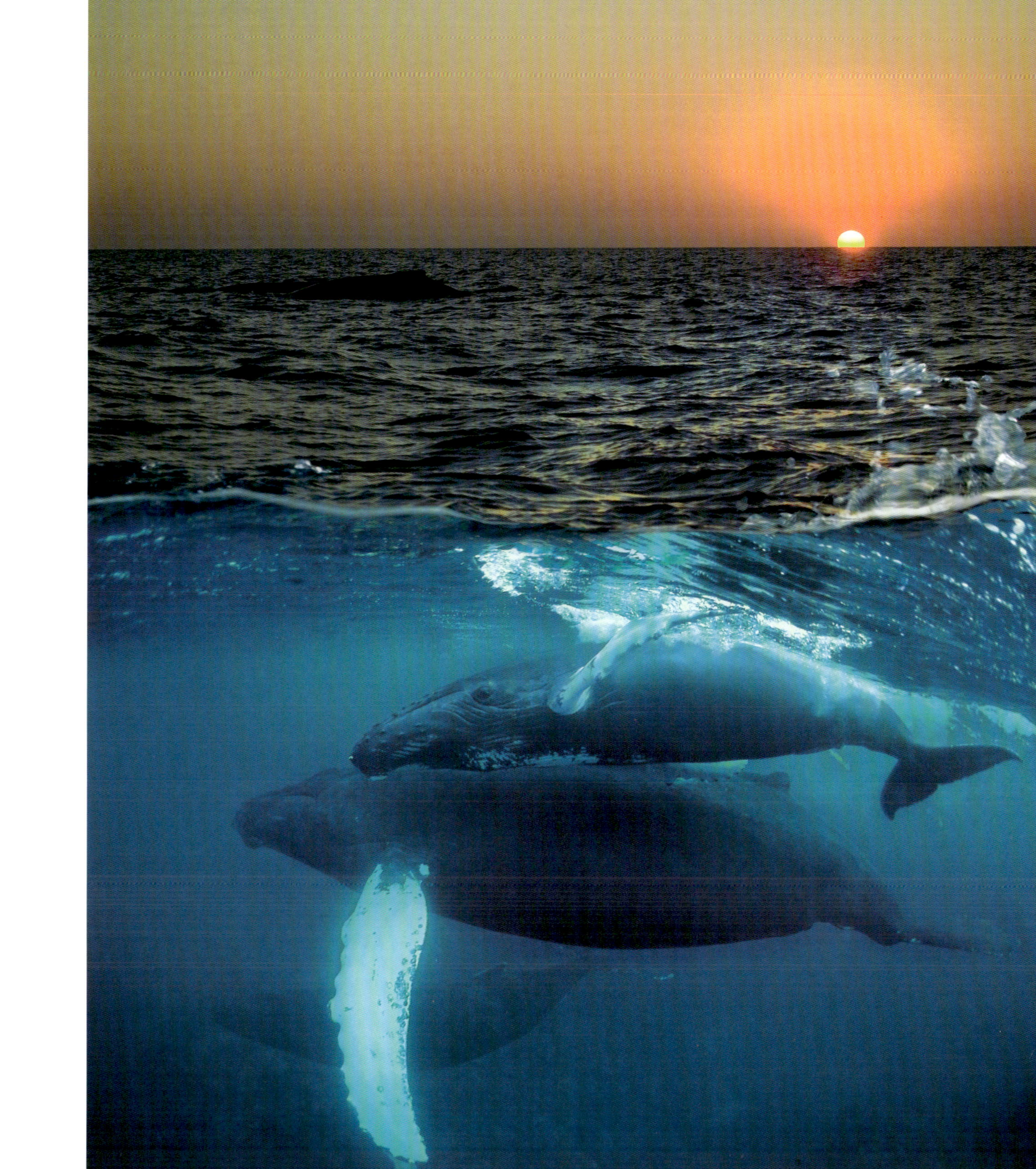

the survival of the planet depends on abundant clean water...

WYLAND

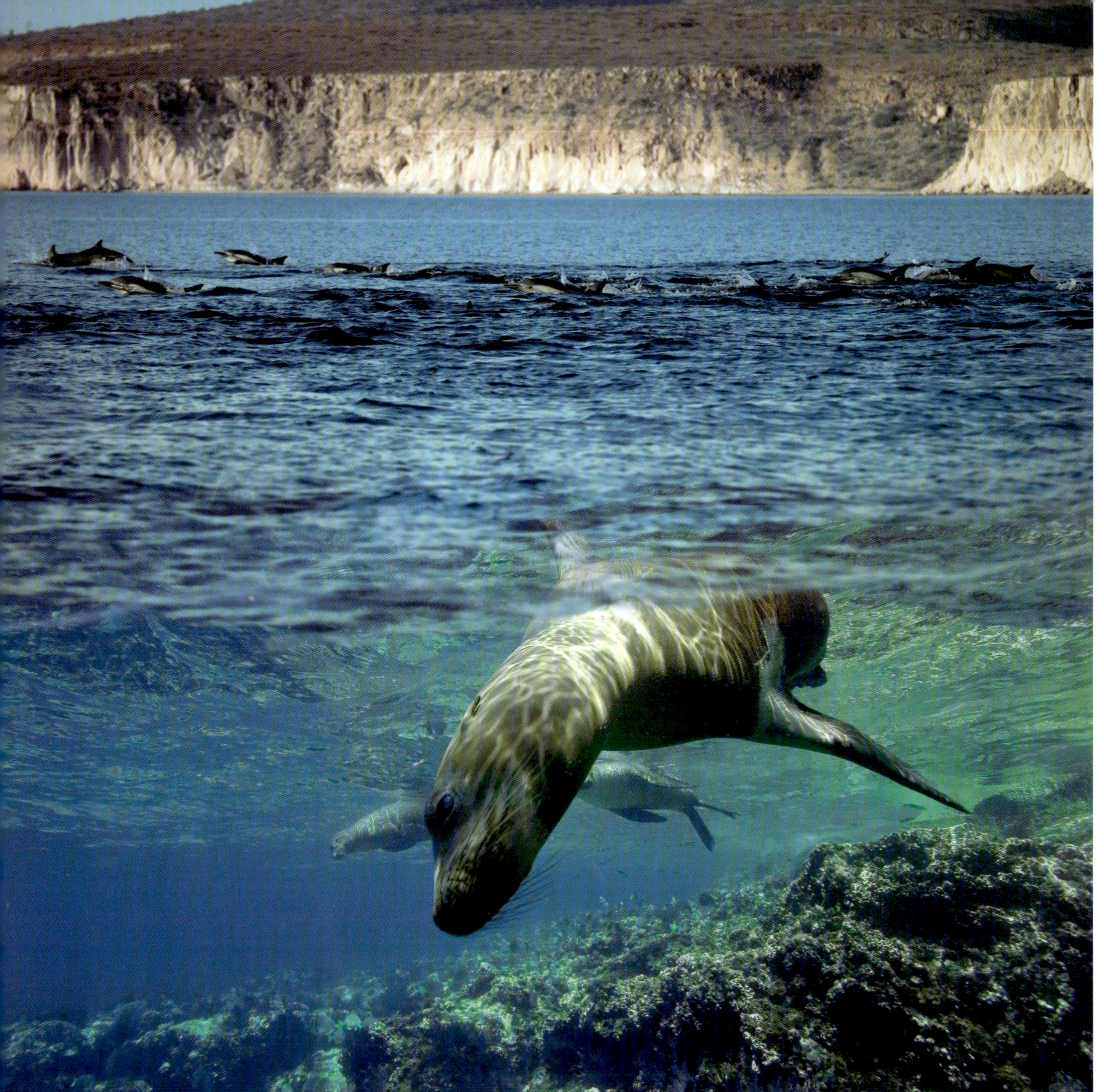

◀ baja sea of cortez
▶ sting ray city view

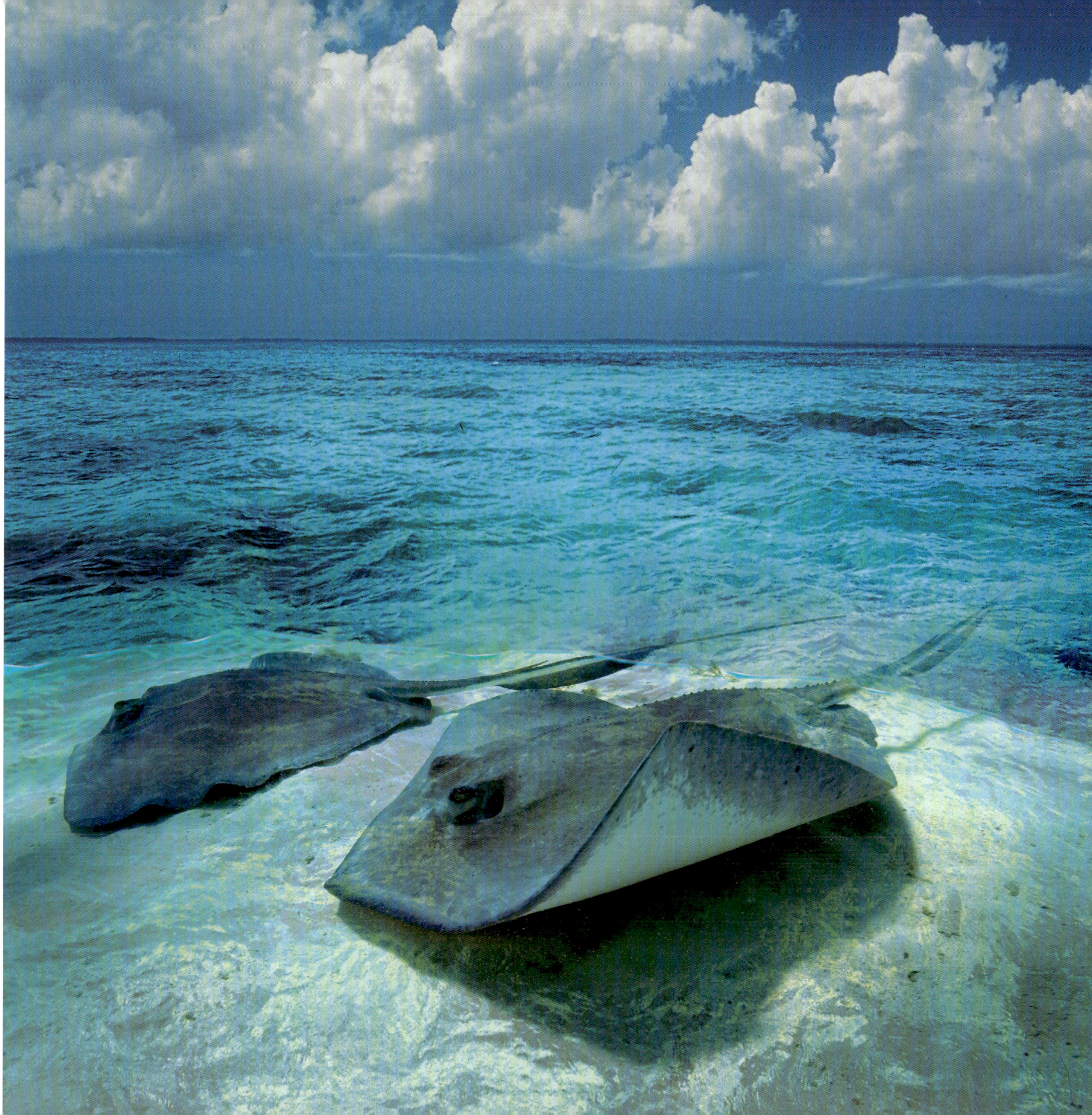

every drop counts...

WYLAND

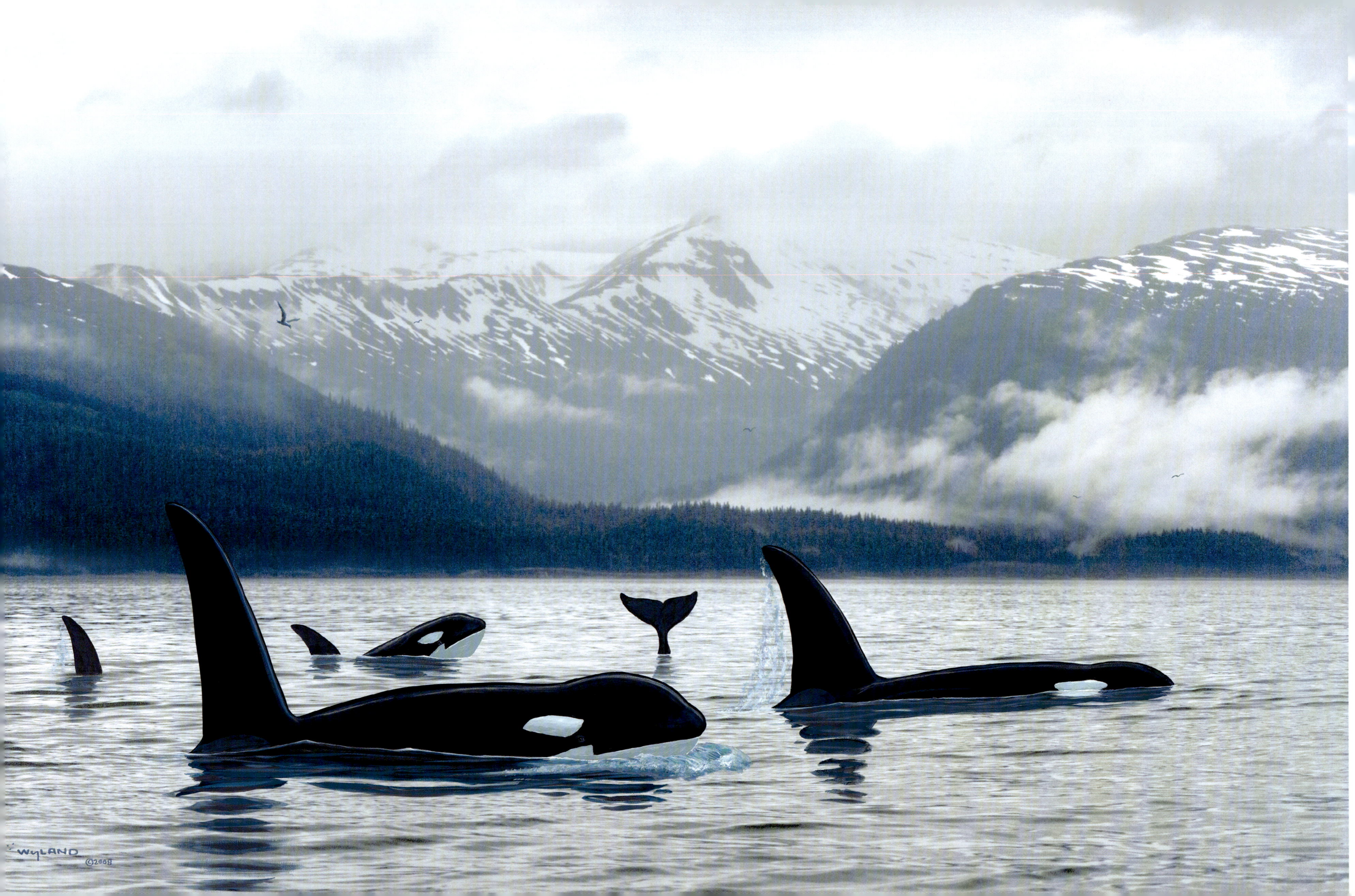

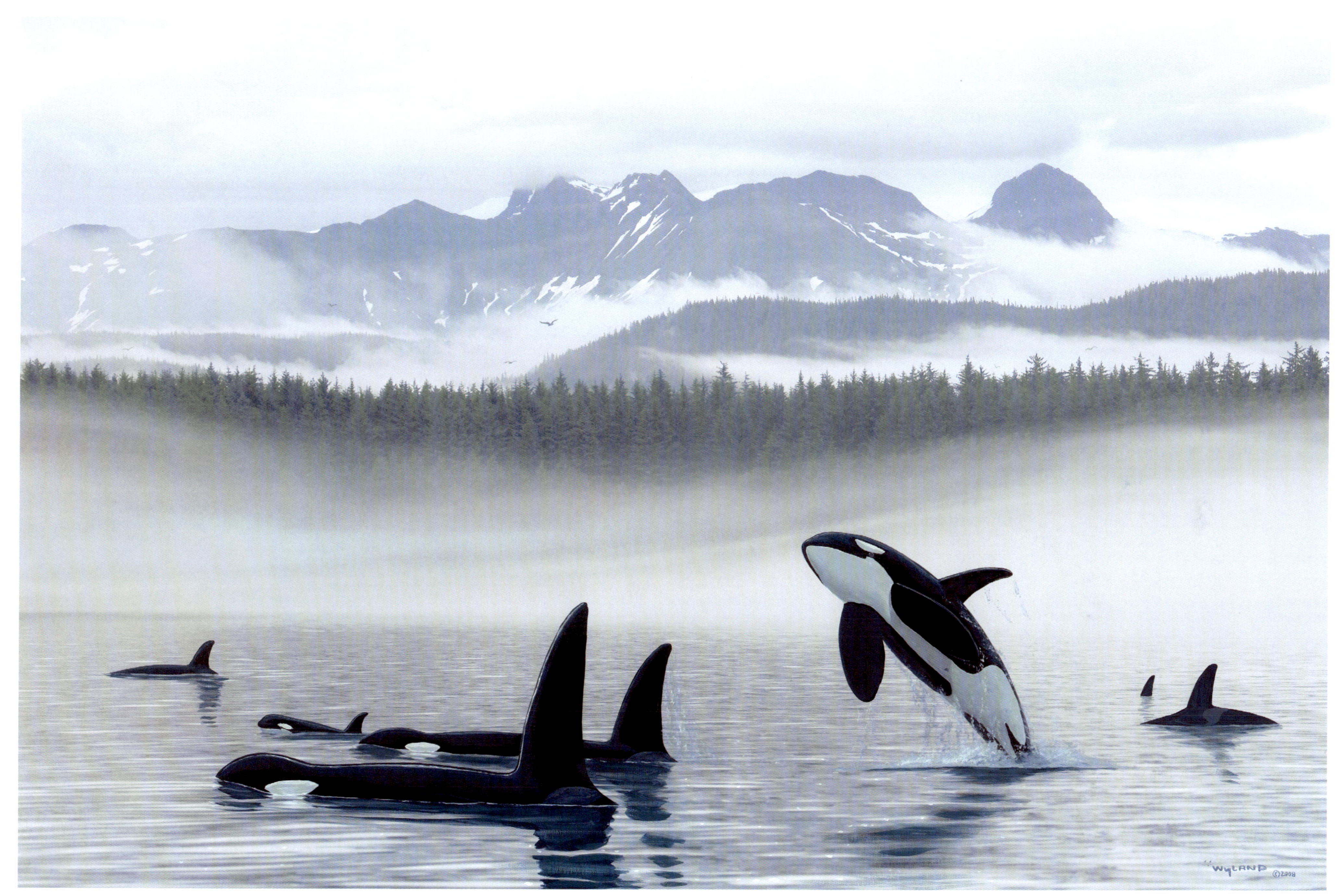

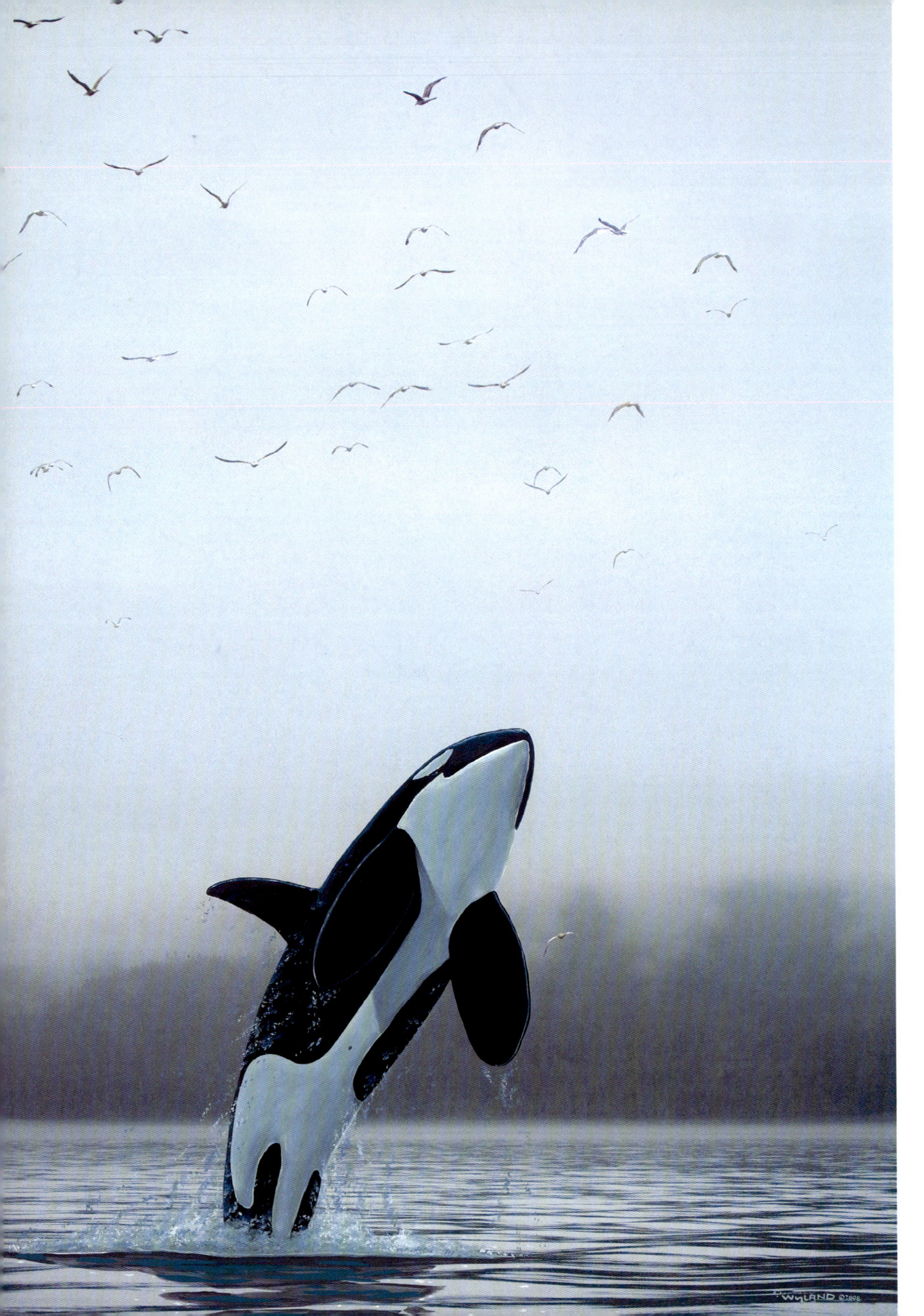

◀ orca calling
▶ sea otter sea

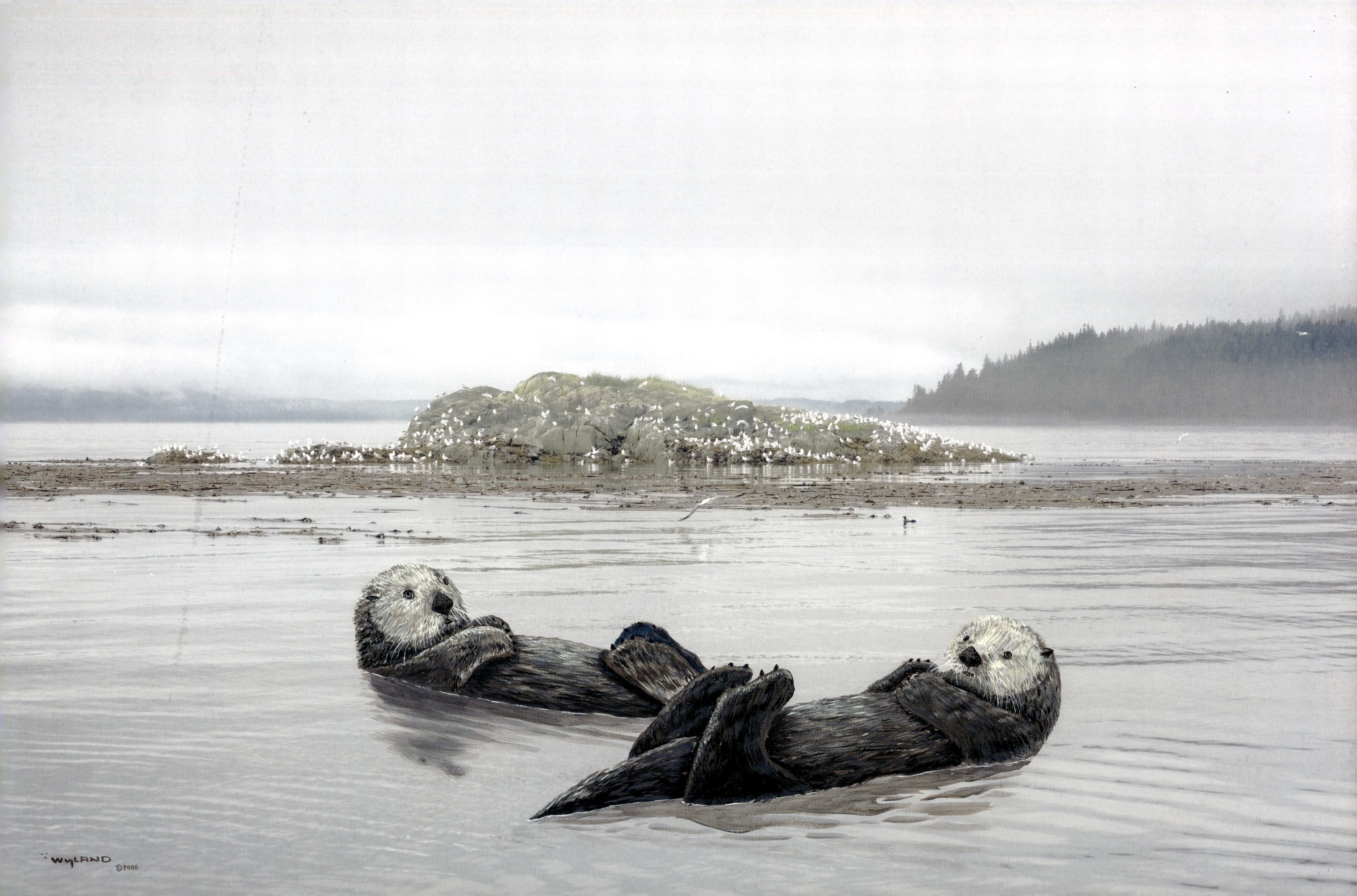

WYLAND
©2008

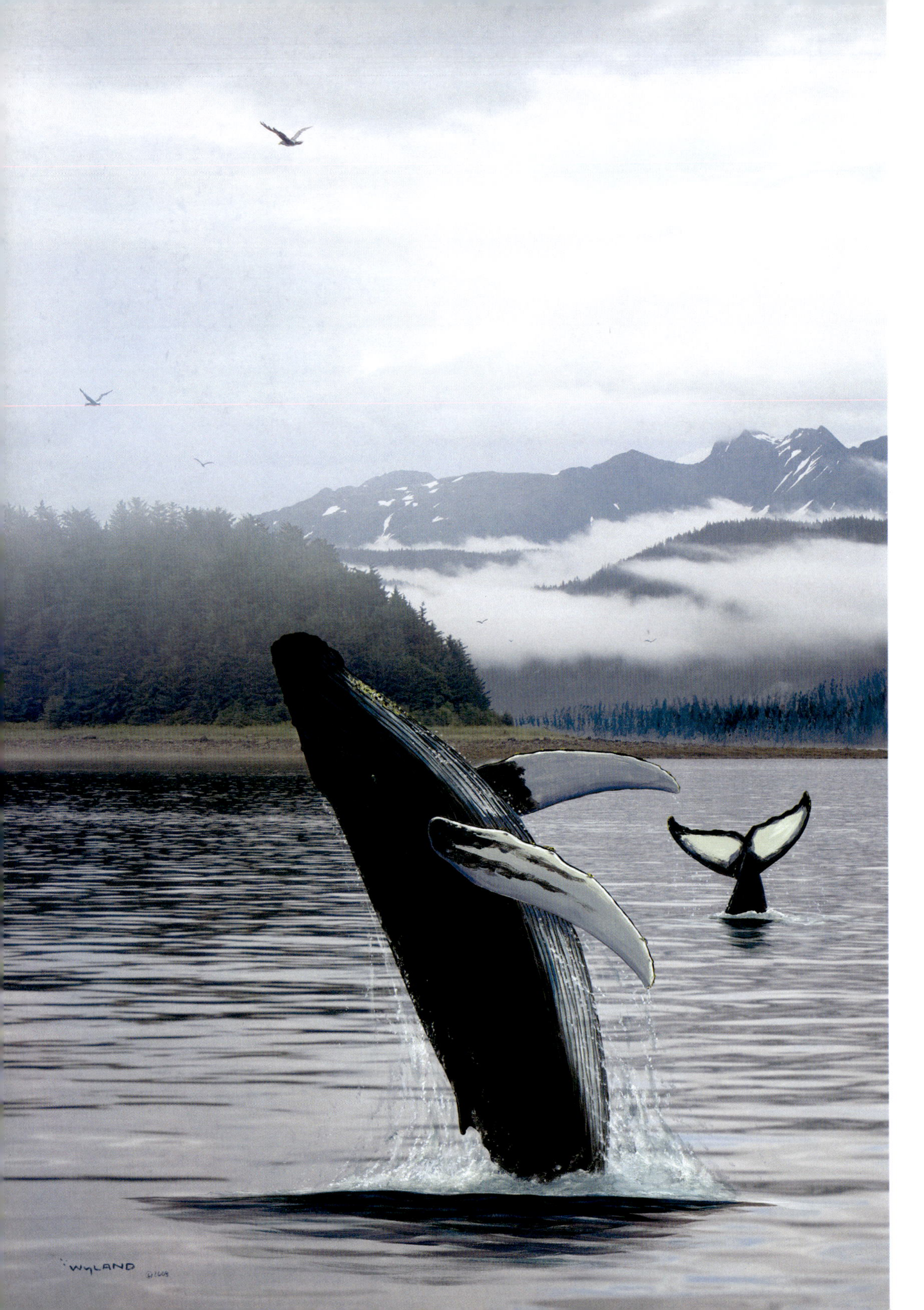

◄ breach for life
► northern pacific sacred waters

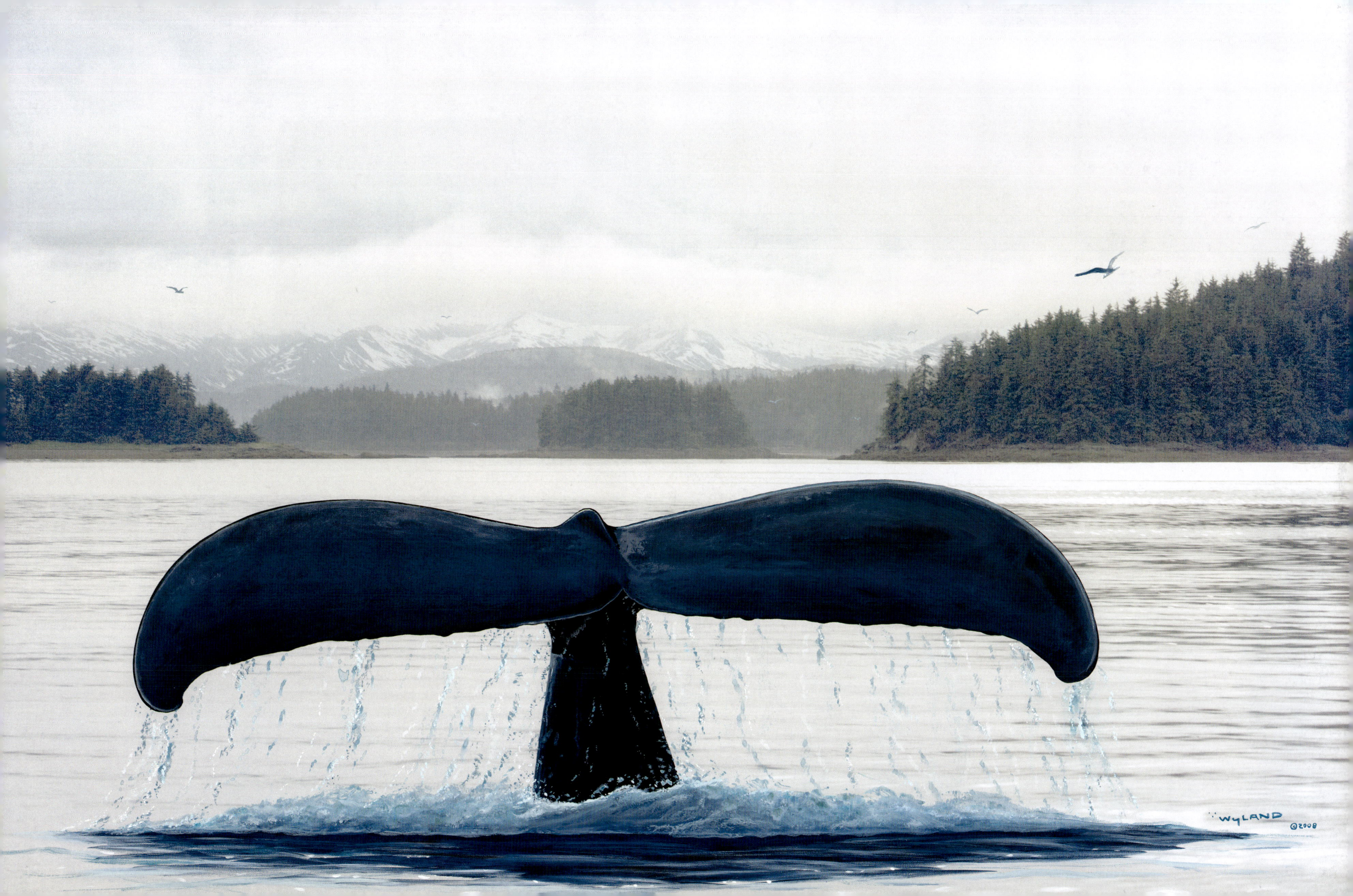

WYLAND ©2008

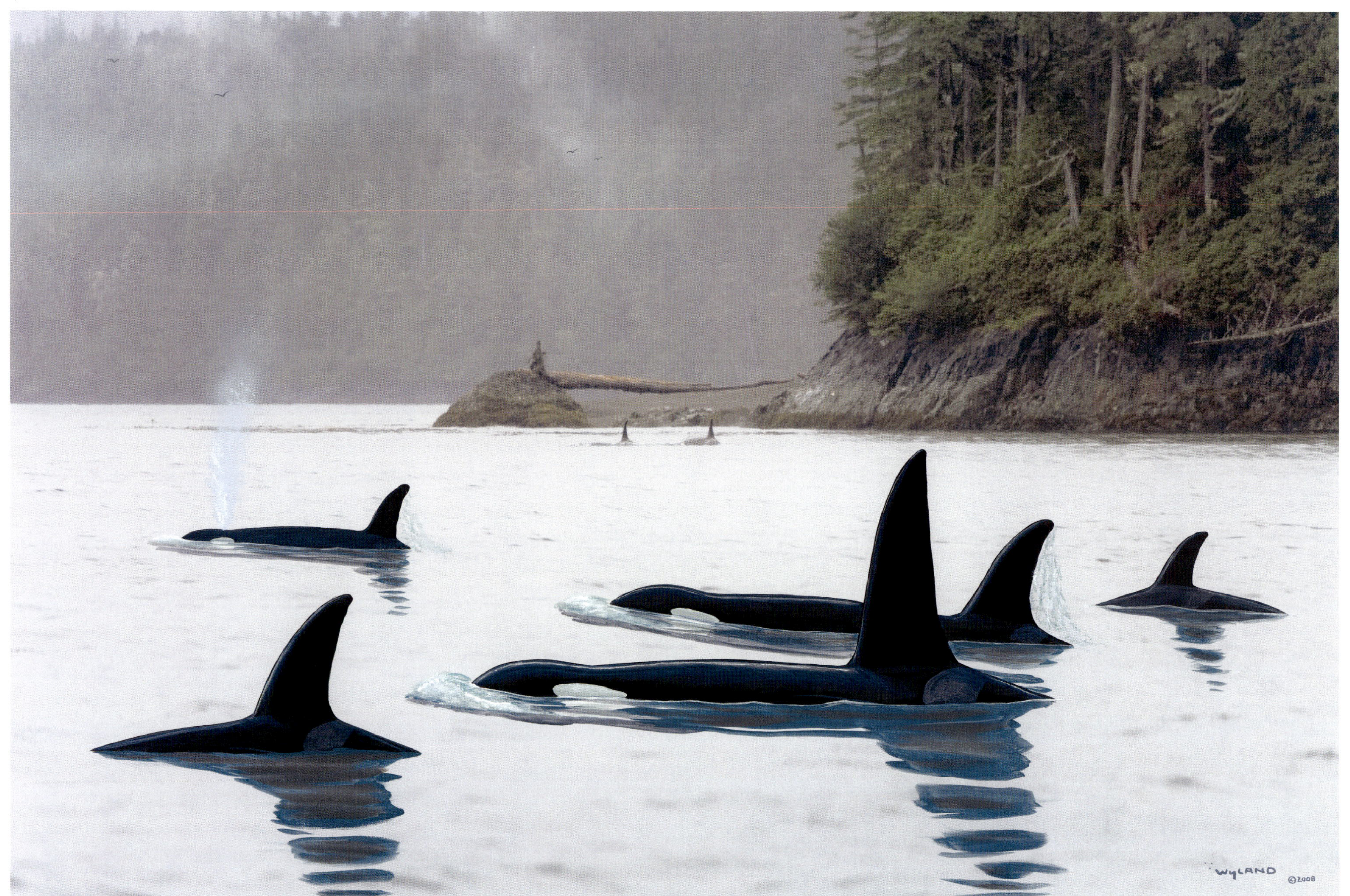

◀ pacific northwest call
▶ peaceful orca

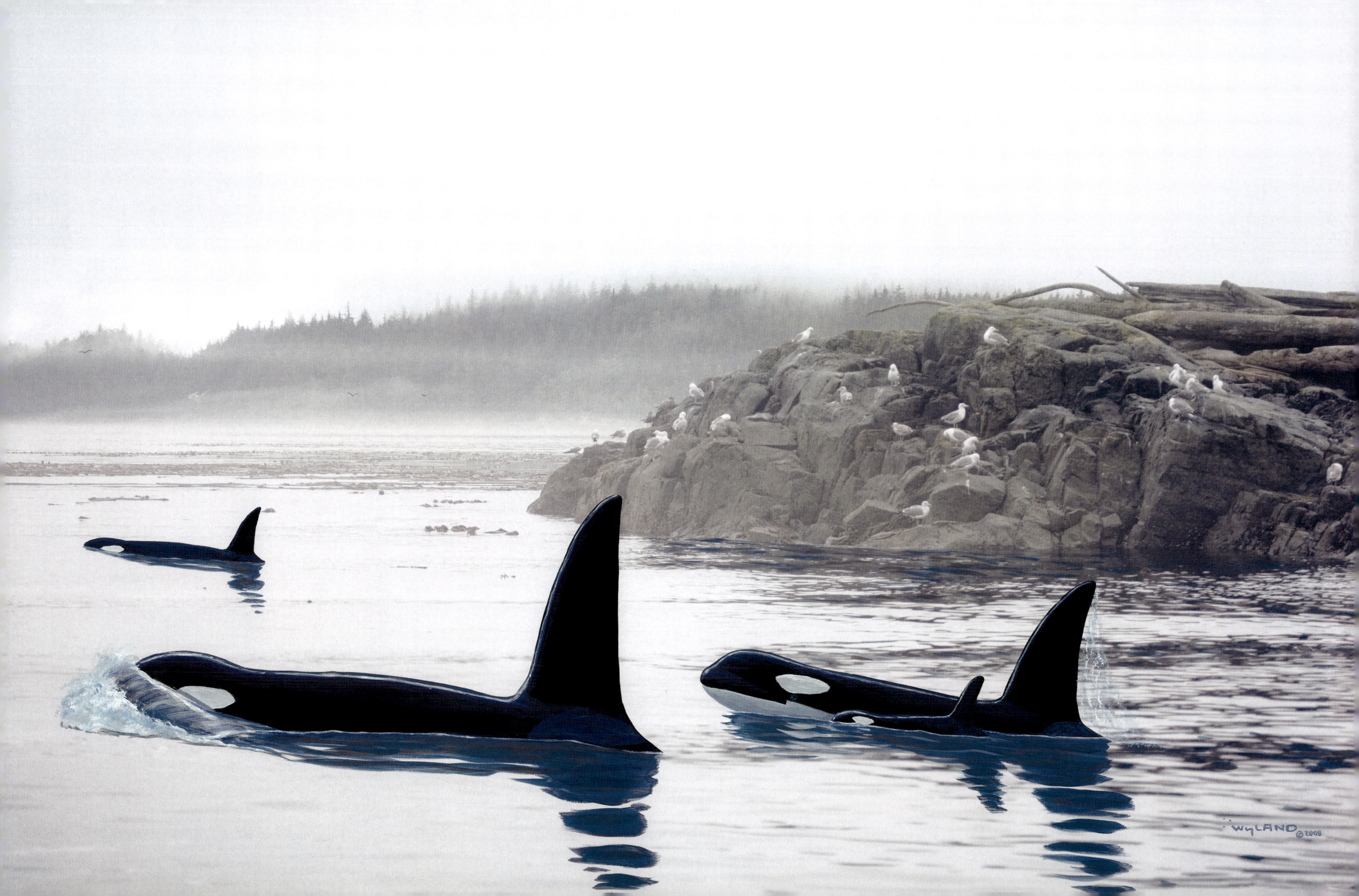

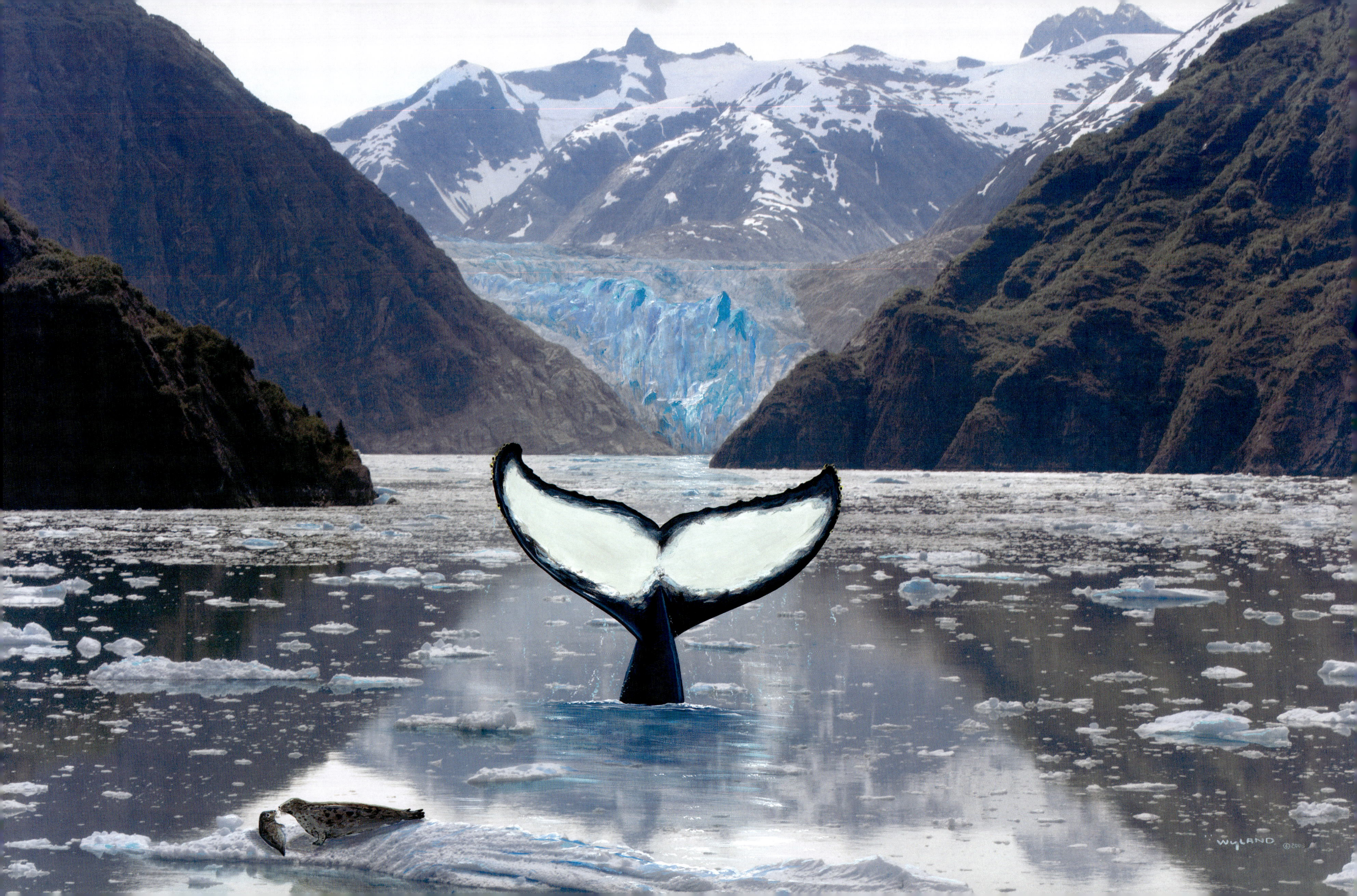
Wyland ©2001

thank you for celebrating my vision of the sea …

best fishes!

WYLAND

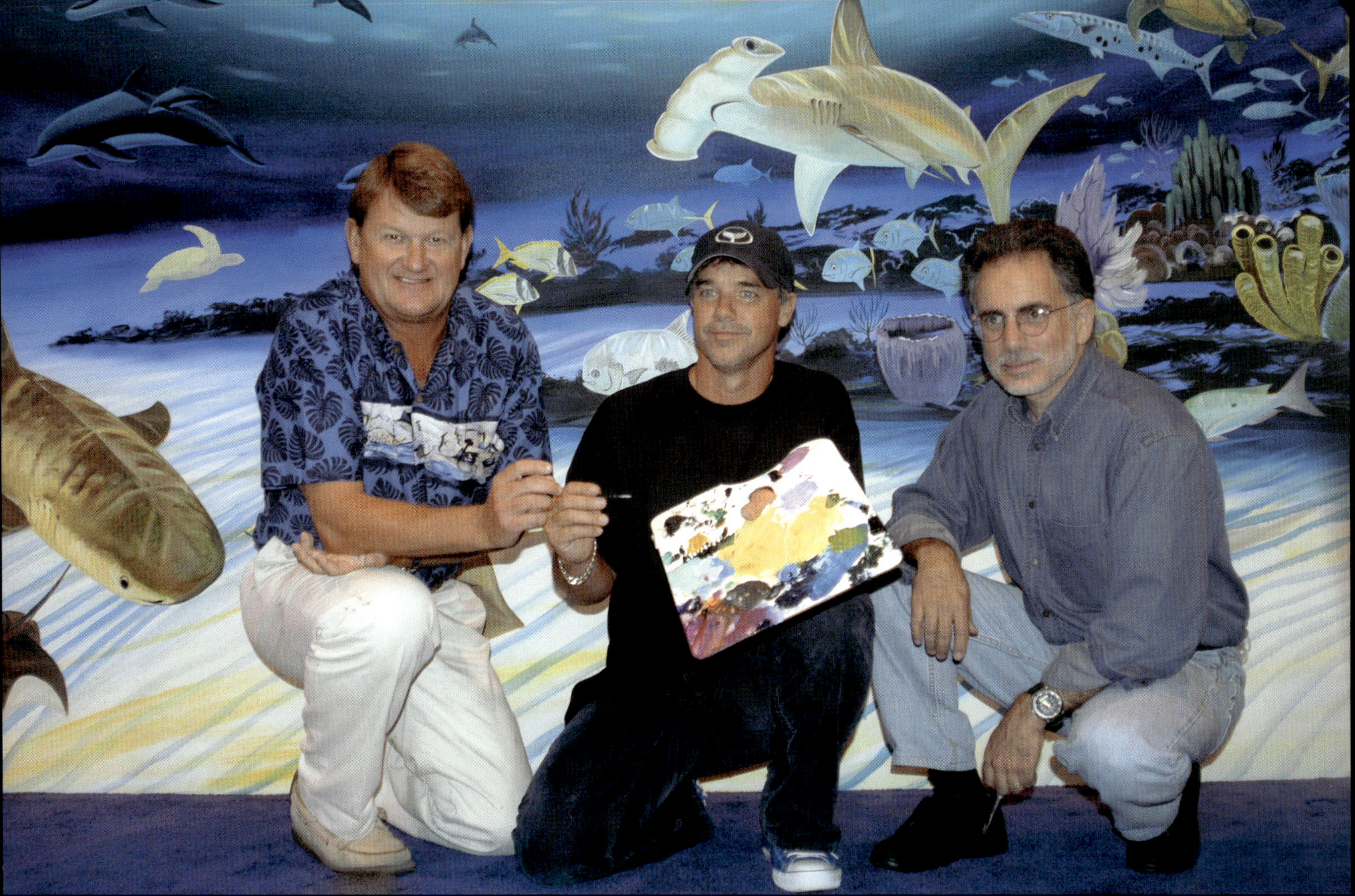

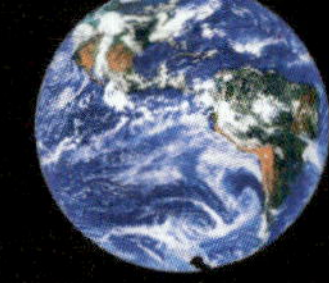

OCEAN ARTISTS SOCIETY™

MICHAEL AW	PASCAL JAGUT
AL BARNES	DENIS LAGRANGE
ERNIE BROOKS	PASCAL LECOCQ
JAMES CAMERON	GREG MACGILLIVRAY
TOM CAMPBELL	SIMON MORRIS
PATRICK CHEVAILLER	CHRIS NEWBERT
CATHY CHURCH	CHARLES "FLIP" NICKLIN
IAN COLEMAN	DOUG PERRINE
BILL CURTISINGER	ROGEST
DAVID DOUBILET	DOUGLAS DAVID SEIRFERT
RICHARD ELLIS	MARTY SNYDERMAN
TODD ESSICK	BOB TALBOT
BOB EVANS	VIKTOR
DAVID FLEETHAM	STAN WATERMAN
STEPHEN FRINK	BRIGETTE WILMS
AL GIDDINGS	WYLAND
HOWARD HALL	
MICHELE HALL	
ERIC HANAUER	IN LOVING MEMORY OF
GUY HARVEY	STANLY MELTZOFF
JENNIFER HAYES	JOHN STEEL
	JAMES D. WATT

◀ Founders of the Ocean Artists Society
Guy Harvey, Wyland, and Bob Talbot

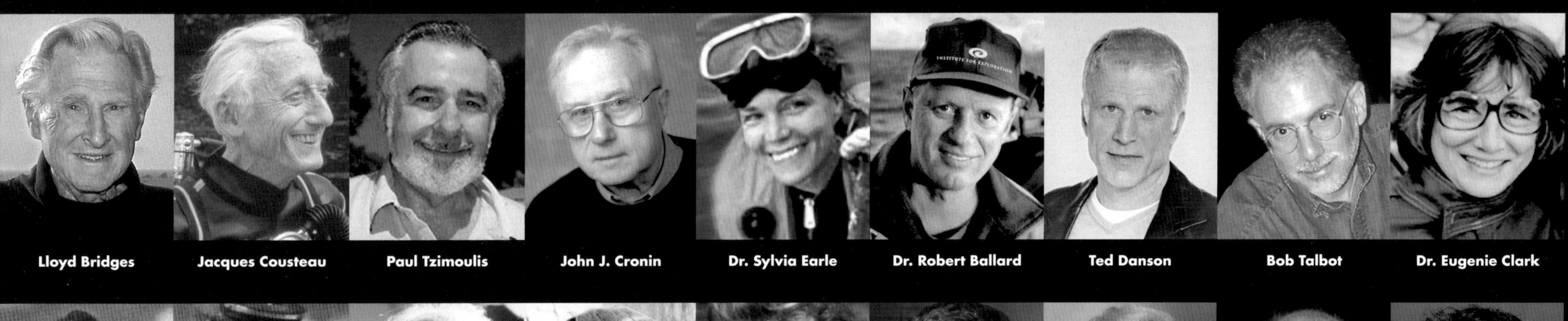

Lloyd Bridges   **Jacques Cousteau**   **Paul Tzimoulis**   **John J. Cronin**   **Dr. Sylvia Earle**   **Dr. Robert Ballard**   **Ted Danson**   **Bob Talbot**   **Dr. Eugenie Clark**

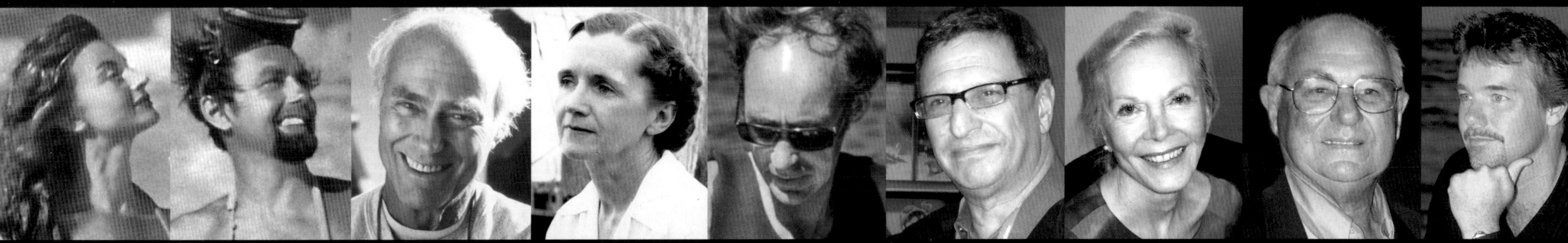

Lottie Hass   **Hans Hass**   **Stan Waterman**   **Rachel Carson**   **Ernie Brooks**   **David Doubilet**   **Zale Parry**   **Rodney Fox**   **Wyland**

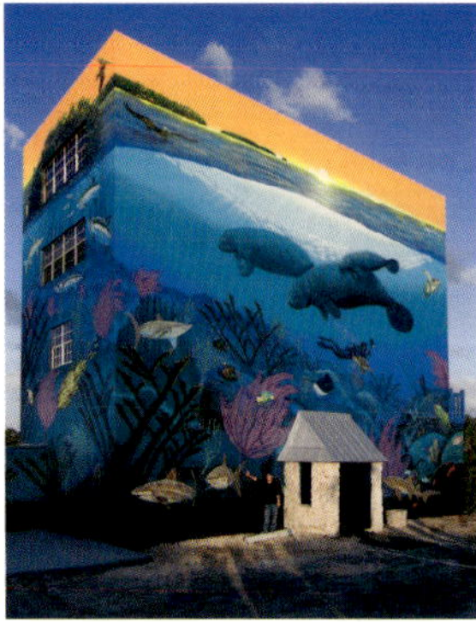 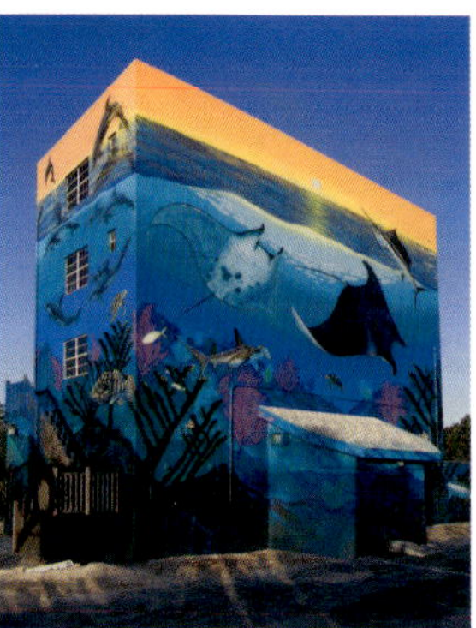

accomplishments

I felt strongly that art could play an important roll in the twenty-first century.
We need a sea change, an environmental renaissance.

The one thing I am most proud of is painting environmental murals with
over one million kids in all fifty states over the last thirty years.

With our help they will change the world.

WYLAND

December 1, 2007, Islamorada, FL

- Founded Wyland Galleries, 1978

- Founder – Wyland Foundation, a 501c3 non-profit, 1993

- The Inc. 500: "The Fastest-Growing Private Companies"
Wyland Studios, Inc. Magazine (September 1995)

- Who's Who in American Art, 1995

- Guinness Book of World Records, Largest Mural, March 1992

- Diving Hall of Fame, Academy of Underwater Arts & Sciences, 1998

- Earth Day Peace Bell Award, United Nations, New York City, 1998

- United Nations Official Artist "International Year of the Ocean", 1998

- NOGI Award, Underwater Arts & Sciences, January 1998

- NEA Magazine "Innovator" Spotlight, 1999, Wyland Ocean Challenge

- Honorary Doctorate / Humanities, 2001, American Intercontinental University,
Atlanta, Ga.

- John M. Olguin Marine Environment Award, 2002, Cabrillo Marine Aquarium,
San Pedro, Calif.

- Founder, Ocean Artists Society, 2002

- Honorary Chairman, Orange County March of Dimes, Walk America 2002

- Official Artis, Dive Equipment Marketing Association (DEMA) Annual Trade
Show, Las Vegas, 2002

- Artist in Residence, Academy of Underwater Arts & Sciences, 2002

- Grand Marshall/ Earth Day Hawaii

- Friends of Israel Disabled Veterans, Los Angeles Humanitarian Honoree

• Founder Wyland ICON Award - winners include Jacques Yves Cousteau, Lloyd Bridges, Paul Tzimoulis, John J. Cronin, Dr. Sylvia Earle, Dr. Robert Ballard, Ted Danson, Bob Talbot, Lottie and Hans Hass, Dr. Eugenie Clark, Stan Waterman, Rachel Carson, Earnie Brooks, David Doubilet, Zale Parry, and Rodney Fox

• Diver of the Year, Beneath the Sea, 2004

• Advisory Board, Cousteau Society

• Creator, Wyland Clean Water Challenge, classroom educational program, in partnership with Scripps Institution of Oceanography and the Birch Aquarium

• Wyland Ocean Challenge of America Tour, "50 States in 50 Days." Celebrating the United Nations "International Year of the Ocean." Painting Ocean Murals with students in all fifty states, 1998

• 95 Life-size Whaling Wall Murals, 1981-2007

• Presentations to over 1,000,000 children, schools and environmental groups

• Official Artist, National Geographic World Magazine Ocean Art Contest

• Wyland Ocean Challenge 17-City East Coast Tour, 2004
17 murals, in 17 cities, in 17 weeks

• Wyland Ocean Challenge West Coast Tour, 2005
12 murals in 8 cities in 8 Weeks

• Host of "Wyland: A Brush With Giants," a one-hour documentary about whales in the Sea of Cortez for Animal Planet Network, 2006

• Opened, "The Wyland Waikiki", a 406 room boutique hotel featuring all aspects of Wyland art in downtown Waikiki, 2006

• Wyland Clean Water Challenge "Barging Down the Mississippi" Ten State Community Art and Conservation Tour, 2006

• Creator, Clean Water Mobile Learning Center Project

• Wyland Clean Water Challenge "Every Drop Counts" National Tour, 2007

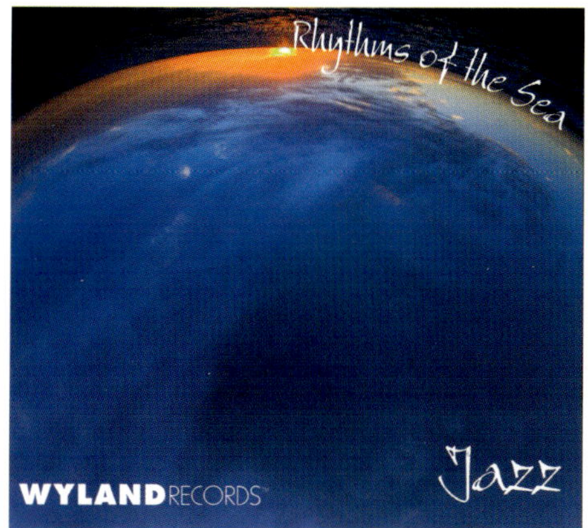

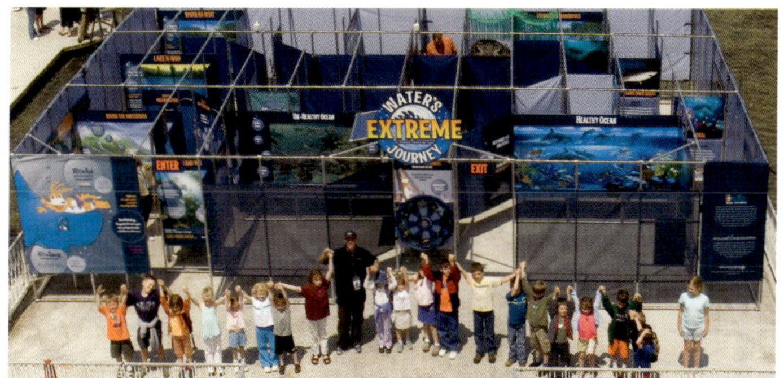

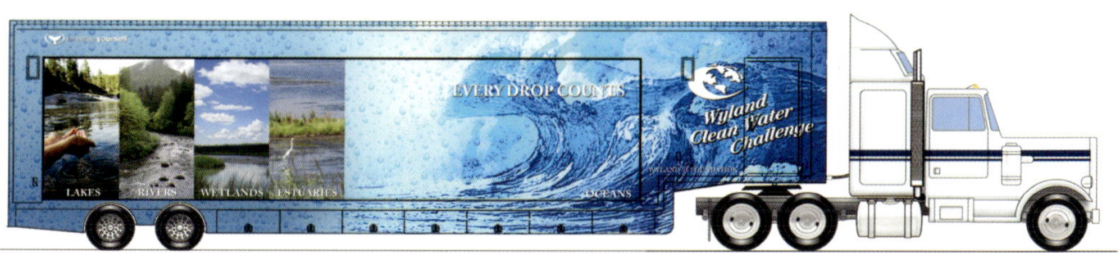

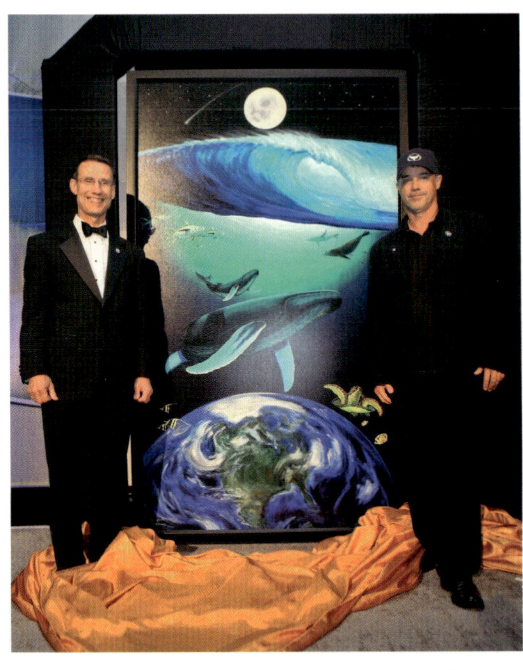

Artist with Vice Admiral Conrad Lautenbacker, Jr, for the unveiling of "Water Planet" official painting for NOAA's 200 Year Celebration

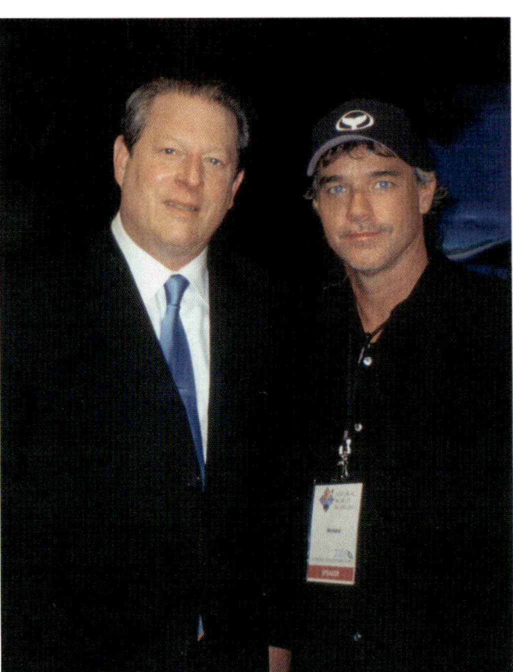

Wyland with Al Gore at a United Nations panel during World Environment Day, San Francisco, 2005. Wyland discussed the role of children in addressing future environmental issues.

• Wyland Clean Water Challenge 204 Country World Tour 2008, Afghanistan to Zimbabwe

• Official artist for the 2008 United States Olympic Team. for the Green Olympics in Beijing, China

• Official artist for NOAA's 200th Celebration of Science And Service to the Nation

• Creator, annual student art scholarship, Center for Creative Studies, Detroit, MI

• Creator, "Water's Extreme Journey," traveling maze exhibitions to promote watershed and wildlife education

• Creator, "Whale Tail" license plates for the State of California, raising over six million dollars for California Coastal Commission education programs and outreach, and new Protect Florida Whales license plate

• Honorary Doctorate, Art, Laguna Beach College of Art and Design, 2007

• Hand Painted, Boeing 737-700 aircraft for Aloha Airlines, featuring life-size endangered Hawaiian marine life. Signature plane was named Flying Whale, 2007

• Milestone: 30th Anniversary of Wyland Galleries will be celebrated in 2008, with latest locations, including Hawaii, California, North Carolina, Florida, Las Vegas, Seattle, Ocean City, Maryland, Niagara Falls, and Long Island, NY.

• Milestone: Wyland art collected in 70 countries by over 700,000 people

• Milestone: 15th Anniversary of Wyland Foundation will be celebrated in 2008 with conclusion of five-year Wyland Clean Water Challenge Tour, presented to 204 Olympic and U.N.-member countries from Afghanistan to Zimbabwe

• Painted last wall in America, Whaling Wall 95, in Key Largo, Fla., 2007 "Gateway to the Florida Keys"

• Scheduled, Whaling Wall 100 is scheduled for July 7 – July 21, 2008, in Beijing, China, for the Green Olympics, where he will paint nearly three miles of canvas with kids from 204 Olympic and U.N. Member countries. The project is titled "Hands Across the Ocean" and will be a pre-Olympic event celebrating Whaling Wall 100

• Founded Wyland Records, 2007

• Released, *Rhythms of the Sea*, 2007, a new jazz CD featuring some of the greatest jazz artists in the world, with music and melodies written by Wyland

• Reached milestone of painting with one million children with the completion of his "Barging Down the Mississippi" 10-state tour

• Wyland Foundation donates to 100 U.S. environmental organizations annually

• Wyland Foundation has supported 500 charity groups and organizations worldwide with art donations annually

• Featured: Wyland brand at the New York Licensing Show, 2007

• Completed HD filming of 26 half-hour episodes for his new public television series and PBS, "Wyland's Art Studio," scheduled to air nationally in April 2008

• Launched a complete line of non-toxic water-based oil paint, brushes, and art supplies with Martin F. Weber to be distributed worldwide in an effort to protect artists, kids, and parents with environmentally sensitive art supplies

• Completed series "How-to-Paint and Draw Marine Life" kits with Walter Foster art books

• Founded by Wyland, Guy Harvey and Bob Talbot with a membership of the "Who's Who" of ocean artists, the Ocean Artists Society hosted its second annual meeting and group show at DEMA in Orlando to discuss the distinguished group's objectives to support conservation efforts, October, 2007

• Presented, Wyland ICON Awards to ocean icons David Doubilet, Zale Parry, and Rodney Fox at NOGI Awards at the DEMA Trade Show in Orlando, 2007

• "Beneath the Sea" dive show in New Jersey will again feature Wyland in a major Wyland fine art exhibition and fundraiser for the Historic Diving Society, NOGI Awards, and Beneath the Sea charities. Wyland was honored by BTS with the Diver of the Year award

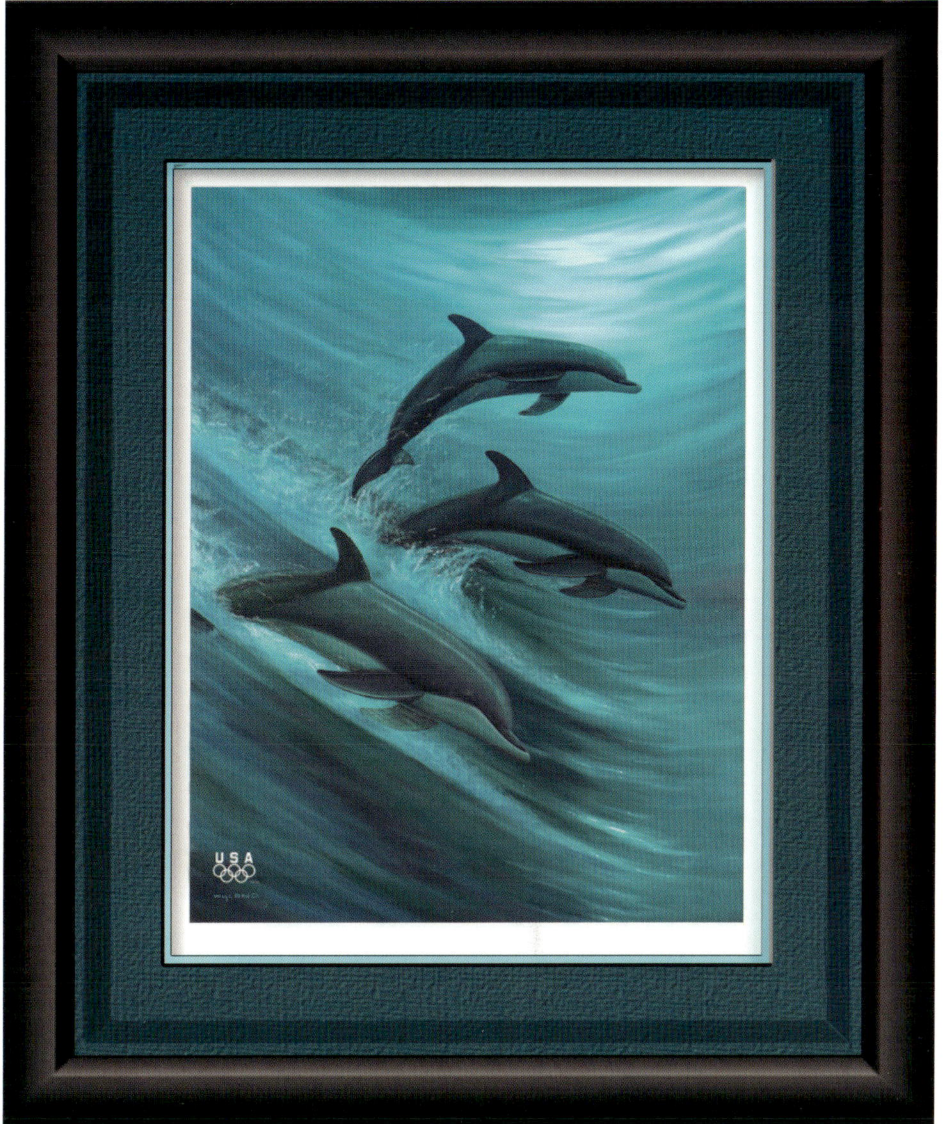

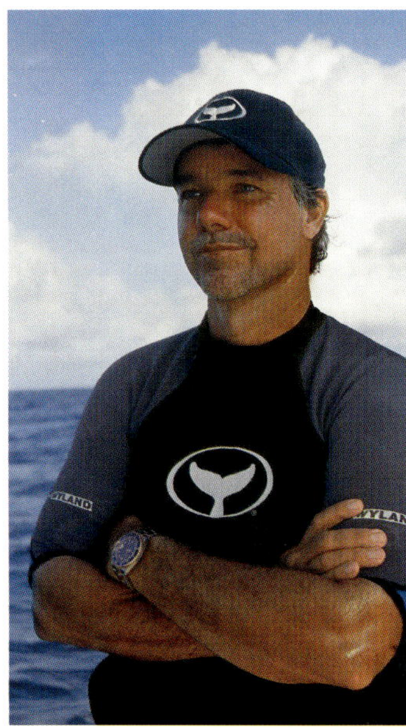

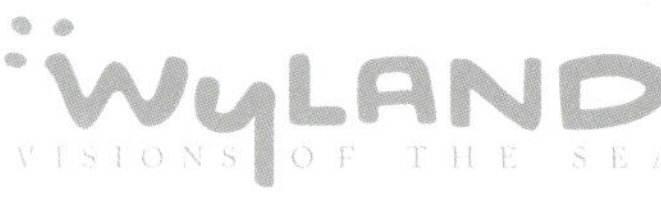

Many of the fine art images are also available in hand signed and numbered limited editions. For more information visit www.wylandgalleries.com